25 CENTS
FEBRUARY
The RING
Max Schmeling
Leading Foreign Heavyweight
In this issue
Jack Dempsey's Ranking of Boxers

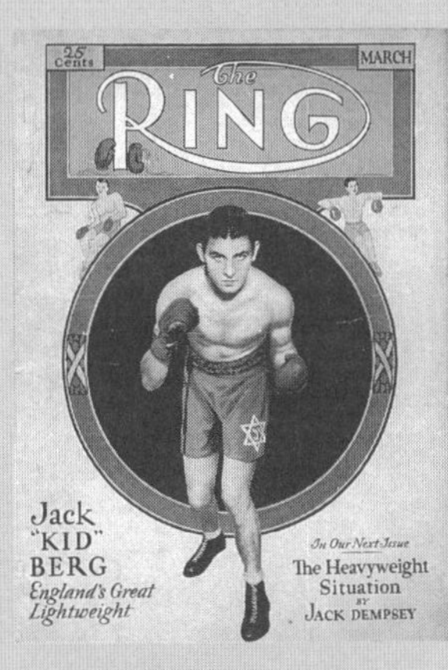
25 Cents
MARCH
The RING
Jack "KID" BERG
England's Great Lightweight
In Our Next Issue
The Heavyweight Situation
BY JACK DEMPSEY

25 CENTS
JULY
The RING
SOUVENIR
HEAVYWEIGHT CHAMPIONSHIP NUMBER

BOXING - WRESTLING - FIGHT FICTION
15 CENTS
FEBRUARY
The RING
The RING'S RANKING for 1932
HEAVYWEIGHT PICTORIAL ISSUE
25 CENTS
AUGUST
The RING
JOE LOUIS
THE BROWN BOMBER

BOXING - WRESTLING - FIGHT FICTION
25 CENTS
SEPTEMBER
The RING
JAMES J. BRADDOCK
WORLD HEAVYWEIGHT CHAMPION
THE LOUIS-CARNERA BATTLE REVIEWED
IN STORY AND PICTURES

LOUIS-SCHMELING FIGHT REVIEWED
25 CENTS
AUGUST
The RING

COMEBACK BRIGADE by HYPE IGOE
25 CENTS
OCTOBER
The RING
MAX SCHMELING
THE MAN OF THE HOUR

LOUIS-SIMON FIGHT PICTURES
25 Cents
JUNE
The RING
BAER-NOVA BOUT REVIEWED

ANNUAL RATING OF BOXERS
25 Cents
FEBRUARY
The RING

THE FIGHTING FILIPINOS
25 Cents
JULY
The RING
BOXING LEADS IN U. S. CAMPS

LEADING MATCHES for 1946
25 Cents
MARCH
The RING
SULLIVAN-KILRAIN BOUT

LOUIS-WALCOTT "INSIDE"
25 Cents
SEPTEMBER
The RING
LOUIS
WALCOTT
LOUIS
WALCOTT

INDOOR SEASON GETS UNDER WAY
25 Cents
NOVEMBER
The RING
Freddie Mills of Great Britain
WORLD LIGHT-HEAVYWEIGHT
CHAMPION

NEW YEAR BRINGS NEW DEAL
25 Cents
JANUARY
The RING
Marcel Cerdan,
World's Middleweight Champion

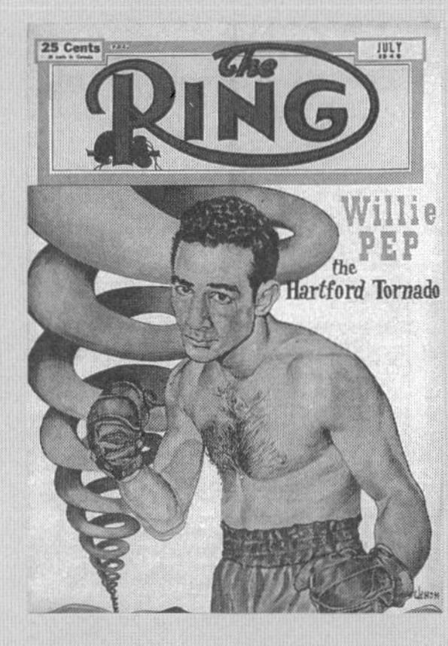
25 Cents
JULY
The RING
Willie PEP
the Hartford Tornado

SEASON'S GREETINGS
25 Cents
JANUARY
The RING
Merry Christmas

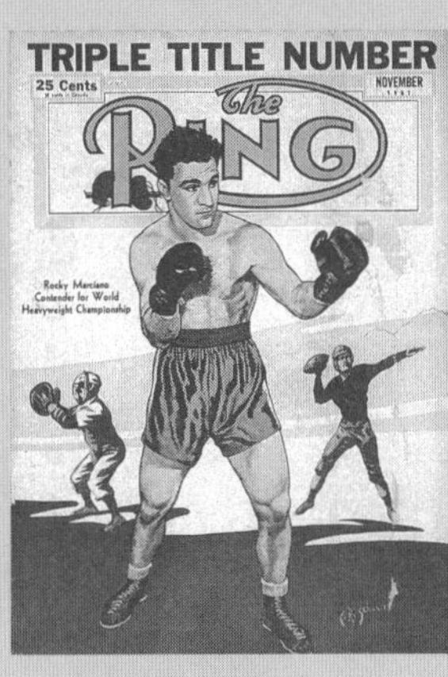
TRIPLE TITLE NUMBER
25 Cents
NOVEMBER
The RING

ANNUAL RATING OF BOXERS
25 Cents
FEBRUARY
The RING
Ray Robinson
FIGHTER OF THE YEAR
BOXING'S THRILLS IN 1951

GALA CELEBRATION
25 Cents
MARCH
The RING
30th
Anniversary
1922 to 1952

CHRONICLE OF BOXING

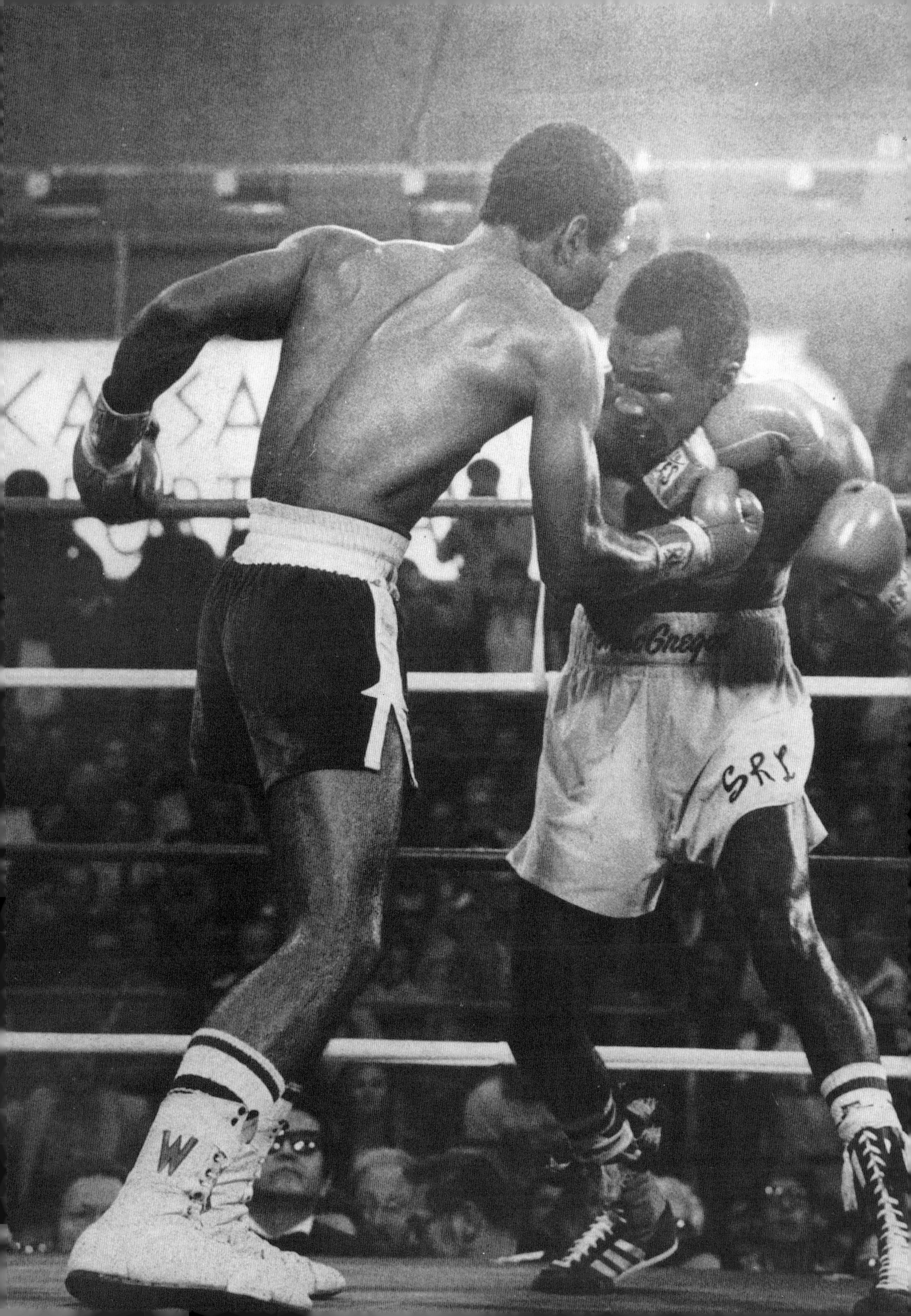
SRL
W

CHRONICLE OF BOXING

STANLEY WESTON
Publisher, The Ring

STEVEN FARHOOD
Editor-in-Chief, The Ring

HAMLYN

DEDICATION

For Marcia, who learned to differentiate between
Vicente Saldivar, Richard Sandoval, and Baltazar Sangchili, whether
she wanted to or not. Her support was unwavering, and
her smile made all the work worthwhile.
SF

THANKS

Thanks to those who provided information for this project,
including Frank Thornton, Col. Robert Thornton, Hank Kaplan,
Bob Yalen, Carlos Irusta, Joe Koizumi, and Jack Fiske.
And special thanks to Dave Gerhardt, who made England
seem much closer than it really was.
SF

First published in 1993
by Hamlyn
an imprint of Reed Consumer Books
Michelin House, 81 Fulham Road, London SW3 6RB
and Auckland, Melbourne, Singapore and Toronto

ISBN 0 600 57743 0

A catalogue record for this book is available from the
British Library

DTP Design: T. Truscott Designs, Henfield, Sussex

Set in 9.5 on 12pt Linotron Goudy

Produced by Mandarin Offset
Printed in Hong Kong

CONTENTS

Stanley Weston, Publisher, *The Ring*. (*Opposite*) Steve Farhood Editor-in-Chief, *The Ring*

INTRODUCTION

When I'm killing time before a fight, whether it be in the press room at Caesars Palace or ringside at a clubshow in Brooklyn, I enjoy talking to veteran sportswriters. Most have covered everything from baseball to badminton, so I invariably ask them which sport is their favorite. "Boxing," they answer, unhesitatingly, and almost to a man. "Definitely boxing."

For 15 years, I've covered almost nothing but boxing, and I'm in no rush to diversify. Writing this book was hardly a leisure activity – my regular work on *The Ring* leaves time for little else. That aside, I can't imagine having tackled a more fascinating and energizing subject.

At times, the project bordered on the bizarre. Spending seven days a week editing, researching, and writing boxing left me somewhat punchdrunk. I remember wondering why Pat Clinton, the Scottish flyweight, was running for president. And more than once I referred to my boss as Harold Weston.

Nonetheless, reliving almost 100 years of the sweet science was a wonderful experience. *The Ring*'s files are a treasure, and without them I could not have even approached the task. I still don't consider myself a historian – many, many others know much, much more – but I did learn a great deal. This book is meant to provide an overview of the fights and fighters that made boxing the most thrilling sport in the world. Hopefully, I got my facts right and did my subjects justice.

How has the game changed since 1900? It hasn't changed anywhere near as much as you might think. First and foremost, money remains the driving force. History tells us that heavyweight champion Tommy Burns ran from Jack Johnson. When the dollars were right, however, the fight was made. Eighty-five years later, we await a heavyweight showdown between world champions Riddick Bowe and Lennox Lewis. Be sure that the fight will happen because there are millions – and lots of them – to be earned.

Are today's fighters better than their predecessors? That's a much harder question to answer. For years, *The Ring* founder and publisher Nat Fleischer and manager and fight film collector Jim Jacobs debated that very point. Fleischer touted the masters from the turn of the century, like Joe Gans and Jim Corbett. Jacobs dismissed them as unsophisticated and flawed. For my taste, lightweight legend Benny Leonard was the first champion to turn boxing into a sweet science. Since his reign, fighters have gotten bigger, stronger, and better conditioned. Especially heavyweights. I've always maintained that Muhammad Ali could have beaten any big man in history, including Dempsey, Louis, and Marciano. My argument, of course, will forever be countered by certain historians. Suffice to say that great fighters should be measured only inside the borders of their eras.

Simply put, what makes boxing so attractive is the fights and fighters. Your won't find more intriguing stories than those of Jack Johnson and Mike Tyson. Or more fascinating personalities than Archie Moore and Muhammad Ali. The courage of Mickey Walker... the tenacity of Rocky Marciano... the emotion of Roberto Duran...

You'll find it all inside these pages. Here's to hoping you enjoy each and every one of them.

Steve Farhood 23.2.93

RING DECADE

1900-1909

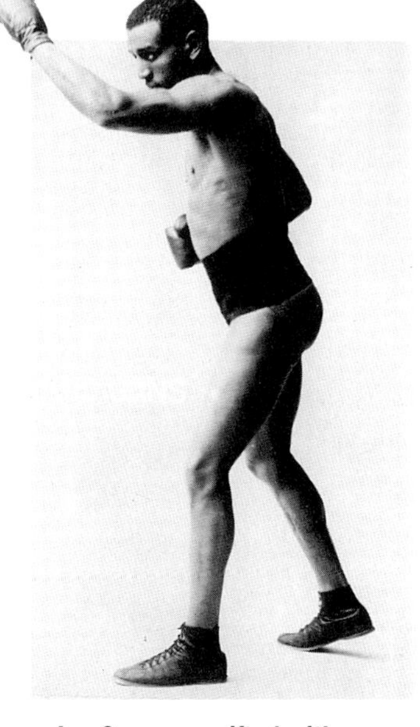

Joe Gans was gifted with every inborn skill to be a super boxer. He truly deserved his nickname "The Old Master."

Bob Fitzsimmons, the remarkable Cornishman, had been heavyweight champion before the turn of the century. In 1903, at age 40, he won the light heavyweight championship, and continued boxing until he was 50.

WHAT boxing will be like in the 21st century is anyone's guess. But as long as men can curl their fingers into their palms, tighten their wrists, and swing their arms, how much can change?

Boxing is basic, which is why it endures. Thousands of years before there were padded gloves, gladiators traded blows wearing iron-studded hand bindings. Circa 1100 B.C., Homer wrote of prize fighting in the *Iliad*, his main event featuring Epeus vs. Euryalus. (Which corner was worked by Ray Arcel has never been established.) Bare-knuckle fighting peaked in the late-18th and mid-19th centuries, and the modern era began in September 1892, when James J. Corbett dethroned the reigning heavyweight champion John L. Sullivan.

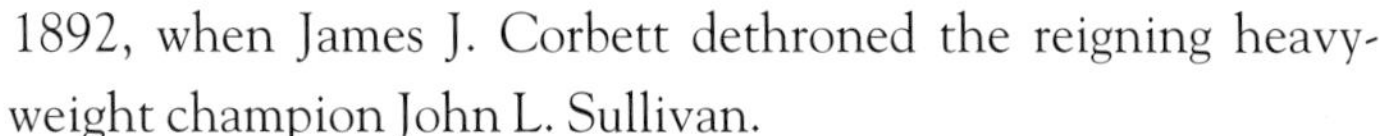

With the Marquis of Queensberry rules in effect, boxing was ready to move forward. In 1900, the game was evolving slowly, taking one step back for every two forward. The new century began on a negative note, when New York State Governor Theodore Roosevelt repealed the Horton Law, which had legalized boxing. Fighters in search of riches were wise to head west. From 1900 to 1910, there were 10 world title fights in New York State, and six in England, the birthplace of the modern game.

California hosted 60 such bouts.

The decade began with six recognized divisions, and concluded with what would come to be known as the original eight. In January 1900, the roll call of world champions included James J. Jeffries at heavyweight, Tommy Ryan at middleweight, Mysterious Billy Smith at welterweight, Frank Erne at lightweight, George Dixon, boxing's first black world champion, at featherweight, and Terry McGovern at bantamweight. (Jeffries, Ryan, and McGovern were American, Smith and Dixon Canadian, and Erne Swiss.)

In 1903, Lou Houseman, a sportswriter from Chicago, introduced the light heavyweight

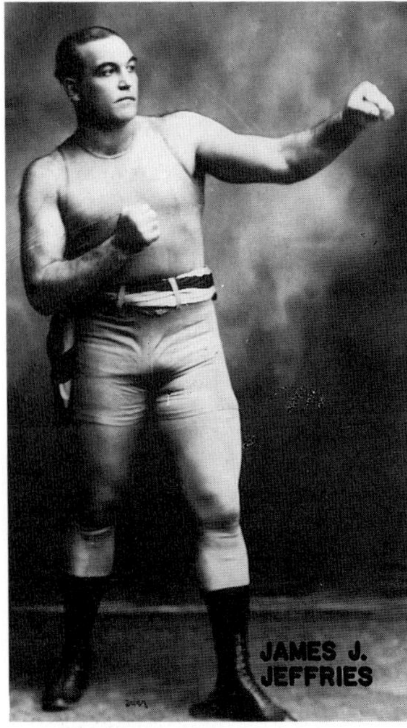

James J. Jeffries lost only one fight in his entire career, and that lone defeat came when he was 35 years old.

Jack Johnson, considered by many to be the greatest heavyweight champion of all-time, was 19 when he had his first fight and 50 when he finally quit.

division. Houseman's motives were selfish; he represented the Austrian-born Jack Root, who was too big to challenge middleweights and too small to face heavyweights. Houseman managed to sell his idea to promoters and fellow sportswriters, and on April 22, 1903, Root became the first light heavyweight champion when he outpointed former middleweight king Kid McCoy.

Sandwiched between the more popular heavyweight and middleweight divisions, the light heavyweight class would struggle. None of the first four champions, Root, George Gardner, Bob Fitzsimmons, and Philadelphia Jack O'Brien, made a successful defense. After O'Brien dethroned Fitzsimmons in December 1905, title fight activity ceased. O'Brien moved up to try the heavyweights, and the throne remained vacant until 1914. It would become a recurring theme for the remainder of the century: light heavyweight champions as heavyweight wannabes. All, of course, in the name of money.

The Ring Record Book lists Chicago's Jimmy Barry as the first world flyweight champion. But the division was universally recognized for the first time in 1909, when England's National Sporting Club established the class. (Until then, a 112-pound boxer was considered a bantamweight.) Four years later, London's Sid Smith outpointed France's Eugene Criqui and became the world champion.

Stanley Ketchel was only 24 when he was murdered in 1910, but he had enough time to establish himself as a true immortal.

As significant as the triumphs of any of the decade's fighters was the emergence of Tex Rickard, who filled a glaring void by becoming the sport's first power promoter. In the '20s, Rickard would gain everlasting fame by hosting Jack Dempsey's million-dollar title bouts. His start came in September 1906, when the former prospector convinced champion Battling Nelson and former titlist Joe Gans to battle in the gold mining boom town of Goldfield, Nevada. Rickard not only signed and staged big fights, but he promoted them by cunningly cultivating fighters' images and manipulating the newspapers.

Rickard's influence cannot be underplayed, but as would always be the case, boxing's appeal was simple: fights and fighters. Easily the dominant single figure was Jack Johnson.

The Texan was not the first black world champion, but he was the first black heavyweight champion, and that made all the difference. Cocky, arrogant, and bitter, Johnson was intent not only on building his own legend, but tearing down those that preceded him. At the start of the decade, when Jeffries was champion, there was a simplicity to the throne. By the time Johnson had established himself as the titlist, however, he had rewritten all the rules.

There had never before been a heavyweight who combined strength, power, speed, and mobility. Though he was despised during the course of his reign, even his most passionate critics had to acknowledge the champion's extraordinary skills. *The Ring* publisher Nat Fleischer would come to rate Johnson as the best heavyweight of all, ahead of Dempsey, Louis, Marciano, Ali, and the rest.

While the newly created light heavyweight division stuttered and stumbled, Bob Fitzsimmons made history when, in November 1903, he won the world title. Having captured the middleweight and heavyweight crowns in the 1890s, the 40-year-old Englishman became the first fighter to capture titles in three divisions.

Michigan's Stanley Ketchel, another kayo victim of Johnson, became the first star at middleweight, and a fighter whose reckless style and punching power would come to symbolize boxing's second most spotlighted division. Ketchel also became a symbol of unrealized potential when, in October 1910, he was shot to death at age 24.

The welterweight and bantamweight classes failed to produce reigns of significant length, but at lightweight, Baltimore's Joe Gans shined throughout the decade. The most prolific champion of the day was featherweight king Abe Attell, a San Franciscan of exceptional defensive skill who made a total of 24 defenses over the course of two reigns. Attell regularly bet on himself to augment his purses, a common practise at the time. In 1909, Monte Attell won the bantamweight crown, marking the first time that brothers held world titles.

Stylewise, Terry McGovern, who won the featherweight crown nine days into the new century, was the antithesis of Attell. But as a pure puncher with frightening power, "Terrible Terry" was the first champion from among the lighter weights to prove, kayo by sensational kayo, that the little guys could hit, too.

Clearly, champion for champion, the heroes of the years 1900-1909 stand proudly with the best of the later decades.

At the completion of the second decade of the modern era, boxing was fragmented and uneven, but also growing in every way. Change was good, and though the players in the game didn't know it at the time, also inevitable.

JANUARY

1900

DECEMBER

TEENAGE SENSATION

Just some of what Brooklyn-based Terry McGovern accomplished at the Broadway Athletic Club:

* He scored eight knockdowns in one round against Canada's George Dixon, a fighter who hadn't previously been downed over the course of a 14-year career.
* He won the world featherweight title at age 19, and in doing so, dethroned a legendary champion who had reigned for 10 years.
* He joined Bob Fitzsimmons and Tommy Ryan as the only fighters to have won world titles in two weight classes. (McGovern was bantamweight titlist.)

Over the first five rounds of their eagerly anticipated contest – fans were paying up to $40 per seat – Dixon outboxed McGovern. But when Dixon tired, "Terrible Terry" swarmed. He almost finished his foe in the sixth and eighth. Finally, after eight knockdowns Dixon's corner tossed a wet sponge into the ring.

"Terrible" Terry McGovern, world champion.

THE REMATCH THAT WASN'T EASIER

If a fighter knocks out his opponent, he'll have a quicker and easier time in the rematch. That axiom must have been formulated a long time after the welterweight rematch between Matty Matthews and Kid McPartland, held on February 16 at New York City's Broadway Athletic Club.

Only two weeks before, Matthews had crushed McPartland by first-round knockout. This time, the Kid proved a bit more durable. He went down in the second round, twice in the 12th, and once each in the 13th, 16th, and 17th. The final knockdown brought the end.

McPartland had proven his mettle the hard way.

Jim Jeffries (right) kayoed ex-champ Jim Corbett in 23rd round, Coney Island, NY, May 11.

STUDENT SHOWS NO RESPECT

In 1897, world heavyweight champion James J. Corbett hired a crude second-year pro from Carrol, Ohio, named James J. Jeffries as a sparring partner. On May 11, in Coney Island, Jeffries proved that when class was in session, he was paying strict attention.

After cleverly outboxing defending titlist Jeffries in a bout scheduled for 25 rounds, Corbett fell into a single left hook in the 23rd stanza and was instantly flattened. Afterward, he blamed the crowd's bloodlust for his sudden and foolish change in tactics.

It was Jeffries' third defense. Corbett, 33, became the first heavyweight to attempt to regain the title.

RINGSIDE VIEW

MARCH

Flashing boxing's best jab, lightweight champion Frank Erne stops Baltimore's highly touted Joe Gans in the 12th round.

APRIL

In his third defense, heavyweight champion James J. Jeffries retains the crown by knocking out hapless Jack Finnegan at 55 seconds of the first round.

DECEMBER

In what is obviously a dive, Baltimore's Joe Gans falls in two rounds to reigning featherweight champion Terry McGovern in Chicago.

FIGHTING TALK

I'll show them I can fight as well as box

JAMES J. CORBETT

before being knocked out in the 23rd round of his title fight vs. James J. Jeffries

WORLD TITLE FIGHTS

HEAVYWEIGHTS

April 6	**James J. Jeffries** (USA) *KO* 1 Jack Finnegan, Detroit
May 11	**James J. Jeffries** *KO* 23 James J. Corbett, Brooklyn

WELTERWEIGHTS

April 17	**Matty Matthews** (USA) *KO* 19 Mysterious Billy Smith, New York City
June 5	**Eddie Connolly** (CAN) *ref* 25 Matty Matthews, Brooklyn
Aug 13	**James (Rube) Ferns** (USA) *KO* 15 Eddie Connolly, Buffalo
Sept 1	**James (Rube) Ferns** *ref* 15 Matty Matthews, Detroit
Oct 16	**Matty Matthews** *ref* 15 James (Rube) Ferns, Detroit

LIGHTWEIGHTS

March 23	**Frank Erne** (SWI) *KO* 12 Joe Gans, New York City

FEATHERWEIGHTS

Jan 9	**Terry McGovern** (USA) *KO* 9 George Dixon, New York City
Feb 1	**Terry McGovern** *KO* 5 Eddie Santry, Chicago
March 9	**Terry McGovern** *KO* 3 Oscar Gardner, New York City
June 11	**Terry McGovern** *KO* 3 Tommy White, Brooklyn
Nov 2	**Terry McGovern** *KO* 7 Joe Bernstein, Louisville

BANTAMWEIGHTS

May 26	**Dan Dougherty** (USA) *ref* 20 Tommy Feltz, Brooklyn
Aug 4	**Danny Dougherty** *ref* 25 Tommy Feltz, Brooklyn

WHEN THE COPS RUSHED THE RING

On March 4, at the Southern Atlantic Club in Louisville, world middleweight champion Tommy Ryan and Tommy West engaged in one of the most violent and bloody title fights in history. Ryan emerged victorious when Terry McGovern, the reigning world featherweight champion and West's chief second, tossed a sponge into the ring as a sign of surrender.

The rivals were familiar; in 1898, Ryan, then the world welterweight titlist, stopped West in 14 rounds. This time, however, the fight was much more demanding. In round two, a right split the lip of the slick-boxing champion and downed him. When West scored a followup knockdown, Ryan took a nine-count. Those moments aside, Ryan eluded most of West's rushes, and after a dozen rounds, the challenger's eyes were battered and swollen.

A bizarre moment highlighted the fight: in round nine, with West seemingly ready to fall, the middleweights fell into a clinch and remained locked. A police captain then rushed the ring and separated them. Ringsiders thought he was stopping the fight. Instead, he had intervened because he thought West was trying to choke the champion.

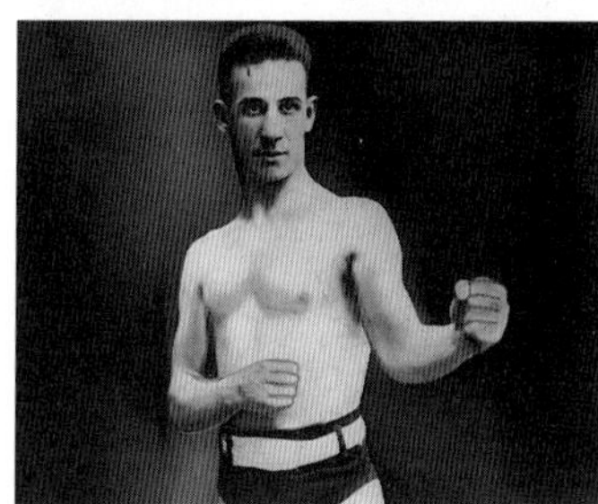

Tommy Ryan kayoed Tommy West to retain his middleweight crown.

RINGSIDE VIEW

APRIL

Terry McGovern extends his reign as world featherweight champion by scoring a fourth-round kayo of Oscar Gardner.

NOVEMBER

Harry Forbes wins the bantamweight title, stopping defending champion Danny Dougherty in the second.

DECEMBER

Joe Walcott, a 5'1½" welterweight from Barbados who is strong enough to have beaten heavyweight Joe Choynski, wins the world title with a fifth-round TKO of James (Rube) Ferns.

JANUARY

1901

DECEMBER

THIS TIME IT'S RUBE'S TURN

It's not unusual for a fighter to climb off the canvas to win a world title. But James (Rube) Ferns had to climb back into the ring.

In October 1900, Ferns had lost the welterweight title to Matty Matthews, whom he had defeated six weeks before. Ferns-Matthews III came on May 24 at the Crescent Athletic Club in Toronto. It was a close affair.

Before the 10th round, Matthews made a critical mistake when he chose to stand during the rest period. He seemed fatigued in the 10th, and Ferns capitalized. So eager was the challenger that he rushed at Matthews and went flying through the ropes and onto the press table. Upon climbing back into the ring, he resumed his attack. Seconds later, a left hook dropped Matthews for the count.

In the future, the pair would meet three more times, with Ferns winning twice. The final scorecard in the division's first great rivalry: Ferns four, Matthews two.

COCKY CORBETT ROCKS McGOVERN

A round for the ages, a major upset, and a title change, all in one fight!

Denver's cocky Young Corbett won the world featherweight title on November 28 in Hartford, Connecticut, knocking reigning king Terry McGovern out cold after 1:44 of the second round. What was truly remarkable, however, was that Corbett, 21, beat the champion at his own game.

The first round was fairly even, but in the second, Corbett, a 5-1 underdog, and the rugged McGovern clashed toe to toe. Corbett broke through first, scoring a knockdown with a counter right. Upon rising, the champion fearlessly attacked, and the featherweights resumed their frenetic pace. Succumbing to McGovern's reckless blows, Corbett fell to one knee. But figuring it was his turn, he fought back, and another right exploded on McGovern's chin. The champion crashed hard, his head hitting the canvas with a thud. He was counted out, and revived moments later with a smelling bottle.

"You can keep the title, Terry," an indignant Corbett said afterward. "I'm satisfied just to be known as the guy who kayoed Terry McGovern."

Young Corbett II (right) scored a startling upset by knocking out featherweight champion Terry McGovern to win the crown, Hartford, Connecticut, November 28.

WORLD TITLE FIGHTS

HEAVYWEIGHTS

Nov 15	**James J. Jeffries** *KO* 6 Gus Ruhlin, San Francisco

MIDDLEWEIGHTS

March 4	**Tommy Ryan** (USA) *KO* 17 Tommy West, Louisville

WELTERWEIGHTS

April 29	**Matty Matthews** *ref* 20 Tom Couhig, Louisville
May 24	**James (Rube) Ferns** *KO* 10 Matty Matthews, Toronto
Sept 23	**James (Rube) Ferns** *KO* 9 Frank Erne, Ft. Erie, Ontario
Dec 18	**Joe Walcott** (BAR) *KO* 5 James (Rube) Ferns, Ft. Erie, Ontario

FEATHERWEIGHTS

April 30	**Terry McGovern** *KO* 4 Oscar Gardner, San Francisco
May 29	**Terry McGovern** *KO* 5 Aurelio Herrera, San Francisco
Nov 28	**Young Corbett** *KO* 2 Terry McGovern, Hartford

BANTAMWEIGHTS

Nov 11	**Harry Forbes** (USA) *KO* 2 Dan Dougherty, St. Louis

JANUARY

1902

DECEMBER

A CHAMP WHO CAN'T BE HURT

Before challenging heavyweight champion Bob Fitzsimmons in 1899, James J. Jeffries bet $5,000 against himself. He wasn't planning to throw the fight, but, as he explained, if he lost, he would need the money, and if he won, he wouldn't miss it.

Jeffries lost his bet but won the title via 11th-round kayo. His fifth defense, on July 25, was a long-awaited rematch with Fitzsimmons, who was 39 and seemingly at the end of an extraordinary career.

For eight rounds, Fitz pounded the champion, breaking Jeffries' nose and opening deep cuts on both cheeks and over each eye. But Jeffries was as close as there's ever been to a fighter who could not be hurt, and in the eighth, he knocked out Fitz with a left hook.

DAILY SPARRING WITH A MIRROR

Immortal Joe Gans won in one round.

In 1900, world lightweight champion Frank Erne dominated Baltimore's Joe Gans, stopping him on a cut in the 12th round. The Swiss-born boxer's method was predictable: he controlled Gans with his extraordinary jab.

Preparing for a title fight rematch, Gans tried to teach his sparring partners how to jab like Erne. But none of them could master the punch, so Gans spent hour after hour in front of a mirror, first playing the part of Erne, then switching to himself. He was convinced that if he could solve the champion's jab, the rest of the fight would be easy.

The rematch was held May 12 in Fort Erie, Ontario, and Erne lasted 100 seconds. He would never again contest the crown.

Frank Erne never challenged again.

REVENGE IN THE STYLE OF JACK JOHNSON

Jack Johnson's rise to the world title was neither steady nor smooth. Over the first six years of his career, he struggled, crisscrossing the country and spending several homeless nights. He never forgot a single one of them.

Frank Childs, a local heavyweight, housed him for a brief time, but that arrangement ended during the wee hours of a bitterly cold winter night due to the unexpected arrival of a cousin. Johnson pleaded, but Childs only pointed to the door.

With fate as his matchmaker, Johnson squared off with Childs on October 21 in Los Angeles. Far superior, the future champion could have ended the bout as he pleased, but he tortured Childs, punching hard enough to hurt him, but not to knock him out. Knowing that Childs had always boasted of his ability to last the distance, Johnson accelerated in round 12 and forced a stoppage.

RINGSIDE VIEW

JUNE

World welterweight champion Joe Walcott avenges a defeat in 1897 by scoring a 15-round decision over challenger Tommy West.

SEPTEMBER

Fighting in his hometown, Baltimore's Joe Gans retains the lightweight title, knocking out Gus Gardner in the fifth round.

OCTOBER

Defending the featherweight title for the first time since upsetting Terry McGovern, Young Corbett stops Joe Berstein in the seventh round.

DECEMBER

Illinois' Harry Forbes completes a marvelous year by retaining the world bantamweight title for the fourth time, scoring a seventh-round TKO over Frankie Neil.

WORLD TITLE FIGHTS

HEAVYWEIGHTS

July 25	**James J. Jeffries** *KO* 8 Bob Fitzsimmons, San Francisco

MIDDLEWEIGHTS

Sept 15	**Tommy Ryan** *KO* 6 Kid Carter, Ft. Erie, Ontario

WELTERWEIGHTS

June 23	**Joe Walcott** *ref* 15 Tommy West, London

LIGHTWEIGHTS

May 12	**Joe Gans** (USA) *KO* 1 Frank Erne, Ft. Erie, Ontario
June 27	**Joe Gans** *KO* 3 George McFadden, San Francisco
July 24	**Joe Gans** *KO* 15 Rufe Turner, Oakland
Sept 17	**Joe Gans** *KO* 5 Gus Gardner, Baltimore
Oct 13	**Joe Gans** *KO* 5 Kid McPartland, Ft. Erie, Ontario

FEATHERWEIGHTS

Oct 16	**Young Corbett** *KO* 8 Joe Berstein, Baltimore

BANTAMWEIGHTS

Jan 23	**Harry Forbes** *KO* 4 Dan Dougherty, St. Louis
Feb 27	**Harry Forbes** *ref* 15 Tommy Feltz, St. Louis
May 1	**Harry Forbes** *D* 20 Johnny Reagan, St. Louis
Dec 23	**Harry Forbes** *KO* 7 Frankie Neil, Oakland

JANUARY

1903

DECEMBER

YOUTH GIVEN BEATING

Fitzsimmons (right) decisioned Gardner for light heavyweight title.

Having won both the world middleweight and heavyweight titles, Bob Fitzsimmons' place in ring history was secure. But after he was twice kayoed by James J. Jeffries, his retirement seemed certain.

In one final moment of glory, however, "Ruby Robert" scored an upset that fooled even the most astute of ring observers. At age 40, he spotted world light heavyweight champion George Gardner 16 years and proceeded to outfight him over the 20-round distance on November 25 at San Francisco's Mechanics' Pavilion.

Fitz scored four knockdowns and was on the verge of scoring a definitive kayo in several different rounds. But lacking the energy of his youth, he wisely rationed his punches, and over the last five rounds, he cruised.

Fitz' victory brought a particularly exceptional distinction: he became the first fighter in history to capture world titles in three different divisions, with the first and third titles coming more than 12 years apart.

WORLD TITLE FIGHTS

HEAVYWEIGHTS

Aug 14	**James J. Jeffries** *KO* 10 James J. Corbett, San Francisco

LIGHT HEAVYWEIGHTS

April 22	**Jack Root** (AUS) *ref* 10 Charles (Kid) McCoy, Detroit
July 4	**George Gardner** (IRE) *KO* 12 Jack Root, Ft. Erie, Ontario
Nov 25	**Bob Fitzsimmons** (ENG) *ref* 20 George Gardner, San Francisco

WELTERWEIGHTS

April 1	**Joe Walcott** *D* 20 Billy Woods, Los Angeles

LIGHTWEIGHTS

Jan 1	**Joe Gans** *WF* 11 Gus Gardner, New Connecticut
March 11	**Joe Gans** *KO* 11 Steve Crosby, Hot Springs, AK
June 29	**Joe Gans** *KO* 10 Willie Fitzgerald, San Francisco
July 4	**Joe Gans** *KO* 5 Buddy King, Butte, MT

FEATHERWEIGHTS

Jan 14	**Young Corbett** *KO* 18 Austin Rice, Hot Springs, AK
Feb 26	**Young Corbett** *D* 20 Eddie Hanlon, San Francisco
March 31	**Young Corbett** *KO* 11 Terry McGovern, San Francisco
Sept 3	**Abe Attell** (USA) *ref* 20 Johnny Reagan, St. Louis

BANTAMWEIGHTS

Feb 27	**Harry Forbes** *ref* 10 Andy Tokell, Detroit
Aug 13	**Frankie Neil** (USA) *KO* 2 Harry Forbes, San Francisco
Oct 16	**Frankie Neil** *D* 20 Johnny Reagan, Los Angeles

THE BIRTH OF THE LIGHT HEAVIES

It was the idea of a Chicago sportswriter named Lou Houseman: a light heavyweight class for boxers too big to compete at middleweight. (Until 1903, anyone scaling more than 158 was classified a heavyweight.) When Jack Root, 168 pounds, and Charles (Kid) McCoy, 173 pounds, clashed at Detroit's Metropolitan Athletic Club on April 22, the idea became reality.

Root quickly established his superiority, and McCoy repeatedly fell to the canvas. He took a seat at least once in every round, and even squatted without being hit. After 10 rounds, the referee awarded the decision, and the newly created title, to Root. The crowd cheered lustily. For Lou Houseman's brainchild, things could only improve.

RINGSIDE VIEW

FEBRUARY

Jack Johnson outpoints "Denver" Ed Martin over 20 rounds in Los Angeles, winning what is called the Black heavyweight title.

SEPTEMBER

San Francisco's clever Abe Attell claims the vacant world featherweight title after scoring a 20-round decision over Johnny Reagan.

GENTLEMAN JIM'S FAREWELL

It didn't matter to former heavyweight champion James J. Corbett that he hadn't had a fight in three years. Nor that the reigning champion, James J. Jeffries, had already knocked him out. Corbett, 36, wanted one final try.

It came on August 14 at Mechanics' Pavilion in San Francisco. Boxing far more aggressively than was his custom, Corbett physically challenged the champion. But to no one's surprise, Jeffries proved far too strong and powerful. There were four knockdowns in all, the last two in the fateful 10th round. Ironically, the kayo blow was a wallop to the solar plexus. More than six years before, Corbett had lost the title when Bob Fitzsimmons had struck with a similar blow.

Corbett (right) was no match for reigning title-holder Jim Jeffries.

JANUARY

1904

DECEMBER

Battling Nelson.

BRITT'S BATTLING WIN

Few doubted that Joe Gans was the world's best lightweight, but his inability to make the 133-pound division limit convinced him to vacate. Jimmy Britt, whom Gans had defeated on a foul, and Battling Nelson were matched for the title on December 20.

For 20 rounds, "The Durable Dane" attacked, but he was unable to reach the slick-boxing San Franciscan. Round after round, Britt frustrated Nelson and helped create his image as a human sponge by landing hundreds of blows without a visible effect. Britt was given the decision, which was accepted by all in attendance but the loser.

"I scored the only knockdown of the fight," Nelson complained, "and had Britt running away."

As it would turn out, Britt would engage in only 23 career bouts. Four of them, however, would come against Nelson. The final score: 2-1-1 for Britt.

Jimmy Britt.

THE REFEREE TAKES A BEATING

World welterweight champion Joe Walcott wasn't overly concerned about the April 28 title challenge of Aaron L. Brown, aka Dixie Kid. And nothing that happened over the first 19 rounds of their scheduled 20-rounder gave him reason to worry.

In round 18, Walcott pounded his foe, and as the bell rang for the start of the final round, the champion seemed sure to win by decision. But throughout the bout, Walcott had been punching to the kidneys and on the break, and when he committed yet another foul, referee "Duck" Sullivan stopped the fight and crowned Dixie Kid champion by the disqualification of Walcott.

Tom O'Rourke, Walcott's manager, and Alex Greggains, one of the bout's promoters, rushed the ring and attacked Sullivan, knocking out two of his front teeth. They were soon joined by a handful of spectators, all of whom had bet on Walcott. Somehow, Sullivan managed to escape with his life.

No one was happy with a world title won in such a manner, and Dixie Kid never defended the crown. In fact, it took him six years to secure international recognition. By then, five more welterweight champions had come and gone.

WORLD TITLE FIGHTS

HEAVYWEIGHTS

Aug 25	**James J. Jeffries** *KO* 2 Jack Munroe, San Francisco

WELTERWEIGHTS

April 29	**Dixie Kid** (USA) *WF* 20 Joe Walcott, San Francisco

LIGHTWEIGHTS

Jan 11	**Joe Gans** *ref* 10 Willie Fitzgerald, Detroit
Oct 31	**Joe Gans** *WF* 5 Jimmy Britt, San Francisco
Dec 20	**Jimmy Britt** (USA) *ref* 20 Battling Nelson, San Francisco

FEATHERWEIGHTS

Feb 1	**Abe Attell** *KO* 5 Harry Forbes, St. Louis
June 23	**Abe Attell** *ref* 15 Johnny Reagan, St. Louis
Oct 13	**Tommy Sullivan** (USA) *KO* 5 Abe Attell, St. Louis

BANTAMWEIGHTS

Oct 17	**Joe Bowker** (ENG) *ref* 20 Frankie Neil, London

RINGSIDE VIEW

FEBRUARY

Featherweight champion Abe Attell retains the crown for the first time, knocking out former bantamweight titlist Harry Forbes in the fifth round.

APRIL

Jack Johnson retains the Black heavyweight title by knocking out Sam McVey in the 20th round of a memorable encounter in San Francisco.

OCTOBER

Joe Gans keeps the lightweight title when Jimmy Britt is disqualified in the fifth round. Less than one month later, Gans relinquishes the title because of difficulty in making weight.

OCTOBER

In a surprise, "Brooklyn" Tommy Sullivan wins the world featherweight title with a fifth-round knockout of Abe Attell.

CHAMPION JEFF EVENS THE SCORE

With the heavyweight title the most precious prize in sports, it is usually the challenger who campaigns for a try at the champion. But in the case of James J. Jeffries-Jack Munroe, it was the champion who pursued the matchup.

On December 20, 1902, Jeffries had boxed a four-round exhibition against Munroe in Butte, Montana. Jeff had never been knocked to the floor in an official bout – a distinction he would hold until his ill-fated comeback effort against Jack Johnson – but in the second round, Munroe surprised the champion by felling him.

Desperate for worthy opponents during his dominant reign, Jeff suggested a challenge by Munroe. The heavyweights clashed on August 26 at Mechanics' Pavilion in San Francisco.

This time, there were no surprises. Jeffries scored three knockdowns in the first round, and two more in the second. In their exhibition bout, Munroe had earned a $250 bonus for lasting the scheduled four rounds. But when it really counted, Jeff made sure he didn't last two.

CHAMP WHO WAS BLIND IN ONE EYE

History would not be kind to Marvin Hart, but for one day, at least, the workhorse from Jefferson County, Kentucky, proved that he was the best heavyweight in the world.

In a bout to crown a new champion, Hart met former light heavyweight titlist Jack Root on July 3 at the Arena in Reno, Nevada. Hart had outpointed Root in November 1902, and in the rematch, he proved far superior. Rising from a flash knockdown, Hart capitalized on his 19-pound weight advantage and overpowered his 171-pound opponent. Root absorbed a steady battering, and referee James J. Jeffries intervened in the 12th round.

Only seven months after knocking out Root, Hart would be dethroned by Tommy Burns. But it wouldn't be until after his death in 1931 that the strapping Kentuckian's secret would be revealed: Hart had won the heavyweight title despite being blind in his right eye.

Marvin Hart (left) kayoed Jack Root (right) in 12th round and claimed the heavyweight title.

JANUARY

1905

DECEMBER

FIGHTING TALK

Because there's no one left for me to fight

JAMES J. JEFFRIES
on why he retired

KAYOED BY BOREDOM

Having defended the world heavyweight title only once a year since 1901, James. J. Jeffries announced his retirement on May 13. Jeff kayoed Jack Munroe in August 1904. His victim had been considered the most deserving challenger, and the giant titlist could no longer find worthy candidates. He decided to work on his considerable acreage in Burbank, California.

The retiring champion chose the fighters to battle for his crown: Kentucky's Marvin Hart and former world light heavyweight champion Jack Root. He refereed the match himself.

AN INGLORIOUS ENDING FOR A GLORIOUS CHAMP

"Eddie," defending light heavyweight champion Bob Fitzsimmons said to referee Eddie Graney, "he hit me in the stomach, and it's all over."

And with that warning, the 42-year-old legend, exhausted and bleeding from the nose and mouth, doubled over on his corner stool and collapsed.

Before an overflow crowd at Mechanics' Pavilion on December 20, Philadelphia Jack O'Brien overcame the catcalls of the fans and the courage of the champion to win by TKO at the bell starting round 14. It was an easy fight for the challenger, who neutralized Fitz' famed power by alternately moving and clinching. From the start, those in attendance screamed for the champion, and O'Brien's tactics enraged them. But he never changed his game, and as a result, Fitz, ever on the attack, took a sustained beating.

As the years passed, the fight took on added significance: with O'Brien immediately jumping to heavyweight, it was the last title fight at light heavyweight for almost nine years. And while Fitzsimmons' final fight did not come until 1914, the triple-crown champion never again threatened for a world title.

RINGSIDE VIEW

MARCH
Scoring the most impressive victory of his career, heavyweight Marvin Hart outpoints Jack Johnson over 20 rounds in San Francisco.

MAY
Lightweight champion Jimmy Britt makes his first defense and scores a 20th-round TKO over Jabez White.

MAY
At London's National Sporting Club, world bantamweight king and local favorite Joe Bowker decisions Pinky Evans over 20 rounds.

SEPTEMBER
Denmark's Battling Nelson wins the world lightweight title by knocking out arch-rival Jimmy Britt with a left hook in the 18th round.

WORLD TITLE FIGHTS

HEAVYWEIGHTS

July 3	**Marvin Hart** (USA) *KO* 12 Jack Root, Reno

LIGHT HEAVYWEIGHTS

Dec 20	**Phila. Jack O'Brien** (USA) *KO* 14 Bob Fitzsimmons, San Francisco

LIGHTWEIGHTS

May 5	**Jimmy Britt** *KO* 20 Jabez White, San Francisco
July 21	**Jimmy Britt** *ref* 20 Kid Sullivan, San Francisco
Sept 9	**Battling Nelson** (DEN) *KO* 18 Jimmy Britt, Colma, CA

BANTAMWEIGHTS

May 29	**Joe Bowker** *ref* 20 Pinky Evans, London

JANUARY

1906

DECEMBER

RINGSIDE VIEW

FEBRUARY

Abe Attell regains the vacant world featherweight title by scoring a 15-round decision over Jimmy Walsh.

OCTOBER

Heavyweight champion Tommy Burns kayos Fireman Jim Flynn in 15 rounds. It is Burns' first defense.

NOVEMBER

Tommy Burns retains the heavyweight title by holding Philadelphia Jack O'Brien to a 20-round draw.

HONEY AND CHEESE

William J. (Honey) Mellody may have had a mellifluous name, but insiders found his credentials to be distasteful.

On October 16 at the Lincoln Athletic Club in Chelsea, Massachusetts, Mellody recovered from a first-round knockdown and scored a 15-round decision over "The Barbados Demon," Joe Walcott. The victory gave the local favorite the welterweight title, which had been vacated by Dixie Kid.

Mellody was instantly regarded as a cheese champion. Many of his key wins had come over aged competition. (Walcott was a tired 33.) Even after outpointing Walcott, Mellody wasn't universally accepted. Walcott claimed that the winner had scaled above the division limit (then 145 pounds). The welters signed for a rematch, and six weeks after their initial encounter, Mellody scored a 12th-round kayo.

A FIGHT GOOD AS GOLD

Battling Nelson (left) squares off with Joe Gans before the lightweight title bout.

Shortly after a gold prospector named Tex Rickard landed in the boomtown of Goldfield, Nevada, he decided to promote a prize fight. If gold put Goldfield on the map, the title fight between Battling Nelson and former king Joe Gans put Rickard on the map.

Rickard's sense of promotion was unmistakeable: he drew nationwide publicity when he displayed the $30,000 purse in tall, neat stacks of freshly minted $20 gold pieces. Newspapermen arrived by the dozen, and more than 8,000 fans attended the fight. (The gate of $90,000 was the richest in history.)

Gans boxed with the speed, stamina, and cleverness of his youth. His only anxious moment came when he broke his hand after landing a shot to Nelson's temple. But he concealed the injury, and took back the title when the Dane, a notorious low puncher, struck south during a 42nd-round clinch.

CHAMPION NAMED NOAH BRUSSO

Marvin Hart, James J. Jeffries' handpicked successor as world heavyweight champion, was a decent fighter, having beaten Jack Johnson. But after Hart was defeated in his first title defense, he was reduced to a footnote on the pages of heavyweight history.

Tommy Burns, the new champion.

Hart's conqueror was a 5'7" French-Canadian from Ontario named Tommy Burns. (Burns, born Noah Brusso, adopted the name of a successful jockey.) The modern era's sixth heavyweight king was more suited to battles at middleweight and light heavyweight, but his quickness and ring intelligence enabled him to record a respectable reign.

On February 23 at the Naud Junction Pavillion in Los Angeles, Burns intentionally infuriated the hot-tempered Hart with a well-timed shove and then easily outboxed him over 20 rounds. At the final bell, referee Charles Eyton unhesitantly raised Burns' hand in victory.

WORLD TITLE FIGHTS

HEAVYWEIGHTS

Feb 23	**Tommy Burns** (CAN) *ref* 20 Marvin Hart, Los Angeles
Oct 2	**Tommy Burns** *KO* 15 Fireman Jim Flynn, Los Angeles
Nov 28	**Tommy Burns** *D* 20 Phila. Jack O'Brien, Los Angeles

WELTERWEIGHTS

Oct 16	**Honey Mellody** (USA) *ref* 15 Joe Walcott, Chelsea, MA
Nov 29	**Honey Mellody** *KO* 12 Joe Walcott, Chelsea, MA

LIGHTWEIGHTS

Sept 3	**Joe Gans** *WF* 42 Battling Nelson, Goldfield, NV

FEATHERWEIGHTS

Feb 21	**Abe Attell** *ref* 15 Jimmy Walsh, Chelsea, MA
March 15	**Abe Attell** *WF* 3 Tony Moran, Baltimore
May 11	**Abe Attell** *D* 20 Kid Herman, Los Angeles
July 4	**Abe Attell** *ref* 20 Frankie Neil, Los Angeles
Oct 30	**Abe Attell** *ref* 20 Harry Baker, Los Angeles
Nov 16	**Abe Attell** *ref* 15 Billy DeCoursey, San Diego
Dec 7	**Abe Attell** *KO* 8 Jimmy Walsh, Los Angeles

ANYTHING BUT A DRAW REQUIRED

When world heavyweight champion Tommy Burns and Philadelphia Jack O'Brien signed for their May 8 title fight rematch in Los Angeles, they agreed to an unusual clause: if the referee judged the bout to be a draw after the scheduled 20 rounds, he had the right to extend it by one round or more. Everyone wanted a conclusive result because the pair had previously fought to a 20-round draw. There was no reason to believe the fight would end inside the distance. At times a reluctant warrior, and always a cautious one, O'Brien had gone the route in 112 of his previous 159 bouts.

As it turned out, referee Charles Eyton had no trouble determining a winner. Burns hunted down the challenger, won 19 of 20 rounds, and retained the crown for the third time.

Before being dethroned by Jack Johnson, Burns would make a total of 11 successful defenses and score knockouts against every challenger except Philadelphia Jack.

Tommy Burns (left) decisioned Philadelphia Jack O'Brien to retain the heavyweight title.

BEATING UP THE BOSS (TWICE)

When Honey Mellody was preparing for his October 1906 welterweight title showdown with Joe Walcott, he hired Providence, Rhode Island's Frank Mantell as a $5-a-day sparring partner. In one of their sessions, the German-born Mantell scored two knockdowns and was promptly fired.

After Mellody won the world title by decisioning Walcott, Mantell, a protege of Jack Johnson, campaigned for a title try. He was made to wait for more than a year, but when a promoter in Dayton, Ohio, made an offer Mellody couldn't refuse, the bout suddenly materialized on November 1.

It was a see-saw affair, and in the 13th round, the champion, a 5-1 favorite, almost scored a knockout. But Mantell kept up his superior infighting, and finished Mellody with a right-left combination in the 15th.

And he made a lot more than $5 for doing it.

Frank Mantell (left) scored a major upset by knocking out Honey Mellody (right).

DESPERATE FOR A KNOCKOUT

Abe Attell frequently augmented his purses with an occasional wager. And before facing Freddie Weeks he took the gamble of his career. He bet $4,000 at 7-1 that he would knock out Weeks in round four. A TKO or disqualification meant that he would lose the bet.

Attell boxed for three rounds and then, at the start of the fourth, suddenly escalated his attack. His first hook felled Weeks, but as the referee was counting him out, DeWitt Van Court, the challenger's manager, began climbing into the ring. So Attell did what he had to do: he knocked him out, too. The referee reached 10, and Attell was $28,000 richer.

JANUARY

1907

DECEMBER

RINGSIDE VIEW

APRIL

Mike (Twin) Sullivan becomes California welterweight champion after decisioning Honey Mellody over 20 rounds.

APRIL

Owen Moran wins the vacant world bantamweight title by scoring a 20-round decision over Al Delmont.

JULY

Australia's Bill Squires lasts less than one round in his challenge of heavyweight champion Tommy Burns.

SEPTEMBER

World lightweight champion Joe Gans retains the title crown with a sixth-round TKO of former champion Jimmy Britt.

WORLD TITLE FIGHTS

HEAVYWEIGHTS

May 8	**Tommy Burns** *ref* 20 Phila. Jack O'Brien, Los Angeles
July 4	**Tommy Burns** *KO* 1 Bill Squires, Colma, CA
Dec 2	**Tommy Burns** *KO* 10 Gunner Moir, London

WELTERWEIGHTS

April 23	**Mike (Twin) Sullivan** (USA) *ref* 20 Honey Mellody, Los Angeles (California World Title)
Nov 1	**Mike (Twin) Sullivan** *ref* 20 Frank Field, Goldfield, NV
Nov 1	**Frank Mantell** (GER) *KO* 15 Honey Mellody, Dayton, OH
Nov 27	**Mike (Twin) Sullivan** *KO* 13 Kid Farmer, Los Angeles

LIGHTWEIGHTS

Jan 1	**Joe Gans** *KO* 8 Kid Herman, Tonopah, NV
Sept 3	**Joe Gans** *KO* 6 Jimmy Britt, San Francisco
Sept 27	**Joe Gans** *ref* 20 George Memsic, Los Angeles

FEATHERWEIGHTS

Jan 18	**Abe Attell** *KO* 8 Harry Baker, Los Angeles
May 24	**Abe Attell** *ref* 20 Kid Solomon, Los Angeles
Oct 29	**Abe Attell** *KO* 4 Freddie Weeks, Los Angeles

BANTAMWEIGHTS

April 22	**Owen Moran** (ENG) *ref* 20 Al Delmont, London

JANUARY

1908

DECEMBER

END OF AN ERA

On July 4, under a merciless sun at the Mission Street Arena in Colma, California, 33-year-old lightweight king Joe Gans learned that time's march is inexorable. Battling Nelson, 26, was the challenger and attacked from the start. For six rounds, Gans summoned the skills that had earned him the nickname "The Old Master". He moved, jabbed, and frustrated his foe.

But in the 12th round, Nelson floored Gans with a right-left uppercut combination. There were knockdowns in the 13th and 16th round before, in the 17th, Gans crashed three times, and referee Jack Welch counted him out.

ENJOYING EVERY SINGLE PUNCH

On Thanksgiving Day Billy Papke should have given thanks that he escaped the ring with his life.

In Colma, California, Papke answered the opening bell as world middleweight champion, having stopped Stanley Ketchel 10 weeks before. But "The Michigan Assassin" had been infuriated by Papke's tactics, and he became obsessed with a rematch.

At the start of their first bout, Ketchel walked to ring center and offered his hand, as was custom. But Papke skipped the ceremony and fired a crushing hook to the jaw. Ketchel never recovered and sustained a terrific beating.

Dominating the rematch, Ketchel told his rival, "It took you 12 rounds to stop a blind man. I'm gonna let your eyes stay open until the 11th so that you can see me knock you out."

He kept his promise, and Papke saw every punch, until the last.

WORLD TITLE FIGHTS

HEAVYWEIGHTS

Feb 10	**Tommy Burns** *KO* 4 Jack Palmer, London
March 17	**Tommy Burns** *KO* 1 Jem Roche, Dublin
April 18	**Tommy Burns** *KO* 5 Jewey Smith, Paris
June 13	**Tommy Burns** *KO* 8 Bill Squires, Paris
Aug 24	**Tommy Burns** *KO* 13 Bill Squires, Sydney
Sept 1	**Tommy Burns** *KO* 6 Bill Lang, Melbourne
Dec 26	Jack **Johnson** (USA) *KO* 14 Tommy Burns, Sydney

MIDDLEWEIGHTS

May 9	**Stanley Ketchel** (USA) *KO* 20 Jack (Twin) Sullivan, Colma, CA
June 4	**Stanley Ketchel** *ref* 10 Billy Papke, Milwaukee
July 31	**Stanley Ketchel** *KO* 3 Hugo Kelly, San Francisco
Aug 18	**Stanley Ketchel** *KO* 2 Joe Thomas, San Francisco
Sept 7	**Billy Papke** (USA) *KO* 12 Stanley Ketchel, Vernon, CA
Nov 26	**Stanley Ketchel** *KO* 11 Billy Papke, Colma, CA

WELTERWEIGHTS

Jan 23	**Harry Lewis** (USA) *KO* 3 Frank Mantell, New Haven, CT
April 23	**Mike (Twin) Sullivan** *ref* 25 Jimmy Gardner, Vernon, CA
Nov 7	**Jimmy Gardner** (IRE) *ref* 15 Jimmy Clabby, Gretna, LA (Louisiana World Title)
Nov 26	**Jimmy Gardner** *D* 20 Jimmy Clabby, Gretna, LA

LIGHTWEIGHTS

May 14	**Joe Gans** *KO* 11 Rudy Unholz, San Francisco
July 4	**Battling Nelson** *KO* 17 Joe Gans, Colma, CA
Sept 9	**Battling Nelson** *KO* 21 Joe Gans, Colma, CA

FEATHERWEIGHTS

Jan 1	**Abe Attell** *D* 25 Owen Moran, Colma, CA
Jan 31	**Abe Attell** *KO* 13 Frankie Neil, San Francisco
Feb 28	**Abe Attell** *KO* 7 Eddie Kelly, San Francisco
April 30	**Abe Attell** *KO* 4 Tommy Sullivan, San Francisco
Sept 7	**Abe Attell** *D* 23 Owen Moran, Colma, CA

BLACK CORONATION AT RUSHCUTTER'S BAY

It is a myth that reigning heavyweight champion Tommy Burns would have preferred to have avoided Jack Johnson. As shrewd a champion as the game has ever known, Burns intentionally gave the impression that he was ducking Johnson. All he was doing, of course, was holding out for a worthwhile purse.

Johnson-Burns opening round.

Finally, an Australian promoter nicknamed "Huge Deal" McIntosh offered Burns an extraordinary guarantee of $30,000 to defend against the black challenger at Rushcutter's Bay, on the outskirts of Sydney. The bout was made for December 26.

Giving away 24 pounds and seven inches, Burns was sadly outclassed from the start. At one point, Johnson exposed his right side and told Burns to hit him with all his might. The champion complied, and Johnson didn't even wince.

Johnson could have ended the fight at will, but he elected to carry Burns. In the 14th round, the police rushed the ring to stop the slaughter, and Johnson was declared the winner.

The news that boxing's first black heavyweight champion had been crowned sparked race riots and lynchings in America. Clearly, the game was changing.

FIGHTING TALK

Jeffries must emerge from his alfalfa farm and remove the golden smile from Johnson's face

JACK LONDON
New York Herald special correspondent after the Johnson-Burns fight

RINGSIDE VIEW

JANUARY

In one of the most thrilling bouts of the modern era, Abe Attell retains the featherweight title by 25-round draw vs. England's Owen Moran.

MAY

Stanley Ketchel kayos Jack (Twin) Sullivan in the 20th round and becomes the first middleweight champion in almost six years.

World Title Fights

HEAVYWEIGHTS

May 19	**Jack Johnson** *ND* 6 Phila. Jack O'Brien, Philadelphia
June 3	**Jack Johnson** *ND* 6 Tony Ross, Pittsburgh
Sept 9	**Jack Johnson** *ND* 10 Al Kaufman, Colma, CA
Oct 16	**Jack Johnson** *KO* 12 Stanley Ketchel, Colma, CA

MIDDLEWEIGHTS

July 5	**Stanley Ketchel** *ref* 20 Billy Papke, Colma, CA

LIGHTWEIGHTS

May 29	**Battling Nelson** *KO* 23 Dick Hyland, Colma, CA
June 21	**Battling Nelson** *KO* 5 Jack Clifford, Oklahoma City

FEATHERWEIGHTS

Jan 14	**Abe Attell** *KO* 10 Freddie Weeks, Goldfield, NV
Feb 4	**Abe Attell** *KO* 7 Eddie Kelly, New Orleans

BANTAMWEIGHTS

June 19	**Monte Attell** (USA) *KO* 18 Frankie Neil, Colma, CA
Dec 17	**Monte Attell** *D* 20 Danny Webster, San Francisco

COSTLY DOUBLE-CROSS

When it became apparent that there was no legitimate competition for world heavyweight champion Jack Johnson, promoters were forced to be creative. Middleweight king Stanley Ketchel was strong enough to kayo heavyweights, and particularly vicious ("He couldn't get enough blood," said manager Dan Morgan), so he was elected.

Legend has it that the fighters met before their October 16 match and agreed to not only minimize the action, but also extend it for the sake of the motion picture exhibitors. After all, Johnson weighed in at 205½, and Ketchel at only 170¼; "The Michigan Assassin" had no chance.

For 11 rounds, it was a relatively polite match. But at the start of the 12th, Ketchel exploded with a right, and the champion crashed to the canvas. He picked himself up, and only seconds later, struck Ketchel with an uppercut. Johnson was not renowned for his power, but the blow was a terrific one: Ketchel was kayoed, and five of his teeth were ripped off at the roots.

Afterward, Johnson was not apologetic. "I must say, though," he commented, " he has given me a sorer chin than I ever had before."

Middleweight champion Stanley Ketchel shocked both the crowd and Jack Johnson when he dropped the heavyweight king in 12th round with Johnson's title on the line.

THE FOURTH AND FINAL CHAPTER

In the historic four-fight grudge of Stanley Ketchel and Billy Papke, the second and third bouts, with Papke winning the middleweight title, and Ketchel subsequently regaining it, were the most significant. But the most competitive bout was their last.

Held on July 4 at the Mission Street Arena in Colma, California, Ketchel-Papke IV was a spectacular brawl. Ringsiders watched the furious first few rounds and concluded that the fight could never go the distance. But champ Ketchel and challenger Papke just kept punching. "Never did I imagine," referee Billy Roche said afterward, "two human beings could stand such punishment."

Both 160-pounders broke their left hands, Papke in round two and Ketchel in round three. Ketchel held an edge from start to finish and took a well-received decision. Given that Papke never wavered, however, observers couldn't help wondering whether "The Michigan Assassin" had lost his kayo punch. One observer who was still convinced of Ketchel's potential was former heavyweight champion John L. Sullivan, who boldly proclaimed, "Ketchel can whip (Jack) Johnson good and plenty." Three months later, Ketchel got his chance.

JANUARY

1909

DECEMBER

Ketchel (left) and Papke.

BROTHERS AND CHAMPIONS

On June 19, Monte Attell, the younger brother of world featherweight titlist Abe Attell, captured the vacant bantamweight title after knocking out Frankie Neil in 18 rounds. The Attells were the first brothers to win world titles.

Where Abe was a master boxer, Monte was more of a puncher. He overpowered the game Neil from the start, and in the 15th round, dropped him with a left to the body. Neil tried to hold on from there, but in the 18th, a single left hook ended his night.

Neil, the world bantamweight champion from 1902 to 1904, had dropped a decision at featherweight to Abe Attell three months before.

Ringside View

FEBRUARY

World featherweight champion Abe Attell stops Eddie Kelly in the seventh round.

MAY

Heavyweight champion Jack Johnson retains the crown after fighting six no-decision rounds with Philadelphia Jack O'Brien.

Jack Johnson

IT'S OFTEN been said that Jack Johnson was ahead of his time. That's giving the future far too much credit.

Not only does Johnson rate among the most significant ring personalities of the modern era, but also among the most fascinating. Consider that Johnson was not only the heavyweight champion as early as 1908, but a black champion who was despised because he dared flaunt his superiority at every turn.

And consider that Johnson found time to master the bass fiddle, work as a house painter, cook, preacher, coral fisher, professional wrestler, dock hand, and stable groom, develop a keen interest in art, literature, and philosophy, marry four times, buy a restaurant in Chicago, jump bail and live in London and Paris, challenge Rasputin to a vodka-drinking contest in pre-revolution Russia, dabble as a matador and secret agent in World War I Spain, peddle Prohibition whisky, open a gym and train fighters, perform as a spear-carrier in a production of *Aida*, and serve nine months of a one-year federal jail sentence.

Finally, consider that his professional ring career spanned 32 years. According to Nat Fleischer, publisher of *The Ring* for more than half a century, Johnson was the greatest heavyweight of all-time.

Johnson, the son of a janitor, was born Arthur John Johnson in Galveston, Texas, on March 31, 1878. He had one brother and three sisters, one of whom repeatedly bruised her knuckles in his defense; as a boy, Johnson earned a neighborhood reputation as a wimp.

At age 12, and facing little more than the hard life of the Galveston docks, Johnson ran way from home. Hopping trains, he landed in Revere, Massachusetts, and found himself begging famed welterweight Joe Walcott for a job as a sparring partner. Johnson only once before had laced a pair of gloves, but Walcott took an interest. The cowardice of the Texan's youth had long ago vanished.

Johnson, however, was hardly an instant success. Before he established himself, there were many homeless nights and empty pockets, and enough injustice to create a hard, bitter man.

The greatest fights of Johnson's career came before he won the world title. His chief rivals were Sam Langford, Joe Jeannette, and Sam McVey, a trio of black fighters who, had they fought in any era but their own, would surely have been world champions. Johnson won what was called the black heavyweight title in February 1903, and over the next five years, he fought McVey three times, Jeannette nine times, and Langford once. He lost only once, to Jeannette on a second-round foul.

John L. Sullivan, the first modern-era heavyweight champion, refused to defend against black contenders,

Arrogant, proud, and supremely confident, Jack Johnson could back up everything he boasted with his extraordinary boxing skills.

Addicted to fast cars (which led to his death) and shapely women (which led to his imprisonment), Johnson, seated beside his wife, about to speed off in a 1913 racer.

and his successors followed the tradition. Nevertheless, after Tommy Burns dethroned Hart in February 1906, Sam Fitzpatrick, Johnson's manager, campaigned for a try at the title. It became popular belief that Burns was ducking Johnson. In reality, he feared no fighter, white or black, and was simply stalling to maximize his potential purse.

After making 11 defenses, Burns agreed to face Johnson. Australian promoter Hugh D. ("Huge Deal") McIntosh guaranteed the champion the handsome sum of £6,000, and on December 26, 1908, the heavyweights squared off before 20,000 fans at Rushcutter's Bay in Sydney.

Convinced that Johnson had a "yellow streak," Burns spotted the challenger six inches in height, 24 pounds, and immeasurable talent. At 6'1¼" and 192 pounds, Johnson combined speed, strength, and punching power as no heavyweight ever had. His jab was at least the equal of Corbett's, and he featured his best weapon, a right uppercut, in a most unusual way: he failed to pivot or move his feet upon delivery. As a result, the punch was almost indefensible.

Floored in each of the first two rounds, Burns was badly outclassed. After a right uppercut dropped him in round 14, the local police chief confronted McIntosh, who was acting as third man, and the fight was stopped. Boxing had its first black heavyweight champion.

Reporting from ringside for the *New York Herald*, Jack London wrote, "The fight, if fight it must be called, was like that between a pigmy and a colossus. A dew drop had more of a chance than (Burns) with the giant Texan."

London called for former champion Jeffries to emerge from his California alfalfa farm "and remove that golden smile from Jack Johnson's face."

(In America, that sentiment would grow during Johnson's reign. After each of his victories, there would be inner city race riots and lynchings of blacks.)

During the course of his seven-year reign, Johnson scored only two title defense victories of note. On October 16, 1909, he met middleweight king Stanley Ketchel, whom he outweighed by 35 pounds. Johnson agreed beforehand to extend the mismatch, but after Ketchel attempted a double-cross by unleashing a knockdown-producing right hand in round 12, the defending champion picked himself up and landed one of his feared right uppercuts. Ketchel collapsed, and was counted out. The punch was so powerful that afterward, several of his front teeth were found embedded in Johnson's glove.

Professional career dates 1897-1928
Contests 107
Won 86
Lost 10
Drawn 11
No-Decisions 0
Knockouts 40
World Heavyweight Champion 1908-1915

On July 4, 1910, Johnson met Jeffries, who, in his absence, had become "The Great White Hope." Jeffries hadn't fought in six years, and it showed. Johnson won as he pleased, scoring the first knockdown of Jeff's career en route to a 15th-round stoppage victory. It was the highlight of his professional life, but soon after, his personal life began to unravel.

In 1911, Johnson married his second wife, Etta Duryea, who committed suicide one year later. And in 1913, he was convicted of violating the Mann Act for having transported Belle Schreiber, who was white, from Pittsburgh to Chicago "for immoral purposes." He was sentenced to one year in prison, but jumped bail and traveled to Europe. Concentrating on the night life of Paris rather than his training, he defended only three times in four years, and grew sadly out of shape.

Johnson, 37, eventually agreed to defend against yet another White Hope, 6'6" Jess Willard, in Havana, Cuba, on April 5, 1915. Promoter Jack Curley had baited the champion by hinting that federal authorities might provide a pardon, especially if Johnson were to return to the States without the title. Whether Johnson indeed threw the fight or not will remain a topic of debate for the ages.

Johnson dominated early, but by the 20th round, the champion was spent. In the 26th, Willard landed a right uppercut, of all punches, and Johnson was counted out. Though immediately after the bout, he was quoted as saying, "I have no excuses to offer, a better and younger man has taken the championship title," he later pointed to a photo of the fateful knockdown as proof that as he lay on the canvas, he casually shielded his eyes from the harsh Havana sun

Curley had secured no deal, and after Johnson returned to the mainland in July 1920, he was taken to Leavenworth Penitentiary in Kansas. A model prisoner, he served nine months. Though he returned to the ring – he fought his last pro fight at age 50 – he was never a factor again.

Johnson lived the rest of his years without controversy – with the exception of repeated speeding incidents. Almost predictably, he died at age 68 in a car accident on June 10, 1946, in Raleigh, North Carolina. With a smile undoubtedly on his face.

This belt, paid for by his admirers, was presented to the champion Johnson in 1910.

RING DECADE

1910-1919

IN GRADING the 10 completed decades of boxing's modern era, historians share no affinity for the years 1910-1920. At first glance, a 10-year span that begins with Jack Johnson and ends with Jack Dempsey, that features 19 of the 20 bouts in the incomparable rivalry between Jack Britton and Ted (Kid) Lewis, that includes such legendary champions as Jimmy Wilde, Georges Carpentier, Benny Leonard, Johnny Kilbane, and Jim Driscoll, would seem the equal of any other. But the era was cheated of its potential, first by lawmakers who, with few exceptions, allowed only no-decision bouts, and then by the first World War, during which seven of the sport's eight titles were frozen. In 1919, the end of the War marked the beginning of better days, both in and out of the ring.

No-decision bouts were meant to legitimize boxing matches, and rid the ring of crooked referees and judges, fixed fights, and betting scandals. As the decade wore on, however, pressure mounted to permit decisions. The issue became the sport's center of controversy.

"I have always been an advocate of decisions in boxing contests of the proper distance, or even in short bouts," wrote famed recordkeeper Thomas S. Andrews in December 1914, "but just now it seems that the real danger lies in permitting decisions in these short-round affairs. The secret of the whole thing is that decisions are wanted to enable the betting fraternity to gamble on the results of the matches.

Jack Dempsey's ferocious kill-or-be-killed style gave boxing a new dimension as well as an unprecedented attraction.

Jack Johnson dominated the decade as one of the world's most controversial figures. Despised by White America, he was adored in Europe.

"As matters now stand, the bettors must lay off or leave the decisions to the newspaper sporting editors. Horse racing has been killed all over the country by the betting abuse, and that is just what will happen to the boxing game if decisions are to be permitted in these short-round affairs. The boxing commissions in the states where the game is legalized had better consider twice before fooling with the buzz saw; better leave the law as it is."

It is difficult to determine whether no-decision bouts proved more frustrating for the boxers who fought them or the historians who recorded them. The only decisive endings came by knockout; all other fights were declared no-decision, and for the purpose of settling bets, predetermined newspapermen at ringside chose the unofficial winner. A look at the results of the day, however, reveals that in many no-decision bouts, both fighters were recorded as winners.

"The old law had some curious side effects," explained the *New York Herald-Tribune*'s Murray Robinson in June 1963. "For instance: a fight manager would rush to the telegraph office in an upstate town to beat his rival Svengali to the wire with a 'popular verdict' (for his boy) story for the many New York City dailies. A fighter with a manager short of wind or flat of foot was out of luck. The stories, incidentally, were never sent collect.

"Because of deadlines, the first account in the office of a fight in, say, Syracuse, would make the Big Town morning papers – and

Ad Wolgast was remarkable when it came to absorbing punishment. It seemed the more he was battered the stronger he became.

they couldn't very well reverse the 'popular verdict' in later editions. But sometimes, a manager's 'connections' worked for him, and his account was accepted even if it finished second on the wire."

No-decision bouts encouraged caution in the ring; as soon as a fighter realized he was overmatched, he would switch into survival mode and stall until the final bell, saving a defeat. As a result, it was difficult to dethrone a champion. Among the few exceptions: Benny Leonard won the lightweight title in May 1917, knocking out Freddie Welsh in the ninth round of a no-decision bout in New York City.

No other fighter suffered from the no-decision phenomenon as much as bantamweight Memphis Pal Moore, who scored a handful of newspaper decisions over reigning world champions like Joe Lynch, Pete Herman, and Kid Williams, but never himself held a universally recognized title. Had Moore campaigned in a different era, he might have become a two- or three-time champion.

No-decision legislation slowed the decade, but the assassination of Archduke Franz Ferdinand in Sarajevo on June 28, 1914, ultimately crippled it. That fateful day, of course, marked the start of World War I. The United States entered the War in April 1917. At the time, seven of boxing's eight world champions were Americans. (The lone exception was Welsh flyweight champion Jimmy Wilde.) Until the end of the decade, title fight activity was all but halted.

Consider:

- Heavyweight champion Jess Willard failed to defend from March 1916 through July 1919, when he was kayoed by Dempsey.
- Light heavyweight champion Battling Levinsky failed to defend from October 1916 through October 1920, when he was dethroned by Georges Carpentier.
- Middleweight champion Mike O'Dowd failed to defend from November 1917 through March 1920.
- Lightweight champion Benny Leonard failed to defend from May 1917 through November 1920.
- Bantamweight champion Pete Herman failed to defend from November 1917 through December 1920, when he was outpointed by Joe Lynch.
- Flyweight champion Jimmy Wilde failed to defend from April 1917 through June 1923, when he was knocked out by Pancho Villa.

Only welterweights Britton and Lewis, who traded the title throughout the decade, remained active champions.

Freddie Welsh, besides being a master boxer and lightweight champion of the world, brought an air of dignity to the sport. A true gentleman, the Welshman was, in fact, urged to run for Parliament. "I am honored," he said, "but I prefer boxing."

The decade's first and last heavyweight title fights, Johnson-Jim Jeffries on July 4, 1910, and Dempsey-Willard exactly nine years later, were the most memorable. Though reluctant and sadly out of shape, Jeffries was destined to wear the tag of Great White Hope. Johnson cruelly toyed with him for 15 rounds, and though his knockout victory could hardly be regarded as an artistic masterpiece, it served a purpose: once and for all, and to the dismay of the masses, the myth of white supremacy had been obliterated.

Dempsey's annihilation of Willard represented the dawn of a new era. Though not initially accepted as a hero, "The Manassa Mauler" was the ring's first superstar, at least in the current sense of the word. In the Roaring Twenties, he would earn millions, and, in the USA, at least, reach a plateau shared only by the likes of Babe Ruth, John Dillinger, Charles Lindbergh, and Rudolph Valentino.

Though, like Dempsey, Benny Leonard's biggest victories were yet to come, the lightweight king was the decade's best fighter. The ring artist met such outstanding competition as Johnny Kilbane, Rocky Kansas, Johnny Dundee, Willie Ritchie, Richie Mitchell, Jack Britton, and Ted (Kid) Lewis. Almost 60 years after Leonard's prime, historians of the lightweight class would place Roberto Duran by his side. No one else belonged.

In a decade dominated by larger-than-life figures like Johnson and Dempsey, perhaps the most intriguing champion was the smallest of all. Wales' Jimmy Wilde stood 5'2½", and scaled anywhere from 94 to 109 pounds. He was skinny and pale, and the first official to license him was brave indeed. Almost miraculously, however, Wilde possessed the kind of power foreign to all but the heaviest-handed of heavyweights. During a period dominated by no-decision bouts across the ocean, "The Mighty Atom's" record was filled with kayos, most of them coming against far bigger foes.

Wilde's reign spanned from 1916 to 1923. Had he boxed today, no one would ever dare suggest that the fighters of the lighter weight classes carry fists of feather.

JANUARY

1910

DECEMBER

MURDERED WITH HIS OWN RIFLE

Relaxing between fights at the Missouri ranch of his close friend, R.P. Dickerson, middleweight champion Stanley Ketchel couldn't help but notice the attractive kitchen cook, one Daisy Johnson. Trouble was, a farmhand, Walter A. Dipley, was infatuated with Miss Johnson.

On October 15, Ketchel was eating a leisurely breakfast when, striking from behind, Dipley shot him with a rifle that had days before been sent to the fighter by his brother. Bleeding profusely from his back, the champion scrambled to his room. That is where he died.

A short time later, law enforcement officials arrested Dipley. He was subsequently convicted of first-degree murder and sentenced to life imprisonment. Ketchel was 24 years old.

NOPE FOR THE GREAT WHITE HOPE

So anxious was the American public for a white fighter to dethrone heavyweight champion Jack Johnson that they turned to a 300-pound, 35-year-old farmer who hadn't fought in five years. But "Great White Hope" James J. Jeffries had never lost a fight, and the bettors made him the favorite.

Promoter extraordinaire Tex Rickard brought the fight to Reno, Nevada, and sold 15,760 tickets to the most significant fight since the beginning of the modern era. Johnson's total purse was an unprecedented $120,000, and Jeffries' $90,000. (Ironically, a considerable portion came from the sale of the film rights. Because of the emotions the bout's result subsequently stirred, most states forbade the showing of the film.)

In the days preceding the July 4 fight, Jeffries battled bouts of depression, and it showed in the ring. Johnson not only dominated, but taunted the former champion as well.

"I devoutly hope I didn't happen to hurt you, Jeff," he would say after landing a crisp combination.

Jeffries, never before downed, finally fell in the 15th round. He was counted out by referee Rickard after his second trip to the floor.

After the news of Johnson's victory spread, there were riots and lynchings throughout the land, and 11 people were killed. Only Jeffries seemed to accept reality. On his train ride back to California, he told a reporter, "I could never have whipped Jack Johnson at my best. I couldn't have hit him. No, I couldn't have reached him in a thousand years."

Inactive more than five years, Jim Jeffries (left) was no match for Jack Johnson.

RINGSIDE VIEW

FEBRUARY

Italy's 19-year-old Frankie Conley dominates from the start and wins the world bantamweight title with a 42nd-round kayo of Monte Attell.

AUGUST

Former lightweight champion Joe Gans, 35, dies of consumption in his native Baltimore.

TOO TOUGH FOR HIS OWN GOOD

Early in his pro career, Battling Nelson engaged in a most unusual contest: he and a rival tied their hands behind their backs and repeatedly rammed heads. The aptly nicknamed "Durable Dane" not only outlasted his foe, but emerged unmarked.

Perhaps it should have surprised no one, then, when, on February 22, Nelson soaked up an inhuman amount of punishment en route to losing the lightweight title to Ad Wolgast.

It was a fierce and mean struggle during which, under a steady drizzle, the fighters punched, bit, and butted. Wolgast held a clear advantage, and by the later rounds, both of Nelson's eyes were closed, and his face was bloodied. Referee Ed Smith suggested surrender: "Never," Nelson replied. "Not me."

But after Wolgast landed a telling right in round 40, Smith intervened. How tough was Nelson? For several years, he still claimed the title because he hadn't been counted out.

WORLD TITLE FIGHTS

HEAVYWEIGHTS

July 4	**Jack Johnson** *KO* 15 James J. Jeffries, Reno

WELTERWEIGHTS

May 4	**Harry Lewis** *KO* 3 Peter Brown, Paris
June 27	**Harry Lewis** *KO* 8 Young Joseph, London
Sept 5	**Jimmy Clabby** (USA) *KO* 13 Guy Buckles, Sheridan, WY (Australian World Title)
Nov 2	**Jimmy Clabby** *KO* 7 Bob Bryant, Sydney
Dec 26	**Jimmy Clabby** *KO* 1 Gus Devitt, Brisbane, Australia

LIGHTWEIGHTS

Feb 21	**Ad Wolgast** (USA) *KO* 40 Battling Nelson, Richmond, CA

FEATHERWEIGHTS

Aug 21	**Abe Attell** *KO* 3 Eddie Marino, Calgary
Sept 5	**Abe Attell** *KO* 17 Billy Lauder, Calgary
Oct 24	**Abe Attell** *ref* 10 Johnny Kilbane, Kansas City
Nov 13	**Abe Attell** *D* 15 Frankie Conley, McDonoghville, LA

BANTAMWEIGHTS

Feb 21	**Frankie Conley** (ITA) *KO* 42 Monte Attell, Vernon, CA
March 6	**Johnny Coulon** (CAN) *KO* 19 Jim Kendrick, New Orleans
Oct 17	**Digger Stanley** (ENG) *KO* 8 Joe Bowker, London
Dec 5	**Digger Stanley** *ref* 20 Johnny Condon, London

FIGHTING TALK

Put a horseshoe in each of his gloves, and bet him $2,500 he can't knock me out

BATTLING NELSON
before his lightweight title defense against Ad Wolgast

THE BEST BANTY IN WORLD BOXING

It's quite unsettling when a world title is disputed, but it's chaos when the top fighters can't decide on their division's weight limit.

Among those claiming the bantamweight title at the start of the new decade were Canada's Johnny Coulon, England's Digger Stanley, America's Monte Attell, and Italy's Frankie Conley. Shortly after, France's Charles Ledoux and America's Eddie Campi would join the fray. Before a sole champion could be crowned, the fighters had to agree on whether to box at 118 pounds (the British limit), 116 (champion Conley's choice), or 115 (champion Coulon's preference).

Johnny Coulon.

Much of the confusion was cleared up on February 3, when Coulon outpointed Conley in what was almost universally regarded as a world title bout. There wouldn't be an undisputed champion, however, until 1914, when Kid Williams would kayo Coulon.

After his fighting days were over, Coulon would gain a different kind of fame. No matter how they struggled, heavyweight champions, from Jack Johnson and Jack Dempsey to Joe Louis and Rocky Marciano, couldn't lift him off the floor. And the former champion scaled only 120 pounds!

Frankie Conley.

World Title Fights

WELTERWEIGHTS

Jan 25	**Harry Lewis** *KO* 4 Johnny Summers, London

LIGHTWEIGHTS

March 17	**Ad Wolgast** *KO* 9 George Memsic, Vernon, CA
March 31	**Ad Wolgast** *KO* 5 Anton LaGrave, San Francisco
April 26	**Ad Wolgast** *KO* 2 One-Round Hogan, New York City
June 27	**Ad Wolgast** *KO* 17 Frankie Burns, San Francisco
July 4	**Ad Wolgast** *KO* 13 Owen Moran, San Francisco

BANTAMWEIGHTS

Feb 26	**Johnny Coulon** *ref* 20 Frankie Conley, New Orleans
Sept 14	**Digger Stanley** *ref* 20 Ike Bradley, Liverpool

Ringside View

JANUARY

The incomparable Jim Driscoll scores an 11th-round TKO of Spike Robson in London. The master boxer from Wales retains the British featherweight title.

JANUARY

1911

DECEMBER

NUMBER ONE, AND GETTING BETTER

It has become accepted that when a fighter wins a world title, he instantly improves. The first example could well have been lightweight champion Ad Wolgast, who in 1910 had taken the crown by outlasting Battling Nelson. Six weeks before, Wolgast had risked his title try by facing bodypunching specialist George Memsic for a second time. He won, but only after twice rising from knockdowns. (In their first battle, Wolgast was knocked down once and lost on points.)

In the rubber match, held on March 17 at the Arena in Vernon, California, Memsic again aimed strictly for Wolgast's body, and again the champion absorbed a battering. But Wolgast landed his punches, too, and Memsic fell in the ninth round.

"I fought far more famous fighters than George Memsic," Wolgast would say later, "but none gave me the trouble I had with him."

WOLGAST NO CHEESE CHAMPION

Even after he won the world lightweight title by kayoing Battling Nelson, and even after he successfully defended it against George Memsic, Anton LaGrave, One-Round Hogan, and Frankie Burns, Ad Wolgast was called a "cheese champion." But after a July 4 date with England's respected Owen Moran, Wolgast sought respect no more.

Unleashing a devastating, non-stop attack aimed mostly at the challenger's body, Wolgast wore down the former bantamweight champion. In round 12, Moran spit out a tooth, and at the start of the 13th, he doubled over after absorbing a tremendous right to the midsection. Wolgast followed with a hook to the jaw, and Moran fell for the count. It was the first time in more than 80 fights that he had been as much as floored.

Cheese no more.

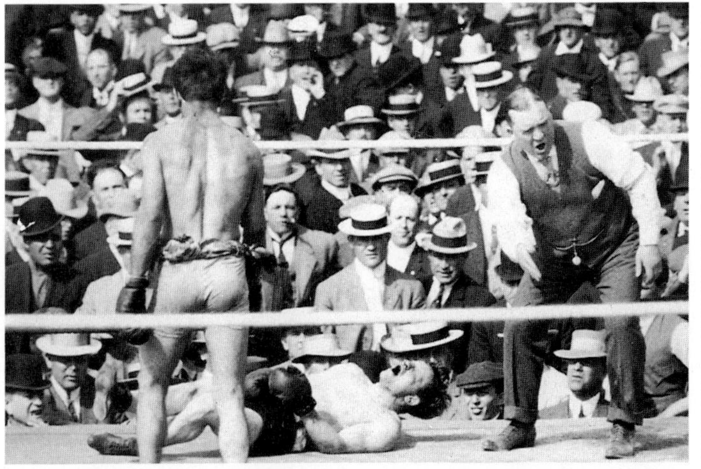

Britain's Owen Moran grimaces in agony after a savage body attack by Ad Wolgast in the 13th.

JANUARY

1912

DECEMBER

RINGSIDE VIEW

JUNE

France's powerpunching Charles Ledoux kayos George (Digger) Stanley in the seventh round and captures the European and British world bantamweight titles.

NOVEMBER

San Francisco's Willie Ritchie takes the world lightweight title from Ad Wolgast by a 16th-round foul. Wolgast is on the verge of a knockout loss when he repeatedly punches low.

DECEMBER

Having taken the featherweight title from Abe Attell in February, Johnny Kilbane successfully defends against former bantamweight king Monte Attell, registering a ninth-round knockout.

WITH A LITTLE HELP

The world lightweight champion Ad Wolgast's defense against Mexico's Joe Rivers was bizarre.

For 12 rounds, Wolgast and Rivers competed evenly. Less than 10 seconds before the end of the 13th, Wolgast delivered a left to the challenger's groin, and, simultaneously, Rivers connected with a hook to the champion's jaw. The punches produced a boxing rarity: a double knockdown!

With many in the crowd screaming that Rivers had been fouled, referee Jack Welsh counted to four. Then he lifted the groggy Wolgast to his feet with his left hand, as he continued to count over Rivers with his right. Trouble was, Rivers had risen at the count of four!

The bell, which Welch later said he never heard, sounded, and the fighters returned to their respective corners. Welch approached Wolgast, raised his arm, and declared him the winner.

Ad Wolgast (right) and Joe Rivers, both groggy, struggle to untangle from the rope.

CAT-NAPPING IN THE CORNER

After Stanley Ketchel's tragic death in October 1910, his archrival, Billy Papke, claimed the middleweight title.

His record didn't support that claim – following Ketchel's passing, Papke won only six of his next 12 bouts. But the veteran nevertheless toured the world, and on December 4, 1912, found himself in Paris, facing local favorite George Bernard.

After six evenly contested rounds, the middleweights returned to their respective corners. Then a most remarkable thing happened: Bernard fell asleep. His cornermen were unable to revive him in time for round seven, and Papke was declared the TKO winner.

Afterward, Bernard claimed he had been drugged. (Given the times, such an excuse could not be easily dismissed.) While the truth was never determined, we can only presume that in his dreams, Bernard knocked Papke out.

A MOST UNWELCOMED BIRTHDAY SURPRISE

Defending the world featherweight title on February 22 (his 28th birthday), Abe Attell figured to outmaneuver Cleveland's Johnny Kilbane, as he had done to dozens of fighters before him. (In October 1910, Attell had scored a 10-round decision over Kilbane.) But on this day, Attell's methods would prove unsatisfactory.

During their first fight, Attell had confused Kilbane with one of his favorite tactics – constant chatter. This time, Kilbane talked back, and in each round, the featherweights traded verbal jabs. All the effective boxing, however, was done by the challenger.

Attell won only one of 20 stanzas, and Kilbane took the title by comfortable 20-round decision. His only scare came in the 16th round, when he fell into a clinch and suddenly felt faint. Pulling back, he asked referee Charley Eaton to wipe down the champion.

Attell, Kilbane later claimed, had a mix of eucalyptus oil and chloroform covering his shoulders. Attell denied the accusation and claimed that it was only cocoa butter.

Abe Attell watches referee raise Johnny Kilbane's hand and proclaim him champion.

WORLD TITLE FIGHTS

HEAVYWEIGHTS

July 4	**Jack Johnson** *W* Disq. 9 Fireman Jim Flynn, Las Vegas, NM

LIGHTWEIGHTS

July 4	**Ad Wolgast** *KO* 13 Joe Rivers, Vernon, CA
Nov 28	**Willie Ritchie** (USA) *WF* 16 Ad Wolgast, Colma, CA

FEATHERWEIGHTS

Feb 21	**Johnny Kilbane** (USA) *ref* 20 Abe Attell, Vernon, CA
May 21	**Johnny Kilbane** *D* 12 Jimmy Walsh, Boston
June 6	**Jim Driscoll** (WAL) *KO* 12 Jean Poesy, London (British World Title)
Oct 14	**Johnny Kilbane** *ref* 12 Ed O'Keefe, Cleveland
Dec 3	**Johnny Kilbane** *KO* 9 Monte Attell, Cleveland

BANTAMWEIGHTS

Feb 3	**Johnny Coulon** *ref* 20 Frankie Conley, Vernon, CA
April 22	**Digger Stanley** *ref* 20 Charles Ledoux, London
June 23	**Charles Ledoux** (FRA) *KO* 7 Digger Stanley, Dieppe, France (British World Title)

FUGITIVE CHAMPION

Jack Johnson never hid his affinity for white women. In fact, he flaunted it, and the heavyweight champion's boldness enraged the white establishment.

In 1910, Congress passed the Mann Act in an effort to crack down on interstate promotion of commercialized vice. In November 1912, law enforcement officials found an excuse to apply the law in regard to Johnson, who was indicted for transporting one Belle Schreiber across several state lines.

Johnson acknowledged that the charges were technically correct. The jury quickly voted for conviction, and Johnson was sentenced by Judge George Carpenter to one year and a day in a federal penitentiary in Joliet, Illinois, as well as a fine of $1,000.

"This defendant," explained Carpenter, "is one of the best-known men of his race, and his example has been far-reaching, and the court is bound to consider the position he occupied among his people. In view of these facts, this case calls for more than a fine."

Johnson subsequently jumped bail and boarded a train for Canada, en route to France.

The world's heavyweight champion was a fugitive.

Johnson when convicted.

JANUARY

1913

DECEMBER

HANGING ON, LIMPLY

With his title defenses seemingly coming as often as Halley's Comet, heavyweight champion Jack Johnson's bout against Battling Jim Johnson, held at Paris' Premierland on December 19, made headlines. While the challenger, a close friend of Johnson's, was only a minor threat, the matchup nonetheless was an historic one. It was the first time in history that two black heavyweights contested for the title.

Without suffering a knockout, Johnson wasn't likely to lose the crown. But the champion received a scare in the third round, when he broke his left arm. For the rest of the fight, he suffered greatly. At various points, he grabbed the top ring rope for support and grimaced as his left arm hung limply at his side. After 10 rounds, referee Emil Maitrot declared the bout a draw. Doubting the validity of Johnson's injury, the crowd booed in disgust.

THE RISE AND FALL OF LUTE

Perhaps no fighter was more representative of the White Hope era than Luther McCarty, a strapping 6'3", 200-pound cowboy from Driftwood Creek, Wild Horse Canyon, Hitchcock County, Nebraska.

McCarty presented questionable credentials – in 1912, he lost to fellow White Hopes Jim Stewart and Jess Willard – but was brilliantly promoted. The public, disgusted by the antics and attitude of world champion Jack Johnson, was desperate for a heavyweight with the proper complexion.

On New Year's Day, Luther McCarty kayoed Al Palzer in a bout recognized by some as a world title fight.

"I will not meet any Negro, but will draw the color line absolutely," he said, sending the message most wanted to hear.

On May 24, McCarty faced the mediocre Arthur Pelkey in Calgary, Alberta. Not a single significant punch was landed. After the fighters separated from a first-round clinch, McCarty, 21, collapsed and was counted out. Eight minutes later, he was dead with a dislocated neck.

RINGSIDE VIEW

JANUARY

Wales' "Peerless" Jim Driscoll retains the British world featherweight crown by holding Owen Moran to a 20-round draw.

APRIL

England's Sid Smith outpoints Eugene Criqui over 20 rounds and captures the world flyweight title, which had been vacant for 16 years.

Luther McCarty (right), the original "Great White Hope", and Arthur Pelkey.

WORLD TITLE FIGHTS

HEAVYWEIGHTS

Dec 19	**Jack Johnson** *D* 10 Battling Jim Johnson, Paris

MIDDLEWEIGHTS

March 5	**Frank Klaus** (USA) *W* Disq. 15 Billy Papke, Paris
Oct 11	**George Chip** (USA) *KO* 6 Frank Klaus, Pittsburgh

LIGHTWEIGHTS

July 4	**Willie Ritchie** *KO* 11 Joe Rivers, San Francisco

FEATHERWEIGHTS

Jan 27	**Jim Driscoll** *D* 20 Owen Moran, London
April 29	**Johnny Kilbane** *D* 20 Joe Dundee, Vernon, CA
Sept 16	**Johnny Kilbane** *ref* 12 Jimmy Walsh, Boston

BANTAMWEIGHTS

June 24	**Eddie Campi** (USA) *ref* 20 Charles Ledoux, Vernon, CA (European World Title)

FLYWEIGHTS

April 11	**Sid Smith** (ENG) *ref* 20 Eugene Criqui, Paris
June 2	**Bill Ladbury** (ENG) *KO* 11 Sid Smith, London

JANUARY

1914

DECEMBER

RINGSIDE VIEW

JANUARY

Denmark's Waldemar Holberg becomes the first universally recognized welterweight champion in three years by scoring a 20-round decision over Ray Bronson.

APRIL

Jack "The Giant Killer" Dillon reigns as the first world light heavyweight champion since 1905 when he outpoints Battling Levinsky over 12 rounds.

TWENTY ROUNDS, AND NO ONE PAID

Acknowledging that no man was capable of unseating heavyweight champion Jack Johnson from the throne, Paris-based promoter/ manager Dan McKetrick thought "Mary Ann" deserved a try. Mary Ann was the pet name given to White Hope Frank Moran's right hand, a powerful blow that could knock out the sturdiest of fighters.

McKetrick thought he managed Moran. When the challenger arrived in Paris with a new handler, the promoter was suspicious.

Acting upon a premise that Moran owed him $25,000 from previous loans, McKetrick ordered his lawyer, Lucien Cerf, to impound the promotion's take at the Bank of France. The money could be withdrawn only upon presentation of a document signed by McKetrick and both fighters. Johnson cooperated, but Moran agreed to sign nothing.

The fight, held on June 27 at the Velodrome d'Hiver, was unexceptional, Mary Ann making few appearances, and Johnson easily winning by 20-round decision. Then came the drama: Cerf died in battle, and McKetrick couldn't find the pertinent papers. As it turned out, the money stayed in the bank.

Johnson, already broke, was out $20,000, and McKetrick was left wondering why he hadn't become an accountant.

IN THE NAME OF BROTHERLY LOVE

Promoter Johnny Weismantel planned an unexceptional club-show for Brooklyn's Broadway Sporting Club on the night of April 6. In the main event, Joe Chip, the younger brother of world middleweight champion George Chip, was to meet Al McCoy, a local southpaw with average skills. Weismantel sold most of the house's tickets, and when Chip pulled out with an injury, he did what he had to do to keep the show alive: he asked George to substitute.

Chip was confident that the work required would be minimal.

McCoy and Chip stood toe to toe for about 90 seconds, at which point the challenger landed a looping left and knocked Chip cold.

Joe Chip would avenge his brother's loss by knocking out McCoy in April 1919. Unfortunately for the Chips, his victory would come almost two years after McCoy had lost the title.

WORLD TITLE FIGHTS

HEAVYWEIGHTS

June 27	**Jack Johnson** *ref* 20 Frank Moran, Paris

LIGHT HEAVYWEIGHTS

April 14	**Jack Dillon** (USA) *ref* 12 Battling Levinsky, Butte, MT
June 15	**Jack Dillon** *ref* 12 Bob Moha, Butte, MT

MIDDLEWEIGHTS

Jan 1	**Eddie McGoorty** (USA) *KO* 1 Dave Smith, Sydney (Australian World Title)
Feb 7	**Eddie McGoorty** *ref* 20 Pat Bradley, Sydney
March 14	**Jeff Smith** (USA) *ref* 20 Eddie McGoorty, Sydney
April 6	**Al McCoy** (USA) *KO* 1 George Chip, Brooklyn
April 13	**Jeff Smith** *KO* 16 Pat Bradley, Sydney
June 6	**Jeff Smith** *ref* 20 Jimmy Clabby, Sydney
Nov 28	**Mick King** (AUT) *ref* 20 Jeff Smith, Sydney
Dec 26	**Jeff Smith** *ref* 20 Mick King, Sydney

WELTERWEIGHTS

Jan 1	**Waldemar Holberg** (DEN) *ref* 20 Ray Bronson, Melbourne
Jan 24	**Tom McCormick** (IRE) *WF* 6 Waldemar Holberg, Melbourne
Feb 14	**Tom McCormick** *KO* 1 Johnny Summers, Sydney
March 21	**Matt Wells** (ENG) *ref* 20 Tom McCormick, Sydney

LIGHTWEIGHTS

April 17	**Willie Ritchie** *ref* 20 Tommy Murphy, San Francisco
July 7	**Freddie Welsh** (WAL) *ref* 20 Willie Ritchie, London

BANTAMWEIGHTS

Jan 31	**Kid Williams** (DEN) *KO* 12 Eddie Campi, Vernon
June 9	**Kid Williams** *KO* 3 Johnny Coulon, Vernon, CA

FLYWEIGHTS

Jan 26	**Percy Jones** (WAL) *ref* 20 Bill Ladbury, London
March 26	**Percy Jones** *ref* 20 Eugene Criqui, Liverpool
May 15	**Joe Symonds** (ENG) *KO* 18 Percy Jones, Plymouth, England

GOOD HOURS, LOUSY PAY

After San Francisco's Willie Ritchie won the world lightweight title in 1912, Frederick Hall Thomas, who had been renamed Freddie Welsh because he hailed from Wales, campaigned for a try at the crown. Welsh had outpointed Ritchie in November 1911, and given his classy skills and boxing-best jab, he saw no reason why he couldn't do it again.

Perhaps Ritchie saw no reason either; when approached about a defense against Welsh at the National Sporting Club in London, he demanded a huge purse. A group of Londoners gathered the money, and Ritchie crossed the ocean for a hefty guarantee of $25,000. The bout took place on July 7.

After 20 rounds, British referee Eugene Corri awarded the title to the challenger by one point, 86½-85½.

The promotion had been a bust, and Welsh wasn't paid a single pound. Legend has it that upon finding out that his $7,000 guarantee had been lost in the promotion, he attacked his manager and bit off part of his ear.

When Ritchie returned to the United States, Welsh followed. He never fought in Britain again.

Welsh (right) beating Ritchie.

END OF A DARK REIGN

A world title fight which remains shrouded in mystery is Jess Willard's 26th-round knockout of defending heavyweight champion Jack Johnson in Havana, Cuba, on April 5.

American promoter Jack Curley convinced Johnson – 37, in debt, and out of shape – to risk the title. He promised $35,000 and, according to Johnson, a guarantee that should Johnson lose, he could return to the United States.

Johnson pounded the 6'6", 230-pound former Kansas farmhand for several rounds. Willard endured, however, and Johnson soon wilted in the 103-degree heat, falling in round 26. He was counted out by referee Jack Welch.

Johnson later claimed that he had taken a dive, pointing to a photograph in which he lay on the canvas while covering his eyes from the brutal sun. Moreover, the Associated Press reported that he rose immediately after Welch had tolled 10. But others reported that he was spent by the 26th round, and had to be revived by his cornermen after the knockout.

Whatever the case, Johnson left Cuba for his native Texas, to visit his 83-year-old mother. Three days later, he was escorted to prison in Leavenworth, Kansas, where he spent 11 months.

Jack Johnson displayed flashes of former brilliance in title-losing bout with Jess Willard.

RINGSIDE VIEW

JUNE

Massachusetts' Mike Glover outpoints London's Matt Wells over 12 rounds to win the world welterweight crown.

JANUARY

1915

DECEMBER

THE GAME'S GREATEST GRUDGE

It was only the second of their 20 tiffs, but on August 31, the world welterweight title fight between defending champion Jack Britton, an Irishman from Clinton, New York, and Ted (Kid) Lewis, a Jew from London, set the tone.

The fighters had met for the first time in March. It was a no-decision affair, but Lewis was the better welter. In the bloody and hotly contested rematch, held at the Armory in Boston, Lewis took the title by decision. It was quite a feat considering that the referee and sole judge had been hand-picked by Britton's manager, "Dumb" Dan Morgan.

WORLD TITLE FIGHTS

HEAVYWEIGHTS

April 5	**Jess Willard** (USA) *KO* 26 Jack Johnson, Havana, Cuba

MIDDLEWEIGHTS

Jan 23	**Jeff Smith** *W* Disq. 5 Les Darcy, Sydney
Feb 20	**Jeff Smith** *ref* 20 Mick King, Melbourne
May 23	**Les Darcy** (AUT) *WF* 2 Jeff Smith, Sydney (Australian World Title)
June 11	**Les Darcy** *KO* 10 Mick King, Sydney
July 31	**Les Darcy** *KO* 15 Eddie McGoorty, Sydney
Sept 4	**Les Darcy** *ref* 20 Billy Murray, Sydney
Oct 9	**Les Darcy** *KO* 6 Fred Dyer, Sydney
Oct 23	**Les Darcy** *ref* 20 Jimmy Clabby, Sydney

WELTERWEIGHTS

June 1	**Mike Glover** (USA) *ref* 12 Matt Wells, Boston
June 21	**Jack Britton** (USA) *ref* 12 Mike Glover, Boston
Aug 31	**Ted (Kid) Lewis** (ENG) *ref* 12 Jack Britton, Boston
Sept 27	**Ted (Kid) Lewis** *ref* 12 Jack Britton, Boston
Oct 26	**Ted (Kid) Lewis** *ref* 12 Joe Mandot, Boston
Nov 2	**Ted (Kid) Lewis** *ref* 12 Milburn Saylor, Boston
Nov 23	**Ted (Kid) Lewis** *KO* 1 Jimmy Duffy, Boston

BANTAMWEIGHTS

Sept 10	**Johnny Ertle** (AUT) *WF* 5 Kid Williams, St. Paul, MN (Claimed World Title)
Dec 6	**Kid Williams** *D* 20 Frankie Burns, New Orleans

FLYWEIGHTS

Oct 18	**Joe Symonds** *KO* 16 Tancy Lee, London

HE MUST'VE SLEPT WELL

The no-decision era was made for Battling Levinsky. A slick boxer, the Philadelphian would be good enough to win the light heavyweight title in 1916. His cautious style allowed him to fight without fear of injury, and he became the most active boxer of his time.

"He'd fight every night if I told him to," said his manager, "Dumb" Dan Morgan.

On January 1, the Battler was ready to go to work. In the morning, he took on Bartley Madden at Brooklyn's Broadway Athletic Club. The 10-round no-decision bout went the distance. In the afternoon, Levinsky crossed the East River to Manhattan and traded with Soldier Kearns in another 10-round no-decision affair. As soon as the bout was over, Levinsky and Morgan motored to Grand Central Station and took a train to Waterbury, Connecticut, for a 12-rounder with White Hope heavyweight Gunboat Smith.

How could Levinsky engage in three fights in one day? He offered a simple explanation: "I never get hurt, and I love money."

Levinsky: three fights in one day.

JANUARY

1916

DECEMBER

THANKS, REF

In June 1914, and only 27 days after Kid Williams won the world bantamweight title, a New Orleans upstart named Pete (Kid) Herman beat up the newly crowned champion over the course of a 10-round no-decision bout. It took Herman 20 months to secure a return, and in order to do so, his manager had to guarantee Williams $5,000. Moreover, Williams was permitted to bring the referee of his choice, Billy Rocap, to New Orleans. As it turned out, that made all the difference.

On February 7, the banties swapped blows for 20 rounds. At the final bell, it was apparent that Herman had done enough to win. But Rocap raised the hands of both fighters, declaring a draw. After all, what were friends for?

RINGSIDE VIEW

FEBRUARY

Wales' Jimmy Wilde, a frail, scrawny flyweight with incredible punching power, wins the world title by kayoing Joe Symonds in 12 rounds.

APRIL

Jack Britton regains the world welterweight title by decisioning arch-rival Ted (Kid) Lewis over 20 rounds.

JULY

Lightweight champion Freddie Welsh retains the title when former champion Ad Wolgast is disqualified in round 11.

WHEN BIG JESS MET MARY ANN

Jack Johnson's reign as heavyweight champion was tarnished by lengthy periods of inactivity. Jess Willard, Johnson's conqueror, did not seem to be in a rush to defend the crown, either. Given the quality of Big Jess' fights, boxing fans may have been fortunate.

At Madison Square Garden on March 25, almost a full year after his victory over Johnson, Willard risked the title against the veteran Frank Moran. It was Tex Rickard's first-ever promotion in New York.

The challenger was still considered dangerous because of his famed right hand, nicknamed "Mary Ann." Willard respected Moran's power, and as a result, their 10-rounder was hideously dull. Aware that he could lose the title only by knockout, the champion was content to box outside of Moran's range, especially after breaking a finger early in the bout.

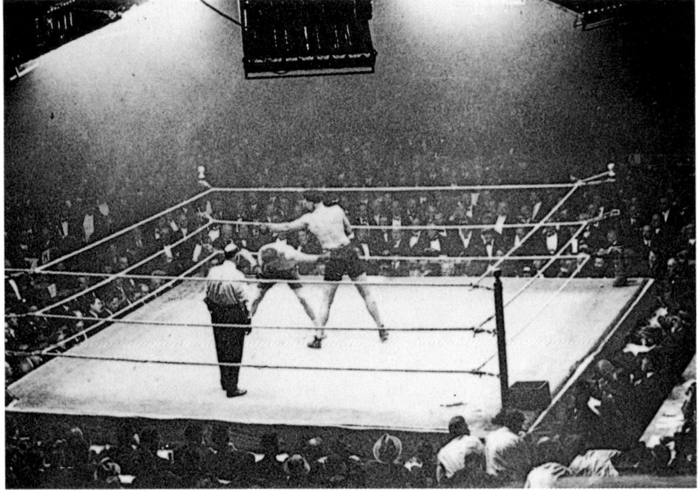

In his first defense, towering Jess Willard (right) decisioned Frank Moran.

Moran never threatened, and by the fifth round, the heavyweights were showered with boos. The bout went the distance, and Willard exited the ring with the title.

If one year seemed like a long time between title fights, Willard's subsequent layoff was interminable. It would be more than two years before he would defend again. But who could blame him for extending the days, weeks, and months before a bout vs. Jack Dempsey?

WORLD TITLE FIGHTS

HEAVYWEIGHTS

March 25	**Jess Willard** *ND* 10 Frank Moran, New York City

LIGHT HEAVYWEIGHTS

April 25	**Jack Dillon** *ref* 15 Battling Levinsky, Kansas City
Oct 24	**Battling Levinsky** (USA) *ref* 12 Jack Dillon, Boston

MIDDLEWEIGHTS

May 13	**Les Darcy** *KO* 5 Alex Costica, Sydney
Sept 9	**Les Darcy** *ref* 20 Jimmy Clabby, Sydney
Sept 30	**Les Darcy** *KO* 9 George Chip, Sydney

WELTERWEIGHTS

March 1	**Ted (Kid) Lewis** *ref* 20 Harry Stone, New Orleans
April 24	**Jack Britton** (USA) *ref* 20 Ted (Kid) Lewis, New Orleans
Oct 17	**Jack Britton** *ref* 12 Ted (Kid) Lewis, Boston
Nov 14	**Jack Britton** *D* 12 Ted (Kid) Lewis, Boston
Nov 21	**Jack Britton** *ref* 12 Charley White, Boston

LIGHTWEIGHTS

July 4	**Freddie Welsh** *WF* 11 Ad Wolgast, Denver
Sept 4	**Freddie Welsh** *ref* 20 Charley White, Colorado Springs, CO

FEATHERWEIGHTS

Sept 4	**Johnny Kilbane** *KO* 3 George (K.O.) Chaney, Cedar Point, OH

BANTAMWEIGHTS

Feb 7	**Kid Williams** *D* 20 Pete Herman, New Orleans

FLYWEIGHTS

Feb 14	**Jimmy Wilde** (WAL) *KO* 12 Joe Symonds, London
April 24	**Jimmy Wilde** *KO* 11 Johnny Rosner, Liverpool
June 26	**Jimmy Wilde** *KO* 11 Tancy Lee, London
July 31	**Jimmy Wilde** *KO* 10 Johnny Hughes, London
Dec 18	**Jimmy Wilde** *KO* 11 Young Zulu Kid, London

A CASE FOR PERSISTENCE

If Jack Britton-Ted (Kid) Lewis was the preeminent grudge series of the era, Battling Levinsky-Jack Dillon was the poor man's version. Both Levinsky and Dillon were accomplished light heavyweights, distinguished by their activity.

On October 24 in Boston, they clashed for the 10th time, with Dillon defending the 175-pound championship. It was Levinsky's 30th fight of the year, and his 173rd over the previous seven years. Dillon hadn't been twiddling his thumbs, either; it was his 164th fight over the same span. In fact, the night before defending against Levinsky, Dillon fought a six-rounder in Philadelphia. Because he had lost only once to Levinsky in their nine previous bouts, the champion was overconfident and ill-prepared, and Levinsky finished with a rush to take the crown.

JANUARY

1917

DECEMBER

IT'S THE KID'S TURN

Jack Britton and Ted (Kid) Lewis always respected each other's abilities, but in the case of their fierce and unique rivalry, familiarity most certainly bred contempt. When Britton defended the world title on June 25, it was the welterweights' 13th meeting, and their fourth in five weeks. Britton and Lewis had grown so accustomed to each other that the latter's corner could no longer offer advice in Yiddish; Britton had long since learned all the phrases.

As per usual, Britton, who labeled Lewis a dirty fighter, refused to shake his opponent's hand before the opening bell.

Promoters across the country were billing the series as English and Jewish (Lewis) vs. Irish and Catholic (Britton), and the participants had begun to believe the hype.

This time around, Lewis' aggressiveness was the difference.

Scoring a 20-round decision victory at Westwood Field, he regained the title that Britton had taken the year before.

Or perhaps more appropriately, he borrowed it back.

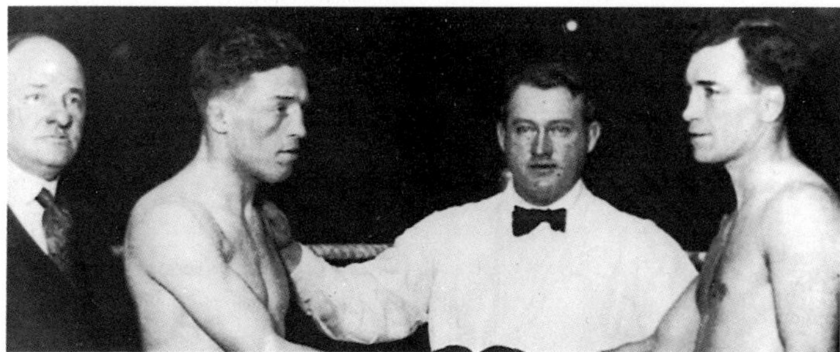

Ted "Kid" Lewis (left) and Jack Britton.

NO REFEREE FAVORS THIS TIME

It wasn't surprising that world bantamweight champion Kid Williams and Pete Herman were rematched in New Orleans. After all, their February 1916 slugfest had ended in controversy. What was surprising, however, was that Herman's camp agreed to allow Williams' hand-picked referee, Billy Rocap, to again serve as third man. Rocap cost Herman the title by declaring the first fight a draw.

In the return on January 9, Herman was even more dominant than he had been 11 months before. He masterfully attacked both the head and body, and Williams couldn't match his work rate.

The bout went the distance once more, but this time, Rocap raised Herman's hand at the final bell. Maybe the fight had been too one-sided for him to hedge.

Or maybe he just wanted to leave New Orleans alive.

FIGHTING TALK

I couldn't sleep at night down there in New Orleans because the bugs kept buzzing around. The bugs were as big as sparrows, and when I got into the ring, I was tired

KID WILLIAMS
after losing his title

HE WASN'T THE "REAL" McCOY

Middleweight contenders were frustrated during Al McCoy's title reign. After winning the crown in April 1914, McCoy fought often, but never while defending the title. In fact, McCoy had 45 non-title bouts, most of the no-decision kind, before risking his championship belt vs. veteran Mike O'Dowd, the "St. Paul Cyclone," at Brooklyn's Clermont Sporting Club on November 14.

Given O'Dowd's credentials – he had mixed with such notables as Jack Britton and Ted (Kid) Lewis – insiders wondered whether the bout was on the level. Had McCoy agreed to sell the title? If he indeed had, he went to extraordinary lengths to make the fight seem legitimate.

In round four, there was a total of six knockdowns, with McCoy falling four times. In the sixth, he crashed five times more, and after knockdown number nine, was counted out.

O'Dowd wouldn't prove to be a particular busy champion either. In fact, he would fail to make a single successful defense. But he had a credible excuse: military service in World War I interrupted his reign, as well as the reigns of boxing's other champions.

Al McCoy.

RINGSIDE VIEW

MARCH

In a tough bout, featherweight champion Johnny Kilbane escapes with a 12-round draw against Eddie Wallace.

MAY

The masterful Benny Leonard kayoes Freddie Welsh in nine rounds and wins the world lightweight title.

WORLD TITLE FIGHT

MIDDLEWEIGHTS			
	Nov 14	**Mike O'Dowd** (USA) *KO* 6	Al McCoy, Brooklyn
WELTERWEIGHTS			
	June 25	**Ted (Kid) Lewis** *ref* 20	Jack Britton, Dayton, OH
LIGHTWEIGHTS			
	May 28	**Benny Leonard** (USA) *KO* 9	Freddie Welsh, New York City
FEATHERWEIGHTS			
	March 26	**Johnny Kilbane** *D* 12	Eddie Wallace, Bridgeport, CT
BANTAMWEIGHTS			
	Jan 9	**Pete Herman** (USA) *ref* 20	Kid Williams, New Orleans
	Nov 5	**Pete Herman** *ref* 20	Frankie Burns, New Orleans
FLYWEIGHTS			
	March 11	**Jimmy Wilde** *KO* 4	George Clark, London
	April 29	**Jimmy Wilde** *KO* 2	Dick Heasman, London

Jimmy Wilde

"IF YOU are one of those little, sawed-off guys, 5-feet-nothing, with arms and legs like broomsticks, don't get that inferiority complex, don't get scared and envious of your lusty brethren, the men with brawn and muscle. Just listen to this story of a little chap who conquered the world – Jimmy Wilde."

—British journalist R. B. Cozzens.

Whether Jimmy Wilde is the best British fighter of all-time will forever remain open to debate. Ted "Kid" Lewis and Benny Lynch will always receive their share of support, and Wilde's mentor and countryman, Jim Driscoll, is also rated at the top. There is little argument, however, concerning Wilde's place among boxing's flyweights. In 1958, *The Ring* editor and publisher Nat Fleischer listed the Welshman as the number-one 112-pounder ever. More than 30 years later, Wilde's status hasn't changed.

No one in the division's 80-year history dominated like Wilde. He was unbeaten in his first 98 fights; he held the crown for seven years and he beat the best on both sides of the Atlantic. But it was not only his accomplishments that made him a remarkable fighter.

Most boxers have a nickname. The special ones might have two. Frail, pale, and skinny, Wilde seemed the prototypical 98-pound weakling. As a result, he collected a handful of monikers, including "The Mighty Atom," "The Human Hairpin," "Indian Famine," and "Ghost With A Hammer." After first meeting Wilde, American manager "Dumb" Dan Morgan noted, "The runt acted more like an office boy than the world champion."

When Wilde first began boxing, he weighed 74 pounds. Promoters repeatedly rejected his requests for fights, fearing they would be held responsible for a serious injury, if not a fatality. (In 1912, Wilde was denied the opportunity to travel to the United States for a series of exhibitions featuring British fighters. Those who made the trip did so on the last voyage of the *Titanic.*) As the Welshman's reputation grew, however, it became apparent that the fighter needing protection was not Wilde, but his opponent. For Wilde was not only an impressive boxer, but also a bone-crackling puncher.

Professional career dates 1910-1923
Contests 145
Won 141
Lost 3
Drawn 1
No-Decisions 0
Knockouts 99
World Flyweight Champion 1916-1923

Welshman Jimmy Wilde is considered the greatest flyweight boxer who ever lived, and, pound for pound, one of the 10 best fighters of all-time. His best fighting weight was about 108 pounds, and he stood just under five feet three inches tall. Wilde's reflexes were uncanny. He seemed to have built-in sensors that alerted him against punches about to be fired his way.

Jimmy Wilde was born on May 5, 1892, in Tylorstown, Glamorganshire, Wales. He grew up in poverty, and followed his father into the coal mines. (At age 15, a mining accident almost cost him his right leg.) He was always drawn to fistfighting; as a child, he fantasized about knocking out Gunner Moir, the top British heavyweight of the day. After marrying Elizabeth Ann Davies at age 18, he was taught boxing's rudimentary skills by his father-in-law, Dai Davies. Among the lessons was bodypunching. Wilde would whale away on his beloved 'Lisbeth, who would be encased in a suit of armor.

Like so many British fighters of the time, Wilde first boxed in booth bouts, which were part of traveling fairs. (It is estimated that when Wilde's booth bouts are added to the 145 bouts on his official record, he engaged in a total of 864 fights.) In Wilde's booth bouts, his promoter, Jack Scarrott, offered one pound to anyone who could last three rounds. It didn't matter that Wilde was regularly matched against men who weighed as much as 170 pounds. Scarrott never had to part with a single pound.

Wilde's first sanctioned bout came in January 1911, when he knocked out Ted Roberts in three rounds. On New Year's Day, 1913, he won his first title, capturing the British 98-pound (or paperweight) crown by stopping Billy Padden in the 18th round. It wasn't until January 1915 that he suffered his first defeat; in a bout for the British and European flyweight titles, he was halted in the 17th round by Scotland's Tancy Lee. He would avenge the loss, and remain unbeaten until the last two bouts of his career.

Wilde's technical skills had been honed by his work with featherweight legend Driscoll. But his exceptional power baffled everyone, including the men of medicine, who regularly studied his body in an effort to unlock the secret. Their examinations revealed nothing.

In February 1916, Wilde won recognition as the world champion with a 12th-round TKO over England's left-hooking Joe Symonds. His first defense was an 11th-round victory over Johnny Rosner. The bout he craved, however, was a return with his sole conqueror.

Wilde (right) squares off with the great Pancho Villa before the 1923 flyweight title fight in New York, in which Jimmy tried, unsuccesfully, to retain the crown. This bout ended Wilde's fabled 13-year career. With a total of 145 bouts, he lost a mere three times, proving that greatness can indeed come in tiny packages.

"If there was a fight I had hankered after..." he said, "it was with Tancy Lee. I wanted to prove beyond all doubt that the previous result had been wrong."

The rematch took place on June 1916, and Wilde gained revenge with an 11th-round stoppage. Before the year was out, he scored one more significant victory, overpowering American champion Zulu Kid, again in 11 rounds.

Over the rest of his career, Wilde would make only one more successful defense. Having eliminated all 112-pound competition, he willingly battled bigger men in lucrative over-the-weight matches. Typical of these bouts was his August 1918 fight with Joe Conn. Spotting his foe almost 20 pounds, Wilde scored six knockdowns in the 10th round and halted Conn in the 12th.

During World War I, sergeant-major Wilde worked as a physical instructor at the Royal Military College at Sandhurst. He also engaged in a handful of top-level contests, including a disputed 15-round decision victory over future world bantamweight champion Joe Lynch, and 20-round verdict over American 118-pound title claimant Memphis Pal Moore.

Toward the end of 1919, Wilde began a six-month tour of the United States, where his reputation was already firmly established. He remained unbeaten over 11 fights, five of which were no-decision affairs.

The first sign that the champion was decelerating came in January 1921, when he squared off against former world bantamweight champion Pete Herman. As usual, Wilde spotted his foe poundage – Herman scaled 121. This time, however, he wasn't able to overcome the handicap, as Herman stopped him in the 17th round.

"I can sincerely say," stated Wilde, "that Herman beat me because he was the better boxer. I do not think there was another bantam to touch him at the time."

Wilde did not fight again until June 1923, when, at age 31, he risked the title against 21-year-old Filipino Pancho Villa before some 40,000 fans at the Polo Grounds in New York City. It is doubtful that Wilde would have triumphed under any circumstances, but after the bell ending round two, Villa drove him to the floor. Wilde never recovered, and sustained a terrific beating until rescued by referee Patsy Haley in the seventh round.

Said Wilde, "I do not recall being knocked out, nor a single thing that happened until, one day three weeks afterwards, I found myself in a little seaside bungalow some distance from New York."

The Villa bout was Wilde's finale. His official record: 141-3-1 (99). His unofficial mark, including booth bouts: 859-4-1.

After leaving the ring, Wilde remained highly visible. Financially secure (despite several failed investments), he became the first president of the National Union of Boxers, and, in his later years, the elder statesman of British boxing.

On March 10, 1969, Wilde died at age 76 in Cardiff. In a sport chock full of great fighters and remarkable stories, he rated with the best on both counts.

This rare photo shows Wilde (right) swarming all over American Joe Lynch during the 1919 bout in London. Although Jimmy appears to be dangerously off-balance, his right foot flying in the air, he was actually in full control, as was almost always the case whenever he plied his trade.

JANUARY

1918

DECEMBER

ALL IN THE SAME CORNER

With World War I severely limiting fight action, action-starved fans flocked to Madison Square Garden on May 24. Among those who helped raise $53,000 were Gunboat Smith, Lew Tendler, Johnny Dundee, Harry Greb, and Battling Levinsky.

Jack Britton and Ted (Kid) Lewis sparked the show. Clashing for the 16th time in a six-round no-decision bout, the welterweights traded punches furiously. In round four, Britton suffered the first knockdown of his career, courtesy of a perfect Lewis left hook.

Britton rose and survived with marvelous ring generalship. However, the consensus was that Lewis had the edge on points.

THE FULTON FOLLY

Minnesota plasterer Fred Fulton stood about 6'3". But in the years to come, as Jack Dempsey's legend would grow, so would Fulton. Hence, historians chronicling Dempsey's rise to the heavyweight title invariably detail his first-round kayo of "the 6'7" Fred Fulton." Talk about tall tales.

On July 27, when Fulton met Dempsey at the old ballpark in Harrison, New Jersey, he was close to a try at reluctant champion Jess Willard. But after 23 seconds with Dempsey, he was close to retirement.

Realizing that he had to crowd his taller foe, Dempsey swarmed from the opening gong. Only 10 seconds into the first round, he exploded with a left and a booming right to the chin. Fulton's knees sagged, his head hit the top rope, and he slid slowly to the canvas. Referee Johnny Eckhardt issued a deliberate count, and at the 23-second mark, Dempsey was declared the winner.

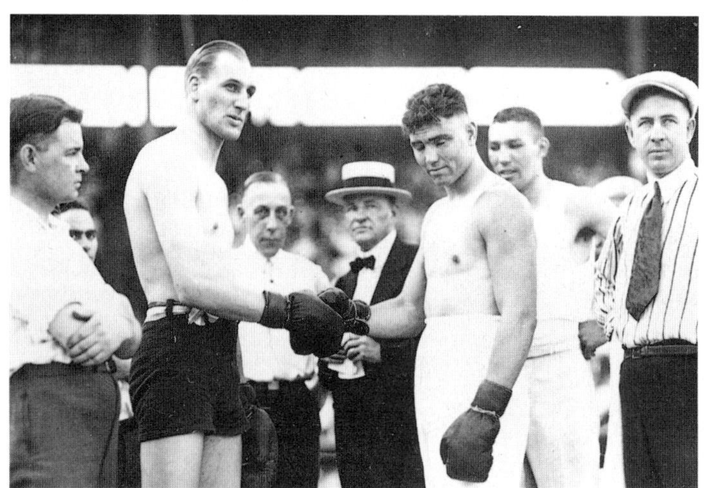

Jack Dempsey pole-axed towering Fred Fulton into senselessness in less than one round.

RINGSIDE VIEW

APRIL

Memphis Pal Moore scores a 15-round referee's decision over Johnny Ertle and claims the world bantamweight title.

MAY

Welterweight champion Ted (Kid) Lewis retains the title by outpointing Johnny Tillman over 20 rounds.

SEPTEMBER

In a disappointingly mild showdown, world champions Benny Leonard (lightweight) and Ted (Kid) Lewis (welterweight) cruise through an eight-round no-decision bout in Newark, New Jersey.

DECEMBER

Heavyweight contender Jack Dempsey completes a fantastic year by knocking out veteran contender Ed (Gunboat) Smith in two rounds in Buffalo.

THE PHAT BOY AND JACK

For one day, at least, boxing bumped World War I off the front page. It happened after the most unlikely of upsets was scored at the Civic Center in San Francisco. Boxing at a benefit for the U.S. Army & Navy Physical Education Fund on September 13, number-one heavyweight contender Jack Dempsey met the flabby, 5'9", cauliflower-eared Willie "Phat Boy" Meehan. California rules limited the bout to a total of four rounds, and so confident of victory was Dempsey's manager, Doc Kearns, that he refused an offer to classify it a no-decision affair.

Dempsey had scored kayos in 11 of his past 12 bouts, and he dropped Phat Boy with a hook to the belly in the second round. As Meehan slumped to the canvas, however, he told his raging foe, "I'm going down, Mr. Dempsey, but I'll be right back up."

Meehan indeed did rise, and proceeded to swing wildly. At the end of the fourth round, referee Eddie Graney raised his hand in triumph, and the 10,000 in attendance howled.

Meehan, a Naval boxing instructor, became an instant cult hero. One cartoon of Phat Boy summed up his popularity. The caption read, "Having polished off the toughest of 'em on this side of the water, he wants to go after the meanest of them all on the other side. 'Now,' he says, 'let me get a crack at the Kaiser!'"

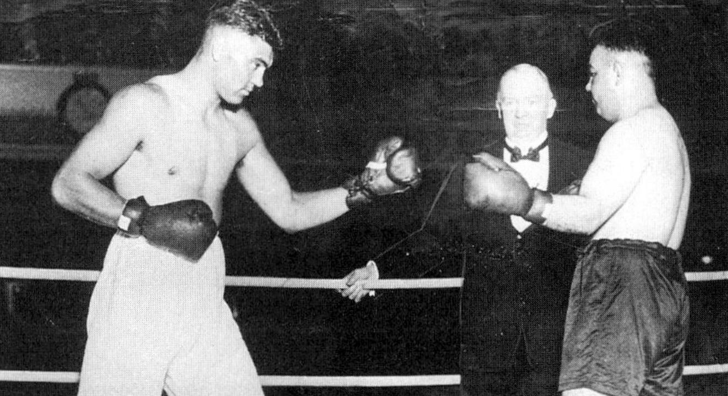

After his knockout of Fulton, Dempsey (left) lost a decision to blubbery Willie Meehan.

WORLD TITLE FIGHTS

WELTERWEIGHTS

May 17	**Ted (Kid) Lewis** *ref* 20 Johnny Tillman, Denver, CO

BANTAMWEIGHTS

April 10	**Memphis Pal Moore** (USA) *ref* 15 Johnny Ertle, Baltimore

UNSPORTSMANLIKE CONDUCT

Perhaps referee Douglas raised the hand of Jimmy Wilde because it had become inconceivable that the Welshman could lose a fight. Before squaring off with American bantamweight Joe Lynch at London's National Sporting Club on March 31, Wilde, the reigning world flyweight champion, had won 29 bouts in a row, including 28 by knockout. He rarely defended the title because of insufficient competition at his weight. As a result, his most challenging battles came against bigger, stronger foes like Lynch. A bone-breaking puncher, Wilde regularly overpowered boxing's best bantams. But over 15 action-packed rounds, Lynch, a future world champion, clearly outworked him.

Douglas' verdict was disputed even by the local scribes.

"No man could have fought more gamely," wrote Edward Wood in England's Daily Sketch, "but (Wilde) was beaten – in my opinion, beaten by every chalk that marks a fight in the ring."

Jimmy "Mighty Atom" Wilde (left) struggled to outpoint America's lanky Joe Lynch in 10 rounds. Wilde's world flyweight crown was not at stake in the London fight on March 31.

ST. PADDY WAS SMILING

As welterweights Jack Britton and Ted (Kid) Lewis engaged in boxing's all-time grudge series, their respective managers, "Dumb" Dan Morgan and Jimmy Johnston, were active participants. Most of the Britton-Lewis bouts were no-decision affairs, and after each one, Morgan and Johnston would race each other to the local telegraph offices and send word of their respective charges' smashing and unequivocal success to newspaper editors across the land.

When Britton regained the title by scoring a ninth-round knockout – the only kayo of the series – on March 17, Morgan was ecstatic. His wires read "Irishman kayos Englishman on St. Patrick's Day!" Among those who were sent the news: the Kaiser, the King of Siam, and King George.

Only the King of Siam, Morgan later reported, took the trouble to reply.

YOUNG AND RUTHLESS ASSASSIN

Ironically, world heavyweight champion Jess Willard was overconfident before his July 4 defense against Jack Dempsey. Willard, 37, had defended the crown only once since kayoing Jack Johnson in 1915, while Dempsey, 24 and active, had scored five consecutive first-round knockouts.

In the most anticipated title fight since Johnson-Jeffries, Willard outweighed Dempsey by 58 pounds. Unsure of the proper approach against such a massive foe, the challenger circled for the first minute of the first round. But caution was foreign to Dempsey, and after Willard missed with a lead, he couldn't help but attack.

What followed was almost beyong belief. Willard fell seven times in the first round, and after nine minutes of combat, the damage included a jaw broken in two places, two fractured ribs, five missing teeth, a closed eye, a squashed nose, and a left ear so battered that Willard would never regain proper hearing.

JANUARY

1919

DECEMBER

Willard retired on his stool at the end of the third round, and boxing had a new champion unlike any it had ever known.

Until his dying day, Willard would maintain that Dempsey's gloves had been loaded. While he could never present any proof, those who had seen Big Jess' face at the Bay View Park Arena in Toledo, Ohio, knew his claim wasn't that far-fetched. Simply put, he had been the victim of the most brutal beating in the modern era's first 20 years.

Dempsey batters Willard to the ropes.

RINGSIDE VIEW

JANUARY

At Albert Hall in London, British and American servicemen, including Memphis Pal Moore, Ted (Kid) Lewis, Harry Greb, Mike O'Dowd, and Eddie McGoorty, engage in exhibition bouts.

APRIL

Lightweight champion Benny Leonard kayes former king Willie Ritchie in the eighth round of a non-title bout in Newark, New Jersey.

JULY

In London, world flyweight champion Jimmy Wilde wins by 20-round decision over Memphis Pal Moore in a non-title bout.

DECEMBER

With ring activity limited by World War I, middleweight contender Harry Greb completes a remarkable 45 fights, outscoring Clay Turner over six rounds in Philadelphia.

WORLD TITLE FIGHTS

HEAVYWEIGHTS

July 4	**Jack Dempsey** (USA) *KO* 4 Jess Willard, Toledo, OH

WELTERWEIGHTS

March 17	**Jack Britton** *KO* 9 Ted (Kid) Lewis, Canton, OH

RING DECADE

1920-1929

BOXING'S personality has always been shaped by the times. Never was this more apparent than in the '20s, a robust decade that was bracketed by the first World War and the Great Depression. As if certain that the good times wouldn't roll forever, the sport packed a handful of critical advances and significant events into a few short years, and by 1930, boxing's enormous potential had been realized.

The unofficial opening of the '20s came on July 4, 1919, in Toledo, Ohio, when Jack Dempsey crushed Jess Willard to win the world heavyweight title. The beginning of Dempsey's reign marked the end of a dark and uncertain decade. While "The Manassa Mauler" was hardly a beloved champion, he became a larger-than-life figure who was as much an integral part of the Roaring Twenties as any other. It is interesting to consider that in his prime, Babe Ruth earned the unheard of sum of $70,000 per year. Dempsey made more than 10 times that for his two bouts with Gene Tunney alone.

Harry Greb overwhelmed opponents with his relentless attacks. Despite ignoring training, he is unquestionably one of the greatest of all-time.

Dempsey carried the kind of punch that thrilled millions, but on May 24, 1920, New York Governor Al Smith flashed the most important right hand in boxing. On that day, Smith signed the Walker Law, which legalized bouts fought to a decision, and also called for a commission to run the sport.

Several states instantly followed New York's lead. The game had taken a large step toward legitimizing itself.

Whether a visionary or an opportunist, Tex Rickard was shrewd enough to capitalize on the ring's growing popularity.

A former prospector, Rickard promoted his first title fight in 1906. But it wasn't until his association with Dempsey and Doc Kearns, the champion's fast-talking manager, that Rickard struck paydirt.

On July 2, 1921, Rickard matched Dempsey with light heavyweight champion and French war hero Georges Carpentier, and boxing was changed forever. Dempsey-Carpentier produced the first million-dollar gate – $1,789,238 to be exact. Though the fight was a predictable mismatch, with Dempsey far bigger and stronger than the 172-pound challenger, no one asked for his money back. Rickard had proved that the event was all that really mattered.

In 1919 came Dempsey's coronation, in 1920, the Walker Law, in 1921, the first million-dollar gate, and in 1922, the perfect complement: the pages on which to chronicle it all.

Dated February 1922, the first issue of *The Ring* magazine was published by Nat Fleischer, the sports editor of the *New York Telegram*, Ike Dorgan, Rickard's press agent, and two additional partners who were soon bought out. *The Ring* was initially limited in scope; Fleischer and Dorgan targeted it for a New York audience. But before long it grew, first nationally, then internationally.

Jack Dempsey's unique magnetism ushered in the era of boxing's million-dollar gates. His war with Luis Firpo in 1923 was outstandingly thrilling.

A few months after launching the magazine, Fleischer awarded Dempsey the first *Ring* championship belt, which remains a universal symbol of fistic supremacy. In 1925, Rickard compiled *The Ring*'s first set of ratings, and the magazine had become "The Bible of Boxing."

Just as Jack Johnson-James J. Jeffries was the biggest bout of the decade past, heavyweight title fights dominated the headlines. Making only six defenses in seven years, Dempsey was the least active long-term champion in history.

Furthermore, he never traded blows with the most deserving contender, Harry Wills, because of Rickard's reluctance to again promote a white-black matchup. Still, Dempsey created magic wherever he fought, from Shelby, Montana, which was bankrupt by his 1923 defense against Tommy Gibbons, to New York City, where, 10 weeks later, he was knocked out of the ring before chopping down Luis Firpo. Dempsey-Tunney I and II, the latter

Gene Tunney was never forgiven for defeating the idolized Dempsey. He was the first to retire as undefeated heavyweight champion.

featuring the long-count controversy, turned Dempsey from antihero to hero, and in the years to come, he would assume his role as the fight fraternity's preeminent statesman.

Smothered in class both in the ring and out, Tunney was a drastically different kind of champion. The erudite New Yorker flaunted considerable talents, but many dismissed him as a fancy dan. The reputation was undeserved; his courage and fighting instincts had been established over the course of his five-fight series with Harry Greb.

Tunney's lone fault, of course, was that he wasn't Dempsey.

Folk hero Will Rogers summed up the public's sentiment when he pined, "Let's have prize fighters with harder wallops and less Shakespeare."

Rogers should have turned to the middleweight division, where champions like Greb, Tiger Flowers, and Mickey Walker were much more thumper than thespian. It was in the '20s that the 160-pounders became boxing's bad boys and brawlers; hours after their title fight in July 1925, Greb and Walker resumed their battle on the streets of Broadway.

Mickey Walker won both the welterweight and middleweight crowns, and in 1929, unsuccessfully challenged light heavyweight king Tommy Loughran. (In the '30s, he would compete evenly with the best of the heavyweight division, too.) "The Toy Bulldog" was managed by Doc Kearns, and in 1961, John Lardner wrote, "Doc would send Mickey up a hill against a ton of sliding rock, if the price was right." Mickey, of course, would've marched without question. Pound for pound, he might've been the toughest fighter in boxing history.

Harry Greb was never described as pretty, either. During the free-wheeling prime of the Prohibition era, he displayed an insatiable appetite for women and liquor. But especially women. Before one of his bouts with Chuck Wiggins, Greb's manager, Red Mason, approached his dressing room from ringside, only to find Greb's door bolted shut. "A woman?" he asked the security guard. "Two," the guard replied.

"The Human Windmill" fought so often that he couldn't possibly ever have partied himself out of condition. Engaging in a total of 299 bouts, the last 90 or so while blind in one eye, he outgutted most of the opponents, and outfouled the rest. His favorite combination, it was said, was a butt under the chin and a left into the groin.

Clever Tommy Loughran often delighted crowds, and frustrated opponents, by finishing rounds in his corner, where all he had to do was sit down.

The middleweights of the '20s were colorful, but also doomed. Both Greb and his conqueror, Tiger Flowers, died at age 32. Oddly, both passed while undergoing facial surgery. Those who believe that tragedies come in threes point to the fact that in 1925, reigning flyweight champion Pancho Villa died at age 23 from blood poisoning. The best of times turned out to be the worst of times, too.

The heavyweights and middleweights weren't the only divisions to produce exceptional talent. Tommy Loughran, who won the light heavyweight title in 1927, was the best fighter in that class' 27-year history. Benny Leonard reigned supreme at lightweight, and Panama Al Brown, who would be a feature player of the 1930s, won the bantamweight crown in 1929.

Perhaps the decade's fastest-rising fighter, however, was Tony Canzoneri, who, from 1927 to 1929, fought for the world title in three divisions. (In the Thirties, he would win the lightweight and junior welterweight titles and become a triple-crown champion.)

If the Dempsey-Willard title fight unofficially opened the decade, the Great Depression closed it. Suddenly, the money of the ring was far too precious to turn down. The desperation of the day was most sadly exemplified by Leonard, who, as 135-pound champion, had retired in 1925 at the request of his mother. At age 35, the greatest lightweight of all time was forced to make a comeback after being wiped out by 1929's stock market crash.

As it turned out, the good times hadn't rolled forever. But in the rings of the Roaring Twenties, there had been enough of them for a lifetime of memories.

Benny Leonard made boxing an art form with his wizardry. He could watch a future opponent spar only one round and know exactly how to whip him.

JANUARY

1920

DECEMBER

RINGSIDE VIEW

MAY

Johnny Wilson, a tough New York City southpaw who brags of his connections to the mob, wins the middleweight title by outpointing Mike O'Dowd over 12 rounds.

DECEMBER

A lethargic Jack Dempsey saves the world heavyweight title with a come-from-behind 12th-round kayo of Bill Brennan.

PAINFUL FAVOR FOR PAL

Jack Dempsey won the heavyweight title in July 1919, and 14 months went by before he defended it for the first time. Doc Kearns, Dempsey's manager, and promoter Tex Rickard couldn't agree on an opponent, and the champion ultimately picked the challenger, the veteran Billy Miske. It would be the last time Dempsey would fight in a bout promoted by someone other than Rickard. A longtime friend of "The Manassa Mauler," Miske was broke and needed the $25,000 payday. But when Dempsey saw Miske before the September 6 fight, he sensed that his buddy's financial situation wasn't all that was troubling him.

Unbeknownst to the champion, Miske was slowly dying from Bright's Disease, which affected his kidneys. Dempsey took him out quickly, but not gently, scoring a third-round knockout.

Incredibly, Miske fought often after losing to Dempsey. His last bout was a kayo of the formidable Bill Brennan in November 1923.

In his first title defense, Dempsey left Billy Miske a helpless wreck.

On New Year's Day 1924, Miske died. He was 29.

"Billy Miske and Benton Harbor (Michigan)..." Dempsey would later say. "Well, I wish it never happened."

TEX RICKARD BUILDS A SUPERFIGHT

Promoter Tex Rickard was sure that a world title fight between heavyweight champion Jack Dempsey and European titleholder Georges Carpentier could bring boxing's first million-dollar gate. But such an attraction had to be carefully constructed, and by matching Carpentier with light heavyweight champion Battling Levinsky on October 12 at International League Park in Newark, New Jersey, Rickard accomplished two things. Firstly, he secured the charismatic Carpentier much-needed exposure in America. And secondly, he made the Frenchman a world champion.

Carpentier overwhelmed Levinsky, who hadn't officially defended the crown since winning it four years earlier. The champion crashed twice in the second round, and for the count in the fourth. Carpentier was so impressive that the pro-Levinsky fans cheered his departure from the ring.

A few days later, Carpentier sailed for Paris, knowing that on his next trip to the United States, Rickard was sure to make him a wealthy man.

Light heavyweight champion Battling Levinsky (left) and Georges Carpentier weigh in for their title bout at Jersey City.

BOXING BECOMES A FAIR GAME, ONCE AND FOR ALL

In New York State, politicians played ping-pong with boxing for more than 60 years. In 1859, the sport was prohibited. In 1896, the state legislature passed the Horton Law, which legalized 25-round gloved contests. But in 1900, Governor – and future President – Theodore Roosevelt repealed the law.

In 1911, the state tried again, passing the Frawley Law, which allowed no-decision bouts. It was repealed in 1917. Which brings us to the Walker Law, signed by Governor Al Smith on May 24, 1920. In the United States, it was the most significant piece of legislation in the history of the modern era. Boxing was legal again, and bouts that didn't end by knockout could be decided by the referee or judges.

The Walker Law called for a state commission to oversee boxing. Other states followed New York's lead, and boxing was soon thriving nationwide.

WORLD TITLE FIGHTS

HEAVYWEIGHTS

Sept 6	**Jack Dempsey** *KO* 3 Billy Miske, Benton Harbor, MI
Dec 14	**Jack Dempsey** *KO* 12 Bill Brennan, New York City

LIGHT HEAVYWEIGHTS

Oct 11	**Georges Carpentier** (FRA) *KO* 4 Battling Levinsky, Jersey City, NJ

MIDDLEWEIGHTS

March 30	**Mike O'Dowd** *KO* 5 Joe Egan, Boston
May 6	**Johnny Wilson** (USA) *ref* 12 Mike O'Dowd, Boston

WELTERWEIGHTS

May 31	**Jack Britton** *ref* 15 Johnny Griffiths, Akron, OH
Aug 23	**Jack Britton** *D* 12 Lou Bogash, Bridgeport, CT

LIGHTWEIGHTS

Nov 26	**Benny Leonard** *KO* 14 Joe Welling, New York City

FEATHERWEIGHTS

April 21	**Johnny Kilbane** *KO* 7 Alvie Miller, Lorain, OH

BANTAMWEIGHTS

Dec 21	**Joe Lynch** (USA) *W* 15 Pete Herman, New York City

JANUARY

1921

DECEMBER

Ringside View

FEBRUARY

Welterweight champion Jack Britton retains the title by outpointing Ted (Kid) Lewis over 15 rounds. It is the last of their 20 meetings.

NOVEMBER

Italian-born Johnny Dundee becomes the first universally recognized junior lightweight champion when he wins fifth-round disqualification over George (K.O.) Chaney.

MILLION-DOLLAR GATE

When world heavyweight champion Jack Dempsey defended against light heavyweight titlist Georges Carpentier on July 2 at Boyles Thirty Acres in Jersey City, New Jersey, boxing was changed forever. The numbers suggested a title fight 50, if not 75 years later: a guarantee of $300,000 for the champion, and a live gate of $1,789,238.

Dempsey drives Carpentier through ropes.

Too big and strong for the 172-pound French challenger, Dempsey emerged victorious by fourth-round kayo. The real winner, however, was Tex Rickard, who had begun promoting by staging the Gans-Nelson title fight 15 years before. Using techniques far ahead of his time, Rickard manipulated the press, meticulously hyping the fight as good guy vs. bad guy. On fight night, no less than 700 reporters were ringside.

The prefight publicity stills featured Dempsey, who had a reputation as a draft dodger, riveting battleships – in patent leather shoes. And if fans were to believe the stories Rickard pushed in the newspapers, the suave and handsome Carpentier had won World War I singlehandedly.

As the Roaring Twenties would progress, Dempsey's image would change. And Tex Rickard, boxing's first great promoter, would remain an outstanding moneymaking machine.

TOP HATS AND HAND WRAPS

On the night that society came to the fights, Benny Leonard and Richie Mitchell put on a show that the diamond rings and fur coats would never forget.

When Miss Anne Morgan's Committee for Devastated France talked Tex Rickard into promoting a show to benefit their post-war cause, Rickard signed the pair for Madison Square Garden. (Miss Morgan was the sister of multimillionaire banker and financier J.P. Morgan.)

In the very first round, Leonard punched the challenger to the canvas. Then he did it again. And again. There were three knockdowns in all.

As Leonard moved in for the coup de grace, Mitchell beat him to the trigger. A left to the stomach staggered Leonard, and a right to the jaw drove him down. Leonard took a nine-count, and barely survived the round.

After absorbing a few more of Mitchell's rights in the second and third rounds, Leonard took command. Mitchell was floored three times in the sixth, and Benny kept the title.

Miss Anne Morgan's friends had never seen anything like it.

World Title Fights

HEAVYWEIGHTS	July 2	**Jack Dempsey** *KO* 4 Georges Carpentier, Jersey City, NJ
MIDDLEWEIGHTS	March 17	**Johnny Wilson** *W* 15 Mike O'Dowd, New York City
	July 27	**Johnny Wilson** *WF* 7 William Bryan Downey, Cleveland
WELTERWEIGHTS	Feb 7	**Jack Britton** *W* 15 Ted (Kid) Lewis, New York City
LIGHTWEIGHTS	Jan 14	**Benny Leonard** *KO* 6 Richie Mitchell, New York City
JUNIOR LIGHTWEIGHTS	Nov 18	**Johnny Dundee** (ITA) *WF* 5 George (K.O.) Chaney, New York City
FEATHERWEIGHTS	Sept 17	**Johnny Kilbane** *KO* 7 Danny Frush, Cleveland
BANTAMWEIGHTS	July 25	**Pete Herman** *W* 15 Joe Lynch, Brooklyn
	Sept 23	**Johnny Buff** (USA) *W* 15 Pete Herman, New York City
	Nov 10	**Johnny Buff** *W* 15 Jack Sharkey, New York City

FIGHTING TALK

Wilde is the greatest little boxer I have ever seen in my life. That's all I can say

PETE HERMAN
after the Wilde fight

IT WASN'T A WILDE NIGHT

Inactive for more than seven months, flyweight champion Jimmy Wilde bulked up to 109 pounds for his January 13 showdown with former bantamweight king Pete Herman. Wilde gave away 8 pounds, which, by his standards, was inconsequential. But against a future legend like Herman, the weight was decisive. The Prince of Wales saw a brilliant, frantically paced bout that both fighters would subsequently label the toughest of their careers.

After 14 rounds, the bout was quite close. In the 15th, however, Wilde was hurt by a blow to the midsection, and in the 17th, he was driven through the ropes three times. Referee Eugene Corri embraced Wilde and escorted him to his corner. It was only the second time in a 144-bout career that the Welshman had been stopped.

Pete Herman (right) and Jimmy Wilde.

JANUARY

1922

DECEMBER

DID HE WANT TO WIN?

It was curious that 37-year-old welterweight champion Jack Britton was defending against lightweight champion Benny Leonard. The smaller titlist wasn't looking to move up in weight – there was more money to be made at lightweight. Nor was Leonard having weight trouble.

Curious, too, was Leonard's lack of effort. On June 26 at the Velodrome in the Bronx, the 3-1 favorite attacked the counter-punching Britton only on occasion, and trailed on points after 10 rounds. In the 13th, Leonard landed a heavy left to the midsection, and Britton crumpled. Referee Patsy Haley ignored Britton's claim of a low blow and began to count. But before he could reach 10, Leonard raced across the ring and hit his fallen rival one more time. He was disqualified.

Had Leonard bet against himself and fouled on purpose? Or had he, for a split second, allowed his emotions to run free? In the years to come, he would maintain that his final punch was one of passion. Nevertheless, the fight would forever be remembered as odd.

Benny Leonard (left) and Jack Britton.

NO WONDER HE NEVER LOST AGAIN

"For God's sake, don't stop it!"

Round after round, defending U.S. light heavyweight champion Gene Tunney pleaded with referee Kid McPartland. And round after round, Tunney fought on in what turned out to be as close to a human sacrifice as the ring had ever seen.

Ten seconds into the first round of his May 23 bout vs. the fierce Harry Greb, Tunney's nose was broken. Later in the round, a huge gash was opened over his left eye. And in the third, Greb busted up Tunney's right eye, too. One postfight estimate suggested that over the course of the 15 rounds, Tunney lost two quarts of blood.

"The gore was so thick on Greb's gloves that he had to step back and hold them out so the referee could wipe them off with a towel," wrote ringside observer James R. Fair. The loss would tell much about Tunney. Two days after, with his face looking "as though he'd taken the wrong end of a razor fight," as Grantland Rice wrote, he marched to the offices of the New York boxing commission and posted a $2,500 bond for a rematch. The bloodbath vs. Greb would be his only loss.

FIGHTING TALK

Not even Dempsey gave me as rough a time as Greb did

GENE TUNNEY

after fighting Harry Greb

RINGSIDE VIEW

JUNE

Georges Carpentier retains the light heavyweight title by scoring a first-round kayo of former welterweight champion Ted (Kid) Lewis, who scales only 157 pounds.

NOVEMBER

Twenty-one-year-old Mickey Walker captures the world welterweight crown with a 15-round decision over veteran Jack Britton.

TRIPPING TO THE WORLD TITLE

Battling Siki lived an extraordinary life. As a teenager, he was brought from his native Senegal to France by a society woman who kept him. He became a hero in World War I, winning the Croix de Guerre for singlehandedly wiping out a machine gun post.

Challenging Georges Carpentier on September 24 in Paris, Siki fell often in the early rounds. But once he hurt the champion, he didn't let up. In the sixth round, Carpentier was rescued by his corner. Referee Henri Bernstein, however, elected to disqualify Siki for tripping. When it looked as if a riot was breaking out, the decision was reversed, and Siki, a hero all over again, was crowned.

Georges Carpentier faces Battling Siki (left).

WORLD TITLE FIGHTS

LIGHT HEAVYWEIGHTS

June 11	**Georges Carpentier** *KO* 1 Ted (Kid) Lewis, London
Sept 24	**Battling Siki** (SEN) *KO* 6 Georges Carpentier, Paris

MIDDLEWEIGHTS

Feb 21	**William Bryan Downey** (USA) *ref* 12 Frank Carbone, Canton, OH (Ohio World Title)
May 15	**William Bryan Downey** *ref* 12 Mike O'Dowd, Columbus, OH
Aug 14	**Dave Rosenberg** (USA) *W* 15 Phil Krug, Bronx, NY (Vacant New York World Title)
Sept 18	**Jock Malone** (USA) *ref* 12 William Bryan Downey, Columbus, OH
Nov 30	**Mike O'Dowd** *WF* 8 Dave Rosenberg, Brooklyn

WELTERWEIGHTS

Feb 17	**Jack Britton** *D* 15 Dave Shade, New York City
June 26	**Jack Britton** *WF* 13 Benny Leonard, Bronx, NY
Nov 1	**Mickey Walker** (USA) *W* 15 Jack Britton, New York City

LIGHTWEIGHTS

Feb 10	**Benny Leonard** *W* 15 Rocky Kansas, New York City

JUNIOR LIGHTWEIGHTS

July 6	**Johnny Dundee** *W* 15 Jack Sharkey, Brooklyn
Aug 28	**Johnny Dundee** *W* 15 Pepper Martin, New York City

FEATHERWEIGHTS

Aug 15	**Johnny Dundee** *KO* 9 Danny Frush, Brooklyn (Vacant New York World Title)

BANTAMWEIGHTS

July 10	**Joe Lynch** *KO* 14 Johnny Buff, Bronx, NY
Dec 21	**Joe Lynch** *W* 15 Midget Smith, New York City

JANUARY 1923 DECEMBER

Ringside View

MARCH

Light heavyweight champion Battling Siki makes the mistake of defending in Dublin against Mike McTigue on St. Patrick's Day. Predictably, he is dethroned via a 20-round decision.

JULY

In the toughest fight of his lightweight title reign, Benny Leonard scores a unanimous 15-round decision over southpaw Lew Tendler.

THE KAYO OF SHELBY, MONTANA

The leaders of Shelby, Montana, (population 2,000) brought heavyweight champion Jack Dempsey to their oil town by promoting a July 4 title defense vs. Tommy Gibbons. When Dempsey and manager Doc Kearns left, they had Shelby in their pockets.

Shelby promised Kearns and Dempsey three separate installments of $300,000. The promoters barely met the first pay date. Then, after spending a small fortune to build a 40,000-seat fight site, they charged $50 for a ringside seat – and sold few tickets. Forced to compromise for installment number two, Kearns agreed to deliver Dempsey only after arranging to secure the fight night box office receipts.

The show was a financial and artistic disaster. Rowdy fans lassoed down the fences, and at least half of the 20,000 were gatecrashers. Gibbons was too fast for Dempsey, who retained the crown after 15 dreadful rounds.

Having collected more than $200,000, Kearns and Dempsey snuck out of town on a specially chartered train. After learning that a shaken Shelby had gone bankrupt, Kearns said, "They're lucky that I didn't sue them for the rest of the dough."

Jack Dempsey (left) and Tommy Gibbons.

A LITTLE HELP FROM THE SCRIBES

No one ever claimed that Argentina's Luis Angel Firpo was a skilled fighter, but he was 6'3" and 216 pounds, and on September 14, before more than 80,000 fans at the Polo Grounds, he proved he could hit. In fact, "The Wild Bull Of The Pampas" nearly took the heavyweight title.

The first round started spectacularly, when Firpo connected with a right that dropped Dempsey to one knee. The champion bounced up and proceeded to explode, scoring knockdown after knockdown, seven in all.

Before the bell, however, Firpo threw a desperation right that found Dempsey's chin. The champion flew through the ropes and out of the ring. Against the rules, he was shoved back by the boxing writers and survived until the round's end.

In the second, Dempsey dropped Firpo three more times, and at the 57-second mark, referee Gallagher counted him out.

Almost 30 years later, Firpo's knockdown of Dempsey would be voted the most dramatic sports moment of the century so far.

Jack Dempsey knocks out Luis Firpo in the second round to retain the crown.

CHAMP WITH STEEL CHIN

Eugene Criqui was on guard duty in the Verdun sector of his native France. Without warning, a German sniper's bullet struck him in the mouth, and passed through his neck. He was lucky to live. After reconstructive surgery – a sheep's rib replaced his jawbone, and skin was grafted over it – he defied his doctors by insisting he'd fight again.

With metal plates lining the inside of his mouth, Criqui suffered only two losses in six years, and at the Polo Grounds on June 2 overpowered featherweight king Johnny Kilbane to complete one of the most improbable comebacks in ring history by winning a world title.

World Title Fights

HEAVYWEIGHTS

July 4	**Jack Dempsey** *ref* 15 Tommy Gibbons, Shelby, MT
Sept 14	**Jack Dempsey** *KO* 2 Luis Angel Firpo, New York City

LIGHT HEAVYWEIGHTS

March 17	**Mike McTigue** (IRE) *ref* 20 Battling Siki, Dublin

MIDDLEWEIGHTS

Jan 9	**Lou Bogash** (ITA) *KO* 11 Charley Nashert, New York City (Vacant New York World Title)
July 24	**Jock Malone** *ref* 12 William Bryan Downey, Columbus, OH
Aug 31	**Harry Greb** (USA) *W* 15 Johnny Wilson, New York City
Dec 3	**Harry Greb** *W* 10 William Bryan Downey, Pittsburgh

LIGHTWEIGHTS

July 23	**Benny Leonard** *W* 15 Lew Tendler, Bronx, NY

JUNIOR LIGHTWEIGHTS

Feb 2	**Johnny Dundee** *W* 15 Elino Flores, New York City
May 30	**Jack Bernstein** (USA) *W* 15 Johnny Dundee, New York City
Dec 17	**Johnny Dundee** *W* 15 Jack Bernstein, New York City

FEATHERWEIGHTS

June 2	**Eugene Criqui** (FRA) *KO* 6 Johnny Kilbane, New York City
July 26	**Johnny Dundee** *W* 15 Eugene Criqui, New York City

FLYWEIGHTS

June 18	**Pancho Villa** (PHIL) *KO* 7 Jimmy Wilde, New York City
Oct 11	**Pancho Villa** *ref* 15 Benny Schwartz, Baltimore

Benny Leonard

PERHAPS the greatest compliment paid to Benny Leonard was that in an era flaunting Jack Dempsey, Harry Greb, Mickey Walker, Jack Britton, Ted (Kid) Lewis, Johnny Kilbane, and Jimmy Wilde, he was considered the greatest champion of all.

During Leonard's prime, an argument was regularly waged as to whether he or Joe Gans was the best lightweight of all-time. In 1969, Gans was unofficially relegated to second place when *The Ring* named Leonard best lightweight in boxing history. Today, Roberto Duran is compared to him, but no one else. Clearly, his legend has not faded.

On April 7, 1896, Benjamin Leinert was born to Gershon and Minny Leinert, a pair of Yiddish-speaking immigrants from Russia who had settled on the Lower East Side of New York City. (The name was changed after a ring announcer introduced the fighter as Benny *Leonard.*) Gershon toiled in a sweat shop to support his eight children. Education was stressed to all of them, but the neighborhood was tough, and a youngster's reputation was established on the streets, not in the classrooms. Leonard's older brother Charlie became an accomplished amateur lightweight. But Benny was frail and skinny, and there was little reason to believe that he would follow. His spirit, however, was a fighting one. At age 11, he had his first "bout," fought on a plot of grass outside the Silver Heel Club, of which two of his uncles were members. His opponent was a local product named Joey Fogarty. They swung wildly, and then split 50 cents.

Leonard would fill out to a solid 5'5" and 135 pounds, but it was his cerebral approach that would ultimately distinguish him from his peers. Leonard studied styles as much as he sparred (rumor was that he honed his reflexes by play-boxing with a tomcat), and capitalized on his opponents' weaknesses as much as his own strengths. As a result, he absorbed a minimal amount of punishment, which, in the beginning, was a good thing; he kept his boxing a secret from the family, and a black eye or fat lip would have been a giveaway.

Leonard could fool his parents for only so long. One day he was confronted by his father, who demanded to know whether he had been fighting. Leonard nodded yes, and then placed a $20 bill into his father's hand.

"When do you fight again?" asked Gershon Leinert.

Leonard turned pro at age 16. In his debut, he was stopped in three rounds by one Mickey Finnegan. Almost all of his bouts were no-decision affairs, but his boxing skills allowed him to outclass all but the most experienced of opponents. One exception was the veteran Joe Shugrue, who, in March 1912, kayoed Leonard in his 11th bout. Toward the end of 1914, however, Leonard teamed with manager Billy Gibson, who began to move him at a proper pace. Within two years, the slick fighter was facing the finest 135-pounders in the world.

Leonard (right) squares off with durable Rocky Kansas before the start of the 1922 bout in which Benny easily retained the lightweight crown.

Before trying for the title, he was tested by Johnny Dundee, whom he would meet a total of eight times, Kilbane, Joe Mandot, Rocky Kansas, Richie Mitchell, and world champion Freddie Welsh.

On May 28, 1917, at the Manhattan Casino in New York City, Leonard clashed with Welsh for the third time. The title was at stake, but because it was a no-decision bout, Leonard could be crowned only by scoring a kayo. The knockout came in round nine. At age 21, Benny Leonard could look forward to a mountain of $20 bills.

Leonard would hold the title for eight years and defend it five times. What marked his reign was his extraordinary skill, but also his confidence and pride. Four months after winning the title, Leonard ignored the color bar by taking consecutive bouts against the best black lightweights of the era, Leo Johnson and Eddie Dorsey. Aware that Leonard was obsessed with the grooming of his hair, Johnson playfully patted him on the head during prefight instructions, then, with one quick swipe, ruined his coiffure. Leonard answered by knocking him out inside of a minute.

During World War I, Leonard taught hand-to-hand combat to soldiers and toured the country in an extended series of over-the-weight matches. His most impressive victory came on July 25, 1917, when he kayoed Kilbane in three rounds. Leonard also squared off against the best of the welterweights, including Britton and Lewis. He remained exceptionally active, but failed to defend the crown for the first three years of his reign. Finally, on July 5, 1920, he risked the championship against powerpuncher Charley White in Benton Harbor, Michigan. He stopped the challenger in the ninth round, but not before being knocked through the ropes by one of White's hooks.

Leonard's most exciting defense came on January 14, 1921, against Richie Mitchell at Madison Square Garden. Before the bout, infamous gambler Arnold Rothstein asked the champion how tough a fight he anticipated. Leonard boasted that he would score a first-round kayo. Rothstein then stated his intentions of betting $25,000 – at generous odds – on that very outcome. And Leonard jumped at the chance for 10 percent of the action.

At the sound of the opening bell, Leonard tore across the ring. His first punch felled Mitchell, and only seconds later, he scored two more knockdowns. Desperate to finish his foe before three minutes had elapsed, Leonard moved in for the *coup de grace*. But Mitchell fired a desperation haymaker that found Leonard's chin, and now it was the *champion* who was lying flat. (He would survive until the end of the round and halt Mitchell in round six.) (The ultimate irony: after the fight, Leonard learned that Rothstein hadn't made the wager after all.)

A handsome, articulate master boxer, Benny Leonard was the most idolized Jewish fighter who ever lived.

Professional career dates 1911-25, 1931-32
Contests 213
Won 180
Lost 21
Drawn 6
No-Decisions 6
Knockouts 69
World Lightweight Champion 1917-1925

Yielding to the prayers of his mother, Leonard retired as undefeated champion in 1925. Six years later, he made an unsuccessful comeback.

On June 26, 1922, Leonard attempted to add the aging Britton's welterweight title to his lightweight crown. He was en route to a comfortable victory when, in round 13, he dropped Britton to one knee with a body blow. With Britton still down, Leonard darted across the ring and released a wallop to his jaw. He was immediately disqualified.

Was Leonard's blatant foul the result of spilt emotion, or a calculated effort to lose the fight? (Those who subscribe to the latter explanation believe that Leonard either bet against himself or figured the 147-pound crown wasn't desirable because it could offer only limited financial opportunities.) The question was never satisfactorily answered.

Leonard's final title defense included his most threatening moment. Slugging with dangerous Philadelphian Lew Tendler on July 23, 1923, the champion was caught by a terrific left. But he stalled Tendler's followup attack by engaging the southpaw in chatter, and by the time Tendler realized he had been conned, the moment was gone.

Concerned with his mother's health – she had fainted during the first round of the Mitchell fight – Leonard retired at her request on January 15, 1925. His investments seemed safe, but 1929's Wall Street crash left him virtually penniless. He returned to the ring in October 1931, and compiled a comeback record of 18-0-1 against limited opposition. But the slow and pudgy Leonard was boxing on memory, and on October 7, 1932, he was kayoed in the sixth round by future welterweight champion Jimmy McLarnin. In an era of ethnic matchups, the baby-faced Irishman had punctuated a long string of victories over Jewish fighters by topping their very best.

Leonard, 36, retired for good with a career mark of 180-21-6 (69) with 6 no-decisions. His life after boxing was rich but short. Leonard made movies, invested in a hockey team in Pittsburgh, served in the Maritime Service during World War II, and became a championship referee. On April 18, 1947, he collapsed and died of a heart attack while working at New York City's St. Nicholas Arena. He was 51. Boxing's greatest lightweight had died in the ring.

JANUARY

1924

DECEMBER

BEATING A LEFTY BY NOT USING A RIGHT

Welterweight champion Mickey Walker knew that his most lucrative defense would come against a challenger from outside the division. His manager, Jack Bulger, and promoter Tex Rickard believed that Walker vs. lightweight king Benny Leonard would produce a second million-dollar gate.

But Leonard didn't seem as anxious to rumble as Walker. To whet the public's appetite (and perhaps Leonard's as well), Walker defended against Lew Tendler, who had given Benny his toughest title fight.

On June 2, Walker-Tendler took place at the Baker Bowl in the challenger's hometown of Philadelphia. A blown-up lightweight, the 142¾-pound Tendler knew he couldn't brawl with Walker. From a distance, however, his southpaw style and considerable skills proved effective.

Walker, a born hooker, stubbornly refused to feature his right hand. He managed to win the fight on his terms. After seven rounds, the bout was even. In the eighth, Walker struck with a big hook. The punch sufficiently weakened Tendler, and Walker eased to a unanimous decision.

However, 29 days later, Leonard left the ring.

WRITER-FIGHTER MAKES HEADLINES

Abe Goldstein grew up as an orphan in New York City. From an early age, he worked at various jobs out of necessity, not choice. Among his assignments was a spell at a local newspaper in the Bronx. At age 15, Goldstein began as a copy boy for $3 a week, and advanced to cub reporter. His favorite beat was boxing.

Though he lacked the temperament of a fighter, Goldstein eventually tried on a pair of gloves and became a skilled pugilist. He turned pro in 1916, and even a 1920 kayo loss to future world champion and fellow New Yorker Joe Lynch didn't put him off

Goldstein slowly advanced into the top 10, and at Madison Square Garden on March 21, he challenged 2-1 favorite Lynch for the title. Lynch had trouble making weight, and Goldstein wisely extended the bout, patiently jabbing in each round. Lynch never threatened, and the title went to Goldstein, even if his pen was mightier than his punch.

WORLD'S TOUGHEST MOMMA'S BOY

Though he wouldn't make the official announcement until January 15, 1925, world lightweight champion Benny Leonard, 28, said goodbye to the ring after a no-decision 10-rounder vs. Pal Moran on August 1.

Abe Goldstein (left) and Joe Lynch.

Leonard's reign began in May 1917, and his successful defenses against such threats as Charlie White, Richie Mitchell, Rocky Kansas, and Lew Tendler had established him as the best boxer in the world. But throughout his glorious days as champion, the New Yorker was guilt-ridden because his mother hated for him to fight.

Against Moran, Leonard sprained his right thumb, and the injury bothered him more than those that had been far more serious.

A big-money welterweight title bout was available against Mickey Walker, but Leonard's mother was ill, and when she made her inevitable request, he couldn't refuse. He would fight no more because his mother had asked him to retire.

Benny Leonard proved to be a great fighter, but a better son.

Benny Leonard retired on his mother's wish. Seven years later, he made a comeback.

WORLD TITLE FIGHTS

MIDDLEWEIGHTS

Jan 18	**Harry Greb** *W* 15 Johnny Wilson, New York City
March 24	**Harry Greb** *KO* 12 Fay Kaiser, Baltimore
June 26	**Harry Greb** *W* 15 Ted Moore, Bronx, NY

WELTERWEIGHTS

June 2	**Mickey Walker** *W* 10 Lew Tendler, Philadelphia
Oct 1	**Mickey Walker** *KO* 6 Bobby Barrett, Philadelphia

JUNIOR LIGHTWEIGHTS

June 20	**Steve (Kid) Sullivan** (USA) *W* 10 Johnny Dundee, Brooklyn
Aug 18	**Steve (Kid) Sullivan** *W* 15 Pepper Martin, Long Island City, NY
Oct 15	**Steve (Kid) Sullivan** *KO* 5 Mike Ballerino, New York City

BANTAMWEIGHTS

March 21	**Abe Goldstein** (USA) *W* 15 Joe Lynch, New York City
July 16	**Abe Goldstein** *W* 15 Charles Ledoux, Bronx, NY
Sept 8	**Abe Goldstein** *W* 15 Tommy Ryan, Long Island City, NY
Dec 19	**Cannonball Martin** (USA) *W* 15 Abe Goldstein, New York City

FLYWEIGHTS

Feb 8	**Pancho Villa** *W* 15 Georgie Marks, New York City
May 30	**Pancho Villa** *W* 15 Frankie Ash, Brooklyn

RINGSIDE VIEW

JANUARY

Middleweight champion Harry Greb repeats his title-winning victory over Johnny Wilson, scoring a one-sided 15-round decision.

JUNE

Brooklyn's Steve (Kid) Sullivan wins the junior lightweight title by decisioning Johnny Dundee over 10 rounds.

HE WON THE TITLE, NO SWEAT

Charley Phil Rosenberg was about 23 years old when he came to a frightening but inevitable metabolic realization: he could no longer eat whatever he wanted without gaining weight.

Reporting for training camp before his bantamweight title challenge of Eddie (Cannonball) Martin, Rosenberg scaled 155, or 37 pounds over the division limit. Off he went to Hot Springs, Arkansas, where the fighter, with the help of trainer Ray Arcel, pulled off an extraordinary feat. For 10 weeks, Rosenberg doubled up his roadwork and took hot baths. At the weigh-in, he scaled 116, two pounds under the limit!

Rosenberg had previously twice lost to Martin, and after five rounds at Madison Square Garden, he appeared en route to a third setback. But he rallied to outbox the Cannonball, and after 15 rounds, Rosenberg captured the title. The weight had been worth it.

THE 16TH ROUND

On July 2, middleweight champion Harry Greb's decision victory over welterweight champion Mickey Walker was as action-packed as a fight between two such warriors would suggest. Outweighing the challenger by seven pounds, Greb was a bit too strong. But Walker had to wait only a couple of hours for revenge.

After the fight, fate reintroduced the free-living combatants inside the taverns of Broadway but it was only after the champions decided to head to Big Bill Duffy's Silver Slipper speakeasy that their talk turned to what had occurred at the Polo Grounds. Feeling no pain, Walker suggested that had Greb not repeatedly thumbed him in the eyes, the outcome would have been different. As an infuriated Greb began to take off his jacket, Walker landed a sucker punch that began a brief gutter brawl.

Eyewitness observers scored unanimously for Walker. After the last punch was thrown, there was no lingering animosity.

Mickey Walker (right) never took a backward step in the entire 15 rounds. But aggression wasn't enough to win Harry Greb's title.

JANUARY

1925

DECEMBER

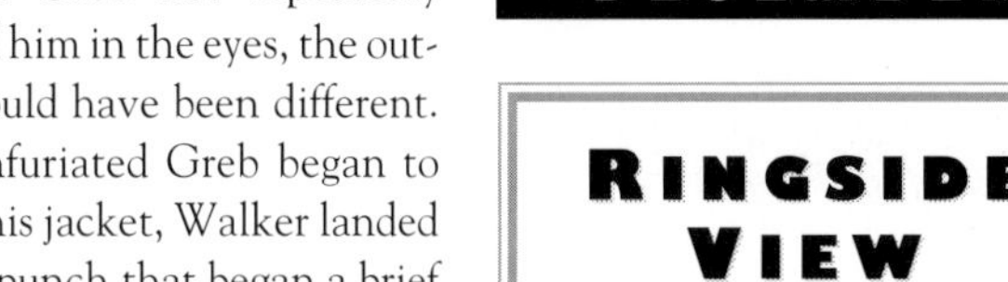

RINGSIDE VIEW

MAY

New York's Paul Berlenbach wins the light heavyweight title by scoring a unanimous 15-round decision over Mike McTigue.

DECEMBER

Headlining the first fight card at the new Madison Square Garden, Paul Berlenbach retains the light heavyweight title by decisioning Jack Delaney.

WORLD TITLE FIGHTS

LIGHT HEAVYWEIGHTS

May 30	**Paul Berlenbach** (USA) *W* 15 Mike McTigue, Bronx, NY
Sept 11	**Paul Berlenbach** *KO* 11 Jimmy Slattery, Bronx, NY
Dec 11	**Paul Berlenbach** *W* 15 Jack Delaney, New York City

MIDDLEWEIGHTS

July 2	**Harry Greb** *W* 15 Mickey Walker, New York City
Nov 13	**Harry Greb** *W* 15 Tony Marullo, New Orleans

WELTERWEIGHTS

Sept 21	**Mickey Walker** *W* 15 Dave Shade, Bronx, NY

LIGHTWEIGHTS

July 13	**Jimmy Goodrich** (USA) *KO* 2 Stanislaus Loayza, Long Island City, NY
Dec 7	**Rocky Kansas** (USA) *W* 15 Jimmy Goodrich, Buffalo

JUNIOR LIGHTWEIGHTS

April 1	**Mike Ballerino** (USA) *W* 10 Steve (Kid) Sullivan, Philadelphia
July 6	**Mike Ballerino** *W* 15 Pepper Martin, Long Island City, NY
Dec 2	**Tod Morgan** (USA) *KO* 10 Mike Ballerino, Los Angeles

FEATHERWEIGHTS

Jan 2	**Louis (Kid) Kaplan** (RUS) *KO* 9 Danny Kramer, New York City
Aug 27	**Louis (Kid) Kaplan** *D* 15 Babe Herman, Waterbury, CT
Dec 18	**Louis (Kid) Kaplan** *W* 15 Babe Herman, New York City

BANTAMWEIGHTS

March 20	**Charley Phil Rosenberg** (USA) *W* 15 Cannonball Martin, New York City
July 23	**Charley Phil Rosenberg** *KO* 4 Eddie Shea, Bronx, NY

FLYWEIGHTS

May 1	**Pancho Villa** *W* 15 Clever Sencio, Manila

A NATIONAL HERO DIES YOUNG

During the week before Pancho Villa's non-title showdown with once-beaten teenage sensation Jimmy McLarnin, the flyweight champion suffered from a terrible toothache. He had grown accustomed to overcoming pain, however, and he answered the opening bell without complaint.

McLarnin easily won on points. Shortly afterward, Villa was hospitalized. The tooth had become ulcerated, and on July 14, he died of blood poisoning.

Pancho Villa, 23, boxing's first world champion from the Philippines, had fought for seven years and made four title defenses.

When Pancho Villa died from blood poisoning, his native Philipines was thrown into mourning. This cartoon appeared on the front page of a Manila newspaper.

JANUARY

1926

DECEMBER

World Title Fights

HEAVYWEIGHTS	
Sept 23	**Gene Tunney** (USA) *W* 10 Jack Dempsey, Philadelphia
LIGHT HEAVYWEIGHTS	
June 10	**Paul Berlenbach** *W* 15 Young Stribling, Bronx, NY
July 16	**Jack Delaney** (CAN) *W* 15 Paul Berlenbach, Brooklyn
MIDDLEWEIGHTS	
Feb 26	**Tiger Flowers** (USA) *W* 15 Harry Greb, New York City
Aug 19	**Tiger Flowers** *W* 15 Harry Greb, New York City
Dec 3	**Mickey Walker** (USA) *ref* 10 Tiger Flowers, Chicago
WELTERWEIGHTS	
May 20	**Pete Latzo** (USA) *W* 10 Mickey Walker, Scranton, PA
July 9	**Pete Latzo** *WF* 4 George Levine, New York City
JUNIOR WELTERWEIGHTS	
Sept 21	**Mushy Callahan** (USA) *W* 10 Pinkey Mitchell, Vernon, CA
LIGHTWEIGHTS	
July 3	**Sammy Mandell** (USA) *ref* 10 Rocky Kansas, Chicago
JUNIOR LIGHTWEIGHTS	
June 3	**Tod Morgan** *KO* 6 Kid Sullivan, Brooklyn
Sept 30	**Tod Morgan** *W* 15 Joe Glick, New York City
Oct 19	**Tod Morgan** *W* 10 Johnny Dundee, San Francisco
Nov 19	**Tod Morgan** *W* 15 Carl Duane, New York City
FEATHERWEIGHTS	
Nov 15	**Dick Finnegan** (USA) *W* 10 Chick Suggs, Boston (Massachusetts World Title)

SO MUCH LIFE, THEN A SUDDEN DEATH

In February, Georgia's Tiger Flowers became the first black middleweight champion when he scored a split 15-round decision over Harry Greb. In August, Flowers repeated the victory. Greb was 32, but there was no reason to think that the living legend was done punching. On September 23, Greb attended the Dempsey-Tunney fight. Less than two weeks later, he was badly hurt in an auto accident.

On October 22 in Atlantic City, Greb underwent surgery that was unrelated to his accident. (Doctors were operating on his nose in an effort to ease his breathing.) During the procedure, Greb went into cardiac arrest and suffered a cerebral hemmorhage. Suddenly he was dead at age 32.

Shortly afterward, his doctor revealed that Greb had been blind in his right eye for the last five years – and 90-plus bouts – of his career. If it were possible, "The Human Windmill" turned out to be even tougher than he seemed.

Gene Tunney, head pall bearer at the funeral.

FIGHTING TALK

Blessed be the Lord my strength, which teacheth my hands to war, and my fingers to fight

TIGER FLOWERS
The 144th Psalm, repeated at the start of each round

A TOOTHLESS TIGER

It was the kind of title fight that was becoming the standard in the middleweight division: two fighters with contrasting styles; hundreds of punches and a couple of knockdowns, but no knockout; a disputable and debatable decision.

On December 3, former welterweight champion Mickey Walker challenged 160-pound titleholder, Tiger Flowers before 11,000 fans at the Coliseum in Chicago. Walker scored a flash knockdown in round one. Then Flowers found his rhythm and began to reach the challenger with long-range combinations.

Walker suffered a cut over his left eye in round four. Falling further and further behind, he kept charging forward, only to be outpunched three to one. "The Toy Bulldog" wasn't easily discouraged, and in the ninth, Flowers fell for the second time. He wisely switched to survival mode.

After 10 brisk rounds, referee Benny Yanger raised Walker's hand. Afterward, he claimed that Walker punched with purpose, Flowers hit with open gloves.

The soft-spoken Flowers was a classy loser. But his manager, Walk Miller, screamed robbery, and the next morning, the Illinois Boxing Commission met to review the verdict. A rematch seemed a safe bet, but it would never happen. Less than one year later, Flowers would be dead.

PICKING TUNNEY – AN EDUCATED GUESS

Both in and out of the ring, heavyweight champion Jack Dempsey and Gene Tunney were opposites. Once a hobo, Dempsey was raw, rugged, instinctive, and as wild as the West. The handsome Tunney, on the other hand, was New York-born and bred, erudite, and as familiar with the characters in Shakespeare as those in the heavyweight top 10.

Feeling pressure to match Dempsey with top black contender Harry Wills, promoter Tex Rickard attempted to first make an elimination bout of Wills-Tunney. But Wills priced himself out of the fight, and Rickard subsequently signed Dempsey and Tunney for Philadelphia's Sesquicentennial Stadium. Despite a steady rain, the attendance was no less than 120,000.

Exhibitions aside, the 31-year-old Dempsey hadn't fought in three years. Lacking the ferocity of his youth, he was no match for the quicker, clever Tunney, who took a unanimous 10-round decision on September 23.

"Honey," Dempsey explained to his wife," I forgot to duck."

Interestingly, the loss turned Dempsey into a fan favorite. He would be the people's choice in the inevitable rematch, and always one to capitalize, Rickard would shamelessly hype it for one full year.

Gene Tunney (left) and Jack Dempsey.

THE BATTLE OF THE LONG COUNT

Jack Dempsey invariably created high drama, so it came as no surprise when his title fight rematch with champion Gene Tunney drew boxing's first $2-million gate. On September 22, Tunney-Dempsey II was fought before 104,493 anxious fans at Chicago's Soldier Field. Tunney's purse was $990,000, and before the fight, he sent promoter Tex Rickard $10,000 so that he, in turn, could be paid a flat $1-million. Dempsey earned $450,000.

The first six rounds were dominated by Tunney's sterling jab. Early in the seventh, however, Dempsey noted that Tunney's guard was low, and attacked with desperation. A right staggered Tunney, and a two-handed volley dropped him near a corner.

Before the opening bell, referee Dave Barry had carefully explained the procedure should either heavyweight score a knockdown. But instead of proceeding to a neutral corner, the challenger stood over Tunney, both his hands grasping the top strand of rope.

Barry shoved Dempsey to a neutral corner, and only then began to count. Tunney rose at nine – he almost surely could have lifted himself up before that – and backpedaled for the remainder of the round. (He had been down for a total of 14 seconds.) He boxed carefully over the last three rounds and kept the crown by unanimous decision.

Heavyweight king Gene Tunney struggles to arise as Jack Dempsey leaps to the attack.

Flyweight champion Fidel LaBarba.

THE FLY AND IVY-COVERED WALLS

Even those who rarely watched fighters outside the heavyweight class acknowledged that Fidel LaBarba was special. In 1924, LaBarba won an Olympic gold medal, and a year later, he outpointed Frankie Genaro to win the American flyweight crown.

LaBarba seemed to be peaking in 1927. (In January, he won the vacant world flyweight crown.) Then in August he retired and enrolled at Stanford University.

As it turned out, the flyweight had been reluctant to turn pro; he did so only to make enough money to pay for college. By the time he was accepted at Stanford, he had earned $250,000 in purses.

LaBarba would remain in school only one year. In July 1928, he returned to the ring as a bantam. But he wasn't smart enough to ever again win a world title.

MIDDLEWEIGHT JINX, PART II

In death, as well as life, Tiger Flowers would forever be linked to Harry Greb. The two biggest victories of the Georgia deacon's career were his 1926 title fight decisions over Greb. Thirteen months after Greb's tragic passing on an operating table in Atlantic City, Flowers met a similar fate.

On November 12, Flowers stopped Leo Gates in four rounds. Four days later, at the Fralick Sanitorium in New York City, he underwent surgery to remove mounting scar tissue from above his eyes. The fighter died of status lymphaticus while under anasthesia – the odds of such a death were estimated as 100,000-1.

When wheeled into the operating room, Flowers, 32, wore his boxing robe and clutched a bible. He repeated, "If I die before I wake, I pray the Lord my soul to take."

WORLD TITLE FIGHTS

HEAVYWEIGHTS

Date	Fight
Sept 22	**Gene Tunney** *W* 10 Jack Dempsey, Chicago

LIGHT HEAVYWEIGHTS

Date	Fight
Aug 30	**Jimmy Slattery** (USA) *ref* 10 Maxie Rosenbloom, Hartford (Vacant NBA Title)
Oct 7	**Tommy Loughran** (USA) *W* 15 Mike McTigue, New York City
Dec 11	**Tommy Loughran** *W* 15 Jimmy Slattery, New York City

MIDDLEWEIGHTS

Date	Fight
June 30	**Mickey Walker** *KO* 10 Tommy Mulligan, London

WELTERWEIGHTS

Date	Fight
June 3	**Joe Dundee** (ITA) *W* 15 Pete Latzo, New York City

JUNIOR WELTERWEIGHTS

Date	Fight
March 14	**Mushy Callahan** *KO* 2 Andy DiVodi, New York City
May 31	**Mushy Callahan** *W* 10 Spug Myers, Chicago

JUNIOR LIGHTWEIGHTS

Date	Fight
May 28	**Tod Morgan** *ref* 12 Vic Foley, Vancouver
Dec 16	**Tod Morgan** *WF* 14 Joe Glick, New York City

FEATHERWEIGHTS

Date	Fight
Sept 12	**Benny Bass** (RUS) *W* 10 Red Chapman, Philadelphia (Vacant NBA Title)
Oct 24	**Tony Canzoneri** (USA) *W* 15 Johnny Dundee, New York City

BANTAMWEIGHTS

Date	Fight
Feb 4	**Charley Phil Rosenberg** *W* 15 Bushy Graham, New York City
March 26	**Bud Taylor** *D* 10 Tony Canzoneri, Chicago (Vacant NBA Title)
May 5	**Teddy Baldock** (ENG) *W* 15 Archie Bell, London (Vacant British World Title)
June 24	**Bud Taylor** (USA) *W* 10 Tony Canzoneri, Chicago (Vacant NBA Title)
Oct 6	**Willie Smith** (SA) *W* 15 Teddy Baldock, London

FLYWEIGHTS

Date	Fight
Jan 21	**Fidel LaBarba** (USA) *W* 12 Elky Clark, New York City (Vacant World Title)
Oct 28	**Johnny McCoy** (USA) *W* 10 Tommy Hughes, Hollywood, CA (Vacant California World Title)
Nov 28	**Frenchy Belanger** (CAN) *W* 10 Frankie Genaro, Toronto (Vacant NBA Title)
Dec 16	**Corp. Izzy Schwartz** (USA) *W* 15 Newsboy Brown, New York City (Vacant New York World Title)
Dec 19	**Frenchy Belanger** *W* 12 Ernie Jarvis, Toronto

Jack Dempsey

It's difficult to rate Jack Dempsey among the larger-than-life legends that made the '20s America's most colorful decade. His competition included Babe Ruth, Al Capone, Rudolph Valentino, Charlie Chaplin, and Charles Lindbergh. Suffice to say that he was, as Paul Gallico described him, "the greatest and most beloved sports hero the country had ever known."

It is equally difficult to rate Dempsey among the best heavyweight champions of all-time. There was Jack Johnson before him, and Joe Louis, Rocky Marciano, and Muhammad Ali who came after. Dempsey's career was best placed in perspective by another heavyweight champion, Jack Sharkey, who, having fought both men, said, "If Joe Louis and Jack Dempsey ever fought in a telephone booth, I'd bet every dime I have that it would be Dempsey who would walk out."

William Harrison Dempsey was born on June 24, 1895, in Manassa, Colorado. He was one of 11 children raised by Hyrum and Celia Dempsey. Hyrum, a one-time West Virginia schoolteacher, had been lured by the promise of the West. But he never managed to realize his dreams, and his family hopped from town to town in an effort to escape poverty.

At age 16, Jack quit school and ran away from home. From 1911 to 1916, he lived as a hobo, hopping freight trains, sleeping in mining camps, begging for food, and using the rudimentary boxing skills he had been taught by his brother Bernie to earn a few dollars. In the mid-teens, he developed a reputation as "Kid Blackie," a rugged middleweight with exceptional strength and an indomitable will. He won most of his fights, but a February 1917 one-round kayo loss to Fireman Jim Flynn confirmed that he remained directionless. Then fate intervened, and Dempsey hooked up with Jack (Doc) Kearns, who had been a saloon keeper, gambler, miner, and middleweight boxer. They would subsequently become the most famous fighter-manager team in boxing history.

Benefiting from Kearns' shrewd manipulations, Dempsey immediately accelerated. In 1918, he scored a string of quick knockouts: Flynn in one; Arthur Pelkey in one; giant contender Fred Fulton in *23 seconds*; the hard-punching Jack Moran in one; reigning light heavyweight champion Battling Levinsky in three; and veteran Gunboat Smith in two. At the age of 23, he was a legitimate threat to dethrone aging world champion Jess Willard.

Dempsey's magic moment came on July 4, 1919, when he challenged Willard at the Bay View Park Arena in Toledo, Ohio. Willard hadn't defended the crown in more than three years; it took promoter Tex Rickard's guarantee of $100,000 to bring him out of hiding.

The fight seemed a physical mismatch: the 6'0¾" Dempsey scaled 187 – he later insisted he weighed no more than 180 – and the 6'6¼" champion 245. It turned out to be a mismatch, all right. Dempsey scored seven first-round knockdowns, broke Willard's jaw, and knocked out six of his teeth. The title changed hands when Willard failed to answer the bell for round four.

Professional career dates 1914-1928
Contests 79
Won 64
Lost 6
Drawn 9
Knockouts 49
World Heavyweight Champion 1919-1926

This classic, candid portrait of Jack Dempsey reveals the inborn killer instinct that made him the most dynamic of all heavyweight champions.

It was a magnificent start to a title reign. But before Dempsey could defend the championship, his image suffered a blow that would take seven years to overcome. In 1917, he had registered for the draft, and was deferred based on his claim that he was the sole supporter of his mother, father, and wife. In the wake of World War I, however, he was indicted for draft evasion, with the government's key witness being his ex-wife Maxine. In June 1920, he was tried and found not guilty. Still, the public viewed him as a "slacker."

As a champion, Dempsey fought his own wars. His first two defenses, kayos of Billy Miske and Bill Brennan, were routine. His third was no more difficult, but it nonetheless made history. Thanks largely to Rickard's brilliant promoting, Dempsey's bout vs. light heavyweight champion Georges Carpentier, held on July 2, 1921, in Jersey City, New Jersey, drew boxing's first million-dollar gate. (A total of $1,626,580, in fact.) Dempsey steamrolled the undersized Frenchman in four rounds.

Two years passed before Dempsey again defended the crown. The wait was worth it; his next two bouts contributed to his legend as much as any others. On July 4, 1923, the champion met yet another blown-up light heavweight, Tommy Gibbons, in the oil town of Shelby, Montana. Shelby's bankers and businessmen promised Kearns a purse of $300,000, to be delivered in three installments. The second payment bankrupted the town, and the third was never made; immediately after Dempsey retained the title by 15-round decision, he and his manager left town with the $60,000 in gate receipts.

"The modern fighter of any distinction," lamented Nat Fleischer, editor and publisher of *The Ring*, "fights for the clang of the cash register, and the clang of the cash register never echoed more loudly than in the recent contest between Jack Dempsey and Tom Gibbons."

In Dempsey's fifth defense, the focus was on the fight. At Madison Square Garden on September 14, the champion faced Argentine bull Luis Angel Firpo. Accustomed to bigger opponents, Dempsey scored no less than seven first-round knockdowns. But shortly before the bell, Firpo connected with a seemingly innocent right, and the champion crashed through the loose ropes and onto the typewriter of the *New York Tribune*'s Jack Lawrence. With the help of telegraph operator Perry Grogan, Lawrence shoved "The Manassa Mauler" back into the ring, and Dempsey lifted himself up at referee Jack Gallagher's count of nine. He recovered to finish Firpo in the second. The sight of Dempsey being hammered out of the ring, however, would become a snapshot of history. In an Associated Press poll, it was voted the most dramatic sports event in the first 50 years of the century.

After the Firpo fight, Dempsey's layoff totalled *three* years. (It should be noted that he never defended against the division's top contender, black heavyweight Harry Wills. The champion was willing, but Rickard, recalling the controversy of Jack Johnson's reign, refused to make the match.) Cashing in on his celebrity, he appeared in motion pictures and on the vaudeville stage; he visited with President Calvin Coolidge at the White House; and in February 1925, he married for the second time. Estelle Taylor was a recycled Hollywood actress, but a beautiful one, and like Firpo had done, she turned Dempsey's legs to jelly.

By the time the champion returned to the ring, he had lost much of his ferocity. On September 23, 1926, he was no match for American light heavyweight champion Gene Tunney, who took his title by one-sided 10-round decision. The rematch came one year later, and brought a $2-million gate. On September 22, 1927, at Soldier's Field in Chicago, master boxer Tunney again defeated Dempsey by 10-round verdict, but not before surviving a terrific scare. In the seventh round, Dempsey combined a right to the body and a hook to the jaw, and Tunney collapsed. Referee Dave Barry instructed Dempsey to advance to a neutral corner, but the challenger didn't respond, and at least four seconds elapsed before the start of the count. Tunney rose at Barry's toll of nine and boxed cautiously until the threat had passed.

The referee's "long count" would be the subject of lengthy debate. In truth, however, Tunney had never been in danger of being kayoed.

"I had my head," he said, "but there was no reason to get up prematurely. Why would anyone want to get up early in the same ring with Jack Dempsey?"

In February 1928, the 32-year-old Dempsey, more popular than ever, but also financially secure, announced his retirement. After losing $3-million in the 1929 stock market crash, he returned for more than 100 exhibitions, but fought no more official bouts. (In his later years, he returned to the ring as a title fight referee.)

Dempsey served in the Coast Guard during World War II, and then opened a popular and successful restaurant in New York City. There were two more marriages, and, finally, tranquility and bliss.

On May 31, 1983, Dempsey, the embodiment of the American Dream, died at age 87.

They just don't make heroes like him anymore.

Ex-champion Dempsey surrounded by autograph-seeking youngsters at a 1950 baseball game. Right up until the time of his death, in 1983 at age 87, the immortal champion's reputation endured.

Dempsey with stablemate Mickey Walker (right), both managed by cunning Jack Kearns, probably the best of all boxing managers. By modern standards, a Dempsey-Walker stable would be valued at more than $100-million.

JANUARY

1928

DECEMBER

THE FRENCH AND THE FEATHERS

What was it about French fighters and the featherweight title? In June 1923, war hero Eugene Criqui kayoed longtime champion Johnny Kilbane, and five years later, stocky former auto mechanic Andre Routis dethroned 3-1 favorite Tony Canzoneri.

On September 28 at Madison Square Garden, Routis used his windmill style, an awkward defense, and an inspired championship-rounds rally to take the crown. It came as no surprise that Canzoneri was the harder puncher. But Routis routinely lifted his elbows while tucking his arms into his chest, and as a result, when Canzoneri punched, he hurt only himself. Behind after 10 rounds, Routis accelerated in the stretch. Canzoneri had trouble making weight, and he couldn't hope to match the Frenchman's volume punching. The decision was unanimous.

On the roll call of featherweight champions, Eugene Criqui would have most unexpected company.

Routis (right) decisioned champ Canzoneri.

THE TOUGHEST FISH IN THE SEA

From the start of his pro career, Benny "Little Fish" Bass was labeled a puncher. By the mid-'20s, the Russian-born, Philadelphia-based featherweight was acknowledged as the hardest hitter in his division. But as is often the case with kayo artists, the critics were not convinced of his heart.

On February 10 at Madison Square Garden, Bass answered them once and for always.

After Kid Kaplan had vacated the throne in July 1926, the 126-pound title had remained fragmented. Bass won the vacant NBA crown in September 1927, and one month later, Tony Canzoneri captured New York State recognition. At the Garden, they clashed to unify the title.

In round three, Canzoneri exploded a hook off Bass' jaw, and the Little Fish collapsed to the canvas. He subsequently absorbed a terrific beating until a brief rally in round 10. But Bass couldn't match Canzoneri's considerable skills, and after the final bell, the announcement of the verdict was a mere formality: Canzoneri by unanimous decision.

Afterward, Bass was taken to hospital, where it was revealed that he had boxed the last 12 rounds with a badly broken collarbone.

Nowhere did it say that punchers couldn't have heart, too.

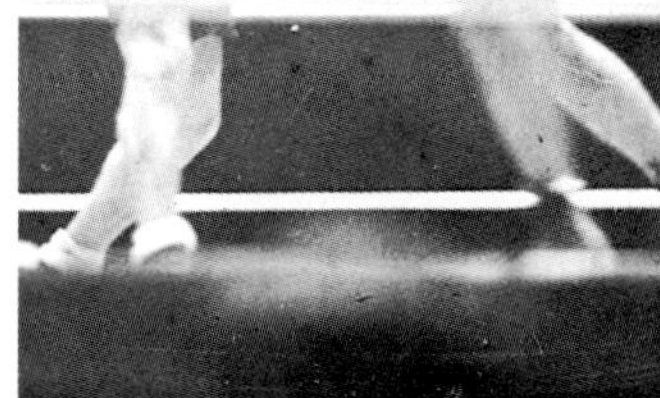

Tony Canzoneri (left) and tough Benny Bass.

WORLD TITLE FIGHTS

HEAVYWEIGHTS

July 26	**Gene Tunney** *KO* 11 Tom Heeney, Bronx, NY

LIGHT HEAVYWEIGHTS

Jan 6	**Tommy Loughran** *W* 15 Leo Lomski, New York City
June 1	**Tommy Loughran** *W* 15 Pete Latzo, Brooklyn
July 16	**Tommy Loughran** *W* 10 Pete Latzo, Wilkes-Barre, PA

MIDDLEWEIGHTS

June 21	**Mickey Walker** *W* 10 Ace Hudkins, Chicago

LIGHTWEIGHTS

June 21	**Sammy Mandell** *W* 15 Jimmy McLarnin, New York City

JUNIOR LIGHTWEIGHTS

May 24	**Tod Morgan** *W* 15 Cannonball Martin, New York City
July 18	**Tod Morgan** *W* 15 Cannonball Martin, Brooklyn
Dec 3	**Tod Morgan** *D* 10 Santiago Zorilla, San Francisco

FEATHERWEIGHTS

Feb 10	**Tony Canzoneri** *W* 15 Benny Bass, New York City
Sept 28	**Andre Routis** (FRA) *W* 15 Tony Canzoneri, New York City

BANTAMWEIGHTS

Feb 25	**Bushy Graham** *W* 15 Corp. Izzy Schwartz, Brooklyn (Vacant New York World Title)

FLYWEIGHTS

Jan 3	**Newsboy Brown** *W* 10 Johnny McCoy, Los Angeles (California World Title)
April 9	**Corp. Izzy Schwartz** *W* 15 Routier Parra, New York City
July 20	**Corp. Izzy Schwartz** *WF* 4 Frisco Grande, Rockaway, NY
Aug 3	**Corp. Izzy Schwartz** *KO* 4 Little Jeff, Rockaway, NY
Aug 29	**Johnny Hill** (SCOT) *ref* 15 Newsboy Brown, London (British & California World Titles)
Dec 3	**Frenchy Belanger** *W* 12 Willie Davies, Toronto

TUNNEY SAYS GOODBYE – ON HIS OWN TERMS

After scoring an 11th-round TKO over game but sadly overmatched New Zealander Tom Heeney, heavyweight champion Gene Tunney grabbed the ring microphone and wished regards to "my friends in Greenwich." Boxing fans assumed Tunney was addressing his acquaintances in the Greenwich Village section of New York City, where he had grown up. But his remarks were meant for those in the affluent town of Greenwich, Connecticut.

The 31-year-old Tunney's public greeting was a subtle message that his fighting days were over. In the next few months, he would announce his retirement from boxing and marry one of Greenwich's wealthiest residents, society heiress Polly Lauder. In subsequent years, Tunney would start several businesses, lecture on Shakespeare at Yale, advance to captain during his service in World War II, and father four children, one of whom would become a U.S. Senator.

Tunney-Heeney was significant for another reason: it would be the last fight promoted by Tex Rickard, who died six months later in Florida. Rickard helped Tunney retire with financial security; the champion was paid $525,000 for the Heeney fight, and left the ring with more than $1-million in the bank.

JANUARY

1929

DECEMBER

LOUGHRAN LOSES MONEY FOR KEEPING TITLE

On March 28, opening night at the sparkling new Chicago Stadium, promoters hoped for a sellout crowd of 25,000. The main event was top-level: light heavyweight champion Tommy Loughran defending against middleweight king Mickey Walker.

The fight was entertaining enough, with the highly skilled Loughran retaining the crown by 10-round decision. Walker, scaling only 165, and spotting the champion 8¼ pounds, attacked throughout. But Loughran boxed with intelligence, holding when necessary and minimizing the toe-to-toe exchanges.

The paid attendance was only 14,554. The disappointing gross, combined with a curious clause in the fight contract, limited Loughran's purse to $15,000. Walker, on the other hand, took home $50,000. Afterward, it was revealed that had Loughran lost the crown, he would've earned an additional $40,000.

Luckily for boxing, the champion valued his title more than his paycheck.

Boxing master Tommy Loughran (left) out classed brave Mickey Walker in a fifth defense that cost him money to win.

SAFE ONLY IN THE RING

When 1924 Olympic gold medalist Jackie Fields signed to face Young Jack Thompson for the vacant NBA welterweight title on March 25 at the Chicago Coliseum, he was sure he had the skills to emerge victorious. His only career losses had come against a trio of championship-caliber fighters, Jimmy McLarnin, Kid Kaplan, and Sammy Mandell. Moreover, he had outpointed the dangerous Thompson six months before.

As it turned out, the key to Fields' triumph was not his considerable ability, but his superb concentration during a most unique crisis. Midway through an unexceptional sixth round, the welterweights almost jumped out of their boots upon hearing what they thought was gunfire. (Remember, this was Al Capone's Chicago.) As it turned out, a row of folding chairs had turned over, causing a domino effect and a loud, extended rat-a-tat noise. One man fell to his death from the balcony. Ten fans were seriously hurt, and 100 more were taken to the hospital. Adding to the chaos, most of the lights went out.

To their credit, Fields and Thompson kept boxing, though at first somewhat tentatively. The bout was fought to its 10-round conclusion, and, never losing his rhythm, Fields was declared the winner by referee Ed Purdy.

Four months later, Fields won the world title when Joe Dundee climbed off the floor and intentionally punched him in the groin.

These things never seemed to happen in the Olympics.

Jackie Fields (right) and Young Jack Thompson.

RINGSIDE VIEW

JUNE

Stylish 5'11" bantamweight Panama Al Brown wins the vacant world title, scoring a unanimous 15-round decision over Vidal Gregorio.

DECEMBER

Former NBA featherweight king Benny Bass takes the world junior lightweight title from longtime king Tod Morgan via second-round kayo. Bass answers the opening bell as a 5-1 favorite, and a betting scandal follows.

WORLD TITLE FIGHTS

LIGHT HEAVYWEIGHTS

Date	Fight
March 28	**Tommy Loughran** *W* 10 Mickey Walker, Chicago
July 18	**Tommy Loughran** *W* 15 James J. Braddock, Bronx, NY

MIDDLEWEIGHTS

Date	Fight
Oct 29	**Mickey Walker** *ref* 10 Ace Hudkins, Los Angeles

WELTERWEIGHTS

Date	Fight
March 25	**Jackie Fields** (USA) *ref* 10 Young Jack Thompson, Chicago (Vacant NBA Title)
July 25	**Jackie Fields** *WF* 2 Joe Dundee, Detroit

JUNIOR WELTERWEIGHTS

Date	Fight
May 28	**Mushy Callahan** *KO* 3 Fred Mahan, Los Angeles

LIGHTWEIGHTS

Date	Fight
Aug 2	**Sammy Mandell** *W* 10 Tony Canzoneri, Chicago

JUNIOR LIGHTWEIGHTS

Date	Fight
April 5	**Tod Morgan** *W* 10 Santiago Zorilla, Los Angeles
May 20	**Tod Morgan** *W* 10 Baby Sal Sorio, Los Angeles
Dec 20	**Benny Bass** *KO* 2 Tod Morgan, New York City

FEATHERWEIGHTS

Date	Fight
May 27	**Andre Routis** *KO* 3 Buster Brown, Baltimore
Sept 23	**Bat Battalino** (USA) *ref* 15 Andre Routis, Hartford

BANTAMWEIGHTS

Date	Fight
June 18	**Panama Al Brown** (PAN) *W* 15 Gregorio Vidal, Long Island City, NY

FLYWEIGHTS

Date	Fight
Feb 7	**Spider Pladner** (FRA) *KO* 6 Johnny Hill, Paris
March 1	**Spider Pladner** *KO* 1 Frankie Genaro, Paris
March 12	**Corp. Izzy Schwartz** *W* 12 Frenchy Belanger, Toronto
April 18	**Frankie Genaro** *WF* 5 Spider Pladner, Paris
Aug 21	**Willie LaMorte** (USA) *ref* 15 Corp. Izzy Schwartz, Newark, NJ
Oct 17	**Frankie Genaro** *ref* 15 Ernie Jarvis, London
Nov 21	**Willie LaMorte** *KO* 7 Frisco Grande, Paterson, NJ

RING DECADE

1930-1939

DURING times of economic depression, the common man needs to escape the hopelessness of everyday life. As a result, the entertainment industry generally flourishes.

Boxing has always been part of that industry, but at the start of the '30s, the roll call of world champions suggested a fistic market not much healthier than the stock market.

Jack Dempsey and Gene Tunney had retired; both the heavyweight and light heavyweight titles were vacant; Mickey Walker, the colorful middleweight champion, was tackling heavyweights, and wouldn't again risk the crown; neither welterweight champion Jackie Fields nor lightweight champion Sammy Mandell would make a successful defense; the flyweight title was fragmented. Only featherweight champion Bat Battalino and bantamweight king Panama Al Brown provided stability. Such lighter-weight champions, however, weren't expected to carry the game.

Joe Louis equaled Dempsey in generating thrills and attracting crowds. He had the power in either fist to flatten a foe with a single blow.

What boxing needed was a dominant heavyweight champion, and a big-time promoter to sell him. In 1934, Joe Louis turned pro, and, coincidentally, Mike Jacobs, a former ticket broker and advisor to Tex Rickard, became a full-time promoter.

Theirs would be a marriage of destiny, and it spearheaded a revival that elevated the entire decade.

It was a wonderfully busy 10 years. Despite inconsistent activity in the junior weight classes, there were 230 world title fights. (In comparison, the '20s had offered only 158 such bouts, and the war-torn '40s would offer 150.) Better yet, the quantity was complimented by quality.

- Tony Canzoneri and Barney Ross became triple-crown champions.
- Henry Armstrong reigned simultaneously as featherweight, lightweight, and welterweight champion, and came within a draw of winning the middleweight title.
- Brown began the longest title reign in bantamweight history.
- Sixto Escobar became the first champion from Puerto Rico, Kid Chocolate from Cuba, Baby Arizmendi from Mexico, and Brown from Panama.
- Legends-to-be such as Jack (Kid) Berg, Billy Conn, Lou Ambers, Jimmy McLarnin, and Benny Lynch scored their greatest triumphs.
- On September 23, 1937, at the Polo Grounds in New York City, Jacobs promoted The Carnival of Champions, the most ambitious card of all-time. The titles in four of the original eight divisions were risked, with Fred Apostoli dethroning middleweight champion Marcel Thil, welterweight king Ross defeating Ceferino Garcia, lightweight leader Ambers decisioning Pedro Montanez, and Harry Jeffra taking the crown from bantamweight champion Escobar.

The decade's highlight, however, was the unprecedented success of Louis. As he carried the sport, an axiom became a truism: how go the heavyweights, so goes boxing.

The first heavyweight title fight of the '30s ended with Max Schmeling writhing on the canvas at Yankee Stadium, the victim of a low blow from Jack Sharkey that made Schmeling a champion of questionable credentials. Eight years later, Schmeling was back on the ballpark floor, put there by a fusillade of Joe Louis' most lethal blows. Sharkey and Louis: the difference made all the difference.

Because of the tumultuous reign of boxing's first black

Barney Ross was often compared with the great Benny Leonard as a boxing master. Holder of three world titles, he later became a war hero.

Tony Canzoneri became a triple-crown champion, collecting the following world championships: featherweight, lightweight, and junior welterweight.

Max Schmeling always went into the ring perfectly trained. An excellent boxer and deadly right-hand hitter, he was the best European heavyweight.

heavyweight champion, Jack Johnson, Louis was scrutinized from the start. In *Joe Louis: Black Hero In White America*, Chris Mead wrote that initially, the press portrayed Louis as either "a savage animal or a sleepy-eyed Southern darkie."

Conversely, the public accepted him from the start, and eventually embraced him.

Unlike Johnson, Louis wasn't abrasive or arrogant. He never taunted opponents, and always remained humble in victory. And when the time would come, he would serve his country in war.

Though Louis and Germany's Schmeling never pretended to be anything more than fighters, fate twice matched them in bouts that transcended the ring. On June 19, 1936, Schmeling punished the heavily favored "Brown Bomber" en route to a 12th-round kayo victory. It was Louis' first loss in 24 bouts. More significantly, it gave Joseph Goebbels, Adolf Hitler's Minister of Propaganda, an opportunity to further hype Aryan supremacy. Boxing insiders knew that Goebbels' words were weak; Joe Jacobs, Schmeling's manager, was Jewish, and the former champion was quite popular in America. But battle lines were being drawn, and even with the Third Reich nothing more than a distant and potential threat to the United States, Schmeling vs. Louis would come to represent Hitler vs. Roosevelt.

After Louis won the world title by knocking out James J. Braddock, a rematch with Schmeling became inevitable. On June 22, 1938, the heavyweights clashed, again at Yankee Stadium. Never before had a prize fight carried such political overtones. Fueled more by pride than patriotism, Louis tore into the challenger and, in 124 seconds, scored one of the most convincing victories in ring history.

It had been only a prize fight, of course, and when the celebration ended, the world remained on the brink of war.

However, the significance of Louis' victory wasn't lost on Heywood Broun, who wrote in the *New York World-Telegram*, "One hundred years from now some historian may theorize, in a footnote at least, that the decline of Nazi prestige began with a left hook delivered by a former unskilled automotive worker who had never studied the policies of Neville Chamberlain and had no opinion whatever in regard to the situation in Czechoslovakia..."

Louis was the most important fighter of the decade, but Henry Armstrong was the best. In August 1929, Armstrong was a teenager working for the Missouri-Pacific Railroad when he saw a newspaper headline that changed his life: "Kid Chocolate Earns $75,000 For Half Hour's Work." Armstrong, who had dreamed of being a doctor, turned pro two years later.

A handful of fighters had thrown as many punches, and others had punched as hard. But no one had ever combined volume and power like "Hammerin' Hank." In October 1937, the 5'5½" whirlwind, who listed movie stars George Raft and Al Jolson among his managers, took the featherweight title by knocking out Petey Sarron. In May 1938, he added the welterweight crown by easily outpointing a spent Barney Ross.

Then, 10 weeks later, in the toughest bout of his career, he decisioned lightweight champion Lou Ambers. From August to November 1938, Armstrong held all three titles. Subsequent rule changes ensured that the feat would never be duplicated.

From 1937 to 1939, Armstrong went 52-1 (44). Given the variety of weight classes and the quality of opposition, his run has to be considered the most brilliant of the modern era.

Louis and Armstrong were the decade's major players, but the '30s flaunted several other great fighters, and several great stories as well. In an era of ethnic matchups, Irish welterweight king McLarnin defeated almost all of the top Jewish fighters, including comebacking lightweight legend Benny Leonard. The erudite Conn brought big-city sophistication to the fight game, and won the light heavyweight title in his first bout at that weight. The controversial and contrived rise, and the predictable fall of Italian giant Primo Carnera made for screaming headlines.

And the sad saga of outstanding Scottish flyweight king Benny Lynch, who died a drunk at age 33, served as a reminder of the fragility of fame. The decade's only disappointment came at middleweight division, where the crown was held by 13 different fighters, none of whom particularly distinguished themselves.

On December 31, 1939, boxing's roll call of titlists included Louis, Conn, Armstrong, and Ambers, special champions all. The world was bracing for war, but at the end of arguably its finest decade, boxing felt no pain.

Henry Armstrong, only man to hold three world titles at the same time, had incredible endurance and a rip-roaring style that demolished opponents.

JANUARY

1930

DECEMBER

CROWNED WHILE FLAT ON HIS BACK

After Gene Tunney retired as undefeated heavyweight champion, a series of elimination bouts was scheduled to crown a new titlist. A pair of veterans, Germany's Max Schmeling and Boston's Jack Sharkey, advanced into the final.

Schmeling featured the harder punch, but Sharkey was far more skilled, and he easily took rounds one, two, and three. In the fourth, however, chaos reigned. Driven to the ropes, Sharkey responded with a heavy hook that landed below Schmeling's beltline. The German fell to the canvas, writhing in pain. Seconds later, his manager, Joe Jacobs, rocketed into the ring screaming "foul!"

After conferring with judge Harold Barnes and then failing in an attempt to convince Schmeling to fight on, referee Jim Crowley announced his decision: Schmeling was the winner and new champion.

For the first time in history, the heavyweight title had changed hands via disqualification. And no one, except Schmeling, was happy about it.

Max Schmeling groans in agony as his manager leaps to his aid in the fourth round.

THE BUSIEST KID IN BOXING

For one year, at least, England's Jack (Kid) Berg was the best fighter in the world. And his best fight came on August 7 at the Polo Grounds vs. Kid Chocolate.

Berg had outpointed Tony Canzoneri in an eliminator for Sammy Mandell's lightweight title. Then he knocked out defending junior welterweight champion Mushy Callahan.

It was Chocolate, however, that represented his toughest test. The Cuban was riding a pro and amateur winning streak of 160 fights. But he wasn't strong enough to discourage "The Whitechapel Windmill," who, according to one report, averaged almost a punch per second.

Berg won by 10-round decision, and kept his form in exciting points wins over Buster Brown, Joe Glick, and the dangerous Billy Petrolle. Boxing's best fighter was also its most exciting.

WORLD TITLE FIGHTS

HEAVYWEIGHTS

Date	Fight
June 11	**Max Schmeling** (GER) *WF* 4 Jack Sharkey, Bronx, NY

LIGHT HEAVYWEIGHTS

Date	Fight
Feb 10	**Jimmy Slattery** *W* 15 Lou Scozza, Buffalo (Vacant World Title)
June 25	**Maxie Rosenbloom** (USA) *W* 15 Jimmy Slattery, Buffalo
Oct 21	**Maxie Rosenbloom** *KO* 11 Abie Bain, New York City

WELTERWEIGHTS

Date	Fight
May 9	**Young Jack Thompson** (USA) *ref* 15 Jackie Fields, Detroit
Sept 5	**Tommy Freeman** (USA) *ref* 15 Young Jack Thompson, Cleveland

JUNIOR WELTERWEIGHTS

Date	Fight
Feb 18	**Jack (Kid) Berg** (ENG) *KO* 11 Mushy Callahan, London

LIGHTWEIGHTS

Date	Fight
July 17	**Al Singer** (USA) *KO* 1 Sammy Mandell, Bronx, NY
Nov 14	**Tony Canzoneri** *KO* 1 Al Singer, New York City

FEATHERWEIGHTS

Date	Fight
July 15	**Bat Battalino** *KO* 5 Ignacio Fernandez, Hartford
Dec 11	**Bat Battalino** *W* 15 Kid Chocolate, New York City

BANTAMWEIGHTS

Date	Fight
Feb 8	**Panama Al Brown** *WF* 4 Johnny Erickson, New York City
Oct 4	**Panama Al Brown** *W* 15 Eugene Huat, Paris

FLYWEIGHTS

Date	Fight
Jan 19	**Frankie Genaro** *KO* 12 Yvon Trevidic, Paris
March 21	**Midget Wolgast** (USA) *W* 15 Black Bill, New York City (Vacant New York World Title)
May 16	**Midget Wolgast** *KO* 6 Willie LaMorte, New York City
June 10	**Frankie Genaro** *W* 10 Frenchy Belanger, Toronto
Dec 26	**Frankie Genaro** *D* 15 Midget Wolgast, New York City

WIN OR LOSE, AL SINGER WAS THE ONE-ROUND WORLD CHAMPION

On November 14 at Madison Square Garden, it took Tony Canzoneri 66 seconds to separate New York's Al Singer from the lightweight title. Ironically, Canzoneri broke Singer's division record for the fastest title fight kayo. Only four months earlier, Singer had ended the five-year reign of Sammy Mandell, scoring a knockout at 1:46 of round one.

Singer's rapid decline was inexplicable. (Sandwiched between his victory over Mandell and his loss to Canzoneri was a third-round kayo defeat vs. Jimmy McLarnin.) Born on the Lower East Side of New York City, he had been billed as a clone of Benny Leonard. But after the loss to Canzoneri, he never recovered.

Singer would fight six times in 1931, and then not again until 1935. He would retire at age 26, providing vivid testimony to the fragility of world-class fighters.

It took Tony Canzoneri 66 seconds to paralyze Al Singer and become lightweight champion, meaning that both of Singer's world title fights had ended in the first round.

THE HEAVYWEIGHT CHAMPION IS GETTING BETTER

Max Schmeling had been heavyweight champion for more than a year, and time had done little to relieve the stench created by his title-winning bout vs. Jack Sharkey. His first defense made everyone feel a bit better.

On July 3, more than 35,000 fans came to Cleveland's newly built Municipal Stadium. Schmeling's opponent was Georgia veteran Young Bill Stribling. Among the most popular fighters in the history of the South, Stribling had scored 18 consecutive kayos. But his record was deceiving; he had been carefully protected by his father/manager.

Stribling boxed strongly for the first four rounds, but Schmeling then began to dominate. Blocking the challenger's jabs and punching accurately, especially with his right hand, he chopped up Stribling, opening cuts over both eyes.

Late in the 15th and final round, Stribling fell. He beat the count of referee George Blake, but could no longer hold off Schmeling. At the 2:46 mark, 14 seconds from the final bell, Blake stopped.

Two years later, Stribling, age 28, would die from injuries suffered in a motorcycle accident near his hometown of Macon, Georgia.

Max Schmeling (right) knocked out Young Stribling with only 14 seconds remaining.

WORLD NUMBER ONE

In 1930, England's indomitable Jack (Kid) Berg had unofficially established himself as boxing's best pound-for-pound fighter by scoring victories over Tony Canzoneri, Mushy Callahan, and Kid Chocolate. In 1931, it was Canzoneri's turn and his key victory was a return with Berg.

At Chicago Stadium on April 24, Canzoneri retained the lightweight title and took Berg's junior welterweight crown with a stunning kayo. Berg walked directly into a booming right hand.

Before the year would conclude, Canzoneri would again defeat Berg, as well as Chocolate. Like Berg the year before, he would become boxing's very best.

Tony Canzoneri (left) and Jackie "Kid" Berg.

JANUARY

1931

DECEMBER

A CROWN FOR THE KID

Kid Chocolate (real name Eligio Sardinias) proved himself a special fighter almost as soon as he arrived in New York in the summer of 1928. It seemed only a matter of time before "The Cuban Bon Bon" would capture a world title.

The tall, classy boxer began 1931 with four straight victories, and on July 15, he was matched with powerpunching junior lightweight champion Benny Bass at the Baker Bowl in Philadelphia.

From the first round, there was no doubt of the outcome. Bass continually stalked, and Chocolate moved cleverly to maximize the distance between them, firing quick, straight combinations.

By the seventh round, Bass' left eye was a hideous sight, and at the 2:58 mark, referee Leo Houck stopped the bloodbath. The Kid was a champion.

WORLD TITLE FIGHTS

HEAVYWEIGHTS

July 3	**Max Schmeling** *KO* 15 Young Stribling, Cleveland

LIGHT HEAVYWEIGHTS

Aug 5	**Maxie Rosenbloom** *W* 15 Jimmy Slattery, Brooklyn

WELTERWEIGHTS

April 14	**Young Jack Thompson** *KO* 12 Tommy Freeman, Cleveland
Oct 23	**Lou Brouillard** (CAN) *W* 15 Young Jack Thompson, Boston

JUNIOR WELTERWEIGHTS

Jan 23	**Jack (Kid) Berg** *W* 10 Goldie Hess, Chicago
April 10	**Jack (Kid) Berg** *W* 10 Billy Wallace, Detroit
April 24	**Tony Canzoneri** *KO* 3 Jack (Kid) Berg, Chicago
July 13	**Tony Canzoneri** *W* 10 Cecil Payne, Los Angeles
Sept 10	**Tony Canzoneri** *W* 15 Jack (Kid) Berg, New York City
Oct 29	**Tony Canzoneri** *W* 10 Phillie Griffin, Newark, NJ
Nov 20	**Tony Canzoneri** *W* 15 Kid Chocolate, New York City

LIGHTWEIGHTS

April 24	**Tony Canzoneri** *KO* 3 Jack (Kid) Berg, Chicago
Sept 10	**Tony Canzoneri** *W* 15 Jack (Kid) Berg, New York City
Nov 20	**Tony Canzoneri** *W* 15 Kid Chocolate, New York City

JUNIOR LIGHTWEIGHTS

Jan 5	**Benny Bass** *W* 10 Lew Massey, Philadelphia
July 15	**Kid Chocolate** (CUBA) *KO* 7 Benny Bass, Philadelphia

FEATHERWEIGHTS

May 22	**Bat Battalino** *W* 15 Fidel LaBarba, New York City
July 23	**Bat Battalino** *W* 10 Freddie Miller, Cincinnati
Nov 4	**Bat Battalino** *W* 10 Earl Mastro, Chicago

BANTAMWEIGHTS

Aug 25	**Panama Al Brown** *W* 15 Pete Sanstol, Montreal
Oct 27	**Panama Al Brown** *W* 15 Eugene Huat, Montreal

FLYWEIGHTS

March 25	**Frankie Genaro** *D* 15 Victor Ferrand, Madrid
July 13	**Midget Wolgast** *W* 15 Ruby Bradley, Brooklyn
July 16	**Frankie Genaro** *KO* 4 Routier Parra, North Adams, MA
July 30	**Frankie Genaro** *KO* 6 Jackie Harmon, Waterbury, CT
Oct 3	**Frankie Genaro** *ref* 15 Valentin Angelmann, Paris
Oct 26	**Young Perez** (TUN) *KO* 2 Frankie Genaro, Paris (NBA Title)

JANUARY

1932

DECEMBER

"WE WUZ ROBBED!"

Cynics called it justice. Everyone else called it the worst decision in heavyweight title fight history. Jack Sharkey's split 15-round decision over defending champion Max Schmeling at the Madison Square Garden Bowl in Long Island City, New York, damaged the credibility of the sport.

Two years earlier, Sharkey's fourth-round low blow had prematurely ended his first title bout vs. Schmeling. For the rematch, he entered the ring a 6-5 favorite. From the start, however, the champion controlled the pace.

After 15 fairly uneventful rounds, it was announced that Sharkey had won on points, prompting Joe Jacobs, Schmeling's incredulous manager, to scream into a radio microphone the immortal words, "We wuz robbed!"

And there had been 61,863 witnesses to the crime.

HE'S THE CHAMP, FAIR OR FOUL

History would remember France's Marcel Thil as the world champion who made victory by disqualification an art form.

Fittingly, his title-winning performance against American Gorilla Jones, which came on June 11 before 60,000 supporters in Paris' open-air Parc des Princes, ended on a foul.

Among those in attendance was Amelia Earhart, and the famed sky rider watched the speedy challenger fly across the ring in an effort to catch the reluctant Jones. In the 11th round, the champion was DQ'ed after repeated warnings for holding and punching low.

For Thil, it would become a familiar formula for triumph.

Max Schmeling (left) and Jack Sharkey.

RINGSIDE VIEW

JANUARY

Philadelphia's Johnny Jadick outpoints Tony Canzoneri in his hometown and wins the junior welterweight title.

SEPTEMBER

Former heavyweight champion Max Schmeling punishes Mickey Walker en route to an eighth-round kayo in New York City.

A PAINFUL BUT PREDICTABLE END

It had been several bad investments, and the stock market crash of 1929, that had prompted legendary lightweight king Benny Leonard to return to the ring. And at a sold-out Madison Square Garden on October 7, it was the bruising power of number-one welterweight contender Jimmy McLarnin that prompted him to retire once more.

Leonard, 36 and flabby, had gone unbeaten in 19 comeback bouts. But his legs began to fail him, and McLarnin, among the ring's hardest hitters, took aim. Though many of the Irishman's punches missed – Leonard still knew plenty of tricks – enough landed to bring the inevitable surrender in round six. As dozens of champions had already learned, time is an ally only to the young.

Finale of Leonard's unparalleled career.

FIGHTING TALK

One of the reasons I want to lick McLarnin is that I want to wipe out his successful record against Jewish fighters

BENNY LEONARD
before fighting McLarnin

WORLD TITLE FIGHTS

HEAVYWEIGHTS

June 21	**Jack Sharkey** (USA) *W* 15 Max Schmeling, Long Island City, NY

LIGHT HEAVYWEIGHTS

March 18	**George Nichols** (USA) *W* 10 Dave Maier, Chicago (Vacant NBA Title)
July 14	**Maxie Rosenbloom** *W* 15 Lou Scozza, Buffalo

MIDDLEWEIGHTS

Jan 25	**Gorilla Jones** (USA) *KO* 6 Oddone Piazza, Milwaukee
April 26	**Gorilla Jones** *W* 12 Young Terry, Trenton, NJ
June 11	**Marcel Thil** (FRA) *WF* 11 Gorilla Jones, Paris
July 4	**Marcel Thil** *ref* 15 Len Harvey, London
Aug 21	**Teddy Yarosz** (USA) *W* 10 Vince Dundee, Pittsburgh

WELTERWEIGHTS

Jan 28	**Jackie Fields** *W* 10 Lou Brouillard, Chicago

JUNIOR WELTERWEIGHTS

Jan 18	**Johnny Jadick** (USA) *W* 10 Tony Canzoneri, Philadelphia
May 20	**Sammy Fuller** (USA) *W* 12 Jack (Kid) Berg, New York City (Claimed World Title)
July 18	**Johnny Jadick** *W* 10 Tony Canzoneri, Philadelphia

LIGHTWEIGHTS

Nov 4	**Tony Canzoneri** *W* 15 Billy Petrolle, New York City

JUNIOR LIGHTWEIGHTS

April 10	**Kid Chocolate** *W* 15 Dave Abad, Havana
Aug 4	**Kid Chocolate** *W* 10 Eddie Shea, Cincinnati

FEATHERWEIGHTS

Jan 27	**Bat Battalino** NC 3 Freddie Miller, Cincinnati
May 26	**Tommy Paul** (USA) *ref* 15 Johnny Pena, Detroit (Vacant NBA Title)
Oct 13	**Kid Chocolate** *KO* 12 Lew Feldman, New York City
Dec 9	**Kid Chocolate** *W* 15 Fidel LaBarba, New York City

BANTAMWEIGHTS

July 10	**Panama Al Brown** *W* 15 Kid Francis, Marseilles
Sept 19	**Panama Al Brown** *KO* 1 Spider Pladner, Toronto

FLYWEIGHTS

Oct 31	**Jackie Brown** (ENG) *KO* 13 Young Perez, Manchester, England (NBA Title)

A GIANT CHAMP OR A GIANT JOKE?

There was an angle to heavyweight champion Jack Sharkey's first title defense, vs. Italy's Primo Carnera on June 29 at the Madison Square Garden Bowl in Long Island City, New York. Given Carnera's reputation as a pretender, the fight needed one.

Sharkey clubbed down by Carnera.

On February 10, Carnera had kayoed Sharkey's protege, Ernie Schaaf, in the 13th round. Schaaf died three days later. His death, it was determined, had been the indirect result of an August 1932 beating issued by Max Baer. Nevertheless, promoters hyped the tragedy as an example of the challenger's power, and the press billed Sharkey-Carnera as a grudge match.

For five rounds, Sharkey dominated, just as he had in registering a 15-round victory over Carnera in October 1931. But in round six, Carnera landed a lunging right uppercut, and the champion crashed. He was promptly counted out by referee Arthur Donovan.

Had the fight been legitimate? There was sufficient reason for suspicion: Carnera's mob connections were common knowlegde. In the years to come, however, Sharkey would maintain that he hadn't taken a dive. But the questions remained.

HOMETOWN DECISION THAT'S BOOED

For the first seven rounds of Tony Canzoneri's double title defense against hometown hero Barney Ross at Chicago Stadium on June 23, the champion attacked with ferocity.

A rally from a bleeding Ross in the last three rounds seemed a bit late. The decision came as a shocker: two judges had Ross ahead, and a new champion was crowned.

"The verdict was an outrage," screamed Canzoneri's manager. His sentiment was echoed by most of the 11,000 fans in attendance; they booed one of their own.

In September, Ross won another split decision in a New York return.

Tony Canzoneri (left)and Barney Ross.

JANUARY

1933

DECEMBER

POWER – IN THE BLINK OF AN EYE

For the first two minutes of welterweight champion Young Corbett III's title defense against Jimmy McLarnin, fought at Los Angeles' Wrigley Field on May 29, it seemed that the division's jinx would be broken. Six consecutive 147-pound champions had lost the crown in their first defense, but Corbett's southpaw jabs were keeping the hard-hitting Irish challenger under control.

Then – boom! McLarnin struck with a right, and Corbett fell hard. Two more knockdowns followed, and when the referee stepped in at 2:37 of round one, Corbett, champion for 97 days, was defenseless.

The jinx lived.

WORLD TITLE FIGHTS

HEAVYWEIGHTS

June 29	**Primo Carnera** (ITA) *KO* 6 Jack Sharkey, Long Island City, NY
Oct 21	**Primo Carnera** *W* 15 Paolino Uzcudun, Rome

LIGHT HEAVYWEIGHTS

March 1	**Bob Godwin** (USA) *W* 10 Joe Knight, West Palm Beach, FL (Vacant NBA Title)
March 10	**Maxie Rosenbloom** *W* 15 Adolf Heuser, New York City
March 24	**Maxie Rosenbloom** *KO* 4 Bob Godwin, New York City
Nov 3	**Maxie Rosenbloom** *W* 15 Mickey Walker, New York City

MIDDLEWEIGHTS

Jan 13	**Ben Jeby** (USA) *KO* 12 Frank Battaglia, New York City (New York World Title)
March 17	**Ben Jeby** *D* 15 Vince Dundee, New York City
July 10	**Ben Jeby** *ref* 15 Young Terry, Newark, NJ
Aug 9	**Lou Brouillard** *KO* 7 Ben Jeby, New York City
Oct 2	**Marcel Thil** *W* 15 Kid Tunero, Paris
Oct 30	**Vince Dundee** (USA) *W* 15 Lou Brouillard, Boston (NBA & New York Titles)
Dec 8	**Vince Dundee** *W* 15 Andy Callahan, Boston

WELTERWEIGHTS

Feb 21	**Young Corbett** III (ITA) *ref* 10 Jackie Fields, San Francisco
May 29	**Jimmy McLarnin** (IRE) *KO* 1 Young Corbett III, Los Angeles

JUNIOR WELTERWEIGHTS

Feb 20	**Battling Shaw** (MEX) *W* 10 Johnny Jadick, New Orleans
May 21	**Tony Canzoneri** *W* 10 Battling Shaw, New Orleans
June 23	**Barney Ross** (USA) *W* 10 Tony Canzoneri, Chicago
July 26	**Barney Ross** *KO* 6 Johnny Farr, Kansas City
Sept 12	**Barney Ross** *W* 15 Tony Canzoneri, New York City
Nov 17	**Barney Ross** *W* 10 Sammy Fuller, Chicago

LIGHTWEIGHTS

June 23	**Barney Ross** *W* 10 Tony Canzoneri, Chicago
Sept 12	**Barney Ross** *W* 15 Tony Canzoneri, New York City

JUNIOR LIGHTWEIGHTS

May 1	**Kid Chocolate** *W* 10 Johnny Farr, Philadelphia
Dec 4	**Kid Chocolate** *W* 10 Frankie Wallace, Cleveland
Dec 25	**Frankie Klick** (USA) *KO* 7 Kid Chocolate, Philadelphia

FEATHERWEIGHTS

Jan 13	**Freddie Miller** (USA) *W* 10 Tommy Paul, Chicago
Feb 28	**Freddie Miller** *ref* 10 Baby Arizmendi, Los Angeles
March 21	**Freddie Miller** *ref* 10 Speedy Dado, Los Angeles
May 19	**Kid Chocolate** *W* 15 Seaman Tom Watson, New York City

BANTAMWEIGHTS

March 18	**Panama Al Brown** *W* 12 Dominic Berasconi, Milan
July 3	**Panama Al Brown** *ref* 15 Johnny King, Manchester

FLYWEIGHTS

June 12	**Jackie Brown** *ref* 15 Valentin Angelmann, London
Sept 11	**Jackie Brown** *ref* 15 Valentin Angelmann, Manchester
Dec 11	**Jackie Brown** *ref* 15 Ginger Foran, Manchester

Mickey Walker

"LIVE today, forget yesterday, and have hope for tomorrow." – the last line of Mickey Walker's autobiography, *Mickey Walker: The Toy Bulldog & His Times.*

Professional career dates 1919-1935
Contests 163
Won 115
Lost 21
Drawn 4
No-Decisions 22
No-Contests 1
Knockouts 61
World Welterweight Champion 1922-1926
World Middleweight Champion 1926-1931

Mickey Walker's life was full of perfect marriages. Foremost, there was the boxer and the ring. "The Toy Bulldog" established his obstinacy at an all-time record age; the product of a difficult delivery, he was born with a black eye. It was his destiny that he fight, and if success can be measured by loving what you do, and doing it well, Walker was a fighter for the ages.

Then there was the boxer and the manager. When Jack (Doc) Kearns and Walker established their handshake agreement in 1925, both were already established celebrities. Walker was the welterweight champion, and the colorful Kearns had recently split with Jack Dempsey, whom he had guided to the heavyweight title. After a start that included two devastating losses, Kearns and Walker began to mesh. They set a frantic pace in an effort to see who could spend the most money in the least amount of time. Moreover, neither liked to drink alone.

Finally, there was the boxer and his times. The end of World War I and the start of Prohibition made the Roaring Twenties a decade like no other. Gangsters were glorified, bootlegging was trendy, and the worlds of sport and movies were overflowing with stars. Walker mixed with Al Capone and Calvin Coolidge, and, as John Lardner wrote, "From Hollywood to Montmartre, he was never outreached for a bar check."

In fact, Walker was so married to life that there wasn't room left for wives. He kept trying, however, taking vows with four different women a total of seven times.

Over the course of his 17-year career, Walker won world titles at welterweight and middleweight, and despite fighting his best at no more than 160 pounds, contended at light heavyweight and even heavyweight. He estimated that he netted about $3-million in purses, and joyfully spent far more than that.

Edward Patrick Walker was born on July 13, 1901, in Elizabeth, New Jersey. He was the oldest of the three children of Mike Walker, a bricklayer who once sparred with John L. Sullivan, and Elizabeth Higgins Walker. By age 14, Walker, a cigarette hanging out the side of his mouth, was tossed out of grammar school. His father sent him to work for an architectural design firm, but Walker was never going to be a nine-to-fiver. He secured work on Elizabeth's docks – until he found that he could make money fighting.

Walker, 17, turned pro on February 10, 1919, engaging in a four-round no-decision draw vs. Dominic Orsini. He was paid $10. By 1921, he was competing against fighters the class of Jack Britton and Dave Shade, and on November 1, 1922, he took Britton's 147-pound crown by unanimous 15-round decision. The thickly built, 5'7" challenger relentlessly pressured his aging foe throughout, but Britton refused to fold. At the final bell, the cheers at Madison Square Garden were for the loser.

Walker made two defenses in 1923, and two more in 1924. His metabolism was changing, however, and his days at welterweight were numbered. On July 2, 1925, he

Walker (left) suffered one of the few losses in his long career to crafty southpaw Young Corbett III, in 1934.

Mickey Walker won the world welterweight and middleweight crowns. His bid to capture the light heavyweight title fell short, but he held future heavyweight champ Jack Sharkey to a draw.

challenged middleweight champion Harry Greb at the Polo Grounds. Giving away seven pounds, he lost a tough 15-round decision.

Late into the night, Greb and Walker partied together in the speakeasys of Broadway. But as soon as the conversation turned to their fight, they opted for the only manly option: a resumption of their brawl on the streets. Walker was the unofficial winner of the rematch.

Teaming with Kearns after the death of his first manager, Jack Bulger, Walker returned to welterweight and successfully defended against Shade. But on May 20, 1926, he was dethroned in Scranton, Pennsylvania, by local favorite Pete Latzo. One month later, he took his worst beating ever, losing by eight-round TKO to Joe Dundee.

Depressed and broke, Walker almost quit the ring. Insiders blamed Kearns, saying that he had created a champion in Dempsey, and destroyed one in Walker. But Walker returned after the summer, and three victories led to a December 3 try at slick middleweight champion Tiger Flowers. The challenger captured a disputed 10-round decision at the Coliseum in Chicago. Once more, Walker was the spirit of Broadway.

He would make three successful defenses of the 160-pound title, and move up to light heavyweight while still king. On March 18, 1929, he challenged world champion Tommy Loughran in Chicago and came within one judge's card of joining Bob Fitzsimmons as boxing's only triple-crown titlist. (Loughran won by split 10-round decision.) By the time Walker relinquished the middleweight title, he had already beaten name heavyweights like Bearcat Wright and Johnny Risko.

Walker would secure one more try at the 175-pound title, losing on points to Maxie Rosenbloom on November 3, 1934. But the fights that helped create his legend were against boxing's big boys. On July 22, 1931, Walker gave away 29 pounds and faced top-rated heavyweight Jack Sharkey. Attacking all the way, he managed a 15-round draw.

Walker followed the draw with wins over a pair of contenders, King Levinsky and Paulino Uzcudun. Observers were fascinated by his success against bigger fighters, but since his days at welterweight, he had always been troubled more by speed than size, strength, or power. When he faced former heavyweight champion Max Schmeling on September 26, 1932, however, Walker couldn't overcome the German's physical advantages. Walker remained competitive for the first half-dozen rounds, but in the eighth, he suffered a knockdown and took a horrible beating. Before the start of the ninth, Kearns elected to surrender.

"I guess this was one we couldn't win, Mick," Kearns said afterward.

"Speak for yourself, Doc," Walker replied. "You threw in the sponge, not me."

In 1934, Walker managed to avenge his title fight defeat to Rosenbloom, but he soon broke with Kearns and quickly faded from the top. His last bout, a kayo loss to Eric Seelig, came on December 1, 1935. He exited with a record of 115-21-4 (61), with 22 no-decisions and 1 no-contest.

Restless in retirement, Walker opened a bar on Broadway and drank the profits. Then one day, he stopped drinking altogether. Just like that. He entertained the troops during World War II, starred in a night club act, made a handful of movies, and wrote a boxing column for the *Police Gazette*. At one point, he even considered running for mayor of Rumson, New Jersey. But in his post-boxing years, Walker was ultimately defined by his artwork.

Inspired by the film *The Moon And Sixpence*, which was based on W. Somerset Maugham's fictionalized biography of the painter Gauguin, the former champion turned to a different kind of canvas. Uncovering a passion for painting, he became obsessed with his brushes and oils. His reward came in May 1944 – a one-man show at the Waldorf-Astoria Hotel.

Unfortunately, Walker did not age gracefully. Suffering from Parkinson's Syndrome, anemia, and arteriosclerosis, he was shuffled from nursing homes to psychiatric hospitals. On April 28, 1981, he died at age 79 in Freehold, New Jersey. "Sober or stiff," he once said, "I belted the guts out of the best of them."

Walker was managed to perfection by the great Jack "Doc" Kearns, who was also the guiding genius behind Jack Dempsey.

JANUARY

1934

DECEMBER

Max Baer eyes the bewildered and helpless heavyweight king, Italian Primo Carnera.

A KNOCKDOWN PER ROUND

It came as no surprise when, on June 14, handsome, talented Max Baer took the heavyweight title from Primo Carnera. But not one of the 52,268 fans at Long Island City's Madison Square Garden Bowl predicted the scenario.

One minute into the first round, the challenger, a feared puncher, scored a knockdown. Before referee Arthur Donovan rescued Carnera in round 11, there would be 10 more. Carnera turned out to be as limited as most observers had suspected. But he had the heart of a champion.

At times, the fight turned comical, with Baer driving Carnera to the canvas, and then falling on top of him. After one such incident, Baer crawled across the ring on all fours.

In hailing the new champion, insiders predicted a lengthy reign. What they would discover was that Baer was indeed good. But he was even more unpredictable.

FIGHTING TALK

He's still a bum. He won because he was in there with a bigger bum

BILL BROWN
New York State Athletic Commission official on Baer's victory over Carnera

REVENGE AT LAST FOR THE JEWISH FACTION

In an era of ethnic matchups, Ireland-born world welterweight champ Jimmy McLarnin had frustrated eight top Jewish fighters.

On May 28, before 45,000 fans at New York City's Polo Grounds, the Jews got their revenge. Scaling only 137¼, lightweight and junior welterweight champion Barney Ross became a triple titlist by dethroning McLarnin via split 15-round decision.

The fight was exciting throughout, and in round nine, both champions scored knockdowns. But there was no explanation for the scoring. Referee Harry Forbes and judge Harold Barnes saw Ross the clear winner in rounds, 13-1-1 and 12-2-1, respectively. Judge Tom O'Rourke, however, had McLarnin ahead by 9-1-5. Presumably, Forbes, Barnes, and O'Rourke agreed on one thing: the need for a rematch. And in September McLarnin gained a split-decision revenge.

McLarnin (right) was outpointed by Jewish fighter Barney Ross in New York.

USING FEET AS WELL AS FISTS

Extending the reign of heavyweight champion Primo Carnera wasn't going to be easy. For defense number two, promoters nominated Tommy Loughran, who six years before had vacated the light heavyweight throne. Squaring off on March 1 at the Madison Square Garden Stadium in Miami, Carnera and Loughran resembled David and Goliath. The champion enjoyed an almost unimaginable 86-pound weight advantage, scaling 270 to Loughran's 184. The bout was uneventful, with Carnera's jab one of two weapons of note. The other was his left foot, which he repeatedly placed over Loughran's foot.

After the champion retained the crown by unanimous decision, Loughran was asked whether he had ever been hurt.

He answered with a shrug: "Only when he stomped on my foot with his size-15 gunboats."

WORLD TITLE FIGHTS

HEAVYWEIGHTS

March 1	**Primo Carnera** *W* 15 Tommy Loughran, Miami
June 14	**Max Baer** (USA) *KO* 11 Primo Carnera, Long Island City, NY

LIGHT HEAVYWEIGHTS

Feb 5	**Maxie Rosenbloom** *D* 15 Joe Knight, Miami
Nov 16	**Bob Olin** (USA) *W* 15 Maxie Rosenbloom, New York City

MIDDLEWEIGHTS

Feb 11	**Teddy Yarosz** *W* 15 Jimmy Smith, Pittsburgh
Feb 26	**Marcel Thil** *W* 15 Ignacio Ara, Paris
May 1	**Vince Dundee** *ref* 15 Al Diamond, Paterson, NJ
May 3	**Marcel Thil** *W* 15 Gustave Roth, Paris
Sept 11	**Teddy Yarosz** *W* 15 Vince Dundee, Pittsburgh
Oct 15	**Marcel Thil** *D* 15 Carmelo Candel, Paris

WELTERWEIGHTS

May 28	**Barney Ross** *W* 15 Jimmy McLarnin, Long Island City, NY
Sept 17	**Jimmy McLarnin** *W* 15 Barney Ross, Long Island City, NY

JUNIOR WELTERWEIGHTS

Feb 7	**Barney Ross** *W* 12 Polo Nebo, New Orleans
March 5	**Barney Ross** *D* 10 Frankie Klick, San Francisco
March 27	**Barney Ross** *W* 10 Bobby Pacho, Los Angeles
Dec 10	**Barney Ross** *W* 12 Bobby Pacho, Cleveland

FEATHERWEIGHTS

Jan 1	**Freddie Miller** *W* 10 Jack Sharkey, Cincinnati
Sept 20	**Freddie Miller** *ref* 15 Nel Tarleton, Liverpool

BANTAMWEIGHTS

Feb 19	**Panama Al Brown** *W* 15 Young Perez, Paris
June 26	**Sixto Escobar** (PR) *KO* 9 Baby Casanova, Montreal (Vacant NBA Title)
Aug 8	**Sixto Escobar** *W* 15 Eugene Huat, Montreal

FLYWEIGHTS

June 18	**Jackie Brown** *D* 15 Valentin Angelmann, Manchester

JANUARY 1935 DECEMBER

HE WAS WORTHY AFTER ALL

Many of boxing's lifers questioned the commitment of light heavyweight Bob Olin. The New Yorker held a position at a Wall Street brokerage firm, and boxed solely because he was good at it. His manager, Harold Scadron, recalled that before fighting for $75 and $100 purses, Olin would go to his pocket and ask him to hold onto $1,000 until he returned to the dressing room.

In November 1934, Olin had benefited from a questionable decision to take Maxie Rosenbloom's world title. For his first defense, he chose a fighter who had already beaten him, John Henry Lewis. The Californian was coming off two straight losses, and Olin thought that he might turn out to be a tad overrated.

No such luck. On October 31 at the Arena in St. Louis, Lewis pounded Olin from ringpost to ringpost. The fans expected referee Walter Heisner to step in, but Olin went the distance.

"Never in my 40 years of covering fights have I seen a man take the kind of punishment Bob Olin took from Lewis," wrote Ed Wray, sports editor of the *St. Louis Post Dispatch*.

Over the rest of his career, Olin won only seven of 11 bouts. But no one ever again dared question his commitment to the ring.

Young Lou Ambers (left) and Tony Canzoneri.

RINGSIDE VIEW

JANUARY

Baby Arizmendi outpoints Henry Armstrong for the second time in two months and captures the vacant California and Mexican featherweight titles.

MAY

Barney Ross regains the welterweight title by unanimous decision over Jimmy McLarnin. Referee Jack Dempsey curiously scores seven of the 15 rounds even.

TAMING A YOUNG TIGER

When Tony Canzoneri, 26, and Lou Ambers, 21, clashed for the lightweight title vacated by Barney Ross, the five years between them might as well have been 15. When Canzoneri fought for his first world title, Ambers was just beginning high school.

Before 17,433 fans at Madison Square Garden, Canzoneri's experience proved critical. Ambers kept running into Canzoneri's still-formidable right hand. There were three knockdowns and Canzoneri regained the crown by unanimous verdict.

Who was it that suggested 26 was so old, anyway?

CINDERELLA TAKES ALL

Long Island City's Madison Square Garden Bowl was a jinx for the champions who defended there, but it seemed unlikely that James J. Braddock would benefit. Braddock was a 10-1 underdog for his June 13 challenge of heavyweight champion Max Baer.

The New Yorker had 24 losses, and in a 1929 bout vs. Tommy Loughran, hadn't even been good enough to win the light heavyweight title. In fact, so directionless was his career that in 1934, Braddock had to apply for relief.

It was expected that Baer's crunching right hand would overwhelm the moderately talented challenger. Braddock, however, outboxed the champion all the way, and in the greatest heavyweight upset in the 45 years of the modern era, took the title by unanimous 15-round decision.

Ringsiders knew that when the frivolous Baer didn't feel like fighting, he was easily beaten. But this time, Maxie had an excuse, though he refused to hide behind it: during the fight, he broke his right thumb, as well as a bone in his left wrist.

As it would turn out, Baer would never be the same. The same could be said for James J. Braddock, boxing's aptly named "Cinderella Man."

Baer (right) wades into Jimmy Braddock.

WORLD TITLE FIGHTS

HEAVYWEIGHTS

June 13	**James J. Braddock** (USA) *W* 15 Max Baer, Long Island City, NY

LIGHT HEAVYWEIGHTS

Oct 31	**John Henry Lewis** (USA) *W* 15 Bob Olin, St. Louis

MIDDLEWEIGHTS

May 4	**Marcel Thil** *KO* 14 Vilda Jaks, Paris
June 3	**Marcel Thil** *W* 15 Ignacio Ara, Madrid
Sept 19	**Babe Risko** (USA) *W* 15 Teddy Yarosz, Pittsburgh (NBA & New York World Titles)

WELTERWEIGHTS

May 28	**Barney Ross** *W* 15 Jimmy McLarnin, New York City

JUNIOR WELTERWEIGHTS

April 9	**Barney Ross** *W* 12 Harry Woods, Seattle

LIGHTWEIGHTS

May 10	**Tony Canzoneri** *W* 15 Lou Ambers, New York City (Vacant World Title)
Oct 4	**Tony Canzoneri** *W* 15 Al Roth, New York City

FEATHERWEIGHTS

Jan 1	**Baby Arizmendi** (MEX) *W* 12 Henry Armstrong, Mexico City (Vacant California & Mexican World Titles)
Feb 17	**Freddie Miller** *KO* 1 Jose Girones, Barcelona
June 11	**Freddie Miller** *ref* 15 Nel Tarleton, Liverpool
Oct 21	**Freddie Miller** *W* 15 Vernon Cormier, Boston

BANTAMWEIGHTS

June 1	**Baltazar Sangchili** (SPA) *W* 15 Panama Al Brown, Valencia, Spain
Aug 26	**Lou Salica** *W* 15 Sixto Escobar, Bronx, NY (NBA Title)
Nov 15	**Sixto Escobar** *W* 15 Lou Salica, New York City

FLYWEIGHTS

Sept 9	**Benny Lynch** (SCOT) *KO* 2 Jackie Brown, Manchester (NBA Title)
Sept 16	**Small Montana** (PHIL) *ref* 10 Midget Wolgast, Oakland (New York World Title)

JANUARY

1936

DECEMBER

POUNDED PURPLE

Only one month after his disappointing title fight loss to Lou Ambers, triple-crown titlist Tony Canzoneri climbed through the ropes for a rematch with former welterweight champion Jimmy McLarnin. (On May 8, Canzoneri had outpointed the baby-faced Irishman over 10 rounds.)

The rise in weight made no difference. On October 5 at Madison Square Garden, Canzoneri never got past his opponent's jab. Long gone was the power that had made McLarnin the most feared puncher in the game.

He was able, however, to easily defeat Canzoneri with his other hand. Left after left found Canzoneri's unprotected face, and by the late rounds, his right eye was cut and purple, and his mouth was bleeding, too. He lasted the distance, but lost by unanimous decision.

Ironically, it was Canzoneri who would elect to keep punching. McLarnin, 29, would fight just once more, decisioning Ambers in a non-title fight. Canzoneri, on the other hand, would campaign for another three years, and even fight once more for the lightweight title.

Lou Ambers (right) and Tony Canzoneri.

A LEGEND STARTS TO FADE

When Tony Canzoneri entered the ring at Madison Square Garden on September 3, he was a prohibitive favorite to defeat Lou Ambers. The oddsmakers had plenty of reasons.

* He was lightweight champion of the world.
* He was the winner of 14 consecutive fights.
* He was coming off a points win over Jimmy McLarnin.
* He had convincingly beaten Ambers in their first title bout.

But Tony Canzoneri turned old overnight. Marching forward and winging punches from the start, Ambers dominated. Canzoneri's right hand, the key weapon in his first fight with Ambers, was rarely featured, and when he did fire it, the challenger easily darted out of reach. Over the course of 15 spirited, albeit unexciting rounds, Canzoneri mustered only two sustained rallies.

After Ambers was crowned by unanimous decision, Canzoneri blamed a four-month layoff. Others pointed to the unusual humidity inside the Garden. His friends, however, knew better.

"Youth licked Tony tonight," former lightweight champion Benny Leonard told the *New York American*. "After all, he's been tossing leather for 11 years."

BROWN BOMBER BLASTED

Joe Louis' route to the heavyweight title was not an unusual one: mixed in with opponents of various styles and skills was a sprinkling of faded former champions. In June 1935, Louis kayoed Primo Carnera, and three months later, he massacred Max Baer.

A try at James J. Braddock's title within his grasp, Louis, 23-0, was matched with another former titlist, Max Schmeling, at Yankee Stadium on June 19. The 30-year-old German was in reasonably good condition, but it seemed he had never recovered from a disheartening stretch during which he lost the title to Jack Sharkey, and then was beaten by Baer and Steve Hamas.

Where Louis was a somewhat mechanical fighter, Schmeling was a student of the game. In studying films of Louis, he detected a potentially critical flaw: because Louis often carried his left hand low, he was a sucker for a counter right.

Over 12 shockingly one-sided rounds, Schmeling landed his right over and over again. Hurt as early as the second round, Louis was unable to adjust. He fell a total of three times, and only his heart allowed him to last as long as round 12 before being kayoed.

Referee Donovan orders Schmeling to neutral corner as Louis struggles to regain his senses.

WORLD TITLE FIGHTS

LIGHT HEAVYWEIGHTS

March 13	**John Henry Lewis** *W* 15 Jock McAvoy, New York City
Nov 9	**John Henry Lewis** *ref* 15 Len Harvey, London

MIDDLEWEIGHTS

Jan 20	**Marcel Thil** *W* Disq. 4 Lou Brouillard, Paris
Feb 10	**Babe Risko** *ref* 10 Tony Fisher, Newark, NJ
July 11	**Freddie Steele** (USA) *W* 15 Babe Risko, Seattle (NBA & New York World Titles)

WELTERWEIGHTS

Nov 27	**Barney Ross** *W* 15 Izzy Jannazzo, New York City

LIGHTWEIGHTS

Sept 3	**Lou Ambers** (USA) *W* 15 Tony Canzoneri, New York City

FEATHERWEIGHTS

Feb 18	**Freddie Miller** *W* 12 Johnny Pena, Seattle
March 1	**Freddie Miller** *W* 15 Petey Sarron, Coral Galbles, FL
May 11	**Petey Sarron** (USA) *W* 15 Freddie Miller, Washington, D.C.
July 21	**Petey Sarron** *W* 15 Baby Manuel, Dallas
Aug 4	**Henry Armstrong** (USA) *W* 10 Baby Arizmendi, Los Angeles (California & Mexican World Titles)
Sept 3	**Mike Belloise** (USA) *KO* 9 Dave Crowley, New York City (New York World Title)
Oct 27	**Henry Armstrong** *W* 10 Mike Belloise, Los Angeles

BANTAMWEIGHTS

June 29	**Tony Marino** (USA) *KO* 14 Baltazar Sangchili, Bronx, NY
Aug 31	**Sixto Escobar** *KO* 14 Tony Marino, Bronx, NY
Oct 13	**Sixto Escobar** *KO* 1 Indian Quintana, New York City

FLYWEIGHTS

Sept 16	**Benny Lynch** *KO* 8 Pat Palmer, Glasgow

MIDNIGHT FOR THE CINDERELLA MAN

In the race to reach heavyweight champion James J. Braddock, Joe Louis outsprinted Max Schmeling. Or perhaps more accurately, he outbid him.

It was a foregone conclusion that either Louis or Schmeling would dethrone the vulnerable Braddock. After seeking the best deal, Joe Gould, Braddock's manager, signed with promoter Mike Jacobs. For defending against Louis, Braddock would receive a guarantee of $300,000, and, should he lose, 10 percent of the net profits from Jacobs' heavyweight title fight promotions for the next 10 years.

Jim Braddock (left) made a valiant attempt to save the heavyweight crown against Joe Louis.

Louis' challenge came on June 22, before 45,500 fans at Chicago's Comiskey Park. Braddock threatened only in the first round, when a right uppercut dropped Louis for a brief count. After that uncomfortable moment, Louis slowly and meticulously destroyed the champion. Upon returning to his corner after the seventh round, Braddock was told by Gould, "I'm going to tell (referee) Thomas to stop it."

"If you do," responded Braddock, his eyes cut and swollen, and his lip split, "I'll never talk to you again."

Braddock had his way, and in the eighth, Louis drove "The Cinderella Man" face-first to the canvas with a straight right. Referee Thomas' toll turned out to be a countdown to history.

A STAND-UP KIND OF A GUY

When seeking horizontal heavyweights, American managers usually telephoned the UK, where even the best of the big men could be counted on to lie down on the job. Such a reputation was best promoted by "Fainting" Phil Scott, who would crumble and scream "foul!" after receiving the most ticklish of blows.

But Tommy Farr, a one-time coal miner from Wales, was tough, as suggested by his victories over Tommy Loughran, Bob Olin, and Max Baer. And when he went 15 rounds with world champ Joe Louis at Yankee Stadium on August 30, he proved just how tough.

Fighting in a crouch that confused the champion, Farr all but eliminated Louis' power weapons. "The Brown Bomber" chopped up his challenger with a steady jab, and won by scores of 13-2, 10-5, and 8-4-3 in rounds. Farr's ability to last the distance against the best puncher of the day, however, dominated the headlines.

The magnitude of Farr's accomplishment wouldn't be realized until the latter stages of Louis' record reign. Louis would kayo 20 of his next 22 opponents. But he never came close to knocking out Farr.

World Title Fights

HEAVYWEIGHTS	
June 21	**Joe Louis** (USA) *KO* 8 James J. Braddock, Chicago
Aug 30	**Joe Louis** *W* 15 Tommy Farr, Bronx, NY
LIGHT HEAVYWEIGHTS	
June 3	**John Henry Lewis** *KO* 8 Bob Olin, St. Louis
MIDDLEWEIGHTS	
Jan 1	**Freddie Steele** *W* 10 Gorilla Jones, Milwaukee
Feb 15	**Marcel Thil** *W* Disq. 6 Lou Brouillard, Paris
Feb 19	**Freddie Steele** *W* 15 Babe Risko, New York City
May 11	**Freddie Steele** *KO* 3 Frank Battaglia, Seattle
Sept 11	**Freddie Steele** *KO* 4 Ken Overlin, Seattle
Sept 23	**Fred Apostoli** (USA) *KO* 10 Marcel Thil, New York City
WELTERWEIGHTS	
Sept 23	**Barney Ross** *W* 15 Ceferino Garcia, New York City
LIGHTWEIGHTS	
May 7	**Lou Ambers** *W* 15 Tony Canzoneri, New York City
Sept 23	**Lou Ambers** *W* 15 Pedro Montanez, New York City
FEATHERWEIGHTS	
Sept 4	**Petey Sarron** *W* 12 Freddie Miller, Johannesburg
Oct 29	**Henry Armstrong** (USA) *KO* 6 Petey Sarron, New York City
BANTAMWEIGHTS	
Feb 21	**Sixto Escobar** *W* 15 Lou Salica, San Juan
Sept 23	**Harry Jeffra** (USA) *W* 15 Sixto Escobar, New York City
FLYWEIGHTS	
Jan 19	**Benny Lynch** *ref* 15 Small Montana, Wembley
Oct 13	**Benny Lynch** *KO* 13 Peter Kane, Glasgow

A NEW CHAMP, FAIR OR FOUL

Some title reigns end by knockout. Others end by decision. Fittingly, middleweight champion Marcel Thil's championship days ended in controversy.

The Frenchman, who was coming off a pair of disqualification victories over Lou Brouillard, was stopped on cuts by San Francisco's Fred Apostoli. Thil cried foul, but no one wanted to listen.

The champion was ahead on two of the three official cards when, in round nine, he suffered a nasty gash over his right eye. During the rest period, Dr. William Walker told referee Arthur Donovan that unless the champion won round 10, the fight should be stopped. Seconds after the start of the round, the cut was reopened, and Donovan intervened.

"It was just my luck that his laces cut me," Thil said afterward. "A punch did not cut me."

Thil had complained once too often; there would be no rematch.

Fred Apostoli (right) stopped Marcel Thil.

JANUARY

1938

DECEMBER

CALL ME CHAMP!

For Joe Louis, a rematch with Max Schmeling was personal. After winning the heavyweight title from James J. Braddock, Louis said, "I don't want to be called champ until I lick Max Smelling."

For millions of others, Louis-Schmeling II represented something much more than a prize fight. With Adolf Hitler promoting the superiority of the Aryan race, Germany's Schmeling became a reluctant symbol.

On June 22, more than 70,000 fans came to Yankee Stadium for a fight that would last 124 seconds – and live forever. The champion showered Schmeling with punches, and after landing a wide right that fractured two vertebrae in the challenger's back, he displayed his murderous finishing touch. There were three knockdowns in all, with referee Arthur Donovan counting Schmeling out.

Symbolism aside, the fight proved only one thing: Joe Louis was superior to Max Schmeling.

THREE TITLES – AND ALL AT ONCE!

The greatest fighter ever? That will be debated for as long as crosses follow jabs. But there can be no argument that in 1938, Henry Armstrong completed the greatest achievement in the history of the ring.

In October 1937, Armstrong had won the featherweight title by knocking out Petey Sarron. On May 31, 1938, he outpointed a lifeless Barney Ross to add the welterweight title. Then, 10 weeks later, he challenged lightweight champion Lou Ambers.

The historic battle took place at Madison Square Garden on August 17. Despite losing three rounds on fouls, Armstrong emerged victorious by split 15-round decision. Ambers' non-stop punching, however, had exacted a heavy toll: "Hammerin' Hank" finished with both eyes cut and swollen, and needed 37 stitches to close a wound inside his mouth. Armstrong was told that if he spat out any more blood, the bout would be stopped. So he intentionally swallowed it.

Upon his coronation, Armstrong reigned as featherweight, lightweight, and welterweight champion of the world. It was a unique accomplishment, and one that would never be matched.

Henry Armstrong (right) and Lou Ambers.

RINGSIDE VIEW

JUNE

Weighing 6½ pounds over the limit, flyweight champ Benny Lynch loses the title on the scales, before his defense against Jackie Jurich. Lynch scores a 12th-round kayo, and the title is declared vacant.

NOVEMBER

Al Hostak breaks both his hands in the early rounds, and Brooklyn's Solly Krieger wins the middleweight title.

PUNCHING THROUGH STEELE

In a summer dominated by Joe Louis and Henry Armstrong, middleweights Freddie Steele and Al Hostak managed to secure a few headlines. Their bout, fought for the NBA title at Seattle's Civic Stadium on July 26, contained enough storylines to sell any fight.

* Upstart challenger Hostak, 22, was once employed as Steele's sparring partner.

* From Washington, Steele was the local number-one hero. Minnesota-born Hostak had moved to Washington as a child, and fought all his pro bouts there.

* Both were big punchers. Steele had kayoed Fred Apostoli and Ceferino Garcia (twice). Hostak had finished his last 14 opponents.

What transpired was almost unbelievable. Steaming out of his corner, Hostak caught Steele with his first counterpunch. Four knockdowns followed, and after only 103 seconds of action, Steele was through. One day later, he announced his retirement at age 25.

"Everyone was saying after the fight that I caught him with a lucky punch," Hostak said later. "It was no lucky punch. I studied Steele's moves for months before I ever got into the ring with him."

WORLD TITLE FIGHTS

HEAVYWEIGHTS

Feb 23	**Joe Louis** *KO* 3 Nathan Mann, New York City
April 1	**Joe Louis** *KO* 5 Harry Thomas, Chicago
June 21	**Joe Louis** *KO* 1 Max Schmeling, Bronx, NY

LIGHT HEAVYWEIGHTS

April 25	**John Henry Lewis** *KO* 4 Emilio Martinez, Minneapolis
Oct 28	**John Henry Lewis** *W* 15 Al Gainer, New Haven, CT

MIDDLEWEIGHTS

Feb 19	**Freddie Steele** *KO* 7 Carmen Barth, Cleveland
April 1	**Fred Apostoli** *W* 15 Glenn Lee, New York City
July 26	**Al Hostak** (USA) *KO* 1 Freddie Steele, Seattle (NBA Title)
Nov 1	**Solly Krieger** (USA) *W* 15 Al Hostak, Seattle
Nov 18	**Fred Apostoli** *KO* 8 Young Corbett, New York City

WELTERWEIGHTS

May 31	**Henry Armstrong** *W* 15 Barney Ross, Long Island City, NY
Nov 25	**Henry Armstrong** *W* 15 Ceferino Garcia, New York City
Dec 5	**Henry Armstrong** *KO* 3 Al Manfredo, Cleveland

LIGHTWEIGHTS

Aug 17	**Henry Armstrong** *W* 15 Lou Ambers, New York City

FEATHERWEIGHTS

June 17	**Leo Rodak** (USA) *W* 15 Jackie Wilson, Baltimore (Vacant Maryland World Title)
Oct 17	**Joey Archibald** (USA) *W* 15 Mike Belloise, New York City (Vacant New York World Title)
Oct 24	**Leo Rodak** *W* 15 Freddie Miller, Washington, D.C.

BANTAMWEIGHTS

Feb 20	**Sixto Escobar** *W* 15 Harry Jeffra, San Juan

FLYWEIGHTS

March 24	**Benny Lynch** *D* 15 Peter Kane, Liverpool
June 29	**Benny Lynch** *KO* 12 Peter Kane, Paisley, Scotland
Sept 22	**Peter Kane** (ENG) *ref* 15 Jackie Jurich, Liverpool (Vacant World Title)
Nov 30	**Little Dado** (PHIL) *ref* 10 Small Montana, Oakland (Vacant California World Title)

THE LOW ROAD TO THE TITLE

The Henry Armstrong-Lou Ambers title fight, held on August 22 before 29,088 fans at Yankee Stadium, was a passionate affair. The busy and brave lightweights hammered each other for all 15 rounds, just as they had one year before, when Armstrong took the title on points. The difference this time was referee Arthur Donovan.

The respected third man of the ring penalized Armstrong for punching low in rounds two, five, seven, nine, and 11. An unprecedented five rounds in all.

Armstrong had outbrawled Ambers in four of those five rounds. He was the more effective infighter in most of the other rounds as well, and as a result, the decision was close, with Ambers regaining the crown by scores of 8-7 (twice) and 11-3-1.

The final bell signaled the start of the second fight, which featured the respective managers and the New York State Athletic Commission. Eddie Mead, Armstrong's handler, was suspended for 13 months after publicly accusing Commissioner Bill Brown of favoring Ambers. And Al Weill, Mead's counterpart, was suspended four months for his unsportsmanlike behavior.

TWO TONS OF TROUBLE

After his retirement, Joe Louis revealed that only two opponents had inspired violent instincts: Schmeling and Tony Galento.

That Galento qualified as a world-class heavyweight was remarkable. He stood 5'9" and, for the Louis fight, scaled an unsightly 233¾. He honed his skills as a bouncer and barkeep. But Galento had a dangerous left hook; after signing to meet Louis at Yankee Stadium on June 28, he promised, "I'll moida da bum."

In the days before the fight, Galento telephoned Louis with threats. Worse yet, newspaperman Barney Nagler reported that during referee Arthur Donovan's final instructions, "Two Ton Tony" informed the champion of his sexual plans for Mrs. Louis.

Galento staggered Louis in the first round. In the second, however, Louis put his punches together from a comfortable distance. Galento opened round three looking like the victim of a horror film, but managed to toss one wild hook in the direction of "The Brown Bomber's" chin. Bullseye! Louis crashed and took a count of two.His moment having come and gone, Galento was massacred in round four. Donovan rescued him at the 2:29 mark.

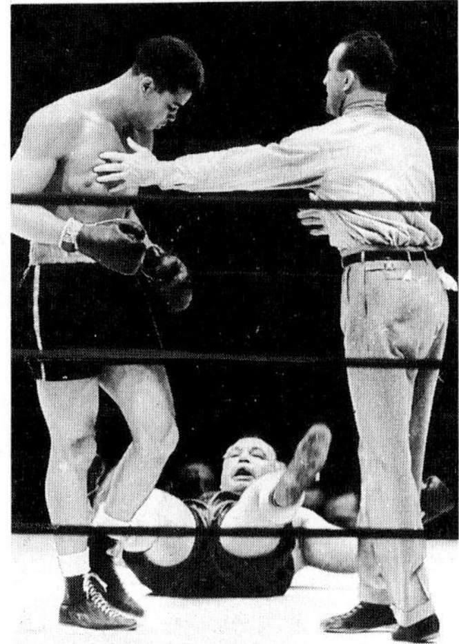

Joe Louis finishes off Tony Galento.

FIGHTING TALK

If it is possible for a colored man to look pale, John Henry did

DAN PARKER
Fight columnist

JANUARY

1939

DECEMBER

SECRET REASON FOR NERVES

When light heavyweight champion John Henry Lewis weighed in for his January 25 try at Joe Louis' heavyweight title, he appeared gaunt and nervous. He scaled only 180¼, about eight pounds less than his recent fighting weight.

Indeed, before a Madison Square Garden crowd of 17,350, Lewis, a 10-1 underdog, fought scared. Thirty seconds into the first round, the champion struck with a right to the jaw, and from that point on, Lewis stumbled on rubbery legs. Three knockdowns later, referee Arthur Donovan stepped in at the 2:29 mark.

"I'm sure glad that I didn't have to hit John again," Louis said.

Lewis would never fight again. Five months later, he retired at 24. For the last three years of his career, a cataract had robbed him of the sight of one eye.

WORLD TITLE FIGHTS

HEAVYWEIGHTS

Jan 25	**Joe Louis** *KO* 1 John Henry Lewis, New York City
April 17	**Joe Louis** KO 1 Jack Roper, Los Angeles
June 28	**Joe Louis** *KO* 4 Tony Galento, Bronx, NY
Sept 20	**Joe Louis** *KO* 11 Bob Pastor, Detroit

LIGHT HEAVYWEIGHTS

Feb 3	**Melio Bettina** (USA) *KO* 9 Tiger Jack Fox, New York City (Vacant New York World Title)
July 10	**Len Harvey** (ENG) *ref* 15 Jock McAvoy, London (Vacant British World Title)
July 13	**Billy Conn** (USA) *W* 15 Melio Bettina, New York City (Vacant World Title)
Sept 25	**Billy Conn** *W* 15 Melio Bettina, Pittsburgh
Nov 17	**Billy Conn** *W* 15 Gus Lesnevich, New York City

MIDDLEWEIGHTS

June 27	**Al Hostak** *KO* 4 Solly Krieger, Seattle
Oct 2	**Ceferino Garcia** (PHIL) *KO* 7 Fred Apostoli, New York City
Dec 11	**Al Hostak** *KO* 1 Eric Seelig, Cleveland
Dec 23	**Ceferino Garcia** *KO* 13 Glenn Lee, Manila

WELTERWEIGHTS

Jan 10	**Henry Armstrong** *ref* 10 Baby Arizmendi, Los Angeles
March 4	**Henry Armstrong** *KO* 4 Bobby Pacho, Havana
March 16	**Henry Armstrong** *KO* 1 Lew Feldman, St. Louis
March 31	**Henry Armstrong** *KO* 12 Davey Day, New York City
May 25	**Henry Armstrong** *ref* 15 Ernie Roderick, London
Oct 9	**Henry Armstrong** *KO* 4 Al Manfredo, Des Moines, IA
Oct 13	**Henry Armstrong** *KO* 2 Howard Scott, Minneapolis
Oct 20	**Henry Armstrong** *KO* 3 Ritchie Fontaine, Seattle
Oct 24	**Henry Armstrong** *ref* 10 Jimmy Garrison, Los Angeles
Oct 30	**Henry Armstrong** *KO* 4 Bobby Pacho, Denver
Dec 11	**Henry Armstrong** *KO* 7 Jimmy Garrison, Cleveland

LIGHTWEIGHTS

Aug 21	**Lou Ambers** *W* 15 Henry Armstrong, Bronx, NY

FEATHERWEIGHTS

April 18	**Joey Archibald** *ref* 15 Leo Rodak, Providence
Sept 28	**Joey Archibald** *W* 15 Harry Jeffra, Washington, D.C.

BANTAMWEIGHTS

April 1	**Sixto Escobar** *W* 15 KO Morgan, San Juan

Henry Armstrong

IF THE violence of boxing were its sole appeal, the game would be little more than a gloved exercise in Darwinism. The legends of the ring are born not of skill and stamina, but character. At the exact moments that championships are won or lost, courage and determination override all else. That's why any list of boxing's 10 best pound-for-pound fighters includes Henry Armstrong.

After Armstrong's death, his heart was found to be one-third larger than average. Historians had a literal explanation for what they had always described figuratively.

Character carried Armstrong to the pantheon. Born Henry Jackson on December 12, 1912, in Columbus, Mississippi, Armstrong was the 11th of 15 children raised by Henry and America Jackson. The fighter's father, a farmer and expert butcher, was a mix of Indian, Irish, and black blood. His mother was half-Cherokee Indian.

When Armstrong was four, the Jacksons moved to St. Louis. America Jackson died only one year later, and Henry was raised by his grandmother. Impressed by the beautiful homes owned by St. Louis' black doctors, Armstrong dreamed of attending medical school. After he graduated high school, however, his father died. Needing money, Armstrong went to work for the Missouri-Pacific Railroad. Every morning, a handcar would pick up the employees for the 10-mile ride from St. Louis to Carondolet, Missouri. Armstrong always chose to run.

While working for the railroad Armstrong came across a newspaper headline that changed his life: "Kid Chocolate Earns $75,000 For Half-Hour's Work." Armstrong reasoned that if a Cuban could make that kind of money during a depression, a hungry American could surely do the same. He immediately resigned, telling his co-workers, "I'm coming back in a Cadillac." It took a while, but Armstrong kept his word. He teamed up with – and took the surname of – a trainer and former fighter named Harry Armstrong, and won 58 of 62 amateur bouts.

On July 27, 1931, Armstrong's pro debut was a disaster: he was kayoed in the third round by a southpaw named Al Iovino. He briefly returned to the amateurs, and then resumed punching for pay. At 5'5½", he was of average height for a featherweight.

Professional career dates 1931-1945
Contests 181
Won 152
Lost 21
Drawn 8
Knockouts 100
World Featherweight Champion 1937-1938
World Welterweight Champion 1938-1940
World Lightweight Champion 1938-1939

But in subsequent years, as he faced bigger and taller opponents, his bobbing, weaving style and fierce infighting turned his inferior reach into an advantage.

Armstrong's abundance of energy allowed him to fight often, and by 1934, he was a feature attraction in Los Angeles. His first major bout came in November 1934, when the judges in Mexico City robbed him of a decision against local favorite Baby Arizmendi – and the promoter robbed him of his $1,500 purse. In January 1935, he and Arizmendi were rematched for the vacant California and Mexico world featherweight titles, and again Armstrong was the victim of a hometown decision. Justice finally prevailed in August 1936, when Armstrong dethroned his rugged rival in Los Angeles. (He would defeat Arizmendi in their fourth and fifth fights as well.)

Legendary entertainer Al Jolson witnessed Armstrong-Arizmendi III and bought the winner's contract. Jolson's front man, Eddie Mead, quickly moved Armstrong toward the top. Incredibly, in 1937 he won all 27 of his fights, and 26 by knockout.

In an attempt to maximize publicity and purses, Jolson and Mead came up with a plan: make history by winning the featherweight, lightweight, and welterweight titles. Step one came on October 29, 1937. Desperate for a significant purse, featherweight champ Petey Sarron gladly defended against Armstrong. The 126-pounders brawled from the opening bell, but Sarron couldn't match "Hammerin' Hank's" unforgiving pace. He fell in round six.

Armstrong wanted the lightweight crown next, but Al Weill, the manager of champion Lou Ambers, proved a stubborn negotiator. As a result, on May 31, 1938, Armstrong challenged welterweight titlist Barney Ross. Doubting that a fighter as small as Armstrong could offer proper competition, the New York State Athletic Commission demanded that the challenger scale at least 138 pounds. Rising from 126, Armstrong trained on beer and, on the morning of the weigh-in, drank glass after glass of water.

"It's a good thing Ross isn't a body-puncher," he said, "because one punch in the belly and the ring will be flooded." As it

Henry Armstrong knocked out 100 of his 181 opponents and decisioned 52 of them on his way to becoming a triple champion.

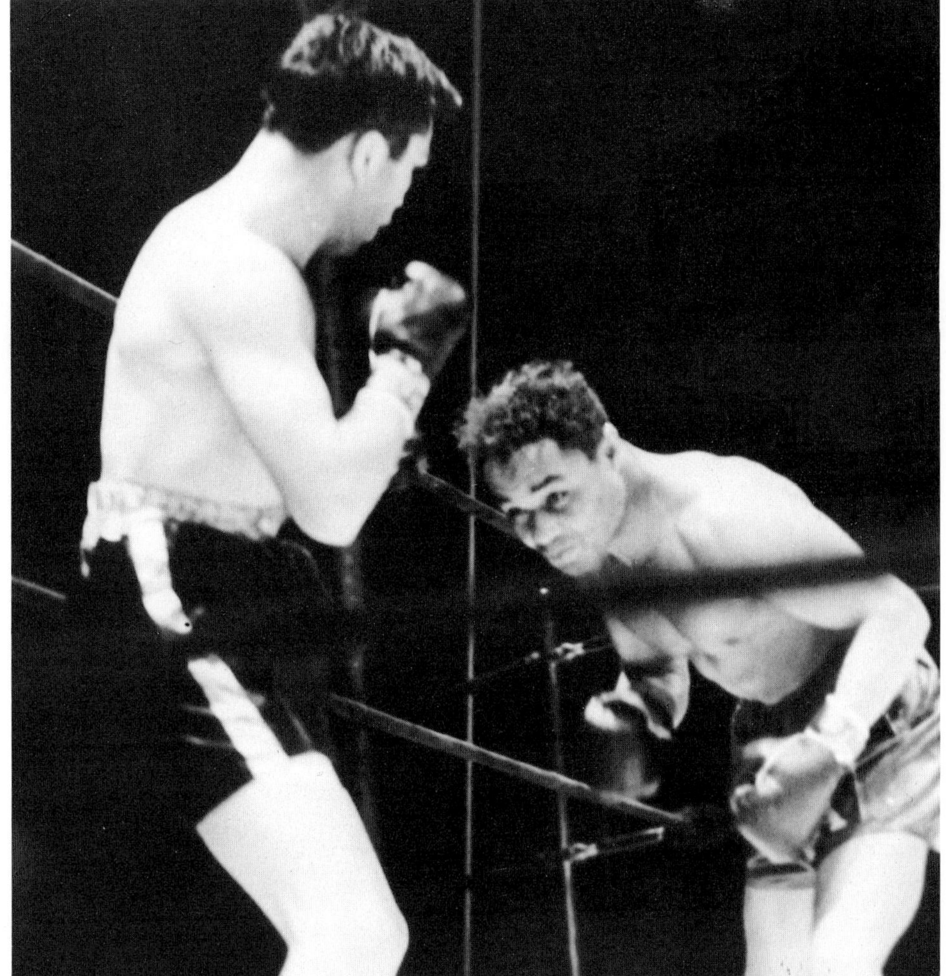

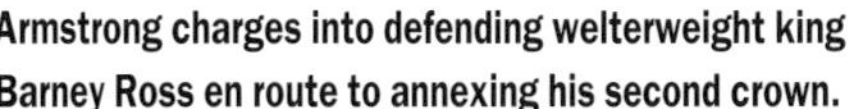

Armstrong charges into defending welterweight king Barney Ross en route to annexing his second crown.

turned out, rain forced a postponement, and it's been estimated that by the time the fighters climbed through the ropes, Armstrong weighed 133 and Ross close to 160.

Overwhelming the shell of a great champion, Armstrong proved more than competitive. In fact, so spent was Ross that the challenger showed mercy. "I carried him the last four rounds," Armstrong said. "I was asked to do it, and he thanked me for it."

Ten weeks after decisioning Ross, Armstrong, the reigning featherweight and welterweight champion, clashed with Ambers. It was a furious fight, and after 10 rounds, a torn bottom lip seemed as if it would cost Armstrong victory.

"If you spit any more blood on that floor," referee Billy Cavanaugh told him, "I'm going to stop this fight."

Armstrong instructed his cornermen to remove his mouthpiece. Over the last five rounds, he swallowed his own blood, and, despite almost blacking out in round 15, captured a split decision. For the first and last time in history, one fighter simultaneously held three world crowns.

After defeating Ambers, Armstrong relinquished the featherweight title. He made only one defense at lightweight, losing an August 1939 decision to Ambers after being penalized *five* rounds for punching low. But as welterweight king, he left an indelible mark, making a record 19 successful defenses, including 11 in 1939. Armstrong's run ended on October 4, 1940, when he was outpointed by the fiendishly clever Fritzie Zivic. On January 17, 1941, he lost the return by 12th-round kayo. It would be his last title fight.

Armstrong's triple crown was amazing, but he actually came close to winning a fourth. On March 1, 1940, the 147-pound king challenged middleweight champion Ceferino Garcia, whom he had already beaten in a 1938 welterweight defense. Armstrong rejected a $75,000 offer to fall in round four and proceeded to clearly outwork the powerpunching Filipino. After 10 rounds, however, referee and sole judge George Blake declared a draw.

Following his second loss to Zivic, Armstrong took off 18 months and then began a lucrative comeback. He won most of his bouts, but lost most of the important ones, including a 10-rounder to Sugar Ray Robinson in August 1943. His last bout was a points loss to Chester Slider on February 14, 1945. He retired at age 32 with a career mark of 152-21-8 (100).

Armstrong's post-boxing years were bittersweet. His purses had totaled between $500,000 and $1-million, but most of the money was gone before his retirement. He financed *Keep Punching*, a movie about himself, opened a bar in Los Angeles, Henry Armstrong's Club, and worked for a company marketing a healing agent for arthritis.

After a brief battle with the bottle, he turned to religion, and, in 1951, was ordained a minister. Returning to St. Louis, he served as an assistant pastor, founded the Henry Armstrong Youth Foundation, and directed the Herbert Hoover Boys Club. In his later years, he and his wife Gussie lived on a monthly $800 Social Security check. Armstrong suffered from various ailments and diseases, including pneumonia, anemia, cataracts, malnutrition, and dementia. On October 24, 1988, he died in Los Angeles. He was 75. Both figuratively and literally, that immense heart had served him well.

Henry waves after winning his first title by kayoing featherweight champ Petey Sarron in 1937.

Ring DECADE

1940-1949

MATCHUP for matchup, there's never been a decade that matched up with the '40s. Fighting for one kind of world title, there was Montgomery vs. Rommel, MacArthur vs. Yamashita, and Hitler vs. Stalin. Fighting for another kind, there was Louis vs. Conn, Zale vs. Graziano, and Pep vs. Saddler. Firepower was maximized; competition was fierce; stakes, whether political or personal, were high. Moreover, no one could be sure who was going to win.

Just like the World War more than 30 years before it, World War II devastated boxing by taking its very best men. Both the Allied Forces, and, to a lesser degree, the Axis, were filled with fighters, the most accomplished of whom taught boxing or appeared in exhibitions.

On the homefront, the first four divisions were most affected.

- Heavyweight champion Joe Louis served in the Army, freezing the title from March '42 to June '46.
- Light heavyweight champion Gus Lesnevich served in the Coast Guard, freezing the title from November '41 to May '46.
- Middleweight champion Tony Zale served in the Navy, freezing the title from November '41 to September '46.
- Welterweight champion Freddie (Red) Cochrane served in the Navy, freezing the title from July '41 to February '46.

Given that the years 1941-1946 were all but erased, the decade provided a surprising amount of history. Most of the magic moments came from five intense rivalries.

The first grudge was born in June 1941, when former light heavyweight champion Billy Conn crashed Joe Louis' Bum of the Month Club and almost won the heavyweight title. Louis-Conn II became the most anticipated bout of the decade, but before it could be made, both fighters were serving in the war.

The inevitable rematch came on June 19, 1946, five years and one day after the original. Promoter Mike Jacobs charged a record $100 per ringside seat, but the fight couldn't match the hype. Both Louis and Conn had slowed. At least the champion had retained his power, and it surfaced in round eight, when he scored what was dismissed as a so-what kayo.

Not all of the decade's best fights occurred either before or after the war. Lightweights Beau Jack and Bob Montgomery fought four times between May 1943 and August 1944, with three of the bouts contested for the New York State world title. The 135-pounders had distinctive styles that meshed perfectly. Jack was the sprinter, starting quickly and fighting furiously for as long as he could. Montgomery was the marathoner, starting slowly and invariably wearing his man down. Neither approach proved superior; they each won twice on points, with the underdog emerging victorious in all four bouts.

Joe Louis was the dominant fighter of the decade. He set the record for heavyweight title defenses, against the best available contenders.

All three of the slugfests between Tony Zale and Rocky Graziano were fought after the war. The middleweights were a study in contrasts: Zale was the hardened veteran from the American heartland, Graziano the young and impetuous street rat from New York City; Zale offered an impenetrable chin, Graziano boxing's most dangerous right hand; Zale had served admirably in the Navy; Graziano had received a dishonorable discharge after punching an officer. Theirs was a series of bouts made partly in heaven, and partly in hell.

Zale-Graziano I and II were unforgettable wars. In both bloody brawls, the winner rallied after barely surviving an extended beating. Zale kept the title by winning the first fight, and Graziano captured it by taking the second. The

Rocky Graziano was an explosive slugger, much like Stanley Ketchel. His three brawls with Tony Zale were unforgettable classics.

Handsome Irishman Billy Conn failed to last the distance in only two of his 75 fights, and it took the murderous power of Joe Louis to do it both times.

third bout was somewhat anticlimactic, with Zale striking early and often and finishing The Rock in three rounds.

Like Zale-Graziano, Willie Pep-Sandy Saddler was a rivalry spiced by differences. Pep was short, white, and technically superior; Saddler was tall, black, and as crushing a puncher as the division had ever seen. Poet Philip Levine described the 126-pounders as "little white perfection, and death in red plaid trunks."

Their first fight came in October 1948. Having lost once in 137 fights, Pep was a 3-1 favorite. Longshot players rejoiced when Saddler scored a brutal fourth-round kayo. Three months later, Pep regained his form, and after jumping to a huge lead, survived the championship rounds, as well as cuts above and below both eyes, to regain the crown in 1949's Fight of the Year.

Sugar Ray Robinson fought Jake LaMotta five times in the '40s, and lost only once. (Their sixth and last fight, the "St. Valentine's Day Massacre," came in February 1951.)

It was during his roller coaster run as middleweight champion that Robinson became known as the best fighter in history.

But Sugar Ray was never more dominant than as a welterweight in the '40s. His talents were displayed in each of his fights against the bigger and stronger LaMotta, and during a title reign that began in December '46, and ended in 1950, only because of a lack a suitable competition.

Ray Robinson averaged 15 fights per year during the decade, losing just once. Like Benny Leonard, he made boxing an art form.

California's Manuel Ortiz wasn't involved in any notable rivalries; the decade provided no bantamweights in his class.

Ortiz reigned from August '42 to May '50, except for a two-month stretch during which he lost the crown to Harold Dade, and quickly won it back. He made a total of 19 successful defenses, and headlines often at Los Angeles' Olympic Auditorium, which would become one of the most celebrated arenas in boxing.

Clearly, the decade belonged to America. But a portion was reserved for a handsome, charismatic, and beloved middleweight who was born in Sidi Bel-Abbes, Algeria, raised in Casablanca, Morocco, and based in Paris. In December 1946, Marcel Cerdan crossed the ocean and debuted in the USA. Less than two years later, the stylish Frenchman dethroned Zale.

Cerdan's reign was all too brief. In his first defense, he injured his left shoulder and took a beating before succumbing to Jake LaMotta. Four months later, while returning to America for a rematch, he was killed in a plane crash at the age of 33. Cerdan's death was the greatest tragedy of the decade.

Perhaps the greatest injustice was the inability of several black fighters to secure championship bouts. Two of them, Ezzard Charles and Archie Moore, won world titles, but only after years of struggle. Among the less fortunate: middleweight Holman Williams, who helped teach Joe Louis how to box; Lloyd Marshall, who beat Charles, Freddie Mills, Joey Maxim, and LaMotta; George Costner, who defeated Ike Williams and Kid Gavilan; Jimmy Bivins, who contended at both light heavyweight and heavyweight; and arguably the best of all, Charley Burley, who was described by legendary trainer Eddie Futch as "the finest all-around fighter I ever saw."

Toward the end of the '40s, the advent of television gave the world's best fighters, no matter their race or color, the opportunity to secure exposure. The Louis-Walcott rematch was the first heavyweight title fight to be nationally televised, and the Gillette-sponsored *Friday Night Fights* became a staple of TV programming.

In the '40s, insiders scoffed at the potential of television. In the '50s, however, they would learn that as popular as boxing was, it was the medium that was becoming the message.

Jake LaMotta rarely took a backward step and his fists rarely stopped flying. But it was incredible durability that was his trademark.

JANUARY

1940

DECEMBER

SOARING FOR FOUR

The first seven times he defended the welterweight title, Henry Armstrong never scaled over the lightweight limit. When he tried for Ceferino Garcia's middleweight title at Gilmore Stadium in Los Angeles, he scaled five pounds below the welter limit.

Armstrong was attempting to become the first ever four-division titlist. In 1938, he had beaten Garcia, but was now nearing the end of his fantastic career.

Fighting true to style, he threw hundreds of punches, opened a cut over Garcia's right eye in round three, and applied pressure from bell to bell. The 153½-pound Garcia, however, shut Armstrong's left eye and retained the crown when referee and sole judge George Blake, influenced by Armstrong's frequent shoulder butting, declared a draw.

BETTER WHEN HE DOES IT AGAIN

Fighters who faced Joe Louis for the first time should have been advised to make the most of their opportunity. Throughout his career, "The Brown Bomber" proved unbeatable in rematches.

That Louis learned from his mistakes was first suggested by his one-round annihilation of Max Schmeling. Further proof came when the heavyweight champion defended for the second time in four months against Chile's awkward Arturo Godoy.

On February 9, Louis had rejected Godoy's challenge by split 15-round decision. Aware that his crowding, crouching style had frustrated the champion, Godoy punctuated the performance by planting a 14th-round kiss on Louis' cheek.

The rematch came at Yankee Stadium on June 20. In his 11th defense, Louis was brilliant. Jack Blackburn had trained him to collide with Godoy at close range and rip him with short hooks and right uppercuts. By the end of the first round, the challenger was bleeding from a cut over his left eye. In the seventh he was down and in the eighth two more knockdowns ended it.

Louis might've offered Godoy a kiss, but the phone number of a plastic surgeon would have been more appropriate.

Joe Louis (left) was awesome in cutting down tough Arturo Godoy in 8th round.

Fritzie Zivic (left) and Henry Armstrong.

A PROMISE KEPT

Welterweight champion Henry Armstrong was decelerating. But no one could have guessed that Fritzie Zivic would beat him.

But the veteran journeyman, best known for his dirty infighting tactics, boxed his way to a close but unanimous 15-round decision victory. (His last punch, a straight right, dropped the champion; Armstrong was saved by the bell.)

Armstrong was the idol of Sugar Ray Robinson, who made his pro debut on the undercard. Robinson visited his hero in the loser's dressing room and tearfully promised that he would one day avenge Armstrong's loss. He did – twice. Only one problem: he beat Armstrong, too.

WORLD TITLE FIGHTS

HEAVYWEIGHTS

Feb 9	**Joe Louis** *W* 15 Arturo Godoy, New York City
March 29	**Joe Louis** *KO* 2 Johnny Paycheck, New York City
June 20	**Joe Louis** *KO* 8 Arturo Godoy, Bronx, NY
Dec 16	**Joe Louis** *KO* 6 Al McCoy, Boston

LIGHT HEAVYWEIGHTS

June 5	**Billy Conn** *W* 15 Gus Lesnevich, Detroit

MIDDLEWEIGHTS

March 1	**Ceferino Garcia** *D* 10 Henry Armstrong, Los Angeles
May 23	**Ken Overlin** (USA) *W* 15 Ceferino Garcia, New York City
July 19	**Tony Zale** (USA) *KO* 13 Al Hostak, Seattle (NBA Title)
Nov 1	**Ken Overlin** *W* 15 Steve Belloise, New York City
Dec 13	**Ken Overlin** *W* 15 Steve Belloise, New York City

WELTERWEIGHTS

Jan 4	**Henry Armstrong** *KO* 5 Joe Ghnouly, St. Louis
Jan 24	**Henry Armstrong** *KO* 9 Pedro Montanez, New York City
April 26	**Henry Armstrong** *KO* 7 Paul Junior, Boston
May 24	**Henry Armstrong** *KO* 5 Ralph Zanelli, Boston
June 21	**Henry Armstrong** *KO* 3 Paul Junior, Portland, ME
Sept 23	**Henry Armstrong** *KO* 4 Phil Furr, Washington, D.C.
Oct 4	**Fritzie Zivic** (USA) *W* 15 Henry Armstrong, New York City
Oct 14	**Izzy Jannazzo** (USA) *W* 15 Cocoa Kid, Baltimore (Vacant Maryland World Title)

LIGHTWEIGHTS

May 3	**Sammy Angott** (USA) *ref* 15 Davey Day, Louisville (Vacant NBA Title)
May 10	**Lew Jenkins** (USA) *KO* 3 Lou Ambers, New York City
Nov 21	**Lew Jenkins** *KO* 2 Pete Lello, New York City

FEATHERWEIGHTS

May 8	**Jimmy Perrin** (USA) *W* 15 Bobby Ruffin, New Orleans (Vacant Louisiana World Title)
May 20	**Harry Jeffra** *W* 15 Joey Archibald, Baltimore
July 10	**Petey Scalzo** (USA) *KO* 15 Bobby (Poison) Ivy, Hartford (NBA Title)
July 29	**Harry Jeffra** *W* 15 Spider Armstrong, Baltimore

BANTAMWEIGHTS

March 4	**Georgie Pace** (USA) *D* 15 Lou Salica, Toronto (NBA Title and Vacant World Title)
Sept 24	**Lou Salica** *W* 15 Georgie Pace, Bronx, NY (Vacant World Title)

BAERING IT

Max Baer may have been a clown, but there was nothing funny about heavyweight champion Joe Louis' defense against Max' younger brother, Buddy. Challenging "The Brown Bomber" on May 23 before a crowd of 23,912 at Washington, D.C.'s Griffith Stadium, the towering, 237½-pound Baer attacked from the start. In the first, he knocked Louis through the ropes with a left hook. Louis, a 10-1 favorite, barely survived until the bell.

The champion slowly gained control, but this time, his power almost cost him the title. In round six, Louis, bleeding from a cut on his left eyelid, scored two knockdowns and then floored Baer for a third time – after the round was over. "I rang the bell and looked up at the fighters," said timekeeper Billy Dechard. "I expected them to go to their corners. Joe hit Baer at least three seconds after the bell had sounded." In Louis' defense, the sound of the bell, which was tucked under the ring floor, had been barely audible. Nevertheless, at the start of round seven, Ancil Hoffman, Baer's manager, refused to allow his fighter to continue. Hoffman demanded a disqualification victory, but it was Baer that was DQ'ed by referee Arthur Donovan.

HIS IRISH BEAT HIM

Joe Louis' career was chock full of famous fights, but the most memorable of all came at the Polo Grounds on June 18, 1941. "This was the best it had ever been and ever would be," *Sports Illustrated*'s Frank Deford would write years later, "the 12th and 13th rounds of Louis and Conn on a warm night in New York, just before the world went to hell."

Former light heavyweight champion Billy Conn, 174, wasn't as strong as defending heavyweight champion Joe Louis, 199½, but he was much quicker. After a tentative start, the challenger began to punch and move in rhythm. By the middle rounds, he took firm control, and in the 12th, he landed at will. Then he stunned Louis with a left hook.

"I miss that," he would later say of the punch, "I beat him." Hurting Louis led Conn to believe he could score a kayo. Entering round 13, he led by scores of 7-5, 7-4-1, and 6-6. But he ignored his corner's instructions to box with caution, and in an instant, he became the latest victim of Louis' awesome power.

A left hook turned the fight, and with two seconds left in the 13th round, Conn was counted out by referee Eddie Joseph. "What's the sense of being Irish if you can't be dumb?" Conn asked.

Joe Louis was lucky to save his crown when flooring Buddy Baer after the bell.

Billy Conn was ahead on points going into the 13th round of his fight with Louis.

JANUARY

1941

DECEMBER

THE FALL OF TEXAS LEW

How could a lightweight good enough to twice knock out Lou Ambers fall so quickly? After winning the 135-pound crown from Ambers in May 1940, tall Texan Lew Jenkins won only five of his next nine bouts. The storyline of his fights never wavered: if Jenkins hit you clean, he knocked you out. But if he missed you, he lost.

Jenkins made his second title defense on December 19 at Madison Square Garden. He couldn't have picked a more difficult opponent. Sammy Angott clinched so effectively that he acquired the nickname "The Clutch." He had scored only 13 kayos in 86 fights.

Angott won almost every stanza en route to a unanimous 15-round decision victory. For Jenkins, it was the second of what would be nine consecutive losses. No world champion had ever fallen quite so quickly.

WORLD TITLE FIGHTS

HEAVYWEIGHTS

Jan 31	**Joe Louis** *KO* 5 Red Burman, New York City
Feb 17	**Joe Louis** *KO* 2 Gus Dorazio, Philadelphia
March 21	**Joe Louis** *KO* 13 Abe Simon, Detroit
April 8	**Joe Louis** *KO* 9 Tony Musto, St. Louis
May 23	**Joe Louis** *W Disq* 7 Buddy Baer, Washington, D.C.
June 18	**Joe Louis** *KO* 13 Billy Conn, New York City
Sept 29	**Joe Louis** *KO* 6 Lou Nova, New York City

LIGHT HEAVYWEIGHTS

Jan 13	**Anton Christoforidis** (GRE) *W* 15 Melio Bettina, Cleveland (Vacant NBA Title)
May 22	**Gus Lesnevich** (USA) *W* 15 Anton Christoforidis, New York City
Aug 26	**Gus Lesnevich** *W* 15 Tami Mauriello, New York City
Nov 14	**Gus Lesnevich** *W* 15 Tami Mauriello, New York City

MIDDLEWEIGHTS

Feb 21	**Tony Zale** *KO* 14 Steve Mamakos, Chicago
May 9	**Billy Soose** (USA) *W* 15 Ken Overlin, New York City
May 28	**Tony Zale** *KO* 2 Al Hostak, Chicago
Nov 28	**Tony Zale** *W* 15 Georgie Abrams, New York City

WELTERWEIGHTS

Jan 17	**Fritzie Zivic** *KO* 12 Henry Armstrong, New York City
April 14	**Izzy Jannazzo** *W* 15 Jimmy Leto, Baltimore
July 29	**Freddy Cochrane** (USA) *W* 15 Fritzie Zivic, Newark, NJ

LIGHTWEIGHTS

Dec 19	**Sammy Angott** *W* 15 Lew Jenkins, New York City

FEATHERWEIGHTS

May 12	**Joey Archibald** *W* 15 Harry Jeffra, Washington, D.C.
May 19	**Petey Scalzo** *D* 15 Phil Zwick, Milwaukee
July 1	**Richie Lemos** (USA) *KO* 5 Petey Scalzo, Los Angeles (NBA Title)
Sept 11	**Chalky Wright** (MEX) *KO* 11 Joey Archibald, Washington, D.C.
Nov 18	**Jackie Wilson** (USA) *W* 12 Richie Lemos, Los Angeles
Dec 16	**Jackie Wilson** *W* 12 Richie Lemos, Los Angeles

BANTAMWEIGHTS

Jan 13	**Lou Salica** *W* 15 Tommy Forte, Philadelphia
April 25	**Lou Salica** *W* 15 Lou Transporenti, Baltimore
June 16	**Lou Salica** *W* 15 Tommy Forte, Philadelphia

JANUARY

1942

DECEMBER

HE ONLY GOT HIT IN THE PAPERS

At Madison Square Garden, New York 21-year-old Willie Pep became the youngest featherweight champion since Terry McGovern when he outpointed defending titlist Chalky Wright over 15 rounds.

The undefeated Pep's 55th consecutive victory wasn't particularly difficult; he boxed smartly and absorbed a minimal amount of punishment. The scores – 11-4 (twice) and 10-4-1 – reflected his dominance. Pep always pleased his fans from his native Connecticut, but his popularity didn't carry over to the New York press.

The New York Daily News' Dick McCann wrote that Pep had retreated "faster and more frequently than Rommel's Afrika Corps." In fact, McCann had scored Wright the winner. Columnist Frank Graham chipped in, "There is, in short, little to distinguish (Pep) from a dozen other featherweights."

Pep would lose once in his next 82 fights. Hey, nobody ever said the experts were experts.

ONE BELL IS ENOUGH

At some point between his 17th and 20th defenses of the heavyweight title, Joe Louis decided he wasn't comfortable as a risk-taking champion. In his first fight against behemoth Buddy Baer, he had risked a disqualification loss after failing to hear the timekeeper's bell. In the rematch, held at Madison Square Garden on January 9, he made sure there was no reason to ring the bell in the first place.

Louis-Baer II was a benefit for the New York Auxiliary of the Naval Relief Society. As a result, the champion fought for free. And for pride. Having been embarrassed by his performance in the first Baer fight, he stormed out of his corner in round one and overpowered his 250-pound foe. Right hands produced the first and seconds knockdowns, and near the end of the round, a left hook-right uppercut combination dropped Baer for referee Frank Fullam's 10-count. When Baer fell for the last time, his head hit the canvas with a thump. Everyone heard it.

Buddy Baer drops like a felled tree after being pole-axed by Louis in the first round.

CONN'S PROGRESS: FROM CHEERS TO BOOS TO WAR

After his knockout defeat to heavyweight champion Joe Louis, it was easy to feel for Billy Conn. The handsome Irishman had fought so brilliantly for so many rounds, until his burning pride got in the way.

On February 13, eight months and two fights after losing to Louis, the former light heavyweight champion was matched with reigning 160-pound king Tony Zale at Madison Square Garden. After 12 one-sided rounds, his arm was raised in victory. Then a most surprising thing happened: exiting the ring, Conn was booed. A 5-1 favorite, Conn, 175¾, was much bigger than Zale, 164¼ . And the 15,033 fans in attendance expected him to hit much harder. But while Zale was staggered in rounds six, seven, and 11, "The Man Of Steel" managed to last the distance.

"I felt ridiculous missing him so much," said a disappointed Conn.

There would be no chance to regain the form that had almost made him heavyweight champion. With World War II beckoning, Conn wouldn't fight again for four years.

Billy Conn (left) had to use all his skill to gain a 12-round decision over Tony Zale.

RINGSIDE VIEW

MARCH

Heavyweight champion Joe Louis faces Abe Simon for the second time and scores a sixth-round kayo. It is his 21st defense.

JUNE

Chalky Wright defends the featherweight title with a 10th-round kayo of former champion Harry Jeffra at Oriole Park, Baltimore.

AUGUST

California's Manuel Ortiz wins the bantamweight title by scoring a unanimous 12-round decision over Lou Salica.

DECEMBER

Beau Jack overwhelms Tippy Larkin in three rounds at Madison Square Garden and wins the vacant New York world lightweight title.

WORLD TITLE FIGHTS

HEAVYWEIGHTS

Jan 9	**Joe Louis** *KO* 1 Buddy Baer, New York City
March 27	**Joe Louis** *KO* 6 Abe Simon, New York City

LIGHT HEAVYWEIGHTS

June 20	**Freddie Mills** (ENG) *KO* 2 Len Harvey, London (British World Title)

LIGHTWEIGHTS

May 15	**Sammy Angott** *W* 15 Allie Stolz, New York City
Dec 18	**Beau Jack** (USA) *KO* 3 Tippy Larkin, New York City (Vacant New York World Title)

FEATHERWEIGHTS

June 19	**Chalky Wright** *KO* 10 Harry Jeffra, Baltimore
Sept 25	**Chalky Wright** *W* 15 Lulu Constantino, New York City
Nov 20	**Willie Pep** (USA) *W* 15 Chalky Wright, New York City

BANTAMWEIGHTS

Aug 7	**Manuel Ortiz** (USA) *W* 12 Lou Salica, Hollywood

SUGAR AND THE BULL, PART II

Having outpointed middleweight Jake LaMotta in October 1942, unbeaten welterweight contender Sugar Ray Robinson was a 3-1 favorite in their rematch, held on February 5 before 18,930 fans at Detroit's Olympia Stadium. In fact, Robinson hadn't only defeated LaMotta, but every other opponent as well. Sugar Ray was unbeaten in 169 bouts, 129 as an amateur and 40 as a pro. But on this night, he would be fortunate to last the 10-round distance.

Despite spotting "The Raging Bull" 16 pounds, Robinson boxed well for seven rounds. Then LaMotta bulled his way inside and stayed there. Toward the end of round eight, Robinson was knocked down and through the ropes; he was saved by the bell. At the end of the 10th, he was hurt for a second time, only to be again rescued by the timekeeper. LaMotta took a unanimous and well-received decision.

Its significance became clear as Robinson did not lose again for more than eight years.

Jake LaMotta (left) decisioned Robinson.

JANUARY

1943

DECEMBER

IT HURT FOR THE WINNER, TOO

With every punch landed came pain, and with every round won came sadness. Early in Sugar Ray Robinson's August 27 points victory over the comebacking Henry Armstrong, it was apparent that one welterweight was fighting on instinct, one on memory.

As a youngster, Robinson had idolized Armstrong. Now, at Madison Square Garden, he was being paid to beat him up. Throughout Armstrong's comeback, his eyes, which were so often bloodied and swollen during the final stages of his remarkable welterweight title reign, had held up. Against Robinson, however, Armstrong had other problems. Sugar Ray boxed neatly, moved with fluidity, and out of respect for his legendary foe, punched just hard and often enough to win all 10 rounds.

After the fight, Armstrong announced his retirement. But he would remain out of the ring only for five months. As Robinson would discover, boxing's legends seemed destined to fade away.

THE BEST OF UNDERDOG BEAU

Perhaps the strangest aspect of the lightweight rivalry between champions Beau Jack and Bob Montgomery was that in all four bouts, the underdog won.

During the war years, boxing boasted of no bigger star than Jack. He regularly sold out Madison Square Garden, and in December 1942, won the vacant New York 135-pound world title.

In his first defense, he was 3-1 favorite to defeat Montgomery. But the Philadelphia "Bobcat" rallied to win on points. The rematch, the second of their four fights, came on November 19 before a Garden crowd of 17,866. Jack started quickly, jabbed strongly, and averaged more than 100 punches per round. The experts had predicted that he would fade and, sure enough, Montgomery powered through in the 14th and 15th stanzas. By the final bell, Jack was drunkenly clinching. Still, in the greatest effort of his career, he won a unanimous decision. Next time, of course, he would be favorite...

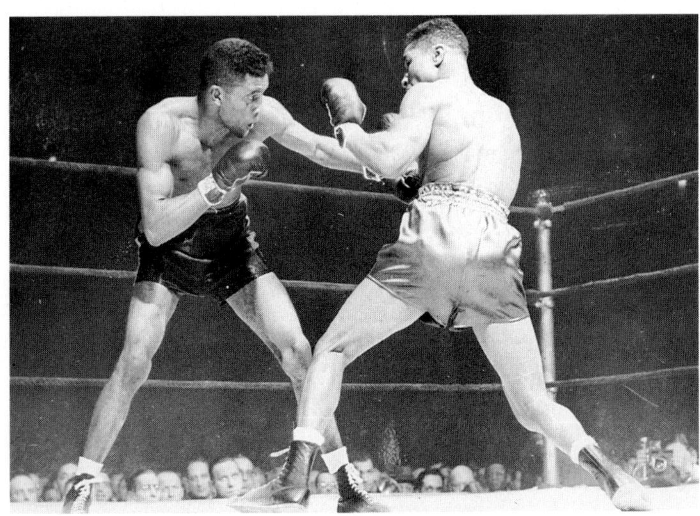
Beau Jack (right) pounded out close 15-round decision over Bob Montgomery to retain title.

WORLD TITLE FIGHTS

LIGHTWEIGHTS

Jan 4	**Luther White** (USA) *W* 15 Willie Joyce, Baltimore (Vacant Maryland World Title)
May 21	**Bob Montgomery** (USA) *W* 15 Beau Jack, New York City (New York World Title)
Oct 27	**Sammy Angott** *W* 15 Slugger White, Los Angeles
Nov 19	**Beau Jack** *W* 15 Bob Montgomery, New York City

FEATHERWEIGHTS

Jan 18	**Jackie Callura** (CAN) *W* 15 Jackie Wilson, Providence (Wins NBA Title)
March 18	**Jackie Callura** *W* 15 Jackie Wilson, Boston
June 8	**Willie Pep** *W* 15 Sal Bartolo, Boston
Aug 16	**Phil Terranova** (USA) *KO* 8 Jackie Callura, New Orleans
Dec 27	**Phil Terranova** *KO* 6 Jackie Callura, New Orleans

BANTAMWEIGHTS

Jan 1	**Manuel Ortiz** *W* 10 Kenny Lindsay, Portland, OR
Jan 27	**Manuel Ortiz** *KO* 11 George Freitas, Oakland
March 10	**Manuel Ortiz** *KO* 11 Lou Salica, Oakland
April 28	**Manuel Ortiz** *KO* 6 Lupe Cardoza, Ft. Worth, TX
May 26	**Manuel Ortiz** *W* 15 Joe Robleto, Long Beach, CA
July 11	**Manuel Ortiz** *KO* 7 Joe Robleto, Seattle
Oct 1	**Manuel Ortiz** *KO* 4 Leonardo Lopez, Hollywood, CA
Nov 23	**Manuel Ortiz** *W* 15 Benny Goldberg, Los Angeles

FLYWEIGHTS

June 19	**Jackie Paterson** (SCO) *KO* 1 Peter Kane, Glasgow

Joe Louis

BEFORE his June 1938 rematch with Max Schmeling, world heavyweight champion Joe Louis was invited to the White House by President Franklin Delano Roosevelt. The United States wouldn't enter World War II for more than three years, but like Louis, Roosevelt was adept at anticipating an opponent's punch.

"Lean over, Joe, so I can feel your muscles," Roosevelt said. "Joe, we need muscles like yours to beat Germany."

"The Brown Bomber," who subsequently kayoed Schmeling in one round, wasn't the only champion to win a title defense, but he was the only one to win a war.

By any measure of greatness, Louis must be rated among the top five fighters in the history of the ring. He had exceptional punching power, especially in his right hand, and above-average boxing skills. He reigned for more than 11 years, and, before retiring as champion, made 25 successful defenses, both records for any division. And, perhaps most significantly, his greatness transcended the ring.

Born Joseph Louis Barrow on May 13, 1914, in Lafayette, Alabama, Louis was one of seven children. After her husband Munroe died in a mental institution, Lillian Barrow married Pat Brooks, a widower with six children of his own. When Louis was 12, the family moved to Detroit.

Lillian Barrow thought she was sending her son to violin lessons, but one day fate brought him to the Brewster Recreation Center. Louis was pummeled in his first amateur bout. He sensed, however, that he belonged. He gave up not only the violin lessons, but school, too.

In 1934, Louis won the National AAU light heavyweight title en route to compiling an overall amateur record of 50-4 (43).

During a 1933 Detroit Golden Gloves tournament, he was spotted by John Roxborough, a wealthy black numbers czar and businessman. Shortly afterward, Roxborough introduced the fighter to another black businessman, Julian Black, who owned a speakeasy and also ran numbers. The partners would sign Louis to a 10-year managerial contract and place their investment under the guidance of Jack Blackburn, a trainer and former world-class fighter who had spent time in jail for manslaughter.

Joe Louis made his professional debut in 1934 as a main event boxer. And not once in his fabled career was he in a preliminary bout.

The handlers quickly realized their fighter was special. Louis turned pro on July 4, 1934, and kayoed Jack Kracken in one round. He went 11-0 over the rest of that year, and 10-0 in 1935, including knockouts over former world champions Primo Carnera and Max Baer.

Roxborough and Black were aware that since Jack Johnson's controversial title reign had ended in 1915, there hadn't been a black heavyweight champion, or even a black title challenger. In an effort to shape the fighter's image, Roxborough publicized the seven commandments he had laid down. Louis was to 1 never have his picture taken

Sergeant Joe Louis is greeted by a London cabbie in 1944. The champion gave countless exhibitions, in every major theatre, during World War II.

with a white woman; **2** never go into a night club alone; **3** never engage in "soft" fights; **4** never engage in fixed fights; **5** never gloat over a fallen opponent; **6** always keep a deadpan expression in front of the cameras; **7** live and fight clean.

Had Louis been similar in personality and temperament to, say, Jackie Robinson, he never could have won over the public. But by the start of World War II, he was the most famous black in American history, and a national hero.

On June 19, 1936, Louis' inexorable march to the title was interrupted by the lethal right hand of former champion Max Schmeling, who stopped him in the 12th round. Rebounding from that miserable beating was the first sign of the heavyweight's greatness.

"Schmeling exposed the fact that Louis has a glass jaw and consequently cannot take a punch," Jack Dempsey was quoted as saying.

"All you have to do to beat him is walk into him and bang him with a solid punch. I don't think he'll ever whip another good fighter."

It took Louis two months to prove Dempsey wrong; in August 1936, he crushed former heavyweight champion Jack Sharkey in three rounds. After five more wins, Louis was again a title threat. The reigning champion, "Cinderella Man" James J. Braddock, was vulnerable, and in order to beat Schmeling to the throne, Mike Jacobs, Louis' promoter, had to sign over 10 percent of his net profits from heavyweight title fight promotions for the next decade, should Braddock lose the fight.

On June 22, 1937, at Comiskey Park in Chicago, Louis recovered from a first-round knockdown and battered Braddock before stopping him in round eight. The son of an Alabama sharecropper was the world's heavyweight champion, but not yet content.

"I don't want to be called champ until I lick Max Smelling," he said.

He received his opportunity in his fourth defense, before more than 70,000 fans at Yankee Stadium on June 22, 1938.

Before the fight, Schmeling, a popular fighter on both sides of the Atlantic, reminded reporters, "I am a fighter, not a politician." But the challenger's attempts to minimize the fight's overtones were futile. In the eyes of the world, Louis-Schmeling II was a prelude to the bitter World War II that lay ahead.

The fight lasted 124 seconds. Attacking with a ferocity not seen since Dempsey dethroned Jess Willard 19 years before, Louis staggered the German with an overhand right and, later in the round, scored with a roundhouse right that broke two vertebrae in Schmeling's back.

"I'm sure enough champion now," Louis said.

Louis made 21 defenses before entering the Army, including a come-from-behind 13th-round kayo of master boxer Billy Conn, and four more defenses after the end of the war. It was during his military service – the champion was inactive from March 27, 1942 through June 19, 1946 – that The Brown Bomber's popularity soared. He toured with the USO and boxed countless exhibitions.

"We won't stop punching," said radio broadcaster Don Dunphy, "just as Louis does, until we win."

The fact that Louis' prime had passed during the war was evident in his penultimate defense, a disputed decision victory over Jersey Joe Walcott on December 5, 1947. Walcott outboxed the slower Louis, and after the final bell, the champion left the ring in disgust. Summoned by his handlers, he returned in time to hear that he had retained the crown.

The verdict may have been a gift, but boxing had no more deserving a recipient.

Remaining dominant in rematches, Louis kayoed Walcott in their return, and then, on March 1, 1949, announced his retirement. Financial problems, however, brought him back 18 months later, and he was beaten on points by his successor, Ezzard Charles. One year after that loss, Louis' comeback – and his career – was ended by future champion Rocky Marciano, who finished the 38-year-old legend in eight rounds.

The rest of Louis' life was plagued by failing mental and physical health, drug use, and battles with the tax man. A free-spender and poor businessman, Louis owed the Internal Revenue Service $1.2-million shortly after his retirement. At the time, his annual income was $20,000, paid by the International Boxing Club.

Louis spent his final years as a greeter at Caesars Palace. In October 1977, he suffered a severe heart attack, and, while hospitalized, a cerebral hemmorhage. On April 12, 1981, he died in Las Vegas at age 66.

Said close friend Frank Sinatra, "It's nice to know that the man who never rested on canvas now rests on clouds."

Although he lacked luster against some foes, the Brown Bomber was unbeatable in return bouts, as was the case with tough Arturo Godoy (right), whom Joe cut to ribbons in their second bout.

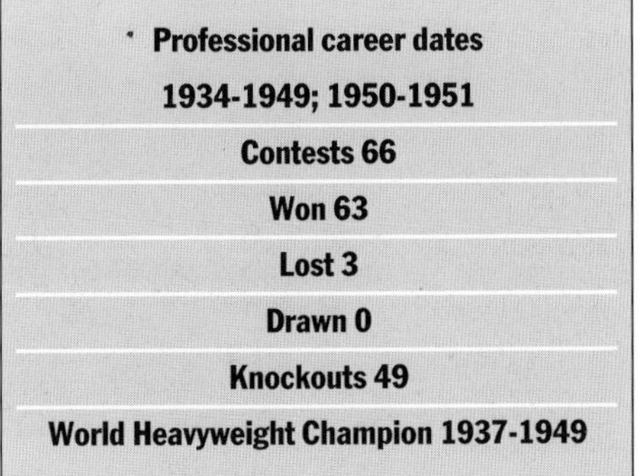

Professional career dates 1934-1949; 1950-1951
Contests 66
Won 63
Lost 3
Drawn 0
Knockouts 49
World Heavyweight Champion 1937-1949

JANUARY

1944

DECEMBER

THE FIGHT FOR SECOND PLACE

That world champion Willie Pep was the finest featherweight in boxing was inarguable.

Pep had established his superiority by dethroning Chalky Wright in 1942, and twice outpointing Sal Bartolo in 1943. When Bartolo took Phil Terranova's NBA crown on March 10, the New Englander moved into sole possession of second place.

The Bartolo-Terranova rematch came on May 5 at Boston Garden. After losing the crown, Terranova had complained that Bartolo, a Pep clone, had bicycled his way to the championship. This time, however, Bartolo fought on the 5'2" New Yorker's terms. Mixing infighting with finesse, Bartolo outboxed and outbrawled him en route to a 15-round split decision victory. (The referee scored for Terranova, 143-141, but the judges had Bartolo ahead, 145-142 and 148-143). Until he could secure a third crack at Pep, second place for Bartolo was better than last in line.

A WAR FOR THE REAL WAR

Their names linked forever in lightweight lore by their four-fight see-saw series, it was thus apt when Beau Jack and Bob Montgomery were drafted the same day.

Before serving their country, the 135-pounders clashed for the final time, on August 4 at Madison Square Garden. Jack won a lackluster 10-round majority decision. (Montgomery's New York world title wasn't at stake.) But the result wasn't important. What really mattered was that the card had produced an all-time record gate of $35,864,000, the result of the sale of war bonds.

When informed that "wounded men are occupying the choice seats", the crowd of 15,822 burst into cheers, applauding for several minutes. Jack and Montgomery had earned their stripes even before being fitted for uniforms.

Montgomery (left) and Jack in army uniform.

RINGSIDE VIEW

MARCH

Bob Montgomery, a 9-5 underdog, regains the New York world lightweight title by split decision over arch-rival Beau Jack.

SEPTEMBER

World featherweight champion Willie Pep defends against former titlist Chalky Wright and scores a unanimous 15-round decision.

NOVEMBER

Manuel Ortiz defends the bantamweight title for the 12th time, knocking out Luis Castillo in the ninth round.

DECEMBER

Sal Bartolo keeps the NBA featherweight crown by scoring a unanimous 15-round decision over Willie Roache.

NORTHERN EXPOSURE

For the first 10 years of his career, veteran lightweight Juan Bautista Zurita Ferrer, better known as Juan Zurita, fought primarily in his native Mexico. But as soon as he established himself as world-class, the southpaw began to travel north for high-profile bouts in California's busy fight towns.

After losing a split decision to Luther (Slugger) White in June 1943, Zurita swore he'd never again leave Mexico. But on March 8, he entered the ring at Hollywood's Legion Stadium for a try at NBA lightweight champion Sammy Angott. If Zurita was uncomfortable fighting on the road, the oddsmakers shared his pessimism; Angott answered the opening bell as a 4-1 favorite.

This time, Zurita was awarded the decision he deserved. Plagued by bad hands and a debilitating struggle to make weight, Angott did very little fighting. More than once, referee and former junior welterweight champion Mushy Callahan instructed him to "pick it up." Zurita landed dozens of right hands, and Angott repeatedly clinched in order to survive.

The victory would turn out to be the highlight of Zurita's career. In his next bout, he would lose on points to Beau Jack, and in his first defense, he would be kayoed in two rounds by Ike Williams. Presumably, he didn't blame that one on the judges.

WORLD TITLE FIGHTS

LIGHTWEIGHTS

March 3	**Bob Montgomery** *W* 15 Beau Jack, New York City
March 8	**Juan Zurita** (MEX) *W* 15 Sammy Angott, Hollywood, CA (Wins NBA Title)

FEATHERWEIGHTS

March 10	**Sal Bartolo** (USA) *W* 15 Phil Terranova, Boston (Wins NBA Title)
May 5	**Sal Bartolo** *W* 15 Phil Terranova, Boston
Sept 9	**Willie Pep** *W* 15 Chalky Wright, New York City
Dec 15	**Sal Bartolo** *W* 15 Willie Roache, Boston

BANTAMWEIGHTS

March 14	**Manuel Ortiz** *W* 15 Ernesto Aguilar, Los Angeles
April 4	**Manuel Ortiz** *W* 15 Tony Olivera, Los Angeles
Sept 12	**Manuel Ortiz** *KO* 4 Luis Castillo, Los Angeles
Nov 14	**Manuel Ortiz** *KO* 9 Luis Castillo, Los Angeles

Juan Zurita (left) relieved hard-to-beat Sammy Angott of his crown in a major upset.

A NEW CHAMP, NO BULL

During World War II, Ike Williams, a 5'9" lightweight with a middleweight's punch, established himself as a world-class contender in New York City, Philadelphia, and Washington, D.C. But when his big moment arrived, he had to travel to Mexico City and learn about life on the road.

Waiting for him was 30-year-old Juan Zurita, the NBA champion and local favorite. They clashed before 35,000 fans at the Circo de Toros bullring. Those in attendance included Williams' supporters, but they were all in the challenger's corner.

Badly outclassed by the 21-year-old future legend, Zurita lasted only two rounds. Then the real fight began. Was Williams tough enough to survive the journey back to his dressing room? He barely managed to make it, but only with the help of a dozen policemen. Along the way, his manager, Connie McCarthy, suffered a nasty gash when a flying beer bottle found his forehead.

Williams would enjoy a lengthy stay at the top. But Zurita never fought again, perhaps realizing that while the road was tough, Mexico City could be downright dangerous.

The fourth Ray Robinson-Jake LaMotta battle; master boxer against bullish aggressor.

SUGAR v BULL: IV AND V

The record book tells us that Jake LaMotta defeated Sugar Ray Robinson only once in six tries. The score, however, belies the competitiveness of their battles.

Robinson-LaMotta IV, held at Madison Square Garden on February 24, featured the best single round of the rivalry. In the sixth stanza, LaMotta pinned Sugar Ray against the ropes, and after Robinson dropped his arms, landed a series of powerpunches to the jaw. Suddenly, Robinson sprung out and staggered "The Raging Bull" with two bolo rights and a lightning flurry. Just when it seemed LaMotta was through, he decided it was his turn once more, and he answered with a blitz that left Robinson covering up. Robinson went on to win by scores of 6-4, 6-3-1, and 7-1-2.

In Battle V, boxer and puncher traded momentum for 12 rounds. This time, Robinson slowed considerably over the last three rounds, drawing boos from the fans at Chicago's Comiskey Park. LaMotta's extended body attack seemed adequate for victory, but again Sugar Ray emerged victorious. The decision was split, with two scores of 61-59 for Robinson, and a 60-57 tally for LaMotta. As LaMotta would say years later, "I fought Sugar Ray so often, I almost got diabetes."

JANUARY

1945

DECEMBER

Ringside View

FEBRUARY

Former triple-crown champion Henry Armstrong fights for the last time, losing a 10-round decision to Chester Slider in Oakland. He exits with a record of 152-21-8 (100).

MAY

Regarded as the best welterweight in the world, Sugar Ray Robinson, 54-1-1, is held to a 10-round draw by Jose Basora in Philadelphia.

AUGUST

The streaking Rocky Graziano scores his second kayo of Freddie Cochrane in three months, stopping the welterweight champion in the 10th round of a non-title bout.

"I WAS TOLD TO LAY DOWN" SAYS HAROLD GREEN

Slick New York City welterweight Harold Green was a tough guy – tough enough to rise from knockdowns in both of his 1944 wars with Rocky Graziano and go on to register two points victories. But on September 28 at Madison Square Garden, Green, riding a 22-bout winning streak, was tough only after his bout was over. Facing Graziano for a third time, he won the first two rounds. But in the third Graziano landed his rockabye right hand, and Green dropped. A split second after being counted out by referee Ruby Goldstein, he leaped to his feet and curiously charged at Graziano.

Green was subsequently fined $1,000 and suspended for one year. It would be 45 years later, however, that he would claim he took a dive.

"I was told to lay down," he would tell *The Ring* magazine. "It wasn't easy. When you're doing it, it hurts."

One can only guess how much it hurt 12 months later, when Graziano was given a shot at the world middleweight title, and Green was left to wonder what a third victory over The Rock might have meant.

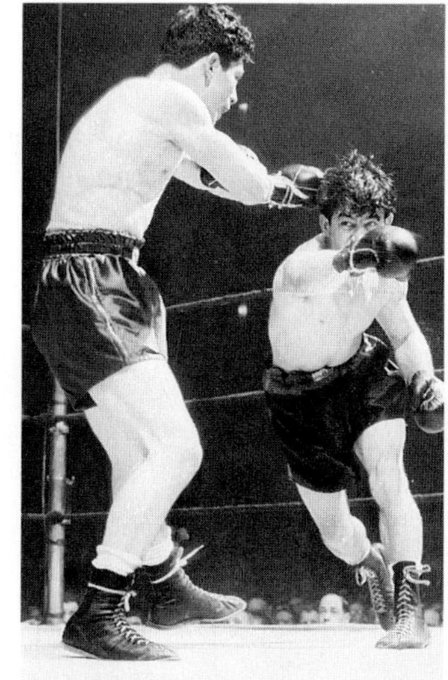

Harold Green (left) and Rocky Graziano.

World Title Fights

LIGHTWEIGHTS		FEATHERWEIGHTS	
April 18	**Ike Williams** (USA) *KO* 2 Juan Zurita, Mexico City (NBA Title)	Feb 19	**Willie Pep** *W* 15 Phil Terranova, New York City

JANUARY

1946

DECEMBER

THE BEST WINS THE BELT

After welterweight champ Marty Servo vacated the throne, officials could have handed Sugar Ray Robinson the crown.

Having defeated Servo, Fritzie Zivic, Tomy Bell, Sammy Angott, Henry Armstrong, and Jake La Motta, Robinson, 73-1-1, had long ago established himself as the world's best 147-pounder.

It was considered a mere formality, then, when Robinson and Bell were matched for the vacant title. They clashed on December 20 at Madison Square Garden, and Robinson won by unanimous 15-round decision. He did, however, have to rise from a second-round knockdown to do so. That night, Robinson celebrated the coronation on opening night at his Harlem pub. The champagne had been chilling for years.

The return Louis-Conn title fight was disappointing. Both men were shells of their glory days.

THE WAIT WASN'T WORTH IT

In June 1941, heavyweight champion Joe Louis and Billy Conn fought a thrilling bout. There was only one problem with a rematch: World War II got in the way.

Louis and Conn returned to the ring after serving their country – and were quickly matched. On June 19, they clashed before a disappointing crowd of 45,266 at Yankee Stadium (promoter Mike Jacobs charged a record $100 for ringside seats). Exhibitions aside, neither had climbed through the ropes for more than four years.

Before the bout, Louis said of the challenger, "He can run, but he can't hide." As it turned out, Conn could do neither. Nor was Louis particularly adept. *The New York Journal American* described the champion as "heavy-legged and far and away slower than ever before." All that remained was Louis' power, and after seven uneventful rounds, he kayoed Conn at the 2:19 mark of round eight. Four years and a World War, however, had proved a bit too much for either to overcome.

GUTS AND A BODY SHOT

They make movies about fights like this: round after round, Rocky Graziano drove boxing's best right hand into the face of middleweight champion Tony Zale, and round after round, Zale marched in for more.

Chapter 1 of the Zale-Graziano trilogy took place on September 27, before 37,827 fans at Yankee Stadium. Blown-up welter Graziano, 154, entered the ring an 11-5 favorite. His first defense in five years, Zale scored a first-round flash knockdown. Graziano won the next four rounds, registering a knockdown of his own. By the end of the fifth, Zale was bleeding from his face, and boxing with a broken thumb. His finish seemed imminent. Midway through the sixth, however, something extraordinary happened: Zale summoned the strength to fire a right to the solar plexus. Graziano froze, and Zale followed with a hook to the chin. Boom! Referee Ruby Goldstein counted to 10, and though Graziano charged back into battle after regaining his breath, the fight had already been waved off.

Although Zale looks a sure loser, he roared back to kayo Rocky Graziano and retain the title.

WORLD TITLE FIGHTS

HEAVYWEIGHTS

June 9	**Joe Louis** *KO* 8 Billy Conn, Bronx, NY
Sept 18	**Joe Louis** *KO* 1 Tami Mauriello, Bronx, NY

LIGHT HEAVYWEIGHTS

May 14	**Gus Lesnevich** *KO* 10 Freddie Mills, London

MIDDLEWEIGHTS

Sept 27	**Tony Zale** *KO* 6 Rocky Graziano, Bronx, NY

WELTERWEIGHTS

Feb 1	**Marty Servo** (USA) *KO* 4 Freddie Cochrane, New York City
Dec 20	**Sugar Ray Robinson** (USA) *W* 15 Tommy Bell, New York City (Vacant World Title)

JUNIOR WELTERWEIGHTS

April 29	**Tippy Larkin** (USA) *W* 12 Willie Joyce, Boston (Vacant World Title)
Sept 13	**Tippy Larkin** *W* 12 Willie Joyce, New York City

LIGHTWEIGHTS

April 30	**Ike Williams** *KO* 8 Enrique Bolanos, Los Angeles
June 28	**Bob Montgomery** *KO* 13 Allie Stolz, New York City
Sept 4	**Ike Williams** *KO* 9 Ronnie James, Cardiff, Wales
Nov 26	**Bob Montgomery** *KO* 8 Wesley Mouzon, Philadelphia

FEATHERWEIGHTS

May 3	**Sal Bartolo** *KO* 6 Spider Armstrong, Boston
June 7	**Willie Pep** *KO* 12 Sal Bartolo, New York City (Unified World Title)

BANTAMWEIGHTS

Feb 25	**Manuel Ortiz** *KO* 13 Luis Castillo, San Francisco
May 18	**Manuel Ortiz** *KO* 5 Kenny Lindsay, Hollywood, CA
June 10	**Manuel Ortiz** *KO* 11 Jackie Jurich, San Francisco

Ringside View

APRIL

Legendary former lightweight champion Benny Leonard, 51, suffers a fatal heart attack while refereeing in New York City.

JUNE

Welterweight champion Sugar Ray Robinson retains the title by knocking out Jimmy Doyle in nine rounds. Doyle subsequently dies from head injuries suffered during the bout.

NOVEMBER

Promised by the mob that he would secure a title shot if he fell, middleweight contender Jake LaMotta takes a dive in the fourth round of his bout against Billy Fox.

CREAM ALMOST RISES

So undistinguished was Arnold Raymond Cream, aka Jersey Joe Walcott, that when heavyweight champion Joe Louis expressed an interest in defending against him, the New York State Athletic Commission ruled that the bout would have to be promoted as an exhibition.

The Commission ultimately relented, and Louis and the 34-year-old Walcott met at Madison Square Garden. This was a slower, more tentative Louis, and in the first and fourth rounds, he walked into counter right hands that drove him to the floor. Walcott, a 10-1 underdog, spent the rest of the fight walking away from the champion, showing different angles, turning his shoulders, and flashing an occasional counterpunch. His was a particularly difficult style to solve. Frustrated and embarrassed, Louis attempted to exit the ring after the final bell, only to be delayed by his handlers. The suddenly aged champion was staring into the crowd when ring announcer Harry Balogh informed the 18,194 in attendance that "The Brown Bomber" had retained the crown by split decision. (The scoring: 8-6-1 and 9-6 for Louis, and 7-6-2 for Walcott.)

"You can't win a fight running away," said Mannie Seamon, Louis' trainer. Perhaps. But at the sound of the final bell, Walcott had convinced Louis otherwise.

The sellout crowd was sure that Jersey Joe Walcott (right) was the new champion.

JANUARY 1947 DECEMBER

ROCKY SOCKS MAN OF STEEL

Chapter II of the Zale-Graziano grudge took place in Chicago.

Incredibly, the middleweights managed to repeat their savage brawl of the year before. This time, however, it was Zale who dashed out of the starting gate, and Graziano who suffered terrible punishment. The Rock was cut over one eye in the first round, and by the third, the other was completely shut.

Graziano began his rally late in round five. The Rock accelerated in the sixth, and with a line of blood dripping down his face, he knocked Zale almost out of the ring. Referee Johnny Behr permitted no more punching and Graziano became world middleweight champion.

Graziano staggers Zale.

VICTORY WITH A VENGEANCE

In 1944, Bob Montgomery knocked out 21-year-old Ike Williams in 12 rounds. Convinced that Montgomery had purposely extended the beating, Williams patiently awaited revenge. It came on August 4 before 30,500 fans.

Their pick-'em rematch unified the lightweight title. The end came in round six, when Montgomery was counted out by referee Charley Daggert.

"I didn't get him as good as I wanted to," Williams said after the fight. "I wanted to murder him. He's no bleeping good."

World Title Fights

HEAVYWEIGHTS

Dec 5	**Joe Louis** *W* 15 Jersey Joe Walcott, New York City

LIGHT HEAVYWEIGHTS

Feb 28	**Gus Lesnevich** *KO* 10 Billy Fox, New York City

MIDDLEWEIGHTS

July 16	**Rocky Graziano** (USA) *KO* 6 Tony Zale, Chicago

WELTERWEIGHTS

June 24	**Sugar Ray Robinson** *KO* 9 Jimmy Doyle, Cleveland
Dec 19	**Sugar Ray Robinson** *KO* 6 Chuck Taylor, Detroit

LIGHTWEIGHTS

Aug 4	**Ike Williams** *KO* 6 Bob Montgomery, Philadelphia

FEATHERWEIGHTS

Aug 21	**Willie Pep** *KO* 12 Jock Leslie, Flint, MI

BANTAMWEIGHTS

Jan 6	**Harold Dade** (USA) *W* 15 Manuel Ortiz, San Francisco
March 11	**Manuel Ortiz** *W* 15 Harold Dade, Los Angeles
May 30	**Manuel Ortiz** *W* 15 Kui Kong Young, Honolulu
Dec 20	**Manuel Ortiz** *W* 15 Tirso Del Rosario, Manila

FLYWEIGHTS

Oct 20	**Rinty Monaghan** (IRE) *W* 15 Dado Marino, London (Vacant NBA Title)

JANUARY

1948

JUNE

A DARK NIGHT IN CHICAGO

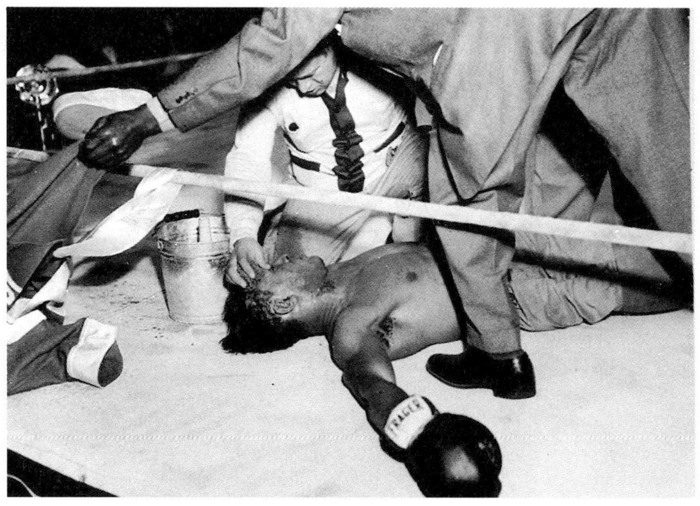

Sam Baroudi lays dying on the ring canvas after being knocked out by Ezzard Charles.

Ezzard Charles would win the heavyweight championship title, make nine defenses, and engage in two memorable shootouts with Rocky Marciano. But those who knew him best claimed he was never the same after defeating Sam Baroudi at Chicago Stadium on February 20.

Charles, the top light heavyweight contender, dominated his 20-year-old opponent before scoring a 10th-round kayo. Baroudi, whose real name was Sammy Crandall, collapsed minutes after the bout. An inhalator squad unsuccessfully worked on him for one hour in his dressing room. He was then taken to a hospital, where, at 5:48 a.m. on February 21, he was pronounced dead of a cerebral hemmorhage. Ironically, in August 1947, Glenn Newton Smith had died from injuries suffered in a bout against Baroudi.

After hearing of Baroudi's fate, Charles immediately retired. He returned to the ring only 10 weeks later, but without the finishing instincts he once possessed.

THE NIGHT HE CAUGHT A RAINBOW

After Ireland's Rinty Monaghan knocked out flyweight champion Jackie Paterson in a 1946 non-title bout, he craved a return for the championship. But after winning world honors in June 1943, the talented Scot froze the title.

Campaigning at bantamweight, he lost 10 times, but kept the crown. (He was stripped after failing to make weight for a scheduled July 1947 defense against Dado Marino, but went to court and regained partial recognition.)

On March 23 at King's Hall in Belfast, Paterson dared risk the title in a rematch vs. Monaghan. Weakened by his fight to make the 112-pound limit, the Scottish southpaw was impotent. Monaghan took the crown by seventh-round knockout, offering a neutral corner jig as referee Tommy Little counted out Paterson. Then, as was his custom, the crooning champion led his fans in a chorus of "When Irish Eyes Are Smiling". The toughest part of Monaghan's night came at his home in the wee hours of the morning, when a particularly enthusiastic well-wisher accidentally knocked him out cold.

GUS GETS STRONGER AS HE AGES

Before serving in World War II, light heavyweight champion Gus Lesnevich had been a strong fighter, but hardly a knockout puncher. In fact, he had scored only 16 kayos in 52 fights.

After the War? They must've fed him extra portions of spinach in the Coast Guard mess halls. In 1946 and '47, Lesnevich registered stoppages over a quartet of world-class light heavyweights, Freddie Mills, Billy Fox, Melio Bettina, and Tami Mauriello. At Madison Square Garden on March 5, he was rematched with Fox, a Philadelphian best known for having TKO'd sturdy Jake LaMotta under questionable circumstances. (In 1960, LaMotta would admit to having thrown the bout.) One minute into the bout, Lesnevich, who had struggled to make weight, dropped Fox for a six-count. He then zeroed in with right hands. Floored for a second time, Fox failed to beat the count of referee Frank Fullam, who counted him out at the 1:58 mark.

At age 33, most fighters are nearing retirement. But after crushing Fox, Lesnevich was being hyped as a legitimate heavyweight title threat.

World light heavyweight champ Gus Lesnevich (right) knocked out Billy Fox in the first round.

RINGSIDE VIEW

JANUARY

Light heavyweight contenders Ezzard Charles and Archie Moore collide in Cleveland, with Charles winning by eighth-round kayo.

FEBRUARY

Featherweight champion Willie Pep retains the crown by stopping Humberto Sierra in the 10th round.

APRIL

Welterweight contender Kid Gavilan outpoints former world title challenger Tommy Bell over 10 rounds in Philadelphia.

MAY

Lightweight champion Ike Williams retains the crown by split and disputed 15-round decision over Mexico's Enrique Bolanos.

.HE ROCK AND STEEL SHOW, FINAL CURTAIN

Middleweight champ Tony Zale kayos Rocky Graziano in the third round.

Their third middleweight title fight lasted only three rounds, but had Tony Zale and Rocky Graziano traded punches for three seconds, they would've found a way to provide thrills.

The final chapter of boxing's most violent trilogy took place on June 10 before 21,479 fans at Ruppert Stadium in Newark, New Jersey. Having knocked out his rival in July 1947, Graziano was made a 12-5 favorite. Handicappers thought the ringworn Zale to be near his end. But "The Man of Steel" was so confident that he predicted a quick victory – by third-round kayo! The bout turned out to be a microcosm of Zale-Graziano I and II.

Zale aggressively answered the opening bell, the immovable object challenging the irresistible force. Strong and sharp, he hooked and hooked some more, and Graziano went down for a three-count. The Rock seemed en route to an embarrassing loss, but for these two, at least one sudden change of momentum was written into every script. Graziano survived until the bell, then rallied in round two with the best right hand in boxing. Zale, however, sponged whatever the champion dished out, and in the third, reestablished his superiority. Graziano suffered his second and third knockdowns, the latter bringing referee Paul Cavalier's full count.

The finish came at the 1:08 mark. In his dressing room, it was determined that Graziano had suffered a concussion. His eyes remained glassy, and he was unable to identify Dr. Vincent Nardiello, whom he knew quite well. "His reflexes are completely shot," Nardiello told reporters. The 26-year-old Graziano was told to go to bed. The 34-year-old Zale celebrated into the night.

WORLD TITLE FIGHTS

HEAVYWEIGHTS

June 25	**Joe Louis** *KO* 11 Jersey Joe Walcott, Bronx, NY

LIGHT HEAVYWEIGHTS

March 5	**Gus Lesnevich** *KO* 1 Billy Fox, New York City

MIDDLEWEIGHTS

June 10	**Tony Zale** *KO* 3 Rocky Graziano, Newark, NJ

WELTERWEIGHTS

June 28	**Sugar Ray Robinson** *W* 15 Bernard Docusen, Chicago

LIGHTWEIGHTS

May 25	**Ike Williams** *W* 15 Enrique Bolanos, Los Angeles

FEATHERWEIGHTS

Feb 24	**Willie Pep** *KO* 10 Humberto Sierra, Miami

FLYWEIGHTS

March 23	**Rinty Monaghan** *KO* 7 Jackie Paterson, Belfast

THE ONE-PUNCH COMEBACK

When Joe Louis and Jersey Joe Walcott weighed in for their rematch, scheduled for June 23 at Yankee Stadium, the champion scaled a career-high 213½ , and the challenger 194¾.

It rained on fight night, and the bout was postponed until the 24th. Then it rained some more, pushing back the confrontation yet another night. By the time Louis and Walcott answered the opening bell on the 25th, reporters had overanalyzed the potential effects of the delay. What they didn't figure was that the 34-year-old champion would further fatten up; it was estimated that he climbed through the ropes weighing as much as 221 pounds. Lacking quickness and timing, Louis boxed even more tentatively than he had during his first defense vs. Walcott. As a result, the bout was a bore, with Walcott characteristically stepping back as he waited to counter, and Louis shuffling forward in seemingly aimless pursuit.

After 10 rounds, Walcott was ahead by the slimmest of margins, leading on two cards (5-4-1 and 6-3-1), and trailing on the third (5-2-3). Late in the 11th, however, Louis struck. A short right froze Walcott, and a furious followup flurry left him on the floor. After referee Frank Fullam counted to 10, Louis had successfully defended the crown for an incredible 25th time.

Wrote *The New York Times'* Arthur Dailey: "With one thunderous punch, Joe Louis retained his world heavyweight title in a thrilling and heartwarming finish to as dreary a championship as ever was held." Everyone sensed it was the end. Louis by knockout – fitting, wasn't it?

Joe Louis (left) retained the title by knocking out Jersey Joe Walcott in the 11th round.

JULY

1948

DECEMBER

LOSING IT ALL IN LONDON

Gus Lesnevich left the ring with tears in his eyes. But it was what he left the ring without that really hurt him.

On July 26 at White City Stadium in London, more than 46,000 fans gathered to see whether Dorsetshire's Freddie Mills could become the first British light heavyweight champion since Bob Fitzsimmons 48 years before. The chances weren't good; in May 1946, Lesnevich, a 4-1 favorite, had beaten Mills by 10th-round kayo. But on this night, Lesnevich, 33, turned old.

For the first nine rounds, almost nothing happened, and referee Teddy Waltham repeatedly warned both fighters to pick up the pace. In the 10th, however, the challenger struck without warning. A roundhouse left felled Lesnevich for a nine-count, and, later in the round, the same punch produced the same result. Lesnevich rallied in the 12th and 13th, but Mills took the last two rounds, and at the sound of the final bell, Waltham, the sole judge, unhesitatingly raised the challenger's arm in victory. "I just didn't have it tonight," said the loser. Lesnevich could have been referring to the 175-pound crown, an all-but-guaranteed try at the heavyweight title, or his form. He'd never regain any of them.

Britain's Freddie Mills drops Gus Lesnevich in the 10th round on his way to the light heavyweight title.

THE OLD BEAU – FOR TWO ROUNDS

At his best, two-time champion Beau Jack set a pace that few lightweights could match. But before challenging world titlist Ike Williams at Philadelphia's Shibe Park on July 12, he spent most of his energy making weight.

Jack scaled 134; it was the first time he had made the division limit in four years. Williams-Jack, which was televised, was delayed for 40 minutes by Senator Alben Barkley, whose speech at the Democratic National Convention, held crosstown, hogged the airwaves. When the opening bell finally sounded, Jack, 27, fought as if in his prime.

Repeatedly pumping his left into the champion's face, he threw punches in bunches. By round three, however, Williams' short, powerful blows were taking effect, and by the fifth, Jack was through. Only 33 seconds of the sixth round were fought, but in that brief time, Jack absorbed a frightful beating. Pounded along the ropes, he bled from the nose and mouth, and made no discernible effort to defend himself. It took the intervention of referee Charley Daggert to save him.

As it turned out, Senator Barkley's speech hadn't been nearly long enough.

WORLD TITLE FIGHTS

LIGHT HEAVYWEIGHTS

July 26 **Freddie Mills** *W* 15 Gus Lesnevich, London

MIDDLEWEIGHTS

Sept 21 **Marcel Cerdan** (FRA) *KO* 12 Tony Zale, Jersey City, NJ

LIGHTWEIGHTS

July 11 **Ike Williams** *KO* 6 Beau Jack, Philadelphia

Sept 23 **Ike Williams** *KO* 10 Jesse Flores, Bronx, NY

FEATHERWEIGHTS

Oct 29 **Sandy Saddler** (USA) *KO* 4 Willie Pep, New York City

BANTAMWEIGHTS

July 4 **Manuel Ortiz** *KO* 8 Memo Valero, Baja, CA

THE MAGIC OF MARCEL

At age 32, Algerian-born Frenchman Marcel Cerdan was only three years younger than defending middleweight champion Tony Zale. But when the fighters began to trade punches, the difference could have been 30 years.

Colliding before a crowd of 19,272 at Roosevelt Stadium in Jersey City, New Jersey, Cerdan and Zale were equally demanding of a sizzling pace. But while the challenger thrived, the champion fell far behind. "...all of a sudden," wrote Frank Graham in the *New York Journal-American*, "the savage had grown worn and tired, and he was just an old prize fighter who had nothing left."

Cerdan kept punching until the end of the 11th round, when a hook dropped the champion. Zale's handlers helped him to his corner stool, and at the start of the 12th, only one fighter was standing. At that very moment, the handsome and charismatic Marcel Cerdan became the most beloved fighter in the history of France. *Vive la difference!*

France's Marcel Cerdan (right) became the new middleweight king by stopping Tony Zale.

A NEW HEADLINER MAKES LOCAL HEADLINES

Harlem-based Sandy Saddler was boxing's best-kept secret. A veteran of 93 fights, the lanky, 5'8" featherweight was a pure puncher who had headlined from Cleveland to Caracas, and Honolulu to Havana.

As improbable as it seemed, his first hometown main event didn't come until his October 29 challenge of world champion Willie Pep at Madison Square Garden. That Pep climbed through the ropes a prohibitive favorite was no insult to the 22-year-old Saddler; at 135-1-1, and with a five-year unbeaten streak, Pep boasted of boxing's best record. Moreover, he had kept the crown for six years, and made six successful defenses.

As the fight drew near, betting was brisk on both sides, and after the noon weigh-in, New York State Athletic Commission Chairman Eddie Eagan warned the fighters, "You are two honest athletes. We are holding you responsible to uphold the good name of boxing."

The fighters heeded Eagan's advice, but the champion forgot to uphold the good name of Pep. He was bloodied by a left to his nose in the first round, twice floored for nine-counts in the third, and downed for referee Ruby Goldstein's full count in the fourth. "I wasn't ready mentally for a tough fight," he said. Eagan agreed. Pep, he decided, never recovered from the "punch shock" Saddler's third-round blitz had brought. Besides, the Chairman reasoned, there were easier ways to dump a fight than swallowing Sandy Saddler's most savage punches for four rounds.

Willie Pep struggles to free himself from Sandy Saddler's headlock. Sandy scored a fourth-round kayo to become the new featherweight king in a shock result.

Ringside View

JULY

Bantamweight champion Manuel Ortiz keeps the crown by kayoing Memo Valero in round eight.

SEPTEMBER

In a non-title 10-rounder, welterweight champion Sugar Ray Robinson outclasses rising contender Kid Gavilan and scores a points victory.

DECEMBER

In Los Angeles, the streaking Maxie Docusen scores a 10-round, non-title victory over reigning world bantamweight champion Manuel Ortiz.

DECEMBER

Rising light heavyweight Joey Maxim is unimpressive in outpointing Jimmy Bivins over 10 rounds in Cleveland.

NO KIDDING FROM THE KID

American fight fans had never seen anything quite like Cuba's Gerardo Gonzalez, better known as Kid Gavilan.

The 5'10½" welterweight wasn't particularly heavy-handed, but his style was pleasing nonetheless. He marched forward against all resistance, delivered punches by the dozen, and featured his signature bolo blows in each and every round.

Gavilan was 20 when he made his U.S. debut. After a brief return to Cuba, he resettled in the States and quickly established himself as a crowd-favorite contender. Even a non-title points loss to world champion Sugar Ray Robinson couldn't halt his momentum.

Gavilan risked his status by signing to face dangerous Tony Janiro on November 12 at Madison Square Garden. But one week before fight night, Janiro fell out with an injury. He was replaced by the capable Tony Pellone.

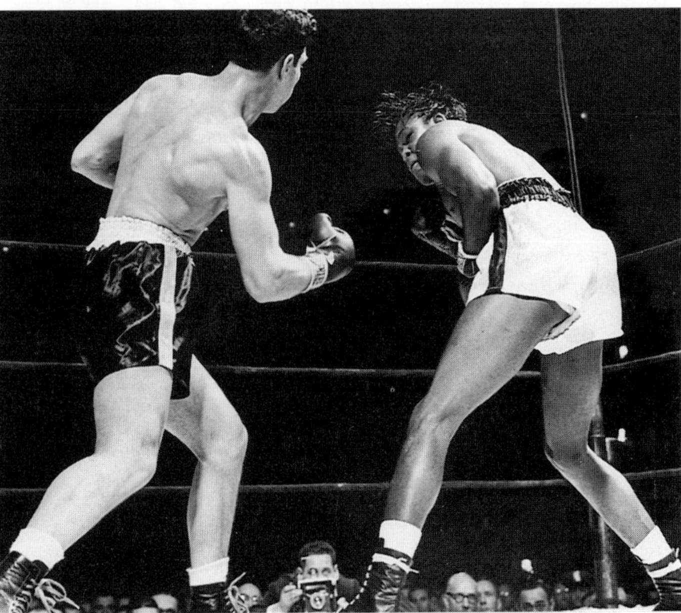

Cuba's colorful Kid Gavilan (right) outpointed Tony Pellone in a tremendous battle and moved closer to a shot at Sugar Ray Robinson's welterweight title.

After a slow start, Gavilan-Pellone turned into a high energy brawl. Gavilan concentrated his attack on the body, and Pellone countered effectively to the head. Round after round the 147-pounders charged into each other, and for the last 30 seconds of the 10th and final round, they engaged in a toe-to-toe trade. At the final bell, none of the 9,408 fans was seated. Gavilan took the decision by 7-3 (twice) and 6-4.

In the months to come, he would secure a title try against Robinson, in no small part due to the effort he had put forth against a most stubborn substitute.

JANUARY

1949

JUNE

FIGHTING TALK

I don't think he'll fight me again

SANDY SADDLER
after his second bout
with Willie Pep

WILLIE WINS THE TITLE BACK

The Fight of the Year was also the fight of Willie Pep's career. On February 11, only three months and 13 days after losing the featherweight title to Sandy Saddler, Pep won it back with a wondrous performance at a sold-out Madison Square Garden.

Jumping in and out, twisting and turning, pushing and pulling, Pep won seven of the first eight rounds. Over the second half of the bout, however, the champion found his rhythm. Saddler struck for the first time in the ninth, and in round 10, he mounted an offensive so fierce that ringsiders were expecting referee Eddie Joseph to intervene.

Pep rebounded in the 11th, but Saddler remained stronger, and at the final bell, a bloodied Pep was doubled over and desperately hanging on to the champion's waist. Saddler's powerpunches had come too late; Pep took a unanimous decision by scores of 10-5, 9-6, and 9-5-1. His face, however, suggested a different outcome. He took three stitches over each eye, three on his left cheek, and two on his right cheek. But he wasn't going to issue a single complaint.

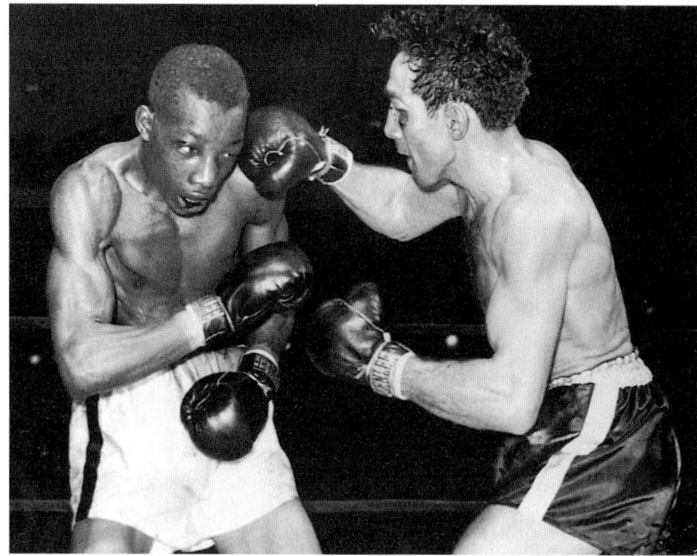

In one of boxing's greatest displays of skill and courage, Willie Pep (right) regained the featherweight crown from Sandy Saddler, who had taken it four months earlier.

AN 11TH-HOUR GAMBLE

On February 28, only one day before heavyweight champion Joe Louis would announce his retirement, top contender Ezzard Charles risked his position by taking on the talented Joey Maxim at the Cincinnati Garden.

Charles was fighting at home, but against a particularly difficult foe; Maxim was tall, strong, and sturdy, and he flashed one of the best jabs in boxing. From the first round to the 15th, Charles-Maxim was a carefully paced boxing match. In the third, Maxim suffered a cut over his right eye, and Charles, scaling a career-high 181¼, began to bleed from the nose. By the middle rounds, both fighters seemed resigned to the fact that a knockout wasn't going to come.

As a result, they contentedly jabbed and clinched until the final bell. Charles took the majority decision by scores of 70-65, 73-69, and 70-70. He hadn't won new supporters, but more importantly, he hadn't lost his status. After all, bigger bouts lay ahead. "We're ready to fight Joe Louis," proclaimed Jake Mintz, one of Charles' managers. He'd have to settle for Joe Walcott.

Ezzard Charles (right) earned a shot at the heavyweight crown by outpointing clever Joey Maxim in his home town, Cincinnati.

THE BROWN BOMBER SAYS GOODBYE

The day was inevitable, but boxing fans couldn't imagine it ever coming.

On March 1 in Miami Beach, world heavyweight champion Joe Louis announced his retirement, in the form of a written statement. Louis had first said goodbye immediately after his 25th defense, a June 1948 knockout of Jersey Joe Walcott. Insiders expected him to change his mind, but defense number 26 was never to come.

"The decision was my own," said the 34-year-old Louis. "I could see that I couldn't fight any more and decided to retire."

NBA boxing commissioner Abe J. Greene gave Louis permission to promote the bout that will determine his successor. Louis, Jim Norris, and Arthur Wirtz, partners in the newly formed International Boxing Club, hope to make a match between Ezzard Charles and Walcott.

"(The title) meant so much to me, I really hated to do it," Louis said. And millions of fans hated for him to do it, too.

THE UNLUCKY ONE-ARMED FIGHTER

Boxing at their best, Marcel Cerdan and Jake LaMotta would have made for a middleweight dream match. Unfortunately, fans will forever wonder who would have won.

On June 16, LaMotta challenged 160-pound king Cerdan before 22,185 fans at Detroit's Briggs Stadium. One of the most eagerly anticipated bouts of the decade was tarnished in the first round, when Cerdan tore a shoulder muscle while delivering a left hook. That the Frenchman lasted until the end of round nine was testimony to his courage and will. Attempting to conceal his injury, Cerdan remained competitive until he again tried to hook in round four. At that point, referee Johnny Weber said he "heard something pop." Cerdan later reported that the excruciating pain convinced him to fight on with one hand. It didn't matter that early in the fight, LaMotta suffered a badly sprained middle knuckle on his left hand. Or that he was cut over the right eye.

Sensing his opponent's handicap, "The Raging Bull" swarmed, and rounds five through nine turned into a carnage. After the ninth, Cerdan's corner asked for Dr. Joseph Calahan to examine the champion. Cerdan stayed on his stool at the bell for round 10, and LaMotta's hand was raised. (After nine rounds, LaMotta led by 51-39, 48-42, and 49-41.)

"The man can't do himself justice," said Lew Burston, Cerdan's American representative. "Why kill him? He has a return bout."

There was no way to know it at the time, of course, but Marcel Cerdan would never fight again.

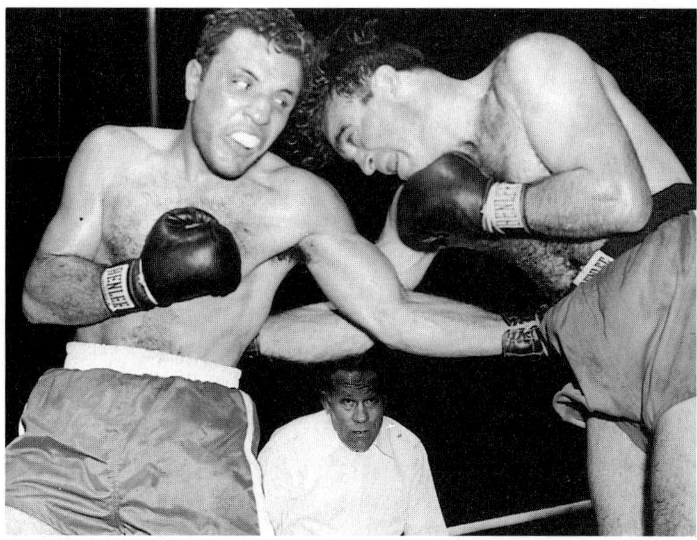

Jake LaMotta (left) used a brutal body attack to stop Marcel Cerdan and win the title.

World Title Fights

HEAVYWEIGHTS

June 21 **Ezzard Charles** (USA) *W* 15 Jersey Joe Walcott, Chicago (Vacant World Title)

MIDDLEWEIGHTS

June 16 **Jake LaMotta** (USA) *KO* 10 Marcel Cerdan, Detroit

FEATHERWEIGHTS

Feb 11 **Willie Pep** *W* 15 Sandy Saddler, New York City

BANTAMWEIGHTS

March 1 **Manuel Ortiz** *W* 15 Dado Marino, Honolulu

FLYWEIGHTS

April 5 **Rinty Monaghan** *W* 15 Maurice Sandeyron, Belfast

Ringside View

JANUARY

Boxing gypsy Archie Moore kayos knockout artist Bob Satterfield in the third round of a light heavyweight contest in Toledo, Ohio.

MARCH

In what would be the last successful defense of his title reign, bantamweight champion Manuel Ortiz scores a unanimous 15-round decision over Dado Marino.

APRIL

Ireland's Rinty Monaghan retains the world flyweight title, scoring a 15-round decision over Maurice Sandeyron.

APRIL

Streaking welterweight contender Kid Gavilan wins his rubber match against lightweight champion Ike Williams in New York City. The 10-round non-title bout goes the distance.

SHADOW OF A LEGEND

Not that the image of Joe Louis needed any boosting, but the NBA heavyweight title fight between Ezzard Charles and Jersey Joe Walcott made "The Brown Bomber" look even better.

Fighting for the title vacated by Louis, Charles, 27, and Walcott, 35, clashed at Chicago's Comiskey Park on June 22. (In favor of an elimination tournament, the powerful New York State Athletic Commission would not recognize the winner as its champion.) Despite spotting Jersey Joe 14 pounds, Charles entered the ring a 7-5 favorite.

Typically cautious, Walcott repeatedly stepped away and waited for counterpunching opportunities. Charles, who had boxed aggressively as a light heavyweight, was careful, too, and action was minimal; between the 12th and 13th rounds, Joseph Triner, Chairman of the Illinois State Athletic Commission, ordered referee Davey Miller to "make Walcott fight."

After 15 rounds, Charles managed to take the title by scores of 78-72 (twice) and 77-73. His performance, however, hadn't been scintillating, either. "...if his winning effort against old Jersey Joe Walcott at Comiskey Park was his best," wrote Al Buck in the New York Post, "he can't hit hard enough to dent a custard pie."

After the bout, ringside reporters couldn't help but wonder whether Charles' unimpressive showing had inspired Louis to contemplate a comeback.

"The only thing I want to fight," said Louis, "is par."

The highlight of the night came when Jake Mintz, one of Charles' managers, fainted in the ring seconds after the decision was announced. Though not contrived, his collapse served to at least temporarily focus the attention away from the fight. The king was dead. God help the new king.

Ezzard Charles (left) and Jersey Joe Walcott.

JULY

1949

DECEMBER

RINGSIDE VIEW

JULY

Lightweight champion Ike Williams registers his third win over Enrique Bolanos, knocking out the Mexican challenger in the fourth round.

SEPTEMBER

Flyweight champion Rinty Monaghan climbs off the floor to retain the title by 15-round draw vs. London's Terry Allen.

DECEMBER

Lightweight champion Ike Williams retains the crown by scoring a unanimous 15-round decision over Freddie Dawson.

DECEMBER

Former featherweight champion Sandy Saddler wins the junior lightweight title, decisioning Orlando Zulueta over 10 rounds. The title had been vacant for 16 years.

SUGAR'S SWEETNESS

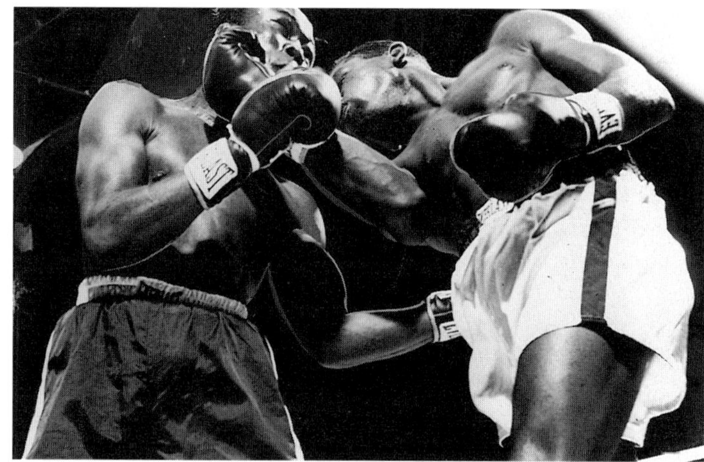

Sugar Ray Robinson gave Kid Gavilan a boxing lesson to retain the welterweight crown.

If Sugar Ray Robinson was this much better than welterweight Kid Gavilan, what were the rest of the world's 147-pounders supposed to do? One idea: move into the middleweight division.

On July 11, before a huge crowd at Philadelphia's Municipal Stadium, world champion Robinson dominated the Cuban over the bout's second half and scored a unanimous 15-round decision. Scores: 9-6 (twice) and 12-3.

The middle rounds provided lots of toe-to-toe exchanges, and in the eighth, Robinson was staggered. But he roared back before the bell, and in the championship rounds, Gavilan couldn't match him. Particularly disheartening to the division's top 10 was the fact that Robinson had made weight on his first trip to the scale. It was anticipated that Sugar Ray would struggle, and trainer George Gainford had kidded about covering him with "reducing salve." Robinson was still a welterweight, and for that, every contender had to toast him – preferably with a high-calorie milkshake.

MORE KILLER INSTINCT THAN SWEETNESS IN THE ROCK

In his autobiography *Somebody Up There Likes Me*, Rocky Graziano described his September 14 crossroads matchup with welterweight contender Charley Fusari, held before a screaming crowd of 31,000 at New York City's Polo Grounds:

"For nine rounds, Fusari ran me ragged. I choked on my own wind and stumbled over my own feet, and when the 10th (round) come up, my corner knew that I was losing the fight."

Fusari, scaling 147½ to The Rock's 159½, needed only to survive for three minutes. It didn't seem difficult; Graziano was tired and frustrated, and blood flowed freely from a cut over his left eye. Then he showed why knockout artists are said to possess "the great equalizer." Early in the 10th, he tore into Fusari with bonecrushing right hands. As Fusari turned limp, Graziano held him by the throat with his left hand and pummeled him with his right. Referee Ruby Goldstein attempted to step in, but even with the third man sandwiched between the fighters, Rocky continued looping in long rights. Only when his handlers rushed the ring did Graziano halt his savage assault. With 56 seconds left in the fight, he was declared the winner by TKO. It had been an awesome victory, but a frightening one as well.

TALKING WITH HIS FISTS

After winning the vacant NBA title by outpointing Jersey Joe Walcott, Ezzard Charles claimed to be the number-one heavyweight in boxing. Acceptance, however, was not universal. Following Joe Louis, Charles was to find, would be most difficult.

Charles made his first defense on August 10 at Yankee Stadium. A 4-1 favorite, he scored an eighth-round stoppage of the former light heavyweight champion Gus Lesnevich. "I'm the heavyweight champion," he said, "with no strings attached."

With fewer strings, anyway. Coming off losses to Freddie Mills and Joey Maxim, the 34-year-old Lesnevich proved the perfect foe. Charles was much sharper and quicker, and he cut Lesnevich over both eyes. With the exception of round six, when the challenger connected with a series of rights, Charles dominated.

After the seventh, Joe Vella, Lesnevich's manager, cried enough. It was Gus' last fight and Charles' first for respect.

Ezzard Charles (left) stopped Gus Lesnevich in eighth round to keep the heavyweight title.

Middleweight champ Jake LaMotta (right) lost by decision to Robert Villemain in New York.

WINNING WITH EMOTION

Middleweight champion Jake LaMotta's first title defense was supposed to be a rematch vs. the fighter he had dethroned, France's Marcel Cerdan. After Cerdan's shocking death, promoters scrambled for a replacement. Fittingly, they chose another Frenchman, Robert Villemain.

At Madison Square Garden on December 9, LaMotta's title was not at stake. Having defeated Villemain in March, "The Raging Bull" climbed through the ropes a 3-1 favorite. In setting the line, however, the oddsmakers forgot to consider emotion. Villemain was similar in style to LaMotta, and on this night, he fought with far more energy. He crowded the champion, worked to the head and body, and all but ignored LaMotta's tepid counters. After 10 rounds, the judges rewarded Villemain by scores of 7-3 (twice) and 5-3-2.

"I did it for my country," he said. "And for Cerdan."

THE $58,000 "WORKOUT"

When Ezzard Charles signed to defend against Pat Valentino, insiders joked that the heavyweight champion was going to be paid $40,000 for a "workout."

Valentino (right) challenges Charles.

As it turned out, the fight, held on October 14 at San Francisco's Cow Palace, was both a financial and artistic success. Charles took home $58,000, and earned every penny. The mop-haired Valentino was initially dismissed as nothing more than a local favorite. As a result, Charles entered the ring a 5-1 favorite. But the challenger stuck to his fight plan – constant pressure and a concentrated body attack – and proved competitive.

Charles-Valentino was the first heavyweight title fight in San Francisco since Jack Johnson-Stanley Ketchel 40 years earlier. And like Johnson-Ketchel, the end came suddenly.

After seven rounds, Valentino held a slim lead on two of the three cards. Early in the eighth, however, Charles struck with a right to the chin, and Valentino fell. Resting on one knee, the Californian tried to rise at referee Jack Downey's count of nine, but fell face-first to the canvas. The bout was waved over at the 35-second mark. For Charles, the "workout" had worked out after all.

A LEGEND DIES YOUNG

On October 27, an Air France Constellation left Paris' Orly Airport for New York City. Scheduled for a fuel stop in the Azores, an island group in the mid-Atlantic, captain Jean de la Neue lost radio contact and veered sharply off course. Seconds later, he crashed into the 3,600-foot Mt. Redondo. All 48 passengers were killed.

The most famous of those on board was former middleweight champion Marcel Cerdan, who was headed for a return bout with Jake LaMotta. Four months before, LaMotta had dethroned Cerdan by 10th-round TKO. The news of Cerdan's death darkened the entire boxing community. No other fighter had been so full of life.

Three days after the tragedy, six of France's all-time great champions, Andre Routis, Eugene Criqui, Emile Pladner, Maurice Holzer, Marcel Thil, and Georges Carpentier, lined up at attention in the ring at the Palais des Sport. A gap was symbolically left between Holzer and Thil. A soldier played Taps, and the timekeeper rang the bell 10 times. Then the fans and fighters sang the Marseillaise. They would never, ever forget.

FIGHTING TALK

They loved him before. Now that he's dead, they'll love him even more. Now they'll realize how great he really was

IRVING COHEN
Fight manager, on the death of Marcel Cerdan

WORLD TITLE FIGHTS

HEAVYWEIGHTS

Aug 10	**Ezzard Charles** *KO* 8 Gus Lesnevich, Bronx, NY
Oct 14	**Ezzard Charles** *KO* 8 Pat Valentino, San Francisco

WELTERWEIGHTS

July 11	**Sugar Ray Robinson** *W* 15 Kid Gavilan, Philadelphia

LIGHTWEIGHTS

July 21	**Ike Williams** *KO* 4 Enrique Bolanos, Los Angeles
Dec 5	**Ike Williams** *W* 15 Freddie Dawson, Philadelphia

JUNIOR LIGHTWEIGHTS

Dec 6	**Sandy Saddler** *W* 10 Orlando Zulueta, Cleveland (Vacant World Title)

FEATHERWEIGHTS

Sept 20	**Willie Pep** *KO* 7 Eddie Compo, Waterbury, CT

FLYWEIGHTS

Sept 30	**Rinty Monaghan** *D* 15 Terry Allen, Belfast

RING DECADE

1950-1959

THE '50s was a time of growth and change. There were ballpark fights and TV fights; champions from New York and Paris, but also Asia, Africa, and Australia; old stars like Archie Moore, and young ones like Floyd Patterson; the perfection of Rocky Marciano, the brilliance of Sugar Ray Robinson, the speed of Kid Gavilan, and the greed of Jim Norris.

By the end of the decade, the '50s resembled the '80s far more than the '40s. Which is either wonderful or tragic.

Throughout the '50s, boxing's powerbroker was blue-blooded millionaire Jim Norris, a sort of Don King, Bob Arum, and Donald Trump all rolled into one. Norris' wealth was pervasive; he owned controlling interest in Madison Square Garden, Chicago Stadium, the Detroit Olympia, and the Chicago Black Hawks hockey team. As head of the International Boxing Club, which he formed in 1949, Norris promoted every single heavyweight, light heavyweight, middleweight, and welterweight title fight for 10 years. He also capitalized on television's infatuation with the sweet science. His muscle was everywhere – the IBC was nicknamed Octopus Inc. – and he dominated the sport even more completely than Mike Jacobs had in the late-'30s and '40s. Whether Norris was a positive or negative force is open to debate. He made many major matches, but his business associates included Frankie Carbo and Blinky Palermo, mobsters who ended up in prison, and boxing's image suffered.

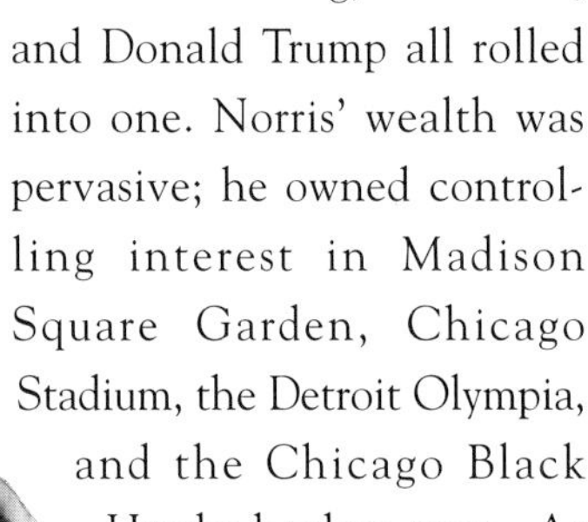

Rocky Marciano earned his immortality before retiring as undefeated heavyweight champion in 1956.

"He alone could have starved the boxing mob into submission, on his terms," wrote the *New York Times'* Arthur Daley. "The cost would have come high, but he had the resources to do it. Instead, he played ball with the hoods, and let the termites eat away the great boxing empire he built."

Sugar Ray Robinson defended the middleweight crown against every worthy contender during the decade, racking up an unsurpassable record.

Conveniently for the IBC, Al Weill, the unofficial manager of heavyweight champion Marciano, was its matchmaker. Marciano's retirement marked the beginning of Norris' decline, in large part because Cus D'Amato, the manager of Marciano's successor, Floyd Patterson, despised the IBC, and chose to remain fiercely independent.

In the mid-'50s, the federal government began an investigation of Norris in regard to anti-trust laws, and in 1958, his empire was dissolved by court order. Until the emergence of King and Arum, there would be no more omnipotent promoters. In one sense, the TV boxing boom reduced the significance of promoters like Norris. As soon as television rights surpassed the live gate as a promoter's primary income, the networks and their advertisers became boxing's major players. A TV series, like the immensely popular Gillette *Friday Night Fights*, brought unprecedented exposure to hundreds of fighters. But the price was considerable: with more boxing offered on TV, fans were less likely to pay for a seat at live cards. As a direct result, the clubshow circuit, which provided invaluable experience for prospects, and fed polished young fighters to the international stage, all but disappeared. TV boxing would slump after the *Friday Night Fights* died in the '60s, but the clubfights would never fully recover.

The decade provided a handful of outstanding champions in the lighter weight classes, including welterweights Gavilan and Carmen Basilio, lightweights Jimmy Carter and Joe Brown, featherweight Sandy Saddler, and flyweight Pascual Perez. But the hottest highlights came at heavyweight, light heavyweight, and middleweight.

Rocky Marciano grew into a ring legend despite a lack of natural ability. He was a creation of trainer Charlie Goldman,

Carl "Bobo" Olson annexed the world middleweight crown and tried for the light heavyweight title. There wasn't one fighter Bobo didn't test.

who recalled watching Marciano for the first time. "I saw a lot of fighters in my time, but I never seen one as clumsy as Rocky," he said. "He had two left feet, he couldn't get out of his own way, and he threw a punch like a bouncer in a gin mill."

Conditioning, persistence, and punching power carried Marciano to the world title. Many historians place him among the top heavyweights of all time, while others dismiss him as a brawler whose biggest wins came against aging opposition. Regardless, as the only champion who never lost a fight, he is unique. After retiring at age 32 ("I got tired of having to be introduced to my daughter," he explained), he resisted the temptation to come back.

Light heavyweight champion Archie Moore was no less unique. Consider:

- He scored 129 knockouts, the most in history.
- He fought from 1936 to 1963, and for 17 years before securing a try at the world title.
- He won the crown at age 39, and kept it until age 48. The key to Moore's longevity remained a secret. The only hints he ever gave: always exercise the mind, and never keep track of time.

Clever with words and fists alike, Moore was a constant source of education and entertainment. His lengthy title reign followed years of neglect, but "The Ol' Mongoose" never looked back. Unfortunately, he failed to achieve his ultimate goal, winning the heavyweight title. In 1955, Marciano proved too strong for him, and one year later, Patterson proved too fast. "Would I have beaten Marciano if I had been 10 years younger?" he said during an interview in 1990. "Why would I want to think about that?"

Where Moore was inimitable, Robinson created a persona that a generation of fighters tried to duplicate. Driving his pink Cadillac through the streets of Harlem, and employing an entourage that included a hairdresser and a masseur, he made sure to leave no doubt that he was a star.

"I went through $4 million, but I have no regrets," he said.

As a champion, Robinson was a promoter's nightmare. Essentially self-managed, he negotiated to maximize every purse and business deal. As a challenger, however, his pride consumed him, and his sole desire, no matter the financial terms, was to regain his former status. Both a quick and mobile boxer, and a hitter with one-punch kayo power, Robinson dominated the welterweight division in the second half of the '40s. But it wasn't until the '50s, during which he won the middleweight crown a record five times, that he established himself as the best fighter, pound for pound, in history.

Robinson's skills and smarts allowed him to adjust to his opponent's style; he outboxed Jake LaMotta, overpowered Bobo Olson, and finished Gene Fullmer with a single hook. And he made sure to do it all with style. Unlike so many of the self-assured entertainers and athletes who followed him, Robinson always made sure to back up his swagger. And when he lost, he did so with class. "You are the real greatest," Muhammad Ali once told him.

While boxing's biggest stars were Americans, the game continued to expand internationally. Bantamweight Vic Toweel became the first world champion from South Africa, and his successor, Jimmy Carruthers, was the first from Australia. Perez gave Argentina its first titlist. Flyweight Yoshio Shirai did the same for Japan, and featherweight Hogan (Kid) Bassey for Nigeria. Still, by the end of the decade, the game was getting dark.

The IBC was gone; Marciano was retired, and Robinson and Moore were decelerating; the clubshows were suffering; and NBC was about to cancel the *Friday Night Fights*, which had been a staple of the network's programming since 1944.

Boxing desperately needed an injection of adrenaline. Fortunately for the sport, a remarkable teenager named Cassius Clay was just turning the corner.

Kid Gavilan brought a new excitement to the welterweight division that he ruled with his aggressiveness and fabled bolo punch.

Jimmy Carter stood out among the large group of brilliant lightweights in the decade. He was always referred to as the "True Professional."

JANUARY

1950

JUNE

Ringside View

FEBRUARY

Welterweight contender Billy Graham outpoints the highly rated Kid Gavilan over 10 rounds in New York.

MARCH

Featherweight champion Willie Pep retains the crown with a unanimous 15-round decision over European champion Ray Famechon.

APRIL

Two-division champion Sandy Saddler retains the junior lightweight title for the first time, stopping Mexico's Lauro Salas.

APRIL

After world flyweight champ Rinty Monaghan's retirement, London's Terry Allen wins the vacant crown, outpointing Honore Pratesi.

AS CLOSE AS A FIGHT CAN GET

Rocky Marciano would retire as the only unbeaten world champion in boxing history. It was at Madison Square Garden on March 24 that he came as close as he ever would to losing.

In a dream matchup, the aggressive and powerful Marciano, 26-0 (24), and rated fifth, faced the clever and technically superior Roland LaStarza, 37-0 (17), and rated sixth. Each round was close, except for the fourth, when Marciano scored a knockdown and opened cuts over both of LaStarza's eyes, and the eighth, when The Rock rallied, but was penalized for punching low.

After 10 rounds, ring announcer Johnny Addie shared the decision with a hushed crowd. Artie Aidala scored for LaStarza, 5-4-1. Arthur Schwartz scored for Marciano, 5-4-1. Referee Jack Watson scored 5-5, but, using the recently instituted supplemental points system, gave Marciano nine points, and LaStarza six. That made Marciano the winner by split decision.

With the judges scoring unanimously in all but two of the rounds, it couldn't have been closer. For LaStarza, however, that would provide little comfort.

"I'm sure as income taxes that I outscored him," he would say years later. Which was more than the rest of Marciano's opponents could say.

Many experts thought Roland LaStarza (left) deserved the decision over Rocky Marciano, but Rocky's hand was raised after 10 rounds, New York, March 24.

MAXIM-IZING HIS POWER

How do you explain a year in which featherfists Willie Pep and Joey Maxim score big-fight knockouts, and bonebreaker Rocky Marciano is forced to go the distance?

When Maxim arrived in London to challenge reigning light heavyweight champion Freddie Mills, British fight fans were expecting world-class skills, but little power. After all, Maxim had scored only 14 kayos in 67 victories. But Doc Kearns, his manager, was hyping a new Maxim.

"He'll stop this limey as sure as you're a foot high," he told a reporter. "Before we left Cleveland, he flattened Jimmy Bivins in the gym with the big mitts."

Mills and Maxim squared off before 18,002 fans (an indoor British record) at Earl's Court. In the first round, the champion scored big with an overhand right. It would turn out to be his only moment. In the fifth, Maxim exploded with 12 unanswered blows, and in the 10th, he dropped his foe for referee Andrew Smyth's full count with a perfect one-two. Afterward, officials discovered four teeth embedded in Mills' gumshield. Doc Kearns had proved prophetic: Mills had been Maxim-ized.

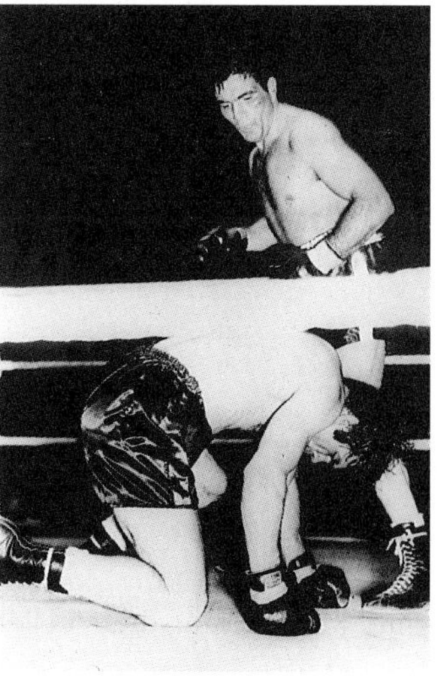

In his first defense of light heavyweight crown, Freddie Mills was kayoed by Joey Maxim in 10th round, London, January 24.

AND A KAYO PUNCH, TOO

Featherweight champion Willie Pep was clearly superior to all of the fighters in his weight class – save one. As a result, most of his title defenses were dismissed as time-killers between slugfests with Sandy Saddler.

Before Pep squared off against Charley Riley on January 16 at Kiel Stadium, The Hartford Courant's Bill Lee described the hometown challenger as "just about the last American featherweight of any particular repute Pep has not beaten." Pep hardly seemed concerned, however, and danced with rhythm over the course of the first four rounds.

At the start of the fifth, the champion was ahead on points and in control. Then he did something unusual: he ended a fight with one punch. With Riley leaning over, Pep fired a right uppercut that landed on the point of the chin. Boom! The challenger fell face-first, and referee Harry Kessler counted him out at the 1:05 mark.

"I think I can beat him; I'd like to fight him again," Riley said after regaining his senses. Though his sentiment suggested he hadn't regained his senses at all.

SOUTH AFRICA'S FIRST CHAMPION

Boxing's longest title reigns are usually ended by the most unlikely of challengers. Never was this more evident than on May 31, when South Africa's Vic Toweel faced bantamweight champion Manuel Ortiz at Rand Stadium in Johannesburg.

On paper, it seemed a horrific mismatch. Though Toweel had engaged in 190 amateur bouts, and represented his country at the 1948 Olympics, his pro record showed only 11 bouts. Ortiz, on the other hand, had answered the opening bell no less than 114 times. Moreover, the Californian had been champion for the better part of eight years. But a look at their recent form hinted at the upset to come.

Toweel, 23, had advanced at breakneck speed, winning the South African bantamweight crown in his fourth fight, the national featherweight title in his seventh bout, and British Empire bantamweight honors in his ninth effort. And five of his 11 fights had gone at least 12 rounds.

Conversely, Ortiz, 33, seemed to be fading. He had lost four non-title bouts in 1949, and was clearly winding down. Ortiz' strategy was to allow the challenger to expend his energy, and then, in the late rounds, rally to victory. It backfired, however, when the speedy Toweel adapted smartly to the slow pace and saved his punches.

The busy middle rounds belonged to the challenger, and Ortiz' desperate flurries in the ninth, 12th, and 15th stanzas weren't enough to salvage referee Willie Corner's verdict.

Before a record crowd of more than 27,000, Toweel was crowned South Africa's first world champion.

"This Vic is so good," commented a very gracious Ortiz, "I guess he'll keep the title for a long time."

South Africa's Vic Toweel (left) ended the reign of great bantamweight champion Manuel Ortiz.

WORLD TITLE FIGHTS

LIGHT HEAVYWEIGHTS

Jan 24 **Joey Maxim** (USA) *KO* 10 Freddie Mills, London

MIDDLEWEIGHTS

June 5 **Sugar Ray Robinson** *W* 15 Robert Villemain, Philadelphia (Vacant Pennsylvania World Title)

JUNIOR LIGHTWEIGHTS

April 18 **Sandy Saddler** *KO* 9 Lauro Salas, Cleveland

FEATHERWEIGHTS

Jan 16 **Willie Pep** *KO* 5 Charley Riley, St. Louis

March 17 **Willie Pep** *W* 15 Ray Famechon, New York City

BANTAMWEIGHTS

May 31 **Vic Toweel** (SA) *W* 15 Manuel Ortiz, Johannesburg

FLYWEIGHTS

April 25 **Terry Allen** (ENG) *W* 15 Honore Pratesi, London (Vacant World Title)

A MESSAGE FOR CHAMPION JAKE

Jake LaMotta had reigned for an entire year without defending the world middleweight title, and on June 5, Sugar Ray Robinson decided to send a message.

At Philadelphia's Municipal Stadium, the reigning welterweight champion faced France's Robert Villemain for the vacant Pennsylvania 160-pound crown. In December '49, Villemain had outpointed LaMotta in a non-title bout. But the oddsmakers weren't impressed; convinced the 29-year-old Robinson was the best fighter at two weights, they made him a 5-1 favorite.

After winning a unanimous 15-round decision, Robinson said, "Nobody has to tell me I'm slower. I can feel it." Then he spoke of retiring on his 31st birthday.

Given the quality of his performance, it was strange talk. Boxing as beautifully as he ever had at welterweight, Robinson, 155, dominated from the outset. Villemain's aggressiveness enabled Sugar Ray to flaunt his jab and combinations, and he only accepted an occasional blow in return. He dropped the Frenchman with an uppercut in round nine, and again with a cross in round 12. Villemain's only moment came in the 13th, when a right deposited Robinson on the canvas. Referee Charley Daggert, however, ruled it a slip. Robinson triumphed by scores of 12-3 (twice) and 10-5. The message was clear: he was rising in weight with ease, while LaMotta was constantly struggling to reduce to the middleweight limit.

Jake would soon have a raging welterweight on his hands. And that was no bull.

Sugar Ray Robinson explodes a perfect right uppercut on Robert Villemain's chin.

JULY

1950

DECEMBER

THE 11TH-HOUR KNOCKOUT

It was the most desperate rally in title fight history. On September 13 at Detroit's Olympia Stadium, middleweight champion Jake LaMotta defended for the second time, facing Laurent Dauthuille.

Tentative and slow, LaMotta quickly fell behind. The challenger boxed strongly, and his jabs began to close "The Raging Bull's" left eye. Still, LaMotta failed to respond. In fact, in the seventh and eighth rounds, referee Lou Handler exhorted him to fight.

In the championship rounds, LaMotta often played possum, pretending that he was hurt in an attempt to sucker Dauthuille into opening up. The tactic finally worked in the last minute of the 15th round, when the champion exploded without warning. His fists rapidly tattooed the Frenchman, and Dauthuille fell for the count. Incredibly, with 13 seconds left in the fight, LaMotta was declared the winner – and still champion. After 14 rounds, Dauthuille was ahead by scores of 72-68, 74-66. and 73-67.

"When he dropped his hands in my corner," LaMotta said, "I knew I had him."

Sure, Jake, you knew it all along.

Jake LaMotta saved his middleweight title in last seconds by kayoing Laurent Dauthuille.

SHOULDERING THE BLAME

The grudge series between Willie Pep and Sandy Saddler is considered the most foul-filled, in-your-face rivalry in boxing history. That reputation, however, wasn't established until the third of their four bouts, on September 8 before 38,781 at Yankee Stadium.

Pep had regained the featherweight crown from Saddler in February '49, but was nonetheless rated as the 8-5 underdog. The odds seemed justified in round three, when Saddler scored a knockdown with a looping left hook. But Pep rebounded in the next three rounds, and the fighting turned salty. Pep pushed, pulled, thumbed, and stepped on Saddler's toes. Saddler wrestled and punched where he wasn't supposed to. Referee Ruby Goldstein was needed in triplicate.

Toward the end of the seventh round, the feathers locked bodies along the ropes, and at the bell, Pep returned to his corner in excruciating pain. Dr. Vincent Nardiello diagnosed a dislocated left shoulder. The bell rang, and when Pep remained seated, Goldstein raised Saddler's hand. At the time of the stoppage, Pep was ahead on all three cards.

"He beat me with a double armlock," Pep complained. "I thought a punch to the kidney did it," answered Saddler. "But if they say I twisted his arm, okay, I twisted it."

Not exactly remorseful, was he?

Saddler drives featherweight champ Pep through ropes on way to regaining crown.

RINGSIDE VIEW

JULY

Middleweight champion Jake LaMotta retains the crown by scoring a unanimous 15-round decision over Italy's Tiberio Mitri, a substitute for Rocky Graziano.

AUGUST

Sugar Ray Robinson drops back down to welterweight and keeps the world title by outpointing Charlie Fusari.

OCTOBER

Randy Turpin wins the British middleweight title, knocking out Albert Finch in round five.

DECEMBER

World bantamweight champion Vic Toweel makes his first defense and stops Danny O'Sullivan in 11 rounds.

THE END OF AN ERA – OFFICIALLY

It was ugly. It was sad. And it was inevitable. More than two years after defending the heavyweight title for the 25th and last time, Joe Louis returned to the ring.

On September 27, the 36-year-old legend challenged reigning champion Ezzard Charles before a disappointing crowd of 13,562 at Yankee Stadium. Charles spotted Louis 34½ pounds, but Louis' bulk served only to slow him.

Charles boxed as he pleased, and by the end, Louis looked 60; he bled from the nose and mouth, squinted through a badly swollen left eye, and punched with a bruised right hand. Charles seemed reluctant to punish his idol and settled for a unanimous 15-round decision victory. (Scores: 13-2, 12-3, and 10-5.) The Louis era, it seemed, had ended the only way it could have.

BOBO WAS ONLY SO-SO

Bobo Olson traveled 5,500 miles from his native Hawaii to challenge Pennsylvania world middleweight champion Sugar Ray Robinson. In the 12th round, his trip to the canvas was considerably shorter.

Robinson-Olson took place on October 26 at Philadelphia's Convention Hall. The 22-year-old challenger was relatively inexperienced, but for a few rounds, at least, he proved troublesome. Boxing out of a crouch and keeping a high guard that left his elbows extended, Olson was difficult – if not painful – to hit. But his gameplan was overly defensive, and Robinson took round after round.

The sudden end came after Robinson connected with a hook to the temple and followed with a right to the side. Olson collapsed and was counted out by referee Charley Daggert. After regaining his senses, Bobo described Robinson as "the greatest fighter I've ever seen."

For his part, Robinson was already thinking ahead. "Well, Jake," he said, referring to world middleweight champion Jake LaMotta, "how about it?"

Sugar Ray Robinson (right) had to call on all his skill to stop Bobo Olson.

WORLD TITLE FIGHTS

HEAVYWEIGHTS

Aug 15	**Ezzard Charles** *KO* 14 Freddie Beshore, Buffalo
Sept 27	**Ezzard Charles** *W* 15 Joe Louis, Bronx, NY
Dec 15	**Ezzard Charles** *KO* 11 Nick Barone, Cincinnati

MIDDLEWEIGHTS

July 11	**Jake LaMotta** *W* 15 Tiberio Mitri, New York City
Aug 25	**Sugar Ray Robinson** *KO* 1 Jose Basora, Scranton, PA
Sept 13	**Jake LaMotta** *KO* 15 Laurent Dauthuille, Detroit
Oct 26	**Sugar Ray Robinson** *KO* 12 Bobo Olson, Philadelphia

WELTERWEIGHTS

Aug 9	**Sugar Ray Robinson** *W* 15 Charley Fusari, Jersey City, NJ

FEATHERWEIGHTS

Sept 8	**Sandy Saddler** *KO* 8 Willie Pep, Bronx, NY

BANTAMWEIGHTS

Dec 2	**Vic Toweel** *KO* 11 Danny O'Sullivan, Johannesburg

FLYWEIGHTS

Aug 1	**Dado Marino** (USA) *W* 15 Terry Allen, Honolulu

FIGHTING THE SHADOWS OF HIS PAST

Didn't Joe Louis have it backwards? His September 1950 loss to world heavyweight champion Ezzard Charles turned out to be the start of his comeback.

Two months after a horrible defeat, the 36-year-old "Brown Bomber" returned to the ring against Argentina's 23-year-old Cesar Brion. Now, it seemed, he was fighting not because he wanted to, but because he had to.

On November 29 at Chicago Stadium, Louis defeated Brion by unanimous 10-round decision, but offered little hope for the future; he scored most of his points with his jab, and even against a slow, plodding opponent, couldn't seem to pull the trigger on his right hand. Ringsiders estimated that in 30 minutes of combat, Louis tried a total of 10 rights.

"It was as if his right hand never knew what his left hand was doing," wrote Arthur Daley of *The New York Times*. Louis scaled 216, or two pounds less than for his try against Charles. He remained optimistic, even though it was clear that he was now reacting and thinking in the ring, instead of anticipating and fighting on instinct.

Looking much older than 36, Joe Louis grimaces under the impact of Cesar Brion's jolting right.

FINDING A PLACE OF HIS OWN

Eighteen months after succeeding Joe Louis as heavyweight champion, Ezzard Charles was finally beginning to secure his own niche.

Defending for the first time in his hometown, "The Cobra" met ex-Marine Nick Barone before a crowd of 10,085 at the Cincinnati Gardens.

For the first time in six title bouts, Charles, 185, enjoyed a weight advantage. Barone was rugged and determined, but at 178½, really a light heavyweight. The challenger's aggressiveness allowed Charles to display all of his skills. He outfought Barone both inside and out, and in round 11, felled him with a barrage that was puncuated with a winging right. Having been floored for the first time in 54 bouts, Barone was counted out by referee Tony Warndorff.

"He's a deceiving guy," Barone said of Charles. "You think you're doing pretty good chasing him and banging him up on the inside. All of a sudden, you're tired. He hits you some sharp raps. You're on the floor and so fogged up, you can't get up."

Following a legend can be futile, but just being Ezzard Charles was becoming good enough.

JANUARY

1951

JUNE

Ringside View

JANUARY

Ezzard Charles retains the heavyweight title for the sixth time, knocking out Lee Oma in 10 rounds.

FEBRUARY

England's Randy Turpin wins the vacant European middleweight crown by scoring a first-round kayo of Luc Van Dam in London.

JUNE

In his first bout since losing the middleweight title, Jake LaMotta is stopped in seven rounds by heavy-hitting light heavyweight Bob Murphy.

ST. VALENTINE'S DAY MASSACRE

At the end, Jake LaMotta, battered and bleeding, lay against the ropes and gazed at Sugar Ray Robinson. The words were muttered in the film *Raging Bull*, but at Chicago Stadium on February 14, the message, perverse and beautiful, was solely with his eyes: "You couldn't put me down, Ray."

Clashing to unify the middleweight title, Robinson and LaMotta met for the sixth and final time. The first seven rounds were both competitive and predictable, with Robinson boxing and LaMotta applying steady pressure. In round eight, however, Robinson began to issue a terrific beating. LaMotta made a final stand in the sizzling 11th, but Sugar Ray regained control before the bell.

"I kept swinging and Jake kept standing," he said. "I didn't think I could knock him out."

After 12 rounds, Robinson led by scores of 63-57, 70-50, and 65-55. At the 2:04 mark of the 13th, referee Frank Sikora intervened, with LaMotta clutching the top rope and absorbing punch after punch without reply. His title having been hammered away, The Bull had only his pride. The scoreboard read Robinson 5, LaMotta 1, but remember, Ray had never put him down.

Sugar Ray Robinson rocks Jake LaMotta with left hook moments before end of a classic fight.

A SMALL STEP BACKWARD

Just when Ezzard Charles was beginning to emerge from Joe Louis' shadow...

On March 7 at Detroit's Olympia Stadium, Charles defended the title against Jersey Joe Walcott, whom he had defeated 21 months before. Walcott was 37, and, on paper at least, hardly a threat. But in the fourth round, he found the champion's jaw with a crippling right hand. The blow bloodied Charles and left him dizzy. He began to box tentatively, and Jersey Joe took the middle rounds. Charles scored his own knockdown with a hook in round nine, and won most of the championship rounds. But Walcott staged a rally in the 15th, and Charles was desperate at the end.

The decision, unanimous for Charles (scores of 80-70, 84-66, and 83-67), was booed by the crowd of 13,852. Walcott milked the moment, parading as he acknowledged the fans' dissatisfaction. He couldn't change the verdict, but it was never too early to begin campaiging for one final title try.

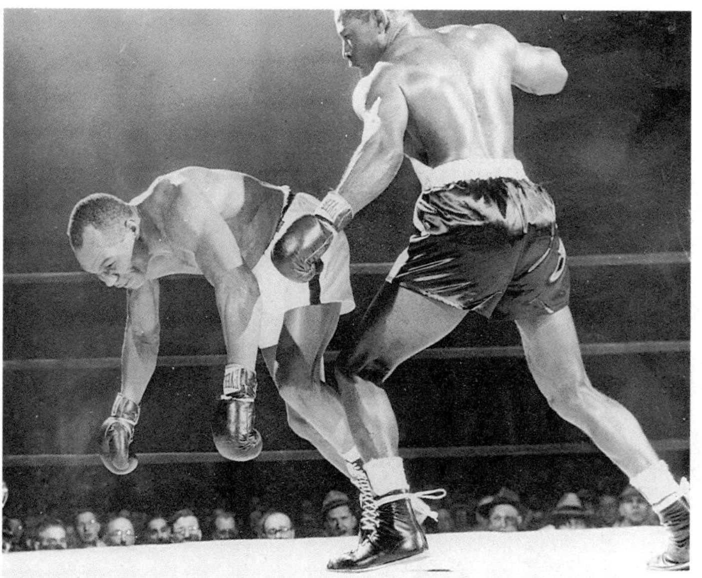

Jersey Joe Walcott falls face-first toward the floor as Ezzard Charles sets to follow up.

SUGAR SUBSTITUTES

One month before, Sugar Ray Robinson, the best welterweight in the world, had won the middleweight title. Four days before, Kid Gavilan, the second best welterweight, had stopped clubfighter Tommy Ciarlo in Havana. That left Johnny Bratton and Charley Fusari to trade blows for the vacant NBA crown.

Perhaps not the best two fighters in their weight class, but it's doubtful that any other 147-pounders could have had a better fight.

Bratton had suffered a broken jaw in losses to Beau Jack and Ike Williams, but on March 14 at Chicago Stadium, it was Fusari whose chin proved soft. After scoring knockdowns in rounds four and 10, Bratton, smooth and strong with his right hand, seemed en route to a comfortable victory. In the last five rounds, however, Fusari managed a furious rally. Badly fatigued, Bratton retreated, covered up, and waited for the final bell. The wait was worth it; Bratton was crowned by split decision (scores of 78-72, 77-73, and 74-76). Robinson and Gavilan could have their reputations; he had the belt.

World Title Fights

HEAVYWEIGHTS

Jan 11	**Ezzard Charles** *KO* 10 Lee Oma, New York City
March 7	**Ezzard Charles** *W* 15 Jersey Joe Walcott, Detroit
May 30	**Ezzard Charles** *W* 15 Joey Maxim, Chicago

MIDDLEWEIGHTS

Feb 14	**Sugar Ray Robinson** *KO* 13 Jake LaMotta, Chicago

WELTERWEIGHTS

March 14	**Johnny Bratton** (USA) *W* 15 Charley Fusari, Chicago (Vacant NBA Title)
May 18	**Kid Gavilan** (CUB) *W* 15 Johnny Bratton, New York City (Vacant World Title)

LIGHTWEIGHTS

May 25	**Jimmy Carter** (USA) *KO* 14 Ike Williams, New York City

OLD FOES, NEW STAKES

Following their consecutive battles in the fall of 1942, Ezzard Charles and Joey Maxim did not imagine that nine years later they would clash for the world heavyweight title.

The fourth and final fight of their series – Charles won the first three – came on May 30 at Chicago Stadium. At 6'1" and 181½, Maxim, the reigning light heavyweight champion, was one inch taller than Charles, and only a half-pound lighter. But Charles-Maxim IV was about speed and skill, not size.

Charles had dominated opponents before, but never with such a savage intensity. He won almost every round. At the end, Maxim's right eye was swollen shut, he was cut in a half-dozen places, and he bled from the nose.

"I was trying to knock him out in every round," said Charles, stating the obvious.

After Charles was declared the winner by unanimous 15-round decision (78-72, and two scores of 85-65), Maxim stretched out in his dressing room and sucked in oxygen. Nine more years before another fight with Charles would be too soon.

FIGHTING TALK

It's the same Charles, only more vicious

JOEY MAXIM
after losing for the fourth time to heavyweight champion Ezzard Charles

Ike Williams falls in the 14th round and Jimmy Carter is the new lightweight king.

BAD BREAK FOR BRATTON

Inside the first five rounds of Johnny Bratton's NBA welterweight title defense vs. Kid Gavilan, fought at Madison Square Garden on May 18, the champion suffered a broken jaw (the third of his career) and a double fracture of his right hand. Otherwise, he remained fighting fit.

Gavilan, a 2-1 favorite, didn't take advantage until the eighth round. He dominated the second half of the fight, during which Bratton threw only a handful of punches. The decision was one-sided, with the challenger taking the title by scores of 11-4 (twice) and 8-5-2.

After "The Kid" was declared the winner, his jubilant supporters wrapped him in a Cuban flag and raised him toward the roof. It was a wonderful time to be young, talented, and champion – especially with Sugar Ray Robinson fighting at middleweight.

Kid Gavilan (right) squares off with Johnny Bratton prior to their welterweight title fight.

DRIED OUT, THEN PUNCHED OUT

As defending lightweight champion Ike Williams dropped weight, boxing bookmakers dropped the odds.

Upon signing for his sixth defense, against the unheralded Jimmy Carter on May 25 at Madison Square Garden, Williams was a 3-1 favorite. But when the sharpies learned that he had three weeks to reduce by 20 pounds, the price fell to 2-1. And after it was learned that at the weigh-in, Williams used one hour and 20 minutes to drop from 135¾ to 135, Carter money flowed.

Carter had begun the year by losing two of three bouts. Williams, however, made the fight easy. Starting slowly and boxing in spurts, the powerpunching champion offered limited resistance.

"It was the weight," he said. "I was all dried out."

Only 3,594 fans, a record low for a title fight at the Garden, saw Carter score four knockdowns and force referee Pete Scalzo to rescue Williams at the 2:49 mark of round 14. Surprisingly, the bout was close at the time of the stoppage, with Carter ahead by scores of 7-5-1 (twice) and 6-6-1. The struggle to make weight seemed like a legitmate excuse, but as it would turn out, Williams was through. He would go 8-7-1 in his last 16 bouts and never again contend for a world crown.

JULY

1951

DECEMBER

THE OLD MAN IS THE BEST MAN

Having lost a pair of heavyweight title fights to both Joe Louis and Ezzard Charles, 37-year-old Jersey Joe Walcott refused to fade away.

On July 18 at Pittsburgh's Forbes Field, he made try number five (an all-time record). Only one week after 7-2 underdog Randy Turpin upset middleweight champion Sugar Ray Robinson, Walcott, a 6-1 longshot, knocked out Charles with one punch and became the oldest heavyweight titlist in history.

"I've tried 21 years for this night," he said. "Now I feel like I'm 16 years old."

Charles forced the fight for four rounds, but in the fifth, Walcott began to score with bold right hands. Early in the seventh, a left hook found the champion's chin, and Charles pitched forward. He was counted out by referee Buck McTiernan.

TURPIN TIME, THEN DO OR DIE

Even the longshot players shied away from backing 23-year-old European and British middleweight champion Randy Turpin's challenge of world titlist Sugar Ray Robinson, held at London's Earl's Court on July 10. Those who took the 7-2 odds, however, were richly rewarded.

Turpin was aggressive from the start, and his awkward style and persistent jab confused Sugar Ray. Referee Gene Henderson repeatedly warned both middleweights for a variety of fouls. But after 15 rounds, he raised only one arm. In one of the biggest upsets of the modern era, Turpin was declared the winner.

The rematch came on September 12, before a swelling crowd of 61,370 at New York City's Polo Grounds. This time, Robinson was fresh and properly prepared. But Turpin proved no easier. After nine rounds, Robinson led by the slimmest of margins. Early in round 10, Robinson suffered a hideous gash over his left eye.

"I was having a tough time anyway," he said afterward. "I figured I gotta do something. So I went at him. It was do or die."

Robinson did, smashing Turpin with a perfectly timed right cross. It would be the most important punch of his entire career. The champion crumpled, then rose at the count of nine.

Robinson's followup was merciless, and at the 2:52 mark, it was halted. Robinson had seized the moment, and the title.

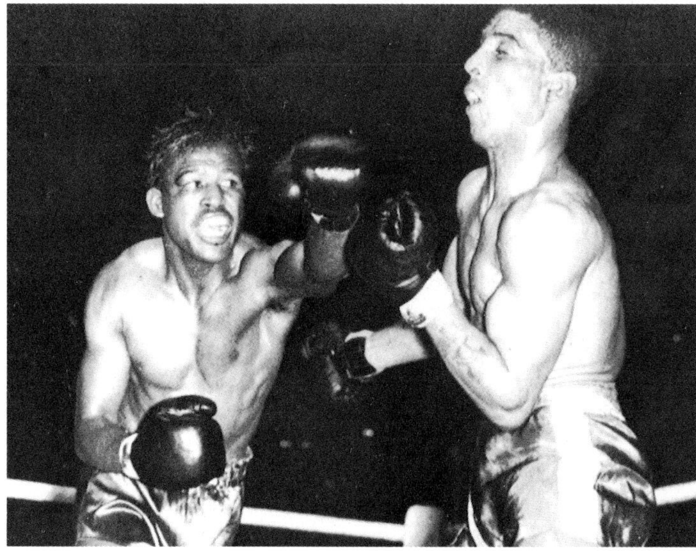

Randy Turpin (left) won the middleweight title by upsetting the great Ray Robinson.

WRESTLING, WITH A BIT OF BOXING THROWN IN

Held on September 26 at New York City's Polo Grounds, Sandy Saddler-Willie Pep IV rated with the nastiest title fights of all-time.

The battle began to degenerate in round two, after defending featherweight champion Saddler cut Pep over the right eye and followed up with the bout's only knockdown. From the third round on, Pep heeled, Saddler thumbed, and both wrestled. In the sixth, the rivals fell to the canvas, and Pep tried to knee Saddler in the throat. In the seventh, they fell again, with hapless referee Ray Miller joining them. After round nine, Pep complained of pain in his hideously swollen right eye, and the bout, dead-even on the cards, was stopped at his request.

Both fighters were subsequently suspended by the New York State Athletic Commission, Pep for life (the suspension would be lifted after 20 months) and Saddler indefinitely.

RINGSIDE VIEW

AUGUST

Making his first title defense 19 months after winning the light heavyweight title, Joey Maxim scores a unanimous 15-round decision over hard-hitting "Irish" Bob Murphy.

AUGUST

Welterweight champion Kid Gavilan retains the crown by unpopular and split 15-round decision over sweet-boxing Billy Graham.

NOVEMBER

Bantamweight champion Vic Toweel retains the crown for the second time, decisioning Luis Romero over 15 rounds.

DECEMBER

Light heavweight Harold Johnson ends the 25-bout unbeaten streak of Archie Moore, outpointing him over 10 rounds.

Willie Pep staggers Sandy Saddler in fourth bout of their classic series. But Pep was stopped in sixth round and Sandy was still featherweight champ, September 26.

The spectacle of the shell of a great champion being tortured was tragic. It happened when 37-year-old Joe Louis spotted Rocky Marciano nine years and was battered into submission.

FUTURE MEETS PAST

Having won eight consecutive bouts following his 1950 title fight loss to Ezzard Charles, 37-year-old former heavyweight champion Joe Louis was seemingly beating the clock. "The Brown Bomber" had gained enough momentum to be made an 8-5 favorite over streaking 28-year-old slugger Rocky Marciano, who was 37-0.

The heavyweights clashed at Madison Square Garden on October 26. The Rock spotted Louis 25¾ pounds – and proved to be the harder hitter. Fighting out of a crouch, he guarded against Louis' right hand while applying three minutes of pressure in each round. Most of Marciano's overhand rights missed, but after seven rounds, he led on all three cards.

In the eighth, Louis succumbed. Marciano felled him with a hook, and later in the round, knocked him through the ropes onto the ring apron with a right. Referee Ruby Goldstein didn't bother to count. Nor did Louis announce his retirement. The clock had done it for him.

WORLD TITLE FIGHTS

HEAVYWEIGHTS

July 18	**Jersey Joe Walcott** (USA) *KO* 7 Ezzard Charles, Pittsburgh

LIGHT HEAVYWEIGHTS

Aug 21	**Joey Maxim** *W* 15 Bob Murphy, New York City

MIDDLEWEIGHTS

July 10	**Randy Turpin** (ENG) *ref* 15 Sugar Ray Robinson, London
Sept 12	**Sugar Ray Robinson** *KO* 10 Randy Turpin, New York City

WELTERWEIGHTS

Aug 29	**Kid Gavilan** *W* 15 Billy Graham, New York City

LIGHTWEIGHTS

Nov 14	**Jimmy Carter** *W* 15 Art Aragon, Los Angeles

FEATHERWEIGHTS

Sept 26	**Sandy Saddler** *KO* 10 Willie Pep, New York City

BANTAMWEIGHTS

Nov 17	**Vic Toweel** *ref* 15 Luis Romero, Johannesburg

FLYWEIGHTS

Nov 1	**Dado Marino** *W* 15 Terry Allen, Honolulu

THE STORY OF THE BOXING GRANDFATHER AND THE GENTLEMAN

At 35, Hawaiian flyweight Dado Marino seemed too old to be a world champion, and too young to be a grandfather. But as he was proving in both his professional and personal lives, age is relative.

On November 1 at Honolulu Stadium, Marino risked the 112-pound crown for the first time, defending against England's Terry Allen, whom he had dethroned 15 months before. The champion, nicknamed the "Little Brown Doll," was the harder puncher, and Allen chose to respect his power. He also chose to respect the fans at ringside, taking time to apologize from his corner for splashing water on them.

The fight was fast-paced throughout. Allen suffered a cut over his right eye, but remained competitive until round 14, when Marino accelerated for the first time. Predictably, the decision went to the local favorite, by scores of 27-15 (twice) and 26-15. The calendar be damned: Grandpa still had a lot of fight left in him.

A CHAMPION WHO PROVED TO BE BETTER THAN GOLD

Many East Coast insiders dismissed California "Golden Boy" Art Aragon as a pretender who had reached the top of the lightweight ranks by crushing carefully selected opposition. But after Aragon outpointed world champion Jimmy Carter in a non-title fight on August 28, even the skeptics had to acknowledge that he had earned a try at the world title.

That try came on November 14 at the Olympic Auditorium in Los Angeles. A free swinger and crowd-pleasing pressure fighter, Aragon started quickly and outpunched the champion over the first five rounds. In the sixth, however, Carter landed a textbook hook that dropped Aragon and turned the fight.

Bleeding from a cut over his left eye, Aragon slowed during the middle rounds, and then stood bravely as Carter issued a beating down the stretch. In both the 13th and 14th rounds, referee Mushy Callahan seemed on the verge of stepping in and stopping the contest, and early in the 15th, Carter scored his second knockdown. But instead of trying once more for the finish, the champion backed off, partly from mercy, and partly from frustration.

The scoring was one-sided, with Carter retaining the crown by 11 points on two cards and 12 points on the third. The East Coast wise guys had been wrong about the Golden Boy. He wasn't the best lightweight in the world, but he turned out to be one of the toughest.

Lightweight champion Jimmy Carter (right) retained the crown by outpointing "Golden Boy" Art Aragon at Los Angeles.

JANUARY

1952

JUNE

WINNING NOT ENOUGH FOR ROCKY

It was no longer enough for unbeaten heavyweight contender Rocky Marciano to win. He had to win impressively. By stopping 36-year-old Lee Savold after six rounds at Philadelphia's Convention Hall on February 13, Marciano advanced to 39-0 (34). But the media wasn't satisfied.

"The bald truth," wrote Jesse Abramson in the *New York Herald-Tribune*, "is that Rocky Marciano never looked worse."

A 3½-1 favorite, Marciano opened cuts above both of Savold's eyes, split his lip, broke his nose, and left red welts all over him. But he failed to register a knockout, or at least a knockdown. (The end came after the sixth round, when Savold's manager, surrendered.) At one point, Marciano missed a wild right and fell to his knees.

Some of the press invariably underlined such moments while dismissing The Rock as a crude brawler. But until he lost for the first time, they would still be unable to say "I told you so."

15 ROUNDS FOR ONE DOLLAR

On March 13, middleweight champion Sugar Ray Robinson made the first defense of his second title reign. He donated all but $1 of his purse to the Damon Runyon Cancer Fund, but failed to give the fans at San Francisco's Civic Auditorium value for their money.

After Robinson topped former kayo victim Bobo Olson by unanimous decision (scores of 86½-78½, 84½-80½, and 85½-79½), some ringsiders blamed his lackluster performance on rust – it was Sugar Ray's first bout in six months. Others suggested he was past his prime. Olson fought aggressively, and after 10 rounds, the bout was even.

"Sometimes," kidded Robinson, "I could feel the breeze from my own misses."

But Robinson, who had prepared by sparring only 15 rounds, rallied down the stretch. At the final bell, Olson was desperately holding on. Sugar Ray was still the king. But he would be considered invincible no more.

WORLD TITLE FIGHTS

HEAVYWEIGHTS

June 5	**Jersey Joe Walcott** *W* 15 Ezzard Charles, Philadelphia

LIGHT HEAVYWEIGHTS

June 25	**Joey Maxim** *KO* 14 Sugar Ray Robinson, Bronx, NY

MIDDLEWEIGHTS

March 13	**Sugar Ray Robinson** *W* 15 Bobo Olson, San Francisco
April 16	**Sugar Ray Robinson** *KO* 3 Rocky Graziano, Chicago

WELTERWEIGHTS

Feb 4	**Kid Gavilan** *W* 15 Bobby Dykes, Miami

LIGHTWEIGHTS

April 1	**Jimmy Carter** *W* 15 Lauro Salas, Los Angeles
May 14	**Lauro Salas** (MEX) *W* 15 Jimmy Carter, Los Angeles

BANTAMWEIGHTS

Jan 26	**Vic Toweel** *ref* 15 Peter Keenan, Johannesburg

FLYWEIGHTS

May 19	**Yoshio Shirai** (JAP) *W* 15 Dado Marino, Tokyo

THE KID AND THE TEXAS SOUTHPAW

In the first racially mixed bout in Florida, welterweight champion Kid Gavilan was made a 4-1 favorite to reject the challenge of Miami-based Texan Bobby Dykes.

The bout was held on February 4 before a crowd of more than 17,000 at Miami Stadium. For the first five rounds, Gavilan justified the odds by crowding the 6-foot southpaw and banging away with his characteristically busy style. The Kid scored a knockdown in round two and seemed en route to a crowd-pleasing victory. But Dykes would prove difficult, if nothing else. Finding the rhythm for his jab, he began to extend the distance between he and his foe. Whenever Gavilan lunged in, the challenger busted him with a straight right. The middle rounds went to the long, tall Texan.

"Feint and back, feint and back," Gavilan said later. "That's the way he goes. Hard to hit."

The championship rounds were close, but the tireless Gavilan was able to accelerate in the 14th and 15th and take a split decision by scores of 142-141, 145-139, and 141-142. Styles make fights, and while Gavilan was torture for certain welters, Dykes had proved that certain welters were torture for The Kid, too.

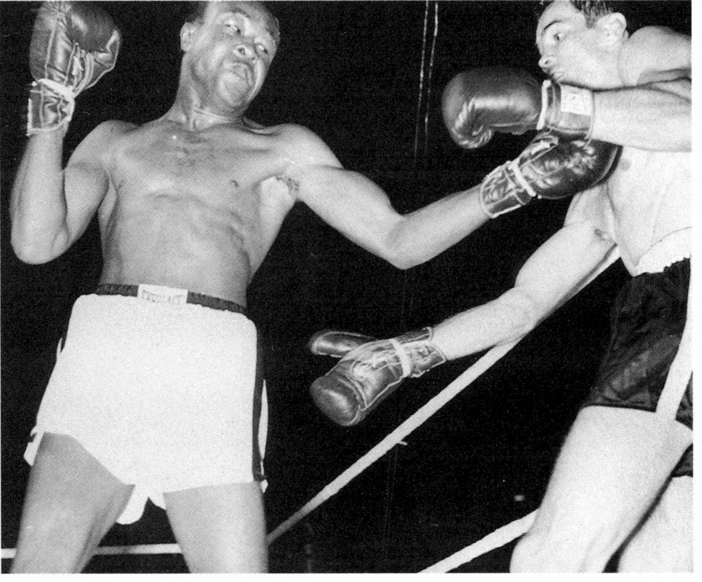

Welterweight champion Kid Gavilan (left) sets up Bobby Dykes for his famous bolo punch.

RINGSIDE VIEW

JANUARY

Avenging a defeat suffered six weeks before, light heavyweight contender Archie Moore scores a 10-round decision over Harold Johnson.

MAY

In a major upset, Mexico's Lauro Salas wins the lightweight title by scoring a split 15-round decision over Jimmy Carter. Only six weeks before, Carter had successfully defended against Salas by unanimous decision.

SUGAR RAY SUCCUMBS TO THE HEAT OF THE NIGHT

First the 104-degree temperature and steaming ring lights claimed referee Ruby Goldstein, who lasted through the 10th round, and was replaced by Ray Miller. Then, between the 13th and 14th rounds, middleweight champion Sugar Ray Robinson succumbed to heat prostration. Light heavyweight champion Joey Maxim was the only one left standing. That simple fact made him the winner and still champion.

On June 25, Maxim and Robinson clashed before a sweaty crowd of 47,963 at Yankee Stadium. Maxim was the slightest of favorites, but it was Sugar Ray, seeking his third title, who shined.

Moving purposefully, firing in combination, and negating the defending champion's 15½-pound advantage, he won almost every round. But he slowed in the 12th, and in the 13th, he backtracked on failing legs in a desperate effort to stall. After the bell, Robinson was examined by Dr. Alexander I. Schiff, who determined the fighter's condition and waved the bout off. (After 13 rounds, Robinson had led by scores of 10-3, 9-3-1, and on the combined card of Goldstein and Miller, 7-3-3.

"The heat didn't beat me, God did," was all he could say in his dressing room.

A strange alibi, but fitting, perhaps, for a strange ending.

Defending light heavyweight champion Joey Maxim stands over exhausted Ray Robinson.

IT WAS UNANIMOUS, BUT FOR WHOM?

Attempting to become the first heavyweight in history to regain the world title, Ezzard Charles challenged familiar rival Jersey Joe Walcott on June 5 at the Municipal Stadium in Philadelphia.

Like chapters I, II, and III, Charles-Walcott IV wasn't particularly eventful. During certain stretches, neither fighter landed more than one punch at a time. During others, neither fighter landed any punches at all. The fight wasn't easy to score. As it turned out, on two of the three cards, the 38-year-old Walcott needed the 15th round, and he won it. That resulted in a unanimous decision, with scores of 8-7, 7-6-2, and 9-6. (The bout was nationally televised, and seconds before the decision was announced, technical difficulties temporarily left millions of viewers without picture or sound.) But had the champion deserved the verdict?

The *New York Times*' Arthur Daley wrote that on his side of the ring, "not one reporter scored Jersey Joe as the winner," with the consensus 11-3-1 for Charles! "Could we all have been viewing the same fight?" he asked.

The only possible answer: from a judge's perspective, a fight without action can be more overwhelming than one with nothing but.

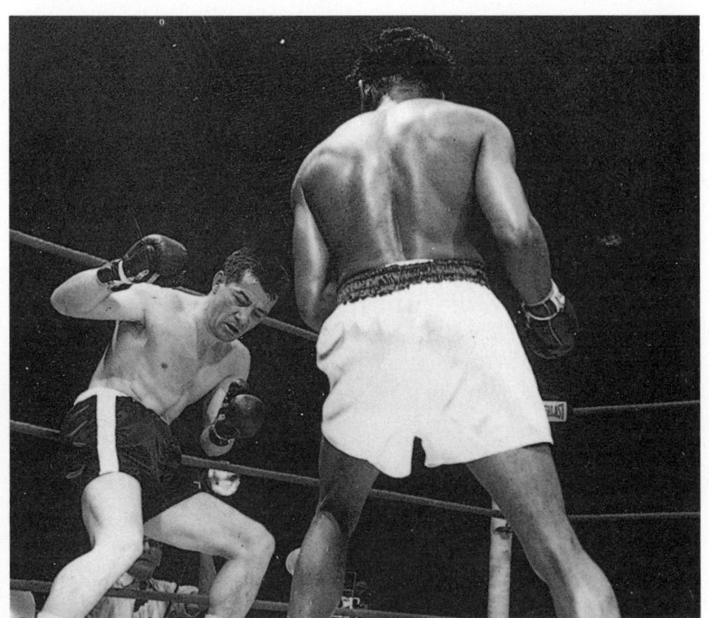

Rocky Graziano made a gallant attempt but was no match for defending champ Ray Robinson.

A SHOOTOUT IN CHICAGO

There were two ways for middleweight champion Sugar Ray Robinson to approach a title defense against a bomber like Rocky Graziano. He could plan to box and look for careful counterpunching opportunities, or decide to dig his boots into the canvas and trade smack for smack.

On April 16 at a sold-out Chicago Stadium, Robinson, 30, still had the skills to execute the former strategy. But he opted for the latter, and that choice made for a short night.

Fighting flatfooted, Robinson became a willing target. At age 29, Graziano was already past his prime, but given a stationary target, he remained a ruthless right-hand puncher. For two rounds, he consistently connected. Then, at the start of the third, he scored a flash knockdown. His trip to the canvas served as Robinson's wakeup call. Midway through the round, he exploded with two hooks and a right. Boom! Just like that, Graziano was counted out by referee Tommy Gilmore.

"I've met many tough fighters in my long career," said Robinson, "but no one ever stung me more than Rocky did."

JULY

1952

DECEMBER

THE GREATEST PUNCH OF ALL

Defending against Rocky Marciano on September 23 at Philadelphia's Municipal Stadium, heavyweight champion Jersey Joe Walcott took little time to prove that he was a level above the challenger's previous competition.

In the very first round, Walcott struck with a short hook, a punch similar to the left he had used to snatch the title from Ezzard Charles. Marciano fell to the canvas, suffering the first knockdown of his career. But The Rock endured, and while Walcott gained the edge in a fierce and bloody battle, the fight was still to be won in the championship rounds.

Walcott led on all three cards after 12 rounds (scores of 7-4-1, 8-4, and 7-5). Early in the 13th, Marciano released a straight right that traveled no more than 18 inches. It would come to be known as the most famous single punch in history. Positioned along the ropes, Walcott was carrying his left hand low. The blow caught him on the side of the chin. He promptly crumbled, and was counted out by referee Charley Daggert.

Just like that, Marciano was crowned champion. He was hardly the perfect fighter, but he had proved that he was capable of landing the perfect punch.

READY FOR THE BIG FIGHT

On July 28, those unacquainted with unbeaten heavyweight Rocky Marciano might have concluded that despite his nickname, "The Brockton Blockbuster" was a safety-first fighter.

The evidence: on a wet night at Yankee Stadium, Marciano, an 11-5 favorite to defeat the 100-fight veteran Harry "Kid" Matthews, made sure to wear his rubbers into the ring. Once the opening bell rang, however, Marciano stormed out of his corner and rained punches until Matthews caved in.

The Rock was characteristically wild in the first round, which was won by Matthews. But in the second, he landed two hooks, and The Kid was counted out by referee Ray Miller. Rain or shine, Marciano, 42-0 (37), was ready for a September challenge of reigning world champion Jersey Joe Walcott.

Hard-hitting Harry Matthews (right) hoped to snap Rocky Marciano's unbeaten streak.

A PHILLY KIND OF FIGHT

Philadelphia's Gil Turner was the kind to magnetize fight fans. He was young (21), good (31-0), and exciting. But on July 7, before 39,025 at Municipal Stadium, he wasn't ready for a veteran champ like welterweight Kid Gavilan.

Over the first four rounds, Turner energized his fans by daring to outGavilan Gavilan. His punches came by the dozen, and the sheer volume pushed back the titlist. But Gavilan knew that time was his ally. In the fifth, he started his rally, and by the 10th, Turner's punches were flat and weak. The challenger made a final stand early in round 11. Then Gavilan took over. A hook and cross sent Turner to the ropes, and a furious followup left him dazed and near-helpless. Referee Pete Tomasco stepped in with 13 seconds remaining in the round. (After 10 rounds, the bout was even on points.)

"I'm young; there's plenty of time for me to win the title," Turner told the press. "Maybe a licking is good for a guy before he becomes a champion."

Perhaps. But as it would turn out, the kayo loss would be the only title fight of Turner's career.

RINGSIDE VIEW

JULY

Former middleweight champion Bobo Olson stays in contention by scoring a 10-round decision victory over France's Robert Villemain in San Francisco.

AUGUST

New York City's Floyd Patterson wins the middleweight gold medal at the Olympic Games in Helsinki, Finland.

OCTOBER

Welterweight champion Kid Gavilan retains the crown for the second time against Billy Graham, scoring a unanimous 15-round decision.

DECEMBER

Reigning middleweight champion Sugar Ray Robinson, 31, announces his retirement from the ring. He plans to begin a career as a dancer.

Gil Turner (right) was given an excellent chance to dethrone welterweight king Kid Gavilan. But he faded in the late rounds and was stopped with 13 seconds of round 11 to go.

FIGHTING TALK

I made up in 15 rounds what I had missed in 16 years

ARCHIE MOORE
after winning the light heavyweight title from Joey Maxim

SETTING THE WRONG RECORDS

Jimmy Carter wasn't the best fighter in the world. But he wasn't the dullest, either.

In May 1951, Carter won the lightweight title by knocking out Ike Williams, and set a record low attendance for a Madison Square Garden title fight (3,594).

On October 15, Carter regained the crown by winning his rubber match against Los Angeles-based Mexican Lauro Salas. He also helped set another dubious record; Carter-Salas drew a crowd of 5,283, a record low attendance for a Chicago Stadium title fight. At least Carter entertained the fans who did show up.

Five months before, Salas had captured the title by cleverly flurrying over the last 30 seconds of each round. He tried a similar strategy as champion, but this time, Carter flurried with him. Salas suffered a cut over one eye in round seven, and while he matched Carter at close range, the challenger proved a superior boxer.

After 15 rounds, the decision was unanimous, with scores of 84-66, 82-68, and 81-69. Carter was a champion again, even if no one seemed to care.

TEN YEARS FOR ARCHIE TO BE KING

It wasn't as if Archie Moore had been denied a try at the light heavyweight title for any significant length of time. After all, he had been the top-rated contender for only 10 years. Shortly after New York State boxing commissioner Bob Christenberry proclaimed, "We are tired of seeing champions make a mockery of their titles by defending against inferior competition," 175-pound champion Joey Maxim signed to defend against the 36-year-old Moore. (It was his third defense in three years.)

The bout took place on December 17 at the St. Louis Arena. The champion was guaranteed $100,000, and Moore 10 percent of the take after Maxim received his share. That would amount to a whopping $800.

From the opening bell, Moore showed why he had been avoided for so long. Moving inside whenever he pleased, he rocked the champion in the first round, and proceeded to cut him over both eyes and the left cheekbone. To his credit, Maxim gutted it out for 15 painful rounds, with Moore taking a unanimous decision by scores of 82-68, 87-63, and 76-74.

In his 108th pro bout, Moore was finally king. Now the world knew what the "Ol' Mongoose" had been sure of all along.

After 18 years of fighting, 39-year-old Archie Moore (right) finally took the world title.

WORLD TITLE FIGHTS

HEAVYWEIGHTS

Sept 23 **Rocky Marciano** (USA) *KO* 13 Jersey Joe Walcott, Philadelphia

LIGHT HEAVYWEIGHTS

Dec 17 **Archie Moore** (USA) *W* 15 Joey Maxim, St. Louis

WELTERWEIGHTS

July 7 **Kid Gavilan** *KO* 11 Gil Turner, Philadelphia

Oct 5 **Kid Gavilan** *W* 15 Billy Graham, Havana

LIGHTWEIGHTS

Oct 15 **Jimmy Carter** *W* 15 Lauro Salas, Chicago

BANTAMWEIGHTS

Nov 15 **Jimmy Carruthers** (AUT) *KO* 1 Vic Toweel, Johannesburg

FLYWEIGHTS

Nov 15 **Yoshio Shirai** *W* 15 Dado Marino, Tokyo

A SWIFT AND THOROUGH BEATING

"Who was that guy?" Defending bantamweight champion Vic Toweel would have been excused had he not remembered Jimmy Carruthers; the fighters had briefly crossed paths at the 1948 Olympic Games in London. (Neither made much of an impression, with Toweel losing in the first round, and Carruthers in the second.) But after defending against Carruthers on November 15 at Johannesburg's Rand Stadium, Toweel would remember the Australian for the rest of his life.

The South African champion presumably set an all-time record by failing to land a single punch. Toweel was a notoriously slow starter, and after Carruthers learned that his foe had struggled to make weight, he shrewdly opted for a sudden strike. Carruthers sped out of his corner and raked Toweel with jabs and hooks. Before he realized that his title was in jeopardy, the local favorite was cut on the bridge of the nose and over his lip. Then Carruthers blasted him out of the ring with a booming right. Toweel attempted to beat the count of referee Willie Smith, but failed.

After 139 of the most brutal seconds in ring history, Carruthers had become the first universally recognized champion in Australian boxing history.

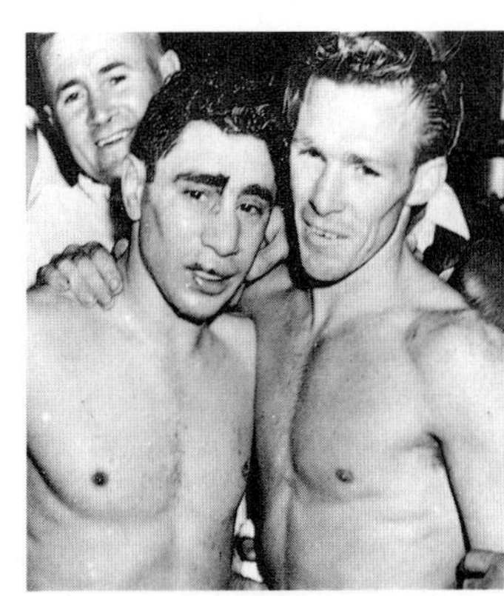

Jimmy Carruthers (right) and Vic Toweel.

JANUARY

1953

JUNE

THE FIGHTER WITH NO FORM

It was impossible to figure lightweight champion Jimmy Carter. When he was good, as in wins over Art Aragon and Lauro Salas, he seemed a solid, well-rounded performer. But when he was bad, as in losses to the same pair of fighters, he seemed both uninterested and outclassed.

On February 16 at the Montreal Forum, Carter met Canadian 135-pound champion Armond Savoie in a non-title bout. It was a close fight throughout, but Savoie's bobbing, weaving style, and roundhouse rights troubled the champion. Carter bled from a cut over his right eye in the fifth, and in the seventh, his left eyebrow was torn. In the 10th and final round, the lightweights went toe to toe, with Carter barely surviving until the bell. Savoie received the split and decision by scores of 5-4-1 (twice) and 4-5-1.

"Savoie will never get a shot at the title as long as we hold it," said Carter's manager. As it would turn out, however, Savoie got revenge over Carter in November.

LOSING BY KAYO BUT IMPROVING

South Africa's boxing fans were certain that Jimmy Carruthers' 139-second demolition of their Vic Toweel had been nothing more than a nightmare. Before believing that Toweel was no longer the best bantamweight in boxing, they would have to see Carruthers repeat his victory.

Carruthers-Toweel II was held at Johannesburg's Rand Stadium on March 21 – four months after the original. The 36,000 fans in attendance thought they were watching an instant replay when the Australian champion exploded in round one and battered Toweel across the ring. This time, however, the South African endured. But that was his only accomplishment.

After a brief mid-rounds rally, Toweel slowed. Carruthers began his big finish in the ninth, with a hook. In the 10th, he followed up with another. Toweel dropped to both knees before rolling over. Referee Willie Smith signalled the end without a count.

Toweel was only 25, but in two bouts Carruthers had ruined him.

THE KID VERSUS KID TELEVISION

The relatively new medium of television couldn't help but embrace welterweight Chuck Davey.

He was an aggressive southpaw, a college graduate, and an unbeaten (37-0-2) performer whose action-packed bouts drew high ratings. They called him "Kid Television." But it was another Kid who proved to be the best 147-pounder in the game.

At Chicago Stadium on February 11, 3-1 favorite Kid Gavilan retained the world title, chopping up Davey, and then stopping him in the 10th round.

"I lick all welterweights," Gavilan said afterward. "I mush 'em like spaghetti mush."

By the finish, Davey's face looked like spaghetti sauce. He was floored by a Gavilan right in round three, cut deeply over one eye, and dropped three more times in round nine. The challenger remained on his stool at the bell for the 10th, claiming he couldn't continue after having caught a punch in the throat. (After nine rounds, Gavilan led by scores of 49-41, 52-38, and 51-39.)

Kid Television had grown up the hard way. And all of America had watched him do it.

Chuck Davey is knocked through ropes by Kid Gavilan in gallant bid to lift world crown.

Vic Toweel (right) failed to prove his knockout loss to Jimmy Carruthers was a fluke.

RINGSIDE VIEW

JANUARY

In a non-title bout, lightweight champion Jimmy Carter is outpointed over 10 rounds by Eddie Chavez.

JANUARY

Former lightweight champion Ike Williams continues his slide, suffering a 10-round points loss to welterweight contender Carmen Basilio in Syracuse, New York.

MAY

Flyweight champion Yoshio Shirai retains the crown for the second time, unanimously outpointing Tanny Campo over 15 rounds.

JUNE

Archie Moore successfully defends the light heavyweight title, scoring a unanimous 15-round decision over former champion Joey Maxim.

ROCKY RUBS OUT ALL DOUBT

Had Rocky Marciano won the heavyweight title by landing a lucky punch? Eight months after rallying to kayo Jersey Joe Walcott, The Rock answered that question in most convincing fashion.

On May 15 at Chicago Stadium, Marciano, 43-0, defended for the first time. Walcott was 39, and before one round elapsed, he had aged another 10 years.

About two minutes into the fight, the champion released a long hook and followed with a right uppercut. Walcott crashed and chose to take referee Frank Sikora's count from a sitting position. He regained his feet a split second after the third man had reached 10, but the bout had been waved over.

Walcott called the kayo "the rottenest deal of my life." He and manager Felix Bocchicchio formally protested, claiming Sikora had issued a fast count, and adding that Marciano hadn't proceeded to a neutral corner. They even tossed in a complaint that the ring had been overpadded.

All their noise, however, couldn't shift the focus from a simple fact: Rocky was for real.

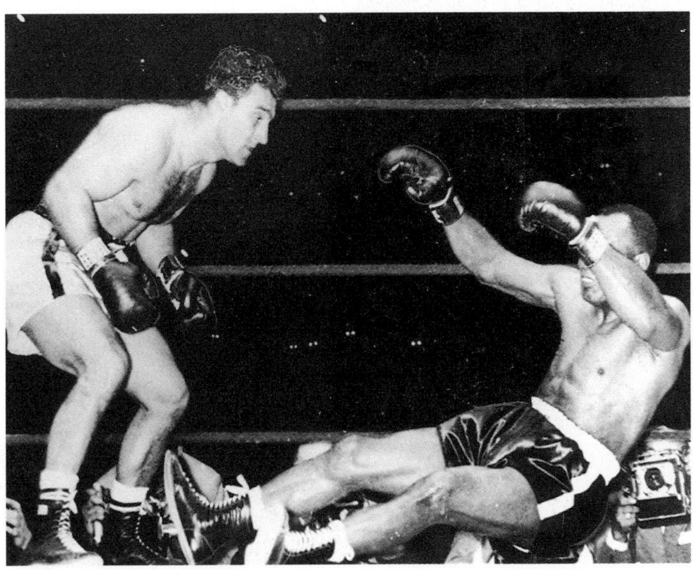

In his first defense of the heavyweight title he won from Jersey Joe Walcott, Rocky Marciano again kayoed Jersey Joe, this time in the first round.

WORLD TITLE FIGHTS

HEAVYWEIGHTS		WELTERWEIGHTS		BANTAMWEIGHTS	
May 15	**Rocky Marciano** *KO* 1 Jersey Joe Walcott, Chicago	Feb 11	**Kid Gavilan** *KO* 10 Chuck Davey, Chicago	March 21	**Jimmy Carruthers** *KO* 10 Vic Toweel, Johannesburg
LIGHT HEAVYWEIGHTS		**LIGHTWEIGHTS**		**FLYWEIGHTS**	
June 24	**Archie Moore** *W* 15 Joey Maxim, Ogden, UT	April 24	**Jimmy Carter** *KO* 4 Tommy Collins, Boston	May 18	**Yoshio Shirai** *W* 15 Tanny Campo, Tokyo
		June 11	**Jimmy Carter** *KO* 13 George Araujo, New York City		

WHEN THE BEST WAS AT HIS BEST

Which Jimmy Carter would appear in the ring for his June 12 lightweight title defense against rising contender George Araujo?

The oddsmakers called the bout pick-'em, which said as much about the champion's inconsistency as the challenger's ability.

The 22-year-old Araujo was 49-2-1 and a legitimate threat. Over the first six rounds, he proved there were no quicker lightweights: cutting Carter over the right eye and jumping to a sizeable lead. But Carter applied steady pressure against his backtracking foe, and by the middle rounds, he began to reach the challenger's body. The turning point came when Carter scored two knockdowns in round nine. Araujo's movement had all but ceased, and the champion captured his prey in the 13th, felling Araujo with a right to the body. Referee Al Berle issued no count.

Only 7,123 fans had come to Madison Square Garden for the fight. Carter was proving to be consistent in only one way: he remained box office poison.

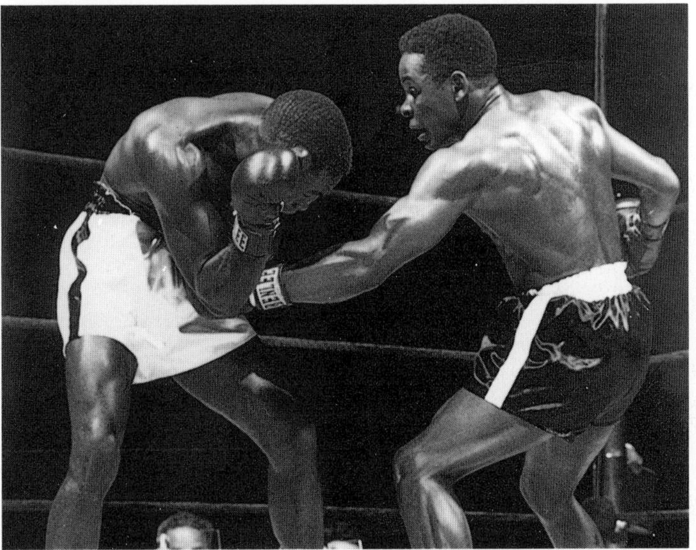

Brilliant challenger George Araujo (right) failed to dethrone veteran Jimmy Carter.

THE FIGHT THEY WOULDN'T STOP

A total of 10 knockdowns over the course of two rounds? Who was the referee, the Marquis de Sade?

Tommy Collins was a good puncher, but not a full-fledged lightweight, a fact that became painfully evident during his April 24 challenge of world champion Jimmy Carter at Boston Garden.

Carter, an 11-5 favorite, shook Collins every time he hit him. The damage was minimal over the first two rounds, but in the third, the bout lost any semblance of competitiveness when Collins was dropped seven times. Round four saw knockdowns eight, nine, and 10, but referee Tommy Rawson gave no sign that he would step in.

The bout was stopped only after the challenger's handlers rushed into the ring to rescue their dizzy fighter. During the fourth round, Collins' yo-yo act enraged Maurice Tobin, who had served as Secretary of Labor under President Harry Truman. Tobin rushed the ring and screamed at Rawson, "Do you want murder?"

Meeting the press after the bout, Rawson was asked why he hadn't called a halt. "Carter never hit him flush," he said. Ouch!

JULY

1953

DECEMBER

HOMETOWN DISADVANTAGE FOR REF

As referee George Walsh made his way from the ring to the dressing rooms at Syracuse's new and sparkling War Memorial Stadium, a dozen policemen accompanied him. Fans shouted insults and tossed programs, and on more than one occasion seemed about to rush at Walsh and his escort. All because the third man had the temerity to score against local favorite Carmen Basilio.

Welterweight champion Kid Gavilan (left) was awarded a highly controversial, title-saving decision over aggressive Carmen Basilio at Syracuse, New York.

On September 18, Basilio, the son of a Canastota, New York, onion farmer, challenged welterweight champion Kid Gavilan.

Making his sixth defense, Gavilan was a 4-1 favorite; most insiders dismissed the challenger as a gutty clubfighter. But Basilio would prove to be much, much more.

From the start, the busy Basilio worked his left hand overtime, and in round two, he found Gavilan's jaw. Boom! Floored for only the second time in his career, the champion took an eight-count. Basilio continued to rally over the next four rounds, landing his hook at will. It looked like a major upset was in the making.

Gavilan, however, was as tough and resilient as any champion of his era. He started to punch in the seventh, scoring with jabs and combinations from the outside, and holding whenever Basilio maneuvered inside. Gavilan had made weight by losing eight pounds in 15 days, but he was the fresher fighter down the stretch. Boxing with a badly swollen left eye, Basilio regained the initiative only in round 15. The ringside press thought the decision to be close, but the partisan fans were sure Basilio had won.

When the split decision was awarded to Gavilan (scores of 8-6-1, 7-6-2, and 5-7-3), their emotion quickly turned from disappointment to anger. That's when George Walsh knew he needed the police.

WORLD TITLE FIGHTS

HEAVYWEIGHTS	Sept 24	**Rocky Marciano** *KO* 11 Roland LaStarza, New York City
MIDDLEWEIGHTS	Oct 21	**Bobo Olson** (USA) *W* 15 Randy Turpin, New York City
WELTERWEIGHTS	Sept 18	**Kid Gavilan** *W* 15 Carmen Basilio, Syracuse
	Nov 13	**Kid Gavilan** *W* 15 Johnny Bratton, Chicago
LIGHTWEIGHTS	Nov 11	**Jimmy Carter** *KO* 5 Armando Savoie, Montreal
BANTAMWEIGHTS	Nov 13	**Jimmy Carruthers** *W* 15 Pappy Gault, Sydney
FLYWEIGHTS	Oct 27	**Yoshio Shirai** *W* 15 Terry Allen, Tokyo

Marciano (left) overpowered LaStarza.

SETTLING AN OLD SCORE

After heavyweight champion Rocky Marciano defended the title for the first time by knocking out Jersey Joe Walcott, there were few doubters remaining.

Those who still questioned The Rock's class pointed to his disputed March 1950 decision over Roland LaStarza as evidence that the undefeated Marciano was vulnerable to a certain style, if not a certain fighter. For that reason, the Marciano-LaStarza II fight was arranged.

It happened on September 24 before a swelling crowd of 44,562 at New York City's Polo Grounds. The fight contributed to the Marciano legend as much as any other.

For the first six rounds, LaStarza boxed strongly, scoring with his jab and making Marciano miss. The champion seemed particularly chippy, and referee Ruby Goldstein repeatedly warned him for hitting low, butting, and punching on the break. Marciano was penalized only once, when Goldstein gave the sixth round to the challenger.

In round seven, Marciano drew close, and LaStarza absorbed a round-long beating. Rocky hit him anywhere and everywhere; LaStarza blocked some of the blows, and was later diagnosed to have suffered broken blood vessels in his left arm. Having established control, Marciano proceeded to bloody LaStarza's nose and cut him under the right eye.

In the 11th, he punished his rival with a right to the jaw and a sweeping hook. Then he followed with a right and a hook, and LaStarza fell, bouncing off the ropes and onto the ring apron. He beat the count, but Marciano was a masterful finisher, and seconds later, Goldstein elected to intervene. After the 10th, Marciano led by scores of 7-3, 6-4, and 5-5.

"He's a 5,000 percent better fighter now," LaStarza said. "The way he counters, the way he makes you miss, he didn't do that before."

Marciano was 45-0. Even the doubters were finding it increasingly difficult argue with such a perfect score.

RINGSIDE VIEW

JULY

Top-rated welterweights Carmen Basilio and Billy Graham struggle to a 12-round draw in Syracuse.

SEPTEMBER

Rising light heavyweight Harold Johnson all but guarantees himself a try at the title by outpointing former heavyweight champion Ezzard Charles over 10 rounds in Philadelphia.

OCTOBER

Flyweight champion Yoshio Shirai retains the crown for the third time, scoring a unanimous 15-round decision over former titlist Terry Allen.

NOVEMBER

Australia's Jimmy Carruthers returns home and keeps the bantamweight title by unanimously outpointing Pappy Gault over 15 rounds.

THE SUGAR RAY ROBINSON WANNABES

Sugar Ray Robinson had knocked out both Bobo Olson and Randy Turpin. After Robinson's retirement, then, his victims were equally qualified to fight for the vacant middleweight title.

On October 21, 10 months after Robinson's exit, Hawaii's Olson and England's Turpin met before 18,869 fans at Madison Square Garden.

In the days preceding the fight, rumors spread that a pending divorce and poor training habits had left former champion Turpin ill-prepared. As a result, Olson climbed through the ropes an 11-5 favorite.

In the first round, an upset seemed imminent when Turpin staggered Olson with a hard hook. The awkward British brawler kept his momentum through round five, but then began to fade. Olson, hardly a potent puncher, scored knockdowns in rounds nine and 10 and forced a furious pace until the final bell.

Ultimately, his superior conditioning made the difference. The Hawaiian was awarded the title by scores of 8-7, 9-4-1, and 11-4.

Olson was the new number one. By default, perhaps, but number one just the same.

Bobo Olson (right) outpointed ex-champion Randy Turpin for world middleweight championship.

PUTTING OUT THE FIRE(FIGHTER)

Armand Savoie was an amateur firefighter who had received citations for a pair of daring rescues.

On November 11 at the Montreal Forum, his fans were certain that he would be cited as the best lightweight in boxing.

In February, Savoie had outpointed world champion Jimmy Carter in a non-title fight. But as often proved, Carter was a different fighter when risking the title.

In the first three rounds, Savoie boxed while backpedaling. Carter was hit by hooks and jabs, and the crowd of 9,136 began to energize. But the champion accelerated in the fourth and then struck suddenly in the fifth. A long, straight right sent Savoie south, and he was counted out by referee Tom Sullivan at the 59-second mark.

Said Carter: "I was just waiting for an opening, waiting to catch him with his hands down." So he could put out the fire.

THE TALE OF THE BRAT, THE KID, AND THE JAW

On November 13 at Chicago Stadium, hometown favorite and former NBA welterweight champion Johnny Bratton challenged world titlist Kid Gavilan.

Bratton's jaw had been broken in three of his previous bouts, including a May 1951 loss to The Kid. Would he hold up through 15 rounds? The skeptics predicted Bratton's doom by pointing to the calendar: it was Friday the 13th.

Bratton lasted from opening to closing bell; no fracture, no knockdowns. But he paid a fearsome price. Gavilan scored at will, and by the seventh round, many of the 19,260 crowd were imploring the referee to stop the slaughter.

Bratton's heart, however, carried him the distance. Throughout the second half of the bout, he was repeatedly cornered, and only Gavilan's lack of power prevented the champion from finishing the job. By the end, Bratton's right eye was closed, and his left eye was badly swollen.

The announcement of the unanimous decision (scores of 85-65, 83-67, and 82-68 for Gavilan) was a mere formality.

"Anyone who says (Gavilan) has slowed down is nuts," said Al Weill, the manager of Rocky Marciano. He might've added the same for anyone who said Bratton had been soft.

If anyone could dethrone Kid Gavilan, it was the brillant Johnny Bratton (left). But Gavilan won.

JANUARY

1954

JUNE

Ringside View

JANUARY

Light heavyweight champion Archie Moore retains the title by outpointing Joey Maxim over 15 rounds. It is Moore's third consecutive title fight victory over the former champion.

MARCH

Archie Moore, the reigning 175-pound champion, rises in weight and kayos highly rated heavyweight Bob Baker in nine rounds.

MAY

Flyweight champion Yoshio Shirai retains the title by split 15-round decision over Leo Espinosa.

JUNE

In a surprise, 1952 Olympic champion Floyd Patterson loses for the first time in 14 pro bouts, dropping an eight-round decision to former light heavyweight champion Joey Maxim.

WAS WILLIE'S LACK OF PEP A FIX?

In the language of gamblers, "late money" is often thought to be "smart money." In other words, bets placed just before the start of a race, game, or fight are presumed to be made by those with inside, or at least up-to-date, information.

After 20-year-old Lulu Perez kayoed former featherweight champion Willie Pep at Madison Square Garden on February 26, boxing's bookmakers had reason to wonder whether the late money had been a bit too smart.

Perez opened as a 6-5 favorite, but between a routine morning weigh-in and the start of the fight, a flood of Perez money was wagered. By the opening bell, the odds had moved to 4-1 for Perez.

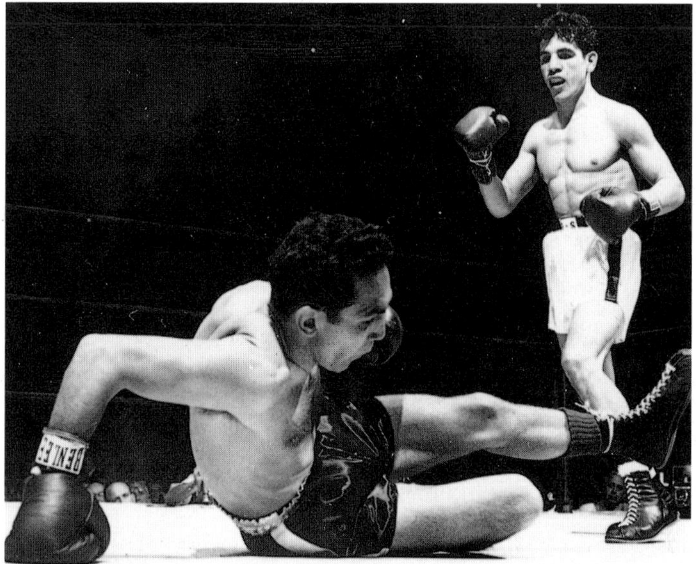

In a fight tainted by controversy, 31-year-old ex-featherweight champion Willie Pep (down) was stopped in the second round by 20-year-old Lulu Perez. It was Pep's 190th pro fight.

Did the bettors know something? After all, Pep was hardly washed up; he was the number-one contender, and 23-1 since losing to world champion Sandy Saddler in September 1951.

The fight supported the late shift in odds. Perez wobbled the 31-year-old Pep with a first-round hook, and then, in the second, scored three knockdowns, which, under New York State rules, brought an automatic stoppage. Postscript: In the July 1981 issue of *Inside Sports*, Paul Good wrote a piece about a fixed bout involving a fighter named "The Champ." All of the details and circumstances were identical to those of the Perez-Pep fight. In the story, "The Champ" took a dive for $16,000. Three years after the article's publication, Pep filed a $75-million libel suit, claiming he loved boxing too much "to do such a thing" as throw a fight. Deliberating for only 15 minutes, a six-person jury voted against him.

NO IFS, ANDS, OR BUTTS

Despite Jimmy Carter's inconsistent form, it was difficult to envision the lightweight champion losing his crown to 10-year-veteran Paddy DeMarco.

"The Brooklyn Billygoat" was a wild swinger who was considered more dangerous with his head than his fists. (In 80 career bouts, the challenger had registered only seven kayos.) Moreover, he had lost six of his previous 11 efforts.

On March 5 at Madison Square Garden, however, DeMarco, a 4-1 underdog, gave the finest performance of his career. He stayed away from Carter's dangerous right hand, jabbed and hooked from a distance, and outscored the champion in most of the desperate flurries.

Carter rallied over the last four rounds, but couldn't salvage the decision, which was unanimous for DeMarco. (Scores of 7-5-3, 9-5-1, and 9-6.) Most incredible of all, referee Ruby Goldstein found it necessary to warn The Billygoat only once for butting!

"I was so sure (of victory) that I made my wife, Betty, come to the fight," said DeMarco. "And this is the first time she's seen me fight since the old four-round days."

Where Carter had been a colorless, albeit competent, champion, DeMarco was a sports-writer's dream. Asked why he had become a fighter, he told the story of a childhood accident in which his nose had been permanently misshaped by a baseball. Another story told of the newly crowned champion's human side. In November 1953, Jimmy Dixon, DeMarco's manager, passed away. Though the fighter had no contractual obligation to do so, he reserved one-third of his title fight purse for Dixon's widow.

New champion Paddy DeMarco.

Beaten champion Jimmy Carter.

World Title Fights

HEAVYWEIGHTS		LIGHTWEIGHTS	
June 17	**Rocky Marciano** *W* 15 Ezzard Charles, Bronx, NY	March 5	**Paddy DeMarco** (USA) *W* 15 Jimmy Carter, New York City
LIGHT HEAVYWEIGHTS		**BANTAMWEIGHTS**	
Jan 27	**Archie Moore** *W* 15 Joey Maxim, Miami	May 2	**Jimmy Carruthers** *ref* 12 Chamrern Songkitrat, Bangkok
MIDDLEWEIGHTS		**FLYWEIGHTS**	
April 1	**Bobo Olson** *W* 15 Kid Gavilan, Chicago	May 24	**Yoshio Shirai** *W* 15 Leo Espinosa, Tokyo

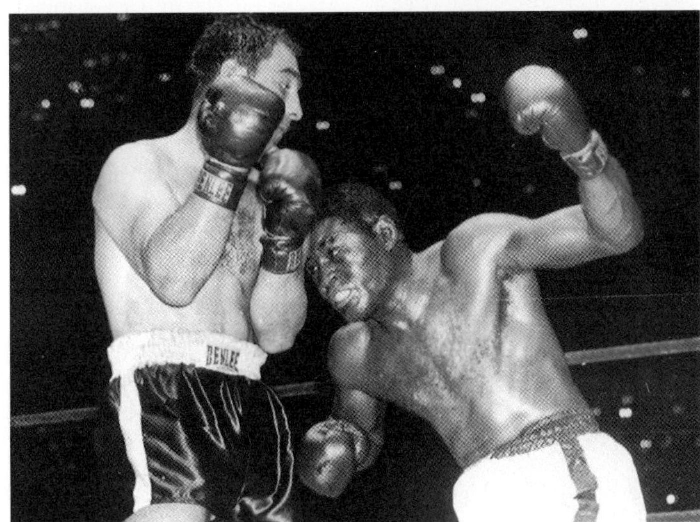

The enormous courage of former champion Ezzard Charles (right) so inspired the huge crowd that they booed the decision in favor of defending heavyweight champion Rocky Marciano.

"IT WAS MY TOUGHEST FIGHT" SAYS MARCIANO

Since losing the heavyweight title to Jersey Joe Walcott, Ezzard Charles had proved to be a hot-and-cold performer. He had beaten Rex Layne, Jimmy Bivins, and Bob Satterfield, among others, but had lost to Walcott, Nino Valdes, and Harold Johnson.

As a result, on June 17, when the former champion climbed through the ropes at Yankee Stadium to challenge reigning king Rocky Marciano, he was a 7-2 underdog. What surprised the 47,585 in attendance was not Charles' effectiveness, but his strategy.

For the first four rounds he boxed as advertised, forcing Marciano to lunge. The Rock fell behind on points, and in doing so, sustained a deep cut at the corner of his left eyebrow. Over the second half of the bout, however, the challenger punched freely with the champion. It became a test of Charles' hook vs. Marciano's right. Charles banged away until weary. Then Marciano took his turn. Marciano called the brutal fight "the toughest of my career."

Ultimately, his strength was the deciding factor. The Rock closed with a rush to take a unanimous decision by scores of 8-5-2, 8-6-1, and 9-5-1. On this night, Charles had been hot, but not quite hot enough.

AN EXTRAORDINARY FAREWELL

On May 2 at Bangkok's National Stadium, bantamweight champion Jimmy Carruthers defended against local slugger Chamrern Songkitrat in the first world title fight ever held in Thailand.

An hour before the bout, the skies opened, and more than one inch of rain fell onto the unprotected canvas. With 50,000 fans already in the stands, the promoters never even considered a postponement. So Carruthers and Songkitrat did what they had to do: both took off their boxing boots and fought barefooted in the torrential downpour.

There were further complications in the third and ninth rounds, when electric ring lights exploded, shattering glass across the ring. At one point, Carruthers hopped on one foot while removing glass from his heel.

A far superior boxer, Carruthers received referee Bill Henneberry's 12-round decision by a score of 32½-27½.

Two weeks later, he shocked the boxing world by announcing his retirement. The Australian southpaw was 19-0 and only 24 years old. As it would turn out, Carruthers, who left the ring for the hotel business, would return six years later. An ill-fated comeback ended after he won only two of six bouts.

MOVING UP IS TOUGH STUFF

After making seven successful defenses, welterweight champion Kid Gavilan had cleaned out his division. Seeking a new challenge, he squared off against middleweight champion Bobo Olson on April 2 at Chicago Stadium.

Before the bout, the Hawaiian-born Olson wrapped a lei around Gavilan's neck. Then he tried to break it. Performing according to form, the fighters set a furious pace. Gavilan was the busier of the two, but jumping a division had failed to transform him into a puncher.

Slower but stronger, Olson applied steady pressure throughout, and banged both the body and head whenever Gavilan allowed him to get inside. Neither fighter came close to scoring a knockdown, but in round 10, they engaged in a minute-long toe-to-toe exchange that *The New York Times*' Joseph C. Nichols described as "one of the most furious and grueling in ring history."

After 15 rounds, Olson was announced the winner by scores of 147-141, 147-139, and 144-144. Both fighters were still champions. All that had been proven was something insiders had known all along: in boxing, bigger is usually better.

Welterweight champion Kid Gavilan (left) failed to strip Bobo Olson of his middleweight crown.

JULY

1954

DECEMBER

ARCHIE'S OVERDUE GARDEN DEBUT

Madison Square Garden's boxing fans may not have been familiar with Archie Moore, but Moore was familiar with Harold Johnson.

On August 11, the 40-year-old Moore fought for the first time at the Garden, defending the light heavyweight title against Philadelphia's Johnson, whom he had beaten in three of four prior meetings. Moore was a 2-1 favorite.

Invariably, fighters who clash in a series of bouts get to know each other all too well. Johnson knew Moore would bob and weave, so he jabbed. Moore knew Johnson would try and keep the fight at a distance, so he worked inside and banged the body.

The 8,327 in attendance were treated to a minimal amount of action. After 13 rounds, Johnson led by scores of 6-5-2, 8-5, and 6-6. In the 14th, however, "The Ol' Mongoose" struck without warning. An overhand right and a followup barrage felled the challenger, and after Johnson rose at referee Ruby Goldstein's count of five, Moore swarmed. Goldstein intervened at the 56-second mark.

Moore had finally played New York, a town that knows a winner when it sees one.

The extraordinary skills of Archie Moore (right) fascinated Madison Square Garden.

HE FOUGHT THE LAW – AND WON

When he wasn't knocking out bantamweights, Thailand's Chamrern Songkitrat worked as a police officer.

On September 19 at Bangkok's Rajadamnern Stadium, he gave an arresting performace against France's Robert Cohen, but lost by split 15-round decision. In the eyes of the 60,000 partisan fans in attendance, including the king and queen of Thailand, the outcome was criminal.

Fighting for the world title that had been vacated by Jimmy Carruthers, Songkitrat and Cohen tested wills and skills. The visitor won the early rounds, breaking Songkitrat's nose in the process. But the Thai rallied, staggering Cohen with two body shots in the seventh, and cutting him above the right eye.

The championship rounds were close, with Cohen's superior class providing the slightest of edges. Cohen was awarded the title by scores of 73½-70½, 73½-72½ , and 71½-72, making Songkitrat 0-for-2 in title tries.

The day job was looking better all the time.

ROCKY MARCIANO THE WINNER – BY A NOSE

For a fighter to remain unbeaten throughout his career, he must not only know how to win, but when to win, too.

On September 17 at Yankee Stadium, heavyweight champion Rocky Marciano defended for the second time against former titlist Ezzard Charles. It brought his most urgent moment as champion.

Having learned from the first fight, Marciano started quickly, knocking Charles down in round two. The Rock maintained control until the end of the sixth, when the tip of his nose was badly split. (Marciano claimed that Charles had done the damage with his elbow; most ringsiders thought it had been two hooks.)

In round seven, Charles added a cut on the champion's left brow. Blood was pouring from both wounds, and Marciano sensed that referee Al Berl might stop the bout. So Marciano did what had to be done. In round eight, he connected with a long right, and Charles dropped. Later in the round, a hook-cross combination again felled the challenger, who pulled himself up a split second after Berl had tolled 10.

Marciano was declared the winner by kayo at the 2:36 mark. His next date would be with a plastic surgeon.

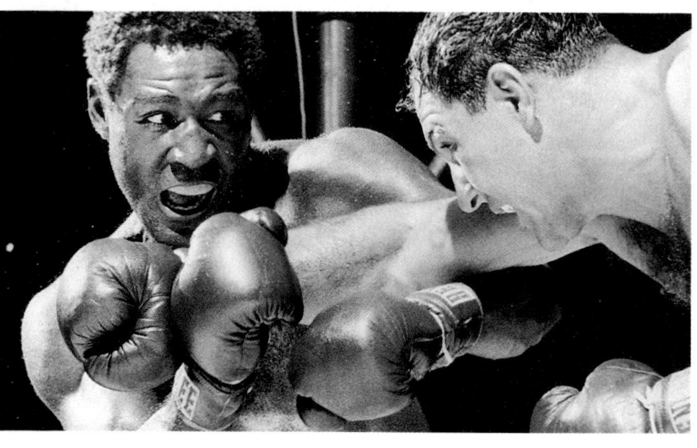

Defending champion Marciano (right) bulls into ex-champion Charles in fifth round.

RINGSIDE VIEW

AUGUST

Middleweight champion Bobo Olson retained the title for the second time, scoring a unanimous 15-round decision over Rocky Castellani.

AUGUST

Mexican favorite Raul (Raton) Macias wins the North American bantamweight title in his 11th fight, decisioning Nate Brooks over 12 rounds in Mexico City.

OCTOBER

Having been inactive since June 1952, former welterweight and middleweight champion Sugar Ray Robinson announced his return to the ring.

DECEMBER

Bobo Olson retains the middleweight title with an 11th-round stoppage of Pierre Langlois.

BAD FIGHT, DECISION

On October 20 at Philadelphia's Convention Hall, Kid Gavilan's welterweight title reign came to a most ugly end.

Only six weeks after a bout with the mumps, the 28-year-old champion defended against New York City's Johnny Saxton. At first glance, neither fighter would benefit from a hometown edge. But Blinky Palermo, Saxton's manager, was from Philadelphia, and prefight whispers suggested that Gavilan would need a kayo.

The bout was dreadful, with Saxton refusing to lead, and Gavilan waiting to counter. The welters grabbed and held more than they boxed and punched.

After 15 tedious rounds, Saxton was declared the new champion by unanimous decision (scores of 9-6, 7-6-2, and 8-6-1). Most of the ringside press disagreed; when polled, 20 of 22 reporters thought Gavilan deserved the verdict.

Pennsylvania Boxing Commission Chairman Frank Wiener couldn't hide his disgust. "I congratulate you," he told Saxton, "on your luck. Take (the title) anywhere you want. If Gavilan made any kind of fight, you wouldn't have won. You disappointed me, and he was worse."

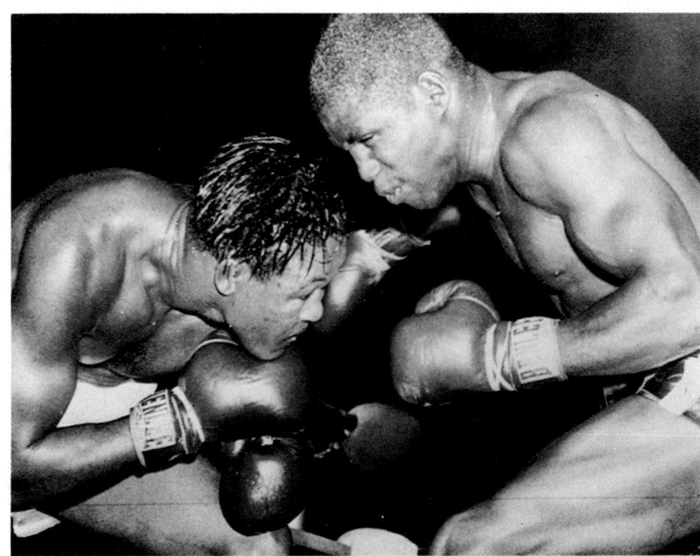

Johnny Saxton (right) ended Kid Gavilan's five-year reign as welterweight champion.

World Title Fights

HEAVYWEIGHTS

Sept 17	**Rocky Marciano** *KO* 8 Ezzard Charles, Bronx, NY

LIGHT HEAVYWEIGHTS

Aug 11	**Archie Moore** *KO* 14 Harold Johnson, New York City

MIDDLEWEIGHTS

Aug 20	**Bobo Olson** *W* 15 Rocky Castellani, San Francisco
Dec 15	**Bobo Olson** *KO* 11 Pierre Langlois, San Francisco

WELTERWEIGHTS

Oct 20	**Johnny Saxton** (USA) *W* 15 Kid Gavilan, Philadelphia

LIGHTWEIGHTS

Nov 17	**Jimmy Carter** *KO* 15 Paddy DeMarco, San Francisco

BANTAMWEIGHTS

Sept 19	**Robert Cohen** (ALG) *W* 15 Chamrern Songkitrat, Bangkok (Wins Vacant World Title)

FLYWEIGHTS

Nov 26	**Pascual Perez** (ARG) *W* 15 Yoshio Shirai, Tokyo

PEREZ PROVES A BULL OF A FLY

On November 26 at Tokyo's Korakuen Stadium, boxing's smallest fighter produced one of the biggest upsets of the year.

Defending 112-pound champion Yoshio Shirai held five-inch height and reach advantages over Argentina's tiny Pascual Perez. He was also far more experienced, with 56 pro bouts to Perez' 23. But the challenger had credentials of his own; he was an Olympic gold medal winner, and in July, he had held Shirai to a 10-round draw in a non-title bout.

Finding the 55-degree temperature a bit uncomfortable, Perez started slowly. But the 4-1 underdog kept pressing, and upon landing, he possessed the power to turn the fight. A 12th-round left uppercut felled Shirai, and Perez' followup attack lasted until the final bell. Perez emerged victorious by scores of 146-139, 143-139, and 146-134.

Japan's first world champion had been dethroned by Argentina's first world champion. Boxing's globe was getting bigger.

CARTER THREE TIMES A CHAMPION

Mother Nature did her best to extend the reign of lightweight champion Paddy DeMarco. Having signed to defend against former champion Jimmy Carter, DeMarco fell out with a virus. Shortly after the fight was rescheduled, DeMarco asked out with inflammation of the elbow. But his (bad) luck ran out, and the bout finally came off November 17 at San Francisco's Cow Palace.

Eight months before, DeMarco had dethroned Carter with a cautious fight plan. This time, he chugged forward in clubfighter fashion, and Carter capitalized.

The first half of the bout was close, but Carter scored a knockdown in round nine, and dominated until the finish. DeMarco fell for a second time at the end of the 14th, and early in the last round, referee Ray Flores determined that the champion was defenseless. At the time of the stoppage, Carter led comfortably on all three cards. Carter had won the 135-pound crown for a record third time.

Apparently, Mother Nature played no favorites.

Jimmy Carter knocked out Tony DeMarco in the 15th round in San Francisco to regain the lightweight title he had lost to Tony earlier in the year.

JANUARY

1955

JUNE

SANDY'S ROUGH AND TOUGH RETURN

Boxing fans didn't know what to make of Sandy Saddler. The featherweight champion had thrice beaten the legendary Willie Pep, but his tactics were more Gorgeous George than Marquis of Queensberry.

On February 25 at Madison Square Garden, Saddler made his first defense in almost 3½ years, or since his fourth bout vs. Pep. (In the interim, he had lost three consecutive bouts to world-rated lightweights, and spent almost two full years in the Army.)

The challenger, Teddy "Red Top" Davis, had earned his title shot by defeating top-rated Percy Bassett. But the 31-year-old Davis held a dubious distinction: with 47 losses in 108 career bouts, he was the losingest fighter to ever try for a world championship.

After scaling a painfully light 124½, the 5'8½" Saddler explained, "The secret is in my legs."

Saddler (right) decisioned "Red Top" Davis.

Seemingly frail, if not sickly, the champion proved to be strong and fit. Davis remained competitive until spraining his right hand in the middle of the fight. Then Saddler assumed command, winning the remainder of the rounds. The decision was unanimous (scores of 11-3-1, 12-3, and 9-3).

"With a good right hand," lamented Davis, "I could have chased him out of the ring."

There were no knockdowns, with the only highlights – or lowlights – being Saddler's various wrestling maneuvers. The crowd of 5,272 booed as the champion held and hit, shoved, heeled, and butted. Saddler was among boxing's most dominant titleholders, but his image was beyond repair.

WORLD TITLE FIGHTS

HEAVYWEIGHTS

May 16	**Rocky Marciano** *KO* 9 Don Cockell, San Francisco

LIGHT HEAVYWEIGHTS

June 21	**Archie Moore** *KO* 3 Bobo Olson, New York City

WELTERWEIGHTS

April 1	**Tony DeMarco** (USA) *KO* 14 Johnny Saxton, Boston
June 10	**Carmen Basilio** (USA) *KO* 12 Tony DeMarco, Syracuse

LIGHTWEIGHTS

June 29	**Bud Smith** (USA) *W* 15 Jimmy Carter, Boston

FEATHERWEIGHTS

Feb 25	**Sandy Saddler** *W* 15 Teddy Davis, New York City

BANTAMWEIGHTS

March 9	**Raul Macias** (MEX) *KO* 11 Chamrern Songkitrat, San Francisco (Wins Vacant NBA Title)

FLYWEIGHTS

May 30	**Pascual Perez** *KO* 5 Yoshio Shirai, Tokyo

Mexico's undefeated Raul Macias kayoed Thailand's Chamrern Songkitrat in 11th round to become new bantamweight king.

THE CROWNING OF THE MIGHTY MEX

Boxing's formula was simple: one division, one champion. But politics was beginning to interfere, and after the NBA stripped world champion Robert Cohen for failing to defend against unbeaten Raul (Raton) Macias, the bantamweight title was split for the first time in 20 years. Cohen had won the vacant world crown in September 1954.

On March 9 at San Francisco's Cow Palace, Macias and Thailand's Chamrern Songkitrat, who had been Cohen's victim, clashed for the NBA version of the title. After substituting for the injured Mario D'Agata, Songkitrat had only two weeks to prepare.

Macias, a 2-1 favorite, popped the Thai with a classy jab and controlled the bout from start to finish. Songkitrat fought in one gear only, marching forward no matter the circumstances. He was knocked down twice in round six, and twice more in round 11, and his nose, rearranged in the Cohen fight, was again broken.

Former middleweight champion and local hero Fred Apostoli, who worked as the third man, halted the slaughter at the 2:38 mark of the 11th, with Macias far ahead on points. The immensely popular Mexican's fans lifted him into the air and paraded him around the ring. Then someone in the crowd released a white bantam cock, who bounced from shoulder to shoulder along with the champion.

Having engaged in only 12 pro bouts, the Mexican, who was recognized as titlist everywhere but California, New York, England, and France, remained relatively inexperienced. But his American representative, George Parnassus, spoke boldly. "We chased Cohen all over the country, trying to get a bout, before the NBA took his title away," he said. "We're through doing the chasing now. He can come to us in Mexico City if he wants the shot."

ARCHIE STARCHES BOBO

Welterweight champion Kid Gavilan moved up and challenged middleweight king Bobo Olson. He lost. Then Olson moved up and challenged light heavyweight champion Archie Moore. He lost. For some reason, Moore was planning to move up and challenge heavyweight champion Rocky Marciano. Didn't he sense a trend?

Moore-Olson came on June 22 at New York City's Polo Grounds. Moore was a 13-5 favorite, but insiders wondered whether a reduction of 21 pounds would weaken him. (In May, Moore had scaled 196½ for a points win over heavyweight contender Nino Valdes.) It was the challenger, however, who lacked strength.

Only an average puncher at 160 pounds, Olson, 170¼, lacked the weapons with which to threaten Moore. He boxed well for two rounds, but in round three, the champion struck with an extended flurry. The final punch was a hook to the chin, and Olson failed to beat the count of referee Ruby Goldstein.

Next up for "The Ol' Mongoose" was Marciano. The trend be damned!

Light heavyweight champ Archie Moore (right) was too much for middleweight king Bobo Olson, winning with third-round kayo.

A SMALL RING AND A BIG BEATING

Before Don Cockell's challenge of heavyweight champion Rocky Marciano, which took place at Kezar Stadium in San Francisco on May 16, the British fighter's handlers complained about the size of the ring.

California rules called for a minimum of 16, and a maximum of 24, square feet. The ring at Kezar was 16½ feet, which, against an aggressive puncher like Marciano, was tantamount to facing him in a phone booth.

Cockell was given little chance; Marciano was a 9-1 favorite, and it was even money that the challenger wouldn't last five rounds. The only real drama concerned Rocky's surgically repaired nose. It had been ripped open by Ezzard Charles eight months before, and would certainly be targeted by Cockell. As it turned out, Marciano emerged unmarked.

After a slow start, he shortened his punches and concentrated on the body. The 205-pound challenger fell at the end of the eighth, and twice in the ninth. Cockell rose each time, but after the third knockdown, referee Frankie Brown stepped in. "He's got a lot of guts," Marciano said of Cockell. "I don't think I ever hit anyone else any more often or harder."

Courageous Don Cockell (left) was holding his own until he was stopped in ninth round.

HOOKING WITH A HOOKER

An age-old boxing axiom says that you box a puncher, and punch a boxer. Both welterweight champion Tony DeMarco and Carmen Basilio were punchers, and because neither intended to change his style, their title fight was among the most anticipated of the year.

Boston's DeMarco, who had dethroned Johnny Saxton seven weeks before, defended against Basilio on June 10 at Syracuse's War Memorial Auditorium.

Hailing from nearby Canastota, New York, the challenger enjoyed the hometown advantage. But in a battle of two hookers, all that would matter would be the ability to dish out punishment and absorb it.

The fight was equal to its hype; DeMarco and Basilio tore at each other from the opening bell. Both fighters stood throughout early-rounds exchanges, but in doing so, paid a price. DeMarco suffered a dangerous gash above his left eye, and Basilio was cut on both eyebrows and on the upper lip. It was DeMarco who wilted first. By the eighth round, he was spent, and the tireless Basilio kept firing.

There were two knockdowns in the 10th, and in the 12th, with DeMarco stumbling on dead legs, referee Harry Kessler called a halt. (At the time of the stoppage, Basilio led by scores of 8-2-1, 8-3, and 7-4.)

DeMarco had taken his chances by punching with a puncher. The result: a third welterweight champion in 2½ months.

RINGSIDE VIEW

JANUARY

Don Jordan retains the California State lightweight title by outpointing former world champion Lauro Salas over 12 rounds in Los Angeles.

FEBRUARY

Middleweight champion Bobo Olson decisions Ralph (Tiger) Jones in a non-title bout in Chicago.

JUNE

Cincinnati's Wallace (Bud) Smith, a lightweight with a mediocre record of 29-12-6, dethrones world champion Jimmy Carter by split 15-round decision.

JULY

1955

DECEMBER

Bantamweight champion Robert Cohen held on to his title with a draw.

BIG BROTHER(S) IS WATCHING WEE WILLIE

Among the 35,000 in attendance on September 3 at Johannesburg's Rand Stadium was Vic Toweel, who, in 1950, had become South Africa's first world champion by winning the bantamweight title. Toweel was ringside for younger brother Willie's challenge of 118-pound champion Robert Cohen. Another brother, Maurice was Willie's manager. Still another, Alan, was his trainer. Same family. Same title. Same stadium.

Different result.

Cohen-Toweel was choppy and unappealing, partly because the champion was off his form. It was Cohen's first defense in almost a year – the layoff was due to minor injuries suffered in a car accident. Moreover, the French-based Algerian fractured his right thumb early in the bout. Toweel was unable to capitalize, however, until the late rounds.

Cohen almost ended the bout in the third, when he scored two flash knockdowns. (Toweel had never before been dropped.) Instead of fighting back, the lanky challenger, unbeaten at 20-0, was content to clinch through the middle rounds. He was warned for holding no less than seven times.

Toweel finally accelerated in the championship rounds. He cut Cohen under the right eye in the 11th, and at the side of the left eye in the 12th. In fact, the champion was fortunate to finish; at the final bell, he was dazed and staggering across the ring.

To the satisfaction of no one, the judges scored the bout a draw. (As was South African custom the scores were not revealed.)

"It was the hardest fight I've ever had," said Toweel, "but I thought I shaded him."

Brothers Vic, Maurice, and Alan could only shrug their shoulders. Despite a strong finish, Willie had fought too cautiously for too long. Too bad, too. It could've been a helluva party at the Toweel's house.

South Africa's Willie Toweel made his effort too late to win the crown.

RINGSIDE VIEW

SEPTEMBER

Welterweight champion Carmen Basilio scores a 10-round decision over Gil Turner in a non-title bout in Syracuse.

SEPTEMBER

Three months after losing the welterweight title, Tony DeMarco kayos Chico Vejar in one round in Boston.

NOVEMBER

Italy's Duilio Loi retains the European lightweight title with a 15-round decision over Seraphin Ferrer in Milan.

DECEMBER

California golden boy Art Aragon scores a 10-round decision victory over state lightweight champion Don Jordan.

THE ROCK'S FANTASTIC FAREWELL?

After defending the heavyweight title against a 41-year-old opponent, Rocky Marciano, 32, was contemplating a sudden exit from the game.

"Yes, it's true that I'm considering retirement," Marciano said after knocking out light heavyweight champion Archie Moore. "My mother and my wife are urging me to retire, strongly. I'm not saying I will retire, though. I just don't know."

Marciano hadn't been uncertain against Moore, who, on September 21, before 61,574 fans at Yankee Stadium, put forth a bold challenge. "The Ol' Mongoose" started with a rush, countering with a second-round right that drove Marciano to the floor. By the end of the round, the champion was bleeding from the nose, as well as a cut on his left brow. Moore's bob-and-weave movement, cross-armed defense, and steady retreat were confusing him. Then The Rock introduced his heavy artillery.

Marciano scored two knockdowns in the sixth, another in the seventh, and still another at the end of the eighth. In the ninth, Moore was dropped for referee Harry Kessler's 10-count by a cross-hook combination. In a classic display of Marciano's unique and effective style, he had systematically battered and beaten a great champion.

Marciano was 49-0. He had made six defenses, and the only challenger to last the distance, Ezzard Charles, was kayoed in the rematch. There had never before been a champion who left the ring without a single loss on his record.

This champion was about to make history.

Archie Moore made a valiant bid to dethrone Rocky Marciano, but was kayoed in ninth round.

AN INSTANT REPLAY, PLUS TWO SECONDS

Insiders labeled the first welterweight title fight between Carmen Basilio and Tony DeMarco a can't-miss brawl. It was. There was no reason for them to think that the rematch would be different. It wasn't.

This time, the roles were reversed: Basilio, and not DeMarco, was the defending champion. And the bout was held at Boston Garden, in DeMarco's backyard, and not Syracuse's War Memorial Auditorium, Basilio's home arena.

The fight was a carbon copy of the original. The 13,373 fans who held tickets – several thousand Bostonians were turned away by local police – were treated to a power punchathon. DeMarco pounced first, and expended much of his energy in trying for an early kayo. In the seventh, he sent Basilio across the ring with a right, and in the eighth, he issued an extended beating.

But then DeMarco decelerated, just as he had in the first fight. Basilio took control in the ninth, and after two 12th-round knockdowns, referee Mel Manning intervened. The time of the stoppage was 1:54; the rematch had lasted exactly two seconds longer than the original.

Carmen Basilio retained welterweight crown by knocking out ex-champ Tony DeMarco in 12th.

CARTER'S MAGIC FAILS AT THE FOURTH TIME OF ASKING

How many times could Jimmy Carter lose and lose again, only to win the fights that mattered most? The New Yorker had captured the lightweight title a record three times. On October 19 at Cincinnati Gardens, he tried for a fourth.

The defending champion, hometown favorite Bud Smith, had dethroned Carter in June. Nonetheless, he climbed through the ropes a 7-5 underdog. The 31-year-old Carter, the bettors believed, could still produce when he had to.

But there would be no more magic. Smith started quickly, hammering Carter with hooks. In round three, the challenger's right brow was cut, and by the ninth, the eye was swollen shut.

Carter's only chance came in the 13th, when he reached Smith with both hands and threatened to finish him. But the champion hung on, and went on to take a unanimous 15-round decision by scores of 143-139 (twice) and 143-135.

There was only problem: Smith was denied his $9,000 purse, which had been attached because of a managerial dispute. Before the bout, he told the local commission that he wasn't sure just who his manager was. Now that he was champion, the list of candidates was sure to grow.

THE BEST ONCE MORE

Sugar Ray Robinson's comeback was six fights old, and no one was quite sure what to make of it. In his second return bout, the former welterweight and middleweight champion had been pounded by Tiger Jones. In his sixth, he had earned a try at the 160-pound crown by edging top-rated contender Rocky Castellani.

The oddsmakers thought Robinson, 35, was too old, so they made world champion Bobo Olson a 3-1 favorite to keep the middleweight crown. Robinson had twice beaten Olson. On December 9 at Chicago Stadium, he scored a hat trick.

It wasn't much of a fight. Moving fluidly, Robinson took the first round. In the second, he gunned a right to the jaw, and the champion slumped to the floor. After Olson was counted out by referee Frank Sikora, Robinson's emotions flowed.

"I had to cry," he told the assembled press. "I just couldn't believe it was all over. It seems almost like a miracle."

The Sugar Ray, the best, was back, which was bad news for the others.

Ray Robinson regained middleweight crown by kayoing Bobo Olson in second round.

World Title Fights

HEAVYWEIGHTS	
Sept 21	**Rocky Marciano** *KO* 9 Archie Moore, Bronx, NY
MIDDLEWEIGHTS	
Dec 9	**Sugar Ray Robinson** *KO* 2 Bobo Olson, Chicago
WELTERWEIGHTS	
Nov 30	**Carmen Basilio** *KO* 12 Tony DeMarco, Boston
LIGHTWEIGHTS	
Oct 19	**Bud Smith** *W* 15 Jimmy Carter, Cincinnati
BANTAMWEIGHTS	
Sept 3	**Robert Cohen** *D* 15 Willie Toweel, Johannesburg

Rocky Marciano

How might Rocky Marciano have reacted had he lost a big fight? He probably would've visited the winner's dressing room, congratulated him on a superb effort, and said all the right things to the press. Then he would've returned to the privacy of his own quarters, punched a hole in the wall, and screamed, "God help that guy if I ever fight him again!"

We can only guess because Marciano never lost a professional prize fight. He won the world title and defended it six times, went 49-0 (43), and exited in his prime. None of the other heavyweight immortals, not Johnson or Dempsey or Louis or Ali, can make the same claim. In fact, Marciano is the only champion *at any weight* to have retired undefeated.

Rocco Francis Marchegiano was born on September 1, 1923, in Brockton, Massachusetts, a suburb of Boston. Perrino and Pasqualena Marchegiano, immigrants from Italy, had six children, and after Rocky, who was their oldest, almost died of pneumonia at age two, they worried most about him. Pasqualena described Rocky as shy and timid. What she didn't know was that when someone made the mistake of aggravating her young son…

In high school, Marciano excelled in baseball and football. He dropped out after his second year, and went to work as a gardener, delivery boy, laborer for the gas company, and, of course, leather tanner at the shoe factory. Brockton was famous for manufacturing footwear, and Marciano's father worked in the factories all his life. Rocky came to despise the smell of leather. His initial motivation was to make enough money so his father would never again have to punch a time clock.

Introduced to boxing by his uncle, John Piccento, Marciano showed natural power, but little speed or skill. He still dreamed of playing catcher in the Major Leagues. It wasn't until lifelong friend Allie Colombo computed Joe Louis' pay per hour that a wide-eyed Rocky was swayed.

After a stint in the Army during World War II, Marciano began his 12-fight amateur career. He won the New England Golden Gloves title, then came to New York for the Eastern Championships. In the first round he was matched with the heavily hyped Coley Wallace. Marciano lost a split decision. No one knew it at the time, but Wallace would become the answer to an oft-asked trivia question.

Professional career dates 1947-1956
Contests 49
Won 49
Lost 0
Drawn 0
Knockouts 43
World Heavyweight Champion 1952-1956

Rocky Marciano was small for a heavyweight. His average fighting weight was only 185 pounds, and he stood a little over five feet 10 inches tall. But what he lacked in size he more than made up for with enormous strength. It was said that the only way to stop Marciano was to kill him.

The next time Marciano came to New York, it was to audition for manager Al Weill and trainer Charley Goldman. The novice was crude but persistent.

"I figured he must want to be a fighter awful bad," said Goldman. "A kid like this deserved a break, and I wanted to make sure he got it."

Marciano became Goldman's pet project. At 5'10¼", The Rock wasn't going to outbox too many heavyweights, so Goldman trained him to fight out of a crouch, punch to the body, and try for a kayo only in the late rounds.

The formula demanded that Marciano remain in prime condition.

"He's in the gym every day before me," said Goldman, "and I have to drive him away from the bags and out of the ring."

Realizing that his fighter was going to develop slowly, Weill shielded Marciano from the New York press by scheduling bouts in New England. (No less than 28 of Marciano's 49 career starts were held in Providence, Rhode Island.) Marciano turned pro on March 17, 1947, scoring a third-round kayo of one Lee Epperson in Holyoke, Massachusetts. He scored 16 straight knockouts before Don Mogard extended him the 10-round distance.

Three bouts highlighted Marciano's climb to the title. In December 1949, he brawled with Carmine Vingo before scoring a terrific sixth-round kayo. Vingo was rushed to the hospital with serious concussion. Doctors initially feared that his injuries would be fatal, but the fighter recovered. The notoriously thrifty Marciano ("He wouldn't pay a nickel to see an earthquake," said Goldman) covered Vingo's hospital bills, gave him $2,500, and, on New Year's Eve, 1950, made him the guest of honor at his wedding.

In March 1950, Marciano squared off against unbeaten (37-0) contender Roland LaStarza. It was a highly competitive bout, with Rocky squeezing by via split verdict. He'd never come closer to losing.

In October 1951, Marciano scored the victory that all but guaranteed a try at the world title. By stopping comebacking 37-year-old Joe Louis in the eighth round, he confirmed the passage of time.

"I'm just lucky," he said, "that I didn't have to fight Joe 10 years ago."

Marciano's magic moment came on September 23, 1952, before 40,000 fans at Municipal Stadium in Philadelphia. Heavyweight champion Jersey Joe Walcott was 38, but also shrewd and shifty. When he opened the bout by dropping Marciano with a hook, it seemed that the challenger would be outclassed. But Marciano's durability surfaced, and his late-rounds rally ended in the 13th, when he kayoed Walcott with a short right. The blow remains the most famous single punch in history.

There was no drama in the rematch; Walcott fell in one round. Marciano's second defense was a long-awaited rematch vs. LaStarza. Again the clever New Yorker proved troublesome, but Marciano hammered away at the challenger's arms and shoulders and scored an 11th-round TKO.

"You know," LaStarza said years later, "the difference in Rocky between the first fight and the second was fantastic; it was much more difficult to land a punch on him."

In 1954, Marciano engaged in a pair of difficult defenses against former champion Ezzard Charles. In the first bout, Charles surprisingly traded with the champion and managed to last the 15-round distance. Three months later, "The Cincinnati Cobra" split open Marciano's nose. Aware that referee Al Berl was contemplating a stoppage, The Rock accelerated with desperation and finished his foe in the eighth.

In 1955, Marciano kayoed England's Don Cockell, then, four months later, rose from the canvas to drop Archie Moore three times en route to a ninth-round kayo victory. It was the last bout of his career; on April 27, 1956, Marciano, age 32, announced his retirement.

Throughout the mid- and late-'50s, there were non-stop rumors of Marciano's return. But The Rock remained different from other ring greats. His only fights were generated by computers. In 1967, Marciano won an all-time heavyweight tournament that was broadcast on radio. (He kayoed Jack Dempsey in the championship match.) In 1969, Marciano and Muhammad Ali climbed through the ropes to spar 70 rounds for a dream fight. Rocky lost 50 pounds for the movie cameras, and won by 13th-round knockout.

On August 31, 1969, Rocky, en route to Des Moines for a birthday party in his honor, was a passenger on a single-engine plane that crashed near Newton, Iowa. There were no survivors. The former heavyweight champion was one day shy of 46.

Marciano was an unlikely candidate for perfection. His legacy, however, was his unbeaten record. The next time you hear someone say that great fighters are born, not made, think of Rocky. Think of his awkward style and his two left feet. Think of Charley Goldman. Then think of those numbers – 49-0 (43) – and you'll realize that anything is possible.

Ezzard Charles (right) brought out Marciano's greatness better than any other opponent. Charles was a vastly superior boxer and, actually, a harder puncher than Rocky. Several times during their two classic brawls, Marciano was on the verge of defeat, but his extraordinary courage and resilience enabled him to snatch victory from defeat.

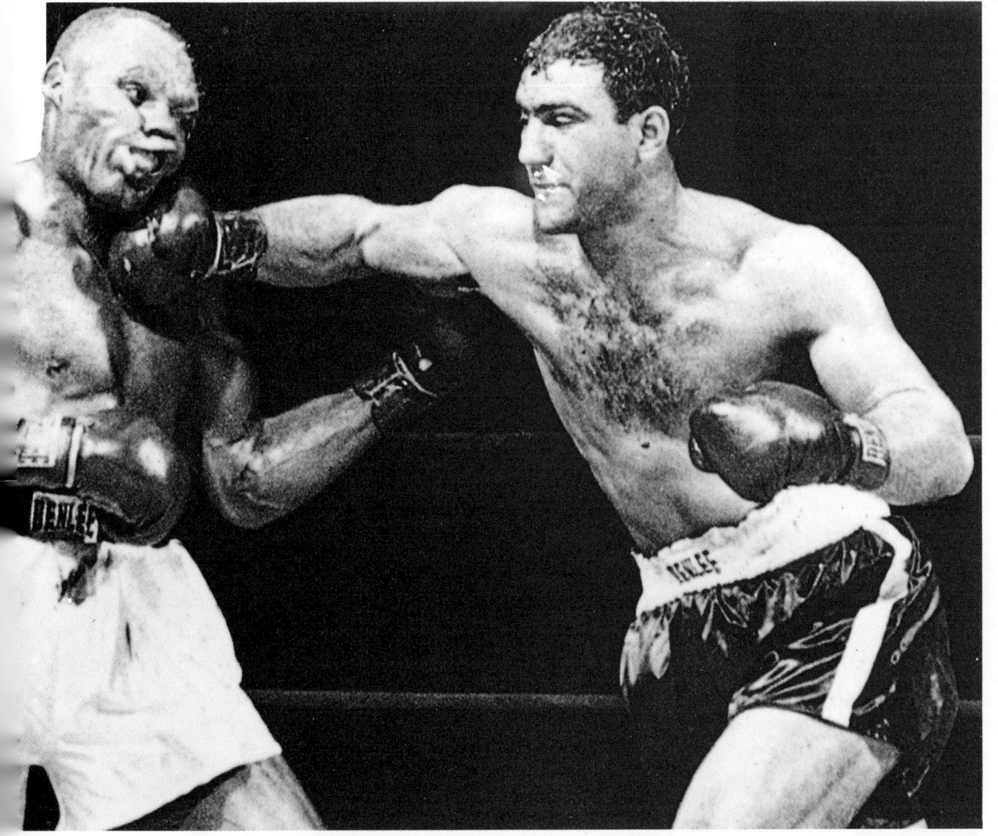

Marciano's awesome power is captured in this remarkable picture as his right fist contorts Jersey Joe Walcott's face into a gruesome mask. The punch set Walcott up for the followup blow that knocked him out in the 13th round and made Rocky the new world heavyweight champion.

JANUARY

1956

JUNE

RINGSIDE VIEW

MARCH

Heavyweight Floyd Patterson remains in title contention by scoring a second-round knockout of Jimmy Walls in New Britain, Connecticut.

MARCH

Fighting for the fourth time this year, light heavyweight champion Archie Moore decisions heavyweight Howard King over 10 rounds in Sacramento.

MAY

Middleweight champion Sugar Ray Robinson keeps the crown by defeating his favorite victim, Bobo Olson. In the first defense of his third reign, Sugar Ray scores a fourth-round knockout.

JUNE

Bantamweight champion Pascual Perez continues to sweep through the division, retaining the title with an 11th-round stoppage of Oscar Suarez.

CHICAGO IS JINX FOR CARMEN

Carmen Basilio liked Chicago the way Napoleon liked Waterloo.

Defending the welterweight title for the second time, Basilio met former king Johnny Saxton on March 14 at Chicago Stadium. The champion agreed to fight in Chicago with trepidation; it was in "The Windy City" that he had lost consecutive 10-round decisions to Chuck Davey and Billy Graham in the summer of 1952.

Basilio-Saxton proved that contrasting styles don't necessarily mesh. Basilio, a hooker, chased, and Saxton, a jabber, ran away. After 15 uneventful rounds, the judges scored unanimously for Saxton, by scores of 144-142, 147-140, and 145-138. The majority of reporters, however, had Basilio ahead.

"I won the fight," said Basilio, who had been a 2-1 favorite. "That's the third time I fought here, and the same thing happened every time. Don't they score double-hooks in this town?"

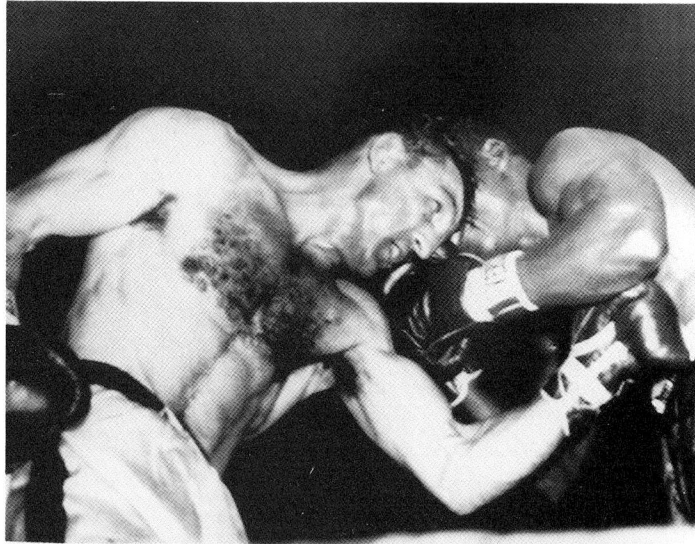

Sleek Johnny Saxton (right) scored a major upset by decisioning Carmen Basilio in 15 rounds.

OVER IN A FLASH

Was it more frustrating to fight featherweight champion Sandy Saddler, or watch him fight? Defending for only the third time in more than five years, Saddler was booed throughout his January bout against Filipino southpaw Flash Elorde in San Francisco. Saddler continually butted, wrestled, and hit on the break.

"I complained to the referee all through the fight," said Lupe Sarreal, the challenger's manager and father-in-law, "but I didn't get any place. He told me that was the only way Saddler could fight, and I had to be satisfied with that."

In a handful of rounds, Elorde scored with lightning flurries. But in the seventh, he suffered a deep cut over his left eye. Dr. Robert Ladden examined the gash during both the 10th and 11th stanzas, and at the 59-second mark of the 13th, referee Ray Flores had seen enough blood – Saddler was leading by 67-65 on all three cards.

For Saddler, winning ugly was becoming an artform.

Sandy Saddler (left) went out a winner in his last title fight by stopping Flash Elorde in 13th.

A DUBIOUS DAILY DOUBLE

What Leo Espinosa accomplished over a 10-week stretch was a unique achievement, but not one for the Filipino stylist's scrapbook.

On January 11, before a crowd of 30,000 at Luna Park in Buenos Aires, Espinosa, the 118-pound champion of the Orient, dropped down to challenge flyweight champion and Argentine idol Pascual Perez. Reminiscent of former titlist Jimmy Wilde, the 5'0" Perez scaled only 107¾, but immediately assumed the role of power-puncher. Espinosa was cut under the left eye in the third round, and bled the rest of the way. He was knocked down in the ninth round, and Perez went on to emerge victorious by unanimous 15-round decision.

Espinosa then moved north to the Plaza Mexico bullring, and on March 25, before a partisan crowd of 60,000, challenged NBA bantamweight champion Raul (Raton) Macias. The Filipino boxed beautifully for five rounds, then wilted at the 7,300-foot altitude. Macias administered a brutal body battering in round nine, and knocked out Espinosa with a right to the jaw in round 10.

Ten weeks, two title tries in two divisions, and two losses. It was time to go home.

A PERFECT TIME TO SAY GOODBYE

Rocky Marciano announces his retirement as undefeated heavyweight champion.

It was hard to believe that Rocky Marciano, 31 years old, 49-0, and the heavyweight champion of the world, would retire in his prime. But on April 27, at the Hotel Shelton in New York City, The Rock confirmed what had been rumored since his kayo of Archie Moore in September 1955.

"I thought it was a mistake when Joe Louis tried a comeback," said Marciano, who was with his wife, Barbara, and his manager, Al Weill. "No man can say what he will do in the future. But, barring poverty, the ring has seen the last of me. I am comfortably fixed, and I am not afraid of the future. Barring a complete and dire emergency, you will never see Rocky Marciano make a comeback."

After acknowledging "I probably have two or three good fights left," Marciano said that his immediate plans included lots of golf. He added that he was considering several business proposals.

The announcement was met with skepticism by Marciano's chief rival, light heavyweight champion Archie Moore.

"Marciano won't quit because he loves the jingle of the American dollar too much," Moore said.

He was wrong. This would turn out to be one fighter who couldn't be bought.

HEAVYWEIGHT TITLE-FIGHT TUNEUP

For 42-year-old Archie Moore, the light heavyweight title had become a secondary consideration. Every few months, the champion would drop 15 or 20 pounds and make a defense. His real concern, however, was the heavyweight division. And with Rocky Marciano having retired, boxing's biggest prize seemed well within his reach.

On June 5 at London's famed Harringay Arena, Moore made his fifth defense of the 175-pound crown, meeting Trinidad-born powerpuncher Yolande Pompey. Moore had reduced 14 pounds in one month, and started as if weak and wasted. Pompey missed more than he landed, but still managed to build a points lead. Then Moore began to fight like a champion. He rallied in the ninth, and one round later, scored three knockdowns over his fatigued foe. Referee Jack Hart stopped the fight at the 2.50 mark.

"Now I want the heavyweight title," Moore said. Only Floyd Patterson, who was half Moore's age, stood in his way.

Defending light heavyweight king Archie Moore (right) was too cunning for Yolande Pompey.

FEELING THE CHEERS

Born a deaf mute, Italy's Mario D'Agata couldn't hear or speak. But as a teenager, he discovered he could punch.

On June 29, D'Agata, the European bantamweight title holder, challenged the world bantamweight champion Robert Cohen at the Foro Italico Soccer Stadium in Rome.

From a human interest angle, at least, the matchup was intriguing; both fighters had overcome career-threatening injuries. In 1954, D'Agata was shot in the stomach during a dispute with a business partner. And earlier in the year, Cohen suffered a broken jaw in an automobile accident.

Cohen enjoyed a big first round, but D'Agata managed to survive. Over the next four rounds, the only development of note was a cut that opened over Cohen's left eye. Toward the end of the sixth, D'Agata dropped the champion with a right hand. At the end of that round, referee Teddy Waltham examined Cohen's wide wound and elected to stop the bout.

Hundreds of fans rushed the ring, and D'Agata, an unlikely hero, was lifted onto the shoulders of his Italian countrymen. He didn't need to hear the cheers; he could *feel* them.

WORLD TITLE FIGHTS

LIGHT HEAVYWEIGHTS

June 5	**Archie Moore** *KO* 10 Yolande Pompey, London

MIDDLEWEIGHTS

May 18	**Sugar Ray Robinson** *KO* 4 Bobo Olson, Los Angeles

WELTERWEIGHTS

March 14	**Johnny Saxton** *W* 15 Carmen Basilio, Chicago

FEATHERWEIGHTS

Jan 18	**Sandy Saddler** *KO* 13 Flash Elorde, San Francisco

BANTAMWEIGHTS

March 25	**Raul Macias** *KO* 10 Leo Espinosa, Mexico City
June 29	**Mario D'Agata** (ITA) *KO* 7 Robert Cohen, Rome

FLYWEIGHTS

Jan 11	**Pascual Perez** *W* 15 Leo Espinosa, Buenos Aires
June 30	**Pascual Perez** *KO* 11 Oscar Suarez, Montevideo

JULY

1956

DECEMBER

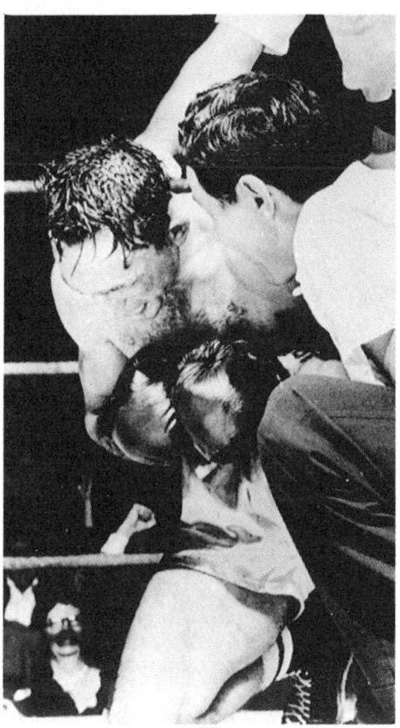

Choked with emotion, Carmen Basilio dropped to his knees and thanked God.

HAS THE REIGN STOPPED?

Featherweight champion Sandy Saddler rarely defended the title, and when he did, he infuriated fans and foes alike with tactics usually reserved for professional wrestling.

On July 27, Saddler's future was clouded when he suffered multiple injuries in an auto accident on the streets of New York City. The champion was riding in a taxi cab when it collided with another automobile. Saddler's head hit against the door. He was taken to the hospital with a concussion, and injuries to his spine and left arm.

It was initially believed that Saddler would be released in a matter of days. But he remained hospitalized for a month. A non-title bout, scheduled against Ike Chestnut on August 8, was scratched, as were negotiations for a defense against Cherif Hamia.

Saddler would fight no more. On January 16, 1957, the NBA would strip him of the title. Five days later, Saddler would announce his retirement. And in February, he would undergo surgery to repair a detached retina. It was an ugly ending to an ugly, albeit dominant, reign.

CHAMPION BUD FORGOT HOW TO WIN

Insiders viewed Cincinnati's oft-beaten Bud Smith as the most unlikely of world champions. After winning the lightweight crown and making one successful defense, Smith seemed determined to validate that view.

On August 24, Smith defended against 30-year-old veteran Joe Brown at the Municipal Arena in the challenger's hometown of New Orleans. In round two, Brown fractured his right wrist, but the break wasn't enough to propel Smith to victory. Boxing with one hand, Brown moved and jabbed. In the late rounds, he sensed he had to do more. He reintroduced his right, accepted the pain when it landed, and scored two 14th-round knockdowns.

"I had to gamble," he explained. "It was the only way to win."

Smith struggled to the final bell, only to learn that the judges had scored against him. The decision was split, with Brown taking the crown by scores of 12-3, 9-3-3, and 6-7-2.

Smith's one successful defense had come in October 1955 against Jimmy Carter. It turned out to be the last victory of his career. He finished with 11 consecutive losses. Never before had a champion's collapse been so complete.

Joe Brown decisioned lightweight champ Bud Smith twice in 1956. The first was a non-title fight, the second made Brown (right) a new champion.

JUSTICE, SWEET AND COMPLETE

The judges had taken the welterweight title from Carmen Basilio. He knew he couldn't depend on them to give it back.

On September 12, at the War Memorial Auditorium in Syracuse, Basilio was rematched with welterweight champion Johnny Saxton. One year before, Saxton had dethroned Basilio by disputed decision. This time, there would be no controversy.

As intense as he had ever been, Basilio marched forward while repeatedly firing his lethal left hook. Surprisingly, Saxton met him in ring center.

"This time," Basilio said, "he fought like a man."

Fighting on Basilio's terms, Saxton couldn't hope to win. He began to utilize lateral movement in the middle rounds, but it was already too late. Basilio hammered his body in the seventh and eighth, and smothered him with punches in the ninth. Referee Al Berl saved Saxton at the 1:31 mark.

"The referee should have let him hit the deck like a champion should," said Frank (Blinky) Palermo, Saxton's manager.

You can be sure that Basilio himself would have liked nothing better.

WORLD TITLE FIGHTS

HEAVYWEIGHTS	
Nov 30	**Floyd Patterson** (USA) *KO* 5 Archie Moore, Chicago
WELTERWEIGHTS	
Sept 12	**Carmen Basilio** *KO* 9 Johnny Saxton, Syracuse
LIGHTWEIGHTS	
Aug 24	**Joe Brown** (USA) *W* 15 Bud Smith, New Orleans

THE MENACE OF LISTON, IN THE RING AND OUT

Brooding and curt, heavyweight prospect Charles (Sonny) Liston counted intimidation among his weapons. Unfortunately, he didn't restrict that intimidation to the ring.

In December, Liston, 14-1 and streaking toward the top 10, was convicted in St. Louis of assault with a deadly weapon, beating up a policeman, and taking his gun. His sentence: nine months in a work house.

The details of the incident, which occurred on May 5, were sketchy. According to the police report, officer Thomas Mellow saw a taxi parked illegally in an alley, and went to an adjacent house to ask if the driver was there. In the house was the cab-driver, Liston, and two women, including Geraldine Chambers, who would subsequently become Liston's wife.

All four had reportedly been drinking. When Mellow asked that the car be moved, Liston argued and then began wrestling with him. Liston and Mellow proceeded outside. Later, Mellow was found lying in the alley badly beaten, his uniform torn, his badge and his revolver missing.

When the police arrested Liston, he admitted fighting with the officer, and told them where the gun was. (He had hid it at his sister's home.) He said he had taken it away in self-defense, because "the man was looking for trouble."

In the seven months between the incident and conviction, Liston was arrested four times, twice for suspicion of theft, once for speeding, and once for failing to answer a summons.

Those coming in contact with Liston should have been issued the standard referee's warning: Protect yourself at all times.

Sonny Liston was sentenced to nine months in prison for assaulting a policeman and stealing the officer's gun. The judge ignored Sonny's self-defense plea.

YOUTH NOT WASTED ON THE YOUNG

On July 14, 1936, Archie Moore turned professional. Floyd Patterson was just one year old at the time.

On November 30, 1956, Moore, 42, became the oldest fighter to ever try for the heavyweight title. And Patterson, 21, became the youngest fighter to ever win it.

At Chicago Stadium, Patterson and Moore clashed for the title that had been vacated by Rocky Marciano. Moore opened as a slight favorite, but the late money was bet on Patterson. Moore had fought Marciano, and Patterson hadn't. The logic was simple: The Rock not only finished his opponents for the night, but for good.

Patterson fought aggressively from the start, and made Moore miss by bobbing and weaving in his familiar peek-a-boo stance. But Moore could figure out any style, and in the third, he began to score. His rally continued in the fourth.In the fifth, the end came in a flash. Patterson leaped in with a power hook and caught Moore flush. The light heavyweight champion rose at referee Frank Sikora's count of nine, but only seconds later Moore was dropped by a right. He was counted out at the 2:27 mark.

"The turning point came in the third round," said Patterson. "I landed a left to Moore's stomach, and I heard him say, 'ugh,' or something like that. I knew then that I could hurt him, and I knew I could beat him."

Before he could absorb the significance of his triumph, Patterson was on a plane heading for New York City. Only hours before the first bell, his wife Sandra had given birth to a daughter. The youngest heavyweight champion in history would also be the first to celebrate his coronation in a maternity ward.

Floyd Patterson (right) became the youngest heavyweight champion in history by stopping Archie Moore in the fifth round of elimination bout to determine Marciano's successor.

RINGSIDE VIEW

SEPTEMBER

Sweden's Ingemar Johansson wins the European heavyweight title by scoring a 13th-round knockout of Francesco Cavicchi in Bologna, Italy.

SEPTEMBER

In his final tuneup before contesting for the vacant heavyweight title, light heavyweight champion Archie Moore knocks out Roy Shire in three rounds.

NOVEMBER

In a non-title bout, middleweight champion Sugar Ray Robinson outpoints Bob Provizzi over 10 rounds in New Haven, Connecticut.

NOVEMBER

Former world middleweight champion Randy Turpin manage to retain the British light heavyweight crown with a fifth-round stoppage of Alex Buxton in Leicester.

JANUARY

1957

JUNE

SUGAR FORCED TO TAKE HIS LUMPS

Gene Fullmer planned to spend Christmas Day, 1956, with his family in West Jordan, Utah, sitting under the tree, sipping egg nog, and filling stockings. Instead, he spent it with sparring partners in training camp, sharing sweat, pounding the bags, and sleeping early.

Fullmer's challenge of middleweight champion Sugar Ray Robinson came before an enthusiastic crowd of 18,134 at Madison Square Garden on January 2. It had been scheduled earlier, but Robinson had pulled out with a virus. First the mild-mannered challenger got angry. Then he got even.

Robinson tried to box, but Fullmer, 25, smothered him from the start. Seemingly impervious to pain, the underdog ignored Sugar Ray's occasional flurries while setting a demanding pace. It was too much for the 36-year-old champion. Sugar Ray suffered a bad cut alongside his right eye in the 14th round, and could summon none of his magic in the final stanza. The title went to Fullmer by well-received scores of 8-5-2, 9-6, and 10-5.

For the family man from the Church of the Latter Day Saints, it hadn't been a merry Christmas. But it was already a happy New Year.

Gene Fullmer (left) used his great strength to dethrone middleweight king Ray Robinson.

RINGSIDE VIEW

JANUARY

Only 26 days after dethroning Sugar Ray Robinson, middleweight champion Gene Fullmer scores a 10-round, non-title decision victory over Wilf Greaves.

MARCH

Defending the flyweight crown before 80,000 fans at Buenos Aires' San Lorenzo Stadium, Pascual Perez knocks out Welshman Dai Dower with a right hand at 2:48 of the first round.

TWO HANDS PROVE BETTER THAN ONE FOR JOE

After losing the lightweight title to Joe Brown, Bud Smith clung to the belief that he had been victimized by a hometown decision. Brown, boxing with a broken right hand, had cautiously circled the ring for most of the fight. Wasn't the challenger supposed to *earn* the title?

The circumstances of Brown-Smith I made a rematch inevitable. The return came at the Miami Beach Auditorium on February 13. Sure that Brown would be twice as dangerous with two hands, the bookies made him a 3-1 favorite.

Brown used his right hand only sparingly, but it didn't matter; Smith was a fighter in decline. By the middle rounds, the champion's jabs cut Smith's lip and closed his left eye. Smith complained to his corner that his eye was "throbbing," but fought on until the bell ending the 10th. At that point, Dr. Alexander Robbins examined the challenger and called a halt. At the time of the stoppage, Brown was far ahead on all three cards.

"It was no contest," said Brown. "I was picking my spots. I was hitting him with anything I wanted to."

Even his right hand.

RUBBER LEGS IN THE RUBBER MATCH

What was it about Johnny Saxton that turned Carmen Basilio into a determined destroyer? There seemed to be no animosity between the two. The welterweights had fought twice, with each winning once. In March 1956, Saxton won a questionable decision; six months later, Basilio gained revenge with a ninth-round kayo. But he wanted more.

He got it in the rubber match, held on February 22 at the Arena in Cleveland. By the opening bell, Basilio was foaming right through his gumshield.

After pummeling the challenger throughout the first, Basilio finished him in the second with a classic hook. Saxton rose at referee Tony LaBranche's count of 10, but wasn't permitted to fight on.

"The fury that Basilio displayed in ripping Saxton to destruction has rarely been duplicated in the prize ring," wrote *The New York Times*.

Basilio's punches had declared the series officially over. Not that Saxton would have wanted a fourth fight anyway.

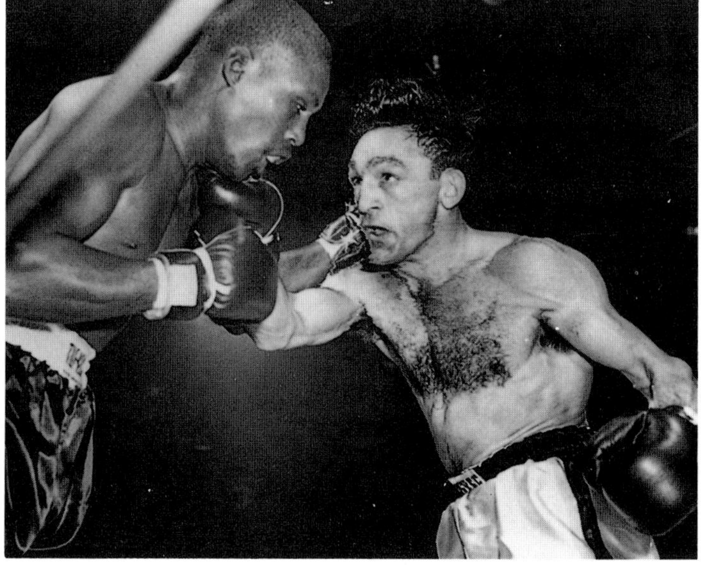

Carmen Basilio (right) retained title by knocking out former champion Johnny Saxton.

THE NIGHT THAT THE SPARKS FLEW IN PARIS

Born a deaf-mute, bantamweight Mario D'Agata had proven his mettle by overcoming his handicap and winning the world title. But his resolve, determination, and courage couldn't have possibly prepared him for the third round of his first defense.

Facing French-based Algerian Alphonse Halimi at the Palais des Sports on April 1, D'Agata began by fighting in his customary aggressive style. With 15 seconds left in the third round, he was digging his head into the challenger's chest when a short circuit caused the ring lights to explode. Burning metal wire and rubber fell across the ring, and D'Agata was scarred on his shoulder and back.

The declaration of a no-contest seemed imminent, but after a 15-minute delay, Belgian referee Philippe de Becker informed both corners that the fight would promptly be resumed. Because of D'Agata's inability to verbalize his thoughts, the press never learned the extent to which the bizarre incident affected him. After the fire, however, the champion was a different fighter. He continued to attack, but Halimi easily countered and took the referee's decision by winning all but one of the remaining rounds.

D'Agata deserved at least a rematch. But he would never again fight for the title.

Halimi is paraded around ring by Parisians.

RAY DELIVERS THE PERFECT PUNCH

It was only appropriate that Sugar Ray Robinson, as close to a perfect fighter as the ring had ever seen, would land what would come to be known as The Perfect Punch.

Having outpointed Robinson in January, middleweight champion Gene Fullmer was a 3-1 favorite to repeat his victory. The rematch came on May 1 at Chicago Stadium. Fullmer took the first three rounds, and Robinson rallied in the fourth.

Then came round five, and The Perfect Punch. Moving toward Robinson, Fullmer held his right hand by his chest. Sensing an opening, Sugar Ray winged a quick hook that found Fullmer's chin. The champion, who had never before been hurt, much less floored, was counted out.

"I just thank God that I got in the punch," said Robinson. "I had no other strategy.

"At age 35, Robinson was middleweight champion for the fourth time. Almost Perfect.

Remarkable Ray Robinson acknowledges thundering ovation after kayoing Gene Fullmer.

FIGHTING TALK

That's the first time I ever got knocked out, and I don't know how it happened

GENE FULLMER
after being knocked unconscious by Sugar Ray Robinson

SHOOTING DOWN THE CHERIF

After Sandy Saddler's retirement, the world's top featherweights engaged in a mini-tournament to crown a new champion. The favorite, France's Cherif Hamia, was given a bye to the final. British Empire champion Hogan (Kid) Bassey earned a spot in the championship match by outpointing Miguel Berrios.

Bassey met Hamia on June 24 at the Palais des Sports. Hamia was made a 7-5 favorite, but the 5'3" Bassey, who had learned to fight on the docks of Lagos, Nigeria, proved far stronger. After rising from a flash knockdown in round two, he proceeded to weaken Hamia with a steady body attack. In the 10th, Hamia was reeling along the ropes when referee Rene Schemann intervened.

Inactivity had tarnished Saddler's reign. Bassey symbolized a fresh start, for which the world's featherweights were grateful.

WORLD TITLE FIGHTS

MIDDLEWEIGHTS

Jan 2	**Gene Fullmer** (USA) *W* 15 Sugar Ray Robinson, New York City
May 1	**Sugar Ray Robinson** *KO* 5 Gene Fullmer, Chicago

WELTERWEIGHTS

Feb 21	**Carmen Basilio** *KO* 2 Johnny Saxton, Cleveland

LIGHTWEIGHTS

Feb 13	**Joe Brown** *KO* 11 Bud Smith, Miami
June 19	**Joe Brown** *KO* 15 Orlando Zulueta, Denver

FEATHERWEIGHTS

June 24	**Hogan (Kid) Bassey** (NIG) *KO* 10 Cherif Hamia, Paris (Wins Vacant Title)

BANTAMWEIGHTS

April 1	**Alphonse Halimi** (ALG) *ref* 15 Mario D'Agata, Paris
June 15	**Raul Macias** *KO* 11 Dommy Ursua, San Francisco

FLYWEIGHTS

March 30	**Pascual Perez** *KO* 1 Dal Dower, Buenos Aires

JULY

1957

DECEMBER

START AT TOP

Pete Rademacher saw it as an omen that he and Floyd Patterson were linked by the calendar. On November 30, 1956, Rademacher knocked out Russia's Lev Moukhine to win the heavyweight gold medal at the Olympic Games in Melbourne, Australia. On the same night, but halfway around the world, Patterson knocked out Archie Moore to win the world title in Chicago.

It was Rademacher's plan to make history by fighting for the heavyweight title in his pro debut. He offered Patterson a guarantee of $200,000. Then Rademacher hyped the bout to the press.

On August 22, Patterson and Rademacher squared off at Seattle's Sicks Stadium. The challenger's all-or-nothing approach floored Patterson in the second. But after that there were no more surprises. Seven knockdowns later, Rademacher was counted out.

BLOWING AWAY THE HURRICANE

Floyd Patterson looked The Hurricane in the eye, braced himself, and started punching. The only way to beat the storm was to attack it.

On July 29 at New York City's Polo Grounds, Patterson defended the heavyweight title for the first time against a familiar foe, Tommy "Hurricane" Jackson. In June 1956, Patterson had qualified for a try at the vacant crown by edging Jackson via split decision. He was a 5-1 favorite to repeat his victory.

This time, it was easier. Standing 6'2½", and boxing in a most unorthodox style, Jackson remained difficult. But he wasn't a hitter, and Patterson controlled almost all of the frequent exchanges. In fact, at the time of the stoppage, the judges had scored a shutout.

Jackson was dropped in the first, second, and ninth rounds, and at 1:52 of the 10th, referee Ruby Goldstein came to his rescue.

Having suffered a bruised kidney, Jackson was hospitalized. The only visitors initially allowed were Patterson and the champion's manager, Cus D'Amato, who were at The Hurricane's bedside as soon as they got wind of his condition. The storm had passed.

In his first title defense, heavyweight king Floyd Patterson knocked out Tommy "Hurricane" Jackson in the 10th round of a one-sided bout in New York.

THIS TIME A GOOD LITTLE ONE BEATS A GOOD BIG ONE

Champ Ray Robinson (right) faded in the late rounds against rugged Carmen Basilio.

On September 23 at Yankee Stadium, heavyweights Ernest Hemingway and Gen. Douglas MacArthur were among those ringside to watch middleweight champion Sugar Ray Robinson defend against welterweight king Carmen Basilio.

Nothing went as expected. Robinson didn't move as much as usual. He surprised Basilio by aiming mostly for the body, and Basilio surprised him by targeting the head. Toward the end, the champion, 36, was fresher than the challenger, 30. Oh, yes, one other thing: Basilio won the fight.

After 15 rounds of furious fighting, Basilio was rewarded by the judges. The decision was split, with scores of 9-5-1 and 8-6-1 for Basilio, and 9-6 for Robinson.

"Robbery!" screamed George Gainford, Robinson's trainer.

"Of course I won," countered Basilio. "I forced the fight, didn't I? I got in the most punches, didn't I? Then I won."

Even Hemingway and MacArthur couldn't argue with that statement.

RINGSIDE VIEW

AUGUST

Lightweight champion Joe Brown is held to a 10-round draw by Joey Lopes in a non-title bout in Chicago.

NOVEMBER

Road warrior Archie Moore travels to Eddie Cotton's hometown of Seattle and outpoints the rising prospect over 10 rounds.

NOVEMBER

Lightweight champion Joe Brown scores a 10-round, non-title decision over Kid Centella in Houston.

WORLD TITLE FIGHTS

HEAVYWEIGHTS

July 29	**Floyd Patterson** *KO* 10 Tommy Jackson, New York City
Aug 21	**Floyd Patterson** *KO* 6 Pete Rademacher, Seattle

LIGHT HEAVYWEIGHTS

Sept 20	**Archie Moore** *KO* 7 Tony Anthony, Los Angeles

MIDDLEWEIGHTS

Sept 23	**Carmen Basilio** *W* 15 Sugar Ray Robinson, Bronx, NY

WELTERWEIGHTS

Oct 29	**Virgil Akins** (USA) *KO* 14 Tony DeMarco, Boston (Vacant Massachusetts World Title)

LIGHTWEIGHTS

Dec 4	**Joe Brown** *KO* 11 Joey Lopez, Chicago

BANTAMWEIGHTS

Nov 6	**Alphonse Halimi** *W* 15 Raul Macias, Los Angeles

FLYWEIGHTS

Dec 7	**Pascual Perez** *KO* 3 Young Martin, Buenos Aires

A HALF-EMPTY STADIUM

Flyweight champion Pascual Perez was not only a dominant titlist, but an exciting one as well. Nonetheless, he couldn't draw in his native Argentina, at least not to the satisfaction of his manager, Lazaro Koci.

On December 7, Perez defended against Spain's Young Martin at the cavernous Boca Juniors Soccer Stadium in Buenos Aires. Koci expected a crowd of 80,000. The fight drew half of that.

Those in attendance were treated to yet another example of the champion's crunching power. Perez and Martin studied each other in rounds one and two. In the third, Perez, having seen enough, landed a right hand. Martin collapsed, and was staggering against the ropes at the count of 10. The bout was halted at the 2:05 mark.

As Perez celebrated, Koci looked toward the future.

"We will fight in Chile, Uruguay, Europe, the United States, anywhere but here," he said. "We cannot get large enough purses, and Perez will not fight here again.

Koci would keep his word; Perez would compete in 112-pound title fights for three more years, but never again would he fight in Argentina.

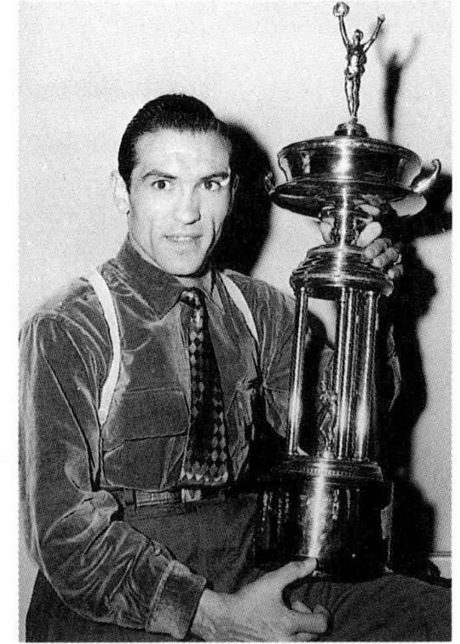

Argentina's great world flyweight champion Pascual Perez (shown with trophy) looked unbeatable in knocking out Young Martin.

WORKING LIKE A CHARM

While dressing for his title defense against Joey Lopes, lightweight champion Joe Brown placed his good luck charm in the pocket of his robe. It was a plastic key that had been made in school by his eight-year-old son. With pun intended, he later claimed it was his key to victory.

Brown-Lopes came on December 4, before a disappointing Chicago Stadium crowd of 4,194. Three months before, the lightweights had fought to a draw in a non-title bout. Lopes would again prove difficult – until the 11th round.

The challenger, a busy fighter without knockout power, took an early lead by attacking behind his jab. Brown counterpunched sharply, and accelerated in the seventh, during which he felled Lopes with a right uppercut.

After 10 rounds, the fight was close, with the champion leading on two of the three cards. In the 11th, he exploded, twice dropping Lopes with rights. At the 1:50 mark, referee Joey White intervened.

"I made the fight," complained the loser. "All he could do was counterpunch."

True, but it had worked like a charm.

Lopes (right) surprised the experts by holding Joe Brown to a 10-round draw in a non-title bout.

HALIMI UNIFIES THE TITLE, QUIETLY

Boxing fans circled the date when it was announced that on November 6 at Wrigley Field in Los Angeles, world bantamweight champion Alphonse Halimi and NBA king Raul (Raton) Macias would unify the title. The local police circled it twice.

Los Angeles' Mexican-Americans were rabid Macias fans, and, fearing the ramifications of an unpopular decision, the city assigned five times the usual number of police to the fight.

"I'm fighting for the glory of Mexico!" Macias declared.

Boxing out of a crouch, Halimi proved quicker and busier.

There were no knockdowns, and neither fighter ever hurt the other. As fate would have it, the bout went the distance, and the decision was split.

When Halimi was declared the winner (scores of 148-141, 143-137, and 141-144), the police braced themselves. To their relief, there were lots of tears, but no violence.

The Rat sent his fans home as meek as mice.

JANUARY

1958

JUNE

A FREAK SHOW IN CHICAGO STADIUM

Apparently, Carmen Basilio wasn't the superstitious type. Despite having lost three disputed decisions in Chicago (to Billy Graham, Chuck Davey, and Johnny Saxton), the middleweight champion signed to defend against Sugar Ray Robinson at Chicago Stadium on March 25. There wasn't a rabbit's foot or a horseshoe to be found.

Six months before, Basilio had dethroned Robinson by unanimous decision. But that had been in New York.

It was predictable that Basilio's fourth fight in Chicago would be controversial. This time the judge who scored for *Basilio* was accused of wearing a blindfold.

Basilio effectively pressured Robinson over the first four rounds. In the fifth, Sugar Ray scored with a hook to the jaw and a right that found the left side of the champion's face. By the sixth, Basilio's left eye was swollen, and before another round had passed, it was closed shut. As the fight progressed, the swelling turned a hideous purple-gray, with Basilio resembling an extra from a grade-B science fiction movie. There was nothing his trainer, Angelo Dundee, could do.

Amazingly, the champion lasted the distance. Forced to advance cautiously, he allowed Robinson to box as he pleased.

But even against a one-eyed fighter, Sugar Ray was unimpressive. He failed to hurt Basilio, and he missed more rights than he landed.

As for the numbers, 30 of 32 ringside reporters had Robinson ahead. Two of the judges agreed, scoring 71-64 and 72-64. But referee Frank Sikora saw Basilio the winner, 69-66.

Sugar Ray didn't mind. At age 36, he had just been crowned middleweight king for the fifth time. How many more times would he break his own record?

With unparalleled resilience, 36-year-old Ray Robinson (left) regained the middleweight crown by decisioning Carmen Basilio in 15 rounds in Chicago.

RINGSIDE VIEW

JANUARY

Boxing for the first time since March 1956, heavyweight contender Sonny Liston scores a second-round knockout of Bill Hunter in Chicago.

JUNE

In his final fight, former welterweight champion Kid Gavilan, 32, is outpointed over 10 rounds by Yama Bahama in Miami Beach. Gavilan exits with a career mark of 107-30-6 (28), and the distinction of having never been kayoed or stopped.

ELIMINATION, ONE BY ONE

When Carmen Basilio won the middleweight title by upsetting Sugar Ray Robinson, among those cheering loudest were Virgil Akins and Isaac Logart. Basilio was the reigning welter champ, and as soon as he was declared the winner, he automatically relinquished the 147-pound crown.

On March 21 at Madison Square Garden, St. Louis' Akins, 30, and Cuba's Logart, 24, squared off in the semifinal of a mini-tournament to determine Basilio's successor. The winner would meet New Jersey's Vince Martinez later in the year.

Akins and Logart had previously met twice, with each welterweight winning once. Akins was the bigger puncher, Logart the quicker boxer. Both had engaged in 64 pro bouts. There was little to choose between the two, and by fight time, Logart was the slightest of betting choices.

Logart opened as advertised, pumping a steady jab and moving fluidly. His style was a flashy one, and Akins seemed a step behind. After five rounds, the Cuban, who hailed from Camaguey, the hometown of Kid Gavilan, was ahead by a score of 4-1 on all three cards.

Midway through the sixth, however, Akins proved that punchers can strike without notice. A right uppercut felled Logart, and later in the round, a straight right again dropped him. The Cuban picked himself up, but seconds later, referee Harry Kessler stopped the fight.

"I knew Logart would have to bob the wrong way eventually," said Akins. "He did, and I really lowered the boom. I'm going to take care of Martinez the same way, maybe quicker."

Tough talk for a fighter with 16 losses. But the unexpected success of Carmen Basilio had suddenly left Akins as boxing's best belter at welter.

Murderous-punching Virgil Akins renders Isaac Logart helpless in the sixth round of his welterweight title elimination bout in New York.

BATTLE OF LOUISIANA

Lightweight champion Joe Brown hailed from Louisiana's state capital, Baton Rouge. Challenger Ralph Dupas was a product of Louisiana's biggest city, New Orleans. Why, then, was their fight held in Houston, Texas?

In boxing, why ask why?

On May 7, at the Sam Houston Coliseum, Brown defended against a 22-year-old fighter with 83 bouts of pro experience. Dupas was quick and clever, and his jab briefly troubled the champion. But Brown flashed his own educated left, then, in round four, introduced his right hand.

Forcing the action, Brown exploded in the eighth. His first knockdown should have ended the fight, but referee Jimmy Webb halted his count at nine because Brown had begun to advance toward his fallen foe. No matter. Two more knockdowns followed, and Webb stopped the fight at the 2:21 mark.

With four kayos in four defenses, Brown was developing into a dominant champion. Certain members of the media had begun to call him "The Black Benny Leonard." It was the ultimate compliment.

Lightweight king Joe Brown bombards Ralph Dupas on his way to a successful defense.

HOGAN KID BASSEY AND THE BIRD

Punchers have a unique mentality, as evidenced by featherweight Ricardo (Pajarito) Moreno's reaction to an 11th-hour controversy concerning the gloves to be used in his challenge of world champion Hogan (Kid) Bassey.

"I don't care what kind of gloves we use," he said, "or if we use any gloves at all."

Having scored kayos in each of his 29 victories, Moreno was as pure a puncher as Bassey had ever faced. As a result, their bout was among the most eagerly anticipated of the year.

The Nigerian champion and Mexican challenger squared off on April 1 at Los Angeles' Wrigley Field. Both sizzled in the first round, with Moreno punching harder, but Bassey more accurately. Bassey controlled the second, then proved his versatility in the third, when he flaunted his own power. An overhand right connected, and Moreno fell face-first. He was counted out by referee Tommy Hart at the 2:58 mark.

Bassey's sensational victory provided a lesson: a good *fighter* will always beat a good *puncher*. With or without gloves.

WORLD TITLE FIGHTS

MIDDLEWEIGHTS		LIGHTWEIGHTS	
March 25	**Sugar Ray Robinson** *W* 15 Carmen Basilio, Chicago	May 7	**Joe Brown** *KO* 8 Ralph Dupas, Houston
WELTERWEIGHTS		**FEATHERWEIGHTS**	
Jan 21	**Virgil Akins** *KO* 12 Tony DeMarco, Boston	April 1	**Hogan (Kid) Bassey** *KO* 3 Ricardo Moreno, Los Angeles
June 5	**Virgil Akins** *KO* 4 Vince Martinez, St. Louis (Vacant World Title)	**FLYWEIGHTS**	
		April 19	**Pascual Perez** *W* 15 Ramon Arias, Caracas

TAKING THE TITLE BY FORCE

Over the course of his 11-year career, Virgil Akins had developed a reputation for being a slow starter. In fact, in 66 fights, he had scored only one first-round knockout.

He picked a helluva night to work up an early sweat.

On June 5, before a crowd of 9,777 at the Arena in St. Louis, Akins, the hometown favorite and 2-1 betting choice, faced Vince Martinez in the final bout of a mini-tournament to fill the vacant welterweight title.

Slow starter?

Before the first round was over, Akins had scored five knockdowns. He added two in round three, and two in round four. After Martinez fell for the ninth time, referee Harry Kessler waved the fight over without issuing a count.

"Vince is the fifth fighter who was never on the floor until meeting Virgil," said Eddie Yawitz, Akins' manager.

The slow starter had turned into a fast finisher.

Virgil Akins (right) knocked out Vince Martinez in the fourth round to gain the undisputed welterweight crown in St. Louis.

JULY

1958

DECEMBER

RINGSIDE VIEW

SEPTEMBER

In a non-title bout, featherweight champion Hogan (Kid) Bassey comes from behind to kayo 36-year-old former titlist Willie Pep in round nine.

SEPTEMBER

London's 22-year-old Terry Downes wins the vacant British middleweight title with a 13th-round stoppage of Phil Edwards.

OCTOBER

Pierro Rollo wins the European bantamweight title, outpointing former world champion Mario D'Agata over 15 rounds in Cagliari, Italy.

NOVEMBER

In a non-title bout in Miami Beach, rugged Johnny Busso earns a title try by decisioning lightweight champion Joe Brown.

HIS TOUGHEST CRITIC IS HIMSELF

For Floyd Patterson, boxing was both a physical and mental discipline. On August 18, before 21,680 fans at Wrigley Field in Los Angeles, the heavyweight champion retained the title for the third time, stopping formerly undefeated Roy Harris, the pride of Cut and Shoot, Texas, after 12 rounds. Patterson scored four knockdowns and lost only one round. But after the fight, reporters found a dissatisfied Patterson doing situps on the floor of his dressing room.

"None of my punches were working tonight," he complained. "I just couldn't get started."

For a flat fighter, Patterson had been overwhelming. Harris scared him in round two, dropping the champion with a right uppercut. But Patterson answered with knockdowns of his own in rounds seven, eight, and 12.

With Harris woozy and bleeding from a bad cut over the left eye, his trainer Bill Gore signalled surrender before the 13th round.

Harris was left to wonder what it might have been like had Patterson been sharp.

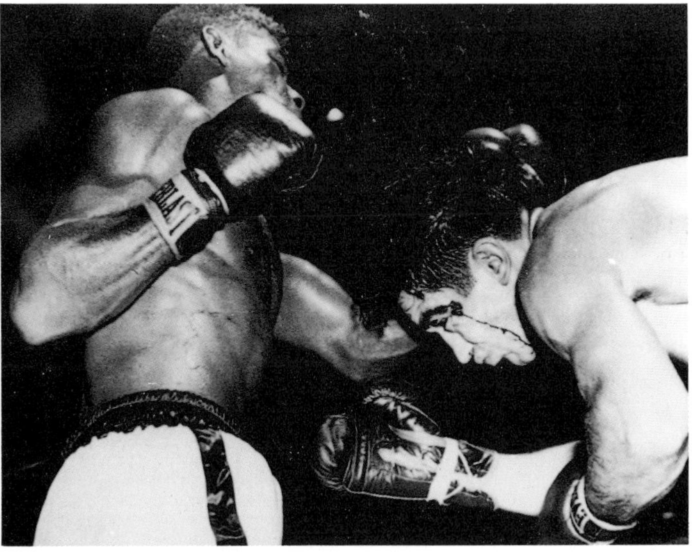

Floyd Patterson's lone title defense in 1958 was his kayo victory over Texan Roy Harris (right).

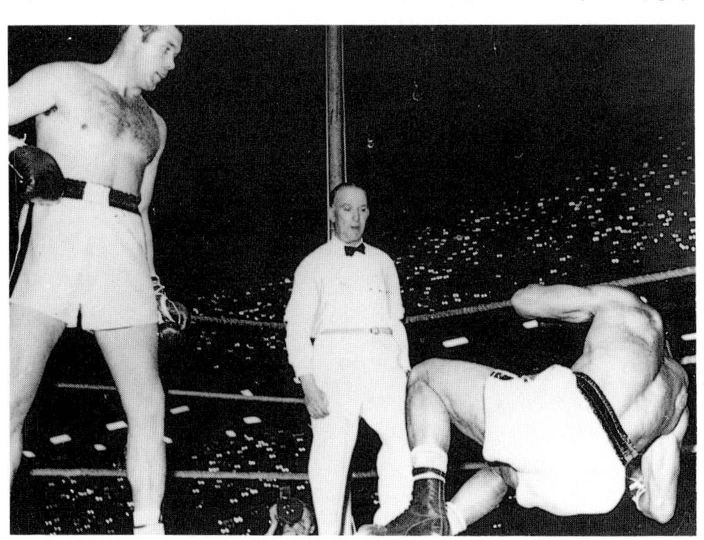

Sweden's Ingemar Johansson knocked out top contender Eddie Machen in one round.

A RIGHT HAND LIKE THUNDER

In the gold medal match at the 1952 Olympics, Ingemar Johansson was disqualified for lack of effort. On September 14, before a partisan crowd of more than 55,000 at Ullevi Stadium in Johansson's hometown of Goteborg, Sweden, the European champion showed the world what he was capable of. In a crossroads matchup of unbeaten 25-year-olds, Johansson squared off against 2-1 favorite Eddie Machen. The USA's Machen, 24-0 (16), was rated second. Johansson, 20-0 (12), sixth.

About a minute into round one, Johansson connected with his primary weapon, a straight right, and Machen collapsed. Forty-five seconds later, he struck again. Same weapon, same result. This time, Irish referee Edward Smythe counted Machen out.

The heavyweight division was alive: Sonny Liston was fighting again, and Ingemar Johansson was trying. Suddenly, Floyd Patterson had plenty to worry about.

BAD ADVICE FROM THE DOC

Lightweight champion Joe Brown had kayoed his first four title challengers. Defense number five, which came on July 23 at Houston's Sam Houston Coliseum, figured to be a bit more difficult. In the opposite corner stood Kenny Lane, an aggressive, albeit featherfisted, southpaw, and the first left-hander to challenge for the 135-pound crown since Lew Tendler 35 years before.

Lane was managed by one of the shrewdest handlers in history, the ageless Jack (Doc) Kearns, who had previously guided Jack Dempsey and Mickey Walker, among other boxers. Ironically, Kearns' advice may have cost Lane the title.

Lane forced the fight and built a sizeable lead. Brown managed to rally in the second half, repeatedly stunning the challenger with counter hooks, and after 14 rounds, the bout was dead-even. It was the champion who accelerated in the 15th, and at the final bell, Lane was dizzy and stumbling.

The decision was close but unanimous for Brown. (Scores of 143-142, 144-143, and 145-141.)

"I lost the fight," said Kearns. "I thought Lane was well in front, and I told him to coast in the last round. I didn't want him to take chances. It is my fault."

AGELESS ARCHIE SETS A RECORD THE HARD WAY

Having twice failed in efforts to win the heavyweight title, Archie Moore would have been excused for fading away. But on December 10 at the Montreal Forum, the 44-year-old light heavyweight champion had plenty of motivation for his defense against French-Canadian fisherman Yvon Durelle.

FIGHTING TALK

I have fought smart men before, but never anyone as smart as that fellow

YVON DURELLE
after being kayoed by light heavyweight champion Archie Moore

Moore climbed through the ropes sharing the all-time record for knockouts (126) with Young Stribling. However, before breaking the tie, the 3-1 favorite flirted with defeat.

Crude and aggressive, Durelle ambushed Moore, scoring three knockdowns in the first round, and one in the fifth. "The Ol' Mongoose" seemed doomed, but Moore found a way to buy time.

With Durelle tiring, the champion began to mount his rally. Moore downed the challenger in the seventh round, at the end of the 10th, and for referee Jack Sharkey's 10-count in the 11th. At the time of the stoppage, Moore was ahead on all three of the cards.

It was a remarkable victory for a remarkable fighter. Ageless Archie Moore had made one thing perfectly clear: he wasn't going to simply fade away.

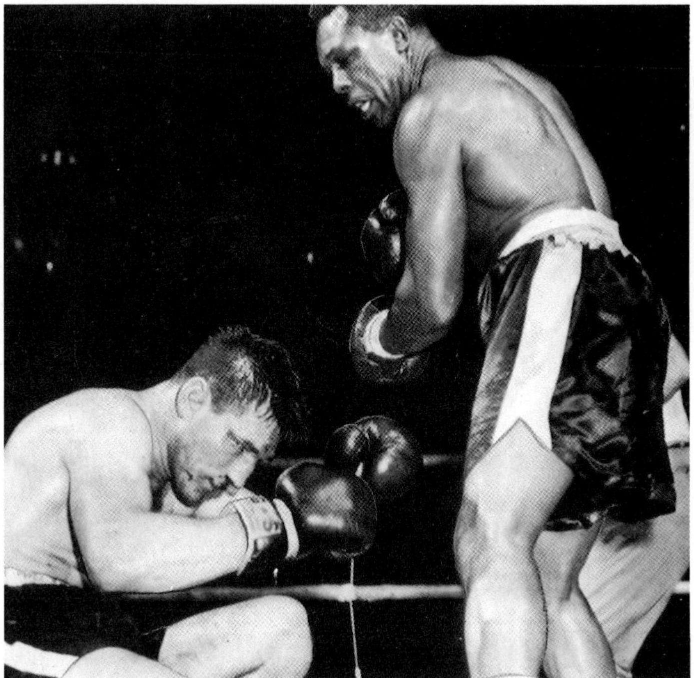

Light heavyweight king Archie Moore watches rugged Canadian Yvon Durelle slump to the floor in the 11th round of a great fight.

PASCUAL PEREZ, THE FLYING FLY

In an effort to maximize purses and defend against fresh competition, Argentine flyweight champion Pascual Perez was turning into boxing's road warrior. On December 15 at the Manila Football Stadium in the Philippines, he defended against local favorite Dommy Ursua. It was the island's first world title fight in 11 years, and 42,000 of the challenger's compatriots, including President Carlos P. Garcia and his entire cabinet, offered their support. It wasn't enough for Ursua.

Argentina's brilliant, undefeated world flyweight champion Pascual Perez (right) retained his title with a dazzling victory over Dommy Ursua of the Philipines.

Had the bout been held anywhere but the Philippines, Ursua would likely have been disqualified. From first round to last, he butted, hit on the break, rabbit punched, and thumbed. Referee Frankie Carter repeatedly warned him, but deducted no points.

Ursua scored big in rounds one and 13. The rest of the fight, however, belonged to Perez. The champion counterpunched with precision and captured a unanimous decision by scores of 149-141, 145-142, and 146-142. It was his 49th bout without a loss.

Next stop: Japan.

THE ARROWS OF GERONIMO

Growing up with 18 brothers and sisters, Los Angeles welterweight Don Jordan never lacked for playmates. His favorite game was bow and arrows, and he became an adept shooter. Hence the nickname "Geronimo."

Because the only weapons allowed were his fists, Jordan was a 3-1 underdog for his December 5 challenge of welterweight champion Virgil Akins. Boxing in front of 7,344 of his hometown fans at LA's Olympic Auditorium, Jordan proved a good marksman.

Round after round was the same: Akins forcing his way inside and punching from all angles, and Jordan countering in his polished style. Referee Lee Grossman penalized Akins for punching low in the eighth and butting in the 14th. The champion's vaunted power never surfaced, and after 15 rounds, Jordan's hometown fans celebrated his unanimous decision triumph. (Scores of 145-138, 145-132, and 146-136.)

Bullseye!

WORLD TITLE FIGHTS

HEAVYWEIGHTS

Aug 18	**Floyd Patterson** *KO* 13 Roy Harris, Los Angeles

LIGHT HEAVYWEIGHTS

Dec 10	**Archie Moore** *KO* 11 Yvon Durelle, Montreal

WELTERWEIGHTS

Dec 5	**Don Jordan** (USA) *W* 15 Virgil Akins, Los Angeles

LIGHTWEIGHTS

July 23	**Joe Brown** *W* 15 Kenny Lane, Houston

FLYWEIGHTS

Dec 15	**Pascual Perez** *W* 15 Dommy Ursua, Manila

Sugar Ray Robinson

IN THE picturebook of boxing's kings, there is no image more regal than Sugar Ray Robinson reigning on Seventh Avenue in Harlem, his flamingo pink Cadillac convertible parked in front of the Sugar Ray Lounge. Everything about him suggested he was The Man. Given the immortals of the ring – Ali and Johnson, Dempsey and Louis, Armstrong and Pep, Duran and Monzon, Benny Leonard and Sugar Ray Leonard, it is telling that Robinson is consistently singled out as the best of them all. He didn't compile a perfect record, as did Rocky Marciano, or transcend the ring and symbolize his era, as did Dempsey and Ali. He won the middleweight title five times, but lost it four times, and fought long past his prime. Still, his credentials are unquestioned. No one before or since has so magnificently combined style, substance, and accomplishment.

Robinson was born Walker Smith Jr. on May 3, 1921, in Detroit. His parents, Walker Smith Sr., a construction worker, and Leila Hurst Smith, separated when Robinson and his two sisters were children. His mother moved the family to New York City – Robinson was 11 – and they eventually settled in Harlem. Sugar Ray's first boxing experience came at the Brewster Center in Detroit, where he watched in wonder as a heavily hyped teenager named Joe Louis banged the bags. In New York, Robinson was 15 when he met trainer George Gainford at the Salem-Crescent Athletic Club. The Gainford-Robinson marriage would last for 30 years.

Walker Smith Jr. changed his name when Gainford entered him into an amateur tournament. Robinson, underage, borrowed the identification of one of Gainford's bootleg fighters. (The real Ray Robinson became a bartender.) The Sugar was added by George Case, a newspaper editor in Watertown, New York. After Robinson had won a bantamweight bout, Case wrote that his boxing was sweeter than sugar. Robinson won all of his sanctioned amateur bouts – 85 in all – and on October 4, 1940, turned pro at Madison Square Garden, scoring a second-round kayo of Joe Echevarria on the undercard of the first Fritzie Zivic-Henry Armstrong title fight.

Flashing fast feet and faster fists, and utilizing his ability to adapt to his opponent's style, Robinson rose at a meteoric pace. He won his first 40 bouts, and in 1941, only his second year as a pro, defeated a former champion in Zivic, a future champion in Marty Servo, and a reigning champion in NBA lightweight king Sammy Angott.

Incredibly, Robinson's first try at a title didn't come until December 1946. There were four reasons: 1) he was black; 2) he was too good; 3) World War II interrupted his momentum – Robinson was inducted into the Army in February 1943; 4) as a self-managed fighter, he refused to do business with the mob, which controlled most of the

Professional career dates 1940-52; 1954-65
Contests 202
Won 175
Lost 19
Drawn 6
No-Contests 2
Knockouts 110
World Welterweight Champion 1946-1951
World Middleweight Champion 1951-1952; 1955-1957; 1958-1960

Welterweight champ Robinson (right) shared the 1947 *Ring* magazine awards with the middleweight king, Tony Zale.

world titles. In the interim, it took a full-fledged middleweight to beat him. On February 5, 1943, Robinson was floored and outpointed by Jake LaMotta. In six bouts vs. "The Raging Bull," it would be his only defeat. In fact, Sugar Ray wouldn't lose again for more than eight years.

On December 20, 1946, Robinson finally received his chance. Welterweight champion Servo was forced to retire after a nose injury, and Robinson and Tommy Bell, whom he had already beaten, were matched to determine the new titlist. Robinson's victory, which came by unanimous decision, was a mere formality. (He did, however, have to rise from a flash knockdown.) Over the next 3½ years, he defended five times, rejecting Jimmy Doyle, Chuck Taylor, Bernard Docusen, Kid Gavilan, and Charley Fusari. Only the Doyle fight was notable; Robinson's ninth-round kayo came easily enough, but one day after the bout, the challenger died from head injuries suffered in the ring. Robinson was torn by the tragedy. Still, when asked whether he had meant to put Doyle "in trouble," he answered honestly. "Mister," he said, "it's my business to get him in trouble."

With nowhere to go but up, Robinson jumped to middleweight. After winning the Pennsylvania world title, he challenged a familiar rival for world honors. Robinson-LaMotta VI, which came at Chicago Stadium on February 13, 1951, came to be known as "The St. Valentine Day's Massacre." As sharp as he would ever be, Robinson pummeled the champion until LaMotta was rescued in round 13. *The New York Times'* James Dawson described the bout as "a struggle that turned into a slaughter."

Steadfastly refusing to fight exclusively for the mob-controlled International Boxing Club, Robinson became among the toughest negotiators in ring history. From 1951 to 1961, he negotiated for 15 title bouts at middleweight, and one at light heavyweight. Before Robinson's first 160-pound defense, vs. England's strong and awkward Randy Turpin, he was softened by a three-month tour of Europe. (Sugar Ray was the first champion to travel with a complete entourage.) Flat and unfocused, Robinson lost on points. Two months later, a cut above his left eye created a sense of urgency, and he kayoed Turpin in round 10.

Robinson was the perfect fighting machine the night he won the middleweight crown from Jake LaMotta.

In 1952, Sugar Ray successfully defended against Bobo Olson and Rocky Graziano. (In his autobiography, he claimed he had turned down $1-million cash to throw the Graziano bout.)

Then, on June 25 at Yankee Stadium, he failed in an effort to capture Joey Maxim's light heavyweight title. Robinson was ahead on all three cards when kayoed by the 100-degree heat. He remained on his stool at the start of the 14th round. It would be the only stoppage defeat in a 202-bout career.

Sugar Ray announced his retirement in December 1952, and spent two years as a tap dancer. But his investments, which included his cafe, a dry cleaning shop, a barber shop, and a bakery, began to suffer, bringing an inevitable return to the ring. In his second return bout, he was badly beaten by Tiger Jones. The loss only stiffened his resolve. Robinson earned a title shot by split decisioning number-one contender Rocky Castellani. On December 9, 1955, he regained the crown by crushing Olson in two rounds.

After yet another victory over Olson (the fourth in seven years), Sugar Ray was dethroned by rugged Gene Fullmer. In the rematch, he knocked out Fullmer with what is still considered the best punch ever thrown, a fifth-round hook that was released without as much as a pivot. "I don't know anything about that punch," Fullmer said, "except I watched it on movies a couple of times." Robinson next dueled with welterweight champion Carmen Basilio, losing the title and then regaining it six months later in two 15-round classics.

On January 22, 1960, Sugar Ray, 38, was dethroned for the final time, losing on points to the clever and cautious Paul Pender. This time he lost the rematch, too, and was subsequently twice beaten by NBA champion Fullmer. Robinson fought as a journeyman until November 10, 1965, when, at age 44, he was decisioned by Joey Archer. His final mark: 175-19-6 (110), with 2 no-contests.

He turned to acting, making movies and starring in television shows, and in 1969, founded the highly successful Sugar Ray Robinson Youth Foundation, which aided underprivileged youngsters in Los Angeles.

Robinson's health soon began to fail him. He suffered from diabetes, hypertension, and Alzheimer's Disease, and in his last years, his second wife, Millie Robinson, shielded him from the public as best she could. Robinson died of natural causes on April 12, 1989. He was 67. Said Rev. Jesse Jackson: "He was as authentic to America as jazz. Sugar Ray Robinson was an original art form." And the best fighter there ever was.

Longtime buddy Joe Louis helps Robinson prepare for his 1951 title bout with Jake LaMotta.

JANUARY

1959

JUNE

ONE FIGHT, AND ALMOST ANOTHER

Sonny Liston may not have been faster than heavyweight champion Floyd Patterson, but he seemed so much bigger and stronger. After watching him destroy Mike DeJohn on February 18 at the Miami Beach Exhibition Hall, a national television audience concluded that he was meaner, too.

Liston bloodied DeJohn's nose over the first two rounds, and later twice sent his mouthpiece flying. The mismatch ended in the sixth, when Liston scored consecutive knockdowns with the same punch, a right to the solar plexus. After DeJohn's second fall, referee Jimmy Peerless called a halt.

When Liston crossed the ring to shake his victim's hand, DeJohn resisted, claiming he had been hit while on one knee. (Liston would later apologize for the blatant foul.)

DeJohn cursed Liston, who responded by swinging and missing. DeJohn's handlers quickly separated the heavyweights, and there was no further activity.

After scoring his 16th straight win, Liston called for Eddie Machen, Zora Folley, or Nino Valdes. "Only rated fighters," he insisted.

Floyd Patterson wasn't on his list. Yet.

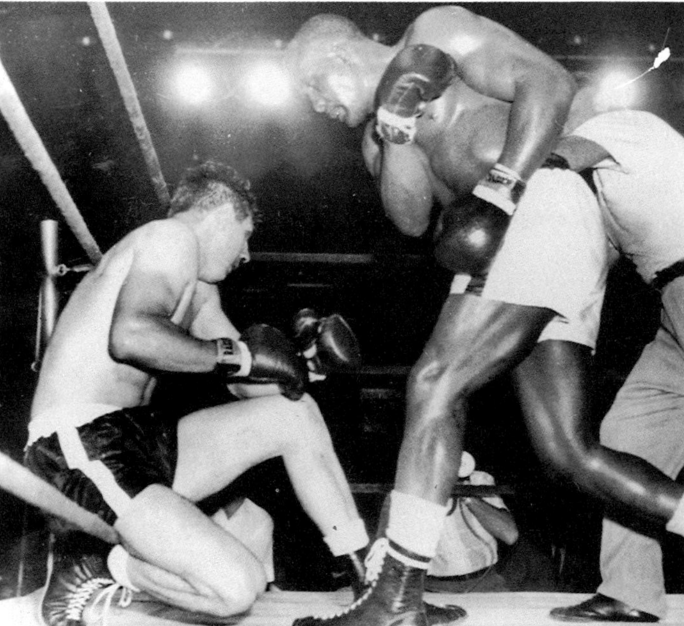

Surging toward a shot at the heavyweight crown, ferocious Sonny Liston destroyed Mike DeJohn in six rounds, and then wanted to fight again.

"WHAT HELD THAT GUY UP?"

Lightweight Joe Brown was still considered one of the best champions in boxing. But were "Old Bones'" bones getting old? Over the second half of 1958, Brown gave hope to challengers by only edging Kenny Lane, and losing a non-title bout to Johnny Busso.

On February 11, at Houston's Sam Houston Coliseum, Brown, making his sixth defense, was rematched with Busso. The New Yorker was dangerous; aside from having already defeated Brown, he was a legitimate puncher. Most of Brown's previous challengers had been featherfists.

Busso fought aggressively, but almost all of his power shots missed. Brown countered with precision, and by the middle rounds, Busso was bleeding from the nose and squinting through a badly swollen left eye.

"What held that guy up?" Brown later wondered.Brown scored a ninth-round knockdown and went on to take a unanimous decision by scores of 148-141, 149-140, and 147-136.

World Title Fights

HEAVYWEIGHTS	
May 1	**Floyd Patterson** *KO* 11 Brian London, Indianapolis
June 26	**Ingemar Johansson** (SWE) *KO* 3 Floyd Patterson, Bronx, NY
WELTERWEIGHTS	
April 24	**Don Jordan** *W* 15 Virgil Akins, St. Louis
JUNIOR WELTERWEIGHTS	
March 12	**Carlos Ortiz** (USA) *KO* 3 Kenny Lane, New York City (Vacant World Title)
LIGHTWEIGHTS	
Feb 11	**Joe Brown** *W* 15 Johnny Busso, Houston
June 3	**Joe Brown** *KO* 9 Paolo Rosi, Washington, D.C.
FEATHERWEIGHTS	
March 18	**Davey Moore** (USA) *KO* 14 Hogan (Kid) Bassey, Los Angeles

A BLOODY BAD BREAK

One week before the biggest fight of his life, Davey Moore ran a fever, the result of infected tonsils. But he decided to keep his date with featherweight champion Hogan (Kid) Bassey, scheduled for March 18 at Los Angeles' Olympic Auditorium. Good choice. He overcame a potentially disastrous case of prefight jitters and chopped up Bassey en route to a 14th-round TKO victory.

Bassey capitalized on the American's tentative start by punching with conviction to both the head and body. But in the third, the champion suffered a deep cut over his right eye, and in the eighth, his left eye was opened, too. His face a hideous mask of blood, Bassey could only inch forward in hopes of finding the challenger.

"I couldn't see, I couldn't see," the Nigerian later complained. "The blood was running in my eyes."

Moore controlled the middle and late rounds with his jab, and between the 13th and 14th, George Biddles, Bassey's manager, surrendered.

"I wouldn't send him out to be murdered, champion or not," he explained.

The newly crowned champion had another date to keep – with the surgeon who would remove his tonsils. That ice cream was sure going to taste good.

Featherweight king Davey Moore (right) after stopping badly battered Hogan "Kid" Bassey.

INGO'S SECRET – BINGO!

Reporters watched Ingemar Johansson's final training sessions in amazement. Only days before the Swede's challenge of heavyweight champion Floyd Patterson, Johansson seemed without a clue. How, the writers wondered, had the European champion ever built a reputation for having a big right hand?

"When I throw my right," Johansson said, "it moves so fast that no one can see it."

So that explained it.

Johansson and Patterson traded punches on June 26 at Yankee Stadium. Ingo threw one right in the first round, and a few close range left-right combos to the body in the second. Then came the third round, during which the ringside press, if not Patterson, saw Johansson's right over and over again.

There were seven knockdowns in all, and after the final flooring, referee Ruby Goldstein saved Patterson from further embarrassment. The time of the stoppage was 2:03.

Boxing had a new heavyweight champion.

"I saw his right plenty of times – after the regular drills were over," said Whitey Bimstein, who had trained Johansson. "I knew he had it."

Let' say the secret was out.

Sweden's Ingemar Johansson floored Floyd Patterson seven times in the third and final round and became the new world heavyweight champion.

WINNING THE WRONG WAY?

Multiple choice question for the top heavyweights of the late-'50s:

Would you rather:
A) Take a barefoot stroll across hot coals
B) Skyjump without a parachute
C) Swim 10 laps in a shark-infested pool
D) Fight Sonny Liston

Correct answer: A, B, or C.

Liston was creating a Catch-22 situation: by crushing all of his opponents, he was convincing the top heavyweights to avoid him.

On April 15 in Miami Beach, the streaking contender easily defeated one of the division's most dangerous punchers, Cleveland Williams. The Texan's jabs bothered Liston in the first round, but as soon as Sonny committed to a body attack, Williams crumbled. There were two knockdowns in round three, and referee Jimmy Peerless halted the slaughter at the 2:04 mark.

Liston was beginning to call for world champion Floyd Patterson. But Cus D'Amato, Patterson's manager, had unplugged the phone.

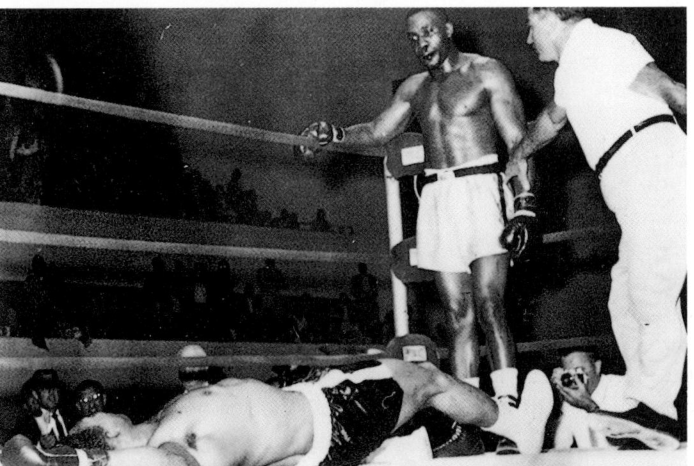

Awesome Sonny Liston paralyzed Cleveland Williams in the third round at Miami Beach, adding to his reputation as the most feared heavyweight on the scene.

WIN FRIENDS, BUT LOSE THE FIGHT

Brian London gave the stereotypical British standup boxer a bad name. London was crude, rude, rough, tough, and naughty. But while in Indianapolis before his May 1 challenge of heavyweight champion Floyd Patterson, the invader charmed the locals. And during the fight, at the Indianapolis Fairgrounds Coliseum, he seemed more intent on mimicking Patterson than maiming him.

London boxed in a poor man's version of Patterson's signature peekaboo style. He held his gloves by his face and kept his elbows tucked in. All he forgot to do was punch. Busy, but not particularly accurate, Patterson took round after round. He exploded at the end of the 10th, and in the 11th, a flurry, puncuated by a picture-book hook, dropped London. The challenger quivered on his back, then twisted over to his side, with his face pressing against the canvas. Referee Frank Sikora could have counted to 50.

Imitation is the sincerest form of flattery. The idea, however, had been for London to *flatten* Patterson, not *flatter* him.

RINGSIDE VIEW

JANUARY

Flyweight champion Pascual Perez loses for the first time in 51 bouts, dropping a 10-round non-title decision to Japan's Sadao Yaoita in Tokyo.

MARCH

At Madison Square Garden, Carlos Ortiz stops Kenny Lane in the third round to win the vacant world junior welterweight title. The throne had been vacant for almost 13 years.

APRIL

Welterweight champion Don Jordan overcomes a badly sprained right hand and scores a unanimous 15-round decision over former titlist Virgil Akins.

JULY

1959

DECEMBER

WHO NEEDS SUGAR RAY ROBINSON?

On August 28, at the Cow Palace in San Francisco, Gene Fullmer and Carmen Basilio, a pair of former world middleweight champions, clashed for the vacant NBA 160-pound crown. Sugar Ray Robinson, who hadn't defended since regaining the crown from Basilio in March 1958, was still recognized in New York and Massachusetts, but nowhere else.

As if trying to punch out the ghost of Robinson, Fullmer and Basilio set a sizzling pace. (The first round was among the best in title fight history.) Basilio charged forward and pumped both fists to the body. But instead of meeting him in ring center, Fullmer retreated and countered. Ringsiders were incredulous; Fullmer had never before banked on finesse.

The battle was competitive, but Fullmer won most of the rounds. In the 14th, he connected with an overhand right, and Basilio slumped toward the canvas until seated on the bottom rope. It counted as a knockdown, the first of his career.

Referee Jack Downey was about to intervene when Angelo Dundee, Basilio's chief second, climbed into the ring and surrendered.

Fullmer had just hammered Basilio, but his best shot came during the postfight press conference. "I'm the champ of 48 states, and he's the champ of two states," Fullmer said of Robinson. "We'll divide the purse that way."

Gene Fullmer (right) stopped Carmen Basilio to win the middleweight championship.

THE MULE AND THE THOROUGHBRED

Boxing's top light heavyweights could only hope that age would conquer champion Archie Moore. They weren't doing a very good job of it.

On August 12 at the Montreal Forum, Moore, 45, defended the 175-pound crown in a rematch against French-Canadian contender Yvon Durelle. In December 1958, Durelle scored three first-round knockdowns before suffering a knockout in round 11.

Yvon Durelle is battered into submission in third round by defending king Archie Moore.

Older, wiser, and no less able, Moore made sure to start quickly. Durelle enjoyed moderate success in the first and second rounds, but in the third, Moore exploded. There were four knockdowns in all, and at the 2:52 mark, referee Jack Sharkey counted out the challenger.

Afterward, Durelle engaged in a display of self-flagellation.

"I am a bum," he said. "I go home. I never fight again. I am heartbroken. Sick. Sick. Sick."

Moore's postfight analysis was a bit more keen. Speaking metaphorically, as he often did, the champion said, "You should not enter a mule in a race at Santa Anita." Spoken like a true thoroughbred.

AVENGING THE LOSS OF THE RAT

Before trying for Alphonse Halimi's bantamweight title, Jose Becerra willingly placed the hopes of an entire nation on his broad shoulders.

"I'm fighting to bring the title back to Mexico," he said.

In November 1957, Halimi had unified the title by outpointing Mexico's top fistic hero, NBA champion Raul (Raton) Macias. He hadn't defended since.

On July 8 at the brand new Sports Arena in Los Angeles, Becerra thrilled the 15,110 in attendance by steamrolling the champion. Becerra initially took three blows to land one, but his intensity soon paid off; Halimi became a stationary target.

"We told him 1,000 times to stay off the ropes," said Joe Rizzo, Halimi's American representative.

In the eighth round, Halimi fell twice. The second knockdown, produced by a thunderous hook, left him stretched motionless on the canvas. Referee Tommy Hart counted him out at the 2:02 mark. At the time of the stoppage, the fight was even on two cards, with Becerra leading on the third.

Becerra's fans gleefully carried him from the ring. Had he so requested, they would've marched all the way to Mexico.

WORLD TITLE FIGHTS

LIGHT HEAVYWEIGHTS

Aug 12	**Archie Moore** *KO* 3 Yvon Durelle, Montreal

MIDDLEWEIGHTS

Aug 28	**Gene Fullmer** *KO* 14 Carmen Basilio, San Francisco (Vacant NBA Title)
Dec 4	**Gene Fullmer** *W* 15 Spider Webb, Logan, UT

WELTERWEIGHTS

July 10	**Don Jordan** *W* 15 Denny Moyer, Portland

LIGHTWEIGHTS

Dec 2	**Joe Brown** *KO* 6 Dave Charnley, Houston

JUNIOR LIGHTWEIGHTS

July 20	**Harold Gomes** (USA) *W* 15 Paul Jorgensen, Providence (Vacant World Title)

FEATHERWEIGHTS

Aug 19	**Davey Moore** *KO* 11 Hogan (Kid) Bassey, Los Angeles

BANTAMWEIGHTS

July 8	**Jose Becerra** (MEX) *KO* 8 Alphonse Halimi, Los Angeles

FLYWEIGHTS

Aug 10	**Pascual Perez** *W* 15 Kenji Yonekura, Tokyo
Nov 5	**Pascual Perez** *KO* 13 Sadao Yaoita, Osaka

Ringside View

JULY

Welterweight champion Don Jordan retains the crown for the second time, scoring a unanimous 15-round decision over Denny Moyer.

DECEMBER

Heavyweight contender Sonny Liston continues his march to the title, knocking out Willi Besmanoff in seven rounds.

DECEMBER

In a non-title bout, lightweight champion Joe Brown scores a 10-round decision over Joey Parks in New Orleans.

BROWN'S IFS AND BUTTS

During the course of his three-year title reign, lightweight champion Joe Brown had proved his versatility. He had beaten southpaws, counterpunchers, infighters, and runners. He had won on points and by knockout. He had featured his left hand in one fight, and his right in the next. In some fights he boxed, and in others he punched. And, at least according to Dave Charnley, he butted, too.

Charnley, the British Empire 135-pound champion, faced Brown on December 2 at Houston's Sam Houston Coliseum. The left-hander figured to trouble Brown, but "Old Bones" controlled the first four rounds. Then came the controversy.

With less than 10 seconds remaining in round five, the fighters crowded each other, and Brown let go a volley. When Charnley returned to his corner, he was bleeding from a horizontal gash on his right brow.

"A right uppercut, followed by a left jab," said Brown.

"A butt," said Charnley.

"A left hook," said referee Jimmy Webb.

Webb's opinion was the only one that mattered, and when Arthur Boggis, Charnley's manager, informed the referee that his fighter was unable to continue, Webb declared Brown the winner by sixth-round TKO.

It had been an ugly fight. Apparently, Brown could win that way, too.

PEREZ MAKES PAYBACK IN ORIENT

Nat Fleischer, publisher of *The Ring*, called it "the heavyweight championship turned upside down." Flyweight champion Pascual Perez' 10th title defense, vs. Japan's Sadao Yaoita, was unlike the previous nine. In January, Yaoita had ruined Perez' perfect record by edging the Argentine in a non-title bout. Yaoita wanted the title; Perez wanted revenge.

The rematch was held on November 5 at the Ogimachi Pool in Osaka. Perez, 53-1, seemed headed for defeat when he was dropped by a right in round two. But referee Juan Notari ruled it a slip, and the champion was never again threatened. A sustained body attack slowed the mobile challenger, and by the championship rounds, Perez was punching for a knockout. The end came in round 13. Yaoita was felled twice, and counted out at the 55-second mark. (After 12 rounds, Perez led by scores of 118-112, 115-113, and 117-117.)

Perez, 33, was no longer perfect. But by stopping his lone conqueror, he proved he was still the best.

BREAKING THE SPIDER'S WEBB

"Who needs Ray Robinson?"

Such was the sentiment of Marv Jensen, the manager of NBA middleweight champion Gene Fullmer. As a result, Team Fullmer looked elsewhere for suitable competition. On December 4, they found it in the champion's backyard.

Fullmer, who hailed from West Jordan, Utah, took on Ellsworth (Spider) Webb, who had won the NCAA boxing title while attending Idaho State University, in Pocatello, Idaho. They agreed to meet somewhere in the middle, at Utah State University's George Nelson Fieldhouse, in Logan, Utah, population 16,000.

Webb had already lost on points to Fullmer (in September 1958). The champion proved no less difficult this time, suckering Webb inside, and then forcing him backward with a free-swinging, two-fisted attack. The sole highlights came in the fourth and eighth rounds, when Fullmer was downed. Both times, however, referee Ken Shulsen ruled slips.

Webb lasted the distance, with Fullmer retaining the crown by scores of 147-141, 148-136, and a ridiculous 150-132.

The fight helped establish Fullmer as a legitimate champion.

That rubber match with Robinson? Who needed it?

Joe Brown (left) retained lightweight crown by stopping Britain's Dave Charnley in the fifth round in Houston, Texas.

Middleweight champion Gene Fullmer (right) had to go the distance to retain his title when he took on a local challenger, the skilled Spider Webb at Logan.

RING DECADE

1960-1969

IN ONE of the most turbulent decades of the century, the British Invasion referred to John Lennon and Mick Jagger, not Henry Cooper and Alan Rudkin. The peace movement protested the war in the jungles of Southeast Asia, not the violence of the rings of Southern California. And the headlines were dominated by JFK and LBJ, not the WBA and WBC.

But boxing still managed to contribute significantly to the fiber of the decade. In fact, Muhammad Ali became as much a symbol of the '60s as any politician, civil rights activist, or pop icon. "The Greatest" ascended the heavyweight throne, and soon after added the unofficial title of the most famous man on the planet.

Fittingly, the decade began with Ali (then Cassius Clay) winning an Olympic gold medal. Before he came to change the way we viewed boxers, however, the U.S. government began to change the way we viewed boxing. The scrutiny began in the late-'50s, when a federal court disbanded the monopolistic International Boxing Club. In 1960 and '61, a Senate Anti-Trust and Monopoly Subcommittee focused on the integrity of the game. Chairman Estes Kefauver spotlighted the alleged underworld connections of number-one heavyweight contender Sonny Liston, as well as some of the dubious characters who had worked closely with IBC president Jim Norris. Kefauver sponsored a bill calling for the Justice Department to form a national boxing commission, but was stonewalled by Attorney General Robert Kennedy, who believed the responsibility of overseeing boxing should lie elsewhere. "The fight game is just about on the way out," testified former heavyweight champion Jack Dempsey. "In other words, it's ready to be buried if something isn't done, and done fast."

Nothing, of course, was done. There were other investigations. In 1962, five days after a national television audience watched Emile Griffith punch Benny Paret into a coma (Paret subsequently died), New York State legislators called for a public hearing.

"Boxing is just a throwback to the old gladiator stuff," said State Senator Max M. Turshen, who proposed a bill banning the sport. "Our present civilization doesn't stand for this kind of thing. We have plenty of other sports."

In 1965, in the wake of the controversial Ali-Liston rematch, Washington returned to the fray when the Senate held three days of hearings.

Said Senator Philip A. Hart: "Time is running out for the boxing industry unless something is done (to end) general public disrespect and distrust."

Slowly, the focus shifted from the sport to its most famous champion. No one had ever before seen anything like Ali, who was part Sugar Ray Robinson, part Gorgeous George, and largely an invention all his own.

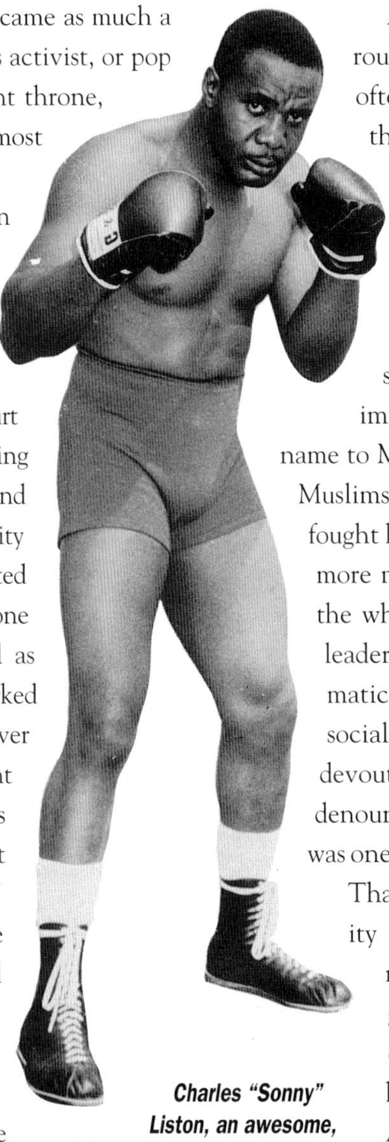

As a rising contender, Cassius Clay predicted the round in which he would stop his opponents. More often than not, he was right. He talked even faster than he punched, hypnotizing the media, and enraging the public. From the beginning he understood how to market himself: while some fans cheered him and others booed him, everyone paid attention to him.

Easy to dismiss when promoting only himself, Clay evoked the reign of Jack Johnson when, immediately after winning the title, he changed his name to Muhammad Ali and began promoting the Black Muslims. Suddenly, he was a threat not only to those who fought him, but to those who watched him as well. The more militant members of the Black Muslims viewed the white man as the devil. A student of movement leader Elijah Muhammad and a protege of the charismatic Malcolm X, Ali recast himself as a controversial social and political force. (While Ali would remain a devout Muslim, by late-'63 and '64, he came to denounce many of the movement's radical beliefs.) This was one champion who wasn't about to play by the rules.

That Ali was secure in his ideals and sense of morality became apparent in the mid-'60s, when he refused induction into the draft. Citing his religious beliefs, he requested – and was denied – exemption as a conscientious objector. America had not yet turned against the war in Southeast Asia, and when the world heavyweight champion said, "Man, I ain't got no quarrel with them Vietcong," he alienated millions of his countrymen.

Charles "Sonny" Liston, an awesome, ill-tempered ex-convict, was unquestionably the most feared fighter of his time.

Cassius Clay revolutionized not only boxing, but sports in general, with his genius for hype and self-promotion. He used wrestler Gorgeous George as his model.

Floyd Patterson became the youngest heavyweight champion and the first to regain the throne. He was taught, trained, and meticulously guided by Cus D'Amato.

Ali's principles cost him dearly. On April 28, 1967, he formally refused induction. Less than one hour later, he was stripped of the title by the New York State Athletic Commission. Soon after, the rest of the commissions followed. (Only Nat Fleischer, the editor and publisher of *The Ring*, continued to recognize Ali as champion.) Without being bested in the ring, and before being convicted of a crime, "The Greatest" was a champion no more.

Ten days later, Ali was indicted for draft evasion by a federal grand jury in Houston. In June, he was tried and convicted.

Bob Foster brought a rare excitement to the light heavyweight division with his devastating punching power. In 65 fights he scored 46 knockouts.

Unbeaten and, at the age of 25, still in his prime, Ali was through for the decade. On June 28, 1971, the U.S. Supreme Court would reverse his conviction. But no one could reverse the calendar. Ali's 3½-year exile cheated boxing of his magic, and, worse yet, cheated the fighter of his potential. With Ali hogging center stage, a handful of other special champions triumphed in relative anonymity. After Floyd Patterson and Ingemar Johansson completed their knockout-filled trilogy, Sonny Liston brought his huge fists and menacing stare to the heavyweight title. But Liston had peaked in the late-'50s, and by the time Ali humbled him, boxing's most intimidating fighter looked like a sad old man.

Youth was again served toward the end of the decade, when the indomitable Joe Frazier emerged as Ali's successor. The middle weights were dominated by Emile Griffith, who, in a decade of rivalries, dueled first with welterweights Paret and Luis Rodriguez, and then with Italian middleweight Nino Benvenuti. Light heavyweight Bob Foster and bantamweight Ruben Olivares brought frightening power to their respective divisions, and at welterweight, Cuba's Jose Napoles provided memories of Sugar Ray Robinson. Classy Carlos Ortiz won world titles in two classes, and only a horrible decision prevented Japan's Fighting Harada from winning titles in three. Flash Elorde earned respect for the junior divisions by dominating at 130 pounds. And in the first half of the decade, bantamweight Eder Jofre, a vegetarian prodigy from Brazil, established himself as the best fighter, pound for pound, in the world.

Champions like Jofre, Harada, Benvenuti, Ismael Laguna, and Nicolino Locche marked a major change: at the start of the '60s, eight of boxing's 11 world champions were from the USA. But then foreign-born fighters began to break through. By the middle of 1970, only two of the game's 15 world champions, Joe Frazier and Bob Foster, would be Americans. It was not coincidental, then, that the balance of power shifted as well. In 1962, the U.S.-dominated National Boxing Association expanded to the World Boxing Association. Its new name aside, the WBA remained void of international representation. In 1963, California promoter George Parnassus, who was seeking to advance his primarily Mexican stable, helped fill that void by bankrolling the World Boxing Council. The WBC established a broad power base by forming federations in North America, South America, the Orient, Africa, Great Britain, Europe, and Central America/the Caribbean. In the '70s, it would surpass the WBA as the most powerful body. Boxing was no longer colored red, white, and blue. But by the end of the decade, Muhammad Ali, that uniquely American phenomenon, was ready to return.

Gene Fullmer's great strength combined with unsurpassed courage and will to win earned him memorable victories over Robinson and Basilio.

JANUARY

1960

JUNE

OLE IN L.A.

It's never been particularly difficult to run a successful boxing show in Los Angeles. All a promoter has to do is pretend he's in Mexico, sign Mexican fighters, draw Mexican fans, hire a Mariachi band, and then get the hell out of the way.

On February 4, at the huge Los Angeles Coliseum, promoter Cal Eaton drew a crowd of 31,830 for a world title fight doubleheader. Puerto Rican junior welterweight champion Carlos Ortiz defended against teenage Mexican kayo artist Battling Torres, and Mexican bantamweight champion Jose Becerra met former titlist Alphonse Halimi of France.

It was estimated that half of the fans in attendance had traveled from south of the border. They went home half-happy. Becerra came from behind to knock out Halimi with a crushing hook in the ninth round, but Ortiz outclassed the 18-year-old Torres, stopping him with a straight right in the 10th.

The Mexicans went one-for-two. Perfect. Something to keep *everyone* happy.

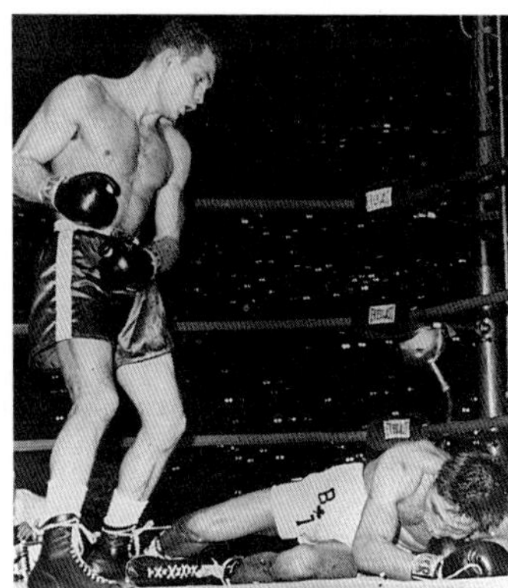

Carlos Ortiz stops Battling Torres.

THE SWEETNESS HAS LEFT THE SUGAR

In the first world title fight of the new decade, Sugar Ray Robinson proved that his time had passed. Having been stripped of the NBA middleweight title for his failure to defend against Carmen Basilio, Robinson was still recognized as champion in New York and Massachusetts. But after defending against Paul Pender on January 22 and the Boston Garden, even that distinction no longer remained. Robinson, 38, was a 4-1 favorite against Pender, a local contender who had once quit boxing to become a fireman. He tried to justify the odds in the first couple of rounds, but Pender was careful, and a sloppy Sugar Ray missed more than he connected.

As he had promised, Pender fought cautiously until the stretch. (During the eighth and ninth rounds, both fighters were content to jab, and the crowd of 10,608 booed them.) The challenger was quicker and busier over the last five rounds, and the judges rewarded him with a split decision. (Scores of 148-142 and 147-138 for Pender, and 146-142 for Robinson.)

When trainer George Gainford complained about the verdict, Robinson said, "No beefs, George. Sometimes we got the best of it in the past."

It was time for the others now, and Sugar Ray's claim to a world title had finally been ended.

Paul Pender (left) outpoints Robinson.

THE FILIPINO FLASH

In boxing, most riots occur after the fights. But on March 16, in Quezon City, The Philippines, the local fans didn't bother to wait.

That night, 24-year-old Filipino favorite Flash Elorde won the world junior lightweight title by knocking down defending champion Harold Gomes a total of six times. The southpaw scored his last two knockdowns in round seven, during which referee Barney Ross counted Gomes out. It was the American's first defense.

Several hours before the fight, chaos reigned when it was announced that all the tickets had been sold. According to *The Manila Times*, "Heads were bashed, people were trampled, property was destroyed, and tempers were frayed as some 50,000 people stormed the Araneta Coliseum..."

Might the ugly scene have been repeated had Gomes retained the crown? Fortunately, Elorde's furious fists made that question moot.

World Title Fights

HEAVYWEIGHTS

June 20	**Floyd Patterson** *KO* 5 Ingemar Johansson, New York City

MIDDLEWEIGHTS

Jan 22	**Paul Pender** (USA) *W* 15 Sugar Ray Robinson, Boston
April 20	**Gene Fullmer** *D* 15 Joey Giardello, Bozeman, MT
June 10	**Paul Pender** *W* 15 Sugar Ray Robinson, Boston
June 29	**Gene Fullmer** *KO* 12 Carmen Basilio, Salt Lake City

WELTERWEIGHTS

May 27	**Benny (Kid) Paret** (CUB) *W* 15 Don Jordan, Las Vegas

JUNIOR WELTERWEIGHTS

Feb 4	**Carlos Ortiz** *KO* 10 Battling Torres, Los Angeles
June 15	**Carlos Ortiz** *W* 15 Duilio Loi, San Francisco

JUNIOR LIGHTWEIGHTS

March 16	**Flash Elorde** (PHI) *KO* 7 Harold Gomes, Quezon City

BANTAMWEIGHTS

Feb 4	**Jose Becerra** (MEX) *KO* 9 Alphonse Halimi, Los Angeles
May 23	**Jose Becerra** *D* 15 Kenji Yonekura, Tokyo

FLYWEIGHTS

April 16	**Pone Kingpetch** (THA) *W* 15 Pascual Perez, Bangkok

Ringside View

MARCH

In Houston, heavyweight contender Sonny Liston scores his second kayo of Cleveland Williams in 11 months, toppling the Texan in two rounds.

MARCH

Lightweight champion Joe Brown is stopped in the sixth round of a non-title bout by Ray Portilla.

KING KINGPETCH

As the longtime editor and publisher of *The Ring* magazine, Nat Fleischer was among the most powerful men in boxing. On April 16, at the Lumpinee Stadium in Bangkok, he elevated that power to new heights by personally crowning a world champion.

Fleischer was the only neutral judge for flyweight titlist Pascual Perez' defense against local favorite Pone Kingpetch. (The second judge was from Perez' native Argentina, and the third was from Thailand.) Perez was a 2-1 favorite to retain the crown for the 10th time, but the 5'6½" challenger stood erect and strong.

After 15 rounds, the fighters were fatigued and scarred; Kingpetch's left eye was closed, and Perez was bleeding from a nasty cut over his right eye. Predictably, the Argentine scored for Perez, and the Thai for Kingpetch. That made Fleischer the deciding vote. His card read 146-140 for Kingpetch, and Thailand had its first world champion.

A deserved decision? Most definitely, at least according to the fight report in *The Ring*.

Flyweight champ Pascual Perez (right) waits his turn to weigh in for bout with Pone Kingpetch.

RINGSIDE VIEW

APRIL

Utha heavyweight Lamar Clark's record kayo streak is broken when he is stopped in nine rounds by Bartolo Soni. Clark had knocked out 44 straight opponents.

JUNE

Paul Pender keeps his share of the middleweight title by scoring a 15-round split decision over legendary five-time champion Sugar Ray Robinson.

FOLLOW THE BOUNCING TITLE

In the early-'50s, the welterweight division was stable. Sugar Ray Robinson was champion, and soon after he jumped to middleweight, Kid Gavilan took over. But when the Cuban was dethroned in 1954, the rush to the throne became a free-for-all. Between 1954 and 1958, the title changed hands no less than seven times.

In December '58, Don Jordan unseated Virgil Akins, and the welterweights had a champion who would seemingly lead them into the new decade. But on May 27, at the Las Vegas Convention Center, Benny (Kid) Paret, another Cuban, outpointed Jordan over 15 rounds. The revolving door was still spinning.

Paret punched mostly to Jordan's body, and before the halfway mark, the smooth-boxing champion was desperate to clinch. When in ring center, he allowed Paret to punch as he pleased. Jordan almost fell in the 12th, and barely lasted the distance. The decision was unanimous (scores of 71-65, 70-68, and 76-67).

For Jordan, the day was a total disaster. He lost his title, and was paid only $2,000 – for expenses – to do so. (He had signed over his $85,000 guarantee in order to void his contract with managers Don Nesseth and Jackie McCoy.)

On the morning of May 28, the welterweight of the '60s woke up with no title, no managers, and no money.

A TWO-TIMER FOR THE FIRST TIME

On June 20, before a crowd of more than 45,000 at New York City's Polo Grounds, Floyd Patterson did what James J. Corbett, Jim Jeffries, Jack Dempsey, and Joe Louis had been unable to accomplish: he became the first heavyweight in the division's 85-year history to regain the title.

In June 1959, Sweden's unbeaten Ingemar Johansson had dethroned Patterson by unleashing his right hand and scoring seven knockdowns in three rounds. During round two of the rematch, Johansson again struck with his best right. This time, Patterson didn't budge. Both physically and psychologically, it turned out to be the fight's key moment.

In the fifth, Patterson took his turn. Early in the round, a hook felled Johansson. He rose at referee Arthur Mercante's count of nine. When Patterson hooked once more, Johansson crashed hard, and Mercante's count was a formality.

Perhaps Patterson was an unlikely champion to make history. Nonetheless, when he exited the ring, the ghosts of the legends made sure to bow.

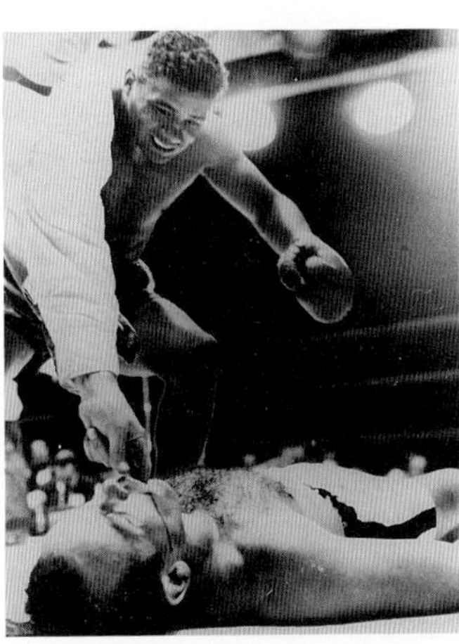

Floyd Patterson became first man to regain the heavyweight crown when he knocked out Ingemar Johansson in New York.

FIGHTING TALK

He was shaking. I've never seen anything like that

FLOYD PATTERSON
on his knockout of defending heavyweight champion Ingemar Johansson

JULY

1960

DECEMBER

RINGSIDE VIEW

JULY

In Denver, number-one heavyweight contender Sonny Liston destroys top-10 contender Zora Folley in two rounds.

SEPTEMBER

Making his first defense, flyweight champion Pone Kingpetch stops former titlist Pascual Perez in eight rounds.

WINNING BY KAYO – AND DECISION

For featherweight champion Davey Moore, it was a long time and a lot of miles between title fights. Moore had made his first defense in August 1959, stopping former champion Hogan (Kid) Bassey. He followed with six non-title bouts, and then traveled to Tokyo. On August 29, at Korakuen Stadium, he risked the crown against Kazuo Takayama.

It was a one-sided, albeit difficult fight. Moore's superior skills enabled him to outscore the local favorite. Takayama bled from the nose and a cut over his left eye, and during the 12th and 13th rounds, he staggered on failing legs. But he charged forward from start to finish, and the champion had to concern himself with the constant threat of butts. After 15 rounds, Moore emerged victorious by scores of 74-62, 73-64, and 73-66. He thought he had halted the Japanese late in round 13, when referee Jimmy Wilson seemingly stopped the fight. (Wilson later claimed he was reacting to the round-ending bell.)

"I heard him stop it," said Moore. "I'm disappointed that I didn't get credited with a knockout." He shouldn't have been; on the road, any win is a good win.

Davey Moore (right) retains the title against Kazuo Takayama before a huge partisan crowd.

THE JOY OF DUILIO LOI

World junior welterweight champion Carlos Ortiz was more brave than smart to defend for a second time against Duilio Loi. (In June, Ortiz had outpointed Loi by split 15-round decision in San Francisco.) The challenger wasn't a threat as a puncher – his record included 102 wins, and only 20 kayos. But fighting at home can turn a toothless tiger into a savage beast.

Ortiz-Loi II came on September 1, before a crowd of 65,000 at San Siro Stadium in Loi's hometown of Milan. Ortiz started quickly, leading to Loi's body and slipping most of the Italian's counters. The middle rounds were fairly even. Then the 31-year-old Loi responded to the cheers of his countrymen and staged a championship-rounds rally. Ortiz could only cover up and wait for the final bell.

The decision was close, but – surprise! – the judges scored for Loi (scores of 72-69, 74-73, and 72-72).

In Milan, Loi was a restaurant owner. That night, the pasta was on the house.

Duilio Loi (left) brought the junior welterweight crown to Italy by decisioning Carlos Ortiz.

GETTING BETTER ALL THE TIME

One of the underlined entries in boxing's book of axioms: a fighter who wins a world title instantly improves by 25 percent. The case of Filipino junior lightweight king Flash Elorde provided evidence.

In March, Elorde had dethroned Rhode Island's Harold Gomes by seventh-round kayo. In the rematch, held on August 17 at the Civic Auditorium in San Francisco, the southpaw improved by 6½ rounds. Elorde's first full-leverage left cross dropped Gomes for a seven-count, and seconds later, a left-right finished him. The challenger was counted out by referee Matt Zidich at the 1:20 mark.

In March, Gomes had blamed the oppressive heat of Manila for his loss. This time, all the heat was generated by Elorde's fists.

The Filipino Flash was a 25-year-old veteran on the rise. After crushing Gomes, he demanded a try at the lightweight title, guaranteeing champion Joe Brown a purse of $60,000. Elorde may have been 25 percent better, but by failing to respond to the offer, Brown proved he was 25 percent smarter.

PART SUGAR RAY, PART JOE LOUIS

After being kayoed by Mexico's Eloy Sanchez in a non-title bout on August 30, bantamweight champion Jose Becerra retired. Sanchez figured to be the logical successor. But only because Eder Jofre was hidden in Brazil.

The 26-year-old Jofre, 34-0-3, was boxing's best-kept secret; he had fought outside of his homeland only once. His second road war came on November 18, at the Olympic Auditorium in Los Angeles, when he clashed with Sanchez for the vacant NBA 118-pound crown.

The New York Times reported that Jofre "boxes like Sugar Ray Robinson and punches like a diminutive Joe Louis." It wasn't false praise; in the fifth round, he floored the Mexican with a straight right, and in the sixth, he landed the same blow. Sanchez was flat long after referee Mushy Callahan counted him out.

In a career of 78 bouts, Jofre would fight outside of Brazil only a handful of times. His performance against Sanchez, however, guaranteed that he'd never sneak up on anyone again.

Eder Jofre knocks out Eloy Sanchez.

THREE FIGHTS, AND STILL TIED

The rubber match between Gene Fullmer and Sugar Ray Robinson was 3½ years in coming. The middleweights had twice squared off in 1957, with each winning once. Their third meeting came on December 3, at the Sports Arena in Los Angeles. For Sugar Ray, the stakes were considerable: he was trying to win the 160-pound crown (at least the NBA version) for a miraculous sixth time, and at age 39, he couldn't count on further chances.

Sugar Ray's best chance seemed a quick kayo. In training camp, George Gainford, his trainer, had spoken of "a secret new punch." It was nothing but hype; fighting in spurts, Robinson hurt the champion only once, in round 11. Fullmer controlled the fight with a steady body attack.

As it turned out, his big finish saved his crown. The bout was declared a 15-round draw, with one judge scoring for Robinson (11-4 on points), one for Fullmer (9-5), and the third calling it even (8-8).

A United Press International press row poll revealed that 14 writers had scored Robinson, and only six for Fullmer. No one, however, asked whether they had voted with their heads or hearts.

Ray Robinson (left) and Gene Fullmer battle to a 15-round draw in NBA middleweight title bout.

World Title Fights

MIDDLEWEIGHTS

Dec 3	**Gene Fullmer** *D* 15 Sugar Ray Robinson, Los Angeles

WELTERWEIGHTS

Dec 10	**Benny (Kid) Paret** *W* 15 Federico Thompson, New York City

JUNIOR WELTERWEIGHTS

Sept 1	**Duilio Loi** (ITA) *W* 15 Carlos Ortiz, Milan

LIGHTWEIGHTS

Oct 28	**Joe Brown** *W* 15 Cisco Andrade, Los Angeles

JUNIOR LIGHTWEIGHTS

Aug 17	**Flash Elorde** *KO* 1 Harold Gomes, San Francisco

FEATHERWEIGHTS

Aug 29	**Davey Moore** *W* 15 Kazuo Takayama, Tokyo

BANTAMWEIGHTS

Oct 25	**Alphonse Halimi** *ref* 15 Freddie Gilroy, Wembley
Nov 18	**Eder Jofre** (BRA) *KO* 6 Eloy Sanchez, Los Angeles

FLYWEIGHTS

Sept 22	**Pone Kingpetch** *KO* 8 Pascual Perez, Los Angeles

"THE KID" MAKES SURE YOUTH IS SERVED

What better place than the world's greatest melting pot, New York City, for a fight between a Cuban and a Argentine-based Panamanian?

On December 10 at Madison Square Garden, welterweight champion Benny (Kid) Paret made his first defense. His opponent, Federico Thompson, was a familiar foe; in March, they had fought to a 12-round draw.

The bout offered a classic contrast in styles. Paret applied constant pressure and aimed for the body, while Thompson counterpunched with smooth combinations. Both were successful in executing their game plans, and the bout was ultimately decided by age. The 23-year-old Paret enjoyed the brisk pace. On the other hand, the 32-year-old Thompson decelerated down the stretch.

After 15 entertaining rounds, Paret kept the title by unanimous decision (scores of 9-6, 9-6, and 7-6-2). It was Thompson's first loss in 33 bouts. Still, he returned home wondering whether his title try had come a few years too late.

Ringside View

OCTOBER

The NBA strips light heavyweight champion Archie Moore, who hasn't defended the title in more than a year.

OCTOBER

In Louisville, 1960 Olympic gold medalist Cassius Clay turns pro, outpointing Tunney Hunsaker over six rounds.

JANUARY

1961

JUNE

RINGSIDE VIEW

FEBRUARY

Harold Johnson wins the vacant NBA light heavyweight title by stopping Jesse Bowdry in nine rounds.

PLAYING ROLE REVERSAL

Stereotypes: British boxers fight in a standup style, pump educated left hands, and present a sound defense. Americans bob and weave, apply pressure, and rely on short left hooks.

Then there were Paul Pender and Terry Downes.

Middleweight champion Pender, who was from Boston, fought in the British mold. Downes, from London, fought like an American. In fact, he had even lived like one, having served from 1954 to 1956 in the U.S. Marine Corps.

On January 14 at the Arena in Boston, the boxer chopped up the fighter and kept the crown via seventh-round TKO. Pender struck early, flooring the challenger with a left-right in the first round. But it was his attack in round four that ultimately determined the outcome. Pender opened a jagged cut on the bridge of Downes' nose, and one over his right eye as well. Always prone to cuts, Downes had undergone plastic surgery in 1959. On this night, however, Pender wielded the scalpel, and 57 seconds into the seventh round, referee Bill Connelly decided that Downes had sacrificed enough blood. (At the time of the stoppage, Pender led on all three cards.) The role of bleeder turned out to be one that Downes couldn't reverse.

Paul Pender (left) stopped game Downes.

THE LEGEND'S LAST TRY

Most fans couldn't begin to imagine boxing without Sugar Ray Robinson. His mortality became painfully apparent on March 4, when he tried for the third and final time to regain the middleweight crown.

At the Las Vegas Convention Center, Robinson met NBA champion Gene Fullmer for a fourth time. Though the 17-foot ring favored the ever-aggressive Fullmer, Robinson boxed neatly over the first two rounds. Late in the third, however, Fullmer struck with an overhand right that drove Robinson into the ropes. He followed with a 20-punch flurry, and Sugar Ray was saved by the bell.

Robinson managed to close and bruise Fullmer's left eye, but never threatened to win. Fullmer piled up points by outworking Robinson, and after 15 rounds, the decision was unanimous for the champion (scores of 70-64, 70-66, and 70-67.)

"I'd have to say this was my best fight of the four with Robinson," said Fullmer.Robinson's best, on the other hand, seemed too long ago to remember.

FLOYD CLOSES THE BOOK (VOL. 3)

The finish of the heavyweight title fight between Floyd Patterson and Ingemar Johansson, held at the Miami Beach Convention Hall on March 13, wasn't quite as conclusive as most ringsiders would have liked. Still, Patterson-Johansson III would be remembered as the best bout of the trilogy.

The results of their first two fights failed to inspire caution. Johansson struck first, twice dropping the champion with right hands. But before round one was over, Patterson sent the Swede down with a leaping hook. The feeling-out process had apparently been waived.

Rounds two through five offered several exchanges, withPatterson gaining an edge. In the sixth, the champion gunned a right to the head, and then another right to the jaw. Johansson crashed, and regained his feet just as referee Billy Regan tolled 10. Afterwards, Regan quelled a minor controversy when he told reporters that if Johansson had beaten the count, he would've stopped the bout anyway.

Patterson and Johansson were done with each other after three fights, two title changes, and almost as many knockdowns (13) as rounds (14).

Patterson knocks out Ingemar Johansson.

WORLD TITLE FIGHTS

HEAVYWEIGHTS

March 13 **Floyd Patterson** *KO* 6
Ingemar Johansson, Miami Beach

LIGHT HEAVYWEIGHTS

Feb 7 **Harold Johnson** (USA) *KO* 9
Jesse Bowdry, Philadelphia
(Wins Vacant NBA Title)

April 24 **Harold Johnson** *KO* 2
Von Clay, Philadelphia

June 10 **Archie Moore** *W* 15
Guilio Rinaldi, New York City

MIDDLEWEIGHTS

Jan 14 **Paul Pender** *KO* 7
Terry Downes, Boston

March 4 **Gene Fullmer** *W* 15
Sugar Ray Robinson, Las Vegas

April 22 **Paul Pender** *W* 15
Carmen Basilio, Boston

WELTERWEIGHTS

June 3 **Emile Griffith** *W* 15
Gaspar Ortega, New York City

JUNIOR WELTERWEIGHTS

May 10 **Duilio Loi** *W* 15
Carlos Ortiz, Milan

LIGHTWEIGHTS

April 18 **Joe Brown** *ref* 15
Dave Charnley, London

FEATHERWEIGHTS

April 8 **Davey Moore** *KO* 1
Danny Valdez, Los Angeles

BANTAMWEIGHTS

March 25 **Eder Jofre** *KO* 10
Piero Rollo, Rio de Janeiro

May 30 **Johnny Caldwell** (IRE) *ref* 15
Alphonse Halimi, Wembley
(Wins Vacant EBU World Title)

FLYWEIGHTS

June 27 **Pone Kingpetch** *W* 15
Mitsunori Seki, Tokyo

Ringside View

APRIL

Harold Johnson retains the NBA light heavyweight title with a second-round stoppage of Von Clay.

APRIL

Lightweight champion Joe Brown keeps the crown for the 10th time, scoring a close 15-round decision over British champion Dave Charnley.

WHY DIDN'T YOU SAY SO SOONER?

Sometimes, a cornerman's words can be just as effective as a fighter's punches. Such was the case on April 1, when 22-year-old Emile Griffith challenged welterweight champion Benny (Kid) Paret at the Convention Hall in Miami Beach.

The 147-pounders struggled evenly, with Griffith blocking most of Paret's signature body-punches, but failing to respond with enough blows of his own. After a dozen rounds, the bout was still to be won; one judge had Paret in front by 117-114; another saw Griffith ahead by 117-116; and a third scoring it even at 115.

"Don't you realize you're fighting for the championship of the world?" co-manager Gil Clancy screamed at Griffith before the start of the 13th. "When are you going to start fighting – after the fight?"

Griffith's answer came early in the 13th, when he stepped inside a Paret right lead and countered with two hooks and a booming right. Paret never threatened to beat the count of referee Jimmy Peerless, who declared Griffith the winner by kayo at the 1:11 mark. Precisely what Clancy had in mind.

IRISH EYES WERE SMILING

It was becoming increasingly evident that NBA champion Eder Jofre was the best bantamweight in boxing. But as long as the title was split, there would be room for a second champion.On May 30, at the Empire Pool in Wembley, France's Alphonse Halimi defended the European version of the title against Belfast's 23-year-old Johnny Caldwell. The continent's flyweight champion, Caldwell flaunted impressive credentials: he won a bronze medal at the 1956 Olmpics, and was unbeaten as a pro (21-0). Nonetheless, the consensus was that Halimi would be too strong for the Irishman.

As it turned out, Caldwell proved too quick for the champion. The bout was competitive for seven rounds. In the eighth, an unintentional butt opened a severe cut over Halimi's left eye. Caldwell subsequently swarmed, and the second half of the bout was a blood-letting. He dropped Halimi in the 15th, and was judged the winner by Dutch referee and sole judge Ben Bril. Caldwell wasn't number one, but being the best of the rest had its rewards, too.

Britain's dynamic, undefeated Johnny Caldwell (left) stripped Alphonse Halimi of the title.

GETTING OLD, BUT STILL BOLD

A lot of light heavyweights had gotten old waiting for Archie Moore to get old. "The Ol' Mongoose" had outlasted the '40s and the '50s, and it was beginning to look like he might fend off Father Time in the '60s as well.

On June 10 at Madison Square Garden, Moore defended his share of the 175-pound crown against Italy's Guilio Rinaldi, who had outpointed him in a non-title fight eight months before. Moore was 47 and Rinaldi was 26. The way Moore saw it, the difference was 21 years of experience.

The bout was boring. The champion started slowly, and Rinaldi failed to capitalize. Over the second half of the bout, Moore began to land crisply. With no answers, Rinaldi was sadly outclassed. Moore cruised to the finish and took the decision by scores of 11-3-1, 11-4, and 9-5-1.

It would be the last title fight of Old Archie's remarkable career. Call his bout with Father Time a draw.

Italy's Guilio Rinaldi (right) attempts to capture Archie Moore's light heavyweight crown.

JULY

1961

DECEMBER

THIS TIME, DOWNES IS UP

Terry Downes' first try at the middleweight title had come in Paul Pender's hometown of Boston. Their rematch was fought on July 11, at the Wembley Pool in London. The jump across the pond made all the difference.

In January, Pender retained the crown by stopping the charismatic Londoner on cuts. This time, it was Pender who bled. Chugging forward, Downes opened gashes over both the champion's eyes, the most dangerous of which was sustained during a trade in the eighth round.

During the rest period between rounds nine and 10, Al Lacey, Pender's chief second, informed Welsh referee Ike Powell of his fighter's surrender. It was a sudden ending; Pender had been jabbing strongly, though Downes had begun to accelerate.

"This proves what I've always said," boasted the winner. "That I can beat anybody if I have the crowd behind me."

Having taken the title, Downes was contractually obligated to a rubber match. It would come nine months later – back on the wrong side of the pond.

Britain's Terry Downes (right) thrilled a hometown crowd by stopping Paul Pender in the ninth.

RINGSIDE VIEW

AUGUST

NBA light heavyweight champion Harold Johnson retains the crown by scoring a split 15-round decision over Eddie Cotton.

SEPTEMBER

Former bantamweight champion Jimmy Carruthers returns to the ring and loses a 12-round decision to Aldo Pravisani in Sydney. It is the Australian's first bout in more than seven years.

TITLE NOBODY WANTED

From 1951 to 1953, Kid Gavilan made seven successful defenses of the welterweight title. Then the crown began to slide from head to head, as if someone had greased it.

At Madison Square Garden on September 30, Emile Griffith made his first defense, meeting Benny (Kid) Paret, whom he had dethroned six months before. Griffith answered the opening bell as a 5-1 favorite. Apparently, the oddsmakers didn't believe that those who ignore history are condemned to repeat it.

It was an uneventful bout, with Griffith punching in combination, and Paret working inside. Griffith threatened to stop the challenger in the 11th, but Paret recovered, and then drove forward to take the last three rounds.

Then the division jinx struck hard; 18 of 22 ringside reporters saw Griffith the winner. But Paret impressed those who counted, regaining the title by split decision (9-6, 8-6-1, and 6-9).

Afterward, Manuel Alfaro, Paret's manager, said his fighter's next few bouts would be over-the-weight non-title matches. At 147 pounds, there seemed no other way to keep the title.

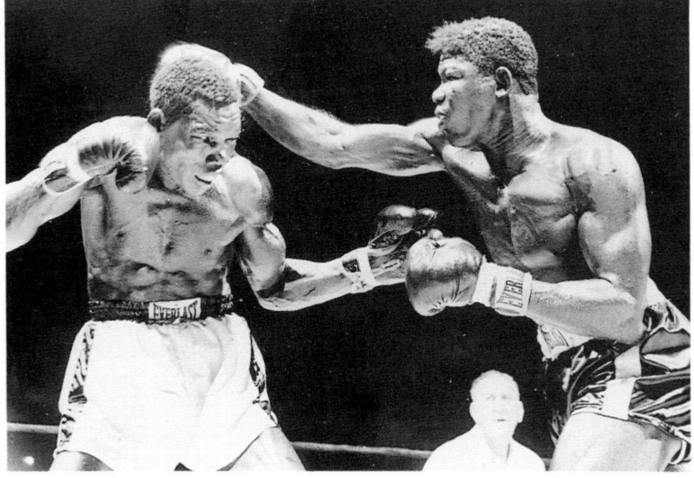

Benny Paret (left) decisioned Emile Griffith to regain the middleweight title.

THE OX KNOWS HOW TO BOX

Making his sixth defense of the NBA middleweight title, Gene Fullmer faced a fighter who boxed better, hit harder, and hadn't yet reached his prime. But having beaten champions like Sugar Ray Robinson and Carmen Basilio, Fullmer enjoyed a huge edge in experience, and he was made a 9-5 favorite to reject the challenge of "The Ox," Cuba's Florentino Fernandez.

The 160-pounders clashed on August 15 at Municipal Stadium in Ogden, Utah. Encouraged by more than 12,000 of his home state fans, Fullmer swept the first four rounds. Fernandez found his rhythm in the fifth, sixth, and seventh, and narrowed the champion's lead. Then Fullmer's experience surfaced. Always aggressive, he began to retreat and counterpunch. It worked, and he took rounds eight through 12.

Fernandez capitalized when Fullmer sprained his right hand in the 13th. The challenger, a converted southpaw, turned lefty and scored with several big crosses. By the finish, Fullmer was bleeding from his eyes, nose, and mouth.

The Ox' rally had come too late; the champion kept the title by split decision (scores of 145-142, 148-140, and 143-145). It could be argued whether Fullmer knew how to box. His ability to win, however, had been established once again.

LOI ANNOYS THE HOI POLLOI

On October 21, at the Sports Palace in Milan, Italian junior welterweight champion Duilio Loi and American challenger Eddie Perkins failed to provide adequate entertainment. As a result, the 15,000 fans in attendance, as well as referee Nello Barrovecchio, decided to entertain themselves.

For 15 painfully dull rounds, Loi and Perkins jabbed at each other from a safe distance. The crowd began to boo and whistle early in the fight, and the noise increased round by round.

In the ninth, Barrovecchio drew cheers by calling time out and urging the fighters to display more enthusiasm. They ignored him, and the fans took to tossing coins into the ring. At one point, Barrovecchio bent down, scooped up a handful, and bowed.

Oh, yes, the fight...It ended in a split draw, with Loi retaining the crown by scores of 70-69, 71-71, and 69-71.

A PAIR OF SLAM-BANGING CHAMPS

NBA middleweight champion Gene Fullmer was 5' 8", and welterweight champion Benny (Kid) Paret 5' 7½"; Fullmer scaled 159¾, Paret 156¾; both fighters had a 69-inch reach, and they shared a slam-bang, infighting style. Why, then, would Fullmer prove to be so much stronger?

On December 9, at the Convention Center in Las Vegas, Fullmer and Paret fought as advertised – in a phonebooth. From the start, Fullmer moved Paret as he pleased, doing most of the pushing and shoving. When Paret initiated an exchange, Fullmer made sure to finish it. In the 10th, Fullmer scored three knockdowns, and Paret was counted out by referee Harry Krause.

"He's tough," Fullmer said. "I never hit a man so many punches."

Typically, Fullmer looked the loser. He showed off his wounds of war to the press: a swollen right eye; a cut over the same eye; another cut at the corner of his left eye; a nick on the middle of his forehead; and a bloody nose. What might he have looked like, the reporters wondered, had he not dominated the fight?

Welterweight champ Benny Paret (left) failed to capture Gene Fullmer's middleweight crown.

NO PETTING, BUT LOTS OF PUNCHING

After weighing in for his challenge of heavyweight champion Floyd Patterson, former football star and 10-1 underdog Tom McNeeley went to the zoo.

"It relaxes him," it was explained.

Patterson-McNeeley came on December 4, at Maple Leaf Gardens in Toronto. (It was the first heavyweight championship match ever held in Canada.) On the night of the fight, the ring was a cage, and McNeeley was a lamb facing a wolf.

Patterson stands over McNeeley.

The challenger was 23-0, and when he dropped Patterson in the first round, ringsiders knowingly traded the standard line, "You can never be sure how good an undefeated fighter really is." But the one-time Michigan State lineman couldn't keep his own feet. Patterson scored eight knockdowns in all – one in the first round, four in the third, and three in the fateful fourth. After the last crash, referee Jersey Joe Walcott counted McNeeley out.

At the postfight press conference, the media lauded McNeeley's courage.

"Courage," he answered, "isn't enough."

At least he hadn't been swallowed whole.

WORLD TITLE FIGHTS

HEAVYWEIGHTS	
Dec 4	**Floyd Patterson** *KO* 1 Tom McNeeley, Toronto
LIGHT HEAVYWEIGHTS	
Aug 29	**Harold Johnson** *W* 15 Eddie Cotton, Seattle
MIDDLEWEIGHTS	
July 11	**Terry Downes** (ENG) *KO* 10 Paul Pender, London
Aug 15	**Gene Fullmer** *W* 15 Florentino Fernandez, Ogden, UT
Dec 9	**Gene Fullmer** *KO* 10 Benny (Kid) Paret, Las Vegas
WELTERWEIGHTS	
Sept 30	**Benny (Kid) Paret** *W* 15 Emile Griffith, New York City
JUNIOR WELTERWEIGHTS	
Oct 21	**Duilio Loi** *D* 15 Eddie Perkins, Milan
LIGHTWEIGHTS	
Oct 28	**Joe Brown** *W* 15 Bert Somodio, Quezon City
FEATHERWEIGHTS	
Nov 13	**Davey Moore** *W* 15 Kazuo Yakayama, Tokyo
BANTAMWEIGHTS	
Aug 19	**Eder Jofre** *KO* 7 Ramon Arias, Caracas
Oct 31	**Johnny Caldwell** *ref* 15 Alphonse Halimi, Wembley

RINGSIDE VIEW

OCTOBER

Lightweight champion Joe Brown retains the title for the 11th time, scoring a unanimous 15-round decision over Bert Somodio.

NOVEMBER

Davey Moore keeps the featherweight crown for the fourth time, outpointing Kazuo Takayama over 15 rounds.

JANUARY

1962

JUNE

Eder Jofre (right) ended Johnny Caldwell's reign as bantamweight champion.

ONE 0 HAS TO GO

It was the kind of fight everyone wanted to see: two world champions, both unbeaten, meeting to unify the title. NBA bantamweight champion Eder Jofre was 37-0-3. On January 18, at Ibirapuera Stadium in his native Sao Paulo, Brazil, he faced Ireland's Johnny Caldwell, 25-0, and recognized as 118-pound champion throughout Europe.

Jofre-Caldwell wasn't so much a unification as a coronation. The Brazilian was a brilliant boxer-puncher, and insiders gave Caldwell almost no chance of winning. The Irishman boxed well for one round, but then lost control and never regained it. He was floored by a hook to the solar plexus in the fifth, and battered in every other round. Shortly after Jofre scored a 10th-round knockdown with a straight right, Sammy Dockerty, Caldwell's manager, tossed a towel into the ring, and referee Willie Pep stopped the fight at the 2:45 mark. Jofre was comfortably ahead on all three cards.

The bantamweight division had one champion. And, just maybe, the best champion in boxing.

CASSIUS IS HUMBLED – BUT NOT REALLY

After only 10 pro bouts, 20-year-old heavyweight Cassius Clay was confirming an age-old belief: it's not important whether the boxing fans like you or hate you, but that they pay to see you.

Boisterous and bold, Clay predicted he would stop his 11th opponent, clubfighter Sonny Banks, before the completion of four rounds. At Madison Square Garden on February 10, he kept his word.

Before he did, however, there was a surprise. In the first round, Banks connected with a short hook, and Clay dropped to the canvas. It was the first knockdown of his career. He rebounded to score two of his own knockdowns in round two, and in round three, his blazing combinations overwhelmed the slower Banks. At the 26-second mark of the fourth round, referee Ruby Goldstein signalled the end.

"All I could think of when Clay was on his fanny," commented Harry Markson, the president of Madison Square Garden Boxing, after the fight, "was that that was a funny place to be for a kid with a big mouth."

THE TRAGIC END OF BENNY PARET

At the weigh-in before Benny (Kid) Paret's welterweight title defense against Emile Griffith, the champion taunted his foe by questioning his manhood. A few hours later, Griffith's opportunity for revenge ended in tragedy.

Paret and Griffith were familiar foes; they had previously met twice, with each having dethroned the other. Griffith was a 7-2 favorite to win the rubber match, held at Madison Square Garden, New York, on March 24.

Paret almost pulled off an upset toward the end of round six, when he pummeled Griffith with an assortment of blows. The challenger was saved by the bell. But when Griffith hurt Paret in round 12, nothing – and no one – came to his rescue.

After driving Paret into the ropes, Griffith exploded with a series of right uppercuts, then left hooks. Veteran championship referee Ruby Goldstein seemed paralyzed, and by the time he intervened, Paret was slumping to the canvas.

Twenty-five minutes later, Paret was taken to Roosevelt Hospital. The next morning, he underwent a three-hour operation to relieve pressure on his brain.

On April 3, 10 days after the fight, Paret died at the age of 25. The brutality of the ring never seemed more cruel.

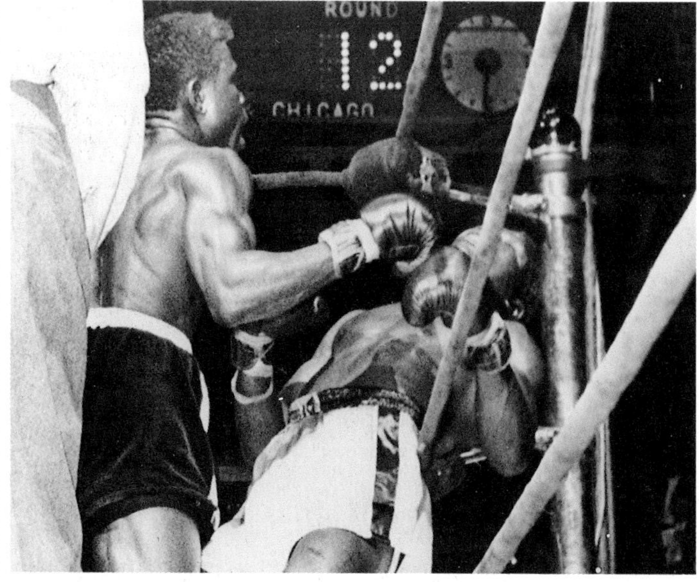

Brave Benny Paret (right) lost both his welterweight title and his life after being knocked out.

WORLD TITLE FIGHTS

LIGHT HEAVYWEIGHTS

May 12	**Harold Johnson** *W* 15 Doug Jones, Philadelphia
June 23	**Harold Johnson** *W* 15 Gustav Scholz, Berlin

MIDDLEWEIGHTS

April 7	**Paul Pender** *W* 15 Terry Downes, Boston

WELTERWEIGHTS

March 24	**Emile Griffith** *KO* 12 Benny (Kid) Paret, New York City

LIGHTWEIGHTS

April 21	**Carlos Ortiz** *W* 15 Joe Brown, Las Vegas

JUNIOR LIGHTWEIGHTS

June 23	**Flash Elorde** *W* 15 Auburn Copeland, Manila

BANTAMWEIGHTS

Jan 18	**Eder Jofre** *KO* 10 Johnny Caldwell, Sao Paulo
May 4	**Eder Jofre** *KO* 10 Herman Marquez, San Francisco

FLYWEIGHTS

May 30	**Pone Kingpetch** *W* 15 Kyo Noguchi, Tokyo

A BOSTON DECISION, AND A FAIR ONE

Paul Pender (left) regained the middleweight crown by outpointing Terry Downes.

Before crossing the ocean for his April 7 title defense against Paul Pender, middleweight champion Terry Downes spoke of anticipating "a Boston decision." In the days preceding the bout, which was held at Boston Garden, he repeated a similar sentiment.

If the Londoner's concern was legitimate, the scoring confirmed his fear; all three judges voted for Pender. But if it was only a psychological ploy, it worked; perhaps compensating for what might be perceived as a natural prejudice, the judges were particularly kind to Downes.

Pender, who emerged triumphant by scores of 144-143, 146-141, and 145-143, controlled the bout with short hooks and straight rights. Downes forced a fast pace, but it worked in the challenger's favor; Pender was in marvelous condition, and he punched often, especially in the early rounds.

Pender's win was significant; it allowed him to join Stanley Ketchel, Tony Zale, and Sugar Ray Robinson as the only middleweights to have regained the title.

"OLD BONES" GOES QUIETLY

Given the quality of his 5½-year title reign, it was difficult to imagine lightweight champion Joe Brown stinking out the house. But that's exactly what he did on April 21, when he defended against former junior welterweight champ Carlos Ortiz at the Las Vegas Convention Center.

Carlos Ortiz (left) decisioned 10-years-older Joe Brown to become lightweight champion.

So flat was the 35-year-old Brown that many ringsiders questioned the legitimacy of his effort. Making his 12th defense, "Old Bones" started slowly – and then decelerated. He waited and waited for an opportunity to fire his counter right, but Ortiz, a heady fighter, presented few openings. As a result, Brown backtracked and allowed the challenger to pile up points.

The fans booed throughout the bout and seemed relieved by the sound of the final bell. Ortiz was declared the winner and new champion by the hideously one-sided scores of 74-60, 74-66, and 74-58.

It was Brown's first loss in almost six years. The veteran would box until age 44, but never regain his form. His post-championship record: 20-23-2.

RINGSIDE VIEW

JANUARY

British Empire middleweight champion Dick Tiger calls for a world title try after a sixth-round knockout of Florentino Fernandez in Miami Beach.

FEBRUARY

The New York State Athletic Commission and the European Boxing Union strip 48-year-old Archie Moore of the light heavyweight title.

WHERE LIFE BEGINS AT 33

With each passing victory, NBA light heavyweight champion Harold Johnson was establishing himself as the logical successor to the division's longtime king, Archie Moore. By traditional standards, 33-year-old Harold Johnson was a senior citizen. But over the course of Moore's title reign, new standards had been established.

On May 12, at the Arena in Philadelphia, Johnson secured universal acceptance as 175-pound king by outpointing the up-and-coming Doug Jones. Well, almost universal; Moore's home state of California still recognized "The Ol' Mongoose."

Jones' youthful energy gave the counterpunching Johnson ample opportunity to shine. His defense tight and his right hand on target, the champion won almost every exchange. The light heavys went toe to toe in the 11th and 12th rounds. Otherwise, Johnson's performance was typically controlled. After 15 rounds, he was given a unanimous decision by scores of 73-64, 71-63, and 74-61.

The way Archie Moore figured, if Johnson were afforded a few more years, he might really become something.

JULY

1962

DECEMBER

BEATING BACK THE DEMONS

Facing his first fight since the Benny (Kid) Paret tragedy four months before, welterweight champion Emile Griffith realized that challenger Ralph Dupas would be only one of his problems.

"I have to fight two persons in the ring that night," he said. "Dupas and myself."Griffith met Dupas at the Las Vegas Convention Center on July 13. The crowd of 5,169 greeted him with a warm ovation, which helped calm his nerves, and co-manager Gil Clancy kept him focused on the task at hand.

Dupas turned out to be extremely difficult. He switched between orthodox and southpaw stances; he moved in and out; he gave the champion tiny targets. But he landed few punches of his own, and Griffith piled up points with aggressiveness.

In the 15th, Griffith broke through, shaking Dupas with a right and a followup flurry. The impressive finish erased any doubts about the decision, and Griffith kept the crown by unanimous scores of 71-64, 74-65, and 73-69.

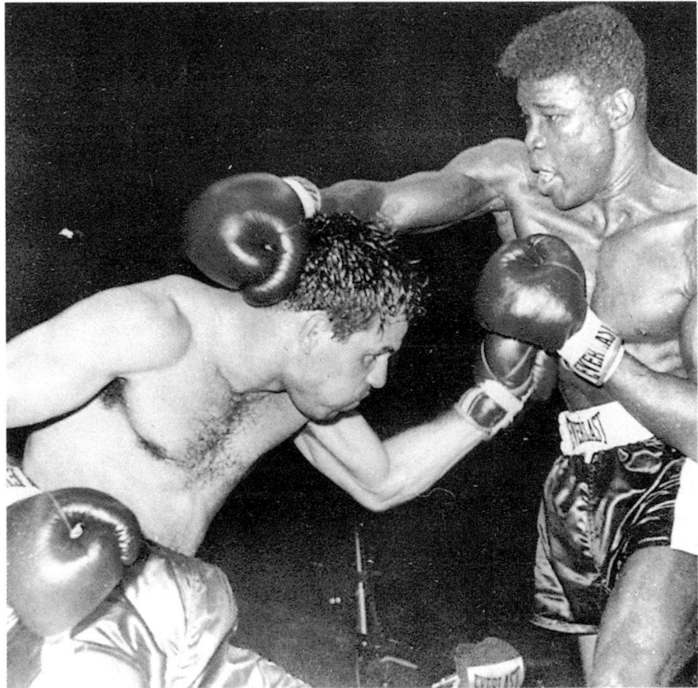

New Orleans hero Ralph Dupas (left) gave defending champ Emile Griffith a hard battle.

Fighters react differently to ring fatalities. Emile Griffith, 23, proved he could overcome the trauma and would fight on.

FINISHING IN FINLAND

Established champions deserve an occasional softie, and 28-year-old featherweight titlist Davey Moore was the longest-reigning king in boxing. On August 17, he risked the crown against Finland's Olli Maeki at Olympic Stadium in Helsinki. It was the first world title fight in Scandinavia.

The NBA considered stripping Moore for failing to meet top contender Sugar Ramos, but the champion nonetheless kept his date with former amateur star Maeki, who was 8-1-1 (1) and unrated. The fight was easier than Moore could have hoped for.

Making his fifth defense, Moore studied Maeki for one round, then attacked. His crisp combinations produced three knockdowns in round two. Referee Barney Ross saved him from further abuse at the 2:35 mark. Soft indeed.

When Moore returned home, the threat of Ramos was greater than ever. The Cuban was knocking out every featherweight placed in front of him, and his title shot was inevitable. Moore could go soft only for so long.

THUD, THUD, BOOM! FLOYD FALLS

Heavyweight champion Floyd Patterson defended against Sonny Liston despite the objection of his manager, Cus D'Amato. The result of the fight proved why boxers should box, and managers should manage.

Patterson met Liston on September 25 at Chicago's Comiskey Park. Liston had been the top contender for two years, during which he leveled every heavyweight foolish enough to face him. Patterson proved to be no less foolish than the rest.

Liston, 214, outweighed the champion by 25 pounds. He opened by pumping the hardest jab since Joe Louis. Patterson crouched and weaved with caution. Midway through the round, Liston hooked to the body, and Patterson fell into the ropes. Liston followed with a hook, a chopping right, and a hook that sent the champion down. At referee Frank Sikora's count of 10, Patterson rose to one knee. The fight had lasted 126 seconds.

"I felt enough of him under my glove on that last hook to know it was a good enough punch to put any man down hard," Liston said.

Cus D'Amato could have guessed.

It took ponderous but powerful Sonny Liston less than one round to win the heavyweight crown from the badly overmatched Floyd Patterson in Chicago.

RINGSIDE VIEW

SEPTEMBER

World bantamweight champion Eder Jofre continues his power play with a sixth-round kayo over Mexico's Jose Medel.

SEPTEMBER

Chicago's Eddie Perkins proves a visitor *can* win by decision in Milan; he captures the junior welterweight title by scoring a unanimous 15-round verdict over local favorite Duilio Loi.

THE FUTURE MEETS PAST

Before leaving his dressing room to face 48-year-old Archie Moore, unbeaten heavyweight Cassius Clay wrote on a blackboard, "Moore In 4." Underneath, he scribbled "Liston In 8."

Presumptuous for a 20-year-old? Clay was that, if nothing else. But on November 15, before a capacity crowd of 16,200 at the Sports Arena in Los Angeles, the cocky Kentuckian kept his promise. Clay scored three knockdowns in round four, and at the 1:35 mark, referee Tommy Hart came to Moore's rescue.

The loss to Clay turned out to be the penultimate effort of Moore's unique career. He would knock out Mike DiBiase in March 1963, and then retire. His final and remarkable mark: 183-22-9 (129) with 1 no-contest.

As for the Liston prediction...Greeting Clay after the fight, the newly crowned world champion told him, "You go eight *seconds* with me and I'll give you the fight."

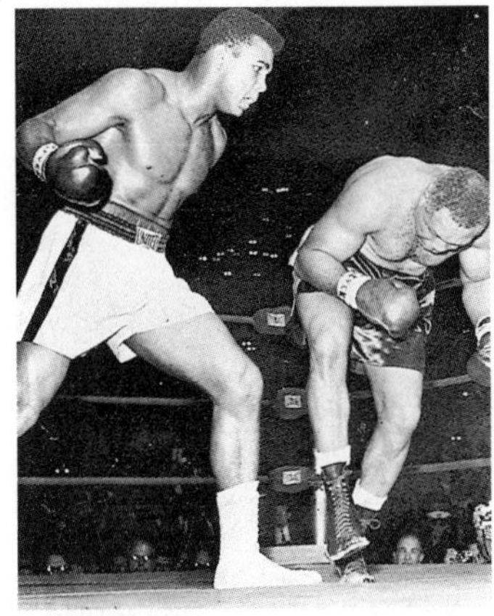

Undefeated 20-year-old Clay beats Moore.

TIGER EARNS HIS STRIPES

Richard Ihetu, better known as Dick Tiger, was a Nigerian-born middleweight by way of Liverpool and Jersey – as in Jersey Jones, his manager. Tiger may have been a world traveler, but until he dethroned WBA (formerly NBA) champion Gene Fullmer, he wasn't world-famous.

A two-time British Empire champion, Tiger challenged Fullmer on October 23 at Candlestick Park in San Francisco. In one of the most entertaining bouts of the year, the middleweights collided in mid-ring and swapped punches for all 15 rounds. Tiger scored with a tremendous right in the first round, but the turning point didn't come until round nine, when Fullmer suffered a 1½-inch cut over his left eye. Tiger capitalized, and in the 10th, he cut the champion over the right eye, too.

Trying to protect his wounds, Fullmer slowed the pace and boxed his way through the championship rounds. Tiger finished unmarked, and, under California's points system, took the title by scores of 10-1, 9-5, and 7-5.

"C'mon, daddy, c'mon," Fullmer's four-year-old son DeLaun, screamed throughout the fight. But to no avail. Man against Tiger proved no contest at all.

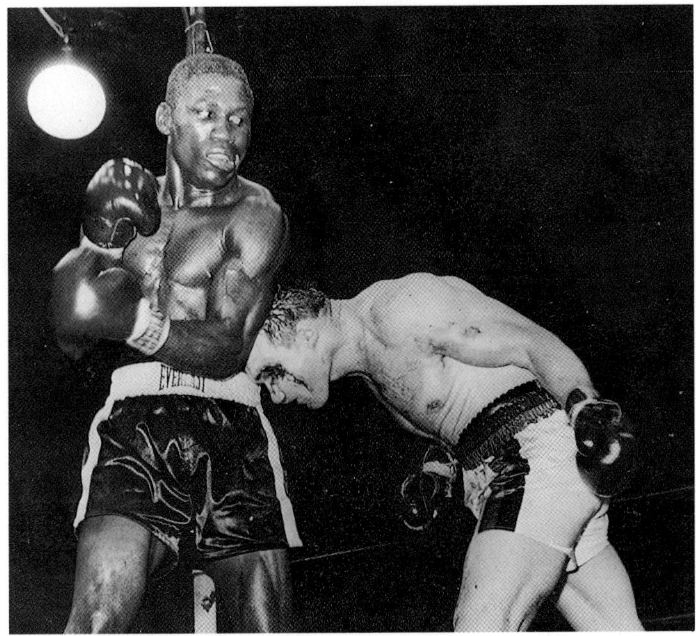

Dick Tiger (left) outpointed bullish Gene Fullmer to capture the middleweight title.

WORLD TITLE FIGHTS

HEAVYWEIGHTS

Sept 25	**Sonny Liston** (USA) *KO* 1 Floyd Patterson, Chicago

MIDDLEWEIGHTS

Oct 23	**Dick Tiger** (NIG) *W* 15 Gene Fullmer, San Francisco

JUNIOR MIDDLEWEIGHTS

Oct 17	**Emile Griffith** *W* 15 Ted Wright, Vienna (Wins Vacant EBU World Title)
Oct 20	**Dennis Moyer** (USA) *W* 15 Joey Giambra, Portland, OR (Wins Vacant World Title)

WELTERWEIGHTS

July 13	**Emile Griffith** *W* 15 Ralph Dupas, Las Vegas
Dec 8	**Emile Griffith** *KO* 9 Jorge Fernandez, Las Vegas

JUNIOR WELTERWEIGHTS

Sept 14	**Eddie Perkins** (USA) *W* 15 Duilio Loi, Milan
Dec 15	**Duilio Loi** *ref* 15 Eddie Perkins, Milan

LIGHTWEIGHTS

Dec 3	**Carlos Ortiz** *KO* 5 Terue Kosaka, Tokyo

FEATHERWEIGHTS

Aug 17	**Davey Moore** *KO* 2 Olli Maeki, Helsinki

BANTAMWEIGHTS

Sept 11	**Eder Jofre** *KO* 6 Jose Medel, Sao Paulo

FLYWEIGHTS

Oct 10	**Fighting Harada** (JAP) *KO* 11 Pone Kingpetch, Tokyo

A CUB OF A SUB

A humble and painfully shy teenager, Tokyo's Masahiko (Fighting) Harada seemed an unlikely candidate for stardom. The 19-year-old flyweight, whose buzzsaw style belied his demeanor, was thrust into the spotlight when countryman and number-one contender Sadao Yaoita was forced to retire because of an injury. Yaoita had been scheduled to challenge Thai world champion Pone Kingpetch.

On October 10, at Tokyo's Kuramae Sumo Arena, Harada substituted for a purse of only $3,000. (Kingpetch was paid $45,000.) The Japanese was a prohibitive underdog; after all, Kingpetch was a 26-year-old veteran who had dethroned the legendary Pascual Perez.

The champion never had a chance. Harada smothered him from the opening round, pushing him to the ropes and banging his body with both hands. Kingpetch's long jab was never a factor, and in round eight, he suffered a 12-stitch cut over his left eye.

Absorbing a monotonous beating, Kingpetch slumped in a corner during round 11 and sat himself on the bottom rope. Referee Sang Hiranyalekha counted him out with one second remaining in the round.

JANUARY

1963

APRIL

A "SPEEDY" WEIGH-IN IN MANILA

Don Elbaum represented Pennsylvania junior lightweight Johnny Bizzaro. On February 16, in Manila, the Philippines, the street-smart manager found himself in the wrong neighborhood.

At 10:15 on the morning of the fight, Bizzaro's opponent, 130-pound world champion and local favorite Flash Elorde, scaled 1¾ pounds over the division limit. Twice more he unsuccessfully tried to make weight. On his fourth attempt, he quickly jumped on and off the scale, and Speedy Cabanela, the local official in charge of the weigh-in, screamed "130 pounds."

Elbaum countered by screaming "fast count," but no one was listening. As a result, Elorde-Bizzaro came off as scheduled, before 40,000 at the Rizal Coliseum.

Bizzaro tried throughout, hitting the titlist as often with his head as with his fists. But Elorde was far sharper, and after 15 rounds, he was declared the winner by scores of 74-64, 72-65, and 72-68. Despite making weight, Bizzaro lost on the scales.

Pone Kingpetch (left) regained the world flyweight title from Japan's dynamic Fighting Harada.

THE THREE KINGS

On January 12, at the National Stadium in Bangkok, a story of three Kings played to an audience of 15,000. Phumipol Adulej, the King of Thailand, sat in a specially erected throne on the ringside floor and watched his countryman, Pone Kingpetch, attempt to become the first flyweight in history to regain the world title. Ultimately, the fighter's fate was was decided by the King of *The Ring*, Publisher Nat Fleischer.Three months before, Kingpetch had been dethroned by teenage upstart Fighting Harada. This time, the tall Thai established his jab, and rallied over the second half of the bout with uppercuts to the body. It was a close fight.

The Thai judge voted 72-67 for Kingpetch, and the Japanese judge scored the bout 69-69. Predictably, the fight was decided by the only "neutral" official, Fleischer, who had Kingpetch ahead by 71-67. (Coincidentally, it had been Fleischer who, in April 1960, had made Kingpetch a champion by casting the deciding vote in the Thai's challenge of Pascual Perez.)

In Thailand, King, Kingpetch, and Kingmaker were heroes all.

FULLMER'S BLOODY, GUTTY TRY

When he was middleweight champion, Gene Fullmer twice rejected the challenge of a desperate and aging Sugar Ray Robinson. On February 23, at the Las Vegas Convention Center, he felt the pain and frustration Robinson had experienced.Fullmer, 31, was trying to regain the WBA 160-pound crown from Dick Tiger, who was two years older, but far fresher. Jabbing and circling, the challenger executed his strategy to near-perfection. But there were occasional slam-bang confrontations, and by the late rounds, Fullmer was bleeding from his nose, as well as cuts above his hairline and left eye.

As it turned out, Tiger's stamina saved his title. He took the 14th and 15th rounds on all three cards, which enabled him to retain the crown with a draw (71-67, 69-69, and 68-70).

"I did everything I was supposed to do," said Fullmer. "I fought according to plan, and things worked out just as planned. Everything but the decision."

RINGSIDE VIEW

FEBRUARY

Emile Griffith retains the European world junior middleweight title with a ninth-round TKO over Chris Christensen in Copenhagen.

Middleweight champion Dick Tiger's face is a bloodied mask as Gene Fullmer bulls in.

World Title Fights

MIDDLEWEIGHTS

Feb 23 **Dick Tiger** *D* 15
Gene Fullmer, Las Vegas

JUNIOR MIDDLEWEIGHTS

Feb 3 **Emile Griffith** *KO* 9
Chris Christensen, Copenhagen

Feb 19 **Dennis Moyer** *W* 15
Stan Harrington, Honolulu

April 29 **Ralph Dupas** (USA) *W* 15
Dennis Moyer, New Orleans

WELTERWEIGHTS

March 21 **Luis Rodriguez** (CUB) *W* 15
Emile Griffith, Los Angeles

JUNIOR WELTERWEIGHTS

March 21 **Roberto Cruz** (PHI) *KO* 1
Battling Torres, Los Angeles

LIGHTWEIGHTS

April 7 **Carlos Ortiz** *KO* 13
Doug Vaillant, San Juan

JUNIOR LIGHTWEIGHTS

Feb 16 **Flash Elorde** *W* 15
Johnny Bizarro, Manila

FEATHERWEIGHTS

March 21 **Sugar Ramos** (CUB) *KO* 11
Davey Moore, Los Angeles

BANTAMWEIGHTS

April 4 **Eder Jofre** *KO* 3
Katsutoshi Aoki, Tokyo

FLYWEIGHTS

Jan 12 **Pone Kingpetch** *W* 15
Fighting Harada, Bangkok

EMILE VS. CUBA, CHAPTER II

Emile Griffith's grudge against Benny (Kid) Paret ended the night he pounded the Cuban into a coma. Luis Rodriguez was also from Cuba, and on March 21, at Dodger Stadium in Los Angeles, he took Griffith's welterweight title. That meant the start of a new grudge.

On a card that featured three coronations (Roberto Cruz won the vacant junior welterweight title by crushing Battling Torres, and Sugar Ramos unseated featherweight king Davey Moore), Rodriguez avenged a December 1960 points loss by clearly outboxing Griffith in the middle rounds, and stealing several other stanzas with flashy flurries. It was Griffith, however, who applied constant pressure, and after the final bell, he paraded around the ring. His celebration came to a sober end when Rodriguez was declared the winner by points scores of 9-5, 8-5, and 8-6.

Rematch, anyone?

Heavily favored welterweight king Emile Griffith (right) couldn't solve Luis Rodriguez' style.

WHO'S CRAZY NOW?

For a fighter to remain unbeaten, he has to be more than just good: he has to be lucky, too. Cassius Clay's red letter day came on March 13, when he faced veteran Doug Jones at Madison Square Garden.

Clay proved to be faster and defensively superior, but he boxed most of the bout with his hands by his sides. Jones capitalized, staggering the 3-1 favorite in the first, eighth, and ninth rounds. The isolated but eye-catching moments made the bout particularly difficult to score, and after 10 rounds, each fighter was confident of victory.

The scoring infuriated Jones, as well as most of the 18,732 fans in attendance; two judges saw it 5-4-1, and the third 8-1-1, all for Clay."Tell my fans I'm sorry," said the winner, who had predicted a fourth-round stoppage.

"Tell them I did my best. And tell them I ain't Superman. If they think I can do everything I say I can do, then they're crazier'n I am."

FIGHTING TALK

He must have been watching the fight in New Jersey

DOUG JONES
on referee Joe LoScalzo's scoring (8-1-1 in rounds) of his fight at Madison Square Garden vs. Cassius Clay

Undefeated Cassius Clay rocks Doug Jones.

LIGHTNING STRIKES TWICE

In November 1958, Ultiminio (Sugar) Ramos, a 16-year-old Cuban, kayoed Jose Blanco in the eighth round. Blanco subsequently died from injuries sustained in the bout.

On March 21, Ramos, 21, challenged featherweight champion Davey Moore on the tripleheader title fight card at Dodger Stadium. Ramos took the crown by 10th-round TKO, but memories of the Blanco tragedy forbade a celebration.

After nearly stopping the number-one contender in the second round, Moore lost control. From the fifth round to the finish, he was battered, and in the 10th, Ramos scored a knockdown with a left hook. As Moore fell, his head hit the bottom rope and snapped forward.

At the end of the round, Willie Ketchum, Moore's manager, instructed referee George Latka to stop the fight. Moore was lucid in his dressing room, but only moments after calling for a rematch, he passed out and fell into a coma. Four days later, he died at White Memorial Hospital. He was 29.

The tragedy came less than one year after the death of Benny (Kid) Paret. Pope John XXIII responded by calling boxing "barbaric." The Golden Age was officially over.

MAY

1963

AUGUST

RINGSIDE VIEW

MAY

Bantamweight champion Eder Jofre continues to dominate the division, stopping Johnny Jamito in the 12th round.

CLOSE, AND GETTING CLOSER

If Emile Griffith and Luis Rodriguez had been rival thoroughbreds, their races would have been a series of photo finishes. If they had been dueling tennis players, all their matches would have ended in fifth-set tiebreakers. If they had been competing sprinters, dash after dash would have been settled by fractions.

But they were boxers, and as such, fated to engage in bouts decided by split decisions.

In March, Rodriguez had taken Griffith's welterweight title by unanimous but disputed decision. Their title fight rematch came on June 8 at Madison Square Garden. In what was becoming a familiar scenario, Griffith forced the fight, and Rodriguez countered with pinpoint accuracy. There were no knockdowns, and few big blows.The verdict – split, of course – went to Griffith, who became the first welter to win the title three times. (Scores of 8-7, 9-6, and 5-10.) A press section poll revealed that 17 of 24 writers favored Rodriguez.

Griffith was apples, and Rodriguez was oranges. It all depended on your taste.

THE UPSET OF THE BOXING YEAR

Light heavyweight champion Harold Johnson was a 5-1 favorite to reject the challenge of Willie Pastrano, and even Las Vegas' most desperate longshot players found little reason to back the underdog. Johnson, 34, was a master counterpuncher from the mold of Archie Moore; he hadn't lost since 1955. Pastrano, 27, had been fighting for 13 years; he lacked power, and had won only four of his last 10 bouts.

Johnson and Pastrano clashed on June 1 at the Convention Center. The 2,970 fans in attendance could have found more action at the craps tables of The Strip. Pastrano won the first five rounds by jabbing, and then began to retreat. His caution gave the champion few openings. Johnson broke through with a big right in round 13, but that punch aside, the bout was void of highlights.

After 15 rounds, the decision was split, with Pastrano taking the crown by scores of 69-68, 69-67, and 68-69.

"I never heard of a fighter winning the title by running," said Johnson, who wouldn't be the last world champion to crap out in Las Vegas.

Underdog Willie Pastrano (right) dethroned "invincible" light heavyweight champ Harold Johnson.

OF TORN SKIN AND GLOVES

When unbeaten heavyweight Cassius Clay arrived in London for his showdown with British Empire champion Henry Cooper, held on June 18 before a crowd of 55,000 at massive Wembley Stadium, the local press referred to him as "Gaseous Cassius." What might happen, they wondered, should "Our 'Enery" connect with one of his patented hooks?

The answer came late in the fourth, a round in which Clay's quick combinations left Cooper's face a bloody mess. With less than 10 seconds remaining, a left found Clay's chin, and the Olympic gold medalist fell through the ropes. He quickly picked himself up, and the bell rang before any further blows could be struck.

During the rest period, Angelo Dundee, Clay's trainer, made referee Tommy Little aware of a rip in Clay's left glove. (The shrewd Dundee didn't cut the glove, but later admitted to widening the tear.) A replacement glove was located and laced, which gave Clay extra seconds to recover.

Early in the fifth, the 1½-inch gash on Cooper's left eye forced Little to intervene. He stopped the fight at the 1:15 mark, with blood pouring from Cooper's cuts. Having survived a sudden scare, Gaseous Cassius was ready to explode.

Cassius Clay won his 19th consecutive fight by stopping Britain's legendary Henry Cooper.

THUD, CRUNCH, SPLAT

For 10 long months, Floyd Patterson went to sleep every night and awoke every morning with the memories of a humiliating first-round kayo loss to Sonny Liston frozen in his mind. He even took to walking the streets in disguise. There could be, he was certain, only one way to exorcise the demons.

Liston-Patterson II came on July 22, at the Convention Center in Las Vegas. Liston was a 4-1 favorite, but even his most confident supporters were shocked by the conclusiveness of his instant replay victory.

Liston opened by pumping his power jab, and then aiming both hands at the challenger's body. When he hooked to the head, Patterson fell, almost politely. He rose at referee Harry Krausse's count of two, and then hammered Liston with his best right hand. No reaction.

There were two more knockdowns, both produced by rights to the head. After Patterson crashed for the third time, Krausse tolled 10 just as he rose from the canvas. The time of the knockout was 2:10 of round one.

The rematch had lasted four seconds longer than the original. At such a rate of improvement, Patterson would need 13 more bouts to last the first round, and 643 more bouts to last the 15-round distance.

Of course, there would be no more slaughters. As Liston's arm was raised, top contender Cassius Clay leaped into the ring and began threatening the champion. In boxing, losers can expect little sympathy; Patterson had already been discarded.

"I feel terrible; I feel disgraced," he said.

He would have to learn how to negotiate those memories.

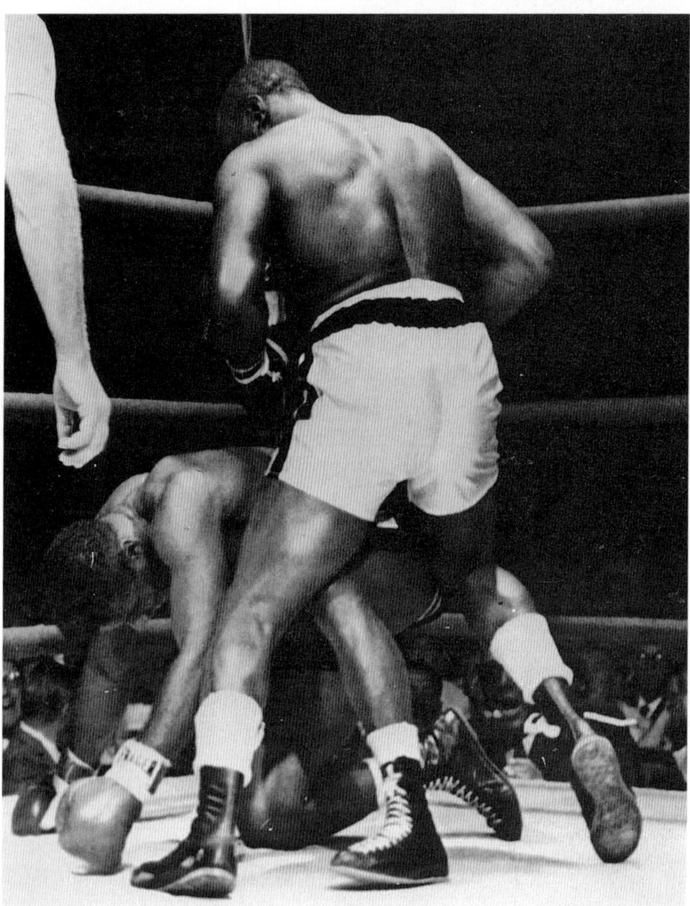

For the second time in a year, Floyd Patterson was knocked out by Sonny Liston.

FULLMER'S FAREWELL

Dick Tiger couldn't possibly have surprised Gene Fullmer; the middleweights had fought twice before. But on August 10, Fullmer was unprepared for the greeting he received from Tiger's fans packed into the Liberty Stadium in Ibadan, Nigeria.

As the challenger, Fullmer entered the ring first. "Fool-mah! Full-mah!" screamed the 35,000 in attendance. Unbeknownst to the Mormon from Utah, he was the second most popular fighter in Nigeria.

Native son Tiger was number one, of course, and the 160-pound titlist's performance served to swell national pride. Attacking from the start, Tiger met minimal resistance. Fullmer, 32, retreated until backed against the ropes. He absorbed an extended beating in round four, and before the fight was half-over, he was bleeding from cuts above and below both eyes.

The most damaging wound was a deep gash on Fullmer's right brow. After the seventh round, manager Marv Jensen informed referee Jack Hart that the challenger would shed no more blood. When Hart raised Tiger's arm, hundreds of fans rushed the ring. It was ten minutes before order was restored.

It would turn out to be the last fight of Fullmer's career. He would exit with a mark of 55-6-3 (24), and victories over, among others, Sugar Ray Robinson, Carmen Basilio, and Benny (Kid) Paret. But none of his triumphs would leave as much of an impression as his visit to Nigeria.

"There were at least a thousand fans waiting outside (the stadium) to cheer goodbye," he said. They were speaking for all of boxing.

RINGSIDE VIEW

JULY

Fighting for the first time since his tragic bout vs. Davey Moore, featherweight champion Sugar Ramos scores a unanimous 15-round decision over Rafiu King.

WORLD TITLE FIGHTS

HEAVYWEIGHTS

July 22 **Sonny Liston** *KO* 1 Floyd Patterson, Las Vegas

LIGHT HEAVYWEIGHTS

June 1 **Willie Pastrano** (USA) *W* 15 Harold Johnson, Las Vegas

MIDDLEWEIGHTS

Aug 10 **Dick Tiger** *KO* 8 Gene Fullmer, Ibadan, Nigeria

JUNIOR MIDDLEWEIGHTS

June 17 **Ralph Dupas** *W* 15 Dennis Moyer, Baltimore

WELTERWEIGHTS

June 8 **Emile Griffith** *W* 15 Luis Rodriguez, New York City

JUNIOR WELTERWEIGHTS

June 15 **Eddie Perkins** *W* 15 Roberto Cruz, Manila

FEATHERWEIGHTS

July 13 **Sugar Ramos** *W* 15 Rafiu King, Mexico City

BANTAMWEIGHTS

May 18 **Eder Jofre** *KO* 12 Johnny Jamito, Quezon City

SEPTEMBER

1963

DECEMBER

World Title Fights

LIGHT HEAVYWEIGHTS

Oct 29 **Eddie Cotton** *W* 15
Henry Hank, Flint, Michigan
(Wins Vacant Michigan World Title)

MIDDLEWEIGHTS

Dec 7 **Joey Giardello** (USA) *ref* 15
Dick Tiger, Atlantic City

JUNIOR MIDDLEWEIGHTS

Sept 7 **Sandro Mazzinghi** (ITA) *KO* 9
Ralph Dupas, Milan

Dec 2 **Sandro Mazzinghi** *KO* 13
Ralph Dupas, Sydney

JUNIOR LIGHTWEIGHTS

Nov 16 **Flash Elorde** *W Disq* 11
Love Allotey, Quezon City

FLYWEIGHTS

Sept 18 **Hiroyuki Ebihara** (JAP) *KO* 1
Pone Kingpetch, Tokyo

Ringside View

OCTOBER

Lightweight champion Carlos Ortiz scores a 10-round non-title decision over Maurice Cullen in London.

THE STANDING COUNT-OUT

In the wake of the ring-related deaths of Benny (Kid) Paret and Davey Moore, boxing officials began to focus on the protection of fighters. One of the results was an ill-fated rule called the safety count-out.

The rule was first used on September 7, when junior middleweight champion Ralph Dupas defended against Italy's 24-year-old Sandro Mazzinghi under a light rainfall at the Vigorelli Velodrome in Milan.

Mazzinghi, a former shoemaker from Florence, was a 2-1 underdog. But he overpowered the American from the start. Dupas was felled by a body blow in the first round. The Italian punished him the rest of the way, and the champion resorted to fouling and clinching.

In round nine, Mazzinghi fired a short right to the chin, and Dupas went down. He rose at the count of eight, but Swiss referee Rolf Neuhold coninued to 10 and then waved the bout over.

"Who ever heard of a champion being counted out on his feet?" complained Dupas. "I had to fight the referee and Mazzinghi tonight."

SOMEBODY UP THERE LIKED HIM

Japanese flyweight Hiroyuki Ebihara grew up poor, and decided to become a professional fighter after watching the Rocky Graziano film biography, *Somebody Up There Likes Me*. On September 18, at the Metropolitan Gymnasium in Tokyo, he became his country's third world titlist in a manner that was pure Rocky.

The 23-year-old Ebihara entered the ring as a favorite because the defending champion, Pone Kingpetch, had appeared sluggish in workouts and had struggled to make the 112-pound limit.

Kingpetch proved impotent against the hard-punching challenger. In fact, he landed only one punch. Ebihara, a southpaw, charged from his corner and released bomb after a bomb. A left knocked down Kingpetch, and later in the round, another left redeposited him on the canvas. He was out cold; referee Sangwein Hiranyalekha could have counted to 100.

For Japan's Rocky, it couldn't have ended any other way.

THEY MADE A TITLE FIGHT AND NOBODY CAME?

The proliferation of world titles is hardly a new phenomenon. On October 29, at the IMA Auditorium in Flint, Michigan, the absurdity of boxing politics was plain for all to see.

All of those who bothered to attend, that is. Only 855 fans paid to watch Seattle's Eddie Cotton and local favorite Henry Hank compete for the vacant Michigan World light heavyweight title. (Having withdrawn from the WBA, the state no longer recognized Willie Pastrano as world champion.)

Rule changes had made boxing a bit different in Michigan. Rounds were two minutes long, though Cotton and Hank fought the conventional three, and fighters rested 90 seconds between.

Cotton controlled the uneventful bout with his sterling jab and emerged victorious by unanimous 15-round decision (two scores of 146-140, and 148-147). The 36-year-old veteran was finally a world champion – in Michigan, if nowhere else.

Eddie Cotton (left) outpointed hard-hitting Henry Hank for Michigan's world light heavy title.

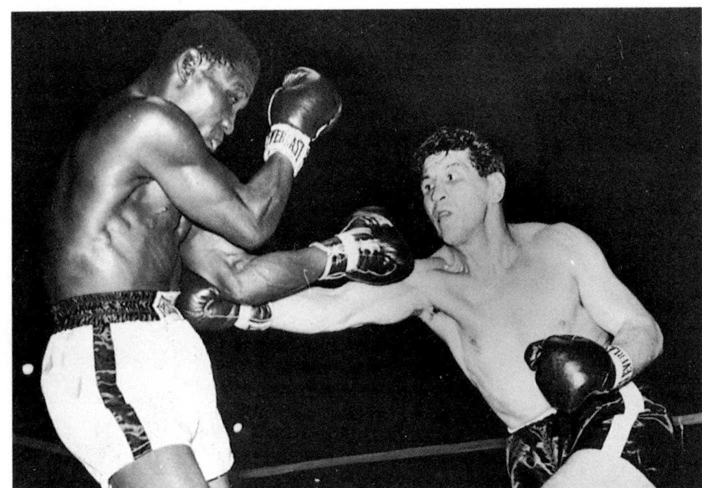

After 15 bruising years, Joey Giardello (right) finally became a middleweight champion.

THE REWARDS OF PERSISTENCE

In 1954, Carmen Telleli, better known as Joey Giardello, was the top-rated middleweight in the world. He signed for a shot at world champion Bobo Olson, but the bout was cancelled after the challenger injured his knee in an auto accident.

In 1960, Giardello finally secured his title try. After being held to a 15-round draw by NBA king Gene Fullmer, however, the Brooklyn-born veteran seemed destined to remain a contender until his last punch was thrown.

His last chance came on December 7, at Convention Hall in Atlantic City. He was a 3-1 underdog vs. champion Dick Tiger, whom he knew quite well; the 160-pounders had split a pair of meetings in 1959.

Giardello knew he couldn't match Tiger's strength, so he kept the bout at a distance, used moved laterally, and clinched when necessary. Tiger became desperate in the later rounds, but Giardello remained disciplined, and showed his confidence by dancing through the last round.

Referee Paul Cavalier, the sole judge, scored 8-5-2 for the challenger. At age 33, Giardello had made it all the way to the top. And no one ever appreciated it more.

HIT BY A HURRICANE

Emile Griffith was the welterweight champion of the world, and the Boxing Writers Association's choice as 1963's Fighter of the Year. Number-two rated middleweight contender Rubin (Hurricane) Carter, however, was unimpressed.

"No welterweight has any business in the ring with me," he said before squaring off with Griffith in a non-title fight. "He won't get up when I knock him down."

On December 20, at the Civic Arena in Pittsburgh, Carter established himself as one of the most dangerous fighters in *any* weight class by scoring the first stoppage of Griffith's career. And he needed only 133 seconds to do it.

Griffith, 151½, opened as the aggressor and controlled the first half of the opening round. But a split second after the fighters broke out of a clinch, Carter, 155, unleashed a hook. Boom! Griffith barely beat the count of referee Buck McTiernan, and was then promptly dropped again. He picked himself up once more, but this time, McTiernan wouldn't allow him to continue. The lesson to be learned: if the Hurricane was heading your way, it was best to relocate.

Rubin "Hurricane" Carter astonished the world by knocking out world champion Emile Griffith in the first round.

GOING QUAZY IN QUEZON CITY

Considering that in August, he had outpointed Emmanuel (Love) Allotey in a non-title bout, junior lightweight champion Flash Elorde would have been excused for denying the London-based Ghanian a try at the title. But on November 16, before 35,000 supporters at the Araneta Coliseum in Quezon City, Elorde risked the title. The challenger displayed his appreciation in a most peculiar way.

From the start, Allotey disregarded the rules. He was effectively aggressive in spurts, but referee Jamie Valencia repeatedly warned him for a variety of infractions. Allotey lost a point for hitting on the break, and another point in round eight for butting.

In the 11th, after Allotey again hit on the break, and then rubbed the laces of his gloves into the champion's face, Valencia separated the fighters and raised Elorde's hand. At the time of the disqualification, Elorde held a slim lead on all three cards.

Hundreds of fans rushed the ring, with some throwing oranges and soda bottles at Allotey.

"I'm sorry it had to happen this way," said Elorde.

Flash Elorde (right) retained the title with a controversial disqualification of Love Allotey.

JANUARY

1964

APRIL

THE KING (PETCH) ONCE MORE

Pone Kingpetch seemed destined to become the Sugar Ray Robinson of the flyweight division. In January 1963, the slender Thai became the first 112-pounder in history to regain the title, only to lose it in his next defense.

On January 23, at Rajdamnern Stadium in Bangkok, Kingpetch won the crown for a third time by edging previous conqueror Hiroyuki Ebihara. In the '50s, Robinson won the middleweight title five times, a record for any division. Kingpetch, 27, was more than halfway there.

In the Thai's first fight with Ebihara, he lasted less than one round. This time, he boxed the 15-round distance without incident. The challenger established his jab by round six, and in the last third of the fight, he added a handful of sizzling right uppercuts. Ebihara flurried, but was outclassed.

With the Thai judge scoring 71-68 for Kingpetch, and the Japanese judge scoring 73-71 for Ebihara, the fight was decided by the card of America's Arch Hindman, who favored Kingpetch by 73-67. Three down, two to go.

RINGSIDE VIEW

FEBRUARY

Featherweight champion Sugar Ramos retains the title for the second time, stopping Mitsunori Seki in the sixth.

"I SHOCKED THE WORLD!"

Before 7-1 underdog Cassius Clay's challenge of heavyweight champion Sonny Liston, held on February 25 at the Miami Beach Convention Hall, 43 of 46 sportswriters picked the defending titlist to win. When Clay's pulse raced to 120 during the chaotic weigh-in, a quick kayo seemed likely.

But destiny would not be denied. Flashing his jab and moving just enough to remain trouble-free, Clay frustrated Liston and opened a cut under the champion's left eye.

The 22-year-old challenger's only scare came at the end of round four, when he was blinded by ointment that had been applied to Liston's cut. He returned to his corner screaming surrender, but trainer Angelo Dundee persuaded him to continue. Clay danced until his vision returned midway through the fifth.

After six rounds, the fight was even on points. At the bell for the seventh round, Liston remained on his stool, citing numbness from his left shoulder down to his forearm. Suddenly and dramatically, the title fight was all over.

"I shocked the world!" Clay shouted over and over again.

It wouldn't be the last time.

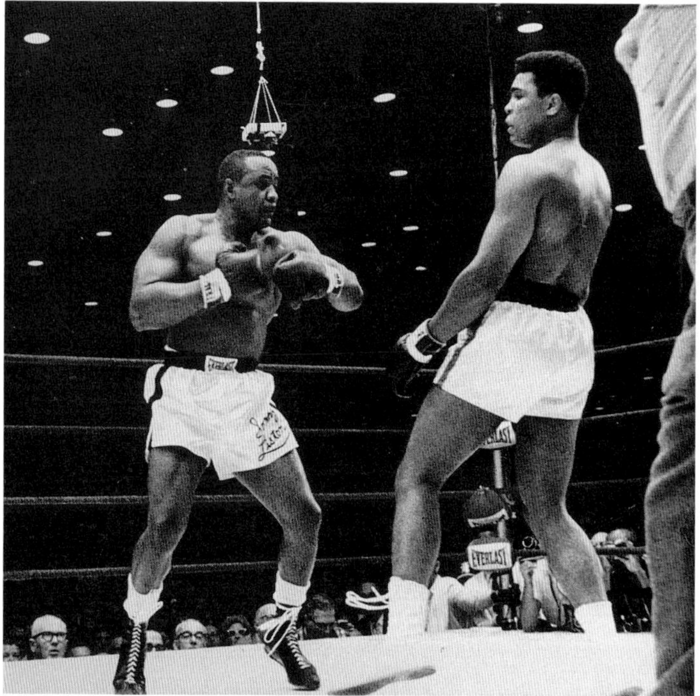

Cassius Clay (right) stopped Sonny Liston in the seventh round to win the heavyweight crown.

JUMPING UP A WEIGHT – AND TRIPPING UP!

Flash Elorde's record as world junior lightweight champion – six successful defenses over four years – was exemplary. But in order to secure lasting greatness, he needed to win the lightweight title. Unfortunately for the Filipino, Carlos Ortiz, who blocked his path, was among the finest fighters in the game.

Elorde challenged the New Yorker on February 15, before 60,000 rabid fans at the Rizal Memorial Coliseum in Manila. The fight was competitive throughout, with Ortiz jabbing and scoring with rights to the body, and Elorde moving in and out and countering. The difference turned out to be the champion's strength; Ortiz dominated the championship rounds.

With Elorde trapped against the ropes in round 14, referee James Wilson stepped in. When the challenger protested, he was told, "I had to stop the fight or he would have killed you."

At the time of the stoppage, Ortiz led on all three cards. For Elorde, the rise had been a futile exercise.

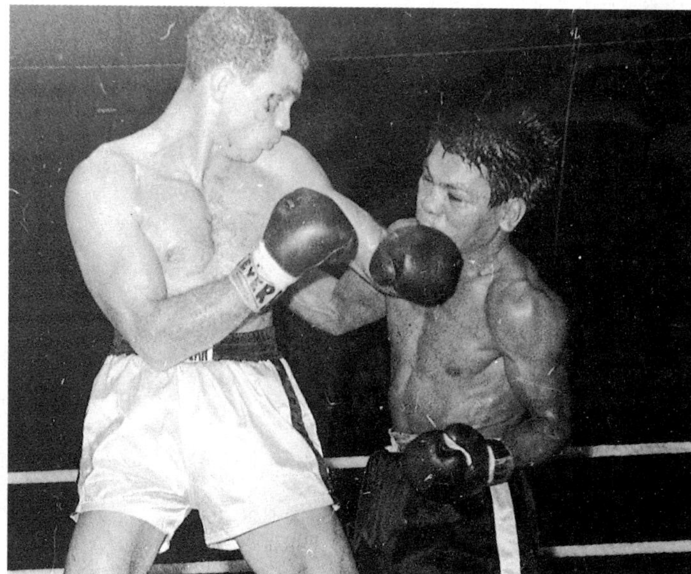

Lightweight champion Carlos Ortiz (left) was brilliant in a title defense against Flash Elorde.

A BLOODY AND BEAUTIFUL TARGET

In Willie Pastrano's second bout after winning the light heavyweight championship from Harold Johnson, he lost a 10-round non-title bout to Argentine bull Gregorio (Goyo) Peralta. Pastrano knew what to expect in the rematch; Peralta was predictable, featuring superior strength and a draining body attack. It would be up to the champion to adjust.

Pastrano-Peralta II came on April 10, at the Municipal Auditorium in the defending titlist's native New Orleans. To Peralta's surprise, Pastrano sprung from his corner and set a hot pace by punching in bunches.

"I was a different boy tonight, wasn't I?" the champion would later say.

The first two rounds belonged to Pastrano, but in the third, Peralta began scoring to the body. He continued his rally in the fourth, but then came the moment that decided the fight: Pastrano landed a right that opened a lengthy gash across the Argentine's left eyebrow. It would take nine stitches to close.

"All that blood gave me a beautiful target," Pastrano said matter of factly. The rhythm of the bout changed drastically in the fifth. Pastrano began to zero in on the cut with his primary weapon, one of boxing's best jabs, and Peralta was forced to switch into a defensive mode. Before the start of round six, referee Pete Giarusso decided that Peralta should not continue.

During the postfight interviews, reporters wanted to know why Pastrano had been so successful the second time around.

"Tonight," he answered, "I cared."

WORLD TITLE FIGHTS

HEAVYWEIGHTS

Feb 25	**Cassius Clay** (USA) *KO* 7 Sonny Liston, Miami Beach

LIGHT HEAVYWEIGHTS

April 10	**Willie Pastrano** *KO* 6 Gregorio Peralta, New Orleans

JUNIOR WELTERWEIGHTS

Jan 4	**Eddie Perkins** *KO* 13 Yoshinori Takahashi, Tokyo
April 18	**Eddie Perkins** *W* 15 Bunny Grant, Kingston

LIGHTWEIGHTS

Feb 15	**Carlos Ortiz** *KO* 14 Flash Elorde, Manila
April 11	**Carlos Ortiz** *W* 15 Kenny Lane, San Juan

FEATHERWEIGHTS

Feb 28	**Sugar Ramos** *KO* 6 Mitsunori Seki, Tokyo

FLYWEIGHTS

Jan 23	**Pone Kingpetch** *W* 15 Hiroyuki Ebihara, Bangkok

ORTIZ IN A BREEZE

It is of paramount importance that before defending his title, a world champion focus solely on his opponent and the task at hand. If his concentration wavers even for a moment, the consequences can be devastating.

Before making his fourth defense of the lightweight title, it was particularly difficult for Carlos Ortiz to focus on his opponent, veteran southpaw Kenny Lane. That's because Ortiz was furious with the WBA, who, ever since he won the title, had threatened to strip him for not defending against Lane. Ortiz had to turn his anger into fight-night energy.

Ortiz and Lane met on April 11, at Hiram Bithorn Stadium in San Juan. They had fought twice before, splitting a pair of bouts in the late-'50s. But Lane was now 32, and when Ortiz set a quick pace, the challenger was forced to retreat.

"He kept telling the world that Carlos was running away from him," said Honest Bill Daly, Ortiz' manager. "And when he got in there, he fought like a scared jackrabbit."

Attacking behind his outstanding jab, Ortiz cut Lane over the left eye in round seven. The only knockdown came in the 14th, when the champion connected with a hook. But Lane leaped to his feet before referee Pete Pantaleo could count.

After 15 rounds, Ortiz was declared the winner by unanimous decision (scores of 144-141, 148-144, and 147-143). "I'll never give him another fight," he said of Lane. "The WBA insisted I fight him, but he's not in my class."

Scoreboard: Ortiz 1, WBA 0.

Carlos Ortiz (right) defended the lightweight title for the second time in two months, decisioning challenger Kenny Lane.

MAY

1964

AUGUST

DAYLIGHT ROBBERY

Choose one:
*Featherweight champion Sugar Ramos retained the title against British and Empire titlist Floyd Robertson.
*Ramos lost to Robertson.
*The bout was a no-contest.

The answer depended on who you cared to listen to. And when.

On May 9, Ramos made his third defense, meeting Robertson at Black Star Stadium in Accra, Ghana, the first title fight held in the challenger's native land.

Ramos controlled the first half of the bout, but Robertson swarmed from round eight until the final bell. In the 13th, he connected with a right, and Ramos dropped. He was saved by the bell.

Toward the end of the 15th round, the 30,000 fans in attendance began to celebrate Robertson's coronation. Referee Jack Hart scored for the Ghanian, but Mexico's Ramon Velasquez and Miami-based WBA president Ed Lassman voted for Ramos, and the Cuban was announced the winner by split decision.

"I've never seen any such thing in my life," said Ginger Addyfio, Robertson's trainer. "I think this is what they call daylight robbery."

"What about the early rounds Ramos won?" countered Angelo Dundee, the champion's trainer.

In the days following the fight, no one was sure exactly who had won. The Ghana Boxing Authority ruled no-contest, then declared Robertson the winner. But the WBA and the British Boxing Board of Control ruled that Ramos remained champion.

EMILE, LUIS, AND KING DAVID

Before facing welterweight champion Emile Griffith for the fourth time, former titlist Luis Rodriguez dreamed of a meeting with King David.

"Come with me into the arena," the king told Rodriguez. "We are matadors, and we will kill the Black Bull."After hearing of the dream, which Rodriguez shared with reporters, Griffith became incensed. He didn't object to the challenger having called him a black bull, but rather that Rodriguez had insensitively used the word *kill.*

"Has he forgotten of my fight with Benny Paret?" Griffith asked.

Perhaps because of the prefight incident, or perhaps because familiarity indeed breeds contempt, Griffith-Rodriguez IV was their messiest, most foul-filled affair. It was held on June 12 at the Las Vegas Convention Center. Rodriguez was an 8-5 favorite, but those inclined to wager might as well have made their selection by flipping a coin; Griffith and Rodriguez were destined to engage in yet another split decision fight.

Referee Harry Krause was busy from the start. Rodriguez was penalized for hitting low in the third stanza, and in three different rounds, the welters traded after the bell. There was also a lot of hitting and holding, butting, and heeling.

Rodriguez moved and boxed less than usual, and he landed more punches than Griffith. But the champion's blows seemed heavier. As had been the case in their first three bouts, the fighters offered the judges 15 rounds of constrasting styles. This time, Griffith was rewarded (scores of 69-67, 70-68, and 70-71).

"I guess I can't ever win the title again," said Rodriguez. "I'll have to go after the middleweight title."

Trouble was, Griffith had the same idea.

RINGSIDE VIEW

JUNE

In a battle of future world champions, Mexican featherweight Vicente Saldivar outpoints Panama's Ismael Laguna in Tijuana.

Emile Griffith (left) solved Luis Rodriguez' puzzling style and retained the welterweight title by decision in Las Vegas.

TALES OF THE TALL

At 6'3", light heavyweight Bob Foster towered over almost all of his opponents. When he wanted bigger challenges, he moved up to heavyweight. But even against boxing's behemoths, he was never forced to look up.

Until July 10, when Foster squared off against 6'6" Ernie Terrell at Madison Square Garden. Terrell, 202½, enjoyed a 19-pound weight advantage. It was 2-1 underdog Foster, however, who was billed as the puncher.

Terrell and Foster engaged in a fast-paced bout, especially by heavyweight standards. When at a distance, Terrell controlled the pace by pumping what his manager, Big Julie Isaacson, called "the best jab in the heavyweight division." But when Foster worked his way inside, the two willingly swapped power hooks.

In round five, referee Arthur Mercante penalized Terrell for leaning on Foster and holding. Later in the round, he took a wayward punch on the chin. The bout had turned into a three-for-all.

The fight was even on points after six rounds. In the seventh, Terrell combined an overhand right and a hook, and, in a delayed reaction, Foster fell. He staggered to his feet at Mercante's count of six, but the referee kept tolling, and after reaching 10, waved the fight over.

Afterward, Mercante explained why he had continued to count. As Foster was struggling to regain his feet, he pushed off the canvas with his glove. That meant that technically, at least, he had not risen from the floor.

But the loser was angry for a different reason.

"I wasn't hit," he complained. "Terrell knocked me down with a push and a shove. He hugged me more than my wife."

Terrell (left) was too big and strong for Bob Foster, kayoing the future light heavy champ.

FLASH AND THE BASH WITH KOSAKA IN TOKYO

During the course of his lengthy title reign, world junior lightweight champion Flash Elorde survived several difficult moments. None of them, however, compared to his defense against top-rated Teruo Kosaka, held on July 27, at Kuramae Sumo Stadium in Tokyo.

Elorde and Kosaka were familiar foes; they had previously tested each other three times in bouts for the Oriental lightweight crown. All of the fights went the distance, with Elorde winning twice.

In the most significant fight of their series, Kosaka consistently beat Elorde to the trigger. The longer the 130-pounders rumbled, the slower the champion seemed. It was Elorde's 14th year as a pro, and as the boxers reached the championship rounds, it appeared that on this night, he would age.

But at age 29, the Filipino proved to have plenty of fight in reserve. He struck in round 12, felling Kosaka with a hook. The Japanese rose, but after Elorde followed with a flurry, referee Jose Padilla stopped the fight at the 1:45 mark.

Certain that Kosaka was headed to victory, the 8,000 fans in attendance exploded. (After 11 rounds, Kosaka was ahead on two of the three cards.) They began tossing seat cushions toward the ring, even as policemen positioned themselves on the apron. A riot was barely averted.

The controversial ending guaranteed that Elorde and Kosaka would meet for a fourth time.

Japan's Teruo Kosaka got back on his feet after being dropped by Flash Elorde.

WORLD TITLE FIGHTS

WELTERWEIGHTS

June 12 — **Emile Griffith** *W* 15 Luis Rodriguez, Las Vegas

JUNIOR LIGHTWEIGHTS

July 27 — **Flash Elorde** *KO* 12 Teruo Kosaka, Tokyo

FEATHERWEIGHTS

May 9 — **Sugar Ramos** *W* 15 Floyd Robertson, Accra

RINGSIDE VIEW

JULY

Two days after his 33rd birthday, former middleweight champion Gene Fullmer announces his retirement. He exits with a career mark of 55-6-3 (24).

SEPTEMBER

1964

DECEMBER

WHEN THEY CARRIED THE WINNER OUT OF THE RING

Emile Griffith was a symbol of strength and durability, the kind of champion whose natural resources allowed him to meet the extraordinary physical demands of boxing. For that reason, the sellout crowd at Wembley's Empire Pool gazed incredulously when the welterweight champion was carried out of the ring following his defense against Welsh southpaw Brian Curvis.

It sounds worse that it was. After 15 rounds, referee and sole judge Harry Gibbs had raised Griffith's hand in victory. But from the 13th round until the finish, the champion suffered from severe cramps in his right leg.

"The situation could have been dangerous," he said. "The cramps got worse in the 15th, and he was hitting me now and then because I could hardly move."

Curvis failed to break a 45-year jinx; there hadn't been a British 147-pound titlist since Ted (Kid) Lewis in 1919. The last fighter to try had been Ernie Roderick, who lost to Henry Armstrong.

The British and Empire champion offered courage, but little else. Both fighters attacked with passion. Griffith, however, was far more accurate and powerful. Curvis was floored in the sixth, 10th, and 13th rounds, each time barely beating Gibbs' count.

Over the last three rounds, when Griffith was handicapped and near-helpless, Curvis found himself far too bloodied and battered to capitalize. They carried Emile out of the ring all right, but he was smiling all the way to his dressing room.

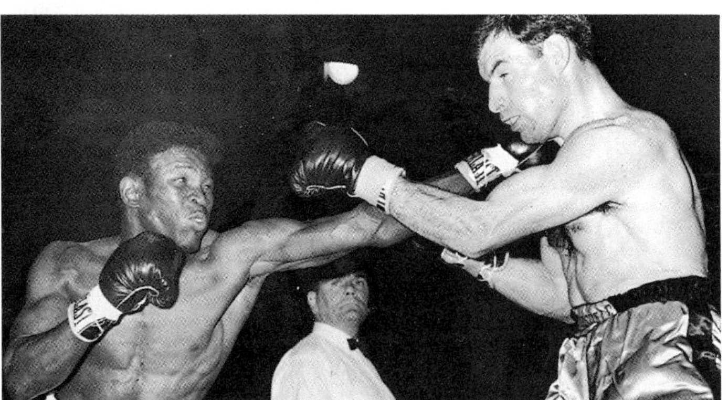

Britain's talented Brian Curvis (right) pressured welterweight king Emile Griffith throughout.

SUGAR'S MOST SOUR NIGHT

In May, featherweight champion Sugar Ramos was declared a split decision winner in his title defense against Ghana's Floyd Robertson. It was among the most controversial decisions of the decade. The postfight focus centered on the verdict, and whether Ramos deserved to continue as champion. What no one addressed was whether he could recover from the beating he had absorbed. It seemed impossible, but at age 22, the Mexico-based Cuban was already spent.

On September 26, 4½ months after edging Robertson, Ramos defended against the number-two contender, southpaw Vicente Saldivar, at Cuatro Caminos in Mexico City. At least he would have the satisfaction of losing his crown to a Mexican. At 5'3", Mexico's Saldivar wasn't the type of fighter who could bounce and wait for counterpunching opportunities. He stood in front of Ramos for the first two rounds and skillfully avoided most of the champion's blows. In the third, the southpaw began to show his speed, darting in and out. By the fifth, the slower Ramos was frustrated, and in the seventh, Saldivar buckled his knees with a left.

Saldivar's chief assets were strength and stamina, and after a final and desperate Ramos rally in round eight, the challenger took over. He scored a knockdown in the 10th – Ramos was saved by the bell – and savagely battered his foe throughout the 11th. Ramos' corner surrendered before the start of round 12.

Saldivar, 21, was the featherweight champion of the world. He might've thanked Floyd Robertson, who after all, had done a wonderful job of clearing his path.

RINGSIDE VIEW

OCTOBER

Italian junior middleweight Sandro Mazzinghi retains the world title for the second time, stopping Tony Montano in the 12th round.

Mexico's Vicente Saldivar (left) won the featherweight crown when Sugar Ramos was unable to answer the bell for the 12th round.

THE BEST IN BOXING

It was a good thing that Bernardo Caraballo's challenge of world bantamweight champion Eder Jofre came in Colombia. Whenever Caraballo learned that he had been scheduled for a bout abroad, he headed for a pub.

The fight site aside, the prospect of facing Jofre was enough to unsettle any bantamweight. Jofre, 45-0-3, had made seven defenses. Most observers considered him the best fighter in boxing.

Jofre risked the crown against Caraballo, who was also unbeaten, on November 27, before 32,000 fans at Bogota's Plaza de Toros. (It was the first world title fight ever held in Colombia.) Despite an 18-month layoff, the champion was aggressive from the start, and Caraballo elected to bob, weave, and dance away.

By round six, there seemed no chance of an upset. In the seventh, the Brazilian softened Caraballo by pounding his body, then dropped him with two rights and a left. Referee Barney Ross tolled 10.

If it was possible, the best was getting better.

WORLD TITLE FIGHTS

LIGHT HEAVYWEIGHTS		**WELTERWEIGHTS**	
Nov 30	**Willie Pastrano** *KO* 11 Terry Downes, Manchester	Sept 22	**Emile Griffith** *ref* 15 Brian Curvis, Wembley
MIDDLEWEIGHTS		**FEATHERWEIGHTS**	
Dec 14	**Joey Giardello** *W* 15 Rubin Carter, Philadelphia	Sept 26	**Vicente Saldivar** (MEX) *KO* 12 Sugar Ramos, Mexico City
JUNIOR MIDDLEWEIGHTS		**BANTAMWEIGHTS**	
Oct 3	**Sandro Mazzinghi** *KO* 12 Tony Montano, Genoa	Nov 27	**Eder Jofre** *KO* 7 Bernardo Caraballo, Bogota
Dec 11	**Sandro Mazzinghi** *ref* 15 Fortunato Manca, Rome		

WINNING HAIR AND SQUARE

For one year, Rubin (Hurricane) Carter had groomed his beard. But before the powerpuncher's challenge of middleweight champion Joey Giardello, which came on December 14 at Philadelphia's Convention Hall, the Pennsylvania State Athletic Commission ordered him to shave off his beard. Carter complied with the order, and then gave a performance reminiscent of Samson. After his haircut.

The fight was unexceptional, which suited the 34-year-old champion. Giardello capitalized on his huge advantage in experience – it was his 127th pro bout, and Carter's 25th – by staying off the ropes and constantly turning Carter. By the middle rounds, the challenger began to tire. Giardello hurt him with hooks in the 13th, 14th, and 15th rounds, and was awarded a unanimous verdict (scores of 72-66, 71-66, and 70-67).

Time would no doubt bring back Carter's beard. There could be no guarantee, however, concerning the loser's damaged reputation.

DOWNES GOES DOWN, AND SAYS GOODBYE

Terry Downes was a 3-1 underdog against light heavyweight champion Willie Pastrano, whom he challenged on November 30, at Belle Vue Stadium in Manchester. Generally, only those with an inclination to gamble were concerned with the odds on a prize fight. But former middleweight champion Downes was a partner in a string of betting shops. That Pastrano was a hot favorite would help business.

Downes tried with all his might to reward the longshot players, but the champion proved a bit too big and strong. The Londoner crowded Pastrano from the start, which nullified his jab. As the rounds mounted, however, Pastrano's muscle surfaced. The end came in the 11th, during which Downes fell twice.

The kayo loss turned out to be Downes' farewell. He retired at age 28, with a career mark of 35-9 (28). A comeback? He advised betting against it.

Ex-middleweight champ Terry Downes failed in a bid for the light heavyweight title when stopped by Willie Pastrano in the 11th round.

JANUARY

1965

APRIL

HIGH AND DRY IN CARACAS

Because he won almost all of his fights, it was easy to dismiss the excessive drinking and poor training habits of Venezuelan junior welterweight Carlos Hernandez. But in December 1964, he went too far; after an extended display of drunkeness on the streets of Caracas, the 24-year-old fighter was suspended and stripped of his national crown. Worse yet, he had jeopardized his title fight against world champion Eddie Perkins.

The bout vs. Perkins was rescheduled for January 18 at the Nuevo Circo. All Venezuela held its breath; it had never spawned a world champion, and Hernandez' neighbors were hoping he wouldn't embarrass them.

As it turned out, he made them proud. Perkins, a 2-1 favorite, sought to stay inside; having risen from the canvas to outpoint Hernandez in June 1961, he was aware of the Venezuelan's right-hand power. In the last third of the bout, Perkins drew boos by repeatedly holding.

The fight went the full 15 rounds and was decided by a controversial split decision. American referee Henry Armstrong scored for Perkins, 150-129, but was outvoted by Venezuelans Dimas Hernandez and Santo Arizmendi, who saw Hernandez ahead by 143-142 and 146-143, respectively. (Upon returning home, Armstrong called the decision "the most brazen demonstration of partiality I've seen in 35.")

Hernandez then swore off liquor. Must've been a boring victory party.

FLOYD AGAIN SHOWS HE HAS GUTS

After Floyd Patterson suffered a pair of humiliating first-round knockouts vs. Sonny Liston, certain fans began to question his courage. Forgotten was the fact that during the New Yorker's heavyweight title reign, he had often risen from the canvas. On February 1, before a huge crowd at Madison Square Garden, Patterson proved his mettle once more.

Unfortunately, Patterson's gutty display went unappreciated; the 19,100 fans in attendance were unaware that the former champion fought 12 rounds against rugged Canadian contender George Chuvalo with a separated bone in his left hand. In fact, only his closest associates knew that on the fight afternoon, he received ultrasonic therapy.

Why hadn't Floyd postponed the fight? Part of the reason was strictly business; bringing in a live gate of $166,423, and a gross of $600,000 from theatre TV, Patterson-Chuvalo was the richest non-title fight in history. But it was more than that. Patterson wanted to prove that he was a warrior, not least to himself.

It was a good, tough fight. Patterson banged away with combinations, and the Canadian responded with a steady body attack. Chuvalo, who suffered cuts on both cheekbones and over his left eye, blamed referee Zack Clayton for his inability to wear Patterson down.

"I planned to work on Floyd's body, then switch to the head," he said. "But every time I got through working his body and went to switch to the head, the referee would step in and break us."

The unanimous decision went to Patterson 6-5-1, 7-5, and 8-4. He was again considered a title threat. And a gutty one at that.

Ex-heavyweight champion Floyd Patterson (right) hammered out unanimous 10-round decision over tough Canadian George Chuvalo.

RINGSIDE VIEW

FEBRUARY

Former welterweight champion Luis Rodriguez scores a 10-round decision victory over Rubin (Hurricane) Carter in New York City.

WORLD TITLE FIGHTS

HEAVYWEIGHTS

March 5	**Ernest Terrell** (USA) *W* 15 Eddie Machen, Chicago (Wins Vacant WBA Title)

LIGHT HEAVYWEIGHTS

March 30	**Jose Torres** (PR) *KO* 10 Willie Pastrano, New York City

WELTERWEIGHTS

March 30	**Emile Griffith** *W* 15 Jose Stable, New York City

JUNIOR WELTERWEIGHTS

Jan 18	**Carlos Hernandez** (VEN) *W* 15 Eddie Perkins, Caracas

LIGHTWEIGHTS

April 10	**Ismael Laguna** (PAN) *W* 15 Carlos Ortiz, Panama City

FLYWEIGHTS

April 23	**Salvatore Burruni** (ITA) *W* 15 Pone Kingpetch, Rome

TOUGH TO FIGHT, BUT WORSE TO WATCH

Heavyweight Ernie Terrell, 6'6" and with an 82-inch reach, was an octopus in a sea of sharks. Nonetheless, on March 5, at the International Amphitheatre in Chicago, he had one of his arms raised as a world champion.

When undisputed champion Muhammad Ali signed to defend against Sonny Liston, the WBA cited its rule prohibiting immediate rematches and stripped him of the title. To fill the vacancy, the organization matched number-one contender Terrell against 32-year-old veteran Eddie Machen, who was rated fourth.

It was among the worst title fights in history. Round after round, Terrell pumped his jab – which Machen generally avoided – feinted once or twice, and then simply leaned on his foe. The heavyweights hugged and wrestled more than they punched. In round six, a shoulder butt closed Terrell's left eye. That aside, the bout was void of highlights.

Someone had to win, and after 15 rounds, Terrell was awarded a unanimous decision (scores of 70-67, 72-66, and 72-67). No one was going to forget Muhammad Ali.

Ernie Terrell (left) beats Eddie Machen.

A DELICIOUS DIVISION DEBUT

Perhaps because he had previously boxed at featherweight, and not lightweight, Panama's Ismael Laguna had escaped the attention of Carlos Ortiz. On April 10, at Anoche Stadium in Panama City, he snuck up on the 135-pound champion, and then slickly snuck past him.

The 21-year-old Laguna defeated Ortiz with speed.

"He doesn't stick around to get hit, and I wasn't fast enough to catch him," explained Ortiz.

After cutting Ortiz with his jab and then eluding the Puerto Rican's late rushes, Laguna was declared champion by majority decision. Referee Jersey Joe Walcott and Panama's Ramon Moynes scored for him by 143-132 and 149-137, respectively. The USA's Ben Greene, hand-picked by Ortiz' manager, Bill Daly, saw it even at 145-145. Greene left ringside under police protection, and later claimed that before the fight, he had been threatened with a lynching if he dared score against Laguna.

Luckily, Laguna hadn't needed his help.

RINGSIDE VIEW

APRIL

Italy's Salvatore Burruni wins the world flyweight title by scoring a unanimous 15-round decision over Pone Kingpetch.

A GARDEN PARTY

It was a sight that New York fight fans would never forget: moments after Jose Torres won the world light heavyweight title by stopping Willie Pastrano at Madison Square Garden, he was carried into the crowd, and passed up and down the aisles by his fans. Somehow, he made the dressing room.

(Torres' triumph came on the same card as welterweight champion Emile Griffith's win over Jose Stable. The show drew a house record gate of $239,556.)

Boxing in a peekaboo stance, Torres hurt Pastrano in the first round with three snapping lefts. By the third, the champion's face was swollen and bloodied, and he began to turn away from Torres' blows. The Puerto Rican scored a knockdown with a body blow in the sixth, but the end didn't come until the rest period between the ninth and 10th, when referee Johnny LoBianco called a halt. Pastrano retired at 63-13-8 (14).

Jose Torres stops Willie Pastrano in ninth round in New York to become the new light heavyweight champion of the world.

MAY

1965

AUGUST

RINGSIDE VIEW

MAY

Featherweight champion Vicente Saldivar makes his first defense, stopping Raul Rojas with 10 seconds remaining in the 15th and final round.

EDER'S NO LONGER THE LEADER

Psychologically, bantamweight champion Eder Jofre was able to match Fighting Harada for 10 rounds. Physically, he remained competitive with the Japanese challenger for 15 rounds. But he lost both fights.

On May 17, at the Aiichi Prefectural Gymnasium in Nagoya, Japan, former flyweight champion Harada scored a huge upset. The 29-year-old Jofre answered the opening bell with a record of 47-0-3, and the reputation as being the best fighter, pound for pound, in boxing. After 15 rounds, he was contemplating retirement.

Formerly boxing's teenage sensation, Harada, 22, sent a message by darting from his corner at the start of every round. Jofre's answer came *between* rounds, when he elected to stand in his corner. By round 10, however, he succumbed to fatigue, and plopped onto his stool.

In the early rounds, Jofre neutralized the challenger's pressure with jabs and straight rights. But Harada never wavered, and by round six, he was swarming. His punching power suddenly inadequate, Jofre was repeatedly forced to fight off the ropes and clinch.

The bout was close throughout the championship rounds, with Harada's superior work rate giving him a slight edge. To the delight of his countrymen, he captured his second world crown by split decision (scores of 71-69, 72-70, and 71-72).

"I was lucky to win," he said. "I really didn't know I had won until the announcement. I was only fighting hard."

Hard enough, it turned out, to defeat a living legend.

Eder Jofre (left) lost to Fighting Harada.

THE MAINE EVENT

The rematch between heavyweight champion Muhammad Ali and Sonny Liston was weird, bizarre, and controversial. And that was *before* the fight.

It started in November 1964, when Ali's emergency surgery for a strangulated hernia brought an 11th-hour postponement. The bout was rescheduled for Boston, but less than three weeks before fight night, the city's district attorney told the heavyweights to look elsewhere because the promoters weren't licensed in Massachusetts. The fight somehow landed in the faded industrial city of Lewiston, Maine.

On May 25, Ali and Liston met before a crowd of 2,434 at the Central Maine Youth Center. After Canada's Robert Goulet set the tone by forgetting the words to the National Anthem, referee Jersey Joe Walcott issued final instructions. Then it was chaos.

There were no significant blows until midway through the first round. When Liston offered a jab, Ali responded with a short chopping right to the head. The counter seemed innocent, but Liston fell. He rolled over, climbed to his knees, and then fell again.

Walcott pointed Ali to a neutral corner. The champion stood over his foe, however, and Jersey Joe failed to pick up the count of timekeeper Frank McDonough. After more than 20 seconds had elapsed, *The Ring* Publisher Nat Fleischer, who was seated next to McDonough, caught Walcott's attention. Jersey Joe was told that Liston had been counted out – twice! By the time the referee returned to the fighters, Liston had regained his feet, and the heavyweights were again trading blows. Walcott jumped between them and raised Ali's hand in victory.

Had Liston taken a dive?

"I didn't quit," he answered. "I just didn't get the count."

And boxing fans the world over just didn't buy the excuse.

Sonny Liston couldn't last one round with defending heavyweight king Muhammad Ali at Lewiston, Maine.

WAITING FOR JAMAICA

Across the globe, world champions were being crowned where they had never been crowned before. Australia. Venezuela. South Africa. Nigeria. Japan. Argentina. Sweden. A title fight victory in a boxer's homeland instantly swelled national pride, and the residents of the Caribbean island of Jamaica were waiting their turn.

In April 1964, they secured their first chance, when world junior welterweight champion Eddie Perkins defended against local favorite Bunny Grant in the capital of Kingston. Accustomed to fighting on the road, Perkins won a unanimous decision.

Thanks to the efforts of promoter Lucien Chen, Jamaica didn't have to wait too long for a second chance. On July 10, before a partisan crowd of more than 17,000 at Kingston's National Stadium, islander Percy Hayles challenged Perkins' successor, Carlos Hernandez.

The challenger was badly overmatched. He climbed through the ropes with a mediocre mark of 19-8-3, which included a loss to countryman Grant. For two rounds, he boxed well, but in the third, the Venezuelan champion connected with a left hook. Boom! Hayles sat on the canvas as referee Willie Pep counted to 10.

From Montego Bay to Negril Beach, the island mourned.

Jamaica had temporarily run out of contenders.

RINGSIDE VIEW

JULY

In a non-title bout, world lightweight champion Ismael Laguna struggles to a 10-round draw vs. Argentina's Nicolino Locche in Buenos Aires.

WORLD TITLE FIGHTS

HEAVYWEIGHTS

May 25	**Muhammad Ali** *KO* 1 Sonny Liston, Lewiston, ME

JUNIOR MIDDLEWEIGHTS

June 18	**Nino Benvenuti** (ITA) *KO* 6 Sandro Mazzinghi, Milan

JUNIOR WELTERWEIGHTS

May 16	**Carlos Hernandez** *KO* 5 Mario Rossito, Maracaibo
July 10	**Carlos Hernandez** *KO* 3 Percy Hayles, Kingston

JUNIOR LIGHTWEIGHTS

June 5	**Flash Elorde** *KO* 15 Teruo Kosaka, Quezon City

FEATHERWEIGHTS

May 7	**Vicente Saldivar** *KO* 15 Raul Rojas, Los Angeles

BANTAMWEIGHTS

May 17	**Fighting Harada** *W* 15 Eder Jofre, Nagoya

THREE JABS AT A TIME

Bob Foster was the fifth-ranked light heavyweight, and Henry Hank was number six. Neither fighter, however, was considered among the division's elite. That status was reserved for a select few: world champion Jose Torres, former champion Willie Pastrano (who hadn't yet officially retired), and top contenders Wayne Thornton and Gregorio Peralta.

Before Foster and Hank could join the upper echelon, they needed to battle for the city of New Orleans. Foster hailed from New Mexico, and Hank Detroit, but both had fought in "The Crescent City," and were seeking to make New Orleans their base.

In December 1964, Foster had stopped Hank in the 10th round.

Ironically, a bout between two of the world's hardest-punching light heavyweights was decided by jabs. Foster, 6'3", and possessing a heavyweight's reach, closed Hank's left eye in the very first round, and later bloodied his nose and mouth.

"I couldn't fight with three jabs coming at me," complained Hank. "I didn't know which one to duck."

Content to dominate with long lefts, Foster kept his distance and minimized the power exchanges. The most exciting moment came after the bell ending round six, when the 175-pounders kept punching. Hank snapped back Foster's head with an uppercut, and Foster answered until referee Pete Giarusso intervened.

The bout went the 12-round distance, with Foster capturing a one-sided verdict (scores of 10-1-1, 10-2, and 9-2-1).

"Hank's the roughest fighter – outside of me – and he's dangerous as long as he's in front of you," said the winner.

Foster wouldn't have to worry about Hank any more; he had run him out of town.

Bob Foster (left) moved closer to shot at the light heavyweight crown by outpointing dangerous Henry Hank in 12 rounds at New Orleans.

SEPTEMBER

1965

DECEMBER

WORTH THE WAIT

Immediately after taking Dick Tiger's middleweight title, Joey Giardello promised his rival a rematch. Tiger didn't think he'd have to wait almost two years.

Payback finally came on October 21, before a crowd of 17,064 at Madison Square Garden. At 36, Tiger was one year older than the champion. It was Giardello, however, who acted his age. Flat from the start – he said he was overtrained – the veteran showed none of the subtle and clever movement that had keyed his championship run. As a result, he was steamrolled.

Pressing from the start, Tiger muscled Giardello to the ropes and issued a steady beating. Hooks that Giardello routinely ducked were finding his chin, and body blows brought no counters. In the seventh round, Giardello swallowed seven straight lefts. He countered with a brief and desperate rally, but in the championship rounds, the only drama was whether he'd last the distance.

"If my corner so much as made a remark about quitting, I'd have fired them all on the spot," he said afterward. "I'm no Liston; I never thought of quitting. They'd have to carry me out of the ring before I'd quit."

Giardello forced Tiger to work for all 15 rounds, and then stood helplessly in his corner as the ring announcer declared the end of his reign. The unanimous decision (scores of 9-5-1, 8-6-1, and 10-5) was well-received.

For Tiger, the wait had been worth it.

EASY FOR SALDIVAR – OR WAS IT?

Sometimes, a boxing match becomes a matter of perception. A good example came on September 7, when featherweight champion Vicente Saldivar defended for the second time, taking on stylish Welshman Howard Winstone at Earl's Court in London. It was either a one-sided drubbing, or an evenly contested match that could have been awarded to either fighter.

The matchup would be the first, and least intriguing, chapter in the classic Saldivar-Winstone trilogy. The 22-year-old Mexican champion was a southpaw and a pressure fighter. Winstone, on the other hand, stood tall and jabbed and crossed in the traditional mode. Over the 15-round distance, Saldivar's style proved more effective.

Leading with a powerful right, Saldivar seemed to confuse the British and Empire champion from the start. The challenger tried to counter with his jab, but failed. By the middle rounds, he was being pushed to the ropes. Winstone bled from a cut over his right eye in round six, from his nose in the 12th, and from a cut over his left eye in the 13th. Though never close to falling, he was staggered in the 10th, and battered and bruised in almost every other stanza. At the final bell, referee and sole judge Bill Williams didn't hesitate to raise Saldivar's arm in victory.

Had it been as simple as that? Not according to the *Daily Mirror*'s Peter Wilson, whose fight story began: "Howard Winstone fought the greatest fight of his life last night at Earl's Court, London – and it was ajudged not to be enough. So, after 15 of the toughest, closest, bitterest rounds, Vicente Saldivar retained the featherweight championship of the world for Mexico."

Perhaps the fight was best summed up by another ringside journalist, who sighed, "Another gallant British defeat."

WORLD TITLE FIGHTS

HEAVYWEIGHTS

Nov 1	**Ernest Terrell** *W* 15 George Chuvalo, Toronto
Nov 22	**Muhammad Ali** *KO* 12 Floyd Patterson, Las Vegas

MIDDLEWEIGHTS

Oct 21	**Dick Tiger** *W* 15 Joey Giardello, New York City

JUNIOR MIDDLEWEIGHTS

Dec 17	**Nino Benvenuti** *W* 15 Sandro Mazzinghi, Rome

WELTERWEIGHTS

Dec 10	**Emile Griffith** *W* 15 Manuel Gonzalez, New York City

LIGHTWEIGHTS

Nov 13	**Carlos Ortiz** *W* 15 Ismael Laguna, San Juan

JUNIOR LIGHTWEIGHTS

Dec 4	**Flash Elorde** *W* 15 Kang Il Suh, Quezon City

FEATHERWEIGHTS

Sept 7	**Vicente Saldivar** *ref* 15 Howard Winstone, London

BANTAMWEIGHTS

Nov 30	**Fighting Harada** *W* 15 Alan Rudkin, Tokyo

FLYWEIGHTS

Dec 2	**Salvatore Burruni** *KO* 13 Rocky Gattellari, Sydney

Dick Tiger (right) outpointed Joey Giardello to regain the middleweight crown he had lost to his rival in 1963.

CAN'T BEAT THAT HOME COOKIN'

Fighters throw the punches, but sometimes managers win the fights. In April, Panama's Ismael Laguna fought before his howling countrymen and won the lightweight title by outpointing New York-based Puerto Rican Carlos Ortiz. It wasn't unusual that his first defense was a return with Ortiz. But manager Bill Daly somehow convinced Laguna's camp to come to San Juan.

When properly prepared, Ortiz was a brilliant fighter, and on November 13, at Hiram Bithorn Stadium, his people saw him at his best. He smartly countered the champion's jabs with hook-cross combinations, and Laguna's speed and mobility were never factors.

Over the championship rounds, Laguna altered his strategy. Realizing he was behind, he tried to attack. But his lack of power was apparent, and in the 12th and 13th rounds, he was almost stopped.

Ortiz regained the title by unanimous decision. The Panamanian judge saw it 145-143, but it wasn't that close, as suggested by the other two scores, 150-138 and 148-143.

"I wasn't tired; that was the difference," said Ortiz.

That, and home cooking.

Panama's Ismael Laguna (left) in the first of his world title fights with Carlos Ortiz.

PATTERSON, SANS BEARD AND MUSTACHE

After suffering a pair of humiliating first-round knockouts at the hands of Sonny Liston, Floyd Patterson took to wearing disguises. Fake beards and mustaches allowed him to shop, see a movie, even go to the fights.

On November 22, at the Las Vegas Convention Center, Patterson challenged heavyweight champion Muhammad Ali. It was a particularly ugly fight; the challenger aggravated a slipped disc in the fourth round, and the injury limited the simplest of movements. Round after round, Ali pumped jabs and crosses into Patterson's face and cruelly taunted him. But Patterson wouldn't quit.

"I begged Floyd to tell the referee that he couldn't fight any longer," said Patterson's personal physician, Dr. Michael Blatt. "He said he would rather die than to ask to have it stopped."

Late in the 12th, referee Harry Krause stopped the hideous slaughter. Patterson was carried to his dressing room, but insisted on meeting the press.

"No more running away," he explained. No more need to.

Heavyweight champ Muhammad Ali stopped former champ Floyd Patterson in 12th round.

RINGSIDE VIEW

NOVEMBER

Sugar Ray Robinson, age 44, fights for the last time, losing a 10-round decision to rising middleweight Joey Archer in Pittsburgh.

FIGHTING A MAN WHO WON'T FIGHT YOU

The first fight telecast in living color turned out to be colorless. On December 10, before a crowd of 12,146 at Madison Square Garden, welterweight champion Emile Griffith defended against Texan Manuel Gonzalez. It figured to be an action bout; Gonzalez had edged Griffith in a non-title affair. But it turned out a dud.

The night began brightly, when the recently retired Sugar Ray Robinson was honored in a moving ceremony. Waiting in the ring for the legendary champion, one in each corner, were Bobo Olson, Gene Fullmer, Carmen Basilio, and Randy Turpin. Griffith and Gonzalez, however, provided no lasting memories. The challenger landed his jab often, but did so while running away. Griffith pursued for all 15 rounds, countering with hooks and rights whenever possible.

"I know everyone thinks I gave a lousy fight," he said. "They're right. But what could I do?"

The champion kept the title by scores of 9-5-1, 11-3-1, and 12-3.

At least his cardinal red trunks had looked good on TV.

JANUARY

1966

APRIL

A SCARE FOR NINO

RINGSIDE VIEW

FEBRUARY

Former lightweight champion Ismael Laguna scores an eighth-round stoppage over reigning junior welterweight king Carlos Hernandez in Panama City.

Boxing fans outside of Italy were unfamiliar with Nino Benvenuti. International acclaim would come in time. But Benvenuti's credentials were already world-class. Consider:

*In 1960, he won the Olympic welterweight gold medal.

*In 1965, he won the world junior middleweight title, and, four months later, the vacant European middleweight crown.

*With a record of 62-0, he had registered an all-time record number of consecutive victories at the start of a pro career.

On February 4, Benvenuti scored his 63rd straight win, outpointing rugged American Don Fullmer over 12 rounds in Rome. It was a rather tame bout, with Nino boxing carefully, and Fullmer rarely rising from his defensive crouch. Wanting to finish strongly, the fighters accelerated over the last couple of rounds. Still, few punches were landed.

At the finish, the winner's face belied the lack of action. Benvenuti bled from several facial cuts, and proceeded to the hospital, where he received 26 stitches.

He remained unbeaten, but not unmarked.

Italy's stylish Nino Benvenuti (left) was marked, but won a 12-round decision over Don Fullmer.

OF DRUGS AND DEATH THREATS

Like a John Le Carre novel, Floyd Robertson's visit to Mexico was filled with secrecy, intrigue, and hidden agendas. On February 12, at the Plaza Mexico bullring, the Ghanian featherweight challenged world champion and local favorite Vicente Saldivar. For Robertson, it was a title try that was more than a year overdue; in May 1964, he had lost a controversial decision to then-champion Sugar Ramos. He was considered by many to be the division's uncrowned king.

Shortly after his arrival in Mexico, Robertson infuriated the local press by minimizing his workouts and refusing interviews. His explanation: he always prepared for a bout in such a manner.

The fight was originally scheduled for February 5, but Robertson was given an extra week to make weight and adjust to the altitude. It didn't help. After an unexceptional first round, Saldivar struck. In the second, the southpaw dropped Robertson with three consecutive lefts, and, moments later, finished him with a flurry. Referee Ramon Berumen tolled 10 at the 2:29 mark.

Offering a unique excuse, Robertson claimed that he had been drugged – *by his own manager!* Scotland's Sam Daugherty, he said, had spiked his prefight beverage, and within minutes, the featherweight was weak and lethargic. But before he could substantiate his charges, Robertson received a death threat, and headed straight for the airport.

At least he hadn't drunk the water.

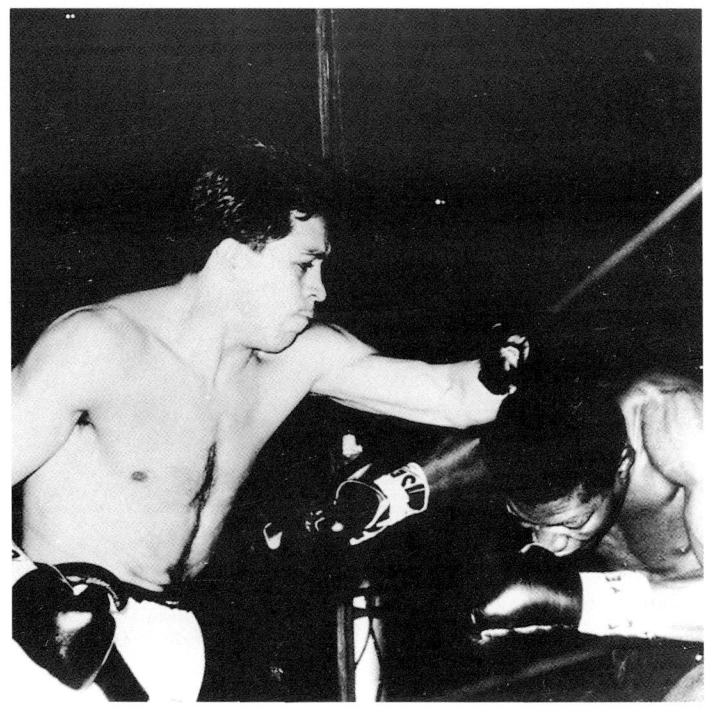

World featherweight king Vicente Saldivar (left) ripped apart Ghana's Floyd Robertson.

RINGSIDE VIEW

APRIL

Italy's Sandro Lopopolo wins the world junior welterweight title, scoring a majority 15-round decision over Carlos Hernandez.

KEEPING A TIGER AT A SAFE DISTANCE

During the course of his welterweight title reign, Emile Griffith was frustrated by his share of runners. On April 25, at Madison Square Garden, he proved he had learned from each and every one of them.

Rising in weight, Griffith challenged 36-year-old middleweight king Dick Tiger. Scaling only 150½, he spotted the defending champion 9½ pounds, and decided that his best chance at victory would be to race, not fight.

Boxing on a left ankle that he had sprained on his last day of training, Griffith jabbed and circled away from Tiger's strong hook. Tiger chased, but as a natural counterpuncher, he was uncomfortable. The only noteworthy moment came in round nine, when Griffith floored the Nigerian with a short right. It was the first knockdown in Tiger's 72-bout career.

The decision, which went to Griffith, was unanimous – and disputed (scores of 9-5-1, 7-6-2, and 7-7-1, but, because of the knockdown, 8-7 on points). In a ringside poll, 17 of 22 sportswriters favored Tiger.

Griffith joined Sugar Ray Robinson and Carmen Basilio as the only welterweight champions to win the middleweight title. And he didn't have to shed a drop of blood to do it.

. . . AND STILL THE KING OF THE JUNGLE

"In a fight between a lion and a Christian," George Chuvalo once said, "I'd rather be the lion."

On March 29, at Maple Leaf Gardens in Toronto, he found himself in a fight between a lion and a Muslim. The lion lost, but was never tamed.

Three weeks before his challenge of heavyweight champion Muhammad Ali, WBA titlist Ernie Terrell pulled out when the bout was moved out of his native Chicago. Chuvalo was summoned as a substitute.

For 15 rounds, the steel-jawed Canadian absorbed Ali's sharpest combinations without a blink. In a futile attempt to trap the swift champion, he chugged forward from start to finish. But his only effective blows landed low.

Ali took the unanimous decision by scores of 73-65, 74-63, and 74-62. He remained the king of boxing's jungle.

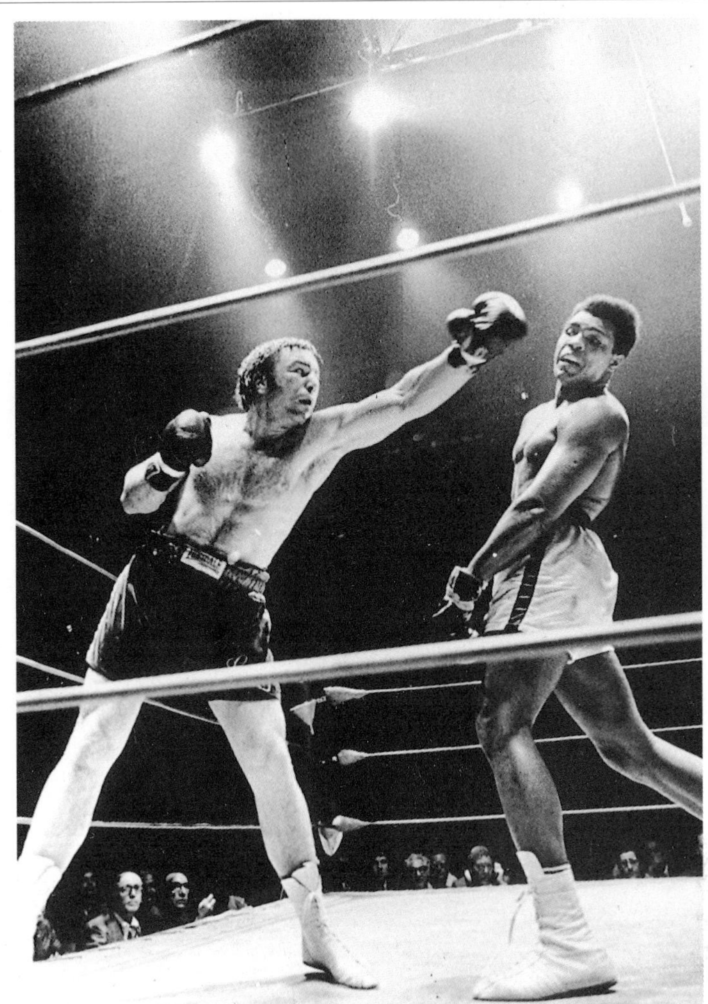

Heavyweight king Muhammad Ali (right) dodges a left from granite-chinned George Chuvalo.

WORLD TITLE FIGHTS

HEAVYWEIGHTS

March 29 **Muhammad Ali** *W* 15 George Chuvalo, Toronto

MIDDLEWEIGHTS

April 25 **Emile Griffith** *W* 15 Dick Tiger, New York City

JUNIOR WELTERWEIGHTS

April 30 **Sandro Lopopolo** (ITA) *W* 15 Carlos Hernandez, Rome

FEATHERWEIGHTS

Feb 12 **Vicente Saldivar** *KO* 2 Floyd Robertson, Mexico City

FLYWEIGHTS

March 1 **Horacio Accavallo** (ARG) *W* 15 Katsuyoshi Takayama, Tokyo (Wins Vacant WBA Title)

THE SPLITTING OF THE FLYS

Salvatore Burruni wasn't the best flyweight in history, but as the division's last unified champion, he remains the answer to the only 112-pound trivia question we've ever heard.

After the WBA stripped Burruni for failing to defend against former champion Hiroyuki Ebihara, Argentina's Horacio Accavallo and Japan's relatively inexperienced Katsuyoshi Takayama clashed to decide his successor. The winner was to face Ebihara in his first defense. (Burruni was still recognized as champion in Australia and Europe, and by *The Ring*.)

Accavallo-Takayama came on March 1, at the Martial Arts Hall in Tokyo. The Argentine overcame a shaky first round, and after 15 evenly contested stanzas, the Japanese judge scored for Takayama (71-70), and the Argentine judge scored for Accavallo (74-66). The deciding vote of the only neutral official, American referee Nick Pope, was Accavallo the winner by 73-69.

Boxing hasn't had a universally recognized flyweight champion since.

MAY

1966

AUGUST

HE SHOULD'VE STAYED HOME

The first 64 bouts of Nino Benvenuti's career came in his native Italy. He won all of them. On June 25, the world junior middleweight champion defended against South Korea's Ki Soo Kim at the Changchung Municipal Gymnasium in Seoul. Benvenuti found himself displaced, disoriented, and, ultimately, dethroned.

En route to winning a gold medal at the 1960 Olympics, Benvenuti had defeated Kim. The Games had been held in Rome. This time, Kim had the house advantage, and he fully capitalized. The 5'8" southpaw attacked behind a tight defense that the quick-fisted Benvenuti never solved. Kim, 23-0-1, hammered the champion's body for all 15 rounds, and emerged victorious by split decision.

South Korea had its first world champion. And Benvenuti had a good excuse to toss his passport in the wastebasket.

WAITING FOR THE RED

Before his challenge of heavyweight champion Muhammad Ali, Britain's Henry Cooper was determined to toughen the skin above his eyes. He sloshed his brows with brine; he rubbed in an alum-based salve; he took special vitamins. But on fight night, nothing short of a helmet and face guard would have saved him.

Cooper's unmatched popularity, and the fact that he had dropped Ali in their first fight, put 46,000 supporters in the seats. It was England's first heavyweight title fight in 58 years.

In the sixth, the champion connected with a short right, and torrents of blood poured from a cut over Cooper's right eye. At the 1:38 mark, referee George Smith called a halt.

"Blood scares me," Ali said afterward. "I was more desperate than anyone else when I saw Cooper bleeding so badly."

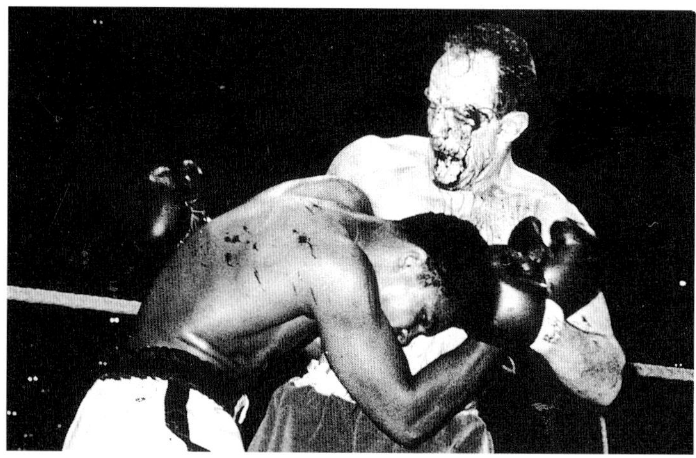

Britain's idolized Henry Cooper (right) was stopped in the sixth round by Muhammad Ali.

RINGSIDE VIEW

JUNE

Bantamweight champion Fighting Harada retains the crown with a unanimous 15-round decision over former titlist Eder Jofre.

Walter McGowan's hand is raised as champ.

GREAT SCOT!

It took Scottish flyweight Walter McGowan two years to avenge his April 1964 European title fight loss to Salvatore Burruni. When he did, his victory came at the optimum time.

After establishing his superiority in Europe, Burruni went on to win the world title, and on June 14, at the Empire Pool in Wembley, he defended against McGowan. Eyebrows were raised when the 32-year-old champion initially weighed five ounces over the division's 112-pound limit. Forty-five minutes later, he returned to the scale at 110. How, observers wanted to know, had he dropped almost 2½ pounds in less than an hour?

It became a moot point after McGowan, 23, cut Burruni over both eyes, and dropped him with a left in the fifth. An unintentional butt cracked the challenger's tender skin in the eighth, but his bleeding never became a factor. Nor did it affect his momentum.

In the championship rounds, McGowan's faithful began to stomp their feet in anticipation of victory. Wee Walter flashed his fast hands until the final bell, at which point referee and sole judge Harry Gibbs declared him the champion.

It was time to celebrate.

WORLD TITLE FIGHTS

HEAVYWEIGHTS

May 21	**Muhammad Ali** *KO* 6 Henry Cooper, London
June 28	**Ernest Terrell** *W* 15 Doug Jones, Houston
Aug 6	**Muhammad Ali** *KO* 3 Brian London, London

LIGHT HEAVYWEIGHTS

May 21	**Jose Torres** *W* 15 Wayne Thornton, Flushing
Aug 15	**Jose Torres** *W* 15 Eddie Cotton, Las Vegas

MIDDLEWEIGHTS

July 13	**Emile Griffith** *W* 15 Joey Archer, New York City

JUNIOR MIDDLEWEIGHTS

June 25	**Ki Soo Kim** (KOR) *W* 15 Nino Benvenuti, Seoul

WELTERWEIGHTS

Aug 24	**Curtis Cokes** *W* 15 Manuel Gonzalez, New Orleans

LIGHTWEIGHTS

June 20	**Carlos Ortiz** *KO* 12 Johnny Bizarro, Pittsburgh

FEATHERWEIGHTS

Aug 7	**Vicente Saldivar** *W* 15 Mitsunori Seki, Mexico City

BANTAMWEIGHTS

June 1	**Fighting Harada** *W* 15 Eder Jofre, Tokyo

FLYWEIGHTS

June 14	**Walter McGowan** (SCO) *ref* 15 Salvatore Burruni, Wembley
July 15	**Horacio Accavallo** *W* 15 Hiroyuki Ebihara, Buenos Aires

GRIFF CHANGES GEARS

Some champions are boxers, and others are punchers. Almost all *outstanding* champions, however, share a common trait: the ability to adapt to their opponents' styles.

In April, Emile Griffith had won the middleweight championship by running from the bigger, stronger Dick Tiger. On July 13, at Madison Square Garden, he kept it by making sure the quicker Joey Archer ran from him.

With only nine kayos in 46 wins, the Bronx' Archer punched with feather fists. Over the first five rounds, Griffith got inside and forced the challenger to fight. But in the sixth, he seemed to lose interest, letting Archer display his considerable skills.

The championship rounds were evenly contested, ensuring a close verdict. The majority decision went to Griffith (scores of 7-7-1, 9-5-1, and 8-7). The difference: he had attacked from opening to closing bell.

Styles indeed make fights. And Griffith proved he had the style for *any* fight.

Clever Joey Archer (left) wasn't quite good enough to capture Emile Griffith's crown.

RINGSIDE VIEW

AUGUST

Curtis Cokes wins the vacant WBA welterweight title by scoring a unanimous 15-round decision over fellow Texan Manuel Gonzalez.

A COTTON TALE

Seattle's Eddie Cotton seemed to fit the description of the prototypical light heavyweight champion: he was a gifted natural boxer, and, by boxing standards, an old man. On August 15, at the Las Vegas Convention Center, he attempted to cap a 21-year career by winning the world title.

Cotton, 40, spotted champion Jose Torres 10 years. In 1961, he had challenged Harold Johnson for the NBA crown, but lost by decision. His record since that disappointing loss was a mediocre 13-8-1. But against Torres, he summoned his best once more.

At the halfway mark, the challenger, a 7-2 underdog, seemed headed for victory. From rounds four through eight, he controlled Torres by whipping his sterling jab. But he lost a point for punching low in round 10.

Cotton's last stand came in the 13th. Torres dominated the last six minutes, and by the final bell, he was issuing a beating. His big finish proved the difference; he kept the title by close but unanimous decision (scores of 70-67, 68-67, and 69-67). Boxing was still a young man's game.

LONDON IS FALLING DOWN

Ten weeks after defending against Henry Cooper, heavyweight champion Muhammad Ali continued his tour of Europe by meeting 32-year-old Briton Brian London. The bout was viewed as a mismatch – Ali was a 15-1 favorite – and on August 6, only 13,000 fans came to Earl's Court. What they saw was a legend-in-the-making who was good enough to win as he chose.

Ali played for the first two rounds, as if believing it rude to send the spectators home without a bit of a show.

In the third, he fired two rights that backed London to a corner. Then came a lightning left-right. Boom! London took referee Harry Gibbs' full count with his head buried on the canvas. Minutes later, he was booed from the ring.

FIGHTING TALK

I'd like a return, but only if you put a 50-pound weight on each ankle

BRIAN LONDON
after being kayoed by heavyweight champion Muhammad Ali

Having made his fifth defense, Ali, 25-0, was leaving the rest of the pack far back. His next stop would be Germany – and a bout with the first southpaw to ever fight for the heavyweight crown.

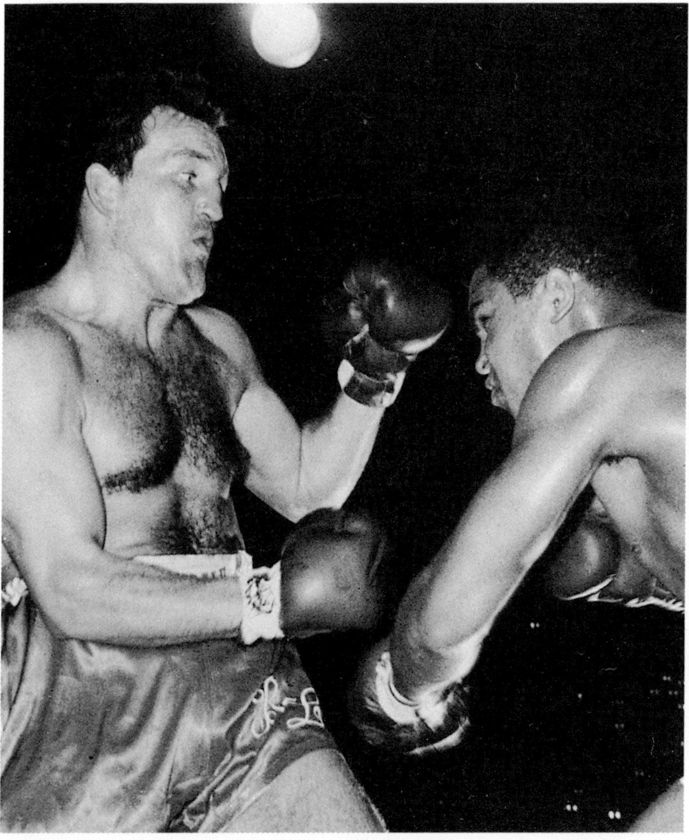

Britain's Brian London (left) was stopped in the third round by heavyweight champ Ali.

SEPTEMBER

1966

DECEMBER

SMOKIN' JOE AND RINGO

With a 1964 Olympic gold medal highlighting his resume, Philadelphia's Joe Frazier easily powered past his first 11 pro opponents. On September 21, at Madison Square Garden, he met resistance.

Argentina's Oscar "Ringo" Bonavena, a fearless, reckless slab of muscle, nearly ruined Frazier's perfect record. Countering sharply, he dropped "Smokin' Joe" twice, first with a cross, then with a hook. Bonavena continued to roll in the third, but Frazier endured, always marching forward.

Over the next seven rounds, Frazier controlled the bout with his hook, which he fired with a grunt. Some of the lefts landed low, but referee Mark Conn deducted no points.

"I didn't do it on purpose," Frazier said.

The pace remained wicked until the final bell, after which Frazier was declared the winner by split decision (scores of 6-4, 5-4-1, and 5-5, but 8-5 in points for Bonavena).

It was far too early to anticipate a showdown between Frazier and world champion Muhammad Ali. But even at this point, a better matchup was hard to find.

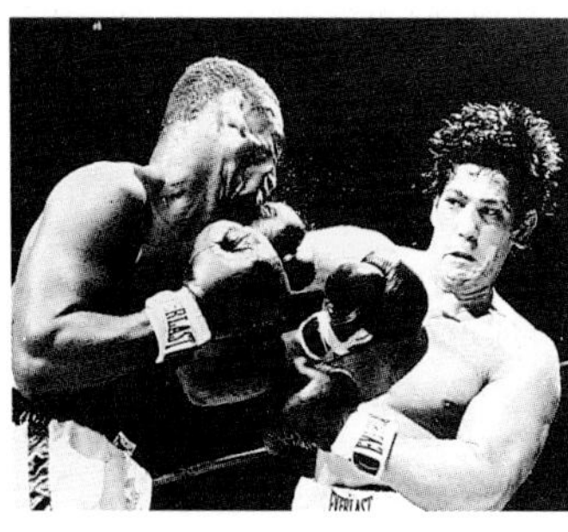

Joe Frazier (left) and Oscar Bonavena.

A LEFT-HANDED COMPLEMENT

In the 66 years of the modern era, a southpaw had never fought for the heavyweight title, much less held it. That changed on September 10, when Germany's Karl Mildenberger and Muhammad Ali met before a crowd of 45,000 at Wald Stadium in Frankfurt.

Ali was made a 10-1 favorite, but insiders labeled Mildenberger, 49-2-3, a live underdog: he was a nimble fighter; he featured a crippling left to the body; he was a surprisingly rugged infighter; he was unbeaten against American heavyweights; and Ali hadn't faced a left-hander as a pro.

Germany's Karl Mildenberger lasted a surprising 12 rounds with defending champion Ali.

For four rounds, Mildenberger's bull-like rushes proved troublesome. At the end of the fifth, however, Ali floored him with a straight right. There was another knockdown in the eighth, and yet another in the 10th. Cut over both eyes, the 28-year-old German had switched to survival mode. Referee Teddy Waltham stepped in at the 1:30 mark of the 11th, with Mildenberger near-defenseless.

Ali wasn't a big puncher, but his blinding flurries were proving just as effective as the power hooks or crosses of a Liston or a Louis.

World Title Fights

HEAVYWEIGHTS

Sept 10	**Muhammad Ali** *KO* 12 Karl Mildenberger, Frankfurt
Nov 14	**Muhammad Ali** *KO* 3 Cleveland Williams, Houston

LIGHT HEAVYWEIGHTS

Oct 15	**Jose Torres** *KO* 2 Chic Calderwood, San Juan
Dec 16	**Dick Tiger** *W* 15 Jose Torres, New York City

JUNIOR MIDDLEWEIGHTS

Dec 17	**Ki Soo Kim** *W* 15 Stan Harrington, Seoul

WELTERWEIGHTS

Nov 28	**Curtis Cokes** *W* 15 Jean Josselin, Dallas
Dec 7	**Charlie Shipes** *KO* 10 Percy Manning, Hayward, CA (Wins Vacant California State World Title)

JUNIOR WELTERWEIGHTS

Oct 21	**Sandro Lopopolo** *KO* 8 Vicente Rivas, Rome

LIGHTWEIGHTS

Oct 22	**Carlos Ortiz** *KO* 5 Sugar Ramos, Mexico City
Nov 28	**Carlos Ortiz** *KO* 14 Flash Elorde, New York City

JUNIOR LIGHTWEIGHTS

Oct 22	**Flash Elorde** *W* 15 Vicente Derado, Quezon City

FLYWEIGHTS

Dec 10	**Horacio Accavallo** *W* 15 Efren Torres, Buenos Aires
Dec 30	**Chartchai Chionoi** (THA) *KO* 9 Walter McGowan, Bangkok

A GORY NIGHT DODGING THE MISSILES IN MEXICO

Lightweight champion Carlos Ortiz' defense vs. Mexico-based Cuban Sugar Ramos, fought on October 22, at the El Toreo bullring in Mexico City, was the most memorable title fight of his career. But for all the wrong reasons.

In the second round, Ramos scored a flash knockdown. But in the third, Ortiz' hooks cut and closed the former featherweight champion's left eye.

During round four, referee Billy Conn signalled for the ringside physician to examine Ramos. The doctor refused. After the bell, Conn repeated his request. Again he was ignored.

In the fifth, Ramos' wound worsened. When the doctor stayed put, Conn declared Ortiz the winner by TKO. Almost instantly, rocks, peso coins, and chairs were thrown at the ring. Ortiz was kicked in the back on his way to the dressing room, and his manager, Bill Daly, suffered two broken ribs.

A few minutes later, Ortiz was told that Conn had been overruled by the Mexican commission, and that if he didn't return to the ring, Ramos would be declared the winner. He called the bluff, and, ultimately, kept the crown.

"THE GREATEST" AT HIS BEST

Even Muhammad Ali's harshest critics acknowledged that on November 14, at the Houston Astrodome, the heavyweight champion was a great fighter. Cleveland William proved it.

Nicknamed "The Big Cat," the 33-year-old Williams was among the hardest hitters in the division.

"He's a real good puncher," Ali said afterward. "But he had nuthin' to punch at."

Ali danced for the first minute of the first round, then sizzled. There were three knockdowns in the second, and another in the third. Referee Harry Kessler intervened at the 1:08 mark, with Williams on his feet, but groggy and helpless.

Ali's jab had never been as blinding; his feet had never seemed so light; his combinations had never flowed so effortlessly. At age 24, he was 27-0 (22), and peaking.

It was time to freeze the moment for the time capsule.

Muhammad Ali was never more impressive than in knocking out Cleveland Williams.

A TIGER CHANGES HIS STRIPES

Two-time middleweight champion Dick Tiger was a good fighter, but also a predictable one. He always started slowly, plodded forward as if wearing ankle weights, and stubbornly limited his attack to the head. On December 16, at Madison Square Garden, he started quickly, darted in and out, and punched primarily to the body. Tiger not only surprised light heavyweight champion Jose Torres, but took his title as well.

Spotting the champion eight pounds, Tiger, 167, realized that his usual style wouldn't necessarily work. Torres expected the Nigerian to force the fight, but, he said, "Every time I tired to press the guy, he moved back."

At 37, Tiger (left) boxed cleverly to take Jose Torres' light heavyweight crown.

Torres landed his share of big blows. Still, he wasn't particularly sharp. (Earlier in the year, he had been hospitalized with a pancreas condition.) Tiger hurt him in the ninth round, and again in the 11th. The bout lasted the distance, with the 37-year-old challenger capturing the crown by scores of 10-5, 10-4-1, and 8-6-1.

An old Tiger had learned some new tricks.

WHAT A DIFFERENCE A YEAR MAKES

In boxing, age is relative. That was never more apparent than on November 28 at Madison Square Garden, where Carlos Ortiz, 30, retained the lightweight title by scoring a 14th-round knockout of junior lightweight champion Flash Elorde.

Wrote Robert Lipsyte in *The New York Times*, "...it was too many punches in too many rounds in too many cities that drove the Filipino to the canvas."

Though the fighters had been born only 18 months apart, Ortiz had fought 470 professional rounds, and Elorde almost 1,000. The challenger was nearing the end, and against a bigger, stronger foe, he proved impotent.

In February 1964, Ortiz had stopped Elorde on a cut. This time, the finish would be far more conclusive. The champion dominated from the start, scoring with jabs and hooks.

"In the corner," he said, "we were saying, 'What's keeping him up?'"

In the 14th, Ortiz cranked up a hook, and Elorde crashed for the first time in his 101-bout career. He remained flat for more than 30 seconds. When he got up, he felt a lot older than 31.

RINGSIDE VIEW

OCTOBER

Light heavyweight champion Jose Torres retains the crown for the third time, stopping Chic Calderwood in the second round.

DECEMBER

Thailand's Chartchai Chionoi wins the flyweight title, stopping Walter McGowan on cuts in the ninth round.

Muhammad Ali

Professional career dates 1960-79; 1980-81
Contests 61
Won 56
Lost 5
Drawn 0
Knockouts 37
World Heavyweight Champion 1964-1967, 1974-1978, 1978-1979

Muhammad Ali's greatness as a fighter can be explained by his God-given talent and championship heart, and the extraordinary competition that demanded he be his best. His greatness as a man is more simply explained: he's never been anything but himself.

Whether Ali was the greatest heavyweight in history is debatable. But over the course of his 50-plus years, he has become the world's most recognized man. And though he long ago shelved his gloves, he remains a symbol to millions.

Born Cassius Marcellus Clay on January 17, 1942, in Louisville, Kentucky, Ali was born to Cassius Marcellus Clay Sr., a sign painter, and Odessa Grady Clay. Ali and his younger brother Rudy grew up in a middle-class environment. But he proved to be as hungry as those fighters rooted in poverty.

Ali first entered a gym at age 12. After his bicycle was stolen, he took the advice of a local policeman and amateur trainer, Joe Martin, who recommended that he vent his frustration in a boxing ring.

Ali first commanded the spotlight in 1959, when he won the National AAU light heavyweight title. He repeated the feat in 1960, and then punctuated his amateur career by winning a gold medal at the 1960 Olympic Games in Rome.

Backed by 11 rich Kentucky businessmen, he turned pro on October 29, 1960, scoring a decision over Tunney Hunsaker. In December 1960, he began a career-long association with trainer Angelo Dundee.

Ali's first high profile bout came on November 15, 1962, when he stopped 48-year-old former light heavyweight champion Archie Moore in four rounds. (As had become his custom, he correctly predicted the round of his triumph.) The brash, cocky contender remained unbeaten through 1963, but survived two scares: at Madison Square Garden, he barely outpointed veteran Doug Jones, and then he rose from the canvas to stop British veteran Henry Cooper.

In 1964, heavyweight champion Sonny Liston was considered invincible. Defending against Ali, he was a 7-1 favorite. But in Miami Beach on February 25, "The Greatest" surprised the world for the first time. He chopped up the champion's face, overcame a mid-rounds scare when temporarily blinded by a foreign substance believed to have been a solution covering Liston's cuts, and became champion when "The Bear" refused to answer the bell for round eight.

The inevitable rematch produced instant controversy because Ali's first-round knockout blow, a short right, seemed relatively harmless. After the chaos created by referee Jersey Joe Walcott's failure to issue a count, Ali, a slight underdog, was declared winner and still champion. It was what happened between the first and second Liston fights, however, that helped shape Ali. After winning the title, he denounced his "slave name" of Cassius Clay, and shortly afterward, proclaimed his devotion to the nation of Islam and declared his name as Muhammad Ali.

At the time of Ali's religious awakening, the establishment viewed the Black Muslims, of which Ali and his spiritual mentor, Malcolm X, were the most visible members, as potentially subversive. As a result, Ali, like Jack Johnson more than 50 years before, had become a symbol.

From 1965 to 1967, Ali successfully defended nine times – and was never threatened. Among his overmatched victims were Patterson, Cooper, George Chuvalo, and Ernie Terrell. The champion proved far too quick and mobile for all of them.

If Ali's conversion to Islam hinted that he would transcend the ring, his April 1967 refusal to be inducted into the U.S. military, which he based on the principles of his religion, came to guarantee that he would represent an entire decade. Ali was subsequently convicted of draft evasion – in June 1971, the Supreme Court would overturn the conviction – but even before the courts had made their

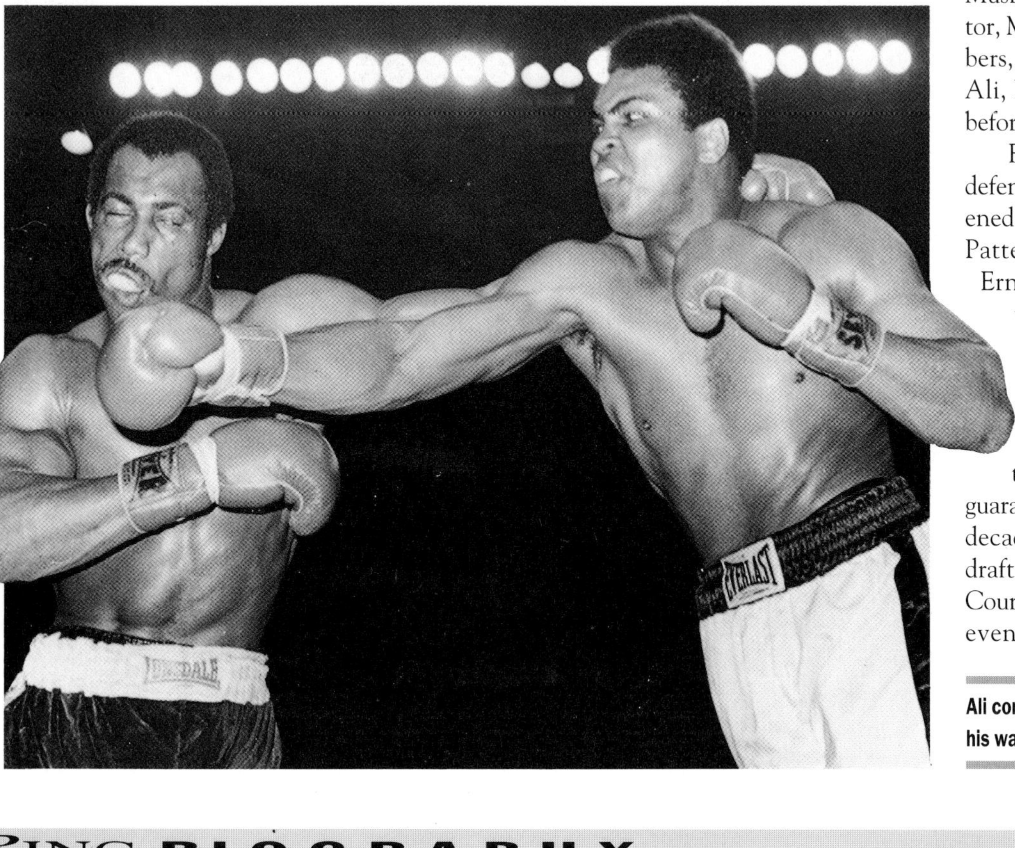

Ali contorts Ken Norton's face with a jolting right on his way to avenging a previous loss.

decision, he was stripped of the title.

During his exile, which extended from March 1967 to October 1970, one development inside the ring, and one outside, helped shape his future. Joe Frazier, a devastating and unbeaten left hooker from Philadelphia, kayoed Jimmy Ellis and gained universal recognition as world champion. And the majority of Americans concluded that the United States' involvement in Vietnam was futile, if not immoral. Ali had been on the right side all along, and his image benefited accordingly.

"Some people thought I was a hero," he said several years later. "Some people said what I did was wrong. But everything I did was according to my conscience."

After comeback victories against Jerry Quarry and Oscar Bonavena, Ali challenged Frazier in what will forever be regarded as the fight of the century. The heavyweights clashed at Madison Square Garden on March 8, 1971. They were both paid the unheard of sum of $2.5-million, and over the course of 15 fantastic rounds, they earned every penny.

Frazier relentlessly imposed his will and dropped the challenger in the final round to cement a convincing points victory.

"I didn't give it away," Ali said. "Joe earned it."

After Ali suffered a broken jaw in a March 1973 loss to Ken Norton, he was dismissed as a title threat. But he won the Norton rematch – all three of their duels were decided by the last round – and, in January 1974, decisioned Frazier in their long-awaited rematch. A top contender again, he signed to face reigning champion George Foreman on October 30, 1974.

The unique setting: four in the morning before 60,000 fans at Twentieth of May Stadium in Kinshasa, Zaire. An overwhelming favorite, Foreman was certain of a first- or second-round knockout victory. But Ali accepted his best punches without as much as a flinch, inventing his rope-a-dope strategy in the process. After Foreman punched himself out, Ali scored an eighth-round kayo.

In the ring, Ali would treasure two more special moments. On October 1, 1975, he and Frazier gave what they had left in "The Thrilla in Manila." Behind on points and badly battered, Frazier wasn't allowed to answer the bell for the final round. "Frazier just quit before I did," Ali said. "I didn't think I could fight anymore."

That should have been the end, but Ali fought on, defending against, among others, Norton, Jimmy Young, and Earnie Shavers. He held onto the title until February 15, 1978, when Leon Spinks, a gold medalist with seven fights of pro experience, outhustled him over 15 rounds. In the rematch, Ali won the title for the third time. It was a just ending to his championship run.

Ali retired on June 27, 1979, but 16 months later returned to challenge WBC champion Larry Holmes. Ali proved impotent and was stopped in 11 rounds. His finale was a decision loss to Trevor Berbick in December 1981.

Today, Ali, the father of eight children, lives on a modest farm in Berrien Springs, Michigan, with his fourth wife, Lonnie. He suffers from Parkinson's Syndrome, and, especially when abandoning his medication, appears slow and lethargic. But he remains active, traveling extensively and worldwide as an opponent of hunger and a promoter of peace and religion.

"People say I had a full life," he told Hauser, "but I ain't dead yet. I'm just getting started."

Cassius Clay joined the Muslims, changed his "slave name" to Muhammad Ali, and refused to be inducted into the U.S. Army.

Ali and Larry Holmes, separated by glib promoter Don King, ham it up after signing for their 1980 bout. Ali, long past his prime, lost by stoppage.

JANUARY

1967

APRIL

WORLD TITLE FIGHTS

HEAVYWEIGHTS

Feb 6 **Muhammad Ali** *W* 15
Ernest Terrell, Houston
(Unifies World Title)

March 22 **Muhammad Ali** *KO* 7
Zora Folley, New York City

LIGHT HEAVYWEIGHTS

Feb 5 **Dick Tiger** *W* 15
Jose Torres, New York City

MIDDLEWEIGHTS

Jan 23 **Emile Griffith** *W* 15
Joey Archer, New York City

April 17 **Nino Benvenuti** *W* 15
Emile Griffith, Flushing, NY

JUNIOR WELTERWEIGHTS

April 30 **Paul Fujii** (USA) *KO* 2
Sandro Lopopolo, Tokyo

FEATHERWEIGHTS

Jan 29 **Vicente Saldivar** *KO* 7
Mitsunori Seki, Mexico City

BANTAMWEIGHTS

Jan 3 **Fighting Harada** *W* 15
Jose Medel, Nagoya

RINGSIDE VIEW

JANUARY

Middleweight champion Emile Griffith defends against Joey Archer for the second time, scoring a unanimous 15-round decision.

"WHAT'S MY NAME?" DEMANDS ALI

On February 5, at the Houston Astrodome, Muhammad Ali wrote one of the ugliest chapters in division history. The heavyweight champion not only punished WBA titleholder Ernie Terrell, but humiliated him as well. Sweeping the last 10 rounds, Ali landed punches as he pleased, all the while shouting "what's my name?" (Terrell had infuriated Ali by stubbornly addressing him as Cassius Clay.)

Standing 6'6", and flaunting an 82-inch reach, Terrell figured to match Ali jab for jab. But Ali's speed made the unification bout a mismatch, and by round six, the WBA champion was covering up or clinching. Terrell managed to keep his feet and last the distance, but both his eyes were cut and closed. (Three days after the fight, he would undergo surgery to repair a broken bone beneath his left eyeball.)

"The only thing I regret is that I didn't knock him out," said Ali, who had won the fight, but lost some friends.

Champion Muhammad Ali (right) was far too fast and clever for big Ernie Terrell. Ali retained the crown with a unanimous decision.

THE LEFT THAT'S GOOD AS GOLD

In August 1966, featherweight champion Vicente Saldivar scored a close decision victory over Japan's Mitsunori Seki. Most titlists would have been content to keep the crown. But the fight had come in his native Mexico, and for Saldivar, a routine victory wasn't enough.

Before the rematch, fought on January 29, at the El Toreo bullring in Mexico City, the soft-spoken southpaw expressed a desire to win more convincingly. And he planned to do it with his "golden left."

As physically dominant as any 126-pounder since Sandy Saddler, Saldivar softened Seki with body blows, then introduced his left in round three. Halfway through the seventh, he struck again, the *coup de grace* being a left uppercut. Seki rose and tried to clinch, but when he turned his back to the champion, officials of the Mexican Boxing Commission ordered referee Ramon Berumen to step in.

"I could defend myself no longer," acknowledged Seki.

The golden left glove had left him limp.

A LITTLE RIOT IN THE BIG APPLE

New York City may be a melting pot, but on February 5, light heavyweight champion Dick Tiger must have felt like he was fighting in San Juan. Every time Puerto Rican title challenger Jose Torres landed a punch, the Madison Square Garden crowd of 12,674 celebrated. And with Torres better than in their first bout, the celebrations came often.

Boxing out of his peekaboo stance, Torres jabbed with conviction and won most of the early rounds. Then Tiger made his move, hurling hammers at Torres' body. Neither fighter gained full control, but after Torres stunned Tiger in the 13th, 14th, and 15th, his supporters were sure that he had done enough to regain the crown.

To their disgust, the split decision went to Tiger. (All three judges scored 8-7, two for the champion, and one for the challenger.) For 20 minutes, the fans tossed wooden chairs, bottles of wine, and other assorted objects toward the ring. It wasn't much of a riot by boxing standards, but it sure ruined what could've been a helluva Garden party.

CRISP WIN, AND THEN...

On March 22, Muhammad Ali made his ninth defense of the heavyweight title, stopping 34-year-old Zora Folley in the seventh round at Madison Square Garden. It would be the champion's last fight for 3½ years.

Folley, who had been rated first in 1958, was well past his prime. Still, the challenger climbed through the ropes with a plan: shake Ali with right hands. It worked until Ali decided to fight back. A left-right to the jaw dropped Folley in the fourth, and a short right drove him face-first to the canvas in the seventh. He was counted out at the 1:48 mark by referee Johnny LoBianco.

Five weeks later, the world watched and waited as Ali arrived at the U.S. Armed Forces Examining and Entrance Station in Houston. When his name was called, he refused induction, claiming exemption "as a minister of the religion of Islam." Only one hour later, the New York State Athletic Commission suspended his license and withdrew recognition of Ali as heavyweight champion. Other state commissions and sanctioning bodies soon followed New York's lead.

"I am proud of the title World Heavyweight Champion," said Ali. "The holder of it should at all times have the courage of his convictions and carry out those convictions, not only in the ring, but in all phases of his life. It is in light of my own personal convictions that I take my stand in rejecting the call to be inducted into the armed services. I do so with full realization of its implications and possible consequences."

On May 8, Ali was indicted for draft evasion, and on June 19, a jury found him guilty. He had once shocked the world. That world had turned upside down.

RINGSIDE VIEW

APRIL

Japan-based former U.S. Marine Paul Fujii wins the world junior welterweight crown by crushing Italy's Sandro Lopopolo in two rounds.

NINO DOES NEW YORK

Italy's Nino Benvenuti was an Olympic gold medalist, a former world champion with a record of 71-1, and a fighter who trained by swinging from tree branches, jumping from cliffs, and sparring without a mouthpiece. With this sort of record, how then could he have possibly snuck up on middleweight champion Emile Griffith?

At Madison Square Garden on March 17, Benvenuti, a 5-2 underdog, took Griffith's crown by unanimous 15-round decision (two scores of 10-5, and 9-6). Featuring quick jabs and quicker feet, the handsome challenger made Griffith lunge and reach, then countered with combinations. His only scare came in round four, when a long right drove him to the floor. He recovered by the sixth, and regained control soon after.

Griffith staged a brief rally in the ninth and 10th, but Benvenuti rebounded down the stretch. The decision was received favorably. New York City had a new hero, even if he lived 3,700 miles away.

Zora Folley fell in the seventh round to become Muhammad Ali's ninth title defense victim.

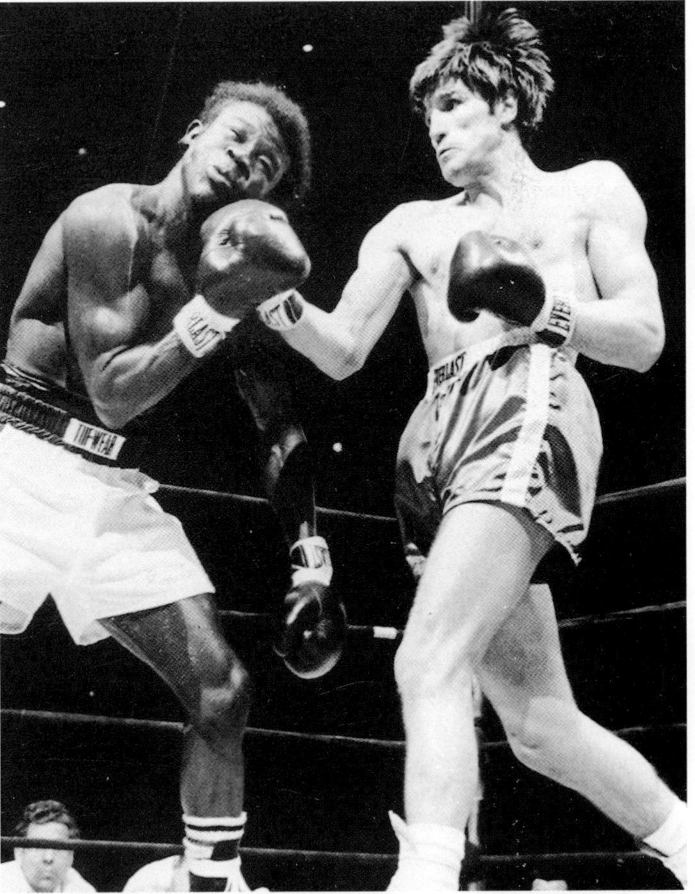

Lanky Nino Benvenuti (right) became Italy's national hero by beating Emile Griffith.

MAY

1967

AUGUST

IT'S OVER IN A FLASH

Since the early-'60s, hundreds of fighters have imitated Muhammad Ali. Japan's Yoshiaki Numata did better than most – he won a world title.

On June 15, at Kuramae Arena in Tokyo, Numata won the world junior lightweight crown by outpointing Flash Elorde. It was the end of an era; the Filipino had made 10 successful defenses, and reigned for more than seven years.

The bout was competitive for a handful of rounds, or until Numata took to boxing like Ali. Somewhat cautious after suffering a flash knockdown in round three, he danced and darted, pumped his jab, and flaunted his hand speed in furious flurries. He even dropped his gloves to his sides and invited the plodding champion to hit him.

Having barely made weight, Elorde slowed over the second half of the bout, and after 15 rounds, Numata was declared the new champion by majority decision (scores of 69-69, 71-66, and 72-66).

How do you say "I shocked the world" in Japanese?

SITTING PRETTY IN SAN JUAN

Lightweight champion Carlos Ortiz' October 1966 defense against Sugar Ramos, which was fought on the challenger's turf in Mexico, ended in a ring riot. Before signing for the July 1 rematch, Ortiz wisely insisted that the bout be held in San Juan. If there was going to be another riot, he wanted the fans on his side.

Ortiz took another precaution: he worked himself into the best condition of his career.

"If training wasn't so hard," he said, "I would fight every day." At Hiram Bithorn Stadium, the dividends came quickly. Ramos was staggered by rights in rounds two and three, and in the fourth, he was backed to the ropes, and then on to one knee. At the 1:18 mark, referee Zack Clayton intervened.

No postfight controversy this time. Complaints by Pancho Rosales, Ramos' trainer, that Clayton had acted hastily were dismissed.

Besides, in San Juan, no one was bothering to listen to him.

Lightweight champion Carlos Ortiz (left) easily stopped Sugar Ramos in their title match before the champion's supporters in San Juan.

THERE'S NO STOPPING SALDIVAR

Joe Frazier helped define Muhammad Ali. Jake LaMotta did likewise for Sugar Ray Robinson. And, on a smaller scale, Howard Winstone served the same purpose for Vicente Saldivar.

Featherweight champion Saldivar and Winstone were rematched on June 15, before 30,000 of the challenger's supporters at Ninian Park Stadium in Cardiff, Wales. In September 1965, the Mexican southpaw had comfortably won their first meeting. This time, he needed a furious rally to keep the crown.

For 10 rounds, Winstone showed all of his skills. He worked his jab overtime, and was careful to slip most of the champion's powerful lefts. But down the stretch, Saldivar, described by one writer as "a pocket version of Rocky Marciano," broke through. Punching non-stop until the final bell, he staggered Winstone on several occasions. Referee and sole judge Wally Thom rewarded him by a score of 75¼-73¼. There were few objections.

"I have to take my hat off to Saldivar," said Winstone. "There just seems no way to stop him.

EVEN IN DALLAS, THINGS BEGIN TO GO A LITTLE BETTER WITH COKES

World welterweight champion Curtis Cokes was fighting in his hometown of Dallas, but everywhere he looked, he was reminded of past failures. On May 19, at the Memorial Auditorium, Cokes defended against Martinique-born Frenchman Francois Pavilla, who, in January, had held him to a draw. And heading the undercard was slick Philadelphian Gypsy Joe Harris, who, in March, had outpointed the champion in a non-title bout.

Cokes would never defend against Harris. He did manage, however, to gain revenge vs. Pavilla. The short, stocky challenger was a pressure fighter and bodypunching specialist, but Cokes countered magnificently with his best weapons, jabs and uppercuts.

The end came suddenly. Late in the 10th, Cokes scored with a right that drove Pavilla to the ropes. A followup hook felled him, and his head hit the canvas with a thud. Pavilla gamely rose, but his manager, George Kanter, tossed a towel into the ring. Referee Pat Riley had no choice but to stop the fight and declare Cokes the winner by TKO.

Those past failures seemed like ancient history.

FOR HARADA, FIGHTING WAS THE EASY PART

Fighting Harada had turned pro as a teenage flyweight. But as a physically mature 24-year-old, he found himself a bantamweight fighting in a featherweight's body. Trouble was, he was the bantamweight champion of the world. That meant that no matter what, he had to make 118 pounds.

The struggle became absurdly difficult before his July 4 defense against Bernardo Caraballo, held at the Martial Arts Hall in Tokyo. Harada began training at 147 pounds. Maybe he was a bantamweight fighting in a *welterweight's* body.

Harada made 118 – not an ounce less – and then made Caraballo suffer. Seeking a quick kayo, he swarmed in the first round, and dropped the Colombian with a right to the chin. But the challenger picked himself up; he was determined to extend Harada into the late rounds.

The fight lasted the distance, with Caraballo countering often enough to remain competitive. Still, the unanimous decision went to the champion (scores of 71-68, 72-66, and 72-68).

Harada's celebration couldn't begin quickly enough. He was relieved that he had retained the title, but even more relieved that he could eat again.

RINGSIDE VIEW

JUNE

Argentina's Carlos Monzon wins the South American middleweight title by outpointing Jorge Fernandez over 12 rounds in Buenos Aires.

AUGUST

Horacio Accavallo retains the WBA flyweight title, scoring a split 15-round decision over former champion Hiroyuki Ebihara.

Japan's bantamweight king Fighting Harada (left) is congratulated by Bernardo Caraballo.

THE SHOWDOWN AT SHEA

With three recent New York fight cards having ended in ring riots, city officials hoped that lightweight champion Carlos Ortiz and former titlist Ismael Laguna would calm the masses before their eagerly anticipated rubber match.

Ortiz: "This won't be close; he'll go by the 10th or 11th round."

Laguna: "I just hope he comes to me like he says he will. I'll stretch him out."

So much for calming the masses.

The August 16 title bout was held before a crowd of 18,160 at Shea Stadium, and early in the night, chants of "Orteez!" and "Lagoona!" filled the ballpark. Unfortunately, the fight failed to match the hype. Ortiz was willing enough, but Laguna danced away for all 15 rounds.

Scoring throughout with his educated left, Ortiz kept the title by unanimous decision (two scores of 10-4-1, and 11-3-1). There was no riot. In fact, there hadn't been much of a fight, either.

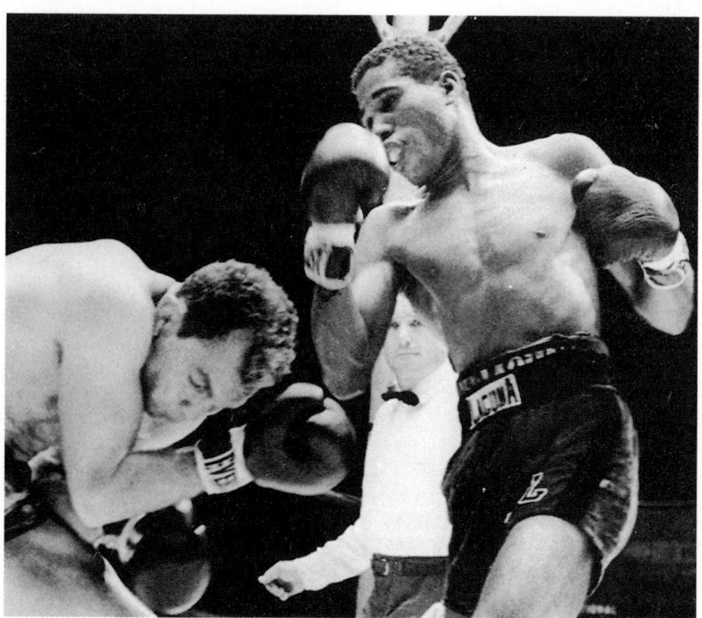

Ismael Laguna (right) lost in valiant attempt to regain lightweight crown from Carlos Ortiz.

WORLD TITLE FIGHTS

WELTERWEIGHTS

May 19 — **Curtis Cokes** *KO* 10 Francois Pavilla, Dallas

LIGHTWEIGHTS

July 1 — **Carlos Ortiz** *KO* 4 Sugar Ramos, San Juan

Aug 16 — **Carlos Ortiz** *W* 15 Ismael Laguna, Flushing, NY

JUNIOR LIGHTWEIGHTS

June 15 — **Yoshiaki Numata** (JAP) *W* 15 Flash Elorde, Tokyo

FEATHERWEIGHTS

June 25 — **Vicente Saldivar** *ref* 15 Howard Winstone, Cardiff

BANTAMWEIGHTS

Aug 4 — **Fighting Harada** *W* 15 Bernardo Caraballo, Tokyo

FLYWEIGHTS

July 26 — **Chartchai Chionoi** *KO* 3 Puntip Keosuriya, Bangkok

Aug 12 — **Horacio Accavallo** *W* 15 Hiroyuki Ebihara, Buenos Aires

SEPTEMBER

1967

DECEMBER

RINGSIDE VIEW

OCTOBER

Junior middleweight champion Ki Soo Kim retains the crown by scoring a split 15-round decision over the USA's Freddie Little.

A TITLE UNIFICATION OF SORTS

When is a title unification fight not really a title unification fight? When one champion is recognized throughout the world, and the other is recognized only in California. After all, California has always had some pretty strange ideas about lots of things.

On October 2, welterweight champion Curtis Cokes clashed with the once-beaten Charlie Shipes. Since the bout was held in Oakland, at the Arena, it was billed as a unification bout. (In December 1966, Shipes had been crowned California world champion after his stoppage of Percy Manning.)

Cokes proved his opponent's title claim to be rather silly. After patiently waiting for counterpunching opportunities, the Texan exploded in round four, dropping Shipes with a right-left. There was another knockdown in the sixth, and after two more in the eight, referee Jack Downey stepped in at the 1:37 mark.

There was one welterweight champion throughout the world.

And in California, too.

RAIN, RIBS, AND A ROUGH REVENGE

Middleweight champion Nino Benvenuti was quite fond of New York City. Certain things, however, seemed to happen to him only when he fought on the road. Like postponements. And injuries. And losing.

Nino's defense against Emile Griffith was originally scheduled for September 28, at Shea Stadium, but rain pushed it back one day. The delay wasn't nearly long enough to allow the Italian champion's injured ribs to heal. Unbeknownst to the press – or Griffith – Benvenuti had been banged up in a sparring session. In the third round of the fight, he felt a wave of pain.

"I couldn't hold up my left after that," he said. "The pain was awful. I could hardly breathe."

Boxing without the spark that had led him to his previous victory over Griffith, Nino was outjabbed and outslugged. Griffith moved forward behind a dominant jab, and by the late rounds, Benvenuti was exhausted, and bleeding from the nose and a cut under his chin.

Griffith clinched victory by flooring his rival in the 14th round. The scores – 9-5-1 twice, and 7-7-1 – suggested a relatively close fight. But Benvenuti knew he was a loser long before the sound of the final bell.

At the end of 15 rousing rounds, both Nino Benvenuti (left) and Emile Griffith think they've won.

VICENTE'S MOST UNEXPECTED EXIT

After conquering his most bitter rival, and doing so in his native Mexico City, featherweight champion Vicente Saldivar appeared to be on top of the world. Two attractive options awaited him: he could jump to lightweight and challenge world champion Carlos Ortiz, or remain at 126 pounds and try to extend his reign into the Seventies. So Saldivar, age 24, announced his retirement.

The southpaw's seventh defense, and his third against Welshman Howard Winstone, came on October 14 at Aztec Stadium. It was a typical Saldivar performance. He banged to the body in the early rounds, which set up a seventh-round knockdown. In the 12th, Winstone fell for a second time, and was subsequently pounded until his manager, Eddie Thomas, surrendered by throwing a towel into the ring. (At the time of the stoppage, Saldivar led by scores of 110-102, 109-106, and 107-107.)

After he was declared the winner, the champion took the ring microphone and said goodbye.

"We've both taken a tremendous amount out of each other," he said of his series with Winstone.

It was as good a reason for retirement as any.

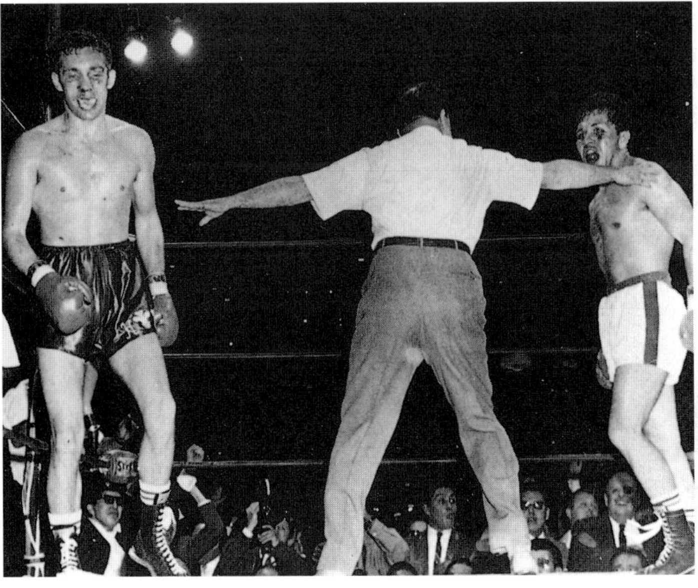
Beaten and dejected, Howard Winstone walks to corner after his seconds threw in the towel.

World Title Fights

LIGHT HEAVYWEIGHTS

Nov 17 **Dick Tiger** *KO* 12
Roger Rouse, Las Vegas

MIDDLEWEIGHTS

Sept 29 **Emile Griffith** *W* 15
Nino Benvenuti, New York City

JUNIOR MIDDLEWEIGHTS

Oct 3 **Ki Soo Kim** *W* 15
Freddie Little, Seoul

WELTERWEIGHTS

Oct 2 **Curtis Cokes** *KO* 8
Charlie Shipes, Oakland
(Unifies World Title)

JUNIOR WELTERWEIGHTS

Nov 6 **Paul Fujii** *KO* 4
Willie Quatour, Tokyo

JUNIOR LIGHTWEIGHTS

Dec 14 **Hiroshi Kobayashi** (JAP) *KO* 12
Yoshiaki Numata, Tokyo

FEATHERWEIGHTS

Oct 14 **Vicente Saldivar** *KO* 12
Howard Winstone, Mexico City

Dec 14 **Raul Rojas** (USA) *W* 15
Antonio Herrera, Los Angeles
(Wins Vacant California State World Title)

FLYWEIGHTS

Sept 19 **Chartchai Chionoi** *KO* 7
Walter McGowan, Wembley

Ringside View

DECEMBER

In the semifinal of the WBA heavyweight tournament, Jimmy Ellis scores a 12-round decision over Oscar Bonavena in Louisville.

TIGER HITS THE JACKPOT

Shortly before arriving at the Las Vegas Convention Center for his November 17 defense against Roger Rouse, light heavyweight champion Dick Tiger received word from his native Nigeria: seven days before, his wife had given birth to their seventh child, a baby girl who had weighed seven pounds. In Las Vegas, three sevens signified a jackpot. Rouse didn't have a chance.

Roger Rouse is downed by Dick Tiger.

The Montana cowboy was hardly a stylist, but in preparing for Tiger, he had been trained to box. His jab-and-move approach worked for a half-dozen rounds. Then Tiger timed his counters and went to work. He opened a 14-stitch cut inside of Rouse's mouth, scored knockdowns in the ninth and 10th rounds, and, in the 12th, dropped the challenger with a right to the head. Having fallen face-first, Rouse rolled over and beat the count. Nonetheless, referee Jimmy Olivas stopped it.

At age 38, Tiger was still a champion. Now it was his turn to send good news back home.

PRIME TIME FOR A POWER PLAY

Hiroshi Kobayashi was given a good chance to dethrone junior lightweight champion Yoshiaki Numata, but even his most loyal supporters couldn't expect a knockout. In 57 fights, Kobayashi had scored only eight kayos.

Numata-Kobayashi came on December 14, at Kuramae Arena in Tokyo. It was Numata's first defense, and the first world title fight in history featuring two Japanese.

For one night, at least, Kobayashi turned into a bone-breaking puncher. He chased the mobile champion from the start, and caught up with him in round six, when he felled Numata with a right to the jaw. There were three more knockdowns in the 12th, the last of which left Numata flat on the canvas for several minutes.

Kobayashi was a pure fighter; he had no car, no girlfriend, and few hobbies. But on December 14, he found a punch. And as a result, he found himself declared a world champion.

In the first world championship bout between two Japanese boxers, Kobayashi kayoed Numata.

A DIFFERENT KIND OF HERO

World junior welterweight champion Paul Fujii was arguably the most popular fighter in Japan. It was an impressive distinction, especially for an American.

Having been born in Hawaii, Fujii was an American citizen of Japanese heritage. He was also a kayo puncher, and while his imperfect Japanese amused the locals, the language he spoke with his fists was universal.

On November 6, at Kuramae Stadium in Tokyo, Fujii made his first defense, meeting the WBA's top contender, southpaw Willi Quatour. The challenger could be sure he wasn't fighting in his native Germany; spectators sat cross-legged on straw mats, and women wearing colorful silk kimonos mingled with businessmen in gray suits. Only Fujii, however, made him feel uncomfortable.

Quatour won the first couple of rounds by landing jabs and body blows, but in the fourth, Fujii fired a right to the jaw, and referee Jay Edson counted to 10. Fujii was communicating just fine.

JANUARY

1968

APRIL

PRELIM TO THE REAL FIGHT

Fighting had always come easy for Welsh featherweight Howard Winstone. Fighting in the ring, that is, not in court.

On January 23, at Royal Albert Hall in London, Winstone won the vacant British world title by stopping Japan's Mitsunori Seki at 1:44 of the ninth round. Given that he had thrice failed to dethrone former champion Vicente Saldivar, it should have been Winstone's greatest moment. But his celebration was tempered by the divorce proceedings that would mark his return to Wales. Winstone had charged his wife Benita with adultery.

Winstone-Seki was a bloody battle, with a one-inch eye cut suffered by Seki ultimately bringing referee Roland Dakin's stoppage.

A world champion at last, Winstone still couldn't be sure he would be tough enough to win the battle that lay ahead.

ROSE THE FIRST OF HIS KIND

Australia's rugged Lionel Rose (standing) scored major upset winning bantamweight title from Japanese idol Fighting Harada in Tokyo.

In October 1962, Fighting Harada, a teenaged substitute, won the world flyweight title by surprising Pone Kingpetch. It was perhaps fitting, then, that on February 26, 1968, at the Martial Arts Hall in Tokyo, Harada lost the world bantamweight title to another teenaged subsitute, Lionel Rose.

Rose, a 19-year-old Aborigine from Australia's bush land, replaced Jesus Pimental. Aware of Harada's struggle to make weight, the challenger made sure to extend the bout into the late rounds by retreating from start to finish. He jabbed with conviction, cut Harada over the right eye, and scored a ninth-round knockdown. After the final bell, he was crowned the new champion by unanimous decision, though a trio of Japanese judges saw the bout closer than it had appeared to be (72-71, 72-70, and 72-69).

The good news was that Rose had become the first Aborigine to achieve fame in any field. The bad news was that he had been paid $7,500, and local custom suggested that he share the money with his close relatives, of which there numbered 2,000.

BLOOD FLOWS FREELY IN THE BULL RING

One of the biggest misconceptions in boxing is that flyweights don't punch as hard, punch for pound, as bigger fighters. On January 28, at the El Toreo bull ring in Mexico City, WBC champion Chartchai Chionoi and local favorite Efren (Alacron) Torres did their part to expose the myth; their title fight was among the most savage and bloody in division history.

Defending the title for the third time, Thailand's Chionoi opened a two-inch gash over the challenger's left eye in the second stanza. As the rounds mounted and the 112-pounders traded powerpunches, the shorter Torres returned the favor; by the midway mark, Chionoi was boxing with one eye swollen almost shut, and the other cut and bruised.

There was no denying that Torres' wound was worse, and in round 13, referee Arthur Mercante stopped the fight. (After 12 rounds, the bout was even on points.) Shocked and overjoyed, Chionoi collapsed to the canvas.

Seemingly so close to victory, Torres had now failed in tries for both the WBA and WBC titles. Five straight victories, however, would lead him to a return with Chionoi, and his destiny.

REVENGE – WHEN IT REALLY COUNTS

The three fights between Joe Frazier and Buster Mathis proved that timing is everything. The heavyweights clashed twice as amateurs, with Mathis winning both times. Buster's second triumph meant a berth on the 1964 U.S. Olympic team, but he late suffered an injury. Frazier went in his stead and won a gold medal.

On March 4, the fighters squared off as pros in the first card at the new Madison Square Garden. (Their bout shared top billing with the middleweight title fight between Nino Benvenuti and Emile Griffith.) Again, Frazier and Mathis met at the crossroads; the winner would be crowned world champion, at least in New York, Illinois, Maine, Pennsylvania, and Massachusetts.

Standing 6'3" and scaling 243½, Mathis was the bigger fighter. But Frazier, 204½, was the bigger hitter. Mathis jabbed and danced for five rounds. As soon as he came off his toes, Frazier unleashed his left hook. In the 11th, a hook busted Buster.

Joe Frazier stopped blubbery Buster Mathis (left) in the 11th round to win New York world title.

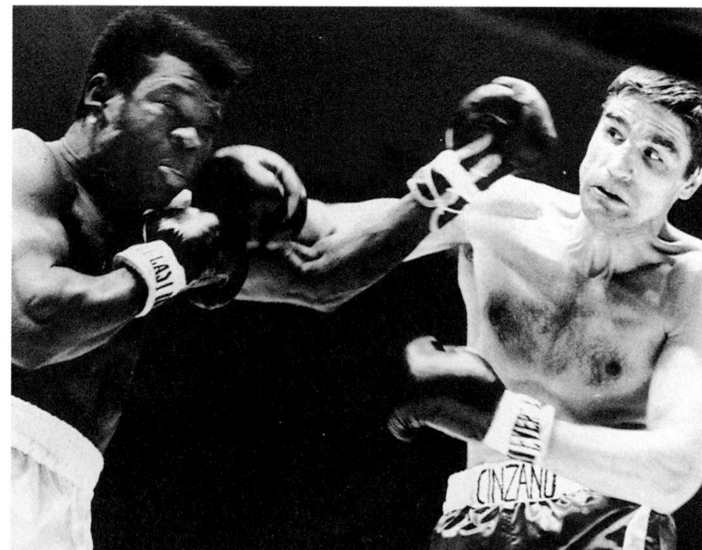

In their third meeting, Nino Benvenuti (right) decisioned Emile Griffith over 15 rounds.

NINO TAKES IT BACK

Throughout the '60s, Emile Griffith's title fights were decided by the slimmest of margins. On March 4, at Madison Square Garden, he defended the middleweight crown against familiar rival Nino Benvenuti. It was hardly surprising that after 15 rounds, a point or two separated the fighters.

It was a fight of shifting momentum. Benvenuti took the first three rounds. Griffith then pulled even by scoring heavily to the body. The key moment came in the ninth, when the Italian connected with a hook that sent Griffith to the floor. The champion recovered easily enough, but on the cards, the knockdown would prove to be critical.

The judges gave Benvenuti rounds nine through 12. Griffith rebounded once more, and at the final bell, he was swarming. But his late rally was insufficient; Benvenuti regained the crown by unanimous scores of 8-6-1 (twice) and 7-7-1 (but 9-7 on points).

Though he would go on to secure title tries in three different divisions, Griffith would never again reign as a world champion.

FIGHTING TALK

I knew what was going on; I even helped the referee pick up the count

EMILE GRIFFITH
on his knockdown

WORLD TITLE FIGHTS

HEAVYWEIGHTS

March 4	**Joe Frazier** (USA) *KO* 11 Buster Mathis, New York City (Wins Vacant New York State World Title)
April 27	**Jimmy Ellis** (USA) *W* 15 Jerry Quarry, Oakland (Wins Vacant WBA Title)

MIDDLEWEIGHTS

March 4	**Nino Benvenuti** *W* 15 Emile Griffith, New York City

WELTERWEIGHTS

April 16	**Curtis Cokes** *KO* 5 Willie Ludick, Dallas

JUNIOR LIGHTWEIGHTS

March 30	**Hiroshi Kobayashi** *D* 15 Rene Barrientos, Tokyo

FEATHERWEIGHTS

Jan 23	**Howard Winstone** (WAL) *KO* 9 Mitsunori Seki, London (Wins Vacant British World Title)
March 28	**Raul Rojas** *W* 15 Enrique Higgins, Los Angeles

BANTAMWEIGHTS

Feb 26	**Lionel Rose** (AUT) *W* 15 Fighting Harada, Tokyo

FLYWEIGHTS

Jan 28	**Chartchai Chionoi** *KO* 13 Efren Torres, Mexico City

RINGSIDE VIEW

APRIL

Welterweight champion Curtis Cokes retains the crown for the third time, stopping Willie Ludick in the fifth round.

WHEN THE UNDERDOGS GOT OVER

After Muhammad Ali was stripped of the heavyweight title, the WBA ran a tournament to crown a successor. Incredibly, all seven bouts were won by the underdogs.

The championship match pitted Jimmy Ellis, who had formerly served as Ali's sparring partner, against 22-year-old Californian Jerry Quarry. Ellis advanced by upsetting Leotis Martin and Oscar Bonavena. Quarry reach the final by topping Floyd Patterson and Thad Spencer.

Ellis-Quarry took place on April 27, at the Oakland Coliseum. It turned out to be a yawner; Quarry liked to counter with hooks off the ropes, but Ellis led only with feints, and kept the bout in ring center. (Afterward, it was revealed that Quarry fought with a broken bone in his back.) After 15 dull rounds, Ellis was rewarded with a majority decision (points scores of 10-5, 7-6, and 6-6).

"The WBA elimination tournament was a total success," commented Madison Square Garden matchmaker Teddy Brenner. "It eliminated all eight fighters."

Jimmy Ellis (right) decisioned Jerry Quarry over 15 rounds to win WBA heavyweight title.

MAY

1968

AUGUST

Ringside View

MAY

Italy's Sandro Mazzinghi regains the world junior middleweight title, scoring a split 15-round decision over defending champion Ki Soo Kim.

"EVERYTHING IS ALL QUIET"

Dick Tiger, who had just suffered his first knockout, and second knockdown, in 77 fights, described his experience this way:

"I do not see anything. I do not hear anything. Everything is all quiet, and it is dark. There is no pain, there is no sound. I do not know I was on the floor. Was I on the floor?"

On May 24, at Madison Square Garden, Tiger, 38, defended the light heavyweight title against 29-year-old Bob Foster.

The long-ignored Foster entered the ring as a 12-5 favorite, and took the title with a single blow. For three rounds, he stuck his jab in the champion's face – Foster enjoyed 7½-and eight-inch advantages in height and reach, respectively. In the fourth, he missed with a right, but followed with a short hook that caught Tiger coming in. Referee Mark Conn reached 10 at 2:05 mark.

Yes, Dick, you were on the floor all right.

Dick Tiger lost the title to Bob Foster.

SMOKE GETS IN MANUEL'S EYES

It was among the most savage first rounds in heavyweight history. For three minutes, New York world champion Joe Frazier and 6'3" Mexican thumper Manuel Ramos played bombs away. That both fighters lasted to the second round was a minor miracle.

The round's most telling blow was a right that staggered Frazier and almost sent him down. Usually a slow starter, "Smokin' Joe" sensed that he needed to turn the flame into a fire. In the second, he hooked, and then hooked some more, and Ramos succumbed.

There were two knockdowns, the second coming late in the round, and after an inspired seven-punch combination. Floored for the first time in his 28-bout career, Ramos rose at referee Arthur Mercante's count of three. Apparently unaware that the bell had sounded, he signalled that he could not continue. "His eyes looked glassy," said Mercante. "I would've stopped it anyway."

Frazier was 21-0 and getting better. In title fights against Buster Mathis and Ramos, he had proven one thing: nobody enjoyed a brawl more than he did.

Mexico's Manuel Ramos (left) disobeyed a warning to stay away from the ropes, and paid when Joe Frazier kayoed him in the second round.

CRUZ HAD PAID HIS DUES

When New York City matchmaker Duke Stefano heard that Carlos Teofilo Rosario (Teo) Cruz had not only dethroned world lightweight champion Carlos Ortiz, but dropped him, too, he commented, "Must've been a shove."

Stefano couldn't help but recall the Cruz who had fought in clubshow prelims in 1962 and '63; who had loads of courage, but little class; who had 12 losses in 49 fights. Regardless, on June 29, at Quisqueya Stadium in Santo Domingo, Cruz, 31, became the first Dominican world champion in history.

The challenger started furiously – he felled Ortiz with a first-round right hand – and finished strongly. Ortiz won his share of the remaining rounds, and the decision figured to be a close one. In some of the oddest scoring in recent memory, Cruz triumphed by split scores of 145-142, 146-121, and 130-131.

Cruz had clearly improved with time. It was clear, however, that one of the judges still needed some work.

A ROSE IS STILL A CHAMP

Australia's Lionel Rose won the world bantamweight title by running from Fighting Harada. On July 2, at the Martial Arts Hall in Tokyo, he kept it by chasing Takao Sakurai.

The Japanese challenger wasn't without credentials. Rated third by the WBA, Sakurai, 26, had won a gold medal at the 1964 Olympics, and was 22-0 as a pro. When the southpaw dropped Rose with a straight left in the second round, ringsiders anticipated an upset. But almost as soon as the champion arose, Sakurai began his sprint.

Round after round, Sakurai circled the ring, and Rose settled for occasional punches to the body. After 15 frustrating rounds, the 20-year-old Australian was awarded a majority decision (scores of 72-70, 72-71, and 72-72).

Afterward, Sakurai was asked about his curious strategy. He explained that he had fought cautiously because his handlers believed him to be ahead on points.

Sounds like they were expecting a hometown decision.

Dynamic Lionel Rose (left) retained his crown by outpointing local hero Takao Sakurai.

THE ALI-LIKE FEATHERWEIGHT

Howard Winstone had sought the world featherweight title for 10 years. He kept it for six months.

On July 24, at Coney Beach Stadium in Porthcawl, Wales, Winstone was dethroned by the fighter who had succeeded him as European champion, Jose Legra.

The Spain-based Cuban talked like Muhammad Ali, and occasionally fought like him, too. Against Winstone, he was particularly vicious; he wanted the title, as well as revenge for a June 1965 defeat. Legra scored two knockdowns in the first round, and opened a cut under Winstone's left eye. By round two, the champion's eye was reduced to a slit.

Legra took advantage by dancing, dropping his hands, popping his jab, and flaunting his speed. Winstone gallantly struggled until the fifth, when, at the 2:02 mark, Gibbs called a halt. "I'm the best in the world today, and will be for a very long time," said the new champion, who sounded just like you-know-who.

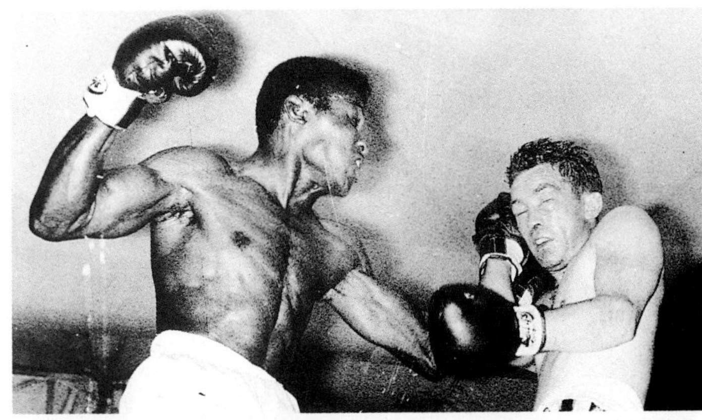

Clever Welshman Howard Winstone (right) lost the title to Jose Legra on a cut eye.

WORLD TITLE FIGHTS

HEAVYWEIGHTS

June 24 **Joe Frazier** *KO* 2
Manuel Ramos, New York City

LIGHT HEAVYWEIGHTS

May 24 **Bob Foster** (USA) *KO* 4
Dick Tiger, New York City

JUNIOR MIDDLEWEIGHTS

May 25 **Sandro Mazzinghi** *W* 15
Ki Soo Kim, Milan

LIGHTWEIGHTS

June 29 **Carlos Teo Cruz** (DR) *W* 15
Carlos Ortiz, Santo Domingo

FEATHERWEIGHTS

July 24 **Jose Legra** (SPA) *KO* 5
Howard Winstone, Porthcawl
(Wins Vacant WBC Title)

BANTAMWEIGHTS

July 2 **Lionel Rose** *W* 15
Takao Sakurai, Tokyo

GRIFF AT THE CROSSROADS

In boxing, you're only as good as your last fight, which, for Emile Griffith, wasn't good at all. For eight years, Griffith had been a championship caliber fighter, winning and defending world titles at both welterweight and middleweight. But in March, he had lost the 160-pound crown to arch-rival Nino Benvenuti. For that reason, insiders viewed his August 6 showdown with undefeated Gypsy Joe Harris as critical.

Griffith, 30, met the 22-year-old Harris before a curious crowd of 13,875 at the Spectrum in Philadelphia. Unbeaten at 24-0, and holding a win over welterweight champion Curtis Cokes, Harris answered the opening bell as a 7-5 favorite. He offered lots of style, but little substance.

Like so many fighters, Harris seemed inspired by Muhammad Ali. He danced around the ring, but instead of outpunching Griffith, tried to unsettle him. Gypsy Joe turned his back on the former champion, wiggled, giggled, and even extended his hands, as if about to touch gloves, and then fired sneak combinations.

"I was told that if Gypsy started boogalooing," said the unflappable Griffith, "I just keep punching."He punched enough to win a unanimous 12-round decision (scores of 58-51, 56-53, and 58-53). Only as good as his last fight, Griffith was pretty good again.

RINGSIDE VIEW

JULY

Fighting for the first time since winning the light heavyweight crown, Bob Foster stops Charley Polite in the third round of a non-title bout.

SEPTEMBER

1968

DECEMBER

THE DAY EIGHT WAS LESS THAN HALF OF 15

On October 25, the Las Vegas-based Freddie Little challenged world junior middleweight champion Sandro Mazzinghi at the Palazzo Dello Sport in Rome. It was his second title try; in October 1967, he had lost a decision – split, of course – to Mazzinghi's predecesor, Ki Soo Kim, in Seoul.

Far quicker than his Italian foe, Little established his jab and opened cuts over both of Mazzinghi's eyes. He widened his lead by scoring a fifth-round knockdown, and after eight rounds, the Associated Press' card read 7-1 for the challenger. Then the bizarre occurred: At the bell for the start of round nine, West German referee Herbert Tomser stopped the fight and ruled it a no-contest.

Tomser later claimed that the ringside doctor called for a halt because of the cuts over Mazzinghi's eyes. "In European rules," said the referee, "if the stoppage is made in the first half, the fight must be a no-contest. For me, the eighth round is also the middle of the fight."

Responded Little's manager, Joe Kiernan, "We were royally robbed in Korea, and this is an international scandal."

Fortunately, a bit of common sense would prevail. Three months later, Mazzinghi would be stripped of the title, and in March 1969, Little would face Stanley (Kitten) Hayward for the vacant crown. That fight would take place in Las Vegas, which, for the road weary – and road *wary* – Little didn't seem like a gamble at all.

WHEN SWEDEN WASN'T SO NEUTRAL

Former world champion Floyd Patterson was among the most popular athletes in Sweden. Scandanavian fans became acquainted with the Brooklyn-born heavyweight by following his thrilling series with local product Ingemar Johansson. Almost three years after knocking out his rival for a second time, Patterson resumed the relationship by fighting three times in Stockholm.

His fourth bout there, however, turned out to be one of the worst experiences of his career.

On September 14, Patterson, 33, challenged WBA heavyweight champion Jimmy Ellis at Stockholm's Raasunda Stadium. Neither fighter proved to be technically superior. Patterson worked best from the outside, leading with leaping hooks, and Ellis countered when he could. But to the uneducated eye, the fight looked like a slaughter; by the middle rounds, Ellis had a broken and misshapen nose, a seven-stitch cut over his right eye, and a fractured left thumb. In fact, from the third round to the end of the fight, he was so handicapped that he couldn't make a fist.

"I used it (anyway)," he said of his left hand. "I had to use it."

When Ellis went down in the 14th, American referee Harold Valan ruled a slip. Valan was also the sole judge, and after 15 rounds, he enraged the local fans, as well as a national TV audience in the USA, by scoring 9-6 for Ellis.

"He landed the most punches," Valan explained, "and you have to score for the man who lands the punches. "Patterson spent most of his time watching."

Something most ringsiders thought Valan should have spent more time doing.

Jimmy Ellis (right) retained WBA heavyweight crown, outpointing Floyd Patterson over 15 rounds.

RINGSIDE VIEW

SEPTEMBER

Attempting to become the youngest lightweight champion in history, 19-year-old Californian Mando Ramos loses a unanimous 15-round decision to defending titlist Carlos (Teo) Cruz.

WORLD TITLE FIGHTS

HEAVYWEIGHTS

Sept 14	**Jimmy Ellis** *ref* 15 Floyd Patterson, Stockholm
Dec 10	**Joe Frazier** *W* 15 Oscar Bonavena, Philadelphia

MIDDLEWEIGHTS

Dec 14	**Nino Benvenuti** *W* 15 Don Fullmer, San Remo

JUNIOR MIDDLEWEIGHTS

Oct 25	**Sandro Mazzinghi** *No Contest* 9 Freddie Little, Rome

WELTERWEIGHTS

Oct 21	**Curtis Cokes** *W* 15 Ramon LaCruz, New Orleans

JUNIOR WELTERWEIGHTS

Dec 12	**Nicolino Locche** (ARG) *KO* 10 Paul Fujii, Tokyo
Dec 14	**Pedro Adigue** (PHI) *W* 15 Adolph Pruitt, Quezon City (Wins Vacant WBC Title)

LIGHTWEIGHTS

Sept 28	**Carlos Teo Cruz** *W* 15 Mando Ramos, Los Angeles

JUNIOR LIGHTWEIGHTS

Oct 6	**Hiroshi Kobayashi** *W* 15 Jaime Valladares, Tokyo

FEATHERWEIGHTS

Sept 28	**Shozo Saijyo** (JAP) *W* 15 Raul Rojas, Los Angeles

BANTAMWEIGHTS

Dec 6	**Lionel Rose** *W* 15 Chucho Castillo, Inglewood

FLYWEIGHTS

Nov 10	**Chartchai Chionoi** *W* 15 Bernabe Villacampo, Bangkok

ROSE AND CHUCHO LEAVE THE FANS LOCO

On December 6, 15,287 fans filed into the Inglewood Forum for Lionel Rose's title defense against Mexico's Chucho Castillo. Almost half of them came from south of the border.

Rose boxed neatly for several rounds, but after Castillo scored a 10th-round knockdown with a roundhouse right, he gained control. Rose rebounded to take the 15th. By then, however, the Mexican fans had already begun their celebrations.

When the decision was announced, the building *really* shook. Referee Dick Young scored for Castillo (9-7), but was outvoted by judges Lee Grossman and John Thomas, who had Rose ahead by identical scores of 7-6.

First fruits and coins were thrown at the ring. Then came the bottles. Finally, fires were set, 10 in all. Fourteen persons were treated at Daniel Freeman Hospital. (Ironically, Young, the sole official to have Castillo ahead, was cut over the right ear by a flying bottle.) In the Forum parking lot, windshields were smashed and cars were overturned. All the while, Rose sat in his dressing room, calmly puffing on a pipe while answering questions.

"Next time I want to defend my title in Australia," he said, "with the fans going crazy for *me*."

Bantamweight champ Lionel Rose (left) was forced to the limit by Mexico's Chuchu Castillo in 15 bruising rounds, but Rose won the decision.

WINNING THE TUSSLE WITHOUT ANY MUSCLE

With 12 kayos in 107 pro bouts, junior welterweight Nicolino Locche seemed as dangerous as a wingless mosquito. But a closer look at his record revealed only two losses in 11 years. A killer bee was more like it.

On December 12, at Kuramae Arena in Tokyo, the 29-year-old Argentine proved to have the perfect style to dethrone power-punching world champion Paul Fujii. Jabbing sharply, and moving only when necessary, the challenger scored as he pleased. By the fourth round, Fujii's right eye was closed. He responded by trying to score a one-punch kayo. Against a defensive wizard like Locche, however, he had almost no chance, and by the eighth round, he was exhausted.

A new champion was crowned after Fujii failed to leave his corner at the start of round 10. Like so many of Locche's victims, he had been stung into submission.

Nicolino Locche (left), the new champion.

A BIT OF A DILLY IN PHILLY

Before defending his share of the title against Oscar Bonavena, Joe Frazier was recognized as heavyweight champion in New York, Maine, Illinois, Pennsylvania, and Massachusetts. After scoring a unanimous 15-round decision, he could add Argentina to the list. Fighting before his fans, Frazier met Bonavena on December 10, at the Spectrum in Philadelphia. At the opening bell, he darted out of his corner and kissed Bonavena with a hook to the chin. Then he *really* got intimate.

Frazier attacked without pause from start to finish. In some rounds he landed low, and in others, he forget to stop punching at the sound of the bell. His left hooks came in waves, and Bonavena, usually an aggressive sort, was repeatedly on the ropes.

His face battered and bleeding, the Argentine staged a mini-rally over the last third of the fight. Somewhat punched out, Frazier nonetheless took a unanimous decision (74-64, 72-64, and 70-67). "When you die," Bonavena told him, "I will be the champion."

Answered Frazier, "I'm afraid I'm going to live for a long time."

RINGSIDE VIEW

DECEMBER

Middleweight champion Nino Benvenuti retains the crown with a unanimous 15-round decision over Don Fullmer.

JANUARY

1969

APRIL

RINGSIDE VIEW

FEBRUARY

Mexico's Efren (Alacran) Torres wins the world flyweight title in his third try, stopping Chartchai Chionoi in the ninth round.

SPANNING THE GLOBE

When French-born Australian Johnny Famechon won the featherweight title by outpointing Jose Legra, it was a triumph shared by his entire family. In March 1950, Famechon's uncle Ray had failed in an attempt to dethrone Willie Pep. Johnny's mission turned out to be a lot easier; despite his arrogance, Legra was no Pep.

Famechon-Legra came on January 21, at Royal Albert Hall in London. The 23-year-old challenger had to overcome Legra's mobility, as well as his own lack of balance. Having chosen the wrong type of boxing shoes, he slipped to the canvas no less than 11 times. (None, however, was ruled a knockdown.)

When upright, Famechon slowed Legra by pounding his body. He also received a major break when, in the second round, Legra fractured his right thumb. This time, the Cuban danced because he had to. He rallied in the 15th round, but it was far too late; Famechon took the crown by referee George Smith's score of 74½-73¼. It's tough to have to try to beat good breeding.

FOSTERING A PUNCHOUT

Like everyone else in boxing, New Jersey's Frankie DePaula had been awed by Bob Foster's one-punch knockout of Dick Tiger. But not so awed that he was going to change his style. After all, DePaula had knocked down Tiger, too. Besides, the former bouncer knew only one way to fight.

"Everybody, including Foster, knows I'm no fancy Dan," he said before his January 23 title opportunity at Madison Square Garden. "So nobody's looking to see me box him. I'm going to start winging from the opening bell."

DePaula's simple but dangerous strategy made for a short and explosive fight. Only seconds into round one, a left to the body dropped the champion. (Foster later claimed he had slipped.) Angry more than hurt, he lifted himself up and used his nine-inch reach advantage to score three knockdowns, bringing an automatic stoppage at the 2:17 mark.

Frank DePaula couldn't last one round with defending light heavyweight king Bob Foster.

MEXICAN FANS GET MANDOMANIA

The fight fans of Southern California needed a break. In a September 1968 title fight doubleheader, a pair of Mexican-Americans, featherweight Raul Rojas and lightweight Mando Ramos, were beaten. In December, Mexican-National Chucho Castillo was edged by Lionel Rose. And on February 15, Rene Barrientos won the WBC junior lightweight crown by from Mexican-American Ruben Navarro.

Three days after Navarro's loss, Ramos ended the losing streak. Rematched with lightweight king Carlos (Teo) Cruz, the 20-year-old from Long Beach became the youngest champion in division history by scoring an 11th-round TKO at the Olympic Auditorium.

For seven rounds, Ramos-Cruz II resembled the original, with the challenger jabbing, and the champion answering with overhand rights. But in the eighth, Cruz suffered a ½-inch cut over his left eye. After several examinations, Dr. Bernhard Schwartz called a halt at the 2:41 mark of round 11. (At the time of the stoppage, the fight was even on points.) It was a long party.

Mando Ramos (right) kayoed Carlos Teo Cruz in the 11th round to win the lightweight title.

World Title Fights

HEAVYWEIGHTS

April 22 **Joe Frazier** *KO* 1
Dave Zyglewicz, Houston

LIGHT HEAVYWEIGHTS

Jan 23 **Bob Foster** *KO* 1
Frank DePaula, New York City

JUNIOR MIDDLEWEIGHTS

March 17 **Freddie Little** (USA) *W* 15
Stanley Hayward, Las Vegas

WELTERWEIGHTS

April 18 **Jose Napoles** (CUB) *KO* 14
Curtis Cokes, Inglewood

LIGHTWEIGHTS

Feb 18 **Mando Ramos** (USA) *KO* 11
Carlos Teo Cruz, Los Angeles

JUNIOR LIGHTWEIGHTS

Feb 15 **Rene Barrientos** (PHI) *W* 15
Ruben Navarro, Quezon City

(Wins Vacant WBC Title)

April 6 **Hiroshi Kobayashi** *W* 15
Antonio Amaya, Tokyo

FEATHERWEIGHTS

Jan 21 **Johnny Famechon** (AUT) *ref* 15
Jose Legra, London

Feb 9 **Shozo Saijyo** *W* 15
Pedro Gomez, Tokyo

BANTAMWEIGHTS

March 8 **Lionel Rose** *W* 15
Alan Rudkin, Melbourne

FLYWEIGHTS

Feb 23 **Efren Torres** (MEX) *KO* 9
Chartchai Chionoi, Mexico City

March 3 **Hiroyuki Ebihara** *W* 15
Jose Severino, Sapporo

CERTIFIABLE GREATNESS

At best, it happens once every few years: a fighter not only wins a world title, but wins in a way that leaves no doubt of his destiny.

On April 18, welterweight champion Curtis Cokes defended against Mexico-based Cuban Jose Napoles at the Inglewood Forum. By the end of the night, every one of the 15,878 fans was sure he had seen something special.

Nicknamed "Mantequilla" (Spanish for butter), Napoles, 29, easily outclassed a classy champion. The first few rounds were uneventful, but the challenger opened up in the fifth, and then treated the fans to an overwhelming performance. Applying pressure, but never at the expense of defense, Napoles hooked with passion. Cokes was forced to the ropes in almost every round, and by midway, he was bleeding from the nose and squinting through a pair of badly swollen eyes.

At the bell for round 14, Doug Lord, Cokes' manager, told referee George Latka that the champion was going to remain on his stool. The surrender marked the beginning of a reign to remember.

Cuba's great Jose Napoles (right) after stopping Curtis Cokes in 13th round.

CURTAINS FOR ZIGGY

Nowhere is a mismatch uglier than in the heavyweight division. When a big man falls, he usually does so with a thud, which accentuates the violence of the knockout.

This was particularly evident on April 22 in Houston, when Joe Frazier risked his share of the world title at the Sam Houston Coliseum against the little-known Dave Zyglewicz, a 25-year-old bricklayer from upstate New York.

At 5'10½" and 190½ pounds, the challenger was both shorter and lighter than Frazier. "Smokin' Joe" wasn't accustomed to such advantages, but he knew how to capitalize on them. His first serious hook hurt Zyglewicz, and a followup left drove the challenger down before 20 seconds had elapsed.

After a few more power-punches, puncuated by a long left, Zyglewicz spun around and crashed. He was leaning on one hand and one knee when referee Jimmy Webb tolled 10 at the 1:36 mark.

"Did he count me out?" Zyglewicz asked 15 minutes later. "Did he *really* count me out? I don't remember being down."

He was better off.

A CORONATION LONG OVERDUE

If a fighter ever deserved to win a world championship, it was Freddie Little, the Rancho High School (Las Vegas) schoolteacher who moonlighted as a top-10 junior middleweight. Twice Little had fought for the title on the road (vs. Ki Soo Kim and Sandro Mazzinghi), and twice he had been robbed.

After Mazzinghi was stripped for refusing an immediate rematch, Little received his third opportunity. It came on March 17, at the Las Vegas Convention Center, where he was matched with Philadelphia's Stanley (Kitten) Hayward.

Bobbing and weaving, Little marched forward and forced Hayward into giving a very un-Philadelphia-like performance. The Kitten showed his claws only in the ninth, when he stunned Little with a series of rights. Then he backed off.

"It's a bad habit of mine," he explained. "When I get ahead, I should just sock it to him."

The crowd of 3,126 booed Hayward's defensive approach, but cheered the decision, which was unanimous for Little (scores of 73-63, 73-64, and 74-62).

Justice sometimes prevails, even in boxing.

MAY

1969

AUGUST

RINGSIDE VIEW

MAY

Former world champion Dick Tiger scores a 10-round non-title decision over middleweight king Nino Benvenuti in New York City.

HITTING HARDER THAN A SHOTGUN

Was light heavyweight champion Bob Foster's punch more lethal than a blast from a shotgun? On May 24, at the Eastern States Coliseum in West Springfield, Massachusetts, he gave evidence.

Top-rated challenger Andy Kendall lacked Foster's credentials, but had proved his toughness two years earlier. During a dispute with his father-in-law, he took a point-blank shotgun blast in the abdomen. His life was saved by eight hours of surgery. During recovery, doctors told him he could never fight again. Of course.

Against Foster, the 5'10" Kendall faced a catch-22 situation: when he boxed from the outside, he swallowed jabs; when he tried to rush inside, the champion caught him with right uppercuts.

In the fourth, Foster caught him with a right to the chin, then poured in punches until Kendall slumped to a sitting position. Referee Bill Connelly called a halt at the 1:15 mark.

After, Kendall thought about retiring. Foster offered the advice: don't retire, just don't ever be the number-one contender again.

GOING TOE TO TOE WITH JOE

The fighters' styles being what they were, Joe Frazier-Jerry Quarry was the most anticipated matchup of the year. Their battle came on June 23 at Madison Square Garden, and no less than 16,570 fans braced themselves for the shootout. Frazier was a pressure fighter, and Quarry a counterpuncher. Both featured thunderous hooks. Someone was sure to fall.

Frazier, who was defending his share of the heavyweight title, seemed eager to feel Quarry's power. The first two rounds were sensational, with enough toe-to-toe exchanges for an entire 15-round fight. Toward the end of the third, "Smokin' Joe" landed a hook that opened an inch-long slice under Quarry's right eye. It would lead to the end of the fight.

From the fourth through the seventh, Frazier methodically backed his bloodied opponent to the ropes. Before the start of the eighth, Quarry told the ringside physician that he could no longer see out of his hideously marked eye. The fight was immediately stopped.

Technically, at least, no one had fallen. But no one had gone home disappointed, either.

Joe Frazier (right) stopped Jerry Quarry in the seventh round to retain the New York title.

FIGHTING TALK

My right hand is all right. My left hand is all right. My back is all right. The only thing was, I had too much fighter in the ring with me

JERRY QUARRY
after being stopped by heavyweight champion Joe Frazier

THE REMATCH IS A REPLAY

Boxing is predictably unpredictable. But after welterweight champion Jose Napoles' conclusive title-winning victory over Curtis Cokes, it was difficult to imagine the rematch being competitive. Indeed, it turned out to be a mismatch.

Napoles-Cokes II came on June 29, at Monumental Plaza in Mexico City. On a cool, drizzly night, more than 25,000 fans saw Napoles start quickly. He established his jab in the second, and began to close Cokes' right eye in the fourth. As in the first fight, Cokes missed with most of his counterpunches. As a result, Napoles did almost all of the scoring, and by the 10th, the challenger was a one-eyed fighter.

Cokes failed to answer the bell for round 11. A champion only three months before, he had been ruined by his defeat by Napoles.

"He's a very good fighter," the loser said, "and sure as hell a better fighter than Curtis Cokes."

Cokes (left) failed in his attempt to regain the welterweight title he had lost to Napoles.

Ringside View

JULY

Fighting for the first time in almost two years, former featherweight champion Vicente Saldivar scores a 10-round decision over another ex-champion, Jose Legra, in Los Angeles.

LEGENDARY PEP BLOWS HIS REPUTATION – AS A REF

As a world champion, Willie Pep was a legend. As a world championship referee, he was legendary, too, but unfortunately for all the wrong reasons.

On July 28, at Sydney Stadium, Pep worked as the third man for Australia-based featherweight champion Johnny Famechon's defense against former flyweight and bantamweight Fighting Harada.

In the fifth round, Harada slipped to the canvas, but Pep ruled it a knockdown. In the 11th, Famechon went down from a punch, but Pep ruled it a slip. (Famechon also crashed in the second and the 14th, and the referee ruled correctly.)

Things got even more confusing after the final bell, when Pep, who was the sole judge, raised both fighters' hands, thus signifying a draw. But after co-promoter Mickey Duff asked the local police to check Pep's card, they noticed an error in his addition. Instead of scoring 71-71, as he thought he had, Pep had Famechon ahead by 70-69.

It seemed a horrible decision; even the local newspapers gave it to Harada. Nonetheless, Famechon kept the title and, Pep's championship days had ended.

"ROCKABYE RUBEN" LEAVES 'EM ALL HAPPY

Painfully aware of what happened to the Inglewood Forum the last time bantamweight champion Lionel Rose had defended there, building owner Jack Kent Cooke was worried. In December 1968, the fans had tossed bottles and lit fires after Rose scored a disputed split decision over Mexican favorite Chucho Castillo. On August 22, Rose was scheduled to return, his opponent another Mexican favorite, 22-year-old knockout artist Ruben Olivares.

"Do not be afraid, Mr. Cooke," Olivares assured him. "I am dedicating my effort to you, and there will be no trouble from my people because I will win by a knockout in nine rounds."

We can't be sure how much comfort Olivares' promises provided, but Cooke sure appreciated his punches. "Rockabye Ruben" sent the sellout crowd of more than 17,000 home happy, and he did so with four rounds to spare.

The first round was close, but in the second, Olivares began to show how he had compiled a record of 50-0-1 (48). Again and again his hook, the lighter-weight equivalent of heavyweight champion Joe Frazier's, thudded against Rose's face and head. Finally, the Australian champion fell. He lasted the round, but not until Olivares sent his mouthpiece flying with yet another hook.

Halfway through the fifth, Olivares struck again. Rose went down three times in the round, and after his third crash, referee Larry Rozadilla stopped the bout.

Everyone went home with a smile, Cooke included. Ruben Olivares, he decided, was his favorite fighter in the whole world.

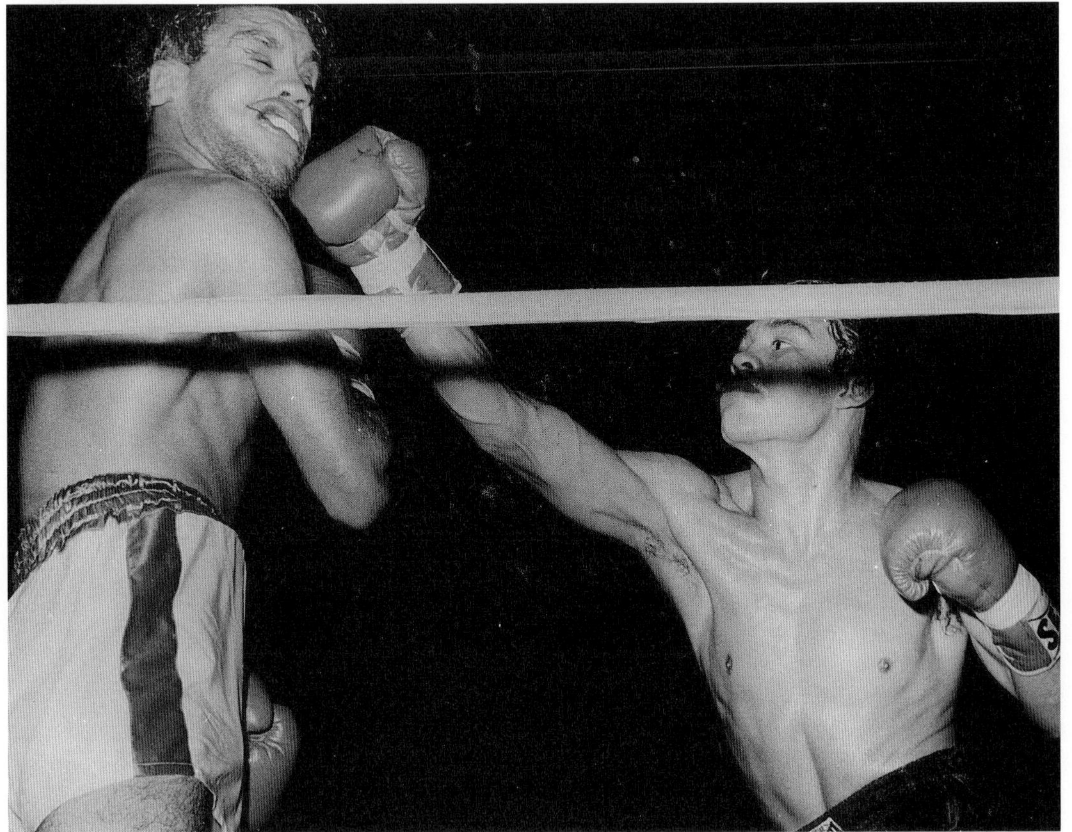

Mexico's undefeated knockout artist Ruben Olivares (right) won the bantamweight title from Lionel Rose in the fifth round at Los Angeles.

World Title Fights

HEAVYWEIGHTS

June 23 **Joe Frazier** *KO* 8 Jerry Quarry, New York City

LIGHT HEAVYWEIGHTS

May 24 **Bob Foster** *KO* 4 Andy Kendall, West Springfield, MA

WELTERWEIGHTS

June 29 **Jose Napoles** *KO* 11 Curtis Cokes, Mexico City

JUNIOR WELTERWEIGHTS

May 3 **Nicolino Locche** *W* 15 Carlos Hernandez, Buenos Aires

FEATHERWEIGHTS

July 28 **Johnny Famechon** *ref* 15 Fighting Harada, Sydney

BANTAMWEIGHTS

Aug 22 **Ruben Olivares** (MEX) *KO* 5 Lionel Rose, Inglewood

SEPTEMBER

1969

DECEMBER

SOMETHING NEW FROM NUMATA

Former 130-pound champion Yoshiaki Numata knew it would be difficult to dethrone world lightweight king Mando Ramos, especially on the champion's home turf. So he studied films and put together a fight plan.

Numata's challenge came on October 4, at the Sports Arena in Los Angeles. (The bout was originally scheduled for June, but Ramos broke his left hand.) The Japanese opened by firing wild overhand rights, which had worked for Carlos Cruz in his September 1968 defeat of Ramos.

"At first," the challenger said afterward, "I hit him so easy, I figured I could knock him out."

The nimble Numata also posed with his hands low, bobbed and weaved in a herky-jerky fashion, and presented Ramos with all sort of weird angles.

His unorthodox tactics worked for four rounds, but in the fifth, Ramos scored a knockdown with two rights. Suddenly exposed, Numata crumbled. He fell three more times in the sixth, and the fight was stopped at the 2:20 mark. Score one for substance over style.

RINGSIDE VIEW

OCTOBER

World junior welterweight champion Nicolino Locche keeps the crown, scoring a unanimous 15-round decision over Joao Henrique.

ULTIMATE HOME COURT ADVANTAGE

It was becoming increasingly apparent that beating Nino Benvenuti in Italy was going to be about as easy as sailing around the world in a dinghy.

On October 4, at Sao Paolo Stadium in Naples, the world middleweight champion defended against America's Fraser Scott, who had been a pro for just 16 months. It began as an ordinary fight, with Benvenuti sticking his jab and Scott maneuvering for openings. But every time the challenger slipped a punch and came up to counter, he was pulled up and warned by referee Tony Gilardi for butting.

"I just couldn't fight Nino by these rules," Scott later complained. "He's like fighting a hurricane. You can stand outside and get butchered, or you can step into the eye."

In the seventh round, Scott tried the latter approach once too often. The fighters tangled and fell to the floor. Gilardi responded by immediately disqualifying Scott.

Said Joe West, the loser's manager, "Man, they can't beat Scott with fists, so they beat him with rules."

For Benvenuti in Italy, whatever it takes.

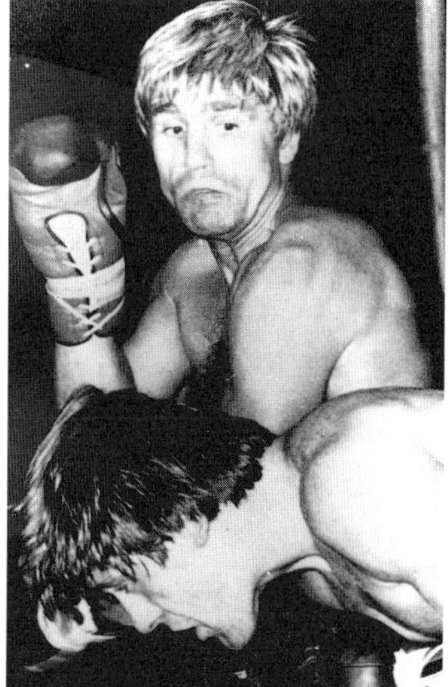

Nino Benvenuti and Fraser Scott.

MANTEQUILLA: TOO SMOOTH, TOO STRONG

Before world welterweight champion Jose Napoles defended against former two-division titlist Emile Griffith, the focus was on the challenger's chances of making weight. Griffith, 31, hadn't made the welter limit of 147 pounds in four years. As it turned out, he scaled 144½, and wasn't at all weakened by the effort. But he still wasn't strong enough to handle Napoles.

The showdown of two of boxing's best came on October 17, before a pro-Napoles crowd of 15,461 at the Inglewood Forum. During his three welterweight title reigns, Griffith had outmuscled most of his foes. Predictably, he tried the same approach against "Mantequilla." But the champion countered brilliantly to the body, and established his superior power by dropping Griffith with a third-round right uppercut. Upon rising, Emile answered only with occasional jabs and hooks.

After 15 rounds, the judges rewarded Napoles with a unanimous decision (scores of 11-4, 11-3-1, and 9-4-2). Having beaten Griffith with relative ease, he seemed, at the relatively advanced age of 29, a long-term proposition.

Former champion Emile Griffith (right) failed in his bid to take Jose Napoles' crown.

World Title Fights

MIDDLEWEIGHTS

Oct 4 **Nino Benvenuti** *W Disq 7* Fraser Scott, Naples

Nov 22 **Nino Benvenuti** *KO 11* Luis Rodriguez, Rome

JUNIOR MIDDLEWEIGHTS

Sept 9 **Freddie Little** *KO 2* Hisao Minami, Osaka

WELTERWEIGHTS

Oct 17 **Jose Napoles** *W 15* Emile Griffith, Inglewood

JUNIOR WELTERWEIGHTS

Oct 11 **Nicolino Locche** *W 15* Joao Henrique, Buenos Aires

LIGHTWEIGHTS

Oct 4 **Mando Ramos** *KO 6* Yoshiaki Numata, Los Angeles

JUNIOR LIGHTWEIGHTS

Nov 9 **Hiroshi Kobayashi** *W 15* Carlos Canete, Tokyo

FEATHERWEIGHTS

Sept 7 **Shozo Saijyo** *KO 2* Jose Luis Pimental, Sapporo

BANTAMWEIGHTS

Dec 12 **Ruben Olivares** *KO 2* Alan Rudkin, Inglewood

FLYWEIGHTS

Oct 19 **Bernabe Villacampo** (PHI) *W 15* Hiroyuki Ebihara, Osaka

Nov 28 **Efren Torres** *W 15* Susumu Hanagata, Guadalajara

THREE YEARS, THEN ONE PUNCH

With victories over the likes of Bennie Briscoe, Vicente Rondon, and Tom Bethea, former welterweight champion Luis Rodriguez had established himself as the world's top-rated middleweight. Nonetheless, it took him three years to secure a try at world champion Nino Benvenuti. Benvenuti would have preferred different opposition. But when the WBA threatened to strip him, the bout was made for November at the Palazzo Dello Sport in Rome.

Both fighters had their moments. Benvenuti scored with his jab, and Rodriguez countered with his right, opening a deep cut on the bridge of the champion's nose. Then came the shocking ending. Early in the 11th, Benvenuti, never considered a big hitter, struck with a hook to the head, and Rodriguez, who had never been stopped, went down for the full count.

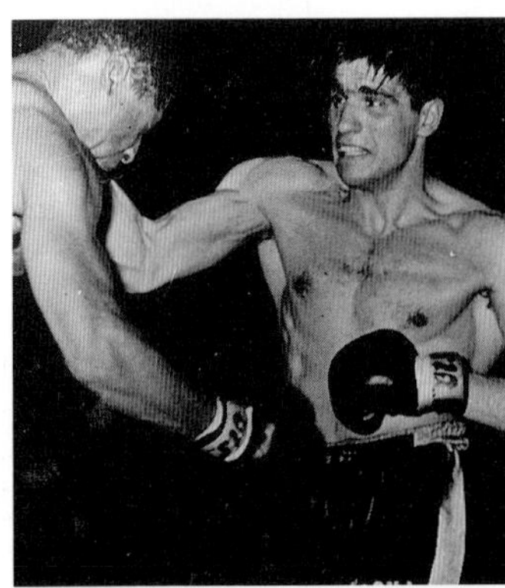

Benvenuti (right) stopped Luis Rodriguez.

THE END OF SONNY'S STREAK

Despite what a large portion of the public might have believed, Sonny Liston didn't disappear after twice losing to Muhammad Ali. Quite the contrary: he built a 14-bout winning streak. But Liston was 37, and in fight number 15, he acted his age.

On December 6, the former heavyweight champion met Leotis Martin at the International Hotel in Las Vegas. Martin, who had been a first-round loser to Jimmy Ellis in the WBA elimination tournament, was a 3-1 underdog. For the first six rounds, he stuck his face into Liston's still-devastating jab. (In the fourth, he also got in the way of a left hook, and suffered a knockdown.) But in the seventh, and especially the eighth, he tried fighting back.

It turned out to be a good idea. In the ninth, he combined a right to the face and a hook to the jaw, and referee Mike Kaplan counted Liston out at the 1:08 mark.

Sonny's quiet comeback had ended with a bang.

RUBEN, RUDKIN, AND REJECTION

Having lost decisions in his first two tries at the world bantamweight crown (vs. Fighting Harada and Lionel Rose), British and Empire champion Alan Rudkin was fortunate enough to secure a third opportunity. But he was unfortunate to do so against a titlist like Ruben Olivares.

Olivares' defense against the Liverpudlian came on December 12, at the Inglewood Forum. It was a brief and brutal fight. In round one, Rudkin suffered the first knockdown of his 43-bout career. And in the second, Olivares punched nonstop until a hook dropped the challenger onto his face. Referee John Thomas tolled 10 at the 2:30 mark.

"There is no one in the world who can stay with him in the bantamweight division," Rudkin said of Olivares. "I know because I've fought all over the world."

The victory lifted Olivares to 53-0-1 (51). At least according to Rudkin, "Rockabye Ruben" was every bit as devastating as his record suggested.

Ringside View

NOVEMBER

Japan's Hiroshi Kobayashi retains the world junior lightweight title for the fourth time, scoring a unanimous decision over Carlos Canete.

Britain's Alan Rudkin (left) was demolished by bantamweight king Ruben Olivares.

RING DECADE

1970-1979

YOU can't point to a specific date, but in the '70s, the name of the game changed from boxing to boxeo. The decade began with unparalleled anticipation; on March 8, 1971, at Madison Square Garden, Joe Frazier whipped Muhammad Ali in The Fight of the Century. It ended with wonderful sentimentality; on September 15, 1978, at the Superdome in New Orleans, Ali won the heavyweight title for the third time by defeating Leon Spinks.

Somewhere in between, boxing began to slip away from the United States. Suddenly, the best fighters came not from Los Angeles, Philadelphia, and New York City, but Buenos Aires, San Juan, Mexico City, Panama City, even Managua. The political power shifted as well, with the Latin-based WBA and WBC gaining almost total control. There were more divisions (the decade saw new junior classes at featherweight and flyweight), more titles, and more champions. Very few of those champions were colored red, white, and blue. In fact, at one point in 1977, Ali and Danny Lopez were the only American-born titlists.

Always, however, there was "The Greatest." At the start of the decade, Ali was viewed by many as a draft-dodging American. By the end, he was a genuine hero worldwide.

George Foreman's crushing power made him seem invincible on his way to becoming champion. It took Muhammad Ali to snap George's long victory streak.

The best fighters of the '70s were Argentinian Carlos Monzon and Panamanian Roberto Duran. But it was Ali and his contemporaries, including Frazier, George Foreman, and Ken Norton, who took center stage. By defeating all of the members of the best class in heavyweight history, and usually in a dramatic fashion, Ali converted the last of those who'd doubted him. In the '60s, his most important fights came outside the ring. Not so in the '70s.

Said television boxing analyst Alex Wallau in Thomas Hauser's biography *Muhammad Ali: His Life And Times*, "Whatever was left of that criticism came to an end in Manila (where Ali fought Frazier for the third time). What Ali did there was take his courage and show it to the world on terms any redneck could understand. Here it is; I'm giving it to you on a silver platter. I'm as tough and brave as any of those tough guys you admire."

It may seem contradictory, but by celebrating the indomitability of the human spirit, Ali ensured his immortality: he climbed off the canvas in the 15th round of his first fight with Frazier; he fought Norton with a broken jaw; he dared stand up to the invincible Foreman; he came back in Manila when the fight was, as he described it, "the closest thing to death"; and, finally, he cheated Father Time by taking back the title from Spinks.

In the final seconds of Ali's historic victory in New Orleans, television announcer Howard Cosell recited the lyrics from Bob Dylan's song "Forever Young." It could have been the perfect ending. But Ali would fight again in the '80s, exposing himself to a light that he once craved, but one that had become far too bright and harsh.

While Ali played off Frazier, and Foreman and Norton, too, Monzon and Duran weren't without worthy adversaries. Had Monzon not made a division-record 14 successful defenses, Rodrigo Valdes would likely have dominated at 160 pounds. And had Duran not kayoed all but one of his 12 title challengers, Esteban DeJesus could have reigned supreme at 135 pounds.

Monzon and Duran were intensely proud and competitive. Both inside the ring and out, however, they were far more different than alike. Tall and surprisingly strong, Monzon was ice, outreaching opponents who chose to box him, and counterpunching those who sought to crowd him. It wasn't long into his reign that he grew bored with the lack of suitable opposition. He eagerly embraced the life of an international playboy, mingling with European movie stars and beautiful actresses. (Duran, on the other hand, was content to play bongos in a band and party with his countrymen.)

Muhammad Ali dominated the 1970s with his extraordinary skills and charisma, twice regaining the heavyweight title.

Carlos Monzon has been called "the best natural fighter who ever lived." He reigned as world middleweight champion through most of the 1970s and retired undefeated in 1977.

Ken Buchanan was the most idolized Scotsman since Benny Lynch. Ken's marvelous boxing skills and courage earned him the lightweight championship of the world.

By the middle of the decade, Monzon seemed a part-time champion. But when it came time for business, he reverted to the hungry streetfighter who had survived the alleyways of Sante Fe, Argentina. At the start of the '70s, and before he dethroned Nino Benvenuti, Monzon was virtually unknown. By the time he retired, he was considered in the class of Stanley Ketchel, Harry Greb, and even Sugar Ray Robinson.

Monzon's last two bouts came against Valdes, a pressure fighter of exceptional energy, strength, and will. Though Monzon's first victory unified the title, it proved little because Valdes was not at his best. In the rematch, however, the Colombian scored an early knockdown and built a sizeable points lead. Needing to rally in the championship rounds, Monzon was forced to push the pace and trade punch for punch. His desperate effort was enough to sway the judges. Unbeaten in 13 years and 80 fights, he had simply forgotten how to lose.

A fighter, and nothing more, Duran was fire. He attacked with a fury unseen since the days of Mickey Walker, Kid Berg, and Henry Armstrong. It was no wonder, then, that he was the only champion of his generation who came to be recognized as the all-time best of his division. (At worst, historians rated him even with Benny Leonard.)

If Valdes turned Monzon into a puncher, DeJesus turned Duran into a boxer. At age 21, Duran won the WBA title by crushing Ken Buchanan. Before defending the crown, he met DeJesus in a non-title bout at Madison Square Garden. The highly skilled Puerto Rican dropped Duran with a counter hook less than one minute into the fight. Duran never fully recovered, and lost a unanimous 10-round decision.

Later that night, hearing screams, Luis Henriquez, Duran's translator and confidant, rushed into the fighter's hotel room. He found the champ in the bathtub, crying and banging his bloodied fists against the wall. Duran would not lose again as a lightweight.

DeJesus again knocked down Duran in the opening round of their second bout. Realizing he wasn't going to intimidate his rival, Duran decelerated and became more selective, outlasting the Puerto Rican. In their third bout, which unified the title, he countered to the body en route to a 12th-round kayo victory. Thanks largely to DeJesus, Duran had become a complete fighter. As the '80s beckoned, he was ready for bigger challenges.

In the '60s, there were 248 world title fights; in the '70s, 530. The added activity gave several outstanding champions the opportunity to shine. Over the first half of the decade, light heavyweight Bob Foster and welterweight Jose Napoles dominated their respective divisions as Monzon and Duran did. But Foster's kayo losses to Ali and Frazier, and Napoles' failure against Monzon, tarnished their records. Eder Jofre completed a marvelous comeback by winning the featherweight title eight years after reigning at bantamweight; junior welterweight Wilfred Benitez became the youngest world champ ever by upsetting Antonio Cervantes at age 17; Alexis Arguello was crowned in two divisions; welterweight champion Pipino Cuevas and featherweight titlist Danny Lopez punched with frightening power; Ruben Olivares, Alfonso Zamora, and Carlos Zarate were among the bantamweight bombers who made their division a national competition for Mexicans only; and, as if to provide balance, slick flyweight king Miguel Canto proved that not all Mexicans looked to hook to the liver.

Toward the end of the '70s, a new cast of champions began to emerge. Larry Holmes established himself as the best big man. Sugar Ray Leonard, part of the 1976 Olympic team that revitalized boxing in the USA, was crowned at welterweight. And Panamanian featherweight Eusebio Pedroza, along with Puerto Rican junior featherweight Wilfredo Gomez, represented the lighter weight classes, as well as the heretofore dominant Latin countries.

Boxing or boxeo, the '70s was a far richer decade than the '60s. And the '80s would prove to be richer yet.

Roberto Duran, with his famed "Hands of Stone," was surely the most electrifying prize fighter of the decade. He went unbeaten in seven years, as one foe after another collapsed at his feet. His thrilling bouts with Esteban DeJesus are classics.

JANUARY

1970

APRIL

Joe Frazier unified the world heavyweight crown when he stopped Jimmy Ellis.

ELLIS IN WONDERLAND

Prior to his February 16 title-unification battle against Joe Frazier at Madison Square Garden, WBA heavyweight champion Jimmy Ellis had been floored only once in his career (by Hurricane Carter). But against "Smokin' Joe," he crashed twice in the fourth round.

"I was down once," he said afterward.

"That's why I stopped the fight," responded Angelo Dundee.

Those who had witnessed the slaughter needed no explanation. Frazier started slowly, losing the first round, and barely edging his cautious opponent in the second. Then he began to beat a steady rhythm with his hook. In the fourth round, his hammer struck twice. The second knockdown came just before the bell, and Ellis returned to his corner solely on instinct.

"He wanted to continue," said chief second Dundee, "but he wasn't responding to my questions. He was fighting the other guy's fight, so I stopped the fight."

There was one heavyweight champion again. Well, sort of. Said Frazier, "I'm gonna sing rock-n-roll until that Muhammad Ali, or Cassius Clay, or whatever his name is, can fight me."

WOULD BUTTER HAVE MELTED OR BEEN SWEET AS SUGAR?

The symbolism was too obvious to miss: in the ring, there was world welterweight champion Jose Napoles picking apart Ernie (Indian Red) Lopez and looking very much like the best fighter in boxing. At ringside, there was Sugar Ray Robinson, the best fighter ever, taking it all in. For Napoles, the ultimate compliment came at the end of the night, when the fans at the Inglewood Forum asked one another, "How do you think Mantequilla would have done against Sugar Ray?"

Napoles rejected the challenge of the top-rated Lopez on February 15. Had the fight taken place one day earlier, it could have been called "The St. Valentine's Day Massacre II." Mantequilla softened Indian Red with his jab, and scored three knockdowns, one each in the first, ninth, and 15th rounds. Lopez rose from his final fall, but referee Larry Rozadilla stopped the fight with 22 seconds to go in the last round. (At the time of the stoppage, the champion was far ahead on points.)

Had Sugar Ray been impressed? He left the Forum with a smile on his face.

In third defense of the welterweight crown, Napoles (left) knocked out Lopez in 15th.

FIGHTING FAMECHON FINDS FIRE

Just when you think you've got boxing figured...

In July 1969, Johnny Famechon defended his share of the world featherweight title by scoring a disputed decision over Japan's Fighting Harada. The bout took place on the champion's home turf in Sydney. The rematch, scheduled for January 6, was held at the Municipal Gymnasium in Tokyo. So Harada was a cinch to gain revenge, right?

The bout was close for nine rounds. The key moment came in the 10th, when the challenger scored a knockdown with a booming right. So Famechon instantly crumbled, right?

Oddly, his trip to the canvas served to invigorate him. The champion took control upon rising, and floored Harada with a hook in the 12th. Two rounds later, he finished his work with a hook that sent the Japanese through the ropes. Harada was counted out at the 1:09 mark.

Seemingly on the verge of winning his third world title, Harada, 26, ended up a hapless kayo victim. It was the last fight of his career. Some things are just hard to figure. Boxing is one of them.

Australia's world featherweight champ Johnny Famechon (left) knocked out ex-bantamweight king Fighting Harada in the 14th round to keep the title.

RINGSIDE VIEW

FEBRUARY

Italy's Bruno Arcari wins the WBC super lightweight title by scoring a 15-round decision over defending titlist Pedro Adigue.

LAGUNA GIVES A LESSON

Before Mando Ramos defended the world lightweight title against former king and number-one contender Ismael Laguna, Jackie McCoy, his manager, sensed that the crown was in jeopardy. "If Mando wins," he said, "he'll hold the title for as long as he wants."

Not *when* Mando wins, or *after* he wins, but *if* he wins.

On March 3, at the Sports Arena in Los Angeles, McCoy's worst fears were realized. Laguna boxed masterfully, quickly opening cuts over both of Ramos' eyes, and then poking at them with one of the division's best jabs. By the middle rounds, the champion was a bloody mess. And before the start of the 10th, McCoy asked ref Lee Grossman to stop the fight. (Laguna led on all three cards.)

"Mando is a 21-year-old kid, and there's no use letting him get banged around like that," explained the manager.

There were no ifs attached.

Ismael Laguna stopped Mando Ramos.

ROUSE GOES AS QUIETLY AS A MOUSE

What seventh-rated light heavyweight Roger Rouse had done to earn a try at world champion Bob Foster was the first mystery of the new decade. In his initial title shot, Rouse was ravaged by Dick Tiger, and in his first bout vs. Foster, he lasted five rounds before being halted on an eye cut.

"He's the only light heavyweight Foster hasn't been able to deck," pointed out Rouse's manager, Pete Jovanovich.

That changed on April 4, when Foster defended the title for the third time. The mismatch was held at the University of Montana Fieldhouse in Missoula. (Rouse hailed from nearby Anaconda.) Given the surroundings, Foster thought it appropriate to display his educated jab. When he followed it with his right, the 34-year-old Rouse went south. There were four knockdowns in three rounds, and before the start of the fourth, the ringside physician decided that Rouse was done. Afterward, Foster called for heavyweight champ Joe Frazier.

For such a dominant champion, a jump in weight seemed to make sense; picking on fighters his own size was turning out to be no fun at all.

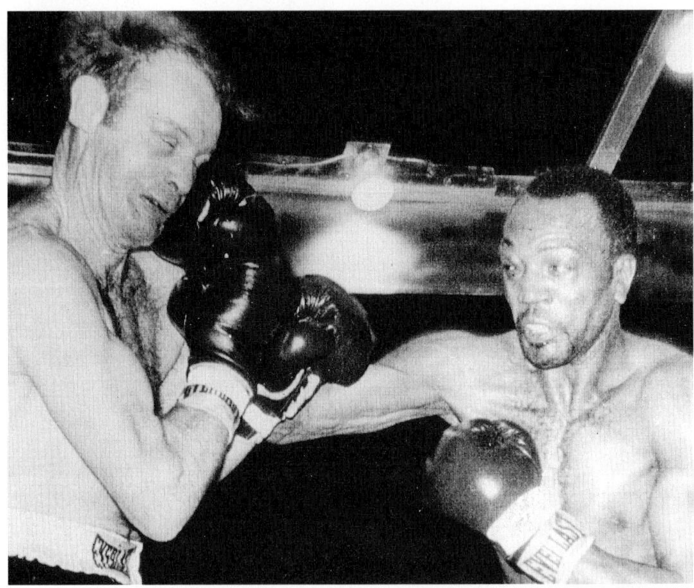

Light heavyweight king Bob Foster (right) annihilated Rouse in four rounds to keep the crown.

THE FIGHT TO BE KING OF MEXICO

When world bantamweight champion Ruben Olivares defended against Chucho Castillo, the two were fighting for something much bigger than the title. At stake was their beloved Mexico.

Olivares-Castillo came on April 18, before 18,762 fans at the Inglewood Forum. Before the heavily hyped bout, the challenger stated: "Winning the title is not important. I'm only interested in beating Olivares. It is all I live for. Olivares is a loudmouth, and not deserving to be champion."

The grudge match lived up to its billing. Castillo scored a knockdown in round three, and combined solid defense and clever counterpunching to frustrate "Rockabye Ruben's" attack. For his part, Olivares proved that he was much more than a kayo artist. He boxed patiently and waited for openings. And while he couldn't drop his arch-rival, he seemed on the verge of a stoppage victory at least five separate times.

After 15 lively rounds, Olivares kept the title by unanimous decision (scores of 7-6, 9-4, and 10-5). Mexico was his forever. Or at least until his next fight with Castillo.

WORLD TITLE FIGHTS

HEAVYWEIGHTS

Feb 16	**Joe Frazier** *KO* 5 Jimmy Ellis, New York City (Unifies World Title)

LIGHT HEAVYWEIGHTS

April 4	**Bob Foster** *KO* 4 Roger Rouse, Missoula, MT

JUNIOR MIDDLEWEIGHTS

March 20	**Freddie Little** *ref* 15 Gerhard Piaskowy, Berlin

WELTERWEIGHTS

Feb 15	**Jose Napoles** *KO* 15 Ernie Lopez, Inglewood

JUNIOR WELTERWEIGHTS

Feb 1	**Bruno Arcari** (ITA) *ref* 15 Pedro Adigue, Rome

LIGHTWEIGHTS

March 3	**Ismael Laguna** *KO* 10 Mando Romos, Los Angeles

JUNIOR LIGHTWEIGHTS

April 5	**Yoshiaki Numata** *W* 15 Rene Barrientos, Tokyo

FEATHERWEIGHTS

Jan 6	**Johnny Famechon** *KO* 14 Fighting Harada, Tokyo
Feb 8	**Shozo Saijyo** *W* 15 Godfrey Stevens, Tokyo

BANTAMWEIGHTS

April 18	**Ruben Olivares** *W* 15 Chucho Castillo, Inglewood

FLYWEIGHTS

March 20	**Chartchai Chionoi** *W* 15 Efren Torres, Bangkok
April 6	**Berkrerk Chartvanchai** (THA) *W* 15 Bernabe Villacampo, Bangkok

MAY

1970

AUGUST

AS IF HE WERE NEVER AWAY

When boxing fans discuss the great comebacks of the ring, Sugar Ray Robinson and Muhammad Ali are mentioned first, then Eder Jofre and George Foreman. For some reason, Vicente Saldivar is almost always overlooked. In fact, his comeback was as impressive as any of the others.

In October 1967, Saldivar retained the featherweight title by stopping Howard Winstone. Almost as soon as his hand was raised, he bid his fans goodbye. He returned almost two years later, outpointing former champion Jose Legra. In only his second comeback bout, the southpaw challenged WBC 126-pound champion Johnny Famechon.

Saldivar scores the only knockdown in his featherweight title fight with Johnny Famechon.

Saldivar's big moment came on May 9, at the Palazzo Dello Sport in Rome. Those who figured the Mexican would be rusty were shocked when he opened with a crisp attack. After suffering a knockdown in round eight, Famechon staged a late charge. Saldivar finished with a pair of puffy eyes, but hung on to take the title by unanimous 15-round verdict (scores of 71-68, 72-68, and 73-70).

It was a wonderful way to say hello again.

NO SOFT TOUCH FOR "THE UNTOUCHABLE"

Afterward, Nicolino Locche said of Adolph Pruitt, "I never met anyone who could punch so hard or who kept pressing so much."

And Pruitt said, "Locche didn't touch me even once. I never felt his hands." So who won the fight? Locche, of course. Easily.

On May 16, the WBA junior welterweight champion defended for the third time, facing Los Angeles-based truckdriver Pruitt at Luna Park Stadium in Buenos Aires. Circling the ring and countering with jabs and hooks, Locche, nicknamed "The Untouchable," frustrated the challenger from start to finish. Pruitt remained aggressive, but the harder he swung, the more he missed. After 15 rounds, the champion was awarded a unanimous decision. You can't beat what you can't touch.

FOR NINO, HOME IS WHERE THE HEART IS

Virtually unbeatable in his native Italy, world middleweight champion Nino Benvenuti always knew *where* to win. Over the first half of 1970, he proved he knew *when* to win as well.

On March 13, Nino faced undistinguished American Tom "The Bomb" Bethea in a non-title fight in Melbourne. (Bethea climbed through the ropes with a record of 9-5-1.) The champion suffered a seventh-round knockdown, and, one round later, surrendered due to bruised ribs.

The title fight rematch came on May 23, in Umag, Yugoslavia, 18 miles southwest of Benvenuti's hometown of Trieste. Boxing carefully, the champion opened a cut above Bethea's right eye. He jabbed at it from a safe distance, then, in the eighth, spotted an opening and capitalized by combining a hook and a straight right. Boom! The Bomb was counted out by referee Georges Gondre at the 2:43 mark.

"It was destiny that I should win in the same round as I had to give up in Melbourne," said Benvenuti, a fighter of destiny if there ever was one.

Nino Benvenuti gives a victory salute after flattening Tom Bethea in the eighth round to retain the middleweight title at Umag, Yugoslavia.

RETURN TO SENDAI

WBA featherweight champion Shojo Saijyo (pronounced Say-Jo) was a ring oddity: he was far more popular in Southern California than in his native land. In 1968, the colorful and handsome boxer fought five times in Los Angeles. He won the title there, decisioning Raul Rojas, and developed a teenybopper rooting section.

"But here," said a Japanese boxing insider, "he's just another fighter."

On July 5, Saijyo indeed looked ordinary in defending against America's sixth-rated Frankie Crawford at the Miyagi Sports Center in Sendai. Making his fourth defense, he was lucky to last the first round. After the 23-year-old champion missed wildly, as he was apt to do, Crawford, 22, stepped in with a short counter hook. He failed to follow up, however, and Saijyo lasted the round.

Usually quick and mobile, Saijyo never found his rhythm. He rebounded to take rounds two, three, and four, but Crawford controlled the middle of the fight. Saijyo regained command in the ninth and 10th. The championship rounds were close but sloppy, with both fighters too tired to inflict significant damage.

Saijyo retained the title by majority decision (scores of 70-67, 71-70, and 69-69). But he hadn't impressed his local fans.

He wished they all could be California girls.

World Title Fights

LIGHT HEAVYWEIGHTS

June 27 **Bob Foster** *KO* 10
Mark Tessman, Baltimore

MIDDLEWEIGHTS

May 23 **Nino Benvenuti** *KO* 8
Tom Bethea, Umag, Yugoslavia

JUNIOR MIDDLEWEIGHTS

July 9 **Carmelo Bossi** (ITA) *ref* 15
Freddie Little, Monza, Italy

JUNIOR WELTERWEIGHTS

May 16 **Nicolino Locche** *W* 15
Adolph Pruitt, Buenos Aires

July 10 **Bruno Arcari** *W Disq* 6
Rene Roque, Lignano Sabaiadoro, Italy

LIGHTWEIGHTS

June 7 **Ismael Laguna** *KO* 13
Ishimatsu Suzuki, Panama City

JUNIOR LIGHTWEIGHTS

Aug 23 **Hiroshi Kobayashi** *W* 15
Antonio Amaya, Tokyo

FEATHERWEIGHTS

May 9 **Vicente Saldivar** *W* 15
Johnny Famechon, Rome

July 5 **Shozo Saijyo** *W* 15
Frankie Crawford, Sendai, Japan

Ringside View

JUNE

World light heavyweight champion Bob Foster continues his reign of terror, stopping the elusive Mark Tessman in the 10th round.

JULY

Italy's Carmelo Bossi wins the world junior middleweight title by scoring a 15-round referee's decision over Freddie Little.

Bob Foster (left) stopped Mark Tessman to retain the light heavyweight title.

TOMORROW'S GEORGE BEATS YESTERDAY'S GEORGE

At the 1968 Olympic Games in Mexico City, George Foreman won the heavyweight gold medal by crushing Russia's Iones Chepulis. Then he won the hearts of his countrymen by waving a tiny American flag.

Following an opening act like that, Big George wasn't about to sneak up on any professionals. But even after Foreman won his first 21 fights – 18 by knockout – no one could be sure how he'd fare against a world-class contender like 32-year-old George Chuvalo. Foreman was made the favorite, but only by the slimmest of odds.

The heavyweights clashed at Madison Square Garden on August 4. Chuvalo stumbled after feeling Foreman's first jab, and then proceeded to flaunt his reputation as a sponge for punches. Jabbing and hooking with thudding power, Foreman landed at will. Both of the Canadian's cheekbones swelled up, and blood trickled from his mouth.

After a third-round hook left Chuvalo hanging halfway through the ropes, Arthur Mercante stopped the slaughter at the 1:41 mark.

"Are you nuts?" Chuvalo screamed at the referee. "Good God. If referees stopped fights that way all my life, I'd have lost a million times!"

"He wasn't defending himself," Mercante later explained. "He didn't do a thing. He was just taking punches."

Foreman was only the second heavyweight to have stopped Chuvalo. The other was world champion Joe Frazier. Was Big George ready to put out Smokin' Joe's fire? Not quite. At age 22, he could afford to take one step at a time.

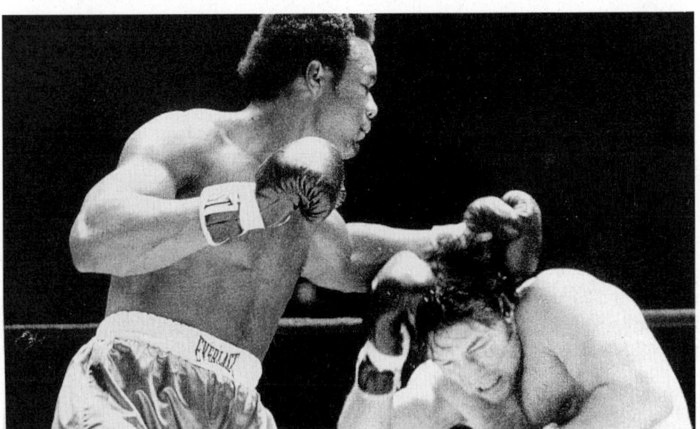

Big George Foreman made it 22 wins in a row by stopping Canada's tough George Chuvalo.

SEPTEMBER

1970

DECEMBER

NO MIRACLES FOR NINO THIS TIME

World middleweight champion Nino Benvenuti was the Houdini of boxing; no matter how hopeless the situation, he managed to escape with the title belt wrapped around his waist.

Benvenuti was particularly difficult to beat in his native Italy. Until November 7, that is, when unheralded Argentine Carlos Monzon came to the Palazzo Dello Sport and took the title in most convincing fashion.

Many insiders questioned Monzon's credentials because he had never fought outside of South America. From the start, however, he displayed world-class skills. Fighting aggressively, he scored with jabs and kept the shorter champion away with straight rights. Benvenuti was staggered in the seventh round, and behind on points when dropped by a perfect right in the 12th. Referee Rudolf Durst counted him out at the 2:00 mark.

"I didn't do anything right," he said. "I hardly threw a single good punch. I wish someone would tell me where I went wrong."

Even Houdini failed to escape that one last time.

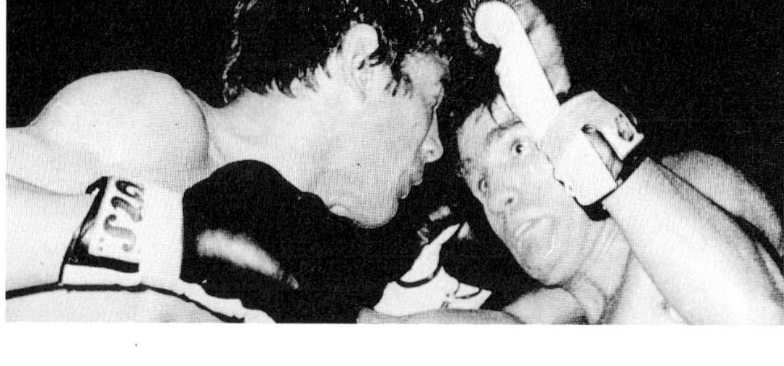

Argentina's great Carlos Monzon (left) knocked out Nino Benvenuti in the 12th round to win the world middleweight crown.

IT'S NOT TOO HOT FOR THE GREAT SCOT

At Hiram Bithorn Stadium in San Juan, it was 100-plus degrees and unbearably humid. The challenger, 25-year-old British champion Ken Buchanan, was from Scotland – pale and about as accustomed to such conditions as a polar bear. The world lightweight champion, Panama's Ismael Laguna, could dance all night. In a distance fight, he figured to cruise to victory.

Laguna, a 5-2 favorite, opened by bobbing and weaving and flaunting his extraordinary speed. By the middle rounds, Buchanan untracked his sterling jab and matched Laguna move for move. The fight tightened until the 12th, when the champion was staggered by a combination. Shockingly, it was Buchanan who finished strongest.

The decision couldn't have been closer, with Buchanan taking the title by split scores of 145-144 (twice) and 144-145. He became the first British world lightweight titlist since Freddie Welsh in 1917.

It was enough to make them turn up the heat in Edinburgh.

WORLD TITLE FIGHTS

HEAVYWEIGHTS

Nov 18	**Joe Frazier** *KO* 2 Bob Foster, Detroit

MIDDLEWEIGHTS

Nov 7	**Carlos Monzon** (ARG) *KO* 12 Nino Benvenuti, Rome

WELTERWEIGHTS

Dec 3	**Billy Backus** (USA) *KO* 4 Jose Napoles, Syracuse

JUNIOR WELTERWEIGHTS

Oct 30	**Bruno Arcari** *KO* 3 Raymundo Dias, Genoa

LIGHTWEIGHTS

Sept 26	**Ken Buchanan** (SCO) *W* 15 Ismael Laguna, San Juan

JUNIOR LIGHTWEIGHTS

Sept 27	**Yoshiaki Numata** *KO* 5 Raul Rojas, Tokyo, Japan

FEATHERWEIGHTS

Dec 11	**Kuniaki Shibata** (JAP) *KO* 14 Vicente Saldivar, Tijuana, Mexico

BANTAMWEIGHTS

Oct 16	**Chucho Castillo** (MEX) *KO* 14 Ruben Olivares, Inglewood

FLYWEIGHTS

Oct 22	**Masao Ohba** (JAP) *KO* 13 Berkrerk Chartvanchai, Tokyo
Dec 7	**Erbito Salavarria** *KO* 2 Chartchai Chionoi, Bangkok

THE GREATEST, PART II

Returning after more than three years, Muhammad Ali (right) stopped Quarry after three rounds.

Muhammad Ali's exile lasted three years, seven months, and four days. To no one's surprise, his return, a 10-rounder vs. Jerry Quarry, created instant controversy.

"We shouldn't let him fight for money if he won't fight for his country," said Georgia Governor Lester Maddox.

Despite such sentiment, the fight came off as scheduled. Ali and Quarry met on October 26, at the Municipal Auditorium in Atlanta. The 28-year-old former champion scaled 211½, or just three pounds more than for his March 1967 defense against Zora Folley. Determined to recreate the glory of his prime, he danced and jabbed for two rounds. But Quarry failed to provide a true test; he suffered a hideous cut over his left eye in round three, and his trainer, Teddy Bentham, wouldn't allow him out for the fourth.

The fight had been anticlimactic, but no one seemed to mind. Ali was back, and that was enough.

IF BOB CAN'T DO IT...

On November 18, Bob Foster reluctantly joined one of boxing's most exclusive clubs. Its membership: Archie Moore, Billy Conn, Joey Maxim, John Henry Lewis, Tommy Loughran, Georges Carpentier, and Philadelphia Jack O'Brien. Each and every one was a light heavyweight champion, and each and every one was a failure in his try at the heavyweight title.

At Detroit's Cobo Arena, Foster was blown away by world champion Joe Frazier. At 209 pounds Smokin' Joe outweighed Foster by 21 pounds, and wasted no time proving he was not only bigger, but better at the weight.

In the first round, Foster, a 5-1 underdog, landed the same hooks and straight rights that had flattened a string of 175-pound contenders. But Frazier walked right through them. In the second, it was the champion's turn. One hook toppled Foster for a nine-count, and another redeposited him on the canvas. Referee Tom Briscoe counted him out at the 49-second mark.

Frazier, 25-0 (22), was peaking. Muhammad Ali, 30-0 (24), was back. For the first time, The Fight of the Century seemed inevitable.

Ringside View

OCTOBER

One day after his 21st birthday, Japan's Masao Ohba wins the WBA flyweight title, scoring a 13th-round kayo over Berkrerk Chartvanchai.

DECEMBER

Muhammad Ali wins his second comeback bout, halting rugged Oscar Bonavena in the 15th and final round at Madison Square Garden.

CHUCHO'S REVENGE

Mexico's Chucho Castillo and his countryman, world bantamweight champion Ruben Olivares, were opposites both in and out of the ring. Castillo was quiet, withdrawn, even sullen; Olivares was amicable, boisterous, and ebullient. Castillo was a study in patience, a counterpuncher who adjusted to his opponent's style; Olivares was an assassin who fired bonebreaking hooks.

Their first battle, fought in April, went to Olivares. The rematch, held on October 16, before 16,007 crazed fans at the Inglewood Forum, brought a surprise ending – and a new champion.

The key moment came in the first round, when a butt opened a cut over Olivares' left eye. The gash didn't become a factor until the middle rounds. Olivares continued to fight gallantly, but the blood began to impair his vision.

After twice stopping the action so that Olivares could be examined, referee Dick Young did what he had to do: at the 2:37 mark of round 14, Castillo was crowned. (At the time of the stoppage, the fight was even on points.)

The opposites had attracted the attention of the world. Rubber match, anyone?

Joe Frazier explodes a knockout blow on Bob Foster's jaw in the second round. Joe's crown was at stake against light heavyweight king Foster.

BACKUS COMES BACK ON TOP

On March 5, 1965, Billy Backus, a southpaw from Canastota, New York, celebrated his 22nd birthday by losing his third fight in a row. His record was 7-7-3, and his future was gloomy. He decided to quit boxing.

If someone had told him that he would someday reign as world welterweight champion, he would've dismissed it as black humor. But 2½ years later, Backus was back in the ring, and on December 3, he challenged titlist Jose Napoles at the War Memorial Auditorium in Syracuse.

Nobody thought Carmen Basilio's nephew would pull off the upset. Napoles, a 9-1 favorite, dominated in the first, and kept beating Backus to the trigger in the second. But the champion suffered cuts over both his eyes, and in the third, Backus managed to match him punch for punch.

After 55 seconds of the fourth, referee Jack Millicent stepped in; Napoles was drenched in blood, and he could barely see.

"It's the greatest thing that's happened to me since I won the title myself," said a jubilant Basilio.

And a much greater surprise.

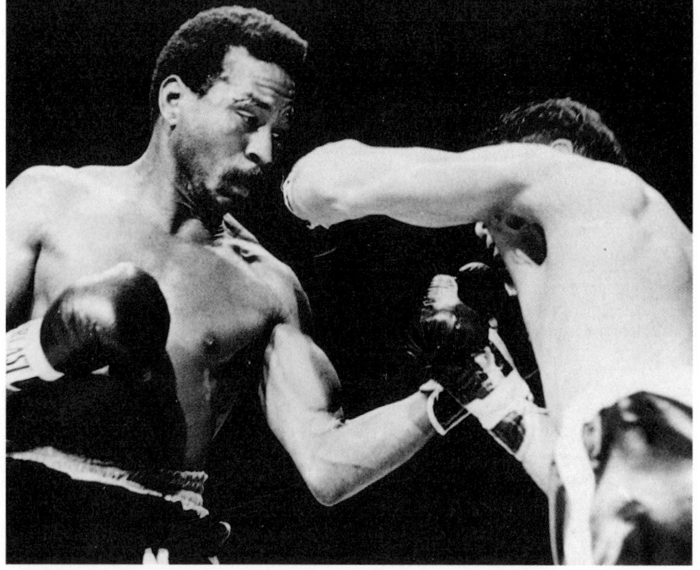

Billy Backus scored one of the decade's major upsets when he stopped Jose Napoles (left).

JANUARY

1971

APRIL

GOING HOME TO VISIT, NOT TO WORK

All over Britain, Ken Buchanan's coronation as lightweight champion was cause for celebration. But before Buchanan's victory over Ismael Laguna, the WBC stripped the Panamanian for failing to honor a contract with a promoter in California. The British Boxing Board of Control was a member of the WBC, so when Buchanan returned to his native Scotland, his status, technically, at least, was no different than when he had left.

Forced back on the road, the champion made his first defense on February 12, vs. Ruben Navarro at the Sports Arena in Los Angeles. (Navarro, rated third, was summoned after Mando Ramos suffered a groin injury three days before fight night.)

Navarro, a native Los Angelino and the North American champion, gave the 10,360 fans in attendance reason for hope when he dropped Buchanan in the first round. (Referee Arthur Mercante ruled it a slip.) From the fifth round through the 15th, however, the champion moved in and out, scored with combinations, and leaned away from counters. Navarro remained willing until the end, but Buchanan proved his master, taking a unanimous decision by 9-4 (twice) and 9-2.

The rest of the world was learning what Great Britain was refusing to acknowledge: Buchanan was the best lightweight in world boxing.

Scotland's pride, lightweight king Ken Buchanan (left), congratulates game loser Navarro.

Ringside View

JANUARY

Yoshiaki Numata retains the WBC 130-pound title with a split 15-round decision over former champion Rene Barrientos.

MARCH

Light heavyweight champion Bob Foster retains the title for the fifth time, halting Hal Carroll in round four.

World Title Fights

HEAVYWEIGHTS

March 8	**Joe Frazier** *W* 15 Muhammad Ali, New York City

LIGHT HEAVYWEIGHTS

Feb 27	**Vicente Rondon** (VEN) *KO* 6 Jimmy Dupree, Caracas (Wins Vacant WBA Title)
March 2	**Bob Foster** *KO* 4 Hal Carroll, Scranton
April 24	**Bob Foster** *W* 15 Ray Anderson, Tampa

JUNIOR MIDDLEWEIGHTS

April 29	**Carmelo Bossi** *D* 15 Jose Hernandez, Madrid

JUNIOR WELTERWEIGHTS

March 6	**Bruno Arcari** *ref* 15 Joao Henrique, Rome
April 3	**Nicolino Locche** *W* 15 Domingo Barrera, Buenos Aires

LIGHTWEIGHTS

Feb 12	**Ken Buchanan** *W* 15 Ruben Navarro, Los Angeles

JUNIOR LIGHTWEIGHTS

Jan 3	**Yoshiaki Numata** *W* 15 Rene Barrientos, Shizuaka, Japan
March 3	**Hiroshi Kobayashi** *W* 15 Ricardo Arredondo, Tokyo

FEATHERWEIGHTS

Feb 28	**Shozo Saijyo** *W* 15 Frankie Crawford, Utsonomiya, Japan

BANTAMWEIGHTS

April 3	**Ruben Olivares** *W* 15 Chucho Castillo, Inglewood

FLYWEIGHTS

April 1	**Masao Ohba** *W* 15 Betulio Gonzalez, Tokyo
April 30	**Erbito Salavarria** *W* 15 Susumu Hanagata, Quezon City

MANUFACTURING A NEW CHAMPION

Boxing's ruling bodies seemed determined to make a point: if a world champion as dominant as Bob Foster could be stripped, no one was safe. Early in 1971, the WBA declared the light heavyweight title vacant because Foster hadn't defended in more than six months. (In November 1970, he had challenged Joe Frazier for the world heavyweight title.)

On February 27, the organization's top-rated contenders, New Jersey's Jimmy Dupree and Venezuela's Vicente Rondon, clashed for the crown at the Nuevo Circo in Caracas. Rondon was tight at the start, and toward the end of the second, he crashed to the canvas. Arising unsteadily, he was saved by the bell.

The veteran rebounded in the third, and by the end of the round, Dupree was bleeding from cuts over both eyes. The momentum quickly shifted; Dupree began to miss, and Rondon zeroed in with his powerpunches.

After the fifth, Dupree was examined by the ringside physician. He was allowed to continue, but not for long. Late in the sixth, Rondon staggered him with a right-left-right, and finished him with a flurry. Referee Zack Clayton tolled 10 at the 2:58 mark.

Rondon's victory aside, almost everyone continued to recognize Foster as champion. But he was no longer a *unified* champion. That was a distinction we would have to get used to.

Bob Foster (right) kayoed Hal Carroll and retained the WBC version of the title.

THE FIGHT OF THE CENTURY

Muhammad Ali managed to climb off the floor after being dropped by heavyweight champ Joe Frazier, but Ali failed in his bid to regain the title.

On March 8 at Madison Square Garden, world heavyweight champion Joe Frazier, 205½, Philadelphia, Pennsylvania, 26-0 (23) defended against former champion Muhammad Ali, 215, Louisville, Kentucky, 31-0 (25). It was the night boxing made the world stop.

Frazier and Ali received record purses of $2.5 million each. Their long-awaited showdown was a social, political, and athletic event rolled into one. Everyone wanted ringside; Frank Sinatra shot pictures for *Life*, and Garden publicist John Condon had to toss Diana Ross out of the press section. But once the opening bell sounded, the focus shifted to two great champions, and The Fight Of The Century.

"I was there to do a job," said Frazier, who seemed unaffected by the significance of the moment. "I was gonna get that job done, and nothing could have stopped me. If he had a couple of nine-millimeters (guns), I would've walked right through them."

Remarkably, the fight lived up to the hype. The heavyweights punched at a furious pace, with Frazier applying unrelenting pressure, and Ali answering with rapid combinations. Frazier took the lead in the middle rounds, when Ali spent long stretches against the ropes. In the 11th, Smokin' Joe buckled Ali's knees with a thunder hook, and followed up with several big lefts. For the first time in his career, "The Greatest" was forced to rely on heart and will. "I don't know how he survived the 11th," said Dr. Ferdie Pacheco, one of Ali's handlers. "It was remarkable."

Frazier clinched victory in the first minute of the 15th. Dipping low, he rose with his best hook. It exploded against Ali's jaw, and the former champion collapsed to the canvas. But Ali refused to be stopped. He rose quickly, took referee Arthur Mercante's mandatory eight-count, and survived until the final bell.

Frazier took a unanimous decision by scores of 8-6-1, 9-6, and 11-4. No matter what the future would bring, he had emerged victorious in the most anticipated fight of all-time.

MAYBE NOT TOUGHER, BUT DEFINITELY BETTER

Having just regained the world bantamweight title from Chucho Castillo, Ruben Olivares bounced into his dressing room, and grabbed a soda bottle, removing the cap with his teeth. He had just spent an hour establishing that he was better than his arch-rival.

The Olivares-Castillo rubber match came on April 3, before a crowd of 18,141 at the Inglewood Forum. (In October 1970, Castillo won the crown by stopping Olivares on a butt-induced cut.) It wasn't a particularly exciting fight; the banties knew each other all too well, and, worse yet, respected each other. The only drama came when Olivares was dropped by a wide hook. (Oddly, in 44 rounds vs. Castillo, "Rockabye Ruben" suffered two knockdowns, while scoring none.)

Olivares was defensively brilliant throughout. Conversely, over the last five rounds, Castillo absorbed a frightful beating. The challenger's late rally cemented a unanimous decision victory (scores of 9-4, 12-4, and 10-3). "This was my best fight," Olivares said. "I used my head." In a different way than Castillo had six months before.

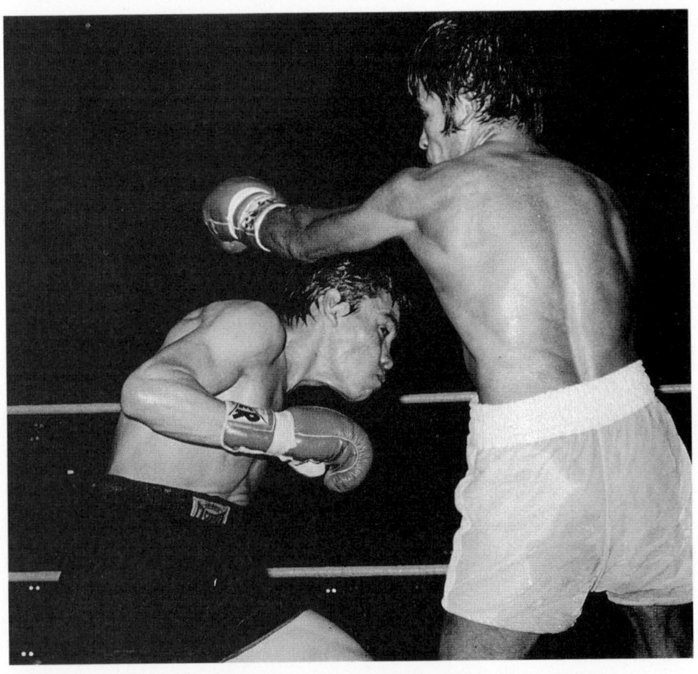

Ruben Olivares (left) avenged his only loss and also regained the bantamweight title.

MAY

1971

AUGUST

A TOWEL FOR TEARS

Everyone in a fighter's life – his handlers, his family, his fans – can tell him he's finished. But he needs to find out for himself.

On May 9, 33-year-old former middleweight champion Nino Benvenuti acknowledged the inevitable after his rematch with world titlist Carlos Monzon. The fight was held at Louis II Stadium in Monte Carlo.

Round one was uneventful, but in the second, Monzon scored a knockdown with a left hook. In the third, Nino began to fall again – both his gloves touched the canvas – when his manager, Bruno Amaduzzi, tossed a towel into the ring. Benvenuti kicked it right out, but referee Victor Avendano stopped the fight. It was Benvenuti's fourth loss in his last six fights.

Benvenuti would not fight again. He finished with a mark of 82-7-1 (35), and a reputation as Italy's greatest fighter of all-time.

Nino Benvenuti is dropped by Carlos Monzon.

A WILTING ROSE

Australia's Lionel Rose was vivid proof that the lighter the weight class, the earlier a fighter's prime. The flyweight, bantamweight, and featherweight divisions simply did not produce senior citizen champions like Archie Moore and Jersey Joe Walcott. Rose would be through before the age of 30. In fact, he would peak before reaching 20.

On May 30, the former bantamweight champion traveled to Hiroshima and, at the Prefectural Gymnasium, challenged WBC 130-pound champion Yoshiaki Numata. The jump in weight seemed severe. Moreover, since losing the bantie crown to Ruben Olivares in August 1969, Rose had been kayoed twice. He had qualified for a title try, however, by outpointing Ishimatsu Suzuki.

Rose was dreadful, and Numata was only slightly better. The Japanese champion utilized his familiar hit-and-run approach, and Rose responded without energy. After 15 unappetizing rounds, the unanimous decision went to Numata (scores of 73-71, 75-73, and 74-72).

It would be the last significant fight of Rose's career. At age 22, he was through, despite a six-fight comeback four years later.

Former bantamweight champ Rose knocked Numata out of the ring in the third round.

COLLECTING A SHORT-TERM LOAN

In December 1970, Jose Napoles suffered one of the biggest upsets of the modern era, losing the welterweight crown on cuts to New York State clubfighter Billy Backus. The classy Cuban was a 2-1 favorite to emerge victorious in the return, which was held on June 4 at the Inglewood Forum .

The rematch began as the original had ended; in the first round, the fighters butted heads, and Napoles returned to his corner with blood trickling down the side of his face. Cutman Angelo Dundee managed to control the wound, and Napoles proceeded to win round after round. Boxing in a tight circle, he peppered the southpaw champion with right hands. By round five, the fight had turned into a mismatch.

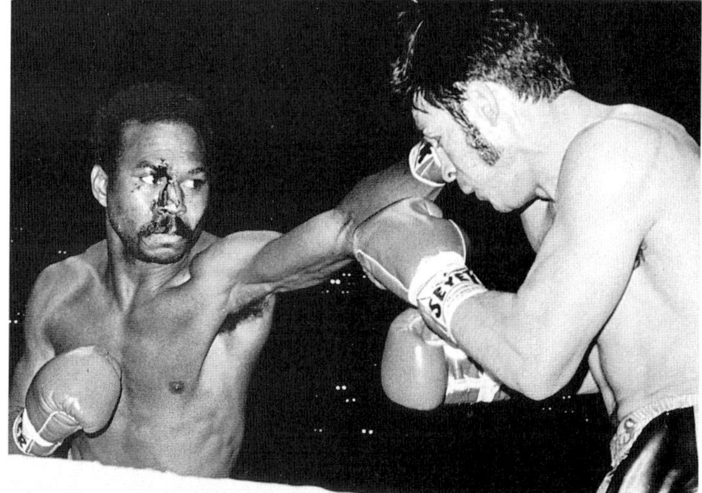

Jose Napoles (left) kayoed Billy Backus in the fourth round to take back the welterweight title.

In the eighth, Napoles scored two knockdowns. After Backus' second fall, referee Dick Young consulted with ringside physician Jack Useem, and they stopped it.

"I thought I never really lost the title," said Napoles. "It was just on loan for six months."

GENTLY BEATING UP AN OLD FRIEND

Having barely survived 15 rounds with heavyweight champion Joe Frazier, Muhammad Ali would have been excused for taking an easy fight. When he signed to face one of his former sparring partners, it seemed he was doing just that. But that former sparring partner, Jimmy Ellis, was a former world champion, too.

Ellis was also a stablemate and a boyhood friend. (Angelo Dundee, who trained both, chose to work Ellis' corner.)

Ali-Ellis came on July 26 at the Houston Astrodome. Ali, who scaled a fleshy 220½, seemed bored. He controlled his one-time employee with a crisp jab, and staggered Ellis with straight rights in the fourth and ninth rounds.

There were no knockdowns, but when Ellis, 189, absorbed several consecutive shots in the 12th and last round, referee Jay Edson intervened.

For Ali, it was a strong comeback performance. Then again, he never seemed the type who would lose once and then fade away.

Muhammad Ali (right) won the NABF heavyweight title by stopping his old friend Jimmy Ellis.

MARCANO SHOWS THAT HE CAN WIN A WORLD CROWN

Boxing has had its share of unlikely kings, but never more of them than since the fragmentation of world titles. As soon as the WBA and WBC began to recognize their own champions, a handful of undeserving fighters secured title shots. Some were even crowned. Among them was Alfredo Marcano.

Before his challenge of long-reigning WBA junior lightweight champion Hiroshi Kobayashi, Venezuela's Marcano was unrated. In fact, he had lost five of his previous nine bouts. His only victory of note: a January 1970 decision over Mexican contender Ricardo Arrendondo.

Marcano-Kobayashi came on July 29, at the Prefectural Gymnasium in Aomori, Japan. The bout was physical and action-packed, but the champion, who had registered only 11 kayos in 72 fights, couldn't match Marcano's power. He finally fell in round 10, and was counted out by referee Yusaku Yoshida at the 1:25 mark.

"I didn't doubt Kobayashi's gameness," said the new champion, "but I knew a few things about his defense, and I did not fear any of his weapons."

In an era of dual champions, that had been more than enough.

Alfredo Marcano won a world title.

CATCHING SOMETHING MORE THAN PUNCHES

Colombia's Rodrigo Valdes was among the most promising middleweights in the world. His drive to the title had been slowed by some of the typical roadblocks – injuries, decision losses, adapting to a new trainer. But after his bout against New Yorker Bobby Cassidy, he would suffer a most unusual setback.

The fight, held on August 9 at Madison Square Garden, seemed unexceptional. Valdes fought aggressively, and by the seventh round, Cassidy was bleeding from no less than four eye cuts. After examining the southpaw in round seven, Dr. Edwin A. Campbell instructed referee Johnny LoBianco to intervene. Just another fight? Hardly. Unbeknownst to Cassidy, he entered the ring suffering from hepatitis. During the course of the bout, the highly contagious disease was passed to Valdes. Soon after, both fighters succumbed to the symptons. Cassidy would miss seven months, and Valdes (who would score two wins during the incubation period), almost six months.

WORLD TITLE FIGHTS

LIGHT HEAVYWEIGHTS	
June 5	**Vicente Rondon** *KO* 1 Piero Del Papa, Caracas
Aug 21	**Vicente Rondon** *W* 15 Eddie Jones, Caracas
MIDDLEWEIGHTS	
May 9	**Carlos Monzon** *KO* 3 Nino Benvenuti, Monte Carlo
WELTERWEIGHTS	
June 4	**Jose Napoles** *KO* 4 Billy Backus, Inglewood
JUNIOR WELTERWEIGHTS	
June 26	**Bruno Arcari** *KO* 9 Enrique Jana, Palermo, Italy
JUNIOR LIGHTWEIGHTS	
May 30	**Yoshiaki Numata** *W* 15 Lionel Rose, Hiroshima
July 29	**Alfredo Marcano** (VEN) *KO* 10 Hiroshi Kobayashi, Aomori, Japan
FEATHERWEIGHTS	
June 3	**Kuniaki Shibata** *KO* 1 Raul Cruz, Tokyo

RINGSIDE VIEW

JUNE

Vincente Rondon defends the WBA light heavyweight title for the first time and scores a first-round kayo of Piero Del Papa.

AUGUST

In a non-title bout, world welterweight champion Jose Napoles scores a fifth-round kayo of Jean Josselin at the Inglewood Forum.

SEPTEMBER

1971

DECEMBER

RINGSIDE VIEW

OCTOBER

Koichi Wajima captures the world junior middleweight crown by split decision over Italy's Carmelo Bossi.

BEATING BACK PAST GHOSTS

The boxing fans who doubted that world champion Carlos Monzon represented the future of the middleweight division were overwhelmed by the evidence presented on September 25, at Luna Park in Buenos Aires. In his title-winning performance and first defense, Monzon crushed Nino Benvenuti. In defense number two, he faced another remnant of the '60s, Emile Griffith.

Monzon, perceived as the fresher fighter, was 29, and had engaged in 85 fights. Griffith, thought to be an old man, was 31, and had fought 83 times. But so much of Griffith's experience had come in world title fights, and the challenger thought he could outsmart Monzon. Despite a five-inch reach disadvantage, Griffith boxed with patience, jabbing strongly and adding occasional hooks. Monzon kept his distance, and countered when he could. It was a very close fight – until the last half of the 14th round.

Monzon struck suddenly, and a shower of punches left Griffith helpless along the ropes. Referee Ramon Berumen came to his rescue at the 2:49 mark.

"I was going good until the 14th round," he said.

Past tense.

Carlos Monzon acknowledges the cheers.

THE NIGHT THAT LAGUNA TURNED GOON

The moment must have come at some point in training camp, during one of those long afternoons when a fighter is kept company only by his thoughts. Envisioning the fight ahead, former lightweight champion Ismael Laguna concluded that he couldn't outbox Ken Buchanan. So he decided to try and outbrawl him.

Ken Buchanan (left) decisioned Ismael Laguna to retain the lightweight championship.

Buchanan-Laguna II came on September 13, at Madison Square Garden. One year before, the Scot had taken Laguna's title by the slimmest of margins. This time, there would be less doubt.

(Before the bout, Buchanan was stripped of the WBC portion of the title for failing to defend against Pedro Carrasco.)

Buchanan started slowly, but instead of capitalizing on his speed, Laguna initiated a streetfight. He punched on the break and hit and held, but drew only warnings from referee Jimmy Devlin. The result: by the fourth round, the champion's left eye was swollen almost shut.

Fighting flatfooted in the middle rounds, Buchanan traded punch for punch. He suffered a cut over his left eye in the 12th, but dominated down the stretch, almost stopping the Panamanian in the 14th and 15th. He took a unanimous decision by scores of 9-6, 8-6-1, and 10-5.

WORLD TITLE FIGHTS

LIGHT HEAVYWEIGHTS

Oct 26	**Vicente Rondon** *KO* 13 Gomeo Brennan, Miami Beach
Oct 29	**Bob Foster** *KO* 8 Tommy Hicks, Scranton
Dec 15	**Vicente Rondon** *KO* 8 Doyle Baird, Cleveland
Dec 16	**Bob Foster** *KO* 3 Brian Kelly, Oklahoma City

MIDDLEWEIGHTS

Sept 25	**Carlos Monzon** *KO* 14 Emile Griffith, Buenos Aires

JUNIOR MIDDLEWEIGHTS

Oct 31	**Koichi Wajima** (JAP) *W* 15 Carmelo Bossi, Tokyo

WELTERWEIGHTS

Dec 14	**Jose Napoles** *W* 15 Hedgemon Lewis, Inglewood

JUNIOR WELTERWEIGHTS

Oct 10	**Bruno Arcari** *KO* 10 Domingo Corpas, Genoa
Dec 11	**Nicolino Locche** *W* 15 Antonio Cervantes, Buenos Aires

LIGHTWEIGHTS

Sept 13	**Ken Buchanan** *W* 15 Ismael Laguna, New York City
Nov 5	**Pedro Carrasco** (SPA) *W Disq* 11 Mando Ramos, Madrid

JUNIOR LIGHTWEIGHTS

Oct 10	**Ricardo Arredondo** (MEX) *KO* 10 Yoshiaki Numata, Sendai, Japan
Nov 7	**Alfredo Marcano** *KO* 4 Konji Iwata, Caracas

FEATHERWEIGHTS

Sept 2	**Antonio Gomez** (VEN) *KO* 5 Shozo Saijyo, Tokyo
Nov 11	**Kuniaki Shibata** *D* 15 Ernesto Marcel, Matsuyama, Japan

BANTAMWEIGHTS

Oct 25	**Ruben Olivares** *KO* 14 Kazuyoshi Kanazawa, Nagoya
Dec 14	**Ruben Olivares** *KO* 11 Jesus Pimentel, Inglewood

FLYWEIGHTS

Oct 23	**Masao Ohba** *W* 15 Fernando Cabanella, Tokyo
Nov 20	**Erbito Salavarria** *D* 15 Betulio Gonzalez, Maracaibo

DOUBLE CHAMPIONS STAR IN A DOUBLEHEADER

Jose Napoles and Ruben Olivares had much in common. They were two-time world champions – Napoles at welterweight, and Olivares at bantamweight – who had regained their crowns after losing them on cuts. They were fan favorites in Mexico and Southern California. And they dominated their respective divisions with crunching left hooks and sterling boxing skills.

On December 14, Napoles and Olivares shared one more thing: top billing on a championship fight card at the Inglewood Forum. Napoles, 31, defended against local contender Hedgemon Lewis. Olivares, 24, faced long-ignored powerpuncher Jesus Pimental, who had been rated first seven years before.

Napoles-Lewis was a close fight, but not an entertaining one. Lewis cautiously circled the ring, jabbing and dancing away. He marked the champion around both eyes and led after seven rounds, but couldn't keep his momentum. Napoles survived a brief scare in the 14th, and went on to take a unanimous decision (scores of 8-6, 8-7, and 9-4).

"Rockabye Ruben's" bout was no easier. For the first five rounds, he and fellow Mexican Pimental traded hooks and crosses without pause. The fight turned in the sixth; Olivares landed a right that drove the challenger through the ropes and down. Pimental subsequently absorbed a frightful beating, and after 11 rounds, his manager, Harry Kabakoff, told referee John Thomas that the damage was enough.

Boxing insiders figured Olivares to keep the title as long as he pleased. Napoles, Cuba-born but Mexico-based, was considered the best 147-pound champion since Sugar Ray Robinson. For Mexican boxing fans, it was never going to get better than this.

Ruben Olivares (left) kaoyed game Jesus Pimental in the 11th round to retain the world bantamweight crown, his 67th victory in 68 fights.

Ex-champion Muhammad Ali (left) easily decisioned blubbery Buster Mathis.

RINGSIDE VIEW

NOVEMBER

Former heavyweight champion Muhammad Ali scores a 12-round decision over Buster Mathis in Houston.

DECEMBER

WBA junior welterweight champion Nicolino Locche retains the crown for the fifth time, scoring a unanimous 15-round decision over Colombia's Antonio Cervantes.

THE REIGN BEGINS IN SPAIN

Unbeaten in 92 consecutive fights, or for 7½ years, Spain's Pedro Carrasco was certainly worthy of a try at the vacant WBC lightweight title. But in extending his unbeaten streak to 93, he needed the help of a tag-team partner.

On November 5, at the Sports Palace in Madrid, Carrasco faced former champion Mando Ramos. It was a one-sided fight from the start; Ramos scored a first-round knockdown, and by the 10th, Carrasco, down a total of four times, was seemingly on the way out.

In the 11th, however, there was chaos after Carrasco crashed to the canvas. Had he been knocked down? Or thrown? After a one-minute delay, Nigerian referee Samuel Odubote, who was working his first world title fight, disqualified Ramos for "hitting on top of the head and below the belt," and raised Carrasco's arm in victory.

Realizing what a farce the fight had been, the WBC ordered an immediate rematch. For some reason, Samuel Odubote was not asked to referee.

JANUARY

1972

APRIL

RINGSIDE VIEW

APRIL

Filipino junior lightweight Ben Villaflor wins the WBA title, scoring a unanimous 15-round decision over Alfredo Marcano.

TERRY FAILED THE EXAM

Terry Daniels wasn't your typical challenger for the world heavyweight title. He came from a family of wealth – his father was a millionaire businessman – and he was nine credits short of a college degree. But before the first heavyweight title fight in New Orleans since Corbett-Sullivan, tough Terry talked the talk.

"Sooner or later, Joe Frazier is going to run into a hard punch," he said. "It's inevitable."

However, on January 15, at the Rivergate Auditorium, Daniels found that he couldn't walk the walk. "Ten seconds after I entered the ring," he said, "game plans went out the window. He was all over me!"

Scaling a surprisingly high 215½, Frazier scored knockdown number one at the end of the first round. He inflicted minimal damage in the second, but dropped Daniels, 195, twice more in the third. After the challenger went down face-first in the fourth, and subsequently lay defenseless against the ropes, referee Herman Dutreix stopped the sacrifice. The end came at the 1:45 mark.

It was Frazier's first fight since his March 1971 epic vs. Muhammad Ali. Daniels could verify that there was lots of fire left in the champion, and plenty of smoke to go with it.

Joe Frazier made his third defense of the undisputed crown by kayoing Terry Daniels.

JUSTICE, AND MANDO, PREVAIL

Sometimes rematches are hard to figure. In November 1971, Mando Ramos was disqualified while on the verge of winning the vacant WBC lightweight title.

An immediate rematch was ordered for February 18, this time at the Sports Arena in Ramos' native Los Angeles. He seemed a cinch to capture the crown. But it wouldn't be that easy. Boxing far better than he had in Madrid, Pedro Carrasco took the early rounds – and marked Ramos' eyes – with jabs and hooks. He also tested the patience of referee Lee Grossman, who warned the Spaniard for head butting, holding and hitting, and shoulder butting.

Ramos unleashed his jab in the middle rounds, and accelerated down the stretch, hurting Carrasco in the 13th and 14th. The rally was enough; he got a split decision by 7-6, 9-5, and 5-8.

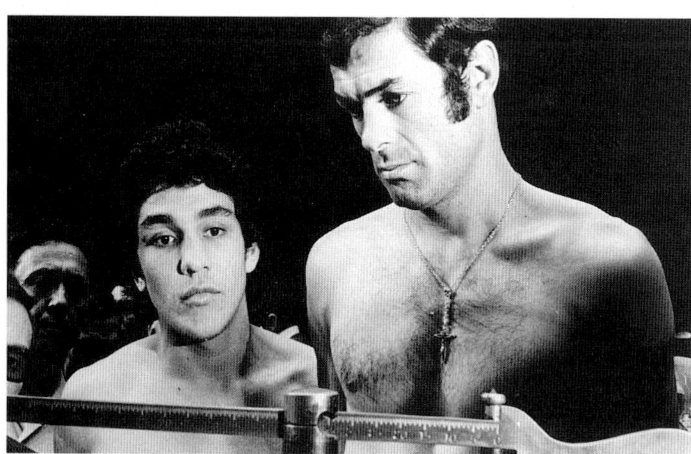

Mando Ramos (left) at the weigh-in before outpointing Pedro Carrasco for the title.

WORLD TITLE FIGHTS

HEAVYWEIGHTS

Jan 15	**Joe Frazier** *KO* 4 Terry Daniels, New Orleans

LIGHT HEAVYWEIGHTS

April 7	**Bob Foster** *KO* 2 Vicente Rondon, Miami Beach (Unifies World Title)

MIDDLEWEIGHTS

March 4	**Carlos Monzon** *KO* 5 Dennis Moyer, Rome

WELTERWEIGHTS

March 28	**Jose Napoles** *KO* 7 Ralph Charles, Wembley

JUNIOR WELTERWEIGHTS

March 10	**Alfonzo Frazer** (PAN) *W* 15 Nicolino Locche, Panama City

LIGHTWEIGHTS

Feb 18	**Mando Ramos** *W* 15 Pedro Carrasco, Los Angeles

JUNIOR LIGHTWEIGHTS

Jan 29	**Ricardo Arredondo** *W* 15 Jose Isaac Marin, San Jose, Costa Rica
April 22	**Ricardo Arredondo** *KO* 5 William Martinez, Mexico City
April 25	**Ben Villaflor** (PHI) *W* 15 Alfredo Marcano, Honolulu

FEATHERWEIGHTS

Feb 5	**Antonio Gomez** *KO* 7 Raul Martinez, Maracay

BANTAMWEIGHTS

March 19	**Rafael Herrera** (MEX) *KO* 8 Ruben Olivares, Mexico City

FLYWEIGHTS

March 4	**Masao Ohba** *W* 15 Susumu Hanagata, Tokyo

THE REINCARNATION OF NINO?

During his title fights in Rome, former middleweight champion Nino Benvenuti occasionally benefited from friendly officiating. But Carlos Monzon? He wasn't even Italian.

On March 4, at the Palazzo Dello Sport in Rome, Monzon met the 32-year-old veteran Denny Moyer. (In the early-'60s, Moyer had reigned as world junior middleweight champion.) Before the bout, the joke was that wherever Monzon fought, he brought along not only his title belt, but his own referee, too. Indeed, for the Moyer fight, the third man was the champion's countryman, Lorenzo Fortunato.

Over the first four rounds, Moyer outboxed Monzon. But in the fifth, the Argentine turned the fight with a hook to the midsection. A knockdown followed, but Moyer had risen and was adequately defending himself when Fortunato called a halt.

The disgusted crowd of 12,000 tossed oranges at the ring, and Monzon, Moyer, and Fortunato returned to their dressing rooms under police protection.

"It was not my fault; I did what I had to do," said Monzon.

A fighter's reputation isn't built in a day.

Monzon was knocked out of the ring by Denny Moyer, but rallied to keep the crown.

THE REAL CHAMP MAKES IT OFFICIAL

When cool and calm, light heavyweight champion Bob Foster was a dangerous puncher. When angry, he was devastating.

Boastful Venezuelan Vicente Rondon, who was recognized as 175-pound champion by the WBA, made Foster angrier than anyone else. After a Rondon exhibition match in Tampa, Foster, seated in the third row, took a swing at his rival. On April 7, at Convention Hall in Miami Beach, he received the opportunity to do it in the ring.

There was controversy even before the first bell. After Rondon weighed in at 177, the Miami Beach commission decided the scale was faulty. Rondon's announced weight: 175 pounds.

The point became moot when Foster took less than six minutes to unify the title. After a quiet first round, Big Bob exploded in the second. A hook dropped Rondon, and later in the round, a left-right-left left him on the canvas, his feet twitching uncontrollably.

"I didn't really want to knock him out," said Foster, who was still angry. "I wanted it to go 15 so I could beat him bad. I hate him, and I hate the WBA."

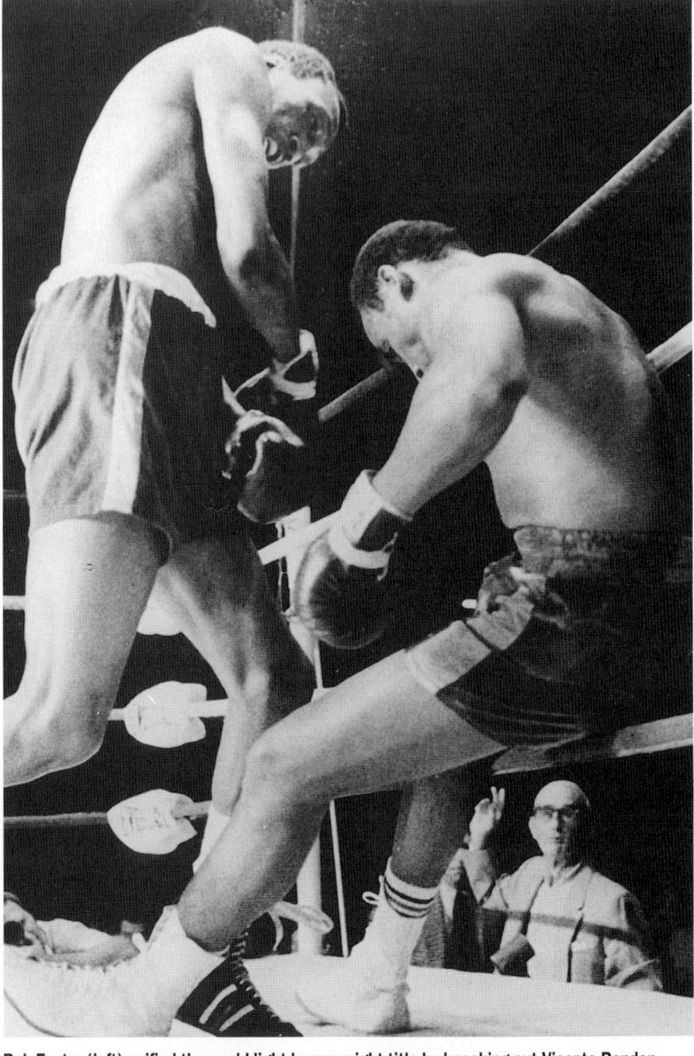

Bob Foster (left) unified the world light heavyweight title by knocking out Vicente Rondon.

THE MEXICAN BANTAMWEIGHT FACTORY

Ruben Olivares became the best bantamweight in the world by winning the title from Lionel Rose. But it wasn't until he won his rubber match vs. Chucho Castillo that he established himself as the best in Mexico.

"Rockabye Ruben" didn't retain the latter title for long. Rafael Herrera was Mexico's new 118-pound sensation. He held wins over Castillo and Rodolfo Martinez, and on March 19, he challenged Olivares at the El Toreo bullring in Mexico City. It was the first world title fight held in Mexico featuring two native fighters.

Olivares struggled to make weight, and when Herrera escalated his attack in the third, the champion responded weakly. Ahead on the cards, Herrera connected with a booming right in round eight. Referee Ray Solis tolled 10 at the 1:20 mark.

The brilliant Olivares had been beaten. But even after winning the world title, Herrera couldn't afford to become complacent. Another future superstar was surely being groomed in the Mexican bantamweight factory.

MAY

1972

AUGUST

STANDER'S NO FALL GUY

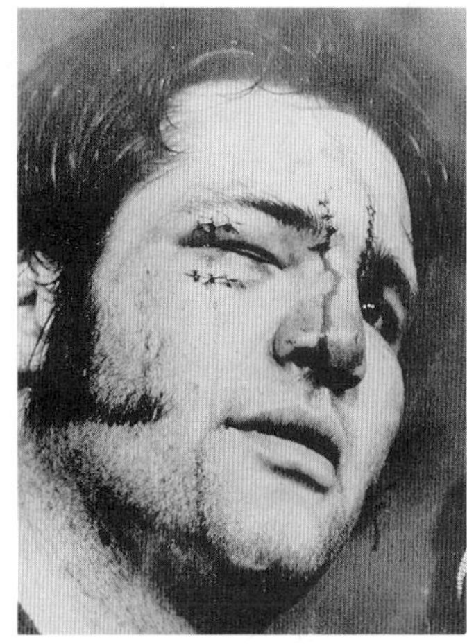

Postfight picture of Ron Stander.

Joe Frazier explains how it's done.

The scene was right out of *Rocky*, only *Rocky* hadn't been written yet. At the start of the fourth round of Ron Stander's million-to-one try at the heavyweight title, the challenger stood on shaky legs and waved champion Joe Frazier toward him. False bravado? Hardly. Bleeding from four fresh cuts, Stander wanted to brawl some more.

Frazier-Stander came on May 25, at the Civic Auditorium in Omaha. (It was the first world title fight ever held in the state of Nebraska.) Stander traded with Smokin' Joe from the start, even stunning him with a right hand in the first round. By the fourth, however, his face resembled a slab of beef. He completed the round, but Dr. Jack Lewis didn't allow him to answer the bell for the fifth. (Following the severe punishment received at the hands of Smokin' Joe, Stander's face later required 32 stitches.)

It had been an action-packed, albeit one-sided, punchathon. Still, one curious question remained unanswered: what had Stander, who ranked no better than 30th, done to earn a shot at the title?

Even his wife Darlene seemed stumped. Said Mrs. Stander: "You don't take a Volkswagen into the Indianapolis 500 unless you know a shortcut."

HE TOOK THE LOW ROAD

While waiting his turn to do battle, a world-class fighter should not concern himself with the preliminary bouts. Perhaps Ken Buchanan should have made an exception before his September 1971 lightweight title defense against Ismael Laguna. On that Madison Square Garden card, a 20-year-old Panamanian lightweight named Roberto Duran energized the crowd by taking all of a minute to destroy the talented Benny Huertas.

On June 26, Buchanan and Duran were back in the Garden, this time to fight each other. Duran proved no less savage than he had been vs. Huertas, rushing from his corner and dropping the Scot with his first strong blow. Amazingly, he never decelerated, backing the champion to the ropes in almost every round, and scoring big with his right hand.

Unfortunately, what would have been a brilliant victory was tarnished by a controversial ending. As the fighters traded after the bell ending the 13th, Buchanan slumped to the canvas and writhed in pain. He told referee Johnny LoBianco that Duran had kneed him in the groin. The third man, however, hadn't seen the foul. Despite Buchanan's protests, the fight was stopped before the start of the 14th.

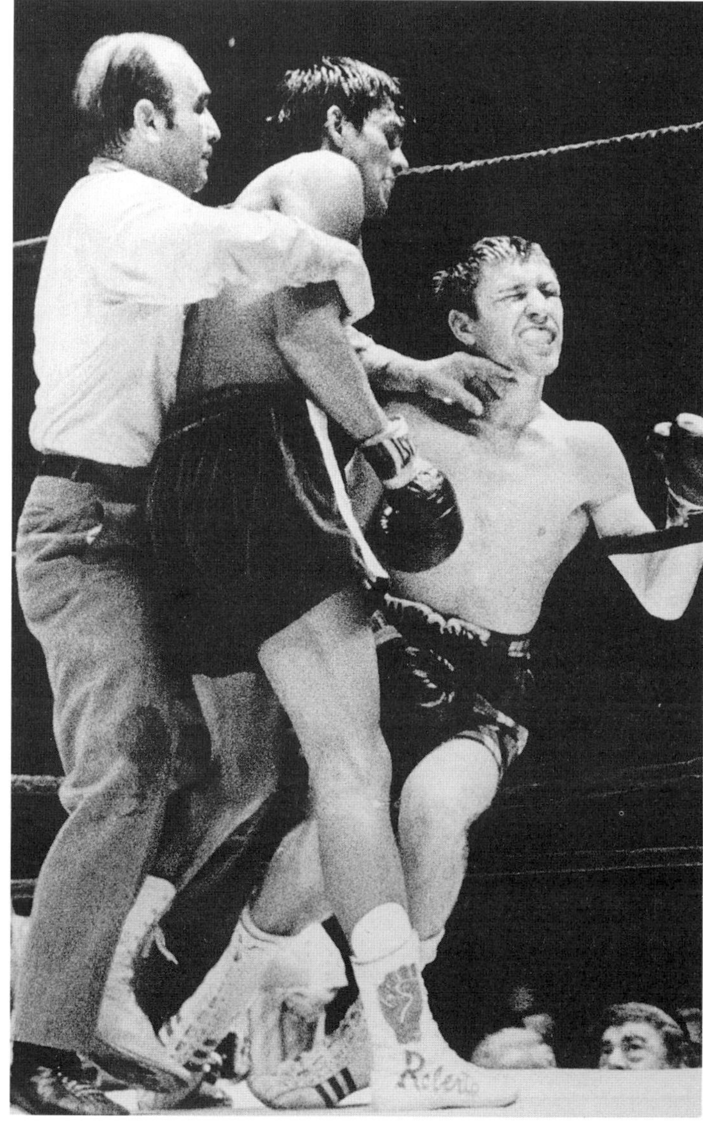

Referee pulls Roberto Duran away from stricken Ken Buchanan in the 13th and final round.

RINGSIDE VIEW

JUNE

Middleweight champion Carlos Monzon makes his fourth defense, stopping Jean-Claude Bouttier in the 13th round.

JUNE

Jose Napoles keeps the welterweight title by halting Adolph Pruitt in two rounds.

AUGUST

Yet another Panamanian world champion is crowned when Ernesto Marcel captures the WBA featherweight title with a majority 15-round decision over Antonio Gomez.

A SWEEP FOR THE SOUL BROTHERS

On June 27, at the Las Vegas Convention Center, light heavyweight champion Bob Foster defended against Mike Quarry, and Muhammad Ali met Mike's big brother Jerry. The card was billed as "The Soul Brothers vs. The Quarry Brothers."

Though he tried, Ali couldn't steal the show. The former champion toyed with Quarry for six rounds, then, after staggering him with combinations at the start of the seventh, implored referee Mike Kaplan to intervene. He did, at the 19-second mark.

Foster's victory was far more spectacular. He connected with a textbook hook a split second before the bell ending the fourth. Quarry crashed and remained motionless for several minutes.

The final score: Soul Brothers 2, Quarry Brothers 0.

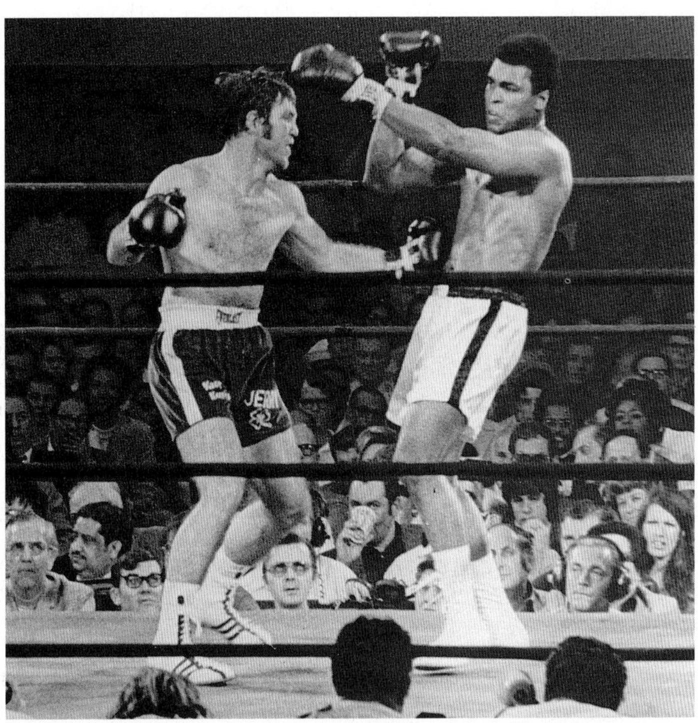

With the NABF heavyweight title at stake, Muhammad Ali (right) pounded game Jerry Quarry.

A PANAMA HAT TRICK

In 1929, bantamweight Al Brown became the first world champion from Panama. But it wasn't until 1972 that the Caribbean nation established itself as a major force in boxing. In March, Alfonzo (Peppermint) Frazer won the WBA junior welterweight title. Three months later, Roberto Duran was crowned lightweight king. And on July 30, Enrique Pinder dethroned bantamweight champion Rafael Herrera.

Pinder's upset of Herrera came at the Nuevo Panama Coliseum in Panama City. He dominated the first eight rounds with jabs and hooks, and after surviving a brief scare in the ninth, regained control. The challenger was in superb condition; he danced until the final bell, and was rewarded with a unanimous decision.

THE MAIN DANE CAN'T REIGN

Boxing was an international game, and Denmark wanted a champion of its own. Its prime candidate was 27-year-old Tom Bogs, who had reigned as European middleweight and light heavyweight champion. On August 9, at Idraets Park Stadium in Copenhagen, he tried for the big prize by challenging world 160-pound king Carlos Monzon.

"I do not believe I can knock him out," Bogs said. "But neither can he stop me."

Bogs was half-right. For three rounds, Monzon seemed bored. But after suffering a cut over his left eye in round four, he displayed a sense of urgency. Bogs fell three times in the fifth, and after his last trip to the canvas, referee Harry Gibbs called a halt.

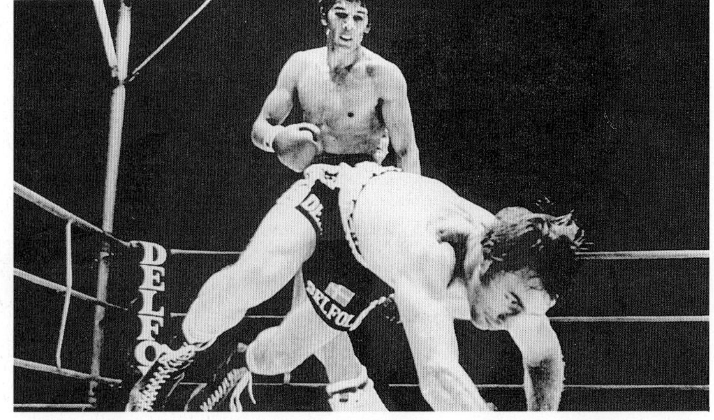

Carlos Monzon stopped Tom Bogs to retain the world middleweight championship.

WORLD TITLE FIGHTS

HEAVYWEIGHTS

May 26 **Joe Frazier** *KO* 5
Ron Stander, Omaha

LIGHT HEAVYWEIGHTS

June 27 **Bob Foster** *KO* 4
Mike Quarry, Las Vegas

MIDDLEWEIGHTS

June 17 **Carlos Monzon** *KO* 13
Jean-Claude Bouttier, Paris

Aug 19 **Carlos Monzon** *KO* 5
Tom Bogs, Copenhagen

JUNIOR MIDDLEWEIGHTS

May 7 **Koichi Wajima** *KO* 1
Domenico Tiberia, Tokyo

WELTERWEIGHTS

June 10 **Jose Napoles** *KO* 2
Adolph Pruitt, Monterrey

June 16 **Hedgemon Lewis** (USA) *W* 15
Billy Backus, Syracuse
(Wins Vacant New York State World Title)

JUNIOR WELTERWEIGHTS

June 10 **Bruno Arcari** *KO* 12
Joao Henrique, Genoa

June 17 **Alfonzo Frazer** *KO* 5
Al Ford, Panama City

LIGHTWEIGHTS

June 26 **Roberto Duran** (PAN) *KO* 14
Ken Buchanan, New York City

June 28 **Mando Ramos** *W* 15
Pedro Carrasco, Madrid

FEATHERWEIGHTS

May 19 **Clemente Sanchez** (MEX) *KO* 3
Kuniaki Shibata, Tokyo

Aug 19 **Ernesto Marcel** (PAN) *W* 15
Antonio Gomez, Maracay

BANTAMWEIGHTS

July 30 **Enrique Pinder** (PAN) *W* 15
Rafael Herrera, Panama City

FLYWEIGHTS

June 3 **Betulio Gonzalez** (VEN) *KO* 4
Socrates Batoto, Caracas
(Wins Vacant WBC Title)

June 20 **Masao Ohba** *KO* 5
Orland Amores, Tokyo

SEPTEMBER

1972

DECEMBER

BINGO! BANGO! CHANGO!

Eudibiel Guillen Chapin, better known as Chango Carmona, spent the better part of his career winning and losing the Mexican lightweight title. On September 15, he expanded his parameters.

Carmona, 27, challenged WBC 135-pound champion Mando Ramos at the Coliseum in Los Angeles. When Ramos scored, the Mexican-Americans cheered, and when Carmona connected, the Mexican-Nationals screamed. The latter group was much louder.The stocky challenger, a former high diver in Acapulco, fought like a miniature Joe Frazier. He attacked from the start, scoring one knockdown in the fourth, and two more in the fifth. When Ramos fell for the fourth time in round eight, referee Rudy Jordan stepped in.

Carmona's celebration lasted well into the night. The world, he had found out, wasn't such a big place after all.

FLOYD'S UNOFFICIAL FAREWELL

It had been more than 20 years since his first fight, and Floyd Patterson still hadn't announced his retirement.

At Madison Square Garden on September 20, Patterson faced Muhammad Ali in a battle of former heavyweight champions. After stopping Floyd on cuts in the seventh round, Ali offered his rival another chance.

"I'll take it," said Patterson. "I'm going back into training tomorrow." Tomorrow never came.

In what turned out to be his farewell performance, Patterson, 37, fought exceptionally well. He pressured Ali throughout, but in the fifth round, his left eye began to puff. By the sixth, the eye was closed, and in the seventh, one of Ali's sharp rights broke open the swelling. Before the start of the eighth, Dr. Harry Kleiman told referee Arthur Mercante to call a halt. (At the time of the stoppage, Ali led by scores of 6-1, 4-2-1, and 3-3-1.)

"The cut was deep and very close to the eyeball," explained Dr. Kleiman.

Patterson exited with a career mark of 55-8-1 (40). Few champions displayed as much heart, provided as many thrills, or claimed more fans.

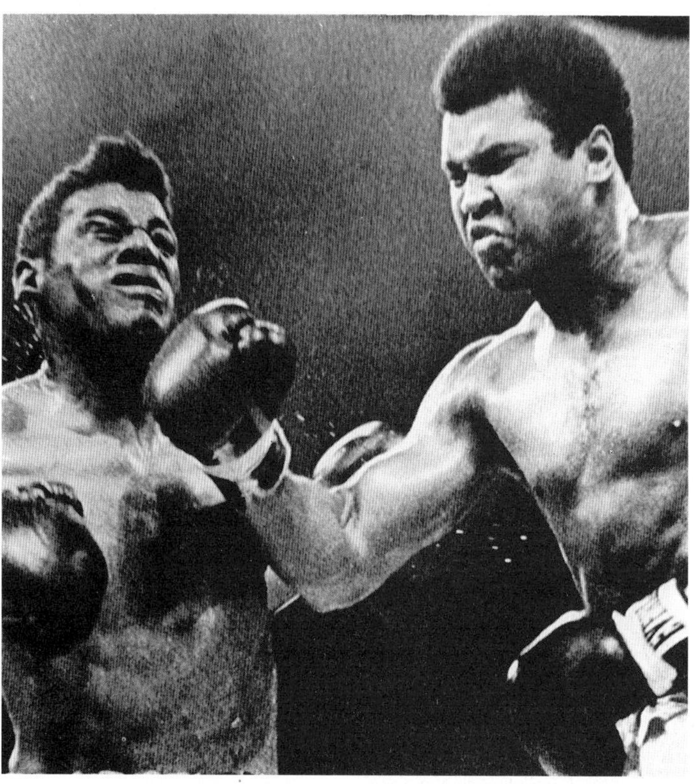

Muhammad Ali (right) retained the NABF heavyweight crown by stopping Floyd Patterson.

RINGSIDE VIEW

OCTOBER

Thought to be washed up, Colombia's Antonio (Kid Pambele) Cervantes wins the WBA junior welterweight title by knocking out Alfonzo (Peppermint) Frazer.

NOVEMBER

Rodolfo Gonzalez captures the WBC lightweight crown, stopping fellow Mexican Chango Carmona.

DECEMBER

Spain's Jose Legra wins the featherweight title for the second time, knocking out WBC champion Clemente Sanchez in round 10.

FINNEGAN SEES FOSTER WIN AGAIN

Picking up paydays while plotting another invasion of the heavyweight ranks, world 175-pound champion Bob Foster decided to take the title on the road. On September 26, he made his 11th defense, facing English southpaw and 1968 Olympic gold medalist Chris Finnegan at the Empire Pool in Wembley.

Finnegan was fearless and had trained hard. The combination allowed him to extend Foster, who was not used to long fights.

Finnegan boxed cautiously, and then, hoping that the 33-year-old champion would tire, accelerated in the middle rounds. Foster scored a 10th-round knockdown with a looping right, but the challenger kept attacking. Behind on points, he tried for a miracle kayo – and never saw the hook that finished him in round 14.

Finnegan had fought with all his heart. But guts wasn't going to be enough to topple Bob Foster.

Bob Foster kayoed game Chris Finnegan and was still light heavyweight champion.

BEATING BACK BAD BENNIE

Carlos Monzon was world middleweight champion, but he still needed to prove he was a better fighter than Philadelphia's Bennie Briscoe, who, in May 1967, had traveled to Argentina and held Monzon to a draw. Monzon was unbeaten since 1964, but that result was viewed as a blemish on his record; insiders concluded that a draw at home vs. an American must really have been a loss.

Monzon-Briscoe II came on November 11, at Luna Park in Buenos Aires. The champion welcomed Bad Bennie's straightforward, bob-and-weave style. In each and every round, Briscoe attacked in an effort to neutralize Monzon's five-inch reach advantage, only to walk into heavy jabs and straight rights. He never got inside, and with the exception of isolated moments in the ninth and 14th rounds, he was battered.

"Any of the punches with which I hit him would have floored another rival," said Monzon, who kept the title by unanimous 15-round decision (scores of 150-139, 149-139, and 149-143). "It was my most difficult defense."

Carlos Monzon had to draw on all his extraordinary skill to save the middleweight crown from the savage attacks of Bennie Briscoe (left).

THE "OTHER" BEST LIGHTWEIGHT IN THE WORLD

If lightweight champion Roberto Duran was boxing's wunderkind, what was Esteban DeJesus? On November 17, at Madison Square Garden, the Puerto Rican proved that the division would have to be big enough for both of them.

DeJesus-Duran, a non-title fight, was decided in the first 30 seconds of the first round, when DeJesus fired a perfect hook. Boom! Duran jumped to his feet at the count of two, but remained respectful of his foe's power.

Punching first, and even forcing Duran to retreat, DeJesus emerged victorious by rounds scores of 6-3-1, 6-2-2, and 5-4-1. He had earned a try at the title.

Legend has it that after losing for the first time in his career, Duran returned to his hotel room and soaked his aching body in a hot bath. Then he began to cry and scream and punch the walls until his hands were bloody.

Clearly, this was a fighter who *had* to win.

Esteban DeJesus (right) shocked the world by beating lightweight champion Roberto Duran.

WORLD TITLE FIGHTS

LIGHT HEAVYWEIGHTS

Sept 26	**Bob Foster** *KO* 14 Chris Finnegan, London

MIDDLEWEIGHTS

Nov 11	**Carlos Monzon** *W* 15 Bennie Briscoe, Buenos Aires

JUNIOR MIDDLEWEIGHTS

Oct 21	**Koichi Wajima** *KO* 3 Matt Donovan, Tokyo

WELTERWEIGHTS

Dec 8	**Hedgemon Lewis** *W* 15 Billy Backus, Syracuse

JUNIOR WELTERWEIGHTS

Oct 28	**Antonio Cervantes** (COL) *KO* 10 Alfonzo Frazer, Panama City
Dec 2	**Bruno Arcari** *W* 15 Everaldo Costa Azevedo, Turin, Italy

LIGHTWEIGHTS

Sept 15	**Chango Carmona** (MEX) *KO* 5 Mando Ramos, Los Angeles
Nov 10	**Rodolfo Gonzalez** (MEX) *KO* 13 Chango Carmona, Los Angeles

JUNIOR LIGHTWEIGHTS

Sept 15	**Ricardo Arredondo** *KO* 12 Susumu Okabe, Tokyo
Sept 25	**Ben Villaflor** *D* 15 Victor Echegaray, Honolulu

FEATHERWEIGHTS

Dec 2	**Ernesto Marcel** *KO* 6 Enrique Garcia, Panama City
Dec 16	**Jose Legra** *KO* 10 Clemente Sanchez, Monterrey

FLYWEIGHTS

Sept 29	**Venice Borkorsor** (THA) *KO* 10 Betulio Gonzalez, Bangkok

JANUARY

1973

APRIL

A CHAMPION DIES YOUNG

WBA flyweight champion Masao Ohba began the year in stunning style, scoring a 12th-round knockout of former two-time titlist Chartchai Chionoi. Three weeks later, he was dead.

On the morning of January 24, Ohba was driving from a friend's house to a gym in Tokyo when his car crossed a highway divider and collided head-on with a truck. He died instantly.

Tall for a 112-pounder (5'5 1/2"), Ohba frustrated opponents with a persistent jab and strong boxing skills. He turned pro at age 17, and, in October 1970, won the title by stopping Berkrerk Chartvanchai in his hometown of Tokyo. Five successful defenses followed (vs. Betulio Gonzalez, Fernando Cabanela, Susumu Hanagata, Orlando Amores, and Chionoi). The champion's career mark: 35-2-1 (15). Ohba was 23.

BRINGING IT BACK TO MEXICO

How dare a Panamanian win the world bantamweight title! Didn't Enrique Pinder know the crown belonged in Mexico, where Jose Becerra, Ruben Olivares, Chucho Castillo, and Rafael Herrera had been among the recent titleholders?

Pinder took the crown in July 1972, when he outpointed Herrera. He paid for it at the start of 1973, when he was stripped of the WBC title for failing to defend against one Mexican, Rodolfo Martinez, and relieved of the WBA version in a defense against another, Romeo Anaya.

Anaya-Pinder came on January 20, at the Gymnasio Nuevo in Panama City. For the first two rounds, Pinder, a blown-up flyweight, boxed cautiously, as he had vs. Herrera. In the third, he gambled – and lost.

After the powerpunching Anaya scored a knockdown with a booming hook, Pinder rose and began trading. Moments later, another hook exploded against his jaw. He was counted out by referee Roberto Lopez at the 2:00 mark.

The title, or at least half of it, was back where it belonged.

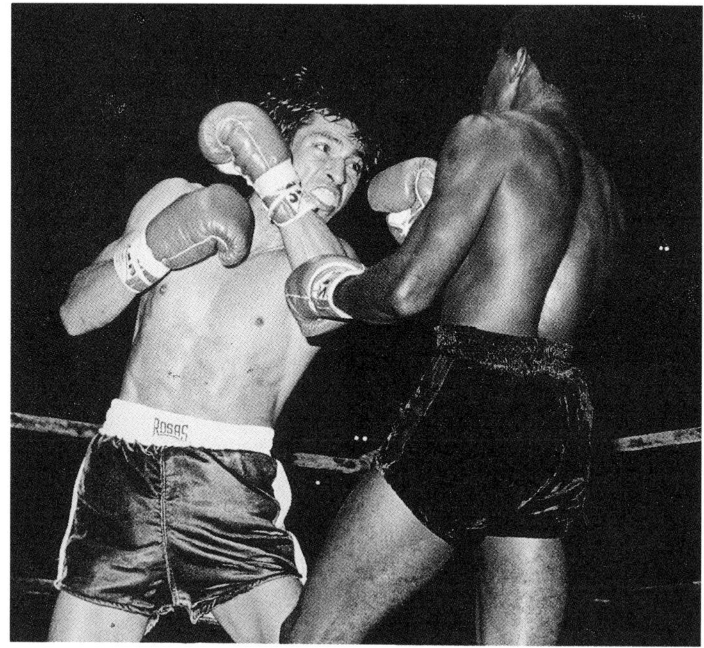

Mexico's murderous-punching Romeo Anaya (left) knocked out Panama's Enrique Pinder.

A STAREOUT, THEN A BLOWOUT

At the weigh-in for heavyweight champion Joe Frazier's defense against George Foreman, the unbeaten fighters engaged in an interminable and intense stareout.

The only words came from Frazier: "I'm gonna sit you on the ground, George." He sounded like he was trying to convince himself, not his opponent.

The showdown came on January 22, at the National Stadium in Kingston, Jamaica. In a beating that was as swift and savage as Dempsey-Willard or Louis-Schmeling II, Foreman, a 3-1 underdog, took the title by second-round knockout. He scored six knockdowns in 4½ minutes.

Frazier's confrontational style helped expedite the matter. In need of punching room, Big George repeatedly caught the champion coming in, or shoved him back before releasing his bludgeoning blows.

Smokin' Joe fell three times in the first round – one of Foreman's punches literally lifted him off the canvas – and three more times in the second. After knockdown number six, referee Arthur Mercante intervened at the 1:35 mark.

There was no stareout after the fight; Frazier couldn't focus.

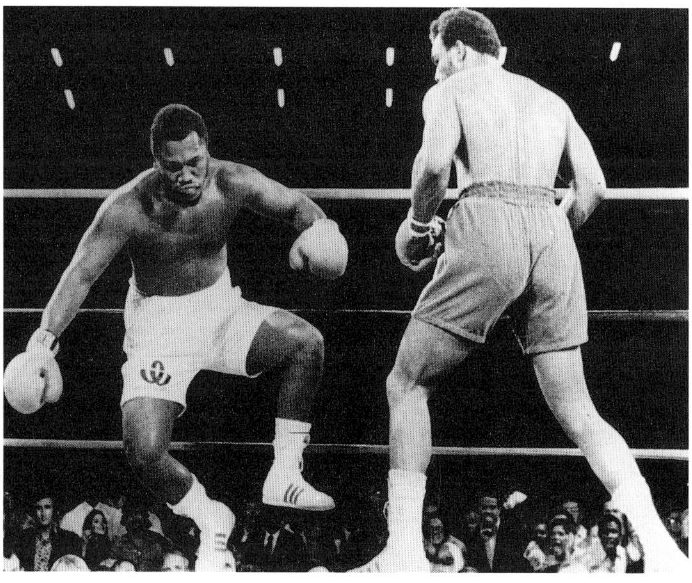

George Foreman (right) ripped Joe Frazier apart before knocking him out in second round.

FIGHTING TALK

I hit him with a punch, and there was a grin on his face, as if he was saying, 'Look, man, you're going to kill me'

GEORGE FOREMAN
after scoring a second-round knockout of Joe Frazier

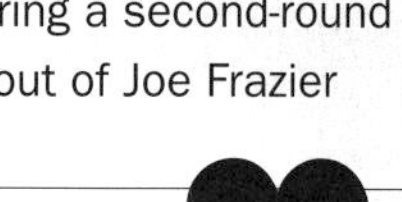

RINGSIDE VIEW

FEBRUARY

Middleweight champion Carlos Monzon is shot twice during a domestic squabble with his wife in Sante Fe, Argentina. He is struck in the right forearm and right shoulder blade, and undergoes two hours of surgery to remove the bullet from his upper arm.

MARCH

WBA junior welterweight champ Antonio Cervantes stops a badly faded Nicolino Locche in the 10th round.

THE BATTLE OF BROKEN JAW

The Punch, a right hand, came in the second round, with Muhammad Ali leaning against the ropes. When he returned to his corner, the former champion's handlers noted that his mouthpiece was covered with blood. Ken Norton had broken Ali's jaw.

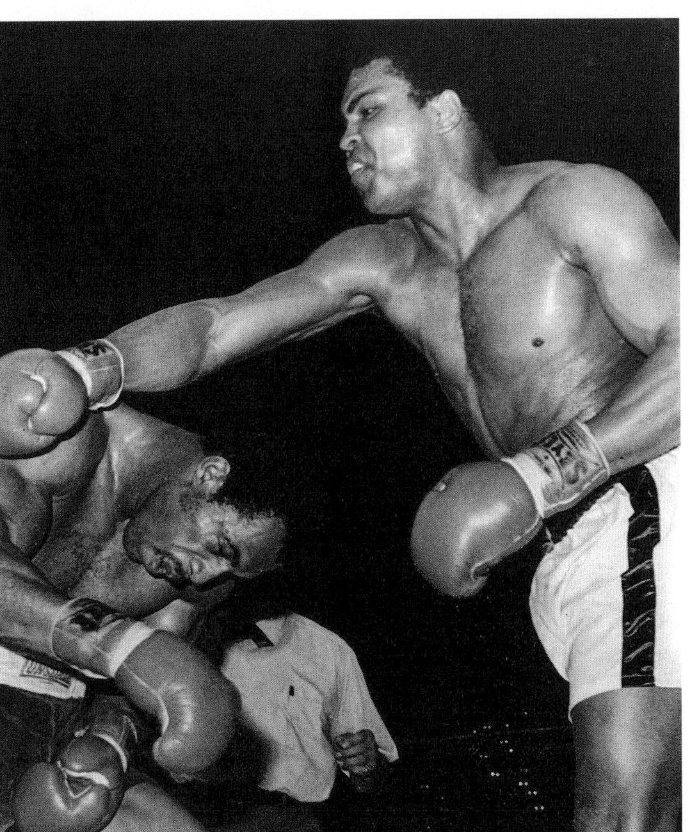

Ken Norton (left) handed Ali his second career defeat, winning a 12-round decision.

"It was a clean break," said Dr. William Lundeen, who would later operate on Ali. "All the way through."

Ali, a 5-1 favorite, met the underpublicized Norton on March 31, at the Sports Arena in San Diego. After The Punch, the fighters fought fiercely, with Ali managing to overcome excruciating pain. Following master trainer Eddie Futch's perfect fight plan, Norton jabbed with Ali, backed him into corners, and then drove both hands to the body. Ali answered with enough quick and sudden flurries to force Norton on the defensive occasionally and to keep the fight close.

As would be the case in each of their three bouts, the last round would determine the winner. Norton swarmed in the 12th, and was rewarded with a split decision (scores of 7-4, 5-4, and 6-5).

Ali, Joe Frazier, and world champion George Foreman had a new playmate among the title-contending heavyweights.

THE FIGHT MEXICO COULDN'T LOSE

Given Mexico's ongoing domination of the bantamweight division, it came as no surprise when the WBC chose a pair of south-of-the-border sluggers, former world champion Rafael Herrera and powerful contender Rodolfo Martinez, to meet for the vacant crown. Two years earlier, Herrera had issued Martinez his only defeat. On April 15, at the Plaza Monumental, they met again.

It was a wild fight, with Herrera's superior skills ultimately proving the difference. Herrera seemed en route to an easy victory when he twice floored Martinez in the fourth round. But the slugger rebounded to score his own knockdown in the eighth. Then Herrera regained control, dropping his foe twice in the 11th, and stopping him in the 12th.

Herrera was a world champion again. But his series with Martinez wasn't over yet.

Rafael Herrera (left) stopped Rodolfo Martinez to win the vacant WBC bantamweight title.

WORLD TITLE FIGHTS

HEAVYWEIGHTS

Jan 22	**George Foreman** (USA) *KO* 2 Joe Frazier, Kingston

JUNIOR MIDDLEWEIGHTS

Jan 9	**Koichi Wajima** *D* 15 Miguel de Oliveira, Tokyo
April 19	**Koichi Wajima** *W* 15 Ryu Sorimachi, Osaka

WELTERWEIGHTS

Feb 28	**Jose Napoles** *KO* 7 Ernie Lopez, Inglewood

JUNIOR WELTERWEIGHTS

Feb 16	**Antonio Cervantes** *W* 15 Josua Marquez, San Juan
March 17	**Antonio Cervantes** *KO* 10 Nicolino Locche, Maracay

LIGHTWEIGHTS

Jan 20	**Roberto Duran** *KO* 5 Jimmy Robertson, Panama City
March 17	**Rodolfo Gonzalez** *KO* 9 Ruben Navarro, Los Angeles

JUNIOR LIGHTWEIGHTS

March 6	**Ricardo Arredondo** *W* 15 Apollo Yoshio, Fukuoka City, Japan
March 12	**Kuniaki Shibata** *W* 15 Ben Villaflor, Honolulu

BANTAMWEIGHTS

Jan 20	**Romeo Anaya** (MEX) *KO* 3 Enrique Pinder, Panama City
April 15	**Rafael Herrera** *KO* 12 Rodolfo Martinez, Monterrey (Wins Vacant WBC Title)
April 28	**Romeo Anaya** *W* 15 Rogelio Lara, Inglewood

FLYWEIGHTS

Jan 2	**Masao Ohba** *KO* 12 Chartchai Chionoi, Tokyo
Feb 9	**Venice Borkorsor** *W* 15 Erbito Salavarria, Bangkok

MAY

1973

AUGUST

GOOD ENOUGH TO BE BORED

Middleweight champion Carlos Monzon never seemed to impress his opponents, but always managed to beat them. The Argentine hadn't lost in nine years. In fact, he was winning so often that boredom had become his most threatening foe.

On June 2, the champion made defense number eight at Louis II Stadium in Monte Carlo. His opponent was former titlist Emile Griffith, whom Monzon had stopped in September 1971. The first sign of Monzon's lack of commitment: in order to make weight, he needed to complete three unscheduled miles of roadwork. The second sign: after 10 rounds, he trailed on points.

Down the stretch, the challenger, 35, began to act his age. Monzon took control, and his rally was enough to salvage a close but unanimous decision (two scores of 147-143, and 147-145).

"I am not really sure that I will fight again," said Monzon, sounding very much like he hoped someone would give him an excuse to continue.

RINGSIDE VIEW

JUNE

Lightweight champion Roberto Duran keeps the crown for the second time, crushing the talented Hector Thompson in the eighth round.

THE GREATEST COMEBACK OF ALL?

If there were doubts concerning the greatness of Eder Jofre, the Brazilian erased them on May 5, when he won the WBC featherweight title eight years after losing the world bantamweight crown. Jofre unseated Spain's Jose Legra, who, at 30, held a seven-year age advantage. But at the end, it was Jofre who was chasing, and Legra who was running.

In 1966, after losing for the second time to Fighting Harada, Jofre retired. His return came three years later, and before challenging Legra at the Municipal Stadium in Brasilia, he registered 15 consecutive wins.

Legra predicted an early kayo, and at the bell ending the third, he left Jofre reeling along the ropes. Before the start of the fourth, the champion turned to the crowd and cockily gave the thumbs-down sign. But Jofre surprised him by attacking, and Legra danced away from then on.

Legra thought his jabs were enough to keep the title. It was Jofre, however, who was rewarded with a majority 15-round decision (146-141, 148-143, and 143-143), as well as a piece of history.

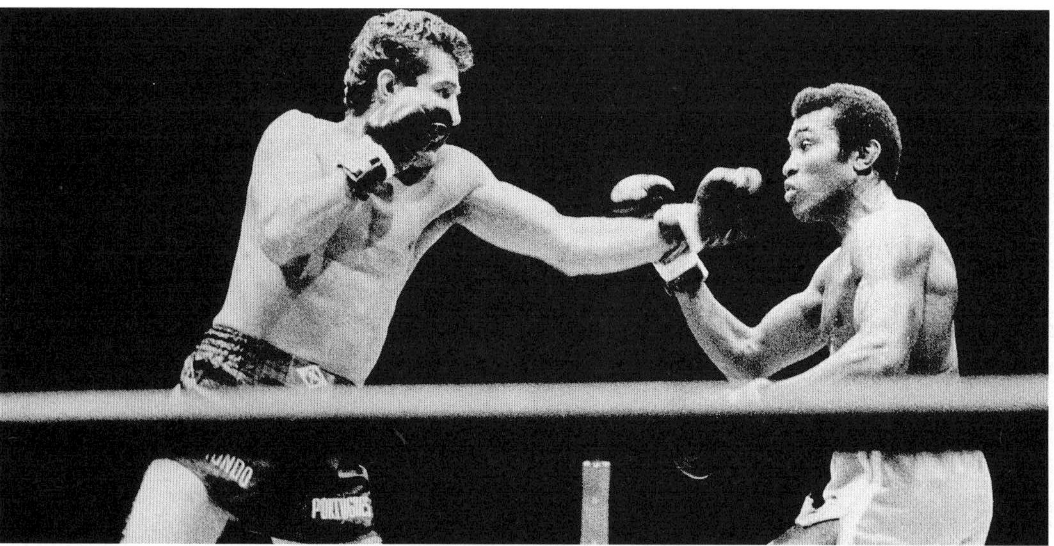

Remarkable 37-year-old Eder Jofre (left), former bantamweight king, outpointed Jose Legra in 15 rounds to capture world featherweight crown.

THE VANILLA ICE CREAM DIET

"What else is left?"

Jose Napoles had just retained the world welterweight title by easily outpointing France's rugged Roger Menetrey. He meant the question to be rhetorical, but his manager, Cuco Conde, needed an answer. As Conde saw it, there was only one viable option: a diet of ice cream, and a jump to middleweight. After all, world 160-pound champion Carlos Monzon was looking down almost as intently as Napoles was looking up.

Said Conde, "We've been trying for the match for two years."

That Napoles needed fresh competition was evident in the Menetrey fight, held on June 23, at the Palais des Sports in Grenoble. "Mantequilla" repeatedly punched first with short and accurate powerpunches, and by the later rounds, the Frenchman was a bloody mess. He refused to fall, however, and Napoles was forced to settle for a one-sided unanimous decision (scores of 149-139, 150-137, and 150-134).

Vanilla, chocolate, or strawberry?

Welterweight king Jose Napoles (left) had to work hard to beat France's Roger Menetrey.

FIRE STILL BURNS IN THE SMOKE

Joe Frazier was through as a world-class heavyweight, at least according to the former champion's critics. Their argument: fighters with Smokin' Joe's style rarely extended their primes. Frazier's classic with Muhammad Ali, the thinking went, sapped him of much of his energy. The evidence was his devastating loss to George Foreman.

On July 2, Frazier fought for the first time since losing the title to Foreman. His opponent was England's Joe Bugner – and each and every one of those who doubted his future. After a slow start, the Mutt and Jeff pair – Frazier was 5'11", Bugner 6'5" – began to test each other. Bugner alternately boxed and slugged, and even staggered Frazier only seconds after rising from a 10th-round knockdown. But Frazier's action style suitably impressed referee and sole judge Harry Gibbs, who scored 59¼-58½ for the Philadelphian.

Frazier left the ring flashing an I-told-you-so smile. There was nothing he enjoyed more than a good fight, and he had a lot to look forward to in boxing's world heavyweight championship.

Joe Bugner uses the ropes to pull himself back to his feet after being dropped by former world heavyweight champion Joe Frazier.

WORLD TITLE FIGHTS

LIGHT HEAVYWEIGHTS

Aug 21 **Bob Foster** *W* 15 Pierre Fourie, Albuquerque

MIDDLEWEIGHTS

June 2 **Carlos Monzon** *W* 15 Emile Griffith, Monte Carlo

JUNIOR MIDDLEWEIGHTS

Aug 14 **Koichi Wajima** *KO* 13 Silvani Bertini, Sapporo

WELTERWEIGHTS

June 23 **Jose Napoles** *W* 15 Roger Menetrey, Grenoble

JUNIOR WELTERWEIGHTS

May 19 **Antonio Cervantes** *KO* 5 Alfonzo Frazer, Panama City

LIGHTWEIGHTS

June 2 **Roberto Duran** *KO* 8 Hector Thompson, Panama City

JUNIOR LIGHTWEIGHTS

June 19 **Kuniaki Shibata** *W* 15 Victor Echegaray, Tokyo

FEATHERWEIGHTS

May 5 **Eder Jofre** *W* 15 Jose Legra, Brasilia, Brazil

July 14 **Ernesto Marcel** *KO* 12 Antonio Gomez, Panama City

BANTAMWEIGHTS

Aug 18 **Romeo Anaya** *KO* 3 Enrique Pinder, Inglewood

FLYWEIGHTS

May 17 **Chartchai Chionoi** *KO* 5 Fritz Chervet, Bangkok (Wins Vacant WBA Title)

Aug 4 **Betulio Gonzalez** *W* 15 Miguel Canto, Maracaibo

FOURIE AND A FURIOUS FOSTER

For a veteran like light heavyweight champion Bob Foster, an insult, whether real or imagined, can provide the motivation for a prime performance.

Before his August 21 defense against the WBA's top-rated Pierre Fourie, fought at University Arena in Albuquerque, Foster thought he heard the South African issue a racial slur.

"He called me 'boy' at the weigh-in," the champion said after the fight. "I wanted to beat him, not knock him out. I didn't hit him with my best punches."

(Fourie claimed he had been misunderstood, and that he had said, "Tonight's the night, Bobby," and not "boy.")

Regardless, Foster controlled the bout with his seven-inch reach advantage. Fourie had won 31 straight bouts, but he couldn't find a way to work inside of Big Bob's jabs. After 15 rounds, Foster kept the title by lopsided scores of 148-120, 149-130, and 149-138.

Fourie joined Ray Anderson as the only challengers to have extended Foster the distance. Unless you believed Foster, who insisted that he had done the extending.

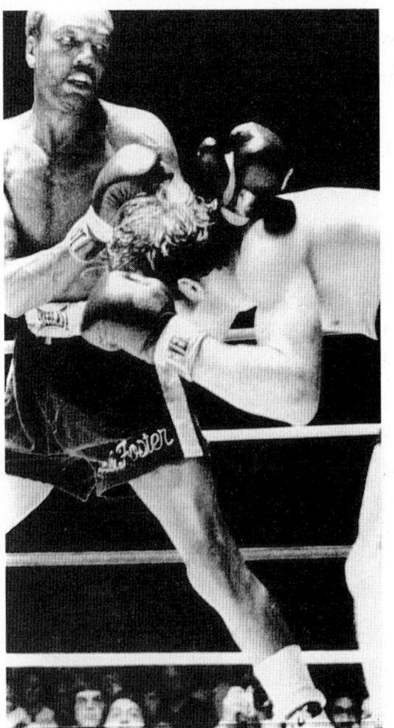

Foster (left) easily decisioned Pierre Fourie.

SEPTEMBER

1973

DECEMBER

BIG GEORGE'S ROMAN HOLIDAY

On September 1, at the Martial Arts Hall in Tokyo, George Foreman continued an age-old tradition: after a heavyweight champion is crowned, his first defense usually comes against an opponent about as dangerous as a storefront mannequin. In a division that boasted of Joe Frazier, Muhammad Ali, and Ken Norton, Puerto Rico's Joe Roman rated among the wannabes. In other words, he was perfect for Big George.

Heavyweight champion George Foreman looms menacingly over challenger Joe "King" Roman.

To no one's surprise, Japan's first heavyweight title fight lasted exactly two minutes.

"It was a 100 percent mismatch," said referee Jay Edson. "You might say it was a 150 percent mismatch."

Roman crashed thrice, and was counted out. His manager, Honest Bill Daly, screamed foul, claiming that Foreman had hit the challenger before Roman had risen from knockdown number two. No one really listened.

In The Land Of The Rising Sun, Foreman wasn't a threat to unseat Godzilla as the number-one box-office attraction. (Only 8,000 fans came to see him fight.) But the champion was 39-0, and in a one-on-one duel, Godzilla figured no better than even money.

RINGSIDE VIEW

SEPTEMBER

Lightweight champion Roberto Duran retains the crown by scoring a 10th-round TKO over Oriental titlist Ishimatsu (Guts) Suzuki.

ALI-NORTON II: NOT A WHISKER BETWEEN THEM

History would remember Muhammad Ali as a great heavyweight, and Ken Norton only as a very good one. When pitted against each other, however, they were as evenly matched as two fighters could be.

In March, Norton broke Ali's jaw en route to an upset decision victory. The rematch, held on September 10, at the Fabulous Forum in Inglewood, California, also went the distance. Again, the bout was decided by the final round.

Far more serious than usual, Ali controlled the first half of the fight by jabbing and dancing. But as soon as his movement stopped, Norton started. He matched Ali jab for jab, and scored with heavy body shots. Still, Ali rallied when he had to. Sharpshooting in round 12, he dominated the last three minutes, and won by split decision (scores of 7-5, 6-5, and 5-6).

"Norton is the best man I ever fought," he said.

He was still being serious.

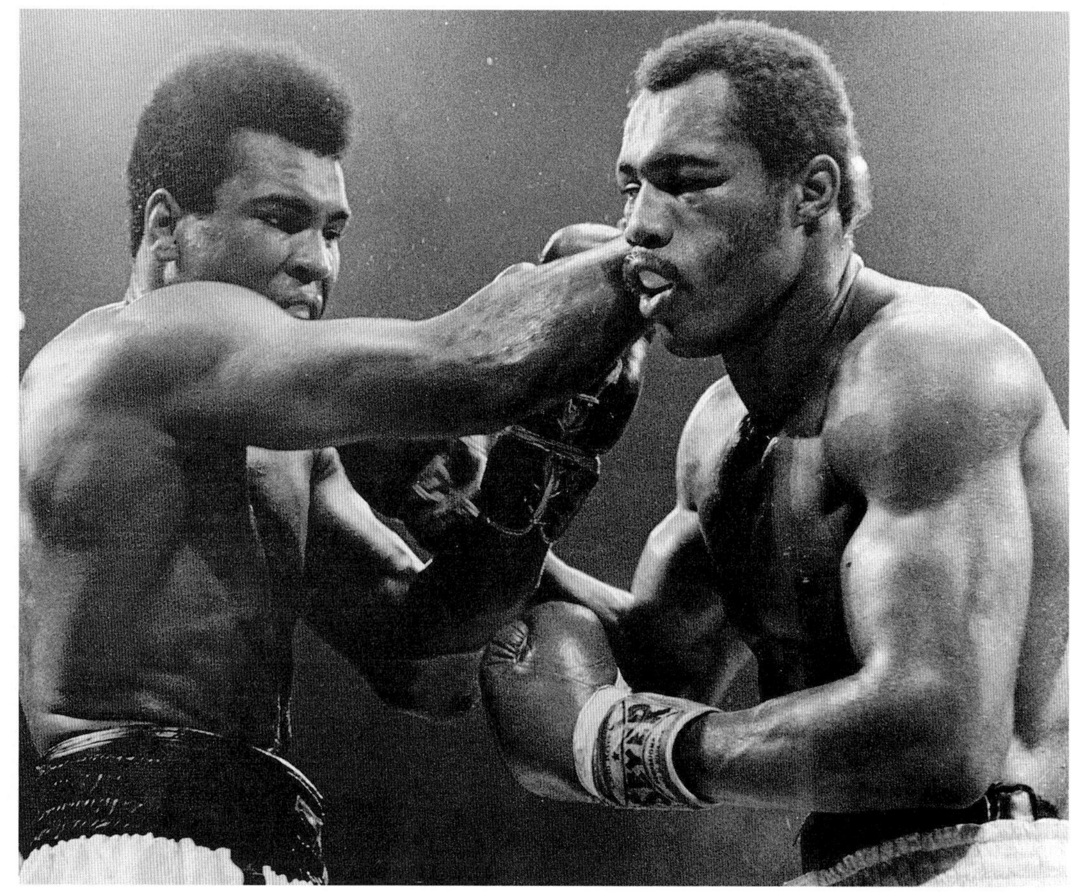

Muhammad Ali (left) avenged a previous loss to Ken Norton and regained the NABF heavyweight title by winning a 12-round decision.

THE BATTLE OF THE COMEBACKS

WBC featherweight champion Eder Jofre and former two-time king Vicente Saldivar had both managed to win the title after retiring from the ring. On October 21, at the Gymnasio Antonio Balbino in Salvador, Brazil, Saldivar staged his second comeback. It proved to be one too many.

Saldivar, 30, was seven years younger than the defending champion. After four rounds, however, he seemed about 10 years older. The first round was quiet, but in the second, Jofre forced the Mexican to the ropes and landed several body blows. The third featured a handful of toe-to-toe exchanges, most of which were punctuated by Jofre's sharper punches.

The end came suddenly in the fourth. A right to the solar plexus froze Saldivar, and a followup flurry dropped him. He was counted out at the 1:40 mark.

Jofre-Saldivar marked the end of the division's Seniors Tour. Saldivar would retire for good, and in June 1974, Jofre would be stripped for failing to defend the crown.

Eder Jofre (right) beat Vicente Saldivar.

WORLD TITLE FIGHTS

HEAVYWEIGHTS

Sept 1	**George Foreman** *KO* 1 Joe (King) Roman, Tokyo

LIGHT HEAVYWEIGHTS

Dec 1	**Bob Foster** *W* 15 Pierre Fourie, Johannesburg

MIDDLEWEIGHTS

Sept 29	**Carlos Monzon** *W* 15 Jean-Claude Bouttier, Paris

WELTERWEIGHTS

Sept 22	**Jose Napoles** *W* 15 Clyde Gray, Toronto

JUNIOR WELTERWEIGHTS

Sept 8	**Antonio Cervantes** *KO* 5 Carlos Giminez, Bogota
Nov 1	**Bruno Arcari** *KO* 5 Jorgen Hansen, Copenhagen
Dec 5	**Antonio Cervantes** *W* 15 Lion Furuyama, Panama City

LIGHTWEIGHTS

Sept 8	**Roberto Duran** *KO* 10 Ishimatsu Suzuki, Panama City
Oct 27	**Rodolfo Gonzalez** *KO* 11 Antonio Puddu, Los Angeles

JUNIOR LIGHTWEIGHTS

Sept 1	**Ricardo Arredondo** *KO* 6 Morito Kashiwaba, Tokyo
Oct 17	**Ben Villaflor** *KO* 1 Kuniaki Shibata, Honolulu

FEATHERWEIGHTS

Sept 8	**Ernesto Marcel** *KO* 9 Spider Nemoto, Panama City
Oct 21	**Eder Jofre** *KO* 4 Vicente Saldivar, Salvador, Brazil

BANTAMWEIGHTS

Oct 13	**Rafael Herrera** *W* 15 Venice Borkorsor, Inglewood
Nov 3	**Arnold Taylor** (SA) *KO* 14 Romeo Anaya, Johannesburg

FLYWEIGHTS

Oct 27	**Chartchai Chionoi** *W* 15 Susumu Hanagata, Bangkok
Nov 18	**Betulio Gonzalez** *KO* 11 Alberto Morales, Caracas

BOXING PUTS ON A BLACK AND WHITE SHOW

It isn't often that a boxing match transcends the ring, but on December 1, at Rand Stadium in Johannesburg, world light heavyweight champion Bob Foster and local challenger Pierre Fourie made history: their title fight was the first integrated bout ever held in South Africa.

(Interestingly, South African Minister of Sport Dr. Piet Koornhof refused to allow an undercard bout featuring Leroy Caldwell, who was black, and Mike Schutte, who was white.)

Upon arriving in South Africa, Foster was immediately embraced by Fourie's countrymen. More than 40,000 of them attended the fight – there was segregated seating – which turned out to be similar to Foster-Fourie I. The champion scaled seven pounds heavier than Fourie, and his sterling jab negated the South African's edge in quickness.

After 15 rounds that featured more clinching than punching, Foster was given a unanimous decision (scores of 103-99, 103-95, and 101-98). But for one night, at least, the outcome wasn't as significant as the fight.

A TAYLOR-MADE VICTORY

Some fighters make great stories. Others make great fights. Bantam weight Arnold Taylor made both.

On November 3, Taylor challenged WBA champion Romeo Anaya at Rand Stadium in Johannesburg. The South African turned pro in 1967, and by 1969, had been crowned national champion in three divisions. Still, he went through five managers, and was forced to moonlight as a baker in order to support his family.

Taylor-Anaya was described by veteran boxing scribe Chris Greyvenstein as "probably the most murderous and dramatic (fight) in South African history." There were six knockdowns, and countless shifts of momentum. Taylor, who scaled only 114, dropped the Mexican in round five, but seemed finished after falling three times in the eighth. He crashed again in the 10th, then staged a remarkable rally.

In the 14th, Taylor landed a right and felt a jolt of power up his arm. "He's gone!" he screamed to his corner. Indeed, Anaya fell hard, and remained on the canvas for two full minutes.

Arnold Taylor's celebration lasted a lot longer than that.

Arnold Taylor (right) stopped Romeo Anaya to become the new WBA bantamweight king.

JANUARY

1974

APRIL

Ringside View

FEBRUARY

WBA featherweight champion Ernesto Marcel makes his fourth defense, scoring a unanimous 15-round decision over a skinny 21-year-old Nicaraguan named Alexis Arguello. Three months later, Marcel retires from boxing.

DISAPPOINTING RERUN OF CLASSIC

Muhammad Ali-Joe Frazier II, held at Madison Square Garden on January 28, was an excellent fight. But in March 1971, "The Greatest" and Smokin' Joe had set new standards. Unlike their first showdown, the rematch failed to justify the hype.

The stakes were high; the winner would get a try at world champion George Foreman.

Ali and Frazier struggled for 12 rounds, but without an error by referee Tony Perez, the end might have come in the second. Only seconds after Ali hurt Frazier with a hook, Perez, thinking the bell had sounded, separated the fighters. When he realized his mistake – about 15 seconds remained – Ali's opportunity had passed.

Ali controlled the remainder of the bout by scoring with combinations and holding whenever Frazier moved inside. He repeatedly pushed down on Joe's neck, but was never penalized.

The scoring, 7-4-1, 8-4, and 6-5-1, was unanimous for Ali.

Said the winner, "I did a little dancing, a little slugging, a little boxing."

And a lot of clinching.

In long-awaited return match, Muhammad Ali (right) outpointed Joe Frazier.

MONZON BEATS TATTOO ON NAPOLES

Boxing's top four divisions were headed by dominant champions. On February 9, welterweight champion Jose Napoles proved that he couldn't compete with the world's best middleweight.

Napoles' long-awaited bout vs. 160-pound champ Carlos Monzon was held under a circus tent in a suburban Paris parking lot. The champions were greeted by trumpets and cymbals. Then Monzon pounded Napoles like a drum.

Capitalizing on his four-inch reach advantage, the Argentine refused to allow Napoles to get close. He controlled the first four rounds with his jab, then hammered the Cuban with extended flurries in both the fifth and sixth. At the start of the seventh, the challenger remained in his corner, claiming that he had been thumbed in the right eye.

"The fight was too easy," said Monzon. "I was hoping to have a good match."

Sorry, Carlos, not with a welterweight. Not even with the best in the world.

Middleweight Carlos Monzon (right) overwhelmed welterweight Jose Napoles in their title bout.

World Title Fights

HEAVYWEIGHTS

March 26 **George Foreman** *KO* 2
Ken Norton, Caracas

MIDDLEWEIGHTS

Feb 9 **Carlos Monzon** *KO* 7
Jose Napoles, Paris

JUNIOR MIDDLEWEIGHTS

Feb 5 **Koichi Wajima** *W* 15
Miguel de Oliveira, Tokyo

JUNIOR WELTERWEIGHTS

Feb 16 **Bruno Arcari** *W Disq* 8
Tony Ortiz, Turin, Italy

March 20 **Antonio Cervantes** *KO* 6
Chang Kil Lee, Cartagena

LIGHTWEIGHTS

March 16 **Roberto Duran** *KO* 11
Esteban DeJesus, Panama City

April 11 **Ishimatsu Suzuki** *KO* 9
Rodolfo Gonzalez, Tokyo

JUNIOR LIGHTWEIGHTS

Feb 28 **Kuniaki Shibata** *W* 15
Ricardo Arredondo, Tokyo

March 14 **Ben Villaflor** *D* 15
Apollo Yoshio, Toyama, Japan

FEATHERWEIGHTS

Feb 16 **Ernesto Marcel** *W* 15
Alexis Arguello, Panama City

FLYWEIGHTS

April 27 **Chartchai Chionoi** *W* 15
Fritz Chervet, Zurich

THE WORLD'S BEST LIGHTWEIGHTS, PART II

WBA lightweight champion Roberto Duran's only career loss had come in a November 1972 non-title bout vs. Esteban DeJesus. In that bout, DeJesus scored a knockdown with a left hook only 30 seconds into the first round. Duran never fully recovered.

The eagerly awaited title fight rematch was held on March 16, at the new Panama Gymnasium in Duran's native Panama City. This time, it took DeJesus 60 seconds before he struck. As the fighters traded toe to toe, the Puerto Rican gunned a long hook, and Duran dropped.

The champion rebounded quickly, however, and then wore down DeJesus. The fast pace, combined with the oppressive heat, drained the challenger, who had experienced difficulty making 135 pounds. (His manager, Gregorio Benitez, had repeatedly asked for postponements, but was denied.) Duran scored a knockdown in round seven, and felled his rival for the count in the 11th with a hook to the jaw and a straight right.

Duran could now unequivocally state that he was the best lightweight in the world. But one more date with DeJesus was yet to come.

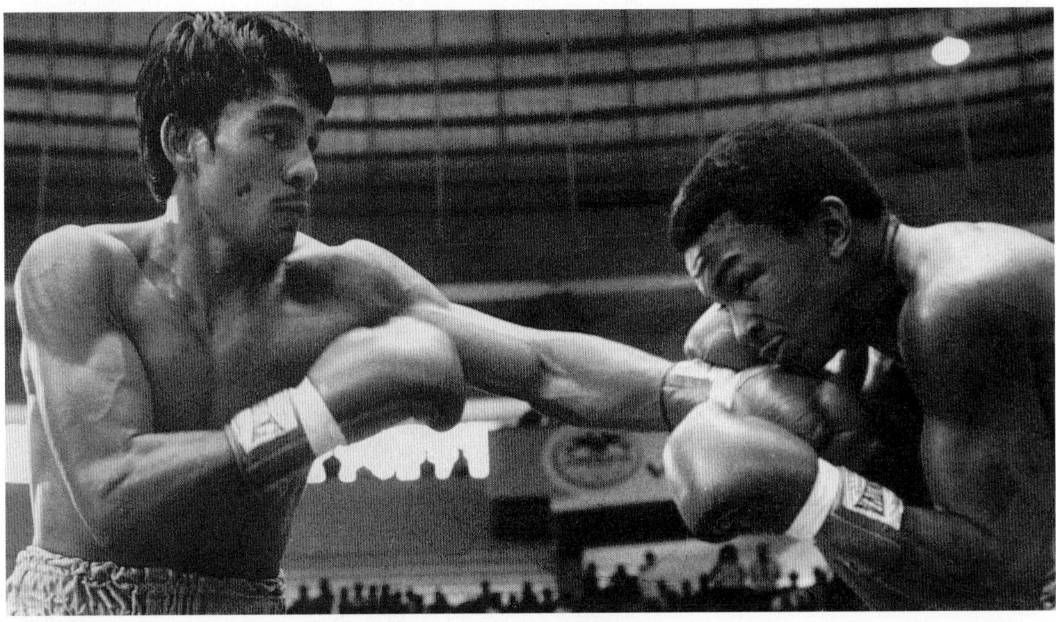

Avenging his only loss, Roberto Duran (left) stopped Esteban DeJesus in the 11th round to retain the world lightweight crown in Panama City.

RINGSIDE VIEW

APRIL

WBA flyweight champion Chartchai Chionoi retains the crown by scoring a split 15-round decision over Fritz Chervet. It is the Thai's 12th world title fight.

NORTON SUCCUMBS TO THE POWER OF SUGGESTION

In unforgettable bouts against some of his era's finest boxers, Ken Norton proved to be a championship-caliber heavyweight. But against the division's biggest punchers, he was little more than a willing target.

Norton's limitations were painfully evident in his first try at the world title, a March 26 challenge of George Foreman at the El Poliedro in Caracas, Venezuela.

As the fighters awaited the opening bell, the menacing champion stared down his foe. Norton wasn't initially intimidated – he boxed reasonably well in the first round – but as soon as he felt Foreman's exceptional power, he folded. Referee Jimmy Rondeau issued two standing eight-counts in the second, and then stopped the bout after Norton suffered a knockdown. The challenger regained his feet as chief cornerman Bill Slayton was signalling his surrender.

"I would've stopped it anyway," said Rondeau.

Norton, who had twice extended Muhammad Ali, hadn't lasted six minutes against Foreman. Big George was 40-0, 25 years old, and seemingly invincible.

Seemingly.

George Foreman (right) knocked out ex-champ Ken Norton to retain the heavyweight title.

GUTS OF THE LIGHTWEIGHTS

The knockouts of heavyweights like George Foreman and Joe Frazier made the loudest noises. Pound for pound, however, the lightweight division contained the hardest hitters in the game. WBA champion Roberto Duran and archrival Esteban DeJesus were the best-known 135-pound knockout artists. But WBC champion Rodolfo Gonzalez (49 kayos in 59 wins) and perennial contender Ishimatsu (Guts) Suzuki were equally dangerous.

On April 11, at Nihon University Auditorium in Tokyo, Gonzalez and Suzuki engaged in a title fight shootout. Predictably, the bout didn't last the distance. It was even on the cards after seven rounds, but in the eighth, Suzuki exploded. Three knockdowns later, he was a world champion.

"I started using my secret weapon – my phantom right," he explained. That right had sure seemed real to Gonzalez.

MAY

1974

AUGUST

PULLING THE TRIGGER IN THE NICK OF TIME

It's happened only seven times in world title fight history: behind on points, a fighter pulls off a miracle with a last-round knockout.

On June 3, at Nihon University Auditorium in Tokyo, world junior middleweight champion Koichi "The Flame" Wajima made his seventh defense, meeting Texan Oscar "Shotgun" Albarado. Three years before, Harry Kabakoff, the challenger's manager, described his powerpunching protege as "a guy who can lose 9½ rounds and then pull out a fight with 18 seconds to go."

Against Wajima, Albarado proved Kabakoff prophetic. For 14 rounds, the 154-pounders traded furiously. With three minutes to go, Wajima led by scores of 67-65 (twice) and 66-67. But The Shotgun unloaded in the 15th. An unrelenting body attack set up three knockdowns, the last bringing referee Yusaku Yoshida's 10-count.

Wajima was counted out at the 1:54 mark. Had Albarado waited any longer, he would had to have scored the kayo at the postfight press conference.

RINGSIDE VIEW

JUNE

Former heavyweight champ Joe Frazier scores a fifth-round stoppage over Jerry Quarry at Madison Square Garden.

THE WAY TO FORCE A SHOWDOWN

Early in 1974, world middleweight champion Carlos Monzon was stripped by the WBC for failing to defend against Rodrigo Valdes. On May 25, at the Louis II Stadium in Monte Carlo, Valdes faced Philadelphia's Bennie Briscoe for the vacant crown. The result of that bout made Monzon look like one smart fighter.

In September 1973, Valdes had outpointed Briscoe in a battle for the North American title. Their rematch was a brutal war. The Colombian staggered his foe in the first round, but Briscoe continued to march forward. He cut Valdes over the left eye in the fourth, and was enjoying his best round in the seventh when the Colombian suddenly struck. A short right and a hook to the jaw dropped Briscoe for referee Harry Gibbs' full count.

(Oddly, Valdes was hospitalized afterward for what doctors diagnosed as "suppressed anxiety.")

By stopping a fighter who had twice extended Monzon to the distance, Valdes instantly elevated his reputation. Perhaps too much so for his own good: it would be two more years before he and Monzon would unify the title.

Colombia's Rodrigo Valdes knocked out Philadelphia's Bennie Briscoe in the seventh round.

A DRAW, AND THEN NO MORE

Once among the most feared punchers in boxing, light heavyweight champion Bob Foster hadn't scored a knockout in almost two years. On June 17, at University Arena in his hometown of Albuquerque, the 35-year-old deputy sherrif defended against Argentina's Jorge Ahumada. He barely kept the title.

The champion was sluggish from the start. Ahumada fought out of a crouch, and Foster's once-dominant jab was ineffective. As the rounds mounted, Ahumada began connecting with hooks. He lost a point for punching low in round 10, but seemed to have fought aggressively enough to take the crown.

However, he was denied by the judges: 148-143 Foster, 145-142 Ahumada, and 144-144.

It turned out to be Foster's last title fight. He would announce his retirement on September 16, officially ending his six-year reign.

Light heavyweight champion Bob Foster (down in 13th round) was lucky to retain the title.

Jose Napoles (left) easily stopped Hedgemon Lewis to retain the welterweight championship.

TAYLOR FINALLY GONGED BY HONG

At least Arnold Taylor was consistent: in winning the WBA bantamweight title from Romeo Anaya, the South African suffered four knockdowns. On July 3, he made his first defense, squaring off against South Korea's Soo Hwan Hong at the West Ridge Park Tennis Stadium in Durban, South Africa. Taylor again fell four times. But there was one big difference: this time, he failed to score any knockdowns of his own.

Both banties struggled to make weight. Hong dominated the first 10 rounds by bobbing and weaving, and scoring with left hooks and right uppercuts. He floored Taylor in the first and fifth, and often dropped his hands and dared the champion to hit him.

In a gutty effort to retain the crown, Taylor attacked throughout the championship rounds. Hong hung in, however, and added knockdowns in rounds 14 and 15 en route to scoring a unanimous decision victory.

Arnold Taylor's unlikely run had been a brief one. But in just two fights, there had been enough thrills and spills for a lifetime.

RINGSIDE VIEW

AUGUST

Fighting for the first time since suffering a kayo loss to Carlos Monzon, 34-year-old world welterweight champion Jose Napoles stops Hedgemon Lewis in the ninth round.

WORLD TITLE FIGHTS

LIGHT HEAVYWEIGHTS

July 17 **Bob Foster** *D* 15 Jorge Ahumada, Albuquerque

MIDDLEWEIGHTS

May 25 **Rodrigo Valdes** (COL) *KO* 7 Bennie Briscoe, Monte Carlo (Wins Vacant WBC Title)

JUNIOR MIDDLEWEIGHTS

June 3 **Oscar Albarado** (USA) *KO* 15 Koichi Wajima, Tokyo

WELTERWEIGHTS

Aug 3 **Jose Napoles** *KO* 9 Hedgemon Lewis, Mexico City

JUNIOR WELTERWEIGHTS

July 28 **Antonio Cervantes** *KO* 2 Victor Ortiz, Cartagena

JUNIOR LIGHTWEIGHTS

June 27 **Kuniaki Shibata** *W* 15 Antonio Amaya, Tokyo

Aug 3 **Kuniaki Shibata** *KO* 15 Ramiro Bolanos, Tokyo

Aug 24 **Ben Villaflor** *KO* 2 Yasutsune Uehara, Honolulu

FEATHERWEIGHTS

July 9 **Ruben Olivares** *KO* 7 Zensuke Utagawa, Inglewood (Wins Vacant WBA Title)

BANTAMWEIGHTS

May 25 **Rafael Herrera** *KO* 6 Romeo Anaya, Mexico City

July 3 **Soo Hwan Hong** (KOR) *W* 15 Arnold Taylor, Durban

FLYWEIGHTS

July 20 **Betulio Gonzalez** *KO* 10 Franco Udella, Lignano Sabbiadoro, Italy

ROCKABYE RUBEN GOES FOR SECOND TITLE

Ruben Olivares' prime figured to be brief. The Mexican often confused training with partying, and lived from fight to fight. When "Rockabye Ruben" lost the bantamweight title in March 1972, even his most loyal supporters figured his championship days were over. But there were nights of glory still to come.

After the retirement of WBA featherweight champion Ernesto Marcel, Olivares, 27, was matched with Japan's top-rated Zensuke Utagawa. They met on July 9, at the Inglewood Forum.

In training, Utagawa had shown a world-class jab. That punch was missing on fight night, however, and Olivares, a 4-1 favorite, landed powerpunches as he pleased. He softened the Oriental champion with rights to the body, and then, in round seven, sought the finish. Utagawa was downed three times. After his third fall, Ruben's arm was raised in victory.

The merry Mexican was back, and for the fans of Southern California, that familiar gap-toothed smile was a most welcomed sight.

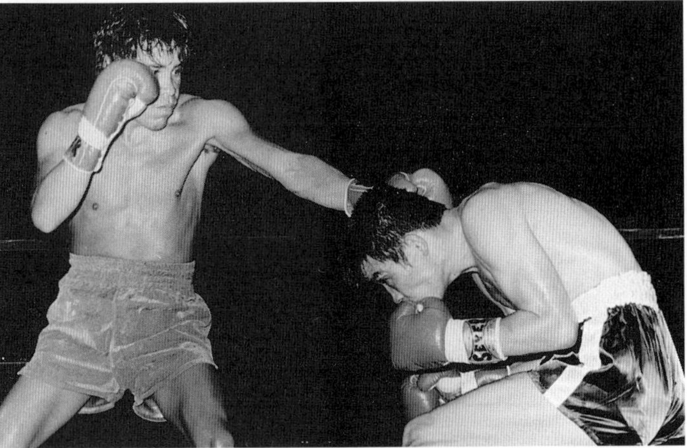

Ruben Olivares (left) won the WBA championship by knocking out tough Zensuke Utagawa.

FIGHTING TALK

I will fight George Foreman if the money is right

RUBEN OLIVARES
after winning the WBA featherweight title with a kayo of Zensuke Utagawa

SEPTEMBER

1974

DECEMBER

THE "PUNK KID" BECOMES A CHAMP

Before meeting Bobby Chacon for the vacant WBC featherweight title, Venezuela's Alfredo Marcano said, "I have fought men. I look at Chacon as a punk kid. He's never fought anybody."

Marcano, of course, was badly mistaken. The 22-year-old Chacon was a kid alright, but he had faced the legendary Ruben Olivares, as well as hot prospect Danny Lopez, who was 23-0 (22) at the time. Those experiences served him well.

The bout came on September 7, at the Olympic Auditorium in Los Angeles. Chacon, a 7-5 underdog, boxed for the first five rounds, scoring with lead rights and wisely resisting the temptation to slug toe to toe. In the sixth, however, Marcano began to zero in. He continued his rally in the seventh, but then Chacon exploded. A cross staggered Marcano, and a right uppercut felled him. After he rose, referee Ray Solis elected to stop the fight.

At least Chacon could say he fought – and knocked out – Alfredo Marcano.

RINGSIDE VIEW

OCTOBER

WBA middleweight champion Carlos Monzon continues to dominate, stopping Tony Mundine in his 10th defense.

CONTEH FACES AHUMADA – AND DUCKS MUM

After world light heavyweight champion Bob Foster announced his retirement, the WBC chose his most recent foe, Argentina's Jorge Ahumada, to battle Liverpudlian John Conteh for the vacant crown.

The bout was the biggest of Conteh's life. If further motivation was needed, it was provided by his mother, who warned, "I'll slug him if he loses."

Ahumada proved tough, though perhaps not as tough as Mrs. Conteh. The veteran offered the bigger blows, but Conteh's punches were sharper, and by the middle rounds, he closed the Argentine's left eye.

The bout remained close until the final three rounds, when Conteh assumed complete command. At the sound of the final bell, referee and sole judge Harry Gibbs raised the handsome Englishman's hand and declared him the winner by a score of 147-142.

"Before the fight," said Ahumada's manager, Gil Clancy, "I heard Conteh couldn't take it on the chin, and that he didn't have heart. I heard wrong."

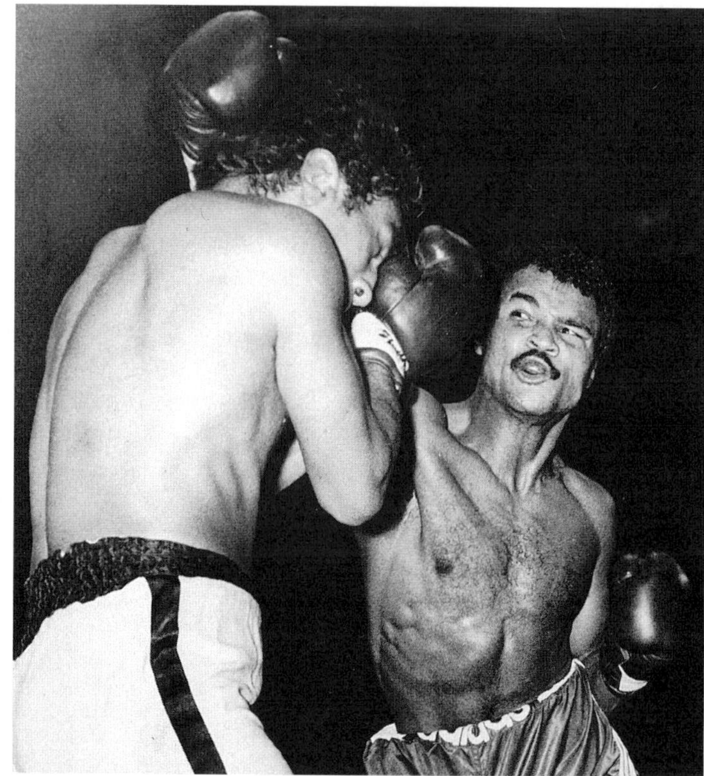

Britain's dynamic John Conteh (right) forces Argentina's Jorge Ahumada on the defensive.

"ALI BOMAYE, ALI BOMAYE!"

After losing the world heavyweight title to Muhammad Ali, George Foreman offered several familiar excuses, and invented some new ones: he had been drugged; excessive weight loss had left him weak; the ropes had been loosened by Ali's handlers; his corner had been overconfident; referee Zack Clayton had issued him a fast count; the canvas had been too slow; the ring had been positioned on a slant.

Foreman left out only one excuse: he had been outfought.

On October 30, in the predawn hours at Stade du Mai in Kinshasa, Zaire, Ali became only the second heavyweight to regain the title. A 7-1 underdog, he upset Big George in an unlikely way: by letting the powerpuncher punch.

Introducing the Rope-a-Dope, Ali stood flatfooted and covered up as Foreman emptied his guns. By the eighth, the champion was exhausted, and the crowd of almost 60,000 was screaming "Ali bomaye!" (Ali kill him!) When "The Greatest" countered with a left and a chopping right, Foreman collapsed. He was counted out with two seconds remaining in the round.

The invincible George Foreman was 41-1. At least he could say that it took a Muhammad Ali to beat him.

Muhammad Ali knocks out undefeated George Foreman in the eighth round to regain the title.

TWO LEGENDS COLLIDE AT THE CROSSROADS

WBA featherweight champion Ruben Olivares was a legend whose prime had recently passed. Nicaraguan challenger Alexis Arguello was a legend in the making. On November 23, at the Inglewood Forum, their paths crossed. Tomorrow knocked out Yesterday in the 13th round.

Defending the title for the first time, Olivares opened cautiously and gave away the first five rounds. As soon as he launched an offensive, however, he gained control. Happily trading with the 5'10" challenger and raking his ribs with hooks, "Rockabye Ruben" seemed en route to win.

"He hurt me in the eighth, ninth, and 10th," Arguello said.

After 12 rounds, Olivares led on points by scores of 8-3, 6-4, and 5-5. But in the 13th, the fighters landed simultaneous lefts, and the champion fell hard. He picked himself up, only to absorb Arguello's followup flurry. After knockdown number two, referee Dick Young counted to 10.

Olivares would be a champion again. But his loss to Arguello was as sure a sign of the passing of time as graying temples and arthritis.

Alexis Arguello (right) scored a startling upset by knocking out Ruben Olivares in the 13th.

RINGSIDE VIEW

DECEMBER

Mexico's Rodolfo Martinez wins the WBC bantamweight title by kayoing countryman and arch-rival Rafael Herrera in the fourth.

DECEMBER

Roberto Duran retains the WBA lightweight crown for the fifth time, crushing Japan's Masataka Takayama at 1:40 of the first.

MOVE OVER, MISTER MONZON

Since the start of the decade, Argentina had flaunted the world's best middleweight, Carlos Monzon. On December 7, Victor Galindez offered his countryman some company.

The 26-year-old Galindez, unbeaten since 1971, was matched with American Len "Stinger" Hutchins at Luna Park in Buenos Aires. The stakes: the vacant WBA light heavyweight title.

Surprisingly, it wasn't much of a contest. The stocky, 5'10" Argentine countered off the ropes with his overhand blows and won almost every round. Hutchins was floored in the first and fourth, pushed to the canvas in the eighth, and issued a standing-eight count by referee Jesus Celis in the 12th. Galindez' only scare was a cut over his right eye, opened by a butt in round four.

Hutchins was unable to answer the bell for the 13th. He subsequently collapsed in his dressing room and spent the night in a local hospital. (He was released the next day.)

Victor Galindez (right) stopped Len Hutchins to win the vacant light heavyweight title.

WORLD TITLE FIGHTS

HEAVYWEIGHTS

Oct 30	**Muhammad Ali** *KO* 8 George Foreman, Kinshasa, Zaire

LIGHT HEAVYWEIGHTS

Oct 1	**John Conteh** (ENG) *ref* 15 Jorge Ahumada, London (Wins Vacant WBC Title)
Dec 7	**Victor Galindez** (ARG) *KO* 13 Len Hutchins, Buenos Aires (Wins Vacant WBA Title)

MIDDLEWEIGHTS

Oct 5	**Carlos Monzon** *KO* 7 Tony Mundine, Buenos Aires
Nov 13	**Rodrigo Valdes** *KO* 11 Gratien Tonna, Paris

JUNIOR MIDDLEWEIGHTS

Oct 8	**Oscar Albarado** *KO* 7 Ryu Sorimachi, Tokyo

WELTERWEIGHTS

Dec 14	**Jose Napoles** *KO* 3 Horacio Saldano, Mexico City

JUNIOR WELTERWEIGHTS

Sept 21	**Perico Fernandez** (SPA) *W* 15 Lion Furuyama, Rome (Wins Vacant WBC Title)
Oct 26	**Antonio Cervantes** *KO* 8 Shinchi Kadoto, Tokyo

LIGHTWEIGHTS

Sept 12	**Ishimatsu Suzuki** *D* 15 Tury Pineda, Nagoya
Nov 28	**Ishimatsu Suzuki** *KO* 13 Rodolfo Gonzalez, Osaka
Dec 21	**Roberto Duran** *KO* 1 Masataka Takayama, San Jose, Costa Rica

FEATHERWEIGHTS

Sept 7	**Bobby Chacon** (USA) *KO* 9 Alfredo Marcano, Los Angeles
Nov 23	**Alexis Arguello** (NIC) *KO* 13 Ruben Olivares, Inglewood

BANTAMWEIGHTS

Dec 7	**Rodolfo Martinez** (MEX) *KO* 4 Rafael Herrera, Yucatan
Dec 28	**Soo Hwan Hong** *W* 15 Fernando Cabanela, Seoul

FLYWEIGHTS

Oct 1	**Shoji Oguma** *W* 15 Betulio Gonzalez, Tokyo
Oct 18	**Susumu Hanagata** (JAP) *KO* 6 Chartchai Chionoi, Yokohama

Roberto Duran

THE ROSTER of the sweet science is comprised of boxers and punchers, and boxer-punchers, so designated because they usually can't do much of either. History has also speckled the game with a handful of what are best called fighters. They are pure and simple; in a different time, they would have been warriors or gladiators. They not only derive joy from the danger of combat and the thrill of victory, but live for them.

When moving his feet and pumping his fists inside a boxing ring, Roberto Duran was the very definition of a fighter. He would have preferred fighting without gloves; he had no respect for his opponents or the rules; and he sneered at displays of sportsmanship.

"He's got them eyes," said Freddie Brown, who, along with Ray Arcel, co-trained Duran for most of his career. "Like an animal. Like he wants to kill you. No matter who fights him, they gotta fear him."

The aura that helped make Duran a four-division world champion and the consensus choice as the greatest lightweight of all-time was pervasive. When asked how he might fare in a streetfight against then-heavyweight champion Muhammad Ali, Duran answered unhesitatingly, "I beat the shit out of him."

Roberto Carlos Duran was born on June 16, 1951, in the Chorrillo section of Panama, the second of nine children born to Clara and Osvaldo Duran. Clara was Panamanian and Osvaldo was Mexican. When Duran was four, the family moved to Guarare, 150 miles from Panama City, but shortly returned to the poverty of Chorrillo.

As a boy, Duran hustled small change by shining shoes, dancing on streetcorners, and catching fish. He stole when he was hungry, and once got caught lifting coconuts from the estate of millionaire industrialist Carlos Eleta. In the type of story that could happen only in boxing, Eleta would become Duran's manager.

Duran dropped out of school at age 14. Two years later, Sammy Medina, a former national champion, brought him to a boxing gym. Duran was raw but eager, and no one ever had to help him develop a killer instinct. He won 13 of 16 amateur fights, and, on March 8, 1967, turned pro in Colon, Panama, scoring a four-round decision over Carlos Mendoza. He was 15 years old.

Professional career dates 1967-present
Contests 96
Won 87
Lost 9
Drawn 0
Knockouts 61
World Lightweight Champion 1972-1979
World Welterweight Champion 1980
World Junior Middleweight Champion 1983-84
World Middleweight Champion 1989

The first half of Duran's 25-year career was marked by one of the most dominant title reigns in history, and the second half by an uncanny ability to summon his skill and rediscover his desire after being dismissed.

The fighter was still a teenager when, on May 16, 1970, he stopped countryman and future world featherweight champion Ernesto Marcel in the 10th round. In September 1971, "Hands of Stone" established himself as a lightweight title threat when he crushed the respected Benny Huertas in 66 seconds. After he followed with wins over former 130-pound champion Hiroshi Kobayashi and Angel Robinson Garcia, he was ready to explode.

On June 26, 1972, Duran challenged WBA lightweight champion Ken Buchanan at Madison Square Garden. The stylish Scot had lost only once in 44 matches, but he had never faced anyone with the fiery style of Duran. The challenger swarmed from the start and scored a 13th-round TKO. (Unfortunately, the bout ended in controversy, with Buchanan writhing in pain after taking a knee in the groin. At the time of the stoppage, the challenger was well ahead on points.)

Duran kept the title for the next 6½ years, risking it 12 times, and, in his final defense, unifying it. For the most part, his competition was demanding. Hector Thompson (KO 8) and Ray Lampkin (KO 14) were outstanding 135-pounders; Ishimatsu (Guts) Suzuki was a future world champion; and Vilomar Fernandez and Edwin Viruet were among the finest defensive fighters of their era. Duran beat them all, chasing down the runners and quickly punching out the brawlers.

The highlight of his reign was his three-fight series with multitalented Puerto Rican Esteban DeJesus. Their first fight came five

Panama's Roberto Duran was only 16 years old when he made his professional debut in 1967. Five years later he was lightweight champion of the world. And so enormous was his popularity that one politician predicted, "Our champion could be elected president of Panama."

months after the Panamanian won the title. Lucky for Duran it was a non-title bout; DeJesus felled the champion with a left hook 30 seconds into round one and went on to win by clear-cut decision.

The title-fight rematch was held in Panama City on March 16, 1974. DeJesus again scored a first-round knockdown, but this time Duran recovered and subsequently issued a terrific beating. The end came in the 11th round.

The rubber match, held on January 21, 1978, in Las Vegas, unified the title. (De Jesus had won WBC honors by outpointing Suzuki in May 1976.) Again the Puerto Rican proved troublesome, and Duran was forced to rely on his oft-underrated technical skills. But his punches remained overwhelming, and DeJesus crashed in round 12.

Duran vacated the title on February 1, 1979, and soon jumped to welterweight. The division was packed with superstars: Wilfred Benitez, Pipino Cuevas, Carlos Palomino, Thomas Hearns, and Sugar Ray Leonard. After brilliantly outfighting Palomino, Duran faced unbeaten WBC champion Leonard in one of the most anticipated bouts ever.

On June 20, 1980, more than 46,000 fans came to Olympic Stadium to see the biggest fight of Duran's life. "The Brawl In Montreal" saw the fighters tearing into each other for 15 rounds, neither backing off or conceding a single punch. The bout was contested at close range, where Duran proved the master. He captured a tight but unanimous and well-received decision.

"I showed I could take a punch," said Leonard. "I didn't want to, but I had to." The rematch came on November 25. Leonard circled the ring this time, and he frustrated Duran by clowning and taunting him. The psychological warfare paid off in round eight, when Duran, only slightly behind on points, did the unthinkable: he quit by turning his back and uttering to referee Octavio Meyran, "No mas."

Perceived by many as a disgrace, the Panamanian nevertheless fought on. Trying yet another division, he jumped to junior middleweight and lost consecutive bouts to WBC champion Wilfred Benitez and Englishman Kirkland Laing. At age 31, he seemed finished. But Top Rank matchmaker Teddy Brenner gave him one more chance, and Duran delivered.

On January 29, 1983, Duran kayoed a faded Cuevas, which earned him a shot at WBA 154-pound champion Davey Moore.

Duran so impressed veteran trainer Ray Arcel (right) that the 73-year old Arcel was inspired to come out of long retirement. But the well-intended relationship was shattered when Duran quit in the 1980 bout with Sugar Ray Leonard.

The fight came on Duran's 32nd birthday, and a sellout crowd filled Madison Square Garden to see if the 5-2 underdog could win his third world title. He did so in spectacular fashion, pounding Moore from the start – the champion's right eye was closed by the third round – and stopping him in round eight.

"I was born again," Duran said. "I've returned to be Roberto Duran. It's been a long time." Duran next faced middleweight champion Marvin Hagler. He proved far more competitive than expected, extending the titlist the 15-round distance, but faded late and dropped a unanimous decision. Then, on June 15, 1984, disaster struck. Matched against co-champion Hearns, Duran suffered the first kayo of his career. A second-round right hand left him face-first on the canvas.

Duran didn't fight again for 18 months. Incredibly, there would be one more comeback. After losing to middleweight contender Robbie Sims, he strung together five modest triumphs. The winning streak earned him a crack at WBC 160-pound champion Iran Barkley.

Barkley-Duran came on February 24, 1989, in Atlantic City. "I knew he was gonna reach down," said Barkley. "This was his last hurrah."

In one of the most thrilling bouts of his career, Duran, 37, dropped "The Blade" in round 11 and went on to take a split 12-round decision. The legend had written his last chapter. On December 7, 1989, Duran fought without spirit in losing his rubber match to defending WBC super middleweight champion Leonard. He's appeared once since, suffering a sixth-round stoppage loss to clubfighter Pat Lawlor. (Duran surrendered after aggravating an injury to his left bicep.) His career mark: 85-9 (60).

When you are born to fight, what do you do after the last bell has sounded? Roberto Duran will likely spend the rest of his life trying to answer that very question.

Strikingly handsome and arrogantly confident, Roberto Duran (left) clowns with Britain's world lightweight champion Ken Buchanan during the press conference prior to the title fight which Duran won by stoppage.

JANUARY

1975

APRIL

RINGSIDE VIEW

MARCH

Unbeaten Mexican sensation Alfonso Zamora wins the WBA bantamweight title at age 21, scoring a fourth-round kayo of Soo Hwan Hong. Zamora advances his record to 21-0 (21).

AN INSULT, THEN A KISS

WBA lightweight champion Roberto Duran was particularly destructive during his March 2 defense against America's Ray Lampkin, held at the New Panama Gymnasium in Panama City. Lampkin jabbed strongly for half the bout, but the oppressive humidity, as well as Duran's relentless attack, wore him down.

Lampkin seemed reluctant to leave his corner at the start of round eight. At that point, Duran took control. He cut Lampkin over both eyes, and finished him with a thunderous hook in the 14th round.

As Lampkin crashed, his head hit the canvas. He was hospitalized at the Caja del Seguro Social Clinic, where he remained unconscious for some 30 minutes.

In a postfight television interview, Duran said "If I had been in normal shape...he would've gone to the morgue instead of the hospital." But later that day, he visited Lampkin and gave him a kiss on the cheek while the American was sleeping.

"Hands of Stone" didn't have a heart of stone after all.

Lightweight king Duran increased his reputation when he kayoed Ray Lampkin in 14th round.

A "TRIP" TO THE CANVAS

The news that Muhammad Ali had retained the heavyweight title by stopping Chuck Wepner was greeted by "So what?" But what had happened in the ninth round had been legitimate "Stop the presses!" material.

Ali-Wepner, the champion's first bout since his upset victory over George Foreman, took place on March 24, at the Coliseum in Richfield, Ohio. Ali scaled an unattractive 223½, and fought only in spurts. He desperately tried to stop "The Bayonne Bleeder," and finally did so when referee Tony Perez intervened with 19 seconds left in the 15th and final round.

But back to round nine. After Wepner tossed a long, sweeping right, Ali fell. Perez ruled a knockdown and issued a mandatory eight-count. Had the champion really been downed by a club-fighter from New Jersey? Officially, yes. But photos would reveal that as Ali leaned away from the punch, Wepner was stepping on his left foot. No matter. Wepner would be able to boast to his grandchildren that he had knocked down Muhammad Ali. And with a straight face, too.

Veteran Chuck Wepner (right) became a hero when he survived until midway in the 15th round against champion Muhammad Ali.

BEER, BUTTER, AND BLOOD

Making the ninth defense of his second reign as world welterweight champion, Jose (Mantequilla) Napoles was not quite as smooth as butter. The Cuban was matched with Armando Muniz, a college-educated part-time beer salesman from California. All that prevented a title change was a controversial ruling from the referee.

Napoles-Muniz came on March 30, at the Convention Center in Acapulco. In the third round, the champion suffered a dangerous cut on his left eyelid. (Muniz was repeatedly warned for butting.) By the 12th, Napoles was bleeding from a cut on his right eyebrow, too. Blood was flowing into both his eyes, and he was near-defenseless.

"The eyelid wound was very deep, and damaged the muscle," said Dr. Federico Soto of the Acapulco Boxing Commission.

When referee Ramon Berumen finally called a halt, he ruled that since the cuts had been caused by butts, the fighter ahead on points would be declared the winner. That fighter was Napoles.

Lamented a bitter Muniz, "I was one millimeter away from becoming a champion."

Welterweight champion Jose Napoles (left) retained the crown in a hotly disputed 12th-round technical victory over talented Armando Muniz.

WORLD TITLE FIGHTS

HEAVYWEIGHTS

March 24 **Muhammmad Ali** *KO* 15
Chuck Wepner, Cleveland

LIGHT HEAVYWEIGHTS

March 11 **John Conteh** *KO* 5
Lonnie Bennett, London

March 28 **Victor Galindez** *KO* 3
Harold Skog, Oslo

April 7 **Victor Galindez** *W* 15
Pierre Fourie, Johannesburg

JUNIOR MIDDLEWEIGHTS

Jan 21 **Koichi Wajima** *W* 15
Oscar Albarado, Tokyo

WELTERWEIGHTS

March 30 **Jose Napoles** *Tech Dec* 12
Armando Muniz, Acapulco

JUNIOR WELTERWEIGHTS

April 19 **Perico Fernandez** *KO* 9
Joao Henrique, Barcelona

LIGHTWEIGHTS

Feb 27 **Ishimatsu Suzuki** *W* 15
Ken Buchanan, Tokyo

March 2 **Roberto Duran** *KO* 14
Ray Lampkin, Panama City

JUNIOR LIGHTWEIGHTS

March 13 **Ben Villaflor** *W* 15
Hyun Chi Kim, Quezon City

March 27 **Kuniaki Shibata** *W* 15
Ould Makloufi, Fukuoka City, Japan

FEATHERWEIGHTS

March 1 **Bobby Chacon** *KO* 2
Jesus Estrada, Los Angeles

March 15 **Alexis Arguello** *KO* 8
Leonel Hernandez, Caracas

BANTAMWEIGHTS

March 14 **Alfonso Zamora** (MEX) *KO* 4
Soo Hwan Hong, Inglewood

FLYWEIGHTS

Jan 8 **Miguel Canto** (MEX) *W* 15
Shoji Oguma, Sendai, Japan

April 1 **Erbito Salavarria** *W* 15
Susumu Hanagata, Toyama, Japan

JUNIOR FLYWEIGHTS

April 4 **Franco Udella** (ITA) *W Disq* 12
Valentin Martinez, Milan
(Wins Newly Created WBC Title)

FOREMAN VS. FIVE

After losing the heavyweight title to Muhammad Ali, George Foreman desperately needed to repair his psyche. He tried to do so by fighting five men in one day.

Foreman's unique exhibition was held on April 26, at Maple Leaf Gardens in Toronto. Only 5,500 fans attended, probably because Big George had selected such laughable opposition.

* Alonzo Johnson had fought only twice in the last 12 years.

* Jerry Judge was a late substitute. He found out he was included by reading the newspapers.

* Terry Daniels had a losing record since being kayoed by Joe Frazier in January 1972.

* Charley Polite had lost 14 of his last 16 bouts.

* Boone Kirkman had been kayoed by Foreman in November 1970. Having broken his collarbone five times, he sparred with shoulder pads.

Combined record: 120-74-5. Total weight: 1,028 pounds.

Foreman was scheduled to box three rounds against each heavyweight. He scored second-round kayos over Johnson, Judge, and Daniels, and went the distance with Polite and Kirkman.

The bouts were sloppy, almost comical. Polite set the tone by kissing Big George during the pre-fight instructions. Worse yet, Foreman had to absorb the taunts of Ali, who was seated ringside.

Ex-champ George Foreman took on five opponents the same day to regain his image.

MAY

1975

AUGUST

WAITING FOR THE INEVITABLE

Ron Lyle was used to waiting. The Denver heavyweight waited until age 29 before turning pro; in 1969, he was paroled after serving 7½ years at Colorado State Penitentiary for murder. He waited for his try at the world title; he lost only one of his first 33 bouts, then watched as clubfighters took their turns before him. And when he finally got his chance, he waited for Ali to start fighting like Ali.

Lyle's opportunity came on May 16, at the Convention Center in Las Vegas. It was Ali's second defense in less than eight weeks, and over the first half of the fight, the champion seemed flat, bored, or both. Employing the rope-a-dope tactics, he lay on the ropes and invited Lyle in. But the challenger declined, anchoring himself at ring center and demanding that Ali fight him there.

Lyle carefully picked his shots, and after 10 rounds, he led on two of the scorecards, with the third card even. Thirty seconds into the 11th, however, Ali exploded with a left-right. He poured in 35 consecutive punches. By the end of the extended flurry, Lyle was groggy, and referee Ferd Hernandez stepped in.The bout was over, and so was Lyle's wait. He'd never again fight for the title.

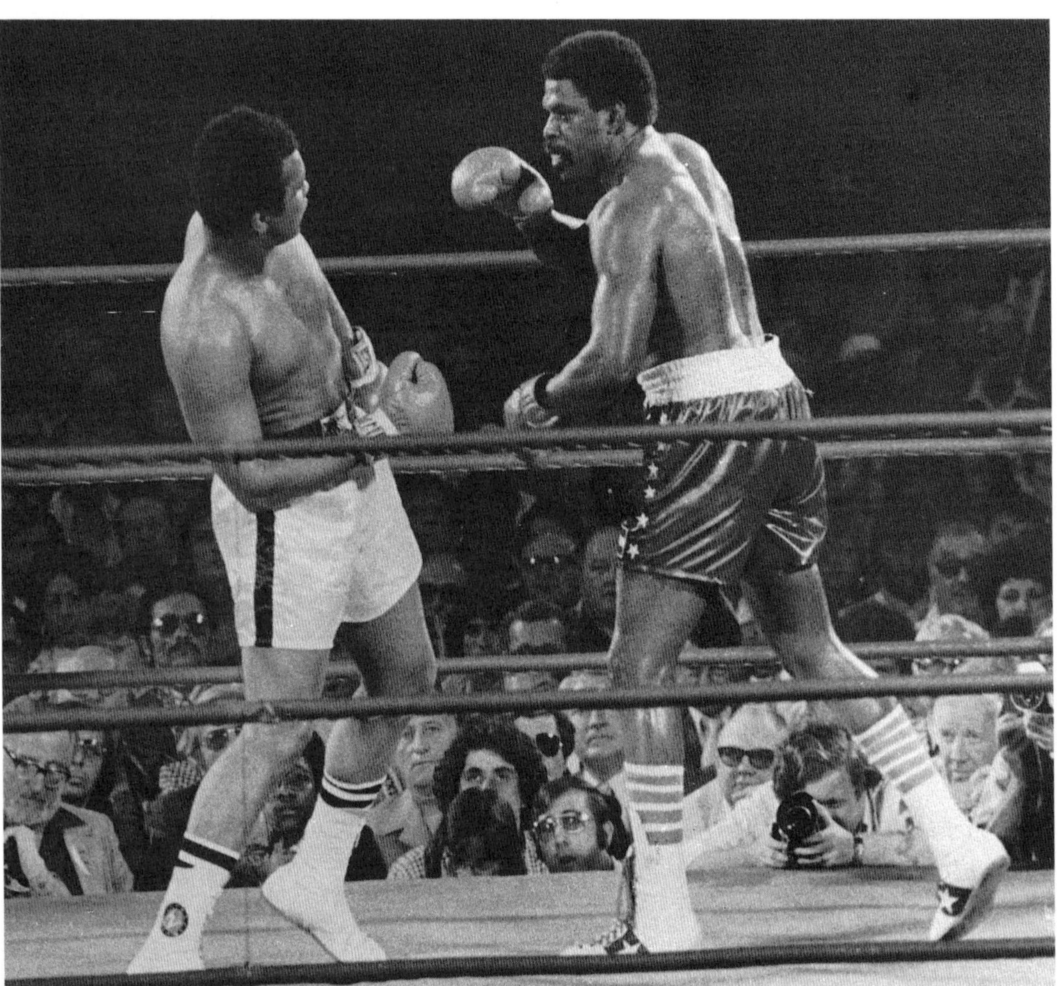

Making his second title defense in less than two months, Muhammad Ali (left) kayoed big Ron Lyle in the 11th round to retain the crown.

RINGSIDE VIEW

JULY

Alfredo Escalera captures the WBC super featherweight title by knocking out Kuniaki Shibata in the second.

CHACON TOO THIN TO WIN

Two weeks before Bobby Chacon defended the WBC featherweight title against Ruben Olivares, the champion scaled 140 pounds. Two days before the fight, he scaled 132. Somehow, he reduced to 124½ by the weigh-in.

"He's so thin, I could wrap my arms around him two or three times," said his wife Valerie.

Predictably, the bout, held on June 20, before a pro-Chacon crowd of 18,770 at the Fabulous Forum in Inglewood, California, was one-sided. Olivares sensed Chacon's lack of strength in the first, and attacked in the second. He scored two knockdowns, and referee Larry Rozadilla stepped in at the 2:29 mark. It was Olivares' second win over the Californian; he had previously kayoed Chacon in June 1973.

"I had nothing," said Chacon. "My legs were too weak. My hands were working too slowly. You could tell that, couldn't you?"

Olivares certainly had.

Ruben Olivares (right) and Bobby Chacon weigh in for their featherweight title fight.

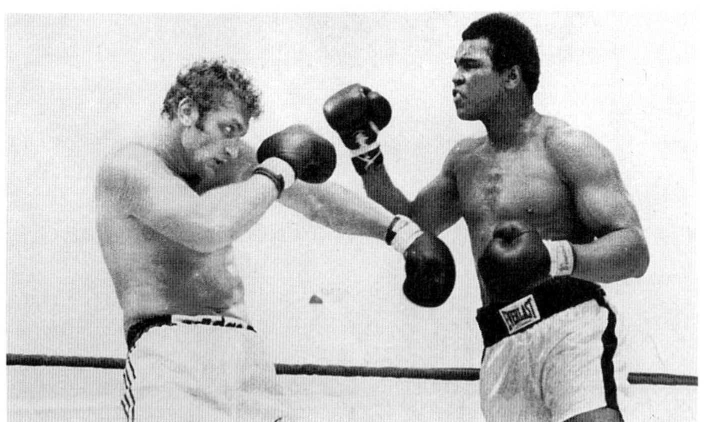

Muhammad Ali (right) retained the heavyweight title by outpointing tough Joe Bugner.

Ringside View

JUNE

World heavyweight champion Muhammad Ali keeps the crown by scoring a unanimous 15-round decision over Joe Bugner.

JUNE

Puerto Rico's Angel Espada wins the vacant WBA welterweight title, outpointing Canadian veteran Clyde Gray over 15 rounds.

World Title Fights

HEAVYWEIGHTS

May 16 **Muhammad Ali** *KO* 11
Ron Lyle, Las Vegas

June 30 **Muhammad Ali** *W* 15
Joe Bugner, Kuala Lumpur

LIGHT HEAVYWEIGHTS

June 30 **Victor Galindez** *W* 15
Jorge Ahumada, New York City

MIDDLEWEIGHTS

May 31 **Rodrigo Valdes** *KO* 8
Ramon Mendez, Cali, Colombia

June 30 **Carlos Monzon** *KO* 10
Tony Licata, New York City

Aug 16 **Rodrigo Valdes** *W* 15
Rudy Robles, Cartegena

JUNIOR MIDDLEWEIGHTS

May 7 **Miguel de Oliveira** *W* 15
Jose Duran, Monte Carlo

June 7 **Jae Do Yuh** (KOR) *KO* 7
Koichi Wajima, Kitakyushu, Japan

WELTERWEIGHTS

June 28 **Angel Espada** (PR) *W* 15
Clyde Gray, San Juan
(Wins Vacant WBA Title)

July 12 **Jose Napoles** *W* 15
Armando Muniz, Mexico City

JUNIOR WELTERWEIGHTS

May 17 **Antonio Cervantes** *W* 15
Esteban DeJesus, Panama City

July 15 **Saensak Muangsurin** (THA) *KO* 8
Perico Fernandez, Bangkok

LIGHTWEIGHTS

June 5 **Ishimatsu Suzuki** *W* 15
Tury Pineda, Osaka

JUNIOR LIGHTWEIGHTS

July 5 **Alfredo Escalera** (PR) *KO* 2
Kuniaki Shibata, Mito, Japan

FEATHERWEIGHTS

May 31 **Alexis Arguello** *KO* 2
Rigoberto Riasco, Managua

June 20 **Ruben Olivares** *KO* 2
Bobby Chacon, Inglewood

BANTAMWEIGHTS

May 31 **Rodolfo Martinez** *KO* 8
Nestor Jiminez, Bogota

Aug 30 **Alfonso Zamora** *KO* 4
Thanomjit Sukhothai, Anaheim

FLYWEIGHTS

May 25 **Miguel Canto** *W* 15
Betulio Gonzalez, Monterrey

Aug 23 **Miguel Canto** *KO* 11
Jiro Takada, Merida

JUNIOR FLYWEIGHTS

Aug 23 **Jaime Rios** (PAN) *W* 15
Rigoberto Marcano, Panama City
(Wins Newly Created WBA Title)

SAENSAK IS NO SAD SACK

When a world champion is judged to be vulnerable, contenders circle around him like vultures scoping a corpse. After capturing the vacant WBC super lightweight title in September 1974, Spain's Perico Fernandez won only one of his next three fights (all non-title bouts). He retained the crown vs. Joao Henrique, and then, for his second defense, picked Thailand's Saensak Muangsurin out of a group of eager contenders. The 23-year-old Muangsurin seemed safe; a veteran of 38 Thai-style bouts, he had fought only twice in the conventional style.

Muangsurin-Fernandez came on July 15, at the Huan Mark Stadium in Bangkok. The challenger turned out to be a dynamo. He swarmed from the start, and by the fourth, the champion was desperately retreating. Fernandez suffered cuts over his left eye and on his bottom lip. At the start of the eighth, he approached Muangsurin and raised his glove to signify the crowning of a new champion.

After three fights, Muangsurin was a world champion. No one had ever reached the top any faster.

THREE STRIKES, JORGE, AND YOU'RE OUT

Jorge Ahumada would never become a world champion despite getting three shots in a year.

After drawing with Bob Foster and losing to John Conteh, he challenged WBA king Victor Galindez. They had met four times, with Galindez winning three.

Galindez-Ahumada IV was held at Madison Square Garden, where Ahumada was a perfect 10-0. At the end of round three Galindez felled the challenger with a hook. Only one problem: the punch landed a split second after the bell. Referee Jimmy Devlin chose not to penalize the champion, claiming the hook "wasn't intentional, more of a reflex, and it didn't do any damage."

Ahumada remained active, and cut the champion over both eyes. But Galindez countered with fury, and after 15 rounds, kept the title by 9-5-1, 10-3-2, and, from the Argentine, a ridiculous 6-2-7.

Ahumada was 0-for-three, and, sadly, forced to believe in fate.

Victor Galindez (right) decisioned Jorge Ahumada over 15 bruising rounds to retain the crown.

SEPTEMBER

1975

DECEMBER

RINGSIDE VIEW

SEPTEMBER

In its infinite wisdom, the WBC fills its vacant light flyweight title by matching Venezuela's Luis (Lumumba) Estaba with Paraguay's Rafael Lovera. Estaba wins by kayo. It is Lovera's *first* pro bout!

SIXTY ROUNDS, NOTHING FOR IT

In June, WBA light heavy champion Victor Galindez retained the crown vs. Jorge Ahumada, who was making his third try for the title. On September 13, at Rand Stadium in Johannesburg, the Argentine defended against local favorite Pierre Fourie, who was making his fourth try.

The bout started slowly, despite the fact that the mobile challenger fought flatfooted. In the eighth, Galindez broke his right hand. But he didn't allow the pain to affect his focus. In fact, the remainder of the bout belonged to him. The champion wobbled Fourie with a right uppercut in the 10th. The 175-pounders brawled with a savage intensity over the last five rounds, with Galindez' body work giving him the edge. He kept the title by split decision. (The point totals were not made public, but USA's Joe Bunsa scored for Fourie by one point.)

Fourie's title fight scoreboard was complete: 30 rounds apiece vs. Bob Foster and Galindez, four losses, and one broken dream.

HERE TODAY, GHANA TOMORROW

On September 20, at the Fabulous Forum in Inglewood, California, the lunatics took over the asylum. Only 8,000 fans attended WBC featherweight champion Ruben Olivares' defense against number-one contender and Commonwealth king David (Poison) Kotey. A sellout crowd, however, couldn't have formed a more intimidating mob.

Kotey, 24, set the tone by dropping the champion with a first-round hook. A strong boxer-puncher, the Ghanian dominated the first 10 rounds. Olivares rallied down the stretch, but the Mexican's fans sensed that the decision would go against him. They began tossing anything and everything into the ring. (Francis Clottey, Kotey's trainer, was hospitalized after being hit on the head by a chair.)

Fearing a full-scale riot, Forum officials decided not to announce the winner. Thirty minutes after the final bell, the verdict was flashed on the overhanging scoreboard: Kotey had indeed taken the title, winning by split scores of 144-143, 143-142, and 143-144.

Fortunately, there was no further trouble, probably because there was nothing left to throw.

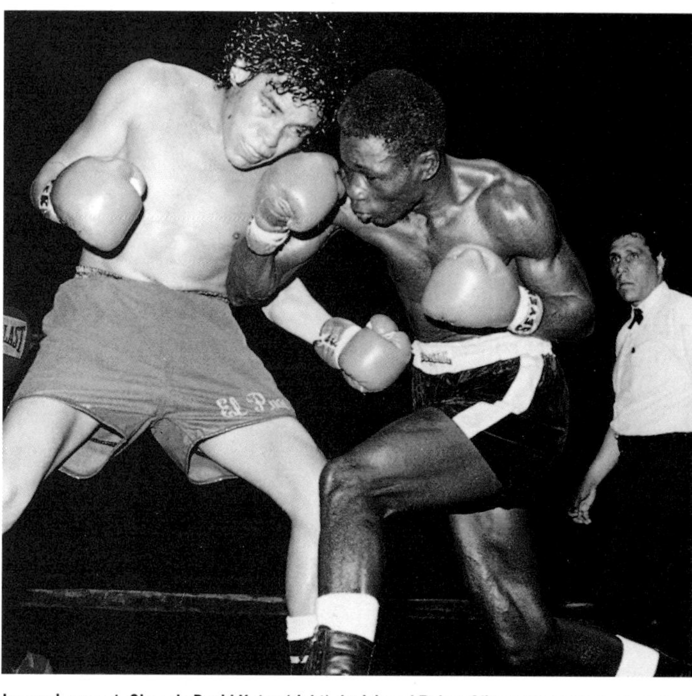

In a major upset, Ghana's David Kotey (right) decisioned Ruben Olivares to become champion.

NEXT TO DEATH IN MANILA "THRILLA"

Though they would both fight on, there is no arguing that on September 30, at the Araneta Coliseum in Quezon City, the Philippines, Muhammad Ali and Joe Frazier left parts of their hearts and souls in the ring. Who better than against each other?

The Ali-Frazier rubber match, known as "The Thrilla In Manila," was one of the greatest bouts in heavyweight history. Ali, the defending champion, easily took the first four rounds. When Smokin' Joe warmed up, however, he forced Ali to the ropes. Hammering the champion to the body, and then the head, Frazier, 31, refused to decelerate. He took six of the next seven stanzas, and was on the verge of a stoppage victory.

Then Ali, 33, summoned his unmatched courage and will. Somehow finding the strength to put together power combinations, "The Greatest" regained control. He staggered Frazier in the 13th, and, with the challenger's right eye swollen shut, pummeled him throughout the 14th. At the bell starting round 15, Eddie Futch, Frazier's trainer, refused to let his game charge continue. (After 14 rounds, Ali led by the off-base scores of 8-5-1, 8-2-4, and 9-3-2.)

"What you saw tonight," said Ali, "was next to death. I felt like quittin'."

In the classic "Thrilla in Manila" Muhammad Ali (right) stopped Joe Frazier after 14 rounds.

A LEGEND MAKES A SMOOTH EXIT IN LAST FIGHT

Jose Napoles said goodbye the way every champion hopes to: while on his feet, and after giving a spirited effort in front of his fans.

On December 6, Napoles, 35, defended the WBC welterweight title against London's John H. Stracey at Monumental Plaza in Mexico City. The champion opened brilliantly, dropping Stracey in the first round with a series of hooks. But this was one challenger who would not be easily discouraged.

"He could have knocked me down in every round," Stracey said, "but I'd have won it anyway."

Napoles battered his foe in the second as well, but finished the round with a cut over his right eye. By the fourth, the eye was swollen shut, and Stracey began to score with jabs and one-twos. In the sixth, Napoles backed to the ropes and weakly defended against an extended onslaught. Referee Octavio Meyron intervened at the 2:30 mark.

"Mantequilla" would fight no more. His final mark: 77-7 (54), with two title reigns and 13 successful defenses. Smooth indeed.

Britain's John Stracey (left) stopped Jose Napoles in the sixth round to become the new world welterweight king and end Napoles' career.

World Title Fights

HEAVYWEIGHTS

Sept 30 **Muhammad Ali** *KO* 14 Joe Frazier, Quezon City

LIGHT HEAVYWEIGHTS

Sept 13 **Victor Galindez** *W* 15 Pierre Fourie, Johannesburg

MIDDLEWEIGHTS

Dec 13 **Carlos Monzon** *KO* 5 Gratien Tonna, Paris

JUNIOR MIDDLEWEIGHTS

Nov 11 **Jae Do Yuh** *KO* 6 Masahiro Misako, Shizuoka, Japan

Nov 13 **Elisha Obed** (BAH) *KO* 11 Miguel de Oliveira, Paris

WELTERWEIGHTS

Oct 11 **Angel Espada** *W* 15 Johnny Gant, Ponce, Puerto Rico

Dec 6 **John H. Stracey** (ENG) *KO* 6 Jose Napoles, Mexico City

JUNIOR WELTERWEIGHTS

Nov 15 **Antonio Cervantes** *KO* 8 Hector Thompson, Panama City

LIGHTWEIGHTS

Dec 4 **Ishimatsu Suzuki** *KO* 14 Alvaro Rojas, Tokyo

Dec 14 **Roberto Duran** *KO* 15 Leoncio Ortiz, Hato Rey, Puerto Rico

JUNIOR LIGHTWEIGHTS

Sept 20 **Alfredo Escalera** *D* 15 Leonel Hernandez, Caracas

Dec 12 **Alfredo Escalera** *KO* 9 Sven-Erik Paulsen, Oslo

FEATHERWEIGHTS

Sept 20 **David Kotey** (GHA) *W* 15 Ruben Olivares, Inglewood

Oct 12 **Alexis Arguello** *KO* 5 Royal Kobayashi, Tokyo

BANTAMWEIGHTS

Oct 8 **Rodolfo Martinez** *W* 15 Hisami Numata, Sendai, Japan

Dec 6 **Alfonso Zamora** *KO* 2 Socrates Batoto, Mexico City

FLYWEIGHTS

Oct 7 **Erbito Salavarria** *W* 15 Susumu Hanagata, Yokohama

Dec 12 **Miguel Canto** *W* 15 Ignacio Espinal, Merida, Mexico

JUNIOR FLYWEIGHTS

Sept 13 **Luis Estaba** (VEN) *KO* 4 Rafael Lovera, Caracas

Dec 17 **Luis Estaba** *KO* 10 Takenobu Shimabukuro, Okinawa

Ringside View

DECEMBER

Middleweight champion Carlos Monzon retains the title for the 12th time, kayoing France's Gratien Tonna in the fifth round.

Carlos Monzon after kayoing Gratien Tonna.

JANUARY

1976

APRIL

LAST ONE DOWN IS THE LOSER

George Foreman's punches broke Ron Lyle's mouthpiece. Lyle's blows drove one of Big George's teeth into his gums. It was that kind of fight.

In a raw and thrilling heavyweight brawl, Foreman and Lyle clashed on January 24, at the Caesars Palace Sports Pavilion. Lyle took a quiet opening round. Nothing was special about the second, either, except that the bell rang after only two minutes.

In the third, Foreman pinned Lyle to the ropes and pounded away. Then came the fantastic fourth. Lyle put together an overhand right and a hook, and boom! Foreman picked himself up and came back punching. A right to the jaw, and boom! Lyle seemed finished, but he, too, rebounded, and at the round's end, connected with another of his big rights. Boom! Big George was down for the second time.

Both fighters were exhausted. In the fifth, Foreman found the energy to fire 17 unanswered blows. Lyle pitched forward and was counted out by referee Charles Roth.

"Man, I don't want to see a replay of this one," he later said.

He probably wouldn't have believed his own eyes, anyway.

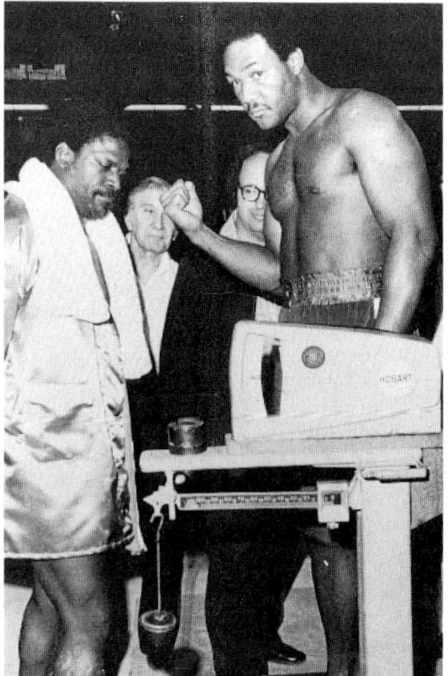

George Foreman (right) and Ron Lyle.

RINGSIDE VIEW

FEBRUARY

Muhammad Ali retains the world heavyweight title by stopping a grossly overmatched Jean Pierre Coopman in the fifth round.

BENITEZ IS MOZART OF THE RING

If you argue that great boxers are born, not made, Wilfred Benitez is your prime piece of evidence. The Puerto Rican boy wonder turned pro at age 15. Two years later, he became the youngest world champion in history.

On March 6, Benitez, 25-0, challenged WBA junior welterweight champion Antonio Cervantes at Hiram Bithorn Stadium in San Juan. He didn't figure to threaten "Kid Pambele"; the Colombian had made 10 successful defenses, and was being mentioned as an opponent for the incomparable Roberto Duran.

Cervantes and his teenage foe boxed evenly until Benitez' extraordinary speed and skill surfaced in the fifth. He took four consecutive rounds, jabbing smartly and making the champion miss with his hooks. Cervantes rallied in the 11th, but couldn't maintain his momentum.

After 15 rounds, Benitez, a clear winner, settled for a split decision victory (scores of 148-144, 147-142, and 145-147). At age 17½, he was too young to appreciate history, but old enough to have made it.

Wilfred Benitez (right) won the junior welterweight crown by outpointing Colombia's Antonio Cervantes in 15 furious rounds.

REMATCH REQUIRED AFTER LULU IN HONOLULU

Sammy Serrano-Ben Villaflor was a classic boxer-puncher matchup that turned out to be anything but a classic fight. Thanks to the three judges, however, it produced classic boxing controversy.

Villaflor, a Filipino based in Hawaii, squared off against Serrano on April 13, at the Blaisdell Center in Honolulu. Defending the WBA 130-pound title for the fifth time in his second reign, he was a 2-1 favorite.

Serrano was trying to become the fourth Puerto Rican world champion crowned over the last 10 months. He kept his distance, pumped his jab, and clinched every time the powerpunching Villaflor moved inside. There was little action. Still, after 15 tedious rounds, the ringside press was almost unanimous in scoring for Serrano. But Villaflor retained the title via split draw (scores of 73-69, 67-72, and 70-70).

Calling the decision "unjust," WBA President Dr. Elias Cordova ordered an immediate rematch.

ALI AT HIS WORST AGAINST YOUNG PRETENDER

FIGHTING TALK

I've had 25 fights up until tonight, and this was one of my easiest

JIMMY YOUNG
after losing by controversial decision to heavyweight champion Muhammad Ali

RINGSIDE VIEW

APRIL

WBA bantamweight king Alfonso Zamora crushes Panamanian challenger Eusebio Pedroza in two rounds. Two years later, Pedroza would begin his record-setting reign at featherweight.

Villaflor (right) drew with Serrano.

Risking the world heavyweight title against defensive specialist Jimmy Young, Muhammad Ali was a 15-1 favorite. But when he scaled a career-high 230 pounds, an upset seemed something more than a remote possibility.

Ali-Young came on April 30, before a crowd of 12,472 at the Capital Centre in Landover, Maryland. Angelo Dundee, Ali's trainer, called the fight "the worst of (his fighter's) career." The champion, flat and uninspired, kept missing and then holding. Young, however, failed to take advantage. Whenever Ali mounted any semblance of an attack, the Philadelphian ducked his head outside the ropes. (Referee Tom Kelly chose not to penalize him for the obvious infraction.)

Someone had to emerge victorious, and while most of the ringsiders saw the bout as too close to call, the judges voted unanimously for Ali (scores of 72-65, 71-64, and 70-68). Call it a reward for the champion's long and meritorious service.

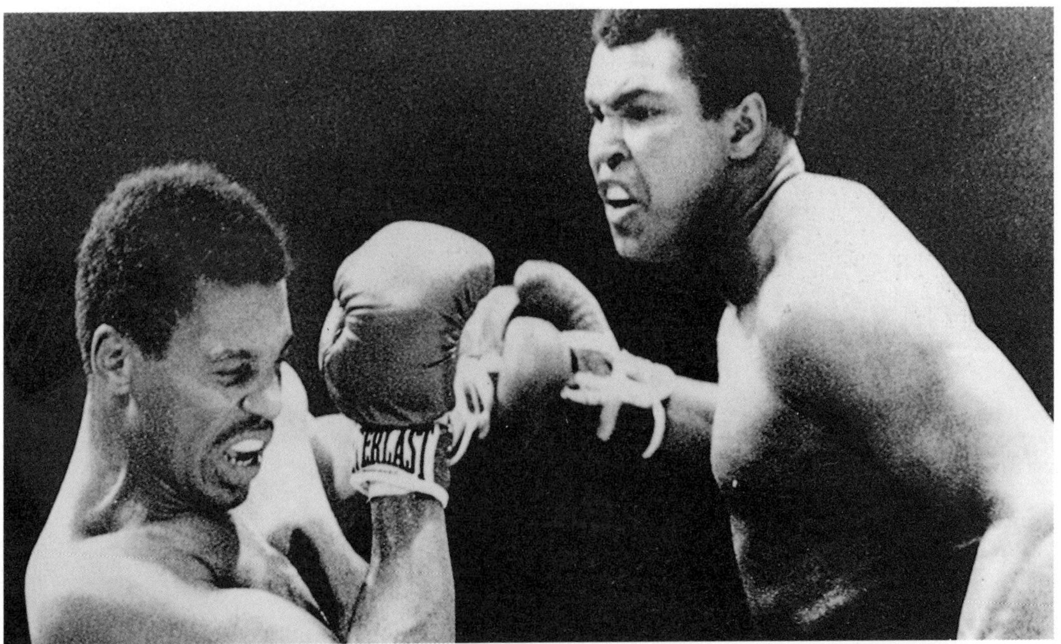

Muhammad Ali was hard-pressed to retain the title against a determined Jimmy Young (left), but took a unanimous decision.

WORLD TITLE FIGHTS

HEAVYWEIGHTS

Feb 20	**Muhammad Ali** *KO* 5 Jean Pierre Coopman, Hato Rey, Puerto Rico
April 30	**Muhammad Ali** *W* 15 Jimmy Young, Landover, MD

MIDDLEWEIGHTS

March 28	**Rodrigo Valdes** *KO* 4 Nessim Cohen, Paris

JUNIOR MIDDLEWEIGHTS

Feb 17	**Koichi Wajima** *KO* 15 Jae Do Yuh, Tokyo
Feb 28	**Elisha Obed** *KO* 2 Tony Gardner, Nassau
April 25	**Elisha Obed** *W* 15 Sea Robinson, Abidjan, Ivory Coast

WELTERWEIGHTS

March 20	**John H. Stracey** *KO* 10 Hedgemon Lewis, Wembley

JUNIOR WELTERWEIGHTS

Jan 25	**Saensak Muangsurin** *W* 15 Lion Furuyama, Tokyo
March 6	**Wilfred Benitez** (PR) *W* 15 Antonio Cervantes, San Juan

JUNIOR LIGHTWEIGHTS

Jan 12	**Ben Villaflor** *KO* 13 Morito Kashiwaba, Tokyo
Feb 20	**Alfredo Escalera** *KO* 13 Jose Fernandez, Hato Rey, Puerto Rico
April 1	**Alfredo Escalera** *KO* 6 Buzzsaw Yamabe, Nara, Japan
April 13	**Ben Villaflor** *D* 15 Samuel Serrano, Honolulu

FEATHERWEIGHTS

March 6	**David Kotey** *KO* 12 Yasutsune Uehara, Accra

JUNIOR FEATHERWEIGHTS

April 3	**Rigoberto Riasco** (PAN) *KO* 10 Waruinge Nakayama, Panama City (Wins Newly Created WBC Title)

BANTAMWEIGHTS

Jan 30	**Rodolfo Martinez** *W* 15 Venice Borkorsor, Bangkok
April 3	**Alfonso Zamora** *KO* 2 Eusebio Pedroza, Mexicali

FLYWEIGHTS

Feb 27	**Alfonso Lopez** (PAN) *KO* 15 Erbito Salavarria, Quezon City
April 21	**Alfonso Lopez** *W* 15 Shoji Oguma, Tokyo

JUNIOR FLYWEIGHTS

Jan 3	**Jaime Rios** *W* 15 Kazunori Tenryu, Kagoshima
Feb 14	**Luis Estaba** *W* 15 Leo Palacios, Caracas

MAY

1976

AUGUST

Ringside View

MAY

Muhammad Ali keeps the heavyweight title, kayoing southpaw Richard Dunn in five rounds.

JUNE

Powerpunching German junior middleweight Eckhard Dagge wins the WBC crown by stopping Elisha Obed in 10 rounds.

World Title Fights

HEAVYWEIGHTS

May 24 **Muhammad Ali** *KO* 5
Richard Dunn, Munich

LIGHT HEAVYWEIGHTS

May 22 **Victor Galindez** *KO* 15
Richie Kates, Johannesburg

MIDDLEWEIGHTS

June 26 **Carlos Monzon** *W* 15
Rodrigo Valdes, Monte Carlo
(Unifies World Title)

JUNIOR MIDDLEWEIGHTS

May 18 **Jose Duran** (SPA) *KO* 14
Koichi Wajima, Tokyo

June 18 **Eckhard Dagge** (GER) *KO* 10
Elisha Obed, Berlin

WELTERWEIGHTS

June 22 **Carlos Palomino** (USA) *KO* 12
John H. Stracey, Wembley

July 17 **Pipino Cuevas** (MEX) *KO* 2
Angel Espada, Mexicali

JUNIOR WELTERWEIGHTS

May 31 **Wilfred Benitez** *W* 15
Emiliano Villa, Hato Rey, Puerto Rico

June 30 **Miguel Velasquez** (SPA) *W Disq* 5
Saensak Muangsurin, Madrid

LIGHTWEIGHTS

May 8 **Esteban DeJesus** (PR) *W* 15
Ishimatsu Suzuki, Bayamon, Puerto Rico

May 22 **Roberto Duran** *KO* 14
Lou Bizzarro, Erie, PA

JUNIOR LIGHTWEIGHTS

July 1 **Alfredo Escalera** *W* 15
Buzzsaw Yamabe, Nara, Japan

FEATHERWEIGHTS

June 19 **Alexis Arguello** *KO* 3
Salvatore Torres, Inglewood

July 16 **David Kotey** *KO* 3
Shig Fukuyama, Tokyo

JUNIOR FEATHERWEIGHTS

June 12 **Rigoberto Riasco** *KO* 10
Livio Nolasco, Panama City

Aug 1 **Rigoberto Riasco** *W* 15
Dong Kyun Yum, Pusan, South Korea

BANTAMWEIGHTS

May 8 **Carlos Zarate** (MEX) *KO* 9
Rodolfo Martinez, Inglewood

July 10 **Alfonso Zamora** *KO* 3
Gilberto Illueca, Juarez, Mexico

Aug 28 **Carlos Zarate** *KO* 12
Paul Ferreri, Inglewood

FLYWEIGHTS

May 15 **Miguel Canto** *W* 15
Susumu Hanagata, Merida, Mexico

JUNIOR FLYWEIGHTS

May 2 **Luis Estaba** *W* 15
Juan Alvarez, Caracas

July 1 **Juan Guzman** (DR) *W* 15
Jaime Rios, Santo Domingo

July 18 **Luis Estaba** *KO* 3
Franco Udella, Caracas

THE COUNTDOWN BEGINS FOR MEXICO'S Z BOYS

WBA bantamweight champion Alfonso Zamora was 25-0 (25). After winning the WBC crown, Carlos Zarate was 33-0 (32). Statistically, Mexico's "Z Boys" were the hardest-hitting titlists in history. And as soon as Zarate joined his countryman at the top, a shootout seemed inevitable.

On May 8, at the Fabulous Forum in Inglewood, California, Zarate, a 3-1 favorite, challenged reigning WBC king Rodolfo Martinez. Neither fighter was particularly sharp, perhaps because they had overtrained. The champion's only chance for victory came in round three, when he wobbled Zarate with a hook. But the 5'8" powerpuncher came back to score a knockdown in round five, and subsequently took control.

Martinez was repeatedly rocked in the eighth, and finished by a right hand in the ninth. As soon as referee Larry Rozadilla reached 10, the countdown began for Zarate-Zamora.

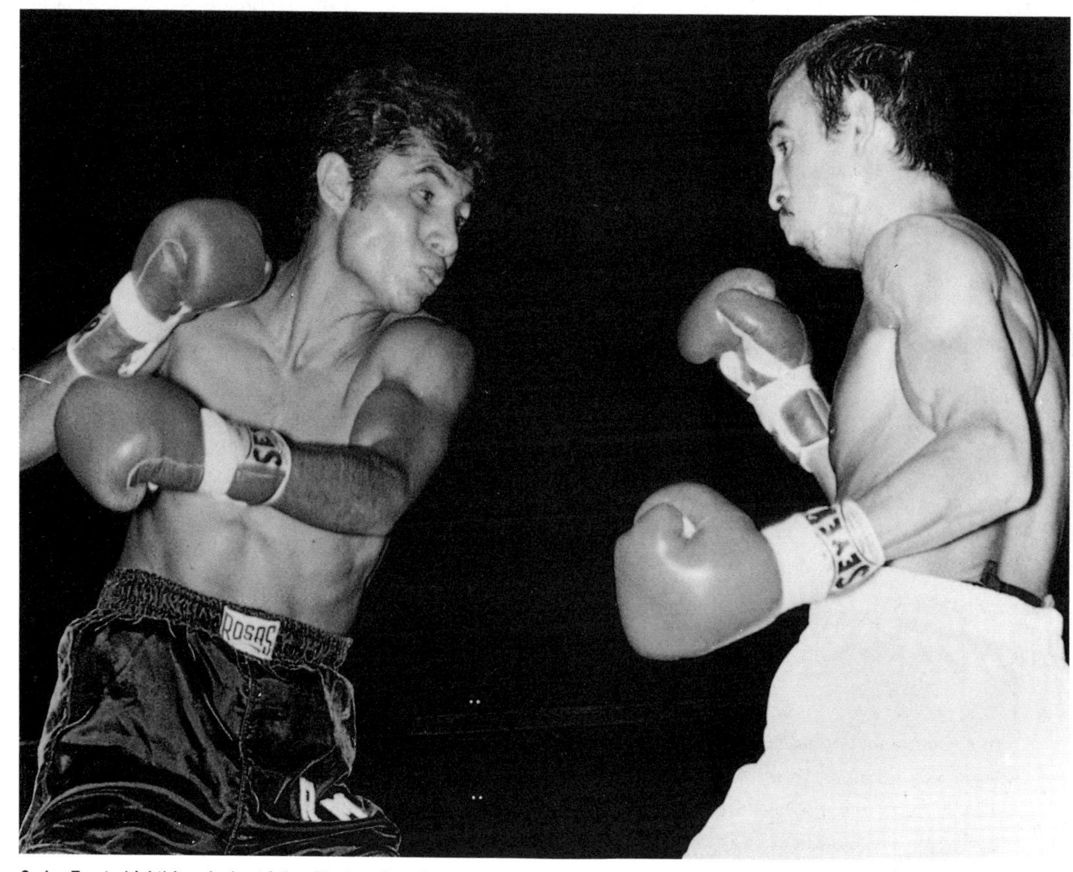

Carlos Zarate (right) knocked out fellow Mexican Rodolfo Martinez in the ninth round to win the bantamweight crown and remain undefeated.

Ringside View

JUNE

In a rematch of former heavyweight champions, George Foreman crushes Joe Frazier in five rounds. Smokin' Joe will not fight again for 5½ years.

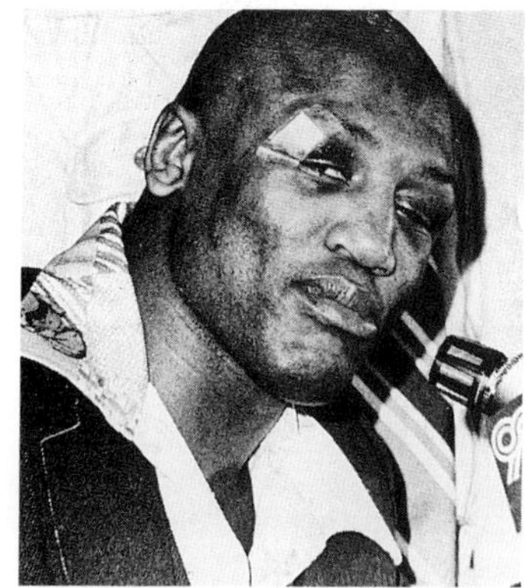

Joe Frazier after being kayoed by Foreman.

THE OTHER WAY TO WIN

Boxing began in England, where fighters were taught to stand erect, jab, and cross with their rights. But some time after James Figg and before Mike Tyson, styles began to change.

On June 22, WBC welterweight champion John H. Stracey, a classic boxer from London's Bethnal Green, defended against Mexico-born Californian Carlos Palomino at the Empire Pool in Wembley. Having lost to Andy Price, and drawn with recent Stracey victim Hedgemon Lewis, the challenger wasn't thought to be much of a threat. For seven rounds, he and Stracey boxed evenly, the only punch of note being a big Stracey hook in the first minute of the fight. In the eighth, however, Palomino began to dip and hook to the body, and the fight quickly turned.

In the 12th, Stracey was felled twice by body blows. After the second knockdown, referee Sid Nathan stepped in.

James Figg never would have understood.

Mexico's Carlos Palomino (left) knocked out Britain's John Stracey in the 12th round.

Ringside View

JULY

In a record-setting performance, five American boxers, Sugar Ray Leonard, Howard Davis Jr., Leo Randolph, and brothers Leon and Michael Spinks, win gold medals at the Olympic Games in Montreal.

THE MIDDLEWEIGHT SUPERFIGHT

What Muhammad Ali-Joe Frazier I was to the heavyweights, Carlos Monzon-Rodrigo Valdes I was to the middleweights. Monzon was the WBA champion, and Valdez the WBC champion. Both were from South America, and their unification match was a battle of personal and national pride.

The fight, the richest middleweight bout in history, didn't match the hype, partly because Valdes couldn't hope to properly focus. One week before the biggest fight of his life, the Colombian's brother Rafael was shot dead in a bar room brawl in Cartagena. Valdes wanted to postpone the bout, but was dissuaded by his handlers. As if he needed further problems, he struggled to make weight, and reduced to 160 pounds with only minutes to spare.

The fight was held on June 26, at Louis II Stadium in Monte Carlo. Valdes applied pressure throughout, but Monzon capitalized on his 5½-inch reach advantage. He countered efficiently and clinched a unanimous 15-round decision – by two points on two cards, and four points on the third – when he dropped his foe with a straight right in round 14.

After 13 title defenses, King Carlos had certified his greatness.

Carlos Monzon (left) needed all his skills to decision Rodrigo Valdes and unify the crown.

WHO WAS THAT KID, ANYWAY?

On New Year's Day, 1972, Mexico's Pipino Cuevas turned pro, five days after his 14th birthday. By the time he climbed into the ring to challenge WBA welterweight champion Angel Espada, he was a hardened veteran of 18. When he climbed back out, he was the youngest 147-pound champion in history.

Cuevas-Espada came on July 17, in Mexicali. The champion, a 5-1 favorite, thought he had scheduled a tuneup for a defense against the top-rated Miguel Campanino; Cuevas had compiled a mediocre record of 16-5, and had lost his most recent effort. Espada quickly learned otherwise.

Espada survived the first round, but in the second, Cuevas zeroed in. There were three knockdowns in all, the last produced by the challenger's awesome hook. Espada was counted out by referee Isidro Rodriguez.

Unfortunately for Espada, he would face Cuevas twice more. The Mexican assassin would singlehandedly destroy his career.

SEPTEMBER

1976

DECEMBER

RINGSIDE VIEW

OCTOBER

Japanese southpaw Yoko Gushiken wins the WBA junior flyweight title by kayoing defending champion Juan Guzman in the seventh round.

OCTOBER

Lanky Argentine Miguel Angel Castellini captures the WBA junior middleweight title by scoring a split 15-round decision over Jose Duran. It is Duran's first defense.

WORLD TITLE FIGHTS

HEAVYWEIGHTS

Sept 28	**Muhammad Ali** *W* 15 Ken Norton, Bronx, NY

LIGHT HEAVYWEIGHTS

Oct 5	**Victor Galindez** *W* 15 Kosie Smith, Johannesburg
Oct 9	**John Conteh** *W* 15 Yaqui Lopez, Copenhagen

JUNIOR MIDDLEWEIGHTS

Sept 18	**Eckhard Dagge** *W* 15 Emile Griffith, Berlin
Oct 8	**Miguel Castellini** (ARG) *W* 15 Jose Duran, Madrid

WELTERWEIGHTS

Oct 27	**Pipino Cuevas** *KO* 6 Shoji Tsujimoto, Kanuzawa, Japan

JUNIOR WELTERWEIGHTS

Oct 16	**Wilfred Benitez** *KO* 3 Tony Petronelli, San Juan
Oct 29	**Saensak Muangsurin** *KO* 2 Miguel Velasquez, Segovia, Spain

LIGHTWEIGHTS

Sept 10	**Esteban DeJesus** *KO* 7 Hector Medina, Bayamon, Puerto Rico
Oct 15	**Roberto Duran** *KO* 1 Alvaro Rojas, Hollywood, FL

JUNIOR LIGHTWEIGHTS

Sept 18	**Alfredo Escalera** *KO* 13 Ray Lunny III, Hato Rey, Puerto Rico
Oct 16	**Samuel Serrano** (PR) *W* 15 Ben Villaflor, San Juan
Nov 30	**Alfredo Escalera** *W* 15 Tyrone Everett, Philadelphia

FEATHERWEIGHTS

Nov 13	**Danny Lopez** (USA) *W* 15 David Kotey, Accra

JUNIOR FEATHERWEIGHTS

Oct 10	**Royal Kobayashi** (JAP) *KO* 8 Rigoberto Riasco, Tokyo
Nov 24	**Dong Kyun Yum,** (KOR) *W* 15 Royal Kobayashi, Seoul

BANTAMWEIGHTS

Oct 16	**Alfonso Zamora** *KO* 12 Soo Hwan Hong, Inchon, South Korea
Nov 13	**Carlos Zarate** *KO* 4 Waruinge Nakayama, Culiacan, Mexico

FLYWEIGHTS

Oct 2	**Guty Espadas** (MEX) *KO* 13 Susumu Hanagata, Los Angeles
Oct 3	**Miguel Canto** *W* 15 Betulio Gonzalez, Caracas
Nov 20	**Miguel Canto** *W* 15 Orlando Javierto, Los Angeles

JUNIOR FLYWEIGHTS

Sept 26	**Luis Estaba** *KO* 11 Rodolfo Rodriguez, Caracas
Oct 10	**Yoko Gushiken** (JAP) *KO* 7 Juan Guzman, Kofu, Japan
Nov 21	**Luis Estaba** *KO* 11 Valentin Martinez, Caracas

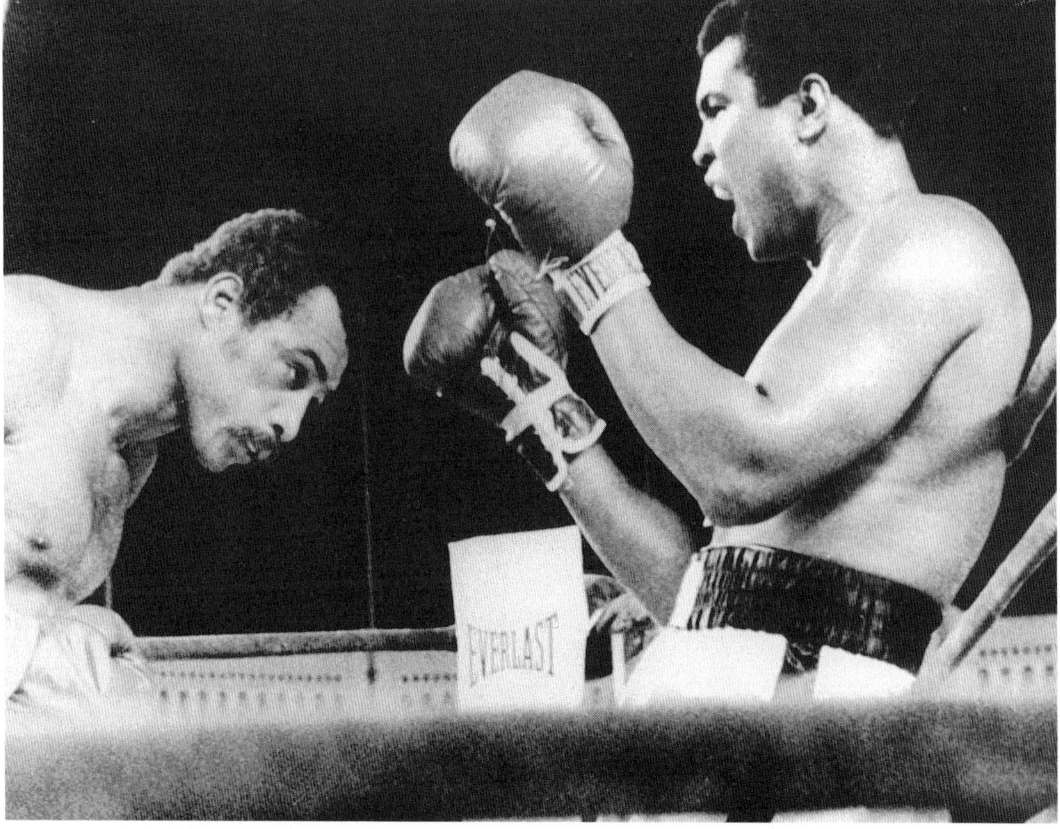

A flabby Muhammad Ali maintained control through most of the 15 rounds against Ken Norton (left) and retained the world title.

ONE LAST NIGHT OF MAGIC

There are fans who will argue until their throats run dry, and then argue some more, that Ken Norton beat heavyweight champion Muhammad Ali in their rubber match, fought on September 28, before 30,298 fans at Yankee Stadium. But whether Ali deserved the decision or not, his performance over the second half of the bout was miraculous.

After eight rounds, Norton led by rounds scores of 5-3 (twice) and 6-2. Then Ali began to peck and poke and steal rounds. And most importantly, he began to dance. At age 34, "The Greatest" still had his legs. As if fated, the bout, like Ali-Norton I and II, came down to the last round.

"I could have fought the whole three minutes all-out and won it easily," said Norton, "but my corner said I had the fight won and don't take any chances."

Norton swarmed over the last 30 seconds, but it wasn't enough; Ali took the round and won the fight by unanimous scores of 8-7 (twice) and 8-6-1.

Said Norton, "I thought I won at least 10 rounds, no less than nine." But he failed to win the only one that counted.

YOU SAY GOODBYE, AND I SAY HELLO

The relativity of age was never more apparent than after WBA junior lightweight champion Ben Villaflor and Puerto Rico's Samuel Serrano fought their rematch, on October 16, at Hiram Bithorn Stadium in San Juan. (The bout was part of a title fight doubleheader featuring Wilfred Benitez vs. Tony Petronelli.)

Villaflor and Serrano, both 23, were born three days apart. But after their bout, Serrano would engage in 16 more title fights, and Villaflor would retire.

In April, Villaflor-Serrano I had been scored a draw, though most ringsiders thought Serrano had won. This time, there was no controversy. Serrano fought more aggressively, and Villaflor, a southpaw, waited to land one big left hand. The judges seemed generous to the champion, scoring unanimously for Serrano by 146-142, 147-141, and a more realistic 147-139.

How old is 23? Old enough to start a championship run. And old enough to end one.

Puerto Rico's Sam Serrano (right) earned a 15-round decision over Ben Villaflor to become the new junior lightweight champion.

LOPEZ DETHRONES KOTEY (AT LEAST THAT'S THE RUMOR)

Apparently, the information explosion never reached Ghana. On November 13, American power-puncher Danny Lopez challenged WBC featherweight champion David (Poison) Kotey before an estimated crowd of 100,000 at the Sports Stadium in Accra. The fight was one-sided from the start, with Lopez cutting Kotey (the Ghanian took 37 stitches, including 17 to close his lower lip), and pummeling him throughout the late rounds.

"Anywhere else the fight would have been stopped," said Lopez. "He wouldn't go down."

Lopez took a unanimous decision, but with Ghana's communications network shut down, word didn't spread until he got home.

"It was strange," said the new champion. "I tried to call after the fight and couldn't. I tried to get the U.S. Embassy to get a message through for me, but they said they couldn't either."

Fortunately, Lopez was able to show off the championship belt. Without it, no one could have been sure that he had really won the title.

THE ROBBERY OF THE DECADE – ASSISTED BY THE HOMETOWN JUDGE!

Having lured WBC super featherweight champion Alfredo Escalera to Philadelphia for a defense against local favorite Tyrone Everett, the challenger's handlers were worried about the officials. The referee, Ray Solis, was Mexican. One of the judges, Ismael Fernandez, was from Escalera's native Puerto Rico. But at least Philadelphia judge Lou Tress would score objectively.

The fight came on November 30, before 16,019 partisan fans at the Spectrum. For 12 rounds, the unbeaten (34-0) Everett, a quick southpaw, boxed brilliantly. And when Escalera's teeth opened a gash in the middle of his forehead, he cruised to the closing bell.

Predictably, Fernandez scored for Escalera, 146-143. Solis had Everett in front, 148-146. It was down to Tress, who scored 145-143 for Escalera!

"That's the only thing that makes me feel bad," complained Everett. "A Philadelphia judge!"

Alfredo Escalera (right) outpointed Tyrone Everett to retain the junior lightweight crown.

JANUARY

1977

APRIL

"ROBERTO WILL CATCH HIM"

Having scored kayos in all nine of his title defenses, WBA lightweight champion Roberto Duran was the most intimidating fighter in the game. On January 29, he met challenger number 10, Dominican veteran Vilomar Fernandez, at the Fountainbleu Hotel in Miami Beach.

"The fellow runs a lot," Carlos Eleta, Duran's manager, said of defensive specialist Fernandez. "But Roberto will catch him."

Eleta proved prophetic. Fernandez boxed reasonably well for seven rounds, but then Duran began to wear him down. The challenger barely survived the 10th, and was downed by a hook to the midsection in the 13th. His will broken, he casually took referee Servio Ley's full count.

Among those in attendance was WBC lightweight champion Esteban DeJesus, who was the last fighter to have beaten Duran. A unification match was greatly anticipated, even by DeJesus, who apparently didn't know better.

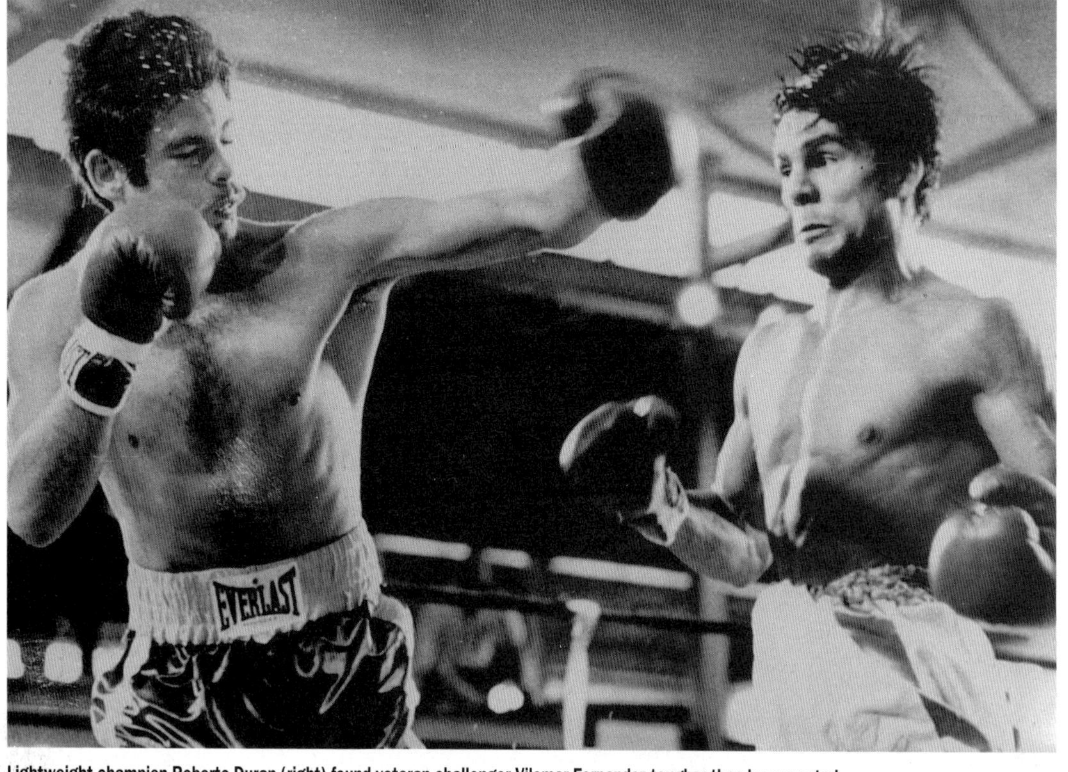

Lightweight champion Roberto Duran (right) found veteran challenger Vilomar Fernandez tougher than he expected.

RINGSIDE VIEW

JANUARY

WBC super lightweight champ Saensak Muangsurin makes the first defense of his second reign, stopping Monroe Brooks.

SCHOOL OF HARD KNOCKS AND DISAPPOINTMENTS

From the Why-We-Shouldn't-Stereotype-Fighters Department: for the first time in history, a pair of college graduates, WBC welterweight champion Carlos Palomino and Armando Muniz, clashed in a world title fight. Their bout came on January 22, at the Olympic Auditorium in Los Angeles.

Making his third try at the title, Muniz began by dropping the champion with a first-round hook. He built a big lead through five rounds. Then Palomino accelerated his attack. He took the sixth through the 12th, but Muniz rallied in the 13th. Entering the last round, the fight was even.

Both fighters were fatigued. Whatever power remained, however, belonged to Palomino. He felled Muniz with a right-left, and then continued his onslaught until referee John Thomas stepped in with 34 seconds left in the fight.

Unfortunately for Muniz, in a boxing match, only one fighter can graduate.

Carlos Palomino (left) knocked out Armando Muniz with only 36 seconds remaining in the 15th round to retain the world welterweight crown.

THE WAR OF THE Z BOYS

There might never be another fight like it: WBC bantamweight champion Carlos Zarate, 38-0 (37), vs. WBA titlist Alfonso Zamora, 29-0 (29). The fellow Mexicans and former stablemates met on April 23, at the Fabulous Forum in Inglewood, California. Due to boxing politics, neither title was at stake. But that didn't lessen the excitement.

Given the fighters' knockout records, no one expected a distance fight. Zamora dominated round one, which was interrupted when a crazed fan ran into the ring. Zarate gained control in the third, landing short hooks inside of Zamora's wider blows. He scored a knockdown late in the round, and finished his foe by twice dropping him in the fourth.

Carlos Zarata (right) kayoed Alfonso Zamora.

IT WAS AN EXPERIENCE, ALRIGHT

George Foreman was one victory away from an eagerly anticipated multimillion-dollar rematch with heavyweight champion Muhammad Ali. Only Jimmy Young blocked his path.

Foreman squared off against Young on March 17, at Roberto Clemente Coliseum in San Juan. For six rounds, Big George boxed cautiously. In the seventh, he connected with a hook, and Young fell against the ropes.

"He really hurt me," Young said. "I didn't think I was going to make it."

He managed to survive, however, and with Foreman tiring by the minute, the fight turned. Young scored a knockdown in the 12th and final round, and took a unanimous decision by scores of 118-111, 116-112, and 115-114.

Then something strange happened in Foreman's dressing room. Suffering from heat prostration, Big George experienced what he later described as a miracle. He felt blood trickling from his forehead, and began babbling passages from the Bible.

"Jesus Christ is coming alive in me!" he shouted. "Hallelujah! I'm clean! Hallelujah! I been born again!"

George was ready to preach. Oh, yeah, he'd finally secure that try at the title – 14 years and one improbable comeback later.

Jimmy Young drops ex-heavyweight champ George Foreman in the 12th and final round on his way to again becoming a leading contender.

WORLD TITLE FIGHTS

LIGHT HEAVYWEIGHTS

March 5 **John Conteh** *KO* 3
Len Hutchins, Liverpool

JUNIOR MIDDLEWEIGHTS

March 5 **Eddie Gazo** (NIC) *W* 15
Miguel Castellini, Managua

March 15 **Eckhard Dagge** *D* 15
Maurice Hope, Berlin

WELTERWEIGHTS

Jan 22 **Carlos Palomino** *KO* 15
Armando Muniz, Los Angeles

March 12 **Pipino Cuevas** *KO* 2
Miguel Campanino, Mexico City

JUNIOR WELTERWEIGHTS

Jan 15 **Saensak Muangsurin** *KO* 15
Monroe Brooks, Chiang Mai, Thailand

April 2 **Saensak Muangsurin** *KO* 6
Ishimatsu Suzuki, Tokyo

LIGHTWEIGHTS

Jan 29 **Roberto Duran** *KO* 13
Villomar Fernandez, Miami Beach

Feb 12 **Esteban DeJesus** *KO* 6
Buzzsaw Yamabe, Bayamon, Puerto Rico

JUNIOR LIGHTWEIGHTS

Jan 15 **Samuel Serrano** *KO* 11
Alberto Herrera, Guayaquil, Ecuador

March 17 **Alfredo Escalera** *KO* 6
Ronnie McGarvey, Hato Rey, Puerto Rico

FEATHERWEIGHTS

Jan 15 **Rafael Ortega** (PAN) *W* 15
Francisco Coronado, Panama City (Wins Vacant WBA Title)

JUNIOR FEATHERWEIGHTS

Feb 13 **Dong Kyun Yum** *W* 15
Jose Cervantes, Seoul

BANTAMWEIGHTS

Feb 5 **Carlos Zarate** *KO* 3
Fernando Cabanela, Mexico City

FLYWEIGHTS

Jan 1 **Guty Espadas** *KO* 7
Jiro Takada, Tokyo

April 24 **Miguel Canto** *W* 15
Reyes Arnal, Caracas

April 30 **Guty Espadas** *KO* 13
Alfonso Lopez, Merida, Mexico

JUNIOR FLYWEIGHTS

Jan 30 **Yoko Gushiken** *W* 15
Jaime Rios, Tokyo

MAY

1977

AUGUST

FINDING A PLACE OF HIS OWN

World bantamweight champions Alfonso Zamora and Carlos Zarate were outstanding fighters. Neither, however, was anxious to defend against Puerto Rican prodigy Wilfredo Gomez. So Gomez moved up and tried for Dong Kyun Yum's WBC super bantamweight crown.

Gomez' moment came on May 21, at Roberto Clemente Coliseum in San Juan. Less than a minute into the fight, Yum, a light-hitting counterpuncher, dropped the challenger with a hook to the jaw. Ironically, it worked against him; he went for the finish and was picked apart.

The Puerto Rican introduced his marvelous boxing skills in the fourth. ("I was in a fog for the first three rounds," he said.) He hit without being hit in return, and quickly caught up on the cards. Yum never again threatened. He was battered throughout the 11th, and finished by a right to the body in the 12th. Referee Dick Young tolled 10 at the 2:40 mark.

Boxing's newest division had its first star.

Wilfredo Gomez (right) beat Dong Kyun Yum.

CHOKING IN THE CLUTCH

May 11th was Duane Bobick's chance to prove he was a legitimate title threat, and not just the latest in a long, sad line of white hopes. Bobick, 38-0 (32), was rated first by the WBA and WBC. A win over Ken Norton would result in a bout with world heavyweight champ Muhammad Ali.

Bobick-Norton was held at Madison Square Garden. The bout lasted less than a minute. It began harmlessly enough, with the fighters approaching each other in ring center. Then Norton landed a right hand to, of all places, Bobick's windpipe. Bobick's eyes teared, and he covered up. (That's a nice way of saying that he fell apart.) Norton rocked him with two overhand rights, and felled him with a third. Bobick barely beat the count, but remained unsteady on his feet, and referee Petey Della halted the bout at the 58-second mark.

Bobick's 38 wins were instantly forgotten. Instead of being regarded as a good fighter, he became known as a bad joke.

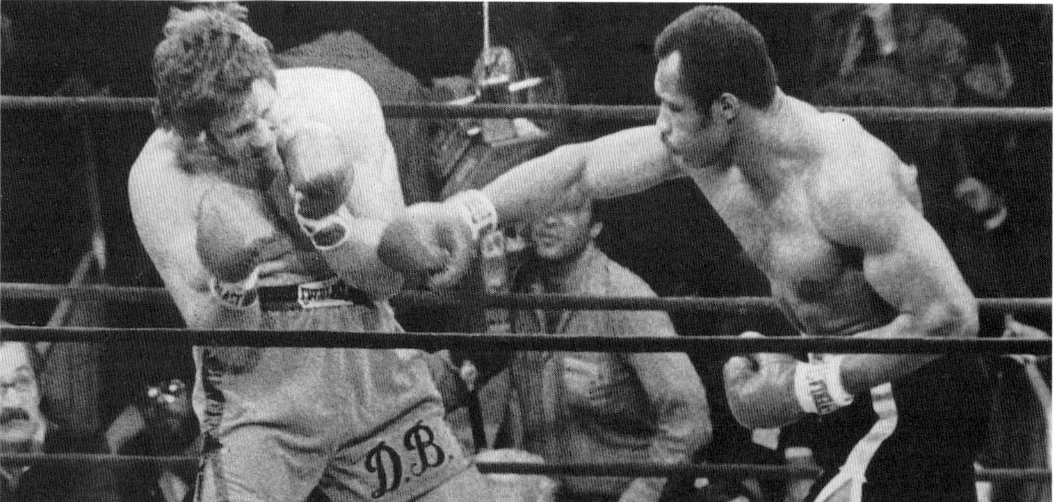

In his first fight since losing to Muhammad Ali, Ken Norton (right) knocked out Duane Bobick in the first round in New York.

WORLD TITLE FIGHTS

HEAVYWEIGHTS

May 16	**Muhammad Ali** *W* 15 Alfredo Evangelista, Landover, MD

LIGHT HEAVYWEIGHTS

May 21	**Miguel Angel Cuello** (ARG) *KO* 9 Jesse Burnett, Monte Carlo (Wins Vacant WBC Title)
June 18	**Victor Galindez** *W* 15 Richie Kates, Rome

MIDDLEWEIGHTS

July 30	**Carlos Monzon** *W* 15 Rodrigo Valdes, Monte Carlo

JUNIOR MIDDLEWEIGHTS

June 7	**Eddie Gazo** *KO* 11 Koichi Wajima, Tokyo
Aug 6	**Rocky Mattioli** (ITA) *KO* 5 Eckhard Dagge, Berlin

WELTERWEIGHTS

June 14	**Carlos Palomino** *KO* 11 Dave (Boy) Green, Wembley
Aug 6	**Pipino Cuevas** *KO* 2 Clyde Gray, Los Angeles

JUNIOR WELTERWEIGHTS

June 17	**Saensak Muangsurin** *W* 15 Perico Fernandez, Madrid
June 25	**Antonio Cervantes** *KO* 6 Carlos M. Gimenez, Maracaibo (Wins Vacant WBA Title)
Aug 3	**Wilfred Benitez** *KO* 15 Guerrero Chavez, New York City
Aug 20	**Saensak Muangsurin** *KO* 6 Mike Everett, Roi-et, Thailand

LIGHTWEIGHTS

June 25	**Esteban DeJesus** *KO* 11 Vicente S. Mijares, Bayamon, Puerto Rico

JUNIOR LIGHTWEIGHTS

May 16	**Alfredo Escalera** *KO* 8 Carlos Becerril, Landover, MD
June 26	**Samuel Serrano** *W* 15 Leonel Hernandez, Puerta La Cruz, Venezuela
Aug 27	**Samuel Serrano** *W* 15 Apollo Yoshio, Hato Rey, Puerto Rico

FEATHERWEIGHTS

May 29	**Rafael Ortega** *W* 15 Yasutsune Uehara, Okinawa

JUNIOR FEATHERWEIGHTS

May 21	**Wilfredo Gomez** (PR) *KO* 12 Dong Kyun Yum, Hato Rey, Puerto Rico
July 11	**Wilfredo Gomez** *KO* 5 Raul Tirado, Hato Rey, Puerto Rico

FLYWEIGHTS

June 15	**Miguel Canto** *W* 15 Kimio Furesawa, Tokyo

JUNIOR FLYWEIGHTS

May 15	**Luis Estaba** *W* 15 Rafael Pedroza, Caracas
May 22	**Yoko Gushiken** *W* 15 Rigoberto Marcano, Sapporo
July 17	**Luis Estaba** *W* 15 Ricardo Estupian, Puerto la Cruz, Venezuela
Aug 21	**Luis Estaba** *KO* 11 Juan Alvarez, Puerto la Cruz, Venezuela

ALI'S LITTLE FOLLY

Heavyweight champ Muhammad Ali toyed with challenger Alfredo Evangelista.

Alfredo Evangelista's career seemed to be unfolding in reverse. Shouldn't the Spain-based heavyweight have won the European title before challenging for the world crown? Shouldn't he have fought for more than 19 months before trying for the most prized possession in sports? Shouldn't he have at least won his previous fight?

On May 16, at the Capital Centre in Landover, Maryland, the lantern-jawed Uruguayan found himself in the ring with world champion Muhammad Ali. He didn't belong, of course, but a guarantee of $100,000 convinced him to try his luck. (Ali made $2.7-million.)

The fight was terribly dull. Ali moved and boxed, and tried to take out Evangelista only once, after stunning him in the sixth. For his part, Evangelista missed with enthusiasm.

Ali won by scores of 72-64, 78-64 and 71-65. It hadn't been much of a fight. Then again, Evangelista hadn't been much of a challenger.

AN EXIT WORTHY OF A MIDDLEWEIGHT LEGEND

If Carlos Monzon-Rodrigo Valdes I was similar to Muhammad Ali-Joe Frazier I, the rematch was very much like "The Thrilla In Manila." World middleweight champion Monzon and former WBC titlist Valdes were aging masters who demanded the best from each other and, in the process, burned every bit of energy they could muster.

Their battle came on July 30, at Louis II Stadium in Monte Carlo. The bout was far more competitive than the original. Valdes opened with fists flying, and in the second round, scored a knockdown with a right cross. (It was the first time Monzon had been felled in 13 years.) Applying constant pressure, he built a slight lead. At the halfway mark, Monzon began his rally. He opened a long cut over the Colombian's left eye in the 10th, and traded with confidence throughout the championship rounds.

The decision, close but unanimous, was taken by Monzon (scores of 144-141, 147-144, and 145-143.) Having made a division-record 14 defenses, the 34-year-old Argentine immediately announced his retirement.

"I think I showed everyone I'm one of the great ones," he said.

After decisioning Rodrigo Valdes in 15 rounds to retain the middleweight title, Carlos Monzon (right) retired after a brilliant 14-year career.

RINGSIDE VIEW

MAY

Unbeaten Argentine knockout artist Miguel Angel Cuello wins the vacant WBC light heavyweight crown by knocking out Jesse Burnett.

JUNE

WBC welterweight champion Carlos Palomino retains the crown by scoring an 11th-round kayo of Briton Dave (Boy) Green.

SEPTEMBER

1977

DECEMBER

FIGHTING TALK

He even cursed my mother, but when I tried to curse his mother, too, the referee stopped me

EDWIN VIRUET
after his unsuccessful challenge of WBA lightweight champion Roberto Duran

IS HANDS OF STONE GETTING SOFTER?

Roberto Duran had become a prisoner of his own competence. On September 17, the WBA lightweight champion retained the crown by scoring a unanimous decision over Edwin Viruet at the Spectrum in Philadelphia. It was the Panamanian's 11th defense, but the first in which he hadn't scored a kayo. Never mind that Viruet had previously extended Duran in a 1975 non-title fight; or that Viruet was both rugged and clever, combining a good chin with a good defense. Duran's fans wanted to know: were the champion's hands of stone getting softer?

Duran worked the body over the first four rounds, and then remained aggressive as the Puerto Rican challenger turned, twisted, held, slipped, and countered. There was never the threat of a knockout, or even a knockdown. After 15 rounds, "Manos de Piedra" was declared the winner by 73-68, 73-65, and 71-65.

It would be the only points victory of his 6½-year reign.

Roberto Duran (left) retained the lightweight crown by outpointing Puerto Rico's Edwin Viruet in 15 hard-fought rounds in Philadelphia.

WORLD TITLE FIGHTS

HEAVYWEIGHTS

Sept 29 **Muhammad Ali** *W* 15 Earnie Shavers, New York City

LIGHT HEAVYWEIGHTS

Sept 17 **Victor Galindez** *W* 15 Yaqui Lopez, Rome

Nov 20 **Victor Galindez** *W* 15 Eddie Gregory, Turin, Italy

MIDDLEWEIGHTS

Nov 5 **Rodrigo Valdes** *W* 15 Bennie Briscoe, Campione d'Italia, Switzerland (Wins Vacant World Title)

JUNIOR MIDDLEWEIGHTS

Sept 13 **Eddie Gazo** *W* 15 Kenji Shibata, Tokyo

Dec 18 **Eddie Gazo** *W* 15 Chae Keun Lim, Inchon, South Korea

WELTERWEIGHTS

Sept 13 **Carlos Palomino** *W* 15 Everaldo Azevedo, Los Angeles

Nov 19 **Pipino Cuevas** *KO* 12 Angel Espada, San Juan

Dec 10 **Carlos Palomino** *KO* 13 Jose Palacios, Los Angeles

JUNIOR WELTERWEIGHTS

Oct 22 **Saensak Muangsurin** *W* 15 Saoul Mamby, Korat, Thailand

Nov 5 **Antonio Cervantes** *W* 15 Adriano Marrero, Maracay

Dec 29 **Saensak Muangsurin** *KO* 14 Jo Kimpuani, Chanthaburi, Thailand

LIGHTWEIGHTS

Sept 17 **Roberto Duran** *W* 15 Edwin Viruet, Philadelphia

JUNIOR LIGHTWEIGHTS

Sept 10 **Alfredo Escalera** *W* 15 Sigfredo Rodriguez, Hato Rey, Puerto Rico

Nov 19 **Samuel Serrano** *KO* 10 Tao Ho Kim, Hato Rey, Puerto Rico

FEATHERWEIGHTS

Sept 12 **Danny Lopez** *KO* 8 Jose Torres, Los Angeles

Dec 17 **Cecilio Lastra** (SPA) *W* 15 Rafael Ortega, Torrelavega, Spain

JUNIOR FEATHERWEIGHTS

Nov 26 **Soo Hwan Hong** *KO* 3 Hector Carrasquilla, Panama City (Wins Newly Created WBA Title)

BANTAMWEIGHTS

Oct 29 **Carlos Zarate** *KO* 6 Danilo Batista, Los Angeles

Nov 19 **Jorge Lujan** (PAN) *KO* 10 Alfonso Zamora, Los Angeles

Dec 2 **Carlos Zarate** *KO* 5 Juan F. Rodriguez, Madrid

FLYWEIGHTS

Sept 18 **Miguel Canto** *W* 15 Martin Vargas, Merida, Mexico

Nov 19 **Guty Espadas** *KO* 8 Alex Santana, Los Angeles

Nov 30 **Miguel Canto** *W* 15 Martin Vargas, Santiago

JUNIOR FLYWEIGHTS

Sept 18 **Luis Estaba** *KO* 15 Orlando Hernandez, Caracas

Oct 9 **Yoko Gushiken** *KO* 4 Montsayarm Mahachai, Oita, Japan

Oct 30 **Luis Estaba** *W* 15 Netrnoi Vorasingh, Caracas

SCORING, AND KNOWING WHAT THE SCORE IS

A good chin almost always beats a good punch. That's why, on September 29, world heavyweight champion Muhammad Ali outpointed Earnie Shavers at Madison Square Garden. Oh, yeah, Angelo Dundee helped, too.

For the benefit of the TV audience, Ali-Shavers featured open scoring. Dundee, as shrewd a cornerman as the game has ever known, had an assistant relay the totals after each round. The fight was quite close, and down the stretch, Dundee knew whether Ali needed to accelerate or stall. On the other hand, Shavers' corner (manager Blackie Gennaro and trainer Frank Luca), was unaware of the scoring. Shavers was told that on their reckoning he was winning the fight.

Arguably the hardest hitter in history, Shavers shook Ali several times. But hurting the champion and finishing him were vastly different tasks. Whenever Shavers struck, Ali clowned, covered up, or moved away. ("When the hour is darkest," he said, "I come through.") After 15 rounds, "The Greatest" was awarded a unanimous verdict by scores of 9-6 (twice) and 9-5-1.

Dundee, of course, knew the score all along.

Muhammad Ali (right) retained the crown against the hard-hitting Earnie Shavers.

15 ROUNDS, BUT BENNY NEEDED 17

Carlos Monzon dominated at middleweight throughout the '70s. But it was Rodrigo Valdes who was responsible for denying Bennie Briscoe a world title. Bad Bennie, considered among the finest 160-pounders to never become a champion, lost three times to Valdes, in an NABF title bout, in a bout for the vacant WBC title, and in a bout for the world title vacated by Monzon.

Their third fight, held in Campioni d'Italia, Italy, came only 13 weeks after Valdes' draining second loss to Monzon. It was rather ordinary, with the only exciting moments coming in the third and fourth rounds, when Valdes battered Briscoe and threatened to stop him. Otherwise, the rivals dueled at close range. Each round seemed to be merely a replay of the one before.

Slower of hand and foot, Briscoe managed to stage a rally near the end. After learning that he had lost by unanimous scores of 149-142, 148-145, and 148-146, he moaned, "Two more rounds and Valdes would have gone to the canvas."

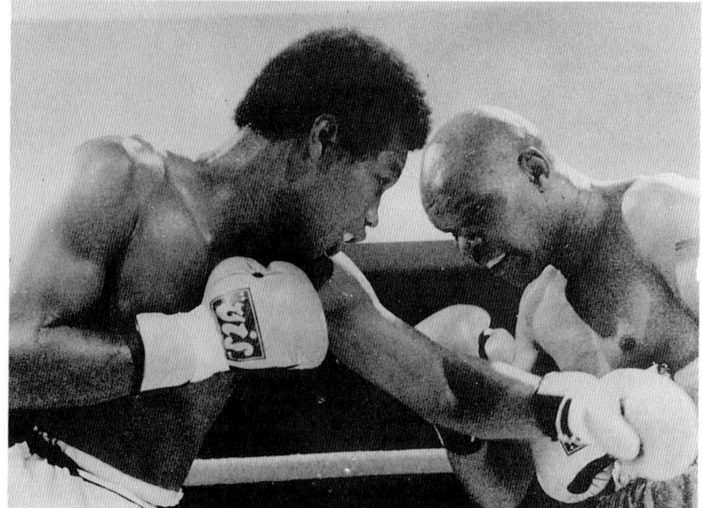

Rodrigo Valdes (left) outpointed Bennie Briscoe in 15 rounds to win the middleweight title.

HAVING LOST MORE THAN A FIGHT

Having suffered a crushing kayo loss in the biggest fight of his life, a non-title showdown with unbeaten countryman Carlos Zarate, Alfonso Zamora remained the WBA bantamweight champion. At 23, he seemed to have a unlimited future. But the Zarate fight proved to be a turning point; he would win half of his last eight.

In his first fight since losing to Zarate, Zamora was a 10-1 favorite to crush inexperienced Panamanian Jorge Lujan. The bout, held on the same card as WBA flyweight champion Guty Espadas' kayo of Alex Santana, came on November 19, at the Sports Arena in Los Angeles. Fighting slickly off the ropes, Lujan survived Zamora's early attack and then accelerated as the champion tired. By the middle rounds, Zamora was being battered, and in the 10th, he was dropped by a straight right. He sat sadly on the bottom rope as referee John Thomas counted to 10.

There was no more fight left.

Zamora after being stopped by Lujan.

RINGSIDE VIEW

OCTOBER

WBC super lightweight champion Saensak Muangsurin retains the crown for the fifth time in his second reign, scoring a controversial and split 15-round decision over New York's Saoul Mamby.

NOVEMBER

In a heavyweight title eliminator, Ken Norton barely outpoints Jimmy Young over 15 rounds in Las Vegas. Four months later, the WBC declares Norton its champion.

JANUARY

1978

APRIL

"PATIENCE WILL WIN THE FIGHT"

The wisdom of co-trainers Freddie Brown and Ray Arcel was the constant in lightweight champion Roberto Duran's formula for victory. Before Duran's January 21 unification battle vs. nemesis and WBC champion Esteban DeJesus, fought at Caesars Palace in Las Vegas, Arcel told the WBA titlist, "Patience will win the fight."

Duran kept his cool when DeJesus mouthed off at the chaotic weigh-in; he remained calm in the early rounds, when DeJesus looked to counter with the hook that had felled Duran in their two previous bouts; he even paced himself after hurting DeJesus for the first time after four rounds.

The fight turned in the fifth, when Duran drew blood with a left uppercut to the mouth. He punched mostly to the body after that, and finished his foe in the 12th. DeJesus dropped from a right to the jaw. After he rose, the Panamanian ended the bout with a seven-punch flurry.

Boxing's only lightweight champion might have been its best of all-time.

Roberto Duran (left) stopped Esteban DeJesus in the 12th round to unify the lightweight crown.

Ringside View

MARCH

After the WBC strips world heavyweight champion Leon Spinks for failing to defend against number-one contender Ken Norton, the organization proclaims Norton its titlist, based on his November 1977 victory over Jimmy Young.

APRIL

Panama's Eusebio Pedroza wins the WBA featherweight title by stopping Cecilio Lastra in the 13th round.

World Title Fights

HEAVYWEIGHTS

Feb 15 **Leon Spinks** (USA) *W* 15
Muhammad Ali, Las Vegas

LIGHT HEAVYWEIGHTS

Jan 7 **Mate Parlov** (YUG) *KO* 9
Miguel Angel Cuello, Milan

MIDDLEWEIGHTS

April 22 **Hugo Corro** (ARG) *W* 15
Rodrigo Valdes, San Remo

JUNIOR MIDDLEWEIGHTS

March 11 **Rocky Mattioli** (AUT) *KO* 7
Elisha Obed, Melbourne

WELTERWEIGHTS

Feb 11 **Carlos Palomino** *KO* 7
Ryu Sorimachi, Las Vegas

March 4 **Pipino Cuevas** *KO* 10
Harold Weston Jr., Los Angeles

March 18 **Carlos Palomino** *KO* 9
Mimoun Mohatar, Las Vegas

JUNIOR WELTERWEIGHTS

April 8 **Saensak Muangsurin** *KO* 13
Francisco Moreno, Hat Yai, Thailand

April 28 **Antonio Cervantes** *KO* 6
Tonga Kiatvayupakdi, Udon Thani, Thailand

LIGHTWEIGHTS

Jan 21 **Roberto Duran** *KO* 12
Esteban DeJesus, Las Vegas
(Unifies World Title)

JUNIOR LIGHTWEIGHTS

Jan 28 **Alexis Arguello** *KO* 13
Alfredo Escalera, Bayamon

Feb 18 **Samuel Serrano** *W* 15
Mario Martinez, Hato Rey, Puerto Rico

April 29 **Alexis Arguello** *KO* 5
Rey Tam, Inglewood

FEATHERWEIGHTS

Feb 15 **Danny Lopez** *KO* 6
David Kotey, Las Vegas

April 15 **Eusebio Pedroza** (PAN) *KO* 13
Cecilio Lastra, Panama City

April 23 **Danny Lopez** *KO* 6
Jose DePaula, Los Angeles

JUNIOR FEATHERWEIGHTS

Jan 19 **Wilfredo Gomez** *KO* 3
Royal Kobayashi, Kitakyushu, Japan

Feb 1 **Soo Hwan Hong** *W* 15
Yu Kasahara, Tokyo

April 8 **Wilfredo Gomez** *KO* 7
Juan Antonio Lopez, Bayamon

BANTAMWEIGHTS

Feb 25 **Carlos Zarate** *KO* 8
Albert Davila, Inglewood

March 18 **Jorge Lujan** *KO* 11
Roberto Rubaldino, San Antonio

April 22 **Carlos Zarate** *KO* 13
Andres Hernandez, San Juan

FLYWEIGHTS

Jan 2 **Guty Espadas** *KO* 7
Kimio Furesawa, Tokyo

Jan 4 **Miguel Canto** *W* 15
Shoji Oguma, Koriyama, Japan

April 18 **Miguel Canto** *W* 15
Shoji Oguma, Tokyo

JUNIOR FLYWEIGHTS

Jan 29 **Yoko Gushiken** *KO* 14
Anaceto Vargas, Nagoya

Feb 19 **Freddy Castillo** (MEX) *KO* 14
Luis Estaba, Caracas

A GAME PLAN GONE BAD

It was difficult to find fault with WBC super featherweight champion Alfredo Escalera's strategies. Having made 10 defenses, the Puerto Rican was among boxing's most successful titlists. Against former featherweight king Alexis Arguello, Escalera planned to smother the long-armed challenger, and then rally.

The fight came on January 28, at Loubriel Stadium in Bayamon. Escalera managed to crowd Arguello, but in the process, absorbed dozens of crushing hooks. After a handful of rounds, the local hero was a bloody mess.

Arguello scored a knockdown in round two, cut the champion over both eyes, and almost tore his upper lip from his face. (It took 30 stitches to repair.) Proving as game as he was good, Escalera briefly rallied. But in the 13th, referee Arthur Mercante decided he had seen enough blood.

Two great fighters had given their all, but Arguello, only one month younger, was still on the way up and improving.

Arguello (left) knocked out Escalera to annex the junior lightweight championship.

AS MONZON, SO HUGO CORRO

As Carlos Monzon had been to Nino Benvenuti, Hugo Corro was to Rodrigo Valdes. Before winning the world middleweight title by dethroning a faded Benvenuti, Monzon was known only in his native Argentina. Likewise, before challenging a slow and tired Valdes (who had succeeded Monzon), Corro, despite only two defeats and a draw in his 46 contests, was recognized only in the land of the Pampas.

Corro-Valdes was held on April 22, at the Ariston Theatre in San Remo, Italy. Making his first defense, Valdes, 31, proved to be all fought out. He missed the majority of his punches, and Corro blocked most of the others. The challenger fought cautiously, which frustrated the crowd. But he repeatedly scored with left-rights in the late rounds, and took the crown by unanimous 15-round decision.

The similarities linking Corro and Monzon were apparent. But only the latter came to be regarded as an all-time great.

Hugo Corro (right) after winning the middleweight championship from Rodrigo Valdes.

NEON LEON PUTS HIS NAME IN VEGAS LIGHTS

Insiders snickered when it was announced that heavyweight champion Muhammad Ali was scheduled to defend against 1976 Olympic gold medalist Leon Spinks, a novice of seven pro bouts. But Sam Solomon, Spinks' trainer, nodded knowingly.

"Ali is a tired, old man," he said. "He's ready to be taken. I know it. He's going back, and somebody's gonna catch him."

Ali got caught on February 15, at the Las Vegas Hilton. Spinks, an 8-1 underdog, was raw and crude, but also vibrant and fearless. When Ali rope-a-doped, he punched freely. And when the champion danced and jabbed, "Neon Leon" chased him down.

After "The Greatest" rallied in the 10th, the crowd of 5,298 began chanting "Ali! Ali!" But this time, there would be no magic. Said Ali, "I was hoping to catch up when he got tired, but he didn't get tired."

Ali tried to save the title by going toe to toe in the 15th. Spinks, however, answered one final time, and took a split decision by scores of 145-140, 144-141, and a sentimental 142-143.

At least this time, Ali had lost the title in the ring.

In a startling upset, Leon Spinks (left) won a split 15-round decision over Muhammad Ali to become the new world heavyweight champion.

MAY

1978

AUGUST

GUARANTEED VICTOR(Y)

About midway through the lengthy reign of WBA light heavyweight champion Victor Galindez, it became apparent that the Argentine wasn't going to lose the title on points. Galindez won his share of rounds, and usually those he lost were scored even.

In a September 1977 try at the title, Yaqui Lopez was edged by Galindez. He screamed robbery loud enough to secure a rematch, which came on May 6, at the Sports Palace in Via Reggio, Italy.

Galindez started slowly, and the lanky Lopez was content to jab. But once the champion got started, one hand wasn't enough to beat him. The Argentine countered with hooks to the body, and by the championship rounds, Lopez was fatigued. It was an uneven and forgettable fight; neither 175-pounder offered a concentrated attack. But at the final bell, there was little doubt that Galindez had done enough to win. He took a unanimous decision by scores of 148-145, 146-144, and 148-146.

In case you were wondering, those totals included lots of even rounds.

Argentina's Victor Galindez (right) was awarded a 15-round decision over Yaqui Lopez.

WORLD TITLE FIGHTS

HEAVYWEIGHTS

June 9	**Larry Holmes** (USA) *W* 15 Ken Norton, Las Vegas

LIGHT HEAVYWEIGHTS

May 6	**Victor Galindez** *W* 15 Yaqui Lopez, Via Reggio, Italy
June 17	**Mate Parlov** *W* 15 John Conteh, Belgrade

MIDDLEWEIGHTS

Aug 5	**Hugo Corro** *W* 15 Ronnie Harris, Buenos Aires

JUNIOR MIDDLEWEIGHTS

May 14	**Rocky Mattioli** *KO* 5 Jose Duran, Pescara, Italy
Aug 9	**Masashi Kudo** (JAP) *W* 15 Eddie Gazo, Akita, Japan

WELTERWEIGHTS

May 20	**Pipino Cuevas** *KO* 2 Billy Backus, Inglewood
May 27	**Carlos Palomino** *W* 15 Armando Muniz, Los Angeles

JUNIOR WELTERWEIGHTS

Aug 26	**Antonio Cervantes** *KO* 9 Norman Sekgapane, Mmbatho, Bophuthatswana

JUNIOR LIGHTWEIGHTS

June 3	**Alexis Arguello** *KO* 1 Diego Alcala, Hato Rey, Puerto Rico
July 8	**Samuel Serrano** *KO* 9 Oh Young Ho, Hato Rey, Puerto Rico

FEATHERWEIGHTS

July 2	**Eusebio Pedroza** *KO* 12 Ernesto Herrera, Panama City

JUNIOR FEATHERWEIGHTS

May 6	**Ricardo Cardona** (COL) *KO* 12 Soo Hwan Hong, Seoul
June 2	**Wilfredo Gomez** *KO* 3 Sakad Porntavee, Korat, Thailand

BANTAMWEIGHTS

June 9	**Carlos Zarate** *KO* 4 Emilio Hernandez, Las Vegas

FLYWEIGHTS

Aug 12	**Betulio Gonzalez** *W* 15 Guty Espadas, Maracay

JUNIOR FLYWEIGHTS

May 6	**Netrnoi Vorasingh** (THA) *W* 15 Freddy Castillo, Bangkok
May 7	**Yoko Gushiken** *KO* 13 Jaime Rios, Hiroshima
July 29	**Netrnoi Vorasingh** *KO* 5 Luis Estaba, Caracas

HE TOOK A 15-ROUND BEATING – IN ONLY THREE MINUTES

Some fights are predictable. Others are ugly. Still others are predictably ugly.

On May 20, WBA welterweight champion Pipino Cuevas made his sixth defense, risking the crown against an unlikely opponent, 35-year-old former world champion Billy Backus, at the Forum in Inglewood, California.

Said Backus, "I was surprised when they called me this time."

When Backus turned pro (in 1962), Cuevas was four years old. Had they fought then, the bout might have been more competitive. Marching out of his corner, the Mexican champion began a fearsome blitz. There was one knockdown, and before three minutes had passed, Backus was bleeding from cuts above and below his swollen right eye.

There would be no extended beating; before the start of round two, referee Carlos Berrocal, acting on the advice of Dr. Roger Thill, called a halt. Backus left the ring looking as if he had finished a 15-round war. He fought no more.

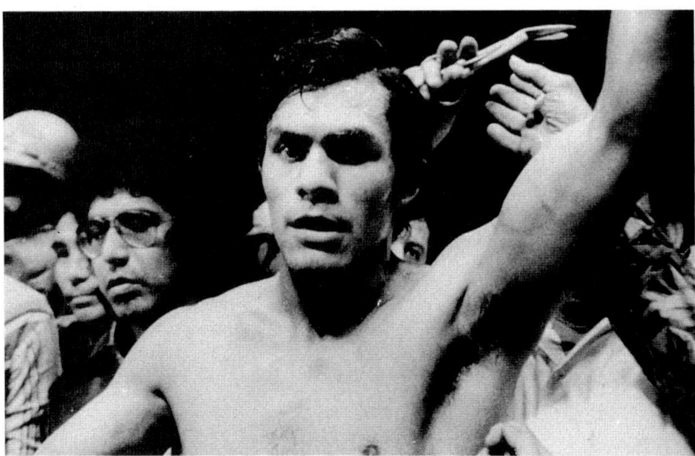

Mexico's Pipino Cuevas raises his hand in victory after knocking out Billy Backus in the first.

THE ROUND FOR HOLMES TO BE CROWNED

After being handed the WBC heavyweight title, Ken Norton tried to earn it. On June 9, he made his first defense, facing the unbeaten (27-0) Larry Holmes. Their battle, at Caesars Palace Sports Pavilion, was among the best in heavyweight history.

Ignoring a torn muscle in his left arm, Holmes built a points lead by pumping his outstanding jab. Norton attacked in the middle rounds, landing several overhand rights to draw even.

With three minutes to go, all three judges had the fight even. And what a round the 15th was! First Norton broke through, pounding Holmes with hooks. Then Holmes answered with rights and uppercuts. Finally, the heavyweights traded toe to toe until the final bell.

"I wanted to take him out," said Holmes. "I hurt him a few times, and he hurt me, but because of his determination and my determination, we both finished."

Two judges scored the round for Holmes, and one for Norton. Both fighters were empty, but only one was richer for the experience.

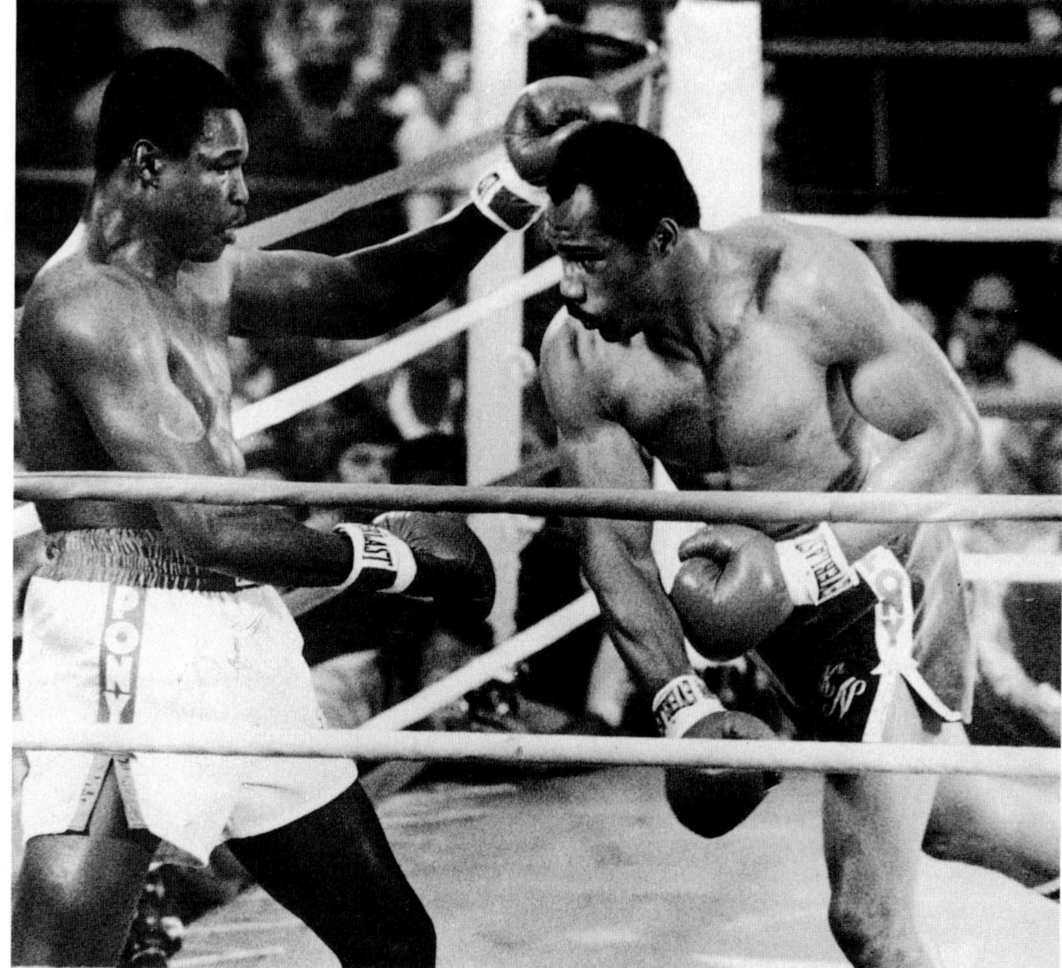

Larry Holmes (left) outpointed Ken Norton in 15 rounds to win the heavyweight championship and remain undefeated in a six-year career.

A FLY WITH STAYING POWER

The smaller the fighter, the shorter the prime. At least so goes conventional wisdom. But there was little conventional about flyweight Betulio Gonzalez.

No less than 11 years separated the remarkable Venezuelan's first and last world title fights. He failed in his first two tries, then won the WBC title twice in 14 months. After being dethroned for the second time (by Shoji Oguma), Gonzalez lost a pair of title fights to the inimitable Miguel Canto. But he was hardly finished. On August 12, at the Maestranza Cesar Giron in Maracay, he won the WBA crown by outpointing Guty Espadas.

Limiting the champion's leverage, Gonzalez smothered Espada, who had scored kayos in all five of his previous title fights. The Mexican broke free only in the 15th and last round, but couldn't finish his foe, and the title changed hands by majority verdict.

Gonzalez would never be considered as skilled as Canto. But at flyweight in the '70s, being second-best wasn't bad at all.

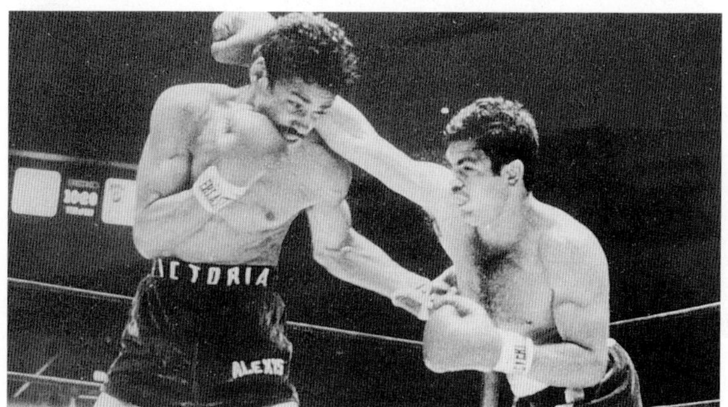

Vilomar Fernandez (right) won a non-title, upset decision over champion Alexis Arguello.

RINGSIDE VIEW

MAY

Performing masterfully, lightly regarded Colombian Ricardo Cardona wins the WBA junior featherweight title by stopping Soo Hwan Hong in the 12th round.

JULY

In a non-title fight, slick Dominican Vilomar Fernandez shocks WBC super featherweight champion Alexis Arguello, taking a 10-round decision at Madison Square Garden.

SEPTEMBER

1978

DECEMBER

FIGHTING TALK

Only in America can an Italian kid turn Jewish to beat up Mexicans

JIMMY DEPIANO
the manager and stepfather of WBA light heavyweight champion Mike Rossman

ONE OF THOSE "OTHER" FIGHTS

If an inventor had patented the world's best corkscrew on the day that Dr. Jonas Salk introduced the polio vaccine, he probably wouldn't have made headlines. Mike Rossman could sympathize: his biggest victory, a TKO over WBA light heavyweight champion Victor Galindez, came on the night that Muhammad Ali triumphed over Leon Spinks.

The Carnival of Champions, held on September 15, at the Superdome in New Orleans, featured Ali-Spinks II, Rossman-Galindez, WBC featherweight titlist Danny Lopez' kayo of Juan Malvarez, and WBA bantamweight champion Jorge Lujan's decision over Albert Davila. Rossman-Galindez was the only real surprise.

The 22-year-old challenger dominated from the second round, when he opened a cut over Galindez' right eye. Rossman subsequently widened the wound with his jab, and in the middle rounds, moved inside. In the 13th, Galindez was pinned against the ropes, bringing referee Carlos Berrocal's intervention. It was the Argentine's first loss in 44 fights.

And after Ali dethroned Spinks, it was quickly forgotten.

Mike Rossman (right) won light heavyweight crown from Victor Galindez with 13th-round TKO.

THE ENDING THAT WAS WRITTEN IN ADVANCE

Father Time might have objected, but fate wasn't about to dismiss Muhammad Ali. Sensing the opportunity to witness history, 70,000 fans filled the New Orleans Superdome for the September 15 rematch with Leon Spinks.

A 2-1 favorite, Ali dominated from the start; Spinks was ill-prepared and unfocused.

The champion chased futilely, eating punches while marching in, and then falling into clinches when Ali needed to rest. Spinks couldn't even find comfort in his corner; his handlers screamed conflicting advice, and after round six, strategist George Benton, disgusted by the chaos, stormed off.

After 15 rounds, Ali was declared the winner by unanimous scores of 10-4-1 (twice) and 11-4. At age 36, he had won the title for a record third time.

Said the living legend, "To outmove, outmaneuver, out-stamina a young man of 25, just seven months after he beat me and they all said I was finished, too old, this is satisfying."

It was satisfying for everybody.

RINGSIDE VIEW

NOVEMBER

World middleweight champion Hugo Corro repeats his title-winning victory over former king Rodrigo Valdes, scoring a unanimous decision.

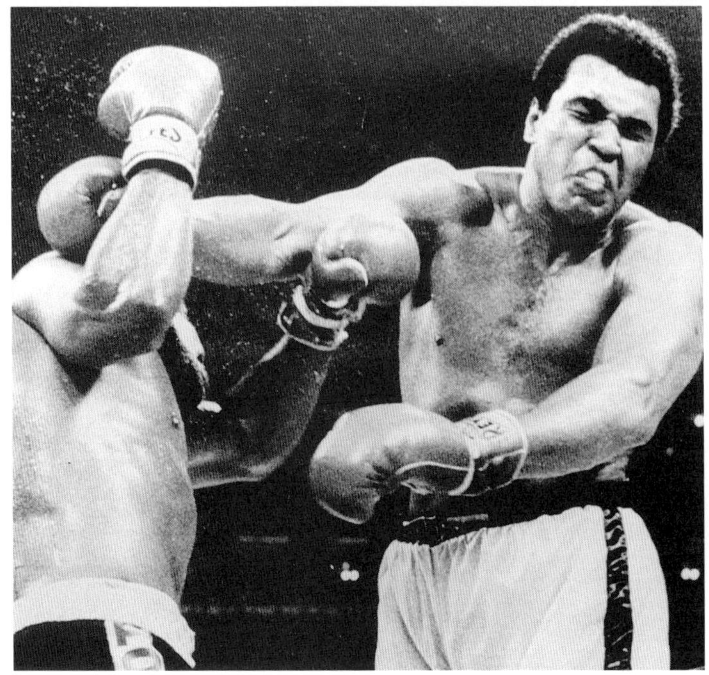

Muhammad Ali regained the heavyweight crown by winning a decision over Leon Spinks.

MATCHUP FOR THE AGES

In hindsight, the matchup pitting defending WBC super bantamweight champion Wilfredo Gomez vs. WBC bantamweight titlist Carlos Zarate might have been the decade's best. The 22-year-old Gomez was 21-0-1 (21) and just beginning to realize his potential; the 26-year-old Zarate was 54-0 (53), and thought by some to be the world's best fighter.

Before a wildly pro-Gomez crowd at the Roberto Clemente Coliseum, Gomez won the first two rounds but Zarate took the third. In the fourth, Gomez exploded. A counter hook dropped the Mexican, and a right redeposited him on the canvas. Gomez also scored an unofficial knockdown after referee Harry Gibbs failed to hear the bell.

After the challenger fell again in the fifth, Gibbs called a halt. Zarate remained a champion, but only Gomez was a king.

Puerto Rico's Wilfredo Gomez knocked out Mexico's Carlos Zarate in the fifth round.

Pipino Cuevas (left) and Pete Ranzany.

RINGSIDE VIEW

SEPTEMBER

WBA welterweight champion Pipino Cuevas makes his seventh defense, crushing Californian Pete Ranzany in two rounds.

FIGHTING FOR A DIFFERENT GOLD

At the 1972 Olympics in Munich, Mate Parlov, a light heavyweight from Yugoslavia, went for the gold and got it. Fellow southpaw Marvin Johnson, a middleweight from the United States, settled for a bronze medal. Six years later, it was Johnson's turn to celebrate – at Parlov's expense.

In January 1978, Parlov won the WBC 175-pound crown by knocking out Miguel Angel Cuello. His second defense came against Johnson at the Sports Palace in Marsala, Italy.

Married six weeks before the fight, Johnson's honeymoon activities included sparring, jumping rope, and roadwork at dawn. At the sound of the opening bell, he took his frustration out on Parlov. The challenger set a torrid pace, and by round four, Parlov was content to clinch.

Round after round belonged to the indefatigable Johnson. After two knockdowns in the 10th, Parlov was rescued by referee Roland Dakin. Johnson's real honeymoon was about to begin.

WORLD TITLE FIGHTS

HEAVYWEIGHTS

Sept 15	**Muhammad Ali** *W* 15 Leon Spinks, New Orleans
Nov 10	**Larry Holmes** *KO* 7 Alfredo Evangelista, Las Vegas

LIGHT HEAVYWEIGHTS

Sept 15	**Mike Rossman** (USA) *KO* 13 Victor Galindez, New Orleans
Dec 2	**Marvin Johnson** (USA) *KO* 10 Mate Parlov, Marsala, Italy
Dec 5	**Mike Rossman** *KO* 6 Aldo Traversaro, Philadelphia

MIDDLEWEIGHTS

Nov 11	**Hugo Corro** *W* 15 Rodrigo Valdes, Buenos Aires

JUNIOR MIDDLEWEIGHTS

Dec 13	**Masashi Kudo** *W* 15 Joo Ho, Osaka

WELTERWEIGHTS

Sept 9	**Pipino Cuevas** *KO* 2 Pete Ranzany, Sacramento

JUNIOR WELTERWEIGHTS

Dec 30	**Sang Hyun Kim** (KOR) *KO* 13 Saensak Muangsurin, Seoul

JUNIOR LIGHTWEIGHTS

Nov 10	**Alexis Arguello** *W* 15 Arturo Leon, Las Vegas
Nov 29	**Samuel Serrano** *W* 15 Takao Maruki, Nagoya

FEATHERWEIGHTS

Oct 21	**Danny Lopez** *W Disq* 4 Fel Clemente, Pesaro, Italy
Nov 27	**Eusebio Pedroza** *W* 15 Enrique Solis, Hato Rey, Puerto Rico

JUNIOR FEATHERWEIGHTS

Sept 2	**Ricardo Cardona** *W* 15 Ruben Valdez, Cartagena
Sept 9	**Wilfredo Gomez** *KO* 13 Leonardo Cruz, San Juan
Oct 28	**Wilfredo Gomez** *KO* 5 Carlos Zarate, Hato Rey, Puerto Rico
Nov 12	**Ricardo Cardona** *W* 15 Soon Hyun Chung, Seoul

BANTAMWEIGHTS

Sept 15	**Jorge Lujan** *W* 15 Albert Davila, New Orleans

FLYWEIGHTS

Nov 4	**Betulio Gonzalez** *KO* 12 Martin Vargas, Maracay
Nov 20	**Miguel Canto** *W* 15 Tacomron Vibonchai, Houston

JUNIOR FLYWEIGHTS

Sept 30	**Sung Jun Kim** (KOR) *KO* 3 Netrnoi Vorasingh, Seoul
Oct 15	**Yoko Gushiken** *KO* 5 Sang Il Chung, Tokyo

JANUARY

1979

APRIL

AN ENCORE – THREE YEARS LATER

After winning the junior welterweight title at age 17, what could Wilfred Benitez possibly have done for an encore? Well, he injured both hands in an auto accident – and was subsequently stripped for failing to defend the title; he suffered three knockdowns in a disputed decision over Bruce Curry; and he contracted hepatitis, resulting in an eight-month layoff. Not exactly what his fans had in mind.

On January 14, the Puerto Rican wunderkind reintroduced his skills during his challenge of WBC welterweight king Carlos Palomino. Benitez won his second world crown, taking a split 15-round decision at the Hiram Bithorn Stadium in San Juan.

The bout was close for six rounds, after which Benitez used his uncanny radar to slip most of the champion's blows. Fighting off the ropes, the challenger sensed when Palomino was going to punch. He countered with blinding speed and triumphed by scores of 148-143, 146-143, and 142-146. (Zack Clayton, who scored for Palomino, claimed the sun had affected his vision.)

Benitez was 20. Incredibly, his prime seemed in front of him.

Puerto Rico's Wilfred Benitez (left) won split 15-round decision over Carlos Palomino.

THE BLOOD-AND-GUTS REMATCH

Over the course of his 19-year career, Alexis Arguello faced several world champions, and even a hall of famer or two. None of his opponents, however, showed more heart than Alfredo Escalera.

In January 1978, Arguello had taken the Puerto Rican's WBC super featherweight title by 13th-round kayo. The rematch came on February 4, at the Sports Palace in Rimini, Italy.

It didn't seem the challenger would survive the early rounds; Escalera suffered cuts over both eyes, and was knocked down in the fourth and fifth. Referee Angelo Poletti allowed him to continue, however, and "The Snake Man" rallied to take most of the middle rounds.

But Arguello was a proud champion, and in the 13th, he saved the crown by dropping his foe with a tremendous hook. Escalera beat the count, then pitched forward, and Poletti stepped in at the 1:24 mark.

The bout ran exactly one minute shorter than the original. And remarkably, it had turned out to be every bit as thrilling.

Alexis Arguello knocked out Alfredo Escalera in the 13th round of a sizzling brawl.

RINGSIDE VIEW

FEBRUARY

In Las Vegas, WBA light heavyweight champion Mike Rossman waits in the ring for Victor Galindez. But the Argentine elects to remain in his dressing room, refusing to fight because of the Nevada State Athletic Commission's selection of officials. Six weeks later, Galindez would regain the crown by stopping Rossman in the 10th round.

MARCH

South Korea's Chan Hee Park, a relative novice, dethrones WBC flyweight champion Miguel Canto via unanimous 15-round decision. It is Park's 11th bout – and Canto's 15th defense.

THE DURAN WANNABES

With Roberto Duran seeking bigger challenges, the world title suddenly became a realistic goal for 135-pounders from Sicily to Seoul. The WBC chose Scottish southpaw and European champion Jim Watt and Mexico-based Colombian powerpuncher Alfredo Pitalua to compete for its vacant title. (In June, Venezuela's Ernesto Espana would win the vacant WBA crown.)

Watt and Pitalua met on April 17, at a highly charged Kelvin Hall in Glasgow. The impressively muscled Pitalua, a step-brother of former world middleweight champion Rodrigo Valdes, started quickly, scoring in the early rounds with heavy hooks. Watt jabbed and remained patient, and in the seventh, scored a knockdown that turned the fight. Punched out, Pitalua was no longer a threat. He lasted only into the 12th.

There could only be one Roberto Duran. But the new champion would do quite well simply by being Jim Watt.

Jim Watt (right) won the vacant WBC lightweight title by stopping Alfredo Pitalua.

Matthew Franklin kayos Marvin Johnson to become the new light heavyweight king.

TAKING A BEATING TO ISSUE ONE

WBC light heavyweight champion Marvin Johnson was perhaps the fastest starter in boxing. Challenger Matthew Franklin was among the slowest. They met on April 22, at the Market Square Arena in Johnson's native Indianapolis. The result: the fight of the year.

In July 1977, Franklin had stopped Johnson in the 12th round of a bout for the North American title. This time, Johnson sought an early knockout. The southpaw swarmed, and by the end of the fifth round, Franklin was cut over both eyes and bleeding from the nose and mouth.

"I could barely see Marvin," he said later. "I kept saying to myself, *I have to do it right now. I have to go for the championship right now.*"

Franklin rallied late in the sixth, and in the seventh, Johnson was saved by the bell. In the eighth, with blood pouring down the faces of both fighters, Franklin scored a knockdown with a right hand. Johnson rose, but referee George DeFabis called a halt.

After the bout, the newly crowned champion changed his name to Matthew Saad Muhammad. He may have needed to work on his starts. But his finishes were surely the stuff of champions.

WORLD TITLE FIGHTS

HEAVYWEIGHTS

March 23 **Larry Holmes** *KO* 7
Osvaldo Ocasio, Las Vegas

LIGHT HEAVYWEIGHTS

April 14 **Victor Galindez** *KO* 10
Mike Rossman, New Orleans

April 22 **Matthew Franklin** (USA) *KO* 8
Marvin Johnson, Indianapolis

JUNIOR MIDDLEWEIGHTS

March 4 **Maurice Hope** (ANT) *KO* 9
Rocky Mattioli, San Remo

March 13 **Masashi Kudo** *W* 15
Manuel R. Gonzalez, Tokyo

WELTERWEIGHTS

Jan 14 **Wilfred Benitez** *W* 15
Carlos Palomino, San Juan

Jan 29 **Pipino Cuevas** *KO* 2
Scott Clark, Inglewood

March 25 **Wilfred Benitez** *W* 15
Harold Weston Jr., San Juan

JUNIOR WELTERWEIGHTS

Jan 18 **Antonio Cervantes** *W* 15
Miguel Montilla, New York City

LIGHTWEIGHTS

April 17 **Jim Watt** (SCO) *KO* 12
Alfredo Pitalua, Glasgow
(Wins Vacant WBC Title)

JUNIOR LIGHTWEIGHTS

Feb 4 **Alexis Arguello** *KO* 13
Alfredo Escalera, Rimini, Italy

Feb 18 **Samuel Serrano** *W* 15
Julio Valdez, San Juan

April 14 **Samuel Serrano** *KO* 8
Nkosana Mgxaji, Capetown

FEATHERWEIGHTS

Jan 9 **Eusebio Pedroza** *KO* 14
Royal Kobayashi, Tokyo

March 10 **Danny Lopez** *KO* 2
Roberto Castanon, Salt Lake City

April 8 **Eusebio Pedroza** *KO* 11
Hector Carrasquilla, Panama City

JUNIOR FEATHERWEIGHTS

March 9 **Wilfredo Gomez** *KO* 5
Nestor Jimenez, New York City

BANTAMWEIGHTS

March 10 **Carlos Zarate** *KO* 3
Mensah Kpalongo, Inglewood

April 8 **Jorge Lujan** *KO* 15
Cleo Garcia, Las Vegas

FLYWEIGHTS

Jan 29 **Betulio Gonzalez** *D* 15
Shoji Oguma, Hamamatsu, Japan

Feb 10 **Miguel Canto** *W* 15
Antonio Avelar, Merida, Mexico

March 18 **Chan Hee Park** (KOR) *W* 15
Miguel Canto, Pusan, South Korea

JUNIOR FLYWEIGHTS

Jan 7 **Yoko Gushiken** *KO* 7
Rigoberto Marcano, Kawasaki, Japan

March 31 **Sung Jun Kim** *D* 15
Rey Melendez, Seoul

April 8 **Yoko Gushiken** *KO* 7
Alfonso Lopez, Tokyo

MAY

1979

AUGUST

Ringside View

JULY

Alexis Arguello retains the WBC super featherweight title for the fifth time, stopping stubborn Mexican southpaw Rafael (Bazooka) Limon in the 11th round.

World Title Fights

HEAVYWEIGHTS

June 22 **Larry Holmes** *KO* 12 Mike Weaver, New York City

LIGHT HEAVYWEIGHTS

Aug 18 **Matthew (Franklin) Saad Muhammad** *W* 15 John Conteh, Atlantic City

MIDDLEWEIGHTS

June 30 **Vito Antuofermo** (USA) *W* 15 Hugo Corro, Monte Carlo

JUNIOR MIDDLEWEIGHTS

June 20 **Masashi Kudo** *KO* 12 Manuel R. Gonzalez, Yokaichi, Japan

WELTERWEIGHTS

July 30 **Pipino Cuevas** *W* 15 Randy Shields, Chicago

JUNIOR WELTERWEIGHTS

June 3 **Sang Hyun Kim** *W* 15 Fitzroy Guisseppi, Seoul

Aug 25 **Antonio Cervantes** *W* 15 Kwang Min Kim, Seoul

LIGHTWEIGHTS

June 16 **Ernesto Espana** (VEN) *KO* 13 Claude Noel, Hato Rey, Puerto Rico (Wins Vacant WBA Title)

Aug 4 **Ernesto Espana** *KO* 10 Johnny Lira, Chicago

JUNIOR LIGHTWEIGHTS

July 8 **Alexis Arguello** *KO* 11 Rafael Limon, New York City

FEATHERWEIGHTS

June 17 **Danny Lopez** *KO* 15 Mike Ayala, San Antonio

July 21 **Eusebio Pedroza** *KO* 12 Ruben Olivares, Houston

JUNIOR FEATHERWEIGHTS

June 16 **Wilfredo Gomez** *KO* 5 Jesus Hernandez, Hato Rey, Puerto Rico

June 23 **Ricardo Cardona** *W* 15 Soon Hyun Chung, Seoul

BANTAMWEIGHTS

June 3 **Lupe Pintor** (MEX) *W* 15 Carlos Zarate, Las Vegas

FLYWEIGHTS

May 20 **Chan Hee Park** *W* 15 Riki Igarishi, Seoul

July 6 **Betulio Gonzalez** *KO* 12 Shoji Oguma, Utsunomiya, Japan

JUNIOR FLYWEIGHTS

July 28 **Sung Jun Kim** *W* 15 Siony Carupo, Seoul

July 29 **Yoko Gushiken** *W* 15 Rafael Pedroza, Kitakyushu, Japan

WHEN THE JUDGES NEEDED JUDGES

Lupe Pintor's 15-round points victory over stablemate and defending WBC bantamweight champion Carlos Zarate may not have been the worst decision of the decade, but it certainly qualified as the oddest.

The bout was held on June 3, at the Caesars Palace Sports Pavilion in Las Vegas. Having sparred together over the years, the Mexicans knew each other too well. Both fought cautiously, though Zarate scored a knockdown in round four, and Pintor buckled him with a hook in the 11th.

Lupe Pintor (left) decisioned fellow Mexican Carlos Zarate in 15 rounds to become the new bantamweight champion at Las Vegas.

Pintor seemed very surprised by the verdict. Two judges saw him the winner by scores of 143-142. However, the third judge had Zarate in front by 145-133! (For reference, Associated Press scored for Zarate by 147-138.)

"How can there be 12 points difference between two judges watching the same fight?" asked Phil Silvers, one of Zarate's handlers. It was a question no one could satisfactorily answer.

Ringside View

AUGUST

In a bout that ushers in the era of casino boxing in Atlantic City, WBC light heavyweight champion Matthew Saad Muhammad scores a unanimous 15-round decision over former titlist John Conteh.

"MIKE WHO" SURPRISES TV

The American television networks thought so little of Mike Weaver that they chose not to air his challenge of WBC heavyweight champion Larry Holmes. Fortunately, the same executives hadn't been responsible for deciding the fate of *Gunsmoke*.

Holmes defended against Weaver on June 22, before 14,136 fans at Madison Square Garden, many of whom came to see the 10-rounder between Roberto Duran and Carlos Palomino. (Duran boxed brilliantly to win on points; it was the last bout of Palomino's career.)

Holmes controlled the early action by pumping his jab. But in the middle rounds, Weaver managed to turn the boxing match into a brawl. He pummeled the champion throughout the 10th, and seemed en route to victory. But one round later, Holmes found the resolve to floor his foe with a savage right uppercut. He finished his work early in the 12th; referee Harold Valan saved Weaver at the 44-second mark.

It had been a great fight. Too bad millions of fans had been denied the opportunity to watch it by the television bosses.

A HERO AND HIS HEROIN

If Matthew Franklin-Marvin Johnson was 1979's fight of the year, Danny Lopez-Mike Ayala was a close runner-up. On June 17, at the San Antonio Audiorium in the challenger's hometown of San Antonio, defending WBC featherweight champion Lopez and the 21-year-old Ayala tested wills. It was an extraordinary bout. What made it almost unbelievable was that Ayala, a heroin addict, had fought so brilliantly while under the influence.

"I shot up after the morning weigh-in," he later revealed, "and went into the ring loaded."

Despite suffering a broken nose, Ayala built a points lead by luring Lopez to the ropes and then countering. The champion roared back in the seventh, scoring a knockdown. When Ayala fell again in the 11th, it appeared referee Carlos Padilla counted him out. But the bout was resumed after the timekeeper claimed a mixup with the count.

Ahead on two of the cards, Lopez finished his foe with a hook in round 15. The end came at the 1:09 mark. Ayala was a hero in defeat. But only he, of course, knew the full story.

Larry Holmes knocks out Mike Weaver in 12th round to retain heavyweight title.

Dynamic Danny Lopez knocked out Mike Ayala in the 15th to retain the featherweight crown.

VITO GETS THE TITLE BY USING HIS HEAD

In planning a strategy for his challenge of world middleweight champion Hugo Corro, Brooklyn's Vito Antuofermo knew what he *wasn't* going to do. In previous title bouts, Corro had not only outboxed Rodrigo Valdes, but also American southpaw Ronnie Harris, who was thought to be the most technically skilled 160-pounder in the world. Finesse had never been Antuofermo's game anyway. That left one approach.

Antuofermo-Corro came on June 30, in a parking lot near the Royal Palace in Monte Carlo. There were few clean hits, but lots of misses, and plenty of butts and low blows. (The challenger was penalized in round six.) "My only problem was his head, not his fists," complained Corro.

The champion proved elusive. He rarely countered, however, and tired badly down the stretch. After 15 rounds, a new champion was crowned by split scores of 146-145, 143-142, and 145-146.

Antuofermo had found the right style: no style at all.

Argentina's Hugo Corro (left) lost a 15-round decision and the world title to Vito Antuofermo.

SEPTEMBER

1979

DECEMBER

READY TO CLAIM THE '80s

At the 1976 Olympics, John Tate wasn't able to celebrate with his gold medal-winning teammates. That's because the USA's representative at heavyweight had been forced to face the most intimidating amateur fighter in the world, Cuba's Teofilo Stevenson. Big John was kayoed in one round.

Three years later, Tate found reason to celebrate all by himself. On October 20, he faced South Africa's Gerrie Coetzee in the final bout of a mini-tournament to fill the WBA heavyweight title that had been vacated by Muhammad Ali. The bout was fought before more than 81,000 fans at the Loftus Versfield Stadium in Pretoria. It was boxing's biggest paying crowd since Dempsey-Tunney II.

Respectful of his opponent's lethal right hand, Tate, 240, started cautiously. Coetzee, 222, threatened over the first half of the bout, then dramatically slowed. Big John swept the last seven rounds by jabbing and crossing, and took the title by unanimous 15-round verdict.

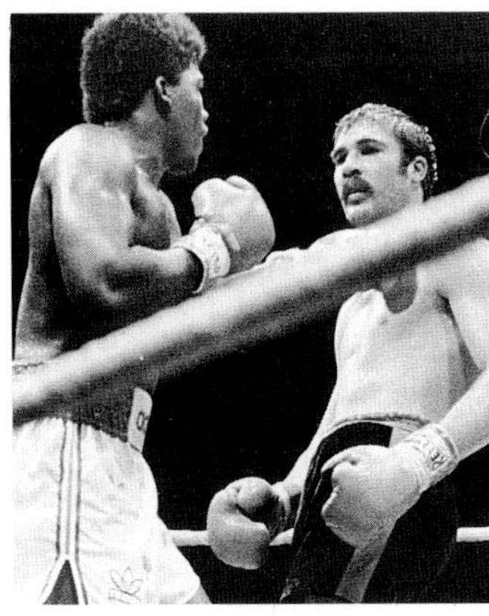

Big John Tate (left) beat Gerrie Coetzee.

CHAMP IS RATTLED TO THE BONE

In 1973, Larry Holmes was paid $145 for a week of sparring with Earnie Shavers. Six years later, he earned $2.5-million in one night.

On September 28, Holmes risked the WBC heavyweight title for the fourth time, dueling with Shavers at Caesars Palace. In 1978, the champion had earned his title try by winning all 12 rounds en route to a decision over "The Acorn." This time, he won every round but one.

The dangerous Shavers struck only once, landing a crushing right late in round seven. Holmes fell on his back, then hit his head on the canvas. A lesser fighter wouldn't have beaten the count. But the champion picked himself up and clinched until the bell.

From the eighth through the 11th, Holmes tortured Shavers. The challenger was exhausted and bloodied; he would take 29 stitches over his right eye. Implored by Holmes, referee Davey Pearl intervened at the 2:00 mark.

Overpaid? In the seventh, Holmes earned every penny.

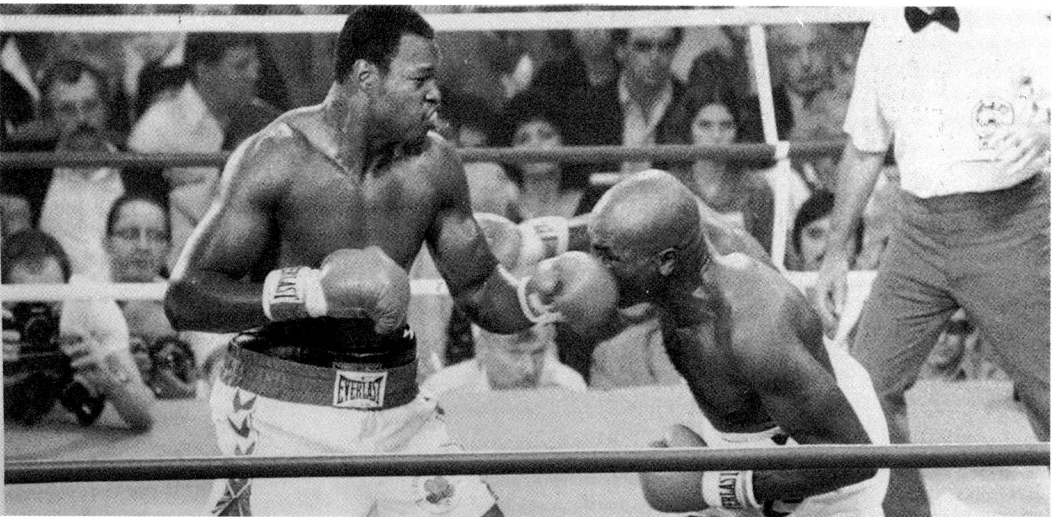

Larry Holmes (left) came back after a seventh-round knockdown to stop Earnie Shavers in the 11th round and retain the heavyweight title.

WORLD TITLE FIGHTS

HEAVYWEIGHTS

Sept 28	**Larry Holmes** *KO* 11 Earnie Shavers, Las Vegas
Oct 20	**John Tate** (USA) *W* 15 Gerrie Coetzee, Pretoria (Wins Vacant WBA Title)

CRUISERWEIGHTS

Dec 8	Marvin Camel *D* 15 Mate Parlov, Split, Yugoslavia (For Newly Created WBC Title)

LIGHT HEAVYWEIGHTS

Nov 30	**Marvin Johnson** *KO* 11 Victor Galindez, New Orleans

MIDDLEWEIGHTS

Nov 30	**Vito Antuofermo** *D* 15 Marvin Hagler, Las Vegas

JUNIOR MIDDLEWEIGHTS

Sept 25	**Maurice Hope** *KO* 7 Mike Baker, Wembley
Oct 24	**Ayub Kalule** (UGA) *W* 15 Masashi Kudo, Akita, Japan
Dec 6	**Ayub Kalule** *W* 15 Steve Gregory, Copenhagen

WELTERWEIGHTS

Nov 30	**Sugar Ray Leonard** (USA) *KO* 15 Wilfred Benitez, Las Vegas
Dec 8	**Pipino Cuevas** *KO* 10 Angel Espada, Los Angeles

JUNIOR WELTERWEIGHTS

Oct 4	**Sang Hyun Kim** *KO* 11 Masahiro Yokai, Tokyo

LIGHTWEIGHTS

Nov 3	**Jim Watt** *KO* 9 Roberto Vasquez, Glasgow

JUNIOR LIGHTWEIGHTS

Nov 16	**Alexis Arguello** *KO* 8 Bobby Chacon, Ingelwood

FEATHERWEIGHTS

Sept 25	**Danny Lopez** *KO* 3 Jose Caba, Los Angeles
Nov 17	**Eusebio Pedroza** *KO* 11 Johnny Aba, Papua, New Guinea

JUNIOR FEATHERWEIGHTS

Sept 6	**Ricardo Cardona** *W* 15 Yukio Segawa, Hacinohe, Japan
Sept 28	**Wilfredo Gomez** *KO* 10 Carlos Mendoza, Las Vegas
Oct 26	**Wilfredo Gomez** *KO* 5 Nicky Perez, New York City
Dec 15	**Ricardo Cardona** *W* 15 Sergio Palma, Barranquilla

BANTAMWEIGHTS

Oct 6	**Jorge Lujan** *KO* 15 Roberto Rubaldino, McAllen, TX

FLYWEIGHTS

Nov 17	**Luis Ibarra** (PAN) *W* 15 Betulio Gonzalez, Maracay
Dec 16	**Chan Hee Park** *KO* 2 Guty Espadas, Pusan, South Korea

JUNIOR FLYWEIGHTS

Oct 21	**Sung Jun Kim** *W* 15 Rey Melendez, Seoul
Oct 28	**Yoko Gushiken** *KO* 7 Tito Abella, Tokyo

HIS MOM GOES DOWN, BUT VITO STANDS TALL

It was toward the end of her son's defense against Marvin Hagler that Vito Antuofermo's mother went down for the count; watching the bout on television in Brooklyn, she fainted, and wasn't revived until after the decision was announced. That's when Hagler almost fainted.

Antuofermo-Hagler was part of a Caesars Palace supercard that featured Benitez-Leonard. Defending the middleweight crown for the first time, boxing's only unified champion was a 4-1 underdog. Hagler was that good.

Jabbing, moving, and switching stances, the challenger won most of the early rounds, and in the process, opened several cuts around Vito's eyes. Antuofermo rallied over the second half, which helped create a thrilling finish. Still, Hagler seemed the clear winner. Two of the judges disagreed, however, and Antuofermo kept the title by split draw (scores of 144-142, 143-143, and 141-144).

Get out the smelling salts.

Middleweight champ Vito Antuofermo (left) and Marvin Hagler battled to a 15-round draw.

FIGHTING TALK

They don't want me to be champion because they know I'll keep the title

MARVIN HAGLER
Middleweight contender after fighting to a disputed draw with world champion Vito Antuofermo

LEONARD ERA: DAY ONE

In the prefight stareout, WBC welterweight champion Wilfred Benitez defeated Sugar Ray Leonard on points. The fighters stood transfixed, eyeball to eyeball, for 30 seconds.

"I was scared senseless," Leonard would later admit.

Once the bout began, he overcame that fear, and the two best young boxers in the world produced a technical classic.

Leonard-Benitez came on November 30, at Caesars Palace. A 7-2 favorite, the 23-year-old Leonard started fast, felling the champion with a third-round jab. For the next few rounds, however, Benitez boxed brilliantly.

"No one, I mean *no one*, can make me miss like that," said Sugar Ray.

A sixth-round butt left Benitez with a nasty gash on his forehead. Otherwise, the welters were mirror images. Both feinted, jabbed, and slipped. Few punches landed, but the pace was sizzling.

Leonard finally broke through in the 15th, dropping Benitez with a left uppercut. The champion rose, but referee Carlos Padilla stopped the fight with only six seconds to go.

(After 14 rounds, Leonard led comfortably on the cards.)

Boxing's future had officially arrived in time for the '80s.

RINGSIDE VIEW

DECEMBER

Marvin Camel and Mate Parlov fight to a 15-round draw in the first-ever (WBC) cruiserweight title fight.

Undefeated Sugar Ray Leonard (right) stopped Wilfred Benitez in the 15th round.

Sugar Ray Leonard

DURING his fantastic 15 years on center stage, there was only one Sugar Ray Leonard, but two very different perceptions of the fighter and the man. The negative perception was Leonard as a creation of the media, a superstar for the '80s who was more Madison Avenue than Bash Boulevard. Before conducting a 1982 interview for *Playboy*, Lawrence Linderman observed, "It seemed to me that Leonard...had become less preoccupied with his sport than with becoming a corporate symbol."

The positive perception was of Leonard as the most dominant boxer of his era, a champion who broke the rules and wrote new ones. Those overrating the past wonder how historians could glorify a fighter who had less than 40 bouts. But Leonard's accomplishments justify his status. He won world titles in five different divisions, made more money than any athlete in history, and was voted the fighter of the '80s. However you see Leonard, he was a fighter of his times, as was Dempsey in the '20s or Ali in the '60s.

Ray Charles Leonard was born on May 17, 1956, in Wilmington, North Carolina (named for the singer Ray Charles, not the fighter Sugar Ray Robinson). One of seven children born to Cicero and Getha Leonard, Ray was 10 when his family moved to Palmer Park, Maryland. The Leonards barely lived above the poverty line.

Leonard was introduced to boxing by his brother Roger (who became a top-10 junior middleweight in the early-'80s). Early in Sugar Ray's amateur career, he hooked up with trainer Dave Jacobs and advisor Janks Morton. "He was a natural," Morton said. "Fast and smart, beautiful to watch."

Leonard narrowly failed to secure a berth on the 1972 Olympic team. Still, his amateur titles were many. He won the National Golden Gloves title three times, the AAU title twice, and a gold medal in 1975's Pan-Am Games. His overall amateur record was 155-5.

On July 31, 1976, came the highlight: Leonard outpointed Cuba's Andres Aldama to win the 139-pound gold medal at the Olympic Games in Montreal. Four of his teammates, Leon and Michael Spinks, Leo Randolph, and Howard Davis Jr., also won gold medals, making the team the most successful in American Olympic history.

After the Games, Leonard planned to enroll at the University of Maryland. But with both parents ailing, and Sugar Ray bitter that his Olympic experience hadn't led to commercial endorsements, he opted to turn pro. Jacobs and Morton would remain. Added to the team were Mike Trainer, as manager, and Angelo Dundee, to select the opponents and work as chief cornerman.

Always keeping his cool no matter how intense the pressure, Ray calmly listens to Janks Morton as he studies his opponent across the ring.

Leonard turned pro on February 5, 1977, outpointing Luis Vega for $40,000, a first-fight record. His rise to contention was rapid. In 1978, he decisioned Randy Shields and kayoed veteran contender Mando Muniz, and in 1979, he won the NABF welterweight title, destroying Pete Ranzany in four rounds. Flashing fast hands and fluid movement, he won as he pleased. His smile, however, belied the hard-edged competitiveness that wouldn't surface until the championship fights to come.

Leonard fought on every television network and signed no long-term promotional deals. His status as a free agent proved invaluable after he became a world champion. On November 30, 1979, he challenged the brilliant and undefeated Wilfred Benitez for the WBC 147-pound crown. It was a classic chess match, with Leonard scoring two knockdowns en route to a 15th-round TKO victory. At 23, he was already the biggest star in boxing.

Sugar Ray was a tactical boxer, but in his first defense, he displayed previously unforseen power, knocking Dave (Boy) Green unconscious with one punch. His next challenger, however, offered far more resistance.

In one of the most eagerly anticipated battles of the ring, Leonard defended against former lightweight champion Roberto Duran. The rivals tested wills in Montreal on June 20, 1980 in a furious 15-round war, with the champion fighting on the challenger's terms. Duran won by close but unanimous decision – one judge, Angelo Potelli, scored 10 rounds even – and, temporarily, at least, took the title of best pound-for-pound boxer in the world.

Five months later, the rematch provided an unimaginable ending. With Leonard slightly ahead on points and outboxing and mocking Duran, the macho Panamanian suddenly uttered the now-infamous words "No mas." What brought Duran's eighth-round surrender would be debated forever, but Leonard was a champion again. "What greater victory could there be," wrote *Sports Illustrated*'s Frank Deford, "than to make the unquittable quit?"

Leonard's greatest victories lay ahead of

Professional career dates 1977-1982; 1984; 1987-1991
Contests 39
Won 36
Lost 2
Drawn 1
Knockouts 25
World Welterweight Champion 1979-1980; 1980-1982
World Junior Middleweight Champion 1981
World Middleweight Champion 1987
World Super Middleweight Champion 1988-90
World Light Heavyweight Champion 1988

him. Building toward a welterweight unification showdown with WBA champion Thomas Hearns, Sugar Ray scored a ninth-round kayo over difficult junior middleweight champion Ayub Kalule. Then, on September 16, 1981, at Caesars Palace in Las Vegas, came the shootout with the unbeaten "Hit Man." In a bout that featured shifting momentums, Leonard and Hearns played role reversal. The 6'2" Hearns jabbed from a distance, and Leonard, his left eye swollen shut, turned hunter. Trailing on all three cards, Sugar Ray managed a pair of knockdowns and scored a TKO in round 14. "I brought it up from the gut," he said. The first chapter of Leonard's career ended with a kayo of Bruce Finch in February 1982. While training for a May defense against Bruce Finch, Leonard suffered from blurred vision. Doctors discovered a detached retina in his left eye. He underwent surgery on May 9, and, at age 26, announced his retirement.

On May 11, 1984, in what turned out to be a one-bout comeback, Leonard rose from the first knockdown of his pro career to stop fringe contender Kevin Howard. He then returned to hibernation for almost three years, until succumbing to the temptation of a try at middleweight champ Marvin Hagler. "The reason I will win," Leonard said, "is because you don't think I can." Sugar Ray was right: no one thought he had a chance against a bigger, more active opponent. But at Caesars Palace on April 6, 1987, Leonard pulled off the upset of the decade, emerging victorious by a split 15-round decision.

After winning the gold in 1976 Olympics, 21-year-old Ray Charles Leonard exploded into professional boxing, where his like had never been seen before.

Like Ali's triumph over Frazier in Manila, the Hagler bout fight would have been a fitting ending. But Leonard fought sporadically for the next four years, drawing in a rematch with Hearns, easily outpointing Duran, winning his fourth and fifth titles (at 168 and 175 pounds) by knocking out Don Lalonde, and, finally, on February 9, 1991, suffering a one-sided points loss to Terry Norris. "It took something like this," he said of the Norris fight, "to make me move on."

Retiring for (presumably) the last time, Leonard exited with a record of 36-2-1 (25). Shortly after his last fight, his already tattered image suffered, first because of a divorce from his wife and teenage sweetheart, Juanita Wilkinson, and then after a public disclosure of a former drug problem. Long after Leonard threw his last punch, fans and foes continued to debate the meaning of the man. The essence of the fighter, however, belongs to history.

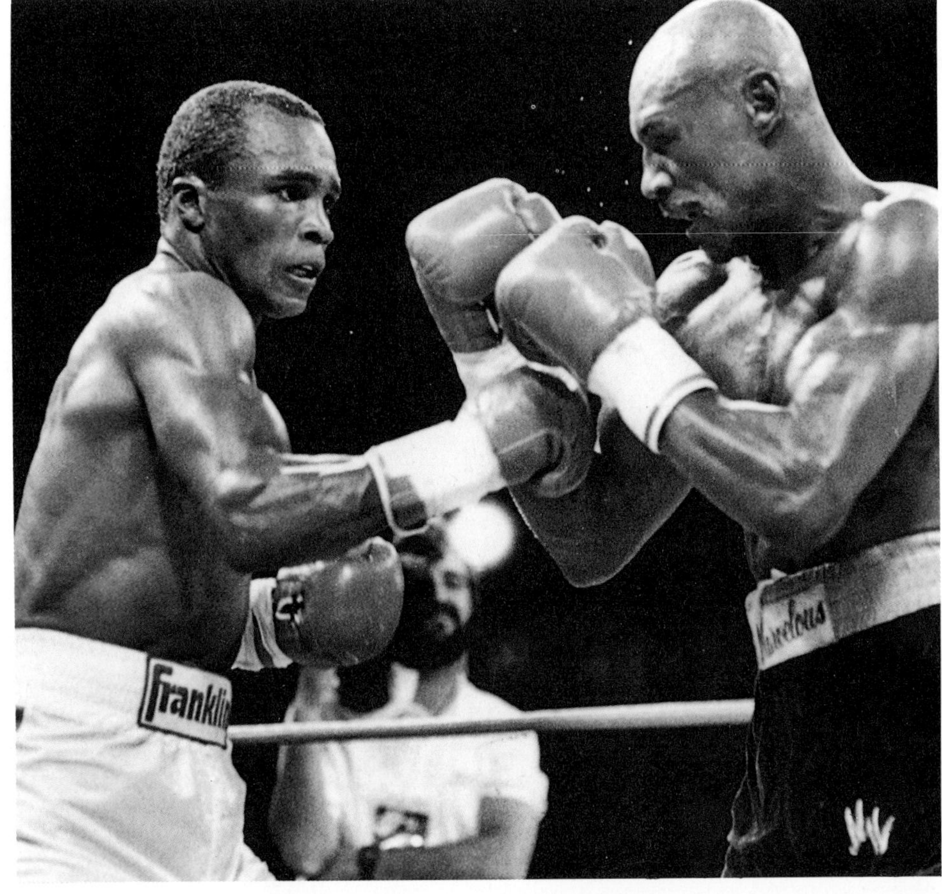

Leonard's hands were so fast that he could snake a damaging punch through a defense as tight as that of Marvelous Marvin Hagler.

RING DECADE

1980-1989

How do you explain a decade which begins with boxing's poster boy of machismo, Roberto Duran, quitting in mid-fight? Or one during which unified welterweight champion Lloyd Honeyghan smiles for photographers while tossing one of his title belts into the trash can? Or one which ends with 17 divisions and, potentially, at least, 51 world champions?

You don't. Boxing proved it was strong enough to succeed despite itself. The decade brought change, confusion, even chaos, but also an exceptional number of superstars and superfights. In 1980, a million-dollar purse made headlines. In 1988, Mike Tyson made $20-million for working 91 seconds.

It was during the '80s that the original eight divisions, and one champ per division, became a distant memory. The cruiserweight class crowned its first champ in 1980. The super middleweights were introduced in '84, and the strawweights in '87. In order to profit from sanctioning fees, each alphabet organization chose to recognize its own titleholder. By the end of the decade, there were enough world champs to fill a small town's phone book.

In 1985 Mike Tyson exploded on the boxing scene like a tornado. Not since Joe Louis had generated similiar excitement almost 50 years before had the world seen any prize fighter as ferocious as this wild dynamo from the streets of Brooklyn. Twenty months after his professional debut, Iron Mike became the youngest heavyweight champion in history.

The intentions of the WBA and WBC, and the IBF, which joined the mix in 1983, became apparent on the rare occasions when promoters attempted to unify titles. Junior bantamweight Jiro Watanabe and middleweight Sumbu Kalambay were among the champions who were stripped for challenging the titlists of a rival organization. The alphabet boys continue to win the battle. Consider:

- In 1985, the welterweight title was unified by Donald Curry. Less than two years later, however, Honeyghan, who succeeded him, gave up the WBA crown for political reasons. It hasn't since been unified.
- The middleweight title was unified until 1987, when Marvin Hagler defended against the comebacking – and unrated – Sugar Ray Leonard. It hasn't since been unified.
- In 1983, Michael Spinks unified the light heavyweight title. He moved to heavyweight in 1985, and shortly after, three different champions were crowned. The title hasn't since been unified.
- In 1988, Evander Holyfield unified the cruiserweight title. He jumped to heavyweight that same year, and shortly after, three different champions were crowned. The title hasn't since been unified.
- In 1987, Mike Tyson unified the heavyweight title, which had been fractured since 1978. It was currently boxing's only unified title.

On the positive side, more alphabet organizations, and more titles, resulted in opportunities for more fighters. It also brought added programming choices for the television networks, which, at the start of the decade, featured a record number of championship bouts.

In the late-'70s, casino gambling was legalized in Atlantic City. High rollers and big fights have always mixed well, and by the early-'80s, the New Jersey beach resort began to rival Las Vegas as the capital of boxing. On almost every weekend, hotel ballrooms were transformed into TV studios, and world champs like Matthew Saad Muhammad, Jeff Chandler, and Aaron Pryor risked their crowns before millions of viewers. With the networks providing most of the purse money, promoters didn't concern themselves with attendance. Live boxing was all but dead.

In November 1982, it was a televised title fight that led to the decade's most significant change. In a grueling

Rather than defend the undisputed world welterweight title in South Africa, as mandated by the WBA, Britain's Lloyd Honeyghan tossed away his championship belt.

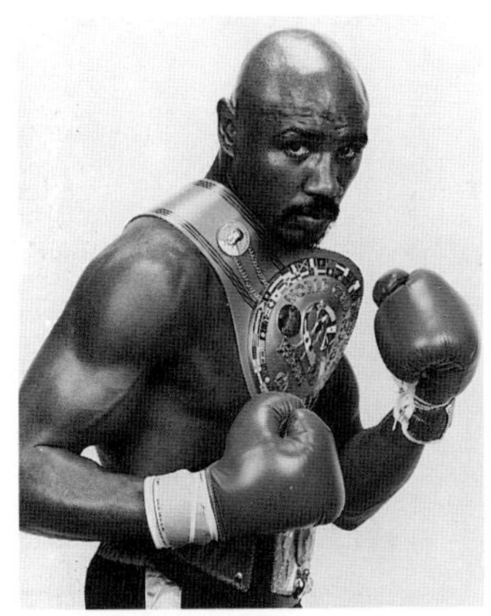

If Marvelous Marvin Hagler's ferocious looks didn't strike fear into his opponents, his whirling, power-packed blows would put them quivering on the canvas.

Sugar Ray Leonard not only borrowed his name from the immortal Sugar Ray Robinson, he equaled the original Ray's matchless skills.

battle, WBA lightweight champion Ray Mancini knocked out South Korea's Duk Koo Kim at the start of the 14th round. Kim subsequently died from head injuries. With a view to reducing the number of ring fatalities, the WBC shortened its title fights from 15 rounds to 12. The WBA quickly followed. Only the IBF resisted, but in 1988, it, too, made the switch.

Sugar Ray Leonard was a brilliantly managed fighter who made his millions from every available form of television (network, closed-circuit, and pay-per-view). By winning world titles in five different divisions, however, he proved that he was anything but a creation of the media. The Fighter of the Decade forced a shift of the spotlight; no longer was boxing dominated by the heavyweights. Sugar Ray, Thomas Hearns, and Duran engaged in an extraordinary round robin, and all three subsequently challenged dominant middleweight king Marvin Hagler. Only Leonard, coming off a three-year retirement, was victorious.

Overshadowed first by Leonard, and then by Hagler, Hearns was the decade's most exciting fighter. An outstanding technician, "The Hit Man" was nonetheless defined by his fight-ending right hand. A single punch ruined steel-chinned Pipino Cuevas, and Duran was left flat and unconscious. But Hearns couldn't topple Leonard, and when he failed against Hagler – their 1985 showdown was spiced by arguably the greatest first round in history – he secured the reputation of a perennial bridesmaid.

Following Duran was like tracing the path of a jumping bean. In the '70s, the fiery Panamanian established himself as perhaps the greatest lightweight of all-time. He opened the '80s by outgunning Leonard in a bout that made him a mainstream star. But all momentum was lost when he said "no mas" in the rematch. In 1982, came consecutive losses to Wilfred Benitez and Kirkland Laing, but Duran was hardly through. He kayoed Cuevas, took Davey Moore's junior middleweight title, and almost upset Hagler. A crushing loss to Hearns was followed by long inactivity, and then one final shining moment: in 1989, the living legend, age 37, won his fourth title by brawling past middleweight champ Iran Barkley.

There were several other lighter-weight marquee attractions. Hector Camacho was bold and supremely gifted; Wilfredo Gomez became the greatest Puerto Rican fighter of all; Salvador Sanchez enjoyed a distinguished, albeit tragically brief, championship run; Julio Cesar Chavez proved dominant in three different divisions; Jeff Fenech overflowed with energy and intensity; Khaosai Galaxy and Myung Woo Yuh were record-setters at junior bantamweight and junior flyweight, respectively; Donald Curry rose brilliantly, and then crashed hard; Eusebio Pedroza made 19 successful defenses at featherweight; and triple-crown champion Alexis Arguello's 1982 classic with Pryor was the Fight of the Decade.

The emergence of the lighter weight classes, of course, didn't preclude the heavyweights from contributing to the storyline. The central figure, Larry Holmes, was an enigma of a champion. He won the bout he had to win – vs. Gerry Cooney – and lost the bout he figured to win – vs. Michael Spinks. By making 20 successful defenses, Holmes secured his place among the century's best big men. But his legacy was tarnished by his loss to Spinks; never before had a heavyweight champion lost the crown to a light heavyweight.

If Holmes' reign was marked by apathy, Mike Tyson brought a maelstrom of emotions. The youngest heavyweight champion in history demanded that we despise him, adore him, fear him, and pity him. Charging through the division with a previously unforeseen combination of speed and power, "Iron Mike" destroyed Spinks, Holmes, and everyone else in his path. Unfortunately, he was destined to also destroy himself.

As the decade drew to a close, our most public of heavyweight kings clinged precariously to his throne. Boxing was easy; it was life Mike Tyson couldn't solve.

The '90s would belong to others.

Larry Holmes dominated the heavyweight division during the 1970s and through most of the 1980s. Big and powerful, he was a master boxer.

JANUARY

1980

APRIL

LITTLE RED'S RUFFLED FEATHERS

WBC featherweight champion Danny Lopez always came back; it was the signature of his title reign. But on February 2, at the Memorial Coliseum in Phoenix, Lopez met an opponent so quick and skillful that he was not only battered and beaten, but embarrassed as well.

Before the bout, 20-year-old Salvador Sanchez' reputation did not extend beyond his native Mexico. But that changed quickly. In the third round, his jabs and counter rights closed Lopez' left eye, and in the fourth, he pinned the champion against the ropes for a brutal 30-second stretch.

Round after round, Lopez walked into punches and bled from a variety of cuts. In the 14th round, with "Little Red" still on his feet but staggering, referee Waldemar Schmidt called a halt.

Having made nine defenses, Lopez was a champion no more. He had established himself as one of the hardest-hitting 126-pounders of all-time. And Sanchez had established that Lopez wasn't going to hit what he couldn't see.

The brilliant Sanchez was having his 36th contest and went 34-1-1, with 26 kayos. It was only a third career defeat for Lopez.

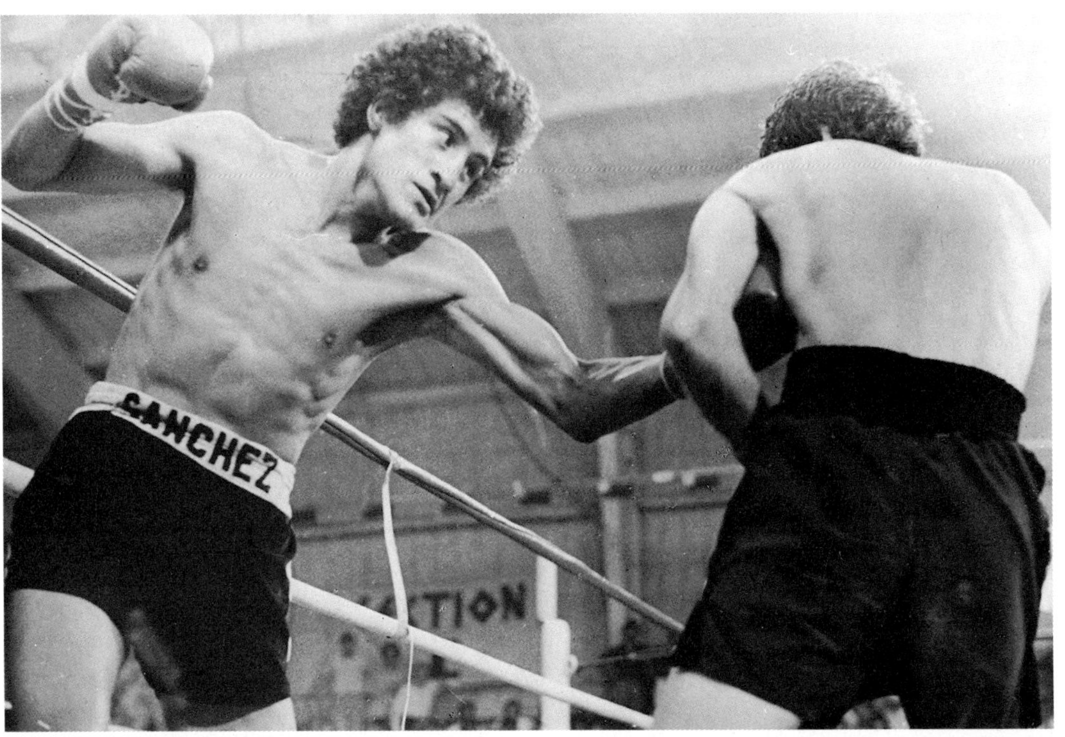

Salvador Sanchez (left) kayoed Danny Lopez in the 13th to win the featherweight crown in an action-packed brawl at Phoenix, Arizona.

WORLD TITLE FIGHTS

HEAVYWEIGHTS

Feb 3 **Larry Holmes** *KO* 6
Lorenzo Zanon, Las Vegas

March 31 **Mike Weaver** (USA) *KO* 15
John Tate, Knoxville

March 31 **Larry Holmes** *KO* 8
Leroy Jones, Las Vegas

CRUISERWEIGHTS

March 31 **Marvin Camel** (USA) *W* 15
Mate Parlov, Las Vegas
(Wins Vacant WBC Title)

LIGHT HEAVYWEIGHTS

March 29 **Matthew Saad Muhammad** *KO* 4
John Conteh, Atlantic City

March 31 **Eddie Gregory** (USA) *KO* 11
Marvin Johnson, Knoxville

MIDDLEWEIGHTS

March 16 **Alan Minter** (ENG) *W* 15
Vito Antuofermo, Las Vegas

JUNIOR MIDDLEWEIGHTS

April 17 **Ayub Kalule** *KO* 12
Emiliano Villa, Copenhagen

WELTERWEIGHTS

March 31 **Sugar Ray Leonard** *KO* 4
Dave (Boy) Green, Landover, MD

April 6 **Pipino Cuevas** *KO* 5
Harold Volbrecht, Houston

JUNIOR WELTERWEIGHTS

Feb 23 **Saoul Mamby** (USA) *KO* 14
Sang Hyun Kim, Seoul

March 29 **Antonio Cervantes** *KO* 7
Miguel Montilla, Cartagena

LIGHTWEIGHTS

March 2 **Hilmer Kenty** (USA) *KO* 9
Ernesto Espana, Detroit

March 14 **Jim Watt** *KO* 4
Charlie Nash, Glasgow

JUNIOR LIGHTWEIGHTS

Jan 12 **Alexis Arguello** *KO* 11
Ruben Castillo, Tucson

April 3 **Samuel Serrano** *KO* 13
Kiyoshi Kazama, Nara, Japan

April 27 **Alexis Arguello** *KO* 5
Rolando Navarette, San Juan

FEATHERWEIGHTS

Jan 22 **Eusebio Pedroza** *W* 15
Spider Nemoto, Tokyo

Feb 2 **Salvador Sanchez** (MEX) *KO* 13
Danny Lopez, Phoenix

March 29 **Eusebio Pedroza** *KO* 9
Juan Malvares, Panama City

April 12 **Salvador Sanchez** *W* 15
Ruben Castillo, Tucson

JUNIOR FEATHERWEIGHTS

Feb 3 **Wilfredo Gomez** *KO* 7
Ruben Valdez, Las Vegas

BANTAMWEIGHTS

Feb 9 **Lupe Pintor** *KO* 12
Alberto Sandoval, Los Angeles

April 2 **Jorge Lujan** *KO* 9
Shuichi Isogami, Tokyo

JUNIOR BANTAMWEIGHTS

Feb 1 **Rafael Orono** (VEN) *W* 15
Seung Hoon Lee, Caracas
(Wins Newly Created WBC Title)

April 14 **Rafael Orono** *W* 15
Ramon Soria, Caracas

FLYWEIGHTS

Feb 10 **Chan Hee Park** *W* 15
Arnel Arrozal, Seoul

Feb 16 **Tae Shik Kim** (KOR) *KO* 2
Luis Ibarra, Seoul

April 13 **Chan Hee Park** *W* 15
Alberto Morales, Taegu, South Korea

JUNIOR FLYWEIGHTS

Jan 3 **Shigeo Nakajima** (JAP) *W* 15
Sung Jun Kim, Tokyo

Jan 27 **Yoko Gushiken** *W* 15
Yong Hyun Kim, Osaka

March 24 **Hilario Zapata** (PAN) *W* 15
Shigeo Nakajima, Tokyo

EDDIE'S NOVACAINE PUNCH

Eddie Gregory becomes new champion.

During the 1972 Olympic Trials, Marvin Johnson and Eddie Gregory roomed together. And on March 31, on the Tate-Weaver undercard at the University of Tennessee, they fought as only roomates can.

Making his first defense of the WBA light heavyweight title, Johnson started quickly – and was quickly floored by a left – right in the third round. Punching mostly to the body, Gregory overcame a nasty cut at the corner of his left eye and wore down the champion. In the 11th, he turned to a crisp left hook, which he called his "novacaine punch." Sufficiently numbed, Johnson was rescued by referee Carlos Berrocal.

We suppose he never felt a thing.

RINGSIDE VIEW

MARCH

Lightweight Hilmer Kenty becomes the first world champion from Detroit's Kronk Gym, dethroning WBA titlist Ernesto Espana by ninth-round TKO.

MARCH

Marvin Camel becomes the first cruiserweight champion in history by winning the vacant WBC title via unanimous 15-round decision over Mate Parlov.

THUMBS UP FOR BRITAIN'S MINTER

Did Vito Antuofermo lose the world middleweight title to Alan Minter, a southpaw from Sussex, or Roland Dakin, a judge, and Minter's countryman?

Antuofermo met Minter on March 16, at Caesars Palace. Theirs was a difficult bout to score; Minter punched smoothly, but inaccurately, and Antuofermo worked his way inside, where Minter quickly clinched. Dakin, however, saw a one-sided bout, scoring for Minter by 149-137. He gave Antuofermo only the 14th round, during which the champion scored a flash knockdown.

According to promoter Bob Arum, Dakin gave the thumbs-up sign to Minter's corner after each round. (An ironic twist: in June 1979, when Antuofermo won the title by scoring a split decision over Hugo Corro, Dakin had voted for him.)

New middleweight champion Alan Minter of England is paraded around the ring in Las Vegas.

While one judge scored 145-143 for Antuofermo, another saw it 144-141 for Minter, which, in conjunction with Dakin's total, made Minter the champion.

Moaned Antuofermo, "This is the only fight I've ever lost where I didn't feel like I was in a fight."

Defending heavyweight champ John Tate is pole-axed by Mike Weaver in Knoxville, Tennessee.

DREAM WEAVER

It was all so perfect: Fighting before his hometown fans at the University of Tennessee's Stokely Athletics Center in Knoxville, WBA heavyweight champion John Tate was cruising to a points victory. Then, with one punch, Mike Weaver ruined him.

Tate-Weaver, fought on March 31, was a typical boxer-puncher matchup. Bigger and more skillful, Tate controlled the early rounds with jabs and right hands. In the 12th, he was staggered by a hook, but there seemed little reason for him to worry; Weaver was as fatigued as he was.

After 14 rounds, Tate led by scores of 137-134, 136-133, 138-133. Needing a knockout to win, Weaver connected with a devastating left hook. Tate fell on his face and lay still as referee Ernesto Magana counted him out only 45 seconds from the final bell.

MAY

1980

AUGUST

DURAN: POUND FOR POUND...

Officially, the June 20 showdown between Ray Leonard and Roberto Duran was fought for Sugar Ray's WBC welterweight crown. Unofficially, the winner would be declared boxing's best.

On a chilly, rainy night, the superstars met before 46,317 fans at Montreal's Olympic Stadium. The action sizzled from the start, and while the fighters held up, Juanita Leonard, the champion's wife, passed out after round eight.

The bout was contested on Duran's terms. He stunned Leonard early, and crowded him throughout. Leonard fought back furiously, producing enough toe-to-toe exchanges to fill a Hollywood western.

At the bell concluding the 13th round, Duran raised his hands in triumph. Indeed, he had clinched victory; he gave away the last two rounds and still won by close but unanimous scores of 146-144, 145-144, and 148-147. (The third card included no less than 10 even rounds.)

"Ray's mistake was that he had it in his head that he was stronger than Duran," said the loser's trainer, Angelo Dundee.

It was a mistake Leonard wouldn't make again.

Sugar Ray Leonard (right) lost his welterweight crown, and the first fight of his career.

TWENTY PUNCHES WEREN'T ENOUGH

Natural talent can take a fighter to the top. But as Matthew Saad Muhammad proved during his riveting reign as WBC light heavyweight champion, there's no substitute for heart.

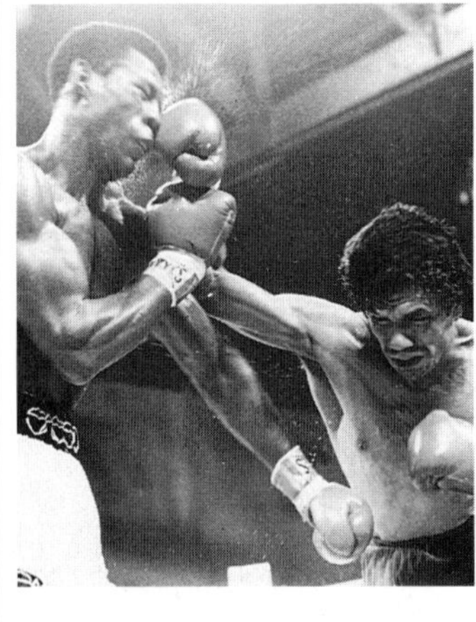

Matthew Saad Muhammad (left) stopped Yaqui Lopez to retain the light heavyweight crown.

On July 13, "Miracle Matthew" defended against Yaqui Lopez at the Playboy Club in McAfee, New Jersey. It was the challenger's fourth try at the title.

The bout was fought in two distinctive stages. Lopez dominated rounds one through eight, after which the champion took over. The turning point came midway through the eighth, when Lopez cornered Saad and poured in 20 unanswered blows. Referee Waldemar Schmidt chose not to call a halt, and before the round's end, Saad was back on the attack.

The champion never lost his momentum. Leading on all cards, he finished his exhausted foe with four knockdowns in the 14th.

"I hit him good, but he didn't go down," said Lopez. "That's why he's champion."

WORLD TITLE FIGHTS

HEAVYWEIGHTS

July 7 — **Larry Holmes** *KO* 7 Scott LeDoux, Minneapolis

LIGHT HEAVYWEIGHTS

May 11 — **Matthew Saad Muhammad** *KO* 5 Louis Pergaud, Halifax, Canada

July 13 — **Matthew Saad Muhammad** *KO* 14 Yaqui Lopez, McAfee, NJ

July 20 — **Eddie (Gregory) Mustafa Muhammad** *KO* 10 Jerry Martin, McAfee, NJ

MIDDLEWEIGHTS

June 28 — **Alan Minter** *KO* 9 Vito Antuofermo, London

JUNIOR MIDDLEWEIGHTS

June 12 — **Ayub Kalule** *W* 15 Marijan Benes, Randers, Denmark

July 12 — **Maurice Hope** *KO* 11 Rocky Mattioli, Wembley

WELTERWEIGHTS

June 20 — **Roberto Duran** *W* 15 Sugar Ray Leonard, Montreal

Aug 2 — **Thomas Hearns** (USA) *KO* 2 Pipino Cuevas, Detroit

JUNIOR WELTERWEIGHTS

July 7 — **Saoul Mamby** *KO* 13 Esteban DeJesus, Bloomington, MN

Aug 2 — **Aaron Pryor** (USA) *KO* 4 Antonio Cervantes, Cincinnati

LIGHTWEIGHTS

June 7 — **Jim Watt** *W* 15 Howard Davis Jr., Glasgow

Aug 2 — **Hilmer Kenty** *KO* 9 Young Ho Oh, Detroit

JUNIOR LIGHTWEIGHTS

Aug 2 — **Yasutsune Uehara** (JAP) *KO* 6 Samuel Serrano, Detroit

FEATHERWEIGHTS

June 21 — **Salvador Sanchez** *KO* 14 Danny Lopez, Las Vegas

July 20 — **Eusebio Pedroza** *KO* 8 Sa Wang Kim, Seoul

JUNIOR FEATHERWEIGHTS

May 4 — **Leo Randolph** (USA) *KO* 15 Ricardo Cardona, Seattle

Aug 9 — **Sergio Palma** (ARG) *KO* 5 Leo Randolph, Spokane, WA

Aug 22 — **Wilfredo Gomez** *KO* 5 Derrik Holmes, Las Vegas

BANTAMWEIGHTS

June 11 — **Lupe Pintor** *D* 15 Eijiro Murata, Tokyo

Aug 29 — **Julian Solis** (PR) *W* 15 Jorge Lujan, Miami Beach

JUNIOR BANTAMWEIGHTS

July 28 — **Rafael Orono** *D* 15 Willie Jensen, Caracas

FLYWEIGHTS

May 18 — **Shoji Oguma** (JAP) *KO* 9 Chan Hee Park, Seoul

June 29 — **Tae Shik Kim** *W* 15 Arnel Arrozal, Seoul

July 28 — **Shoji Oguma** *W* 15 Sung Jun Kim, Tokyo

JUNIOR FLYWEIGHTS

June 1 — **Yoko Gushiken** *KO* 8 Martin Vargas, Kochi, Japan

June 7 — **Hilario Zapata** *W* 15 Chi Bok Kim, Seoul

Aug 4 — **Hilario Zapata** *W* 15 Rey Melendez, Caracas

A HOMEBOY AND HIS HARD-HITTING HAMMER

Thomas Hearns grew up 15 minutes from Detroit's Joe Louis Arena, where, on August 2, he took WBA welterweight champion Pipino Cuevas' title with a straight right that had seemingly been borrowed from "The Brown Bomber's" arsenal.

No one had envisioned a mismatch; Hearns was 28-0 (26), but Cuevas had kayoed 10 of 11 previous challengers.

Capitalizing on his 5½-inch advantage in reach, Hearns, 21, scored heavily in the first, then struck with frightening power in the second. A short cross felled the champion. Cuevas rose, but when he wobbled, his manager, Lupe Sanchez, rushed into the ring.

"A fighter's life is worth more to me than 10 world champions," he explained.

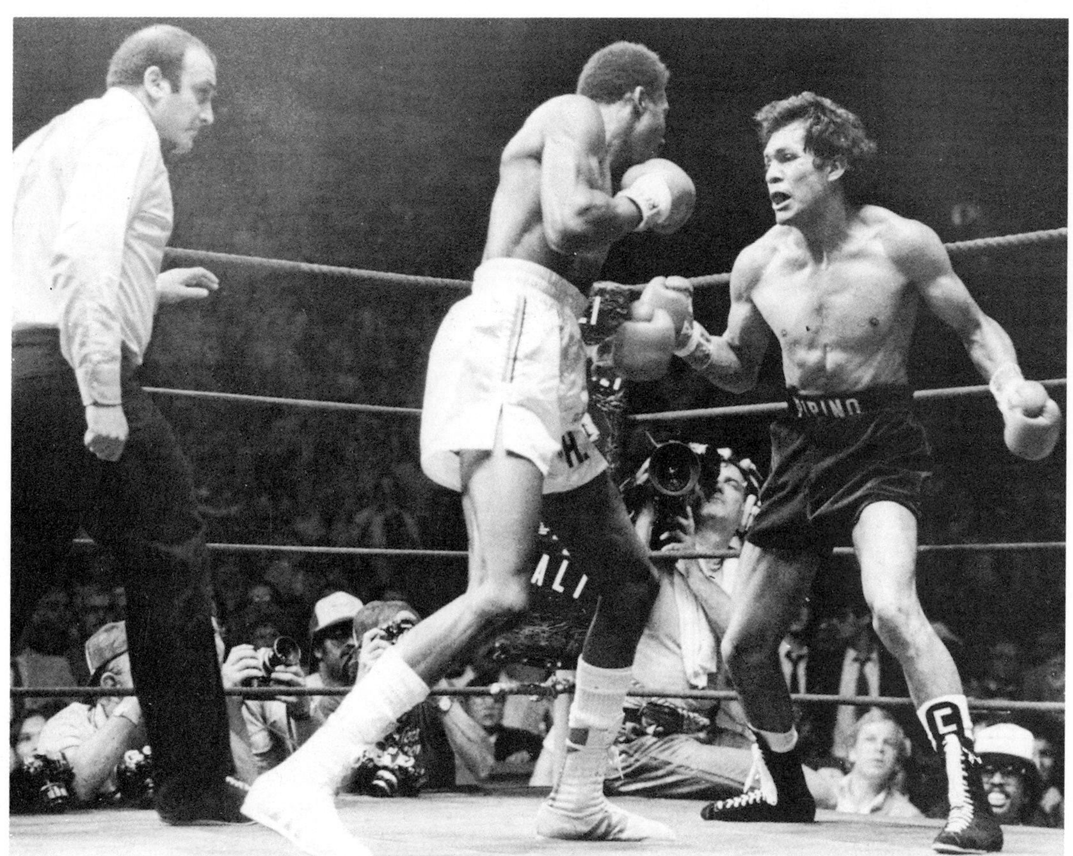

Thomas Hearns (left) knocked out Pipino Cuevas in the second round to win the WBA welterweight title and remain undefeated.

RINGSIDE VIEW

MAY

In a major upset, WBA junior featherweight champion Ricardo Cardona is dethroned by 1976 Olympic gold medalist Leo Randolph via 15th-round TKO.

JUNE

Underdog Jim Watt of Scotland retains the WBC lightweight title by scoring a unanimous 15-round decision over heavily hyped Howard Davis Jr.

TIME FOR THE HAWK – FINALLY

The world's top lightweights had ignored unbeaten dynamo Aaron Pryor for almost two years. So "The Hawk" moved up and took out his frustrations on 34-year-old WBA junior welterweight champion Antonio Cervantes.

Pryor-Cervantes came on August 2, at the Riverfront Coliseum in the challenger's hometown of Cincinnati. In what would become a familiar scenario in Pryor's title bouts, The Hawk began to fight only after suffering a first-round knockdown. Tossing punches in bunches, he cut Cervantes in the third, and dropped him for the count with a right in the fourth.

"This fight," he said, "proves why all the fighters were afraid to get in the ring with me."

Aaron Pryor (left) kayoed Antonio Cervantes to win the junior welterweight title.

SEPTEMBER

1980

DECEMBER

RINGSIDE VIEW

SEPTEMBER

WBC bantamweight champion Lupe Pintor retains the title for the third time, knocking out Welsh challenger Johnny Owen in round 12. Owen, 24, dies 45 days later from head injuries suffered in the bout.

OCTOBER

Only four months after retiring from the ring, former WBA light heavyweight champion Victor Galindez, 31, dies in an auto racing accident in Argentina.

BLOOD, BOTTLES, AND BEER CANS

Middleweight champion Alan Minter had failed to hurt Marvin Hagler, so the sellout crowd of 12,000 at the Wembley Pool tried its luck. But instead of firing fists, the fans opted for bottles and beer cans. In a land of royalty, it was a most unceremonial coronation.

Middleweight champ Minter met Hagler on September 27. Before clashing in the ring, the southpaws traded insults in the press, and by the opening bell, both were angry and ready to brawl. Minter, a smooth boxer, wasn't about to outbrawl Hagler.

In the first round, Minter suffered a pair of cuts around his left eye. Hagler scored often in the second, opening another cut, under Minter's nose. In the third, yet another cut minimized Minter's vision. Hagler punched freely, but when referee Carlos Berrocal stepped in at the 1:45 mark, Minter's countrymen exploded.

The new champion returned to his dressing room, bobbing and weaving all the way.

Middleweight king Alan Minter (left) could not hold off Marvin Hagler's relentless assaults.

LIGHT WASN'T RIGHT FOR WEAK ALI

At the weigh-in for WBC heavyweight champion Larry Holmes' October 2 defense against the comebacking Muhammad Ali, Las Vegas' heavy bettors waited for a sign. When the local commission announced Ali's weight at only 217½, they nodded knowingly and rushed the windows of the Caesars Palace sports book. Their money went on Ali, who hadn't fought in two years. But the challenger's trainer, Angelo Dundee, knew better. "Light isn't right," he said.

Dundee was correct; Ali had reduced from 256 pounds by popping thyroid hormone pills. The medication had badly weakened him, and by fight time, the 38-year-old legend was lifeless.

"All I could think of after the first round," he said, "was Oh, God, I still have 14 rounds to go."

Issuing a reluctant beating, Holmes won every round. Finally, before the start of the 11th, Dundee informed referee Richard Greene of his surrender. Ali would never have quit; his cornerman had done the world a favor.

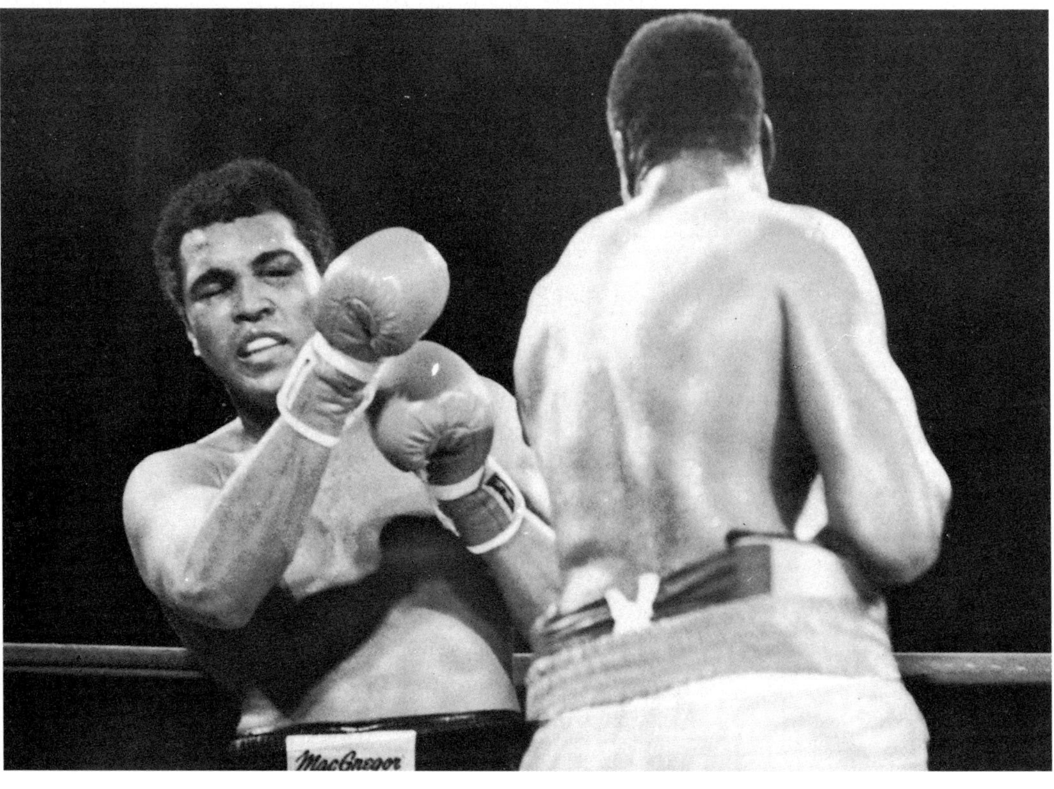

Muhammad Ali (left) showed none of his former brilliance and was stopped by Holmes.

DURAN UTTERS THE UNTHINKABLE

Roberto Duran quitting in the ring? You were more likely to see the Pope sunbathing nude. Or hear Fidel Castro extolling the virtues of democracy.

Until November 25. On that night, at the Superdome in New Orleans, the WBC welterweight champion met Sugar Ray Leonard for the second time in five months.

Before the rematch, Sugar Ray said, "I can change; Duran can't." He was referring to the fierce in-fighting that had favored the Panamanian in the first fight. This time, the bout would be contested on Leonard's terms.

The challenger boxed, jabbed, countered, and stayed off the ropes. After seven rounds, he led by scores of 4-2-1 (twice) and 4-3. More significantly, he was frustrating Duran; in the seventh, he had shuffled, mugged, and taunted him unmercifully.

Late in round eight, Duran pulled back and waved his glove in disgust. "No mas, no mas," he told referee Octavio Meyran. "No mas box."

Just like that, the fight was over. And for millions of fans, so was the myth of Roberto Duran.

Sugar Ray Leonard regained the welterweight crown he had lost to Roberto Duran when Duran suddenly quit in the eighth round.

FIGHTING WITH HIS HEAD

Champions find ways to win. And WBC lightweight titlist Jim Watt was resourceful, if nothing else.

On November 1, at Kelvin Hall in his native Glasgow, Watt, 32, met 21-year-old veteran Sean O'Grady. In order to accommodate American television, the bout started at 2 a.m. By 2:30, it seemed the challenger was en route to victory; he was punching aggressively, and Watt was badly cut over the right brow. But in the 10th, a butt split O'Grady's forehead, and blood poured down his face. At the 2:37 mark of round 12, referee Raymond Baydelrou stepped in and declared Watt the TKO winner.

Watt the Scot had found a way.

Sean O'Grady's face shows the battle scars.

WORLD TITLE FIGHTS

HEAVYWEIGHTS

Oct 2	**Larry Holmes** *KO* 11 Muhammad Ali, Las Vegas
Oct 25	**Mike Weaver** *KO* 13 Gerrie Coetzee, Sun City, Bophuthatswana

CRUISERWEIGHTS

Nov 25	**Carlos DeLeon** (PR) *W* 15 Marvin Camel, New Orleans

LIGHT HEAVYWEIGHTS

Nov 28	**Matthew Saad Muhammad** *KO* 4 Lotte Mwale, San Diego
Nov 29	**Eddie Mustafa Muhammad** *KO* 4 Rudi Koopmans, Los Angeles

MIDDLEWEIGHTS

Sept 27	**Marvin Hagler** (USA) *KO* 3 Alan Minter, London

JUNIOR MIDDLEWEIGHTS

Sept 6	**Ayub Kalule** *W* 15 Bushy Bester, Aarhus, Denmark
Nov 25	**Maurice Hope** *W* 15 Carlos Herrera, Wembley

WELTERWEIGHTS

Nov 25	**Sugar Ray Leonard** *KO* 8 Roberto Duran, New Orleans
Dec 6	**Thomas Hearns** *KO* 6 Luis Primera, Detroit

JUNIOR WELTERWEIGHTS

Oct 2	**Saoul Mamby** *W* 15 Maurice Watkins, Las Vegas
Nov 22	**Aaron Pryor** *KO* 6 Gaetan Hart, Cincinnati

LIGHTWEIGHTS

Sept 20	**Hilmer Kenty** *KO* 4 Ernesto Espana, San Juan
Nov 1	**Jim Watt** *KO* 12 Sean O'Grady, Glasgow
Nov 8	**Hilmer Kenty** *W* 15 Vilomar Fernandez, Detroit

JUNIOR LIGHTWEIGHTS

Nov 20	**Yasutsune Uehara** *W* 15 Leonel Hernandez, Tokyo

FEATHERWEIGHTS

Sept 13	**Salvador Sanchez** *W* 15 Patrick Ford, San Antonio
Oct 4	**Eusebio Pedroza** *W* 15 Rocky Lockridge, McAfee, NJ
Dec 13	**Salvador Sanchez** *W* 15 Juan LaPorte, El Paso

JUNIOR FEATHERWEIGHTS

Nov 8	**Sergio Palma** *KO* 9 Ulises Morales, Buenos Aires
Dec 13	**Wilfredo Gomez** *KO* 3 Jose Cervantes, Miami

BANTAMWEIGHTS

Sept 19	**Lupe Pintor** *KO* 12 Johnny Owen, Los Angeles
Nov 14	**Jeff Chandler** (USA) *KO* 14 Julian Solis, Miami
Dec 19	**Lupe Pintor** *W* 15 Albert Davila, Las Vegas

JUNIOR BANTAMWEIGHTS

Sept 15	**Rafael Orono** *KO* 3 Jovito Rengifo, Barquisimeto, Venezuela

FLYWEIGHTS

Oct 18	**Shoji Oguma** *W* 15 Chan Hee Park, Sendai, Japan
Dec 13	**Peter Mathebula** (SA) *W* 15 Tae Shik Kim, Los Angeles

JUNIOR FLYWEIGHTS

Sept 17	**Hilario Zapata** *KO* 11 Shigeo Nakajima, Gifu, Japan
Oct 12	**Yoko Gushiken** *W* 15 Pedro Flores, Kanazawa, Japan
Dec 1	**Hilario Zapata** *W* 15 Reinaldo Becerra, Caracas

JANUARY

1981

APRIL

BOZA SHOWS HE'S NO CLOWN

Before WBC super featherweight champion Bazooka Limon defended against London-based Ugandan Cornelius Boza-Edwards, the bold Mexican made a tasteless reference to countryman Lupe Pintor's September 1990 victory over Welsh bantamweight Johnny Owen. (Six weeks after that bout, Owen died of brain injuries.)

"I don't know why (Boza) wants to fight me," he said. "He knows what Mexicans do to British fighters. The same thing will happen this time."

On March 8, at the Civic Auditorium in Stockton, California, Limon fought like he talked. A fearless brawler, he butted and punched high, low, and everywhere in between. But Boza, a fellow southpaw, answered in kind. The challenger scored a knockdown in the fifth, and went toe to toe in the thrilling sixth, during which both fighters suffered cuts.

After absorbing a low blow in the 13th, Boza got angry. He finished strong and took the title by scores of 146-140 (twice) and 143-141. Limon's punches were not as threatening as his words.

Cornelius Boza-Edwards (left) stripped Rafael "Bazooka" Limon of the junior lightweight title.

Ringside View

FEBRUARY

Panamanian southpaw Hilario Zapata retains the WBC light flyweight title for the fifth time, scoring a 13th-round TKO over stringbean American contender Joey Olivo.

WHEN A DRAW IS REALLY A LOSS

Call it a statistical oddity: after challenging both WBC bantamweight champion Lupe Pintor and WBA king Jeff Chandler, Japan's Eijiro Murata remained undefeated. Still, he hadn't won a world title.

In June 1980, Murata had fought to a 15-round draw with Pintor. On April 5, he received his second chance, squaring off against Chandler at the Kuramae Arena in Tokyo. The Oriental & Pacific champion nearly scored a first-round stoppage; a right shook Chandler, but "Joltin' Jeff" managed to survive the round. Murata maintained his momentum until the second half of the bout, when Chandler began scoring with counter uppercuts. In the 14th, it was Murata who almost fell.

After 15 rounds, the judges scored a split draw (totals of 145-142 for Chandler, 147-146 for Murata, and 143-143). The Japanese was still undefeated. But not losing won nothing.

Bantamweight king Jeff Chandler (left) and Japan's Eijiro Murata battled to a 15-round draw, with Chandler retaining the crown.

DREAMER O'GRADY BURSTS KENTY'S BUBBLE

While in training for his try at WBA lightweight champion Hilmer Kenty, Sean O'Grady experienced a recurring nightmare. He dreamed of his face covered with blood, and the referee saving him from further punishment. That, of course, is exactly how his first title shot had ended; in November 1980, O'Grady suffered a TKO loss to WBC champion Jim Watt.

O'Grady faced the unbeaten Kenty on April 12, at Bally's Park Place Hotel in Atlantic City. Who says dreams don't come true? In the fifth round, a butt ripped open O'Grady's left brow. This time, however, the blood didn't become a factor.

Pressuring Kenty all the way, "Bubblegum Sean" featured a draining body attack and scored knockdowns in rounds two and eight. Kenty survived the last three rounds on heart alone.

O'Grady took the title by scores of 147-137, 146-139, and 146-138. Only five months after his heartbreaking loss to Watt, he was a world champion. He never could have dreamed it.

Ringside View

APRIL

Forced to go the distance for the first time since winning the title, WBC heavyweight champion Larry Holmes scores a unanimous 15-round decision over awkward Canadian Trevor Berbick.

Larry Holmes (right) was pressed to retain the heavyweight crown against Trevor Berbick.

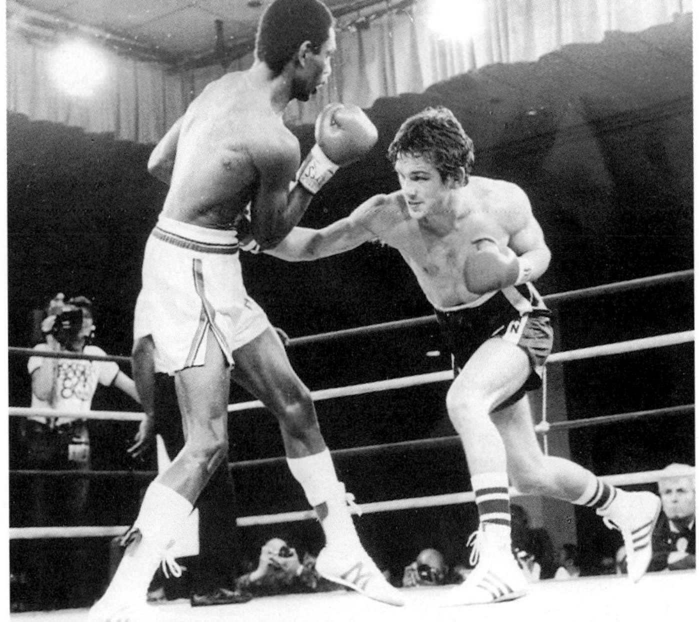

Sean O'Grady (right) captured a 15-round decision over Hilmer Kenty for the lightweight crown.

World Title Fights

HEAVYWEIGHTS

April 11	**Larry Holmes** *W* 15 Trevor Berbick, Las Vegas

LIGHT HEAVYWEIGHTS

Feb 28	**Matthew Saad Muhammad** *KO* 11 Vonzell Johnson, Atlantic City
April 25	**Matthew Saad Muhammad** *KO* 9 Murray Sutherland, Atlantic City

MIDDLEWEIGHTS

Jan 17	**Marvin Hagler** *KO* 8 Fulgencio Obelmeijas, Boston

WELTERWEIGHTS

March 28	**Sugar Ray Leonard** *KO* 10 Larry Bonds, Syracuse
April 25	**Thomas Hearns** *KO* 13 Randy Shields, Phoenix

LIGHTWEIGHTS

April 12	**Sean O'Grady** (USA) *W* 15 Hilmer Kenty, Atlantic City

JUNIOR LIGHTWEIGHTS

Jan 11	**Rafael Limon** (MEX) *KO* 15 Ildefonso Bethelmy, Los Angeles (Wins Vacant WBC Title)
March 8	**Cornelius Boza-Edwards** (UGA) *W* 15 Rafael Limon, Stockton, CA
April 9	**Samuel Serrano** *W* 15 Yasutsune Uehara, Wakayama, Japan

FEATHERWEIGHTS

Feb 14	**Eusebio Pedroza** *KO* 13 Patrick Ford, Panama City
March 22	**Salvador Sanchez** *KO* 10 Roberto Castanon, Las Vegas

JUNIOR FEATHERWEIGHTS

April 4	**Sergio Palma** *W* 15 Leonardo Cruz, Buenos Aires

BANTAMWEIGHTS

Jan 31	**Jeff Chandler** *W* 15 Jorge Lujan, Philadelphia
Feb 22	**Lupe Pintor** *W* 15 Jose Uziga, Houston
April 5	**Jeff Chandler** *D* 15 Eijiro Murata, Tokyo

JUNIOR BANTAMWEIGHTS

Jan 24	**Chul Ho Kim** (KOR) *KO* 9 Rafael Orono, San Cristobal, Venezuela
April 22	**Chul Ho Kim** *W* 15 Jiro Watanabe, Seoul

FLYWEIGHTS

Feb 3	**Shoji Oguma** *W* 15 Chan Hee Park, Tokyo
March 28	**Santos Laciar** (ARG) *KO* 7 Peter Mathebula, Soweto, South Africa

JUNIOR FLYWEIGHTS

Feb 8	**Hilario Zapata** *KO* 13 Joey Olivo, Panama City
March 8	**Pedro Flores** (MEX) *KO* 12 Yoko Gushiken, Gushikawa, Japan
April 24	**Hilario Zapata** *W* 15 Rudy Crawford, San Francisco

THE FLYWEIGHT JINX

No one, it seemed, could hold on to the WBA flyweight title. A fighter would look good in winning it, then look equally bad in his first defense.

On March 28, at Orlando Stadium in the South African township of Soweto, Peter Mathebula became the latest victim of the jinx. His conqueror was Argentina's Santos Laciar, a short pressure fighter with a heavy hook. Boxing tentatively, Mathebula was never in the fight. Laciar weakened him with body blows, dropped him in the fifth, and finished him in the seventh. After falling for a second time, the South African informed referee Stanley Berg that he didn't want to continue.

MAY

1981

AUGUST

RINGSIDE VIEW

JUNE

Larry Holmes retains the WBC heavyweight title for the 10th time, crushing former champion Leon Spinks in three rounds.

JUNE

One month after Wilfred Benitez becomes boxing's fifth three-division champion, Alexis Arguello is crowned number six. The former featherweight and junior lightweight king adds the WBC lightweight crown by scoring a unanimous 15-round decision over Jim Watt.

When Wilfred Benitez knocked out Maurice Hope in the 12th round, he became the first man in 43 years to win titles in three divisions.

A DIFFERENT KIND OF WEDDING PRESENT FOR HOPE

One day after WBC super welterweight titlist Maurice Hope defended against former 140-and 147-pound champion Wilfred Benitez, the Antiguan southpaw got married. Fortunately, he didn't have to switch the ceremony from a church to a hospital. The fight took place on May 23 at Caesars Palace. Hope started strongly, but Benitez gained control in the fifth, when he switched his attack to the body. He punished Hope throughout the 11th, and finished him in the 12th, landing a textbook right to the chin. Hope fell face-first and was out cold for 10 minutes. He was briefly hospitalized – but still managed to get to the altar on time.

A TITLE-FIGHT TUNEUP

Those who dismissed WBC welterweight champion Sugar Ray Leonard as a pampered golden boy chose not to acknowledge that the 1976 gold medalist rarely took the easy road. With a multimillion-dollar unification match vs. WBA king Thomas Hearns scheduled for September, Sugar Ray agreed to a dangerous "tune-up": on June 25, at the Houston Astrodome, he rose in weight and challenged WBA junior middleweight champion Ayub Kalule.

Kalule was a strong and awkward southpaw, and every time Leonard struck, the Denmark-based Ugandan answered.

Leonard was staggered in the seventh. In the ninth, however, he turned the fight with a wild right. His followup blows downed the defending champion, who rose, but then informed referee Carlos Berrocal of his surrender. The bout was stopped at the 2:59 mark.

"If I had known the round was over," said Kalule, "I would have fought more."

It probably wouldn't have made a difference.

It was a first-ever career defeat in his 36th contest for Kalule and took Leonard to 30-1-0.

Sugar Ray Leonard does a somersault after knocking out Ayub Kalule in the eighth round to win the junior middleweight crown.

MICHAEL COMPLETES THE OLYMPIC CYCLE

All four of Michael Spinks' gold medal-winning Olympic teammates, Sugar Ray Leonard, Howard Davis Jr., Leo Randolph, and older brother Leon Spinks, had fought for world titles. And with the exception of Davis, all of them had been crowned.

Spinks' chance came on July 18, when he challenged WBA light heavyweight champion Eddie Mustafa Muhammad at the Imperial Palace Hotel in Las Vegas. The fighters' styles dictated a careful, tactical fight. After seven rounds, neither 175-pounder had taken command. But in the eighth, Muhammad's right eye was closed shut. (He claimed he had been thumbed; Spinks said his jabs had been responsible.)

Said the champion, "I couldn't see, so I had to hold my head up." That cost him in the 12th, when a Spinks right hand sent him to the canvas. Muhammad switched to survival mode after that, and Spinks took the title by unanimous scores of 144-140, 146-138, and 145-139.

And unlike his brother, he was going to keep it for a while.

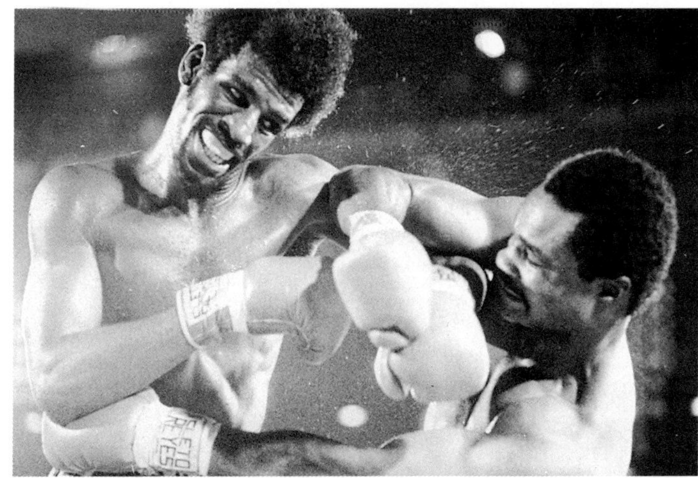

Michael Spinks (left) won a unanimous 15-round decision over Eddie Mustafa Muhammad.

"POUND FOR POUND" IS DOWNED

The symmetry: in 1978, WBC super bantamweight champion Wilfredo Gomez knocked out Mexican bantamweight king Carlos Zarate, who had risen in weight. It was a shocker; Zarate was unbeaten, and thought by many to be boxing's best fighter.

On August 21, WBC featherweight titlist Salvador Sanchez stopped Puerto Rican super bantamweight champ Gomez, who had risen in weight. It was a shocker; Gomez was unbeaten, and thought by many to be boxing's best.

Gomez, who weakened himself by struggling to make weight, was annihilated. A hook felled him 40 seconds into the opening round, and he never fully recovered. Sanchez fractured his right cheekbone and reduced his eyes to slits. In the eighth, Gomez was driven halfway through the ropes, and referee Carlos Padilla stopped it.

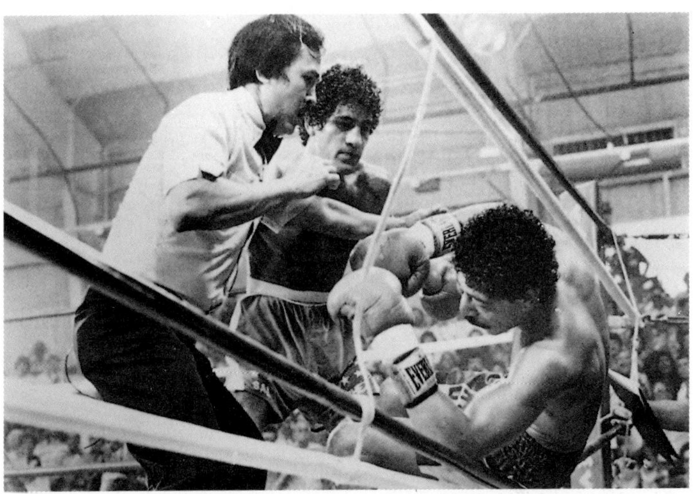

Salvador Sanchez retained the title by stopping previously undefeated Wilfredo Gomez.

WORLD TITLE FIGHTS

HEAVYWEIGHTS

June 12 **Larry Holmes** *KO* 3 Leon Spinks, Detroit

LIGHT HEAVYWEIGHTS

July 18 **Michael Spinks** (USA) *W* 15 Eddie Mustafa Muhammad, Las Vegas

MIDDLEWEIGHTS

June 13 **Marvin Hagler** *KO* 5 Vito Antuofermo, Boston

JUNIOR MIDDLEWEIGHTS

May 23 **Wilfred Benitez** *KO* 12 Maurice Hope, Las Vegas

June 25 **Sugar Ray Leonard** *KO* 9 Ayub Kalule, Houston

WELTERWEIGHTS

June 25 **Thomas Hearns** *KO* 4 Pablo Baez, Houston

JUNIOR WELTERWEIGHTS

June 12 **Saoul Mamby** *W* 15 Jo Kimpuani, Detroit

June 27 **Aaron Pryor** *KO* 2 Lennox Blackmoore, Las Vegas

Aug 29 **Saoul Mamby** *W* 15 Thomas Americo, Djakarta

LIGHTWEIGHTS

June 20 **Alexis Arguello** *W* 15 Jim Watt, London

JUNIOR LIGHTWEIGHTS

May 30 **Cornelius Boza-Edwards** *KO* 14 Bobby Chacon, Las Vegas

June 29 **Samuel Serrano** *W* 15 Leonel Hernandez, Caracas

Aug 29 **Rolando Navarrete** (PHI) *KO* 5 Cornelius Boza-Edwards, Via Reggio, Italy

FEATHERWEIGHTS

Aug 1 **Eusebio Pedroza** *KO* 7 Carlos Pinango, Caracas

Aug 21 **Salvador Sanchez** *KO* 8 Wilfredo Gomez, Las Vegas

JUNIOR FEATHERWEIGHTS

Aug 15 **Sergio Palma** *KO* 12 Ricardo Cardona, Buenos Aires

BANTAMWEIGHTS

July 25 **Jeff Chandler** *KO* 7 Julian Solis, Atlantic City

July 26 **Lupe Pintor** *KO* 8 Jovito Rengifo, Las Vegas

JUNIOR BANTAMWEIGHTS

July 29 **Chul Ho Kim** *KO* 13 Willie Jensen, Pusan, South Korea

FLYWEIGHTS

May 12 **Antonio Avelar** (MEX) *KO* 7 Shoji Oguma, Mito, Japan

June 6 **Luis Ibarra** *W* 15 Santos Laciar, Buenos Aires

Aug 30 **Antonio Avelar** *KO* 2 Tae Shik Kim, Seoul

JUNIOR FLYWEIGHTS

July 19 **Hwan Jin Kim** (KOR) *KO* 13 Pedro Flores, Taegu, Japan

Aug 15 **Hilario Zapata** *W* 15 German Torres, Panama City

SEPTEMBER

1981

DECEMBER

THE FIRST FIGHT OF THE DECADE

In analyzing the welterweight unification battle between WBC champion Sugar Ray Leonard and WBA titlist Thomas Hearns, insiders anticipated a classic boxer-puncher matchup. Sugar Ray was the dancemaster, and Hearns the feared kayo artist. But halfway through their heavily hyped bout, fought on September 16 before 25,000 fans at Caesars Palace, the fighters traded roles.

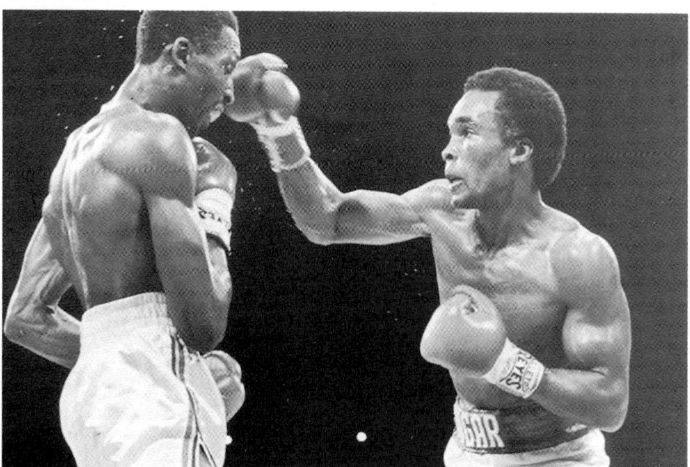
Sugar Ray Leonard (right) proved his greatness with a 14th-round kayo of Thomas Hearns.

For the first five rounds, Leonard, concerned with "The Hit Man's" big right hand, boxed cautiously. But after hurting Hearns in both the sixth and seventh, he turned hunter. And Hearns, capitalizing on his 4-inch reach advantage, began to jab and move.

Hearns was more successful; he closed Sugar Ray's left eye, and built a lead on the cards. However, Leonard broke through in the 13th, scoring a knockdown, and again in the 14th, when an inspired flurry left Hearns helpless and seated on the ropes. Referee Davey Pearl intervened at the 1:45 mark.

Sugar Ray had found a way. Winners always do.

OCTOBER

In a chilling battle, WBC lightweight champion Alexis Arguello stops 20-year-old Ray "Boom Boom" Mancini in the 14th round.

OCTOBER

World middleweight champion Marvin Hagler punishes fellow southpaw Mustafa Hamsho, opening several cuts en route to scoring an 11th-round TKO.

SURVIVING A RIGHT HAND FIRED FROM HELL

In preparing for his 11th defense, WBC heavyweight champion Larry Holmes ordered tapes of his opponent, unbeaten New Yorker Renaldo Snipes. After only a few minutes he turned off his VCR for fear of growing overconfident.

Holmes met Snipes on November 6, at the Civic Arena in Pittsburgh. For six rounds, the awkward challenger tried – and failed – to match skills with the champion. But in the seventh, he fired an overhand right that connected flush. Holmes collapsed as if he had been struck by a cannonball. He rose quickly, then wobbled and crashed into a corner post. He was one punch away from losing the title – and a multimillion-dollar fight vs. Gerry Cooney. But Snipes failed to land that punch.

For Holmes, there were no more anxious moments. In the 11th, he shook Snipes with a right. His followup attack brought a stoppage from referee Ortega – and a smile from Gerry Cooney.

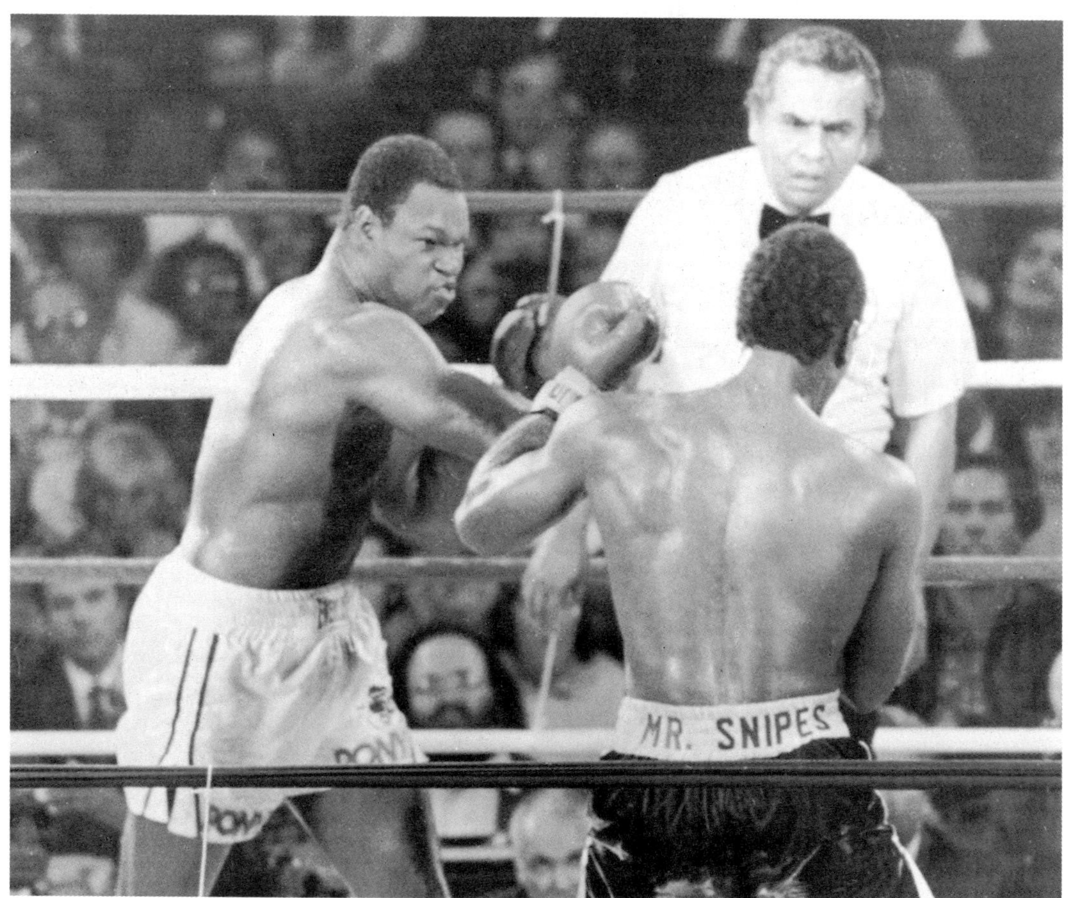

Heavyweight champion Larry Holmes (left) retained the title and remained undefeated by stopping Renaldo Snipes in the 11th round.

A FINAL GOODBYE

Champions demand to exit on their own terms. Joe Frazier, who had been stopped in his last two bouts, didn't want to be remembered as a loser. Muhammad Ali needed to distance the memories of his miserable comeback bout vs. Larry Holmes. So the legends decided to fight just one more time.

On December 3, Frazier, 37, ended a 5½-year retirement by squaring off against Jumbo Cummings at the International Amphitheatre in Chicago. Scaling a blubbery 229, he smoked only in spurts. The judges were kind; after 10 rounds, they scored a majority draw.

Eight days later, Ali, 39, faced contender Trevor Berbick on a baseball field at the Queen Elizabeth Sports Centre in Nassau, the Bahamas. He fought far better than he had against Holmes, but there were few jabs, little hand speed, and no power. The industrious Berbick took a unanimous 10-round verdict.

Forever linked in history, Ali and Frazier had said goodbye.

All smiles as ex-champ Joe Frazier (right) weighs in with opponent Jumbo Cummings.

Dwight Braxton (left) stopped Matthew Saad Muhammad to win the light heavyweight title.

NO MORE MIRACLES FOR MATTHEW

In the fight before the fight, WBC light heavyweight champion Matthew Saad Muhammad won by losing 6½ pounds in 12 hours. After barely making weight for his defense against Dwight Braxton, however, "Miracle Matthew" had no strength left for his opponent.

Muhammad and Braxton traded blows on December 19, at the Playboy Hotel in Atlantic City. Firing overhand rights and vicious body blows, the 5'6¼" challenger started quickly.

"By the fourth round," said Adolph Ritacco, Muhammad's cutman, "(Saad) was spent."

In the 10th, Braxton floored the champion with a right. Seconds later, referee Arthur Mercante stepped in, turning Miracle Matthew into Sad Saad.

WORLD TITLE FIGHTS

HEAVYWEIGHTS

Oct 3	**Mike Weaver** *W* 15 James Tillis, Rosemont, IL
Nov 6	**Larry Holmes** *KO* 11 Renaldo Snipes, Pittsburgh

LIGHT HEAVYWEIGHTS

Sept 26	**Matthew Saad Muhammad** *KO* 11 Jerry Martin, Atlantic City
Nov 7	**Michael Spinks** *KO* 7 Vonzell Johnson, Atlantic City
Dec 19	**Dwight Braxton** (USA) *KO* 10 Matthew Saad Muhammad, Atlantic City

MIDDLEWEIGHTS

Oct 3	**Marvin Hagler** *KO* 11 Mustafa Hamsho, Rosemont, IL

JUNIOR MIDDLEWEIGHTS

Nov 7	**Tadashi Mihara** *W* 15 Rocky Fratto, Rochester (Wins Vacant WBA Title)

WELTERWEIGHTS

Sept 16	**Sugar Ray Leonard** *KO* 14 Thomas Hearns, Las Vegas (Unifies World Title)

JUNIOR WELTERWEIGHTS

Nov 14	**Aaron Pryor** *KO* 7 Dujuan Johnson, Cleveland
Dec 20	**Saoul Mamby** *W* 15 Obisia Nwankpa, Lagos

LIGHTWEIGHTS

Sept 12	**Claude Noel** (TRI) *W* 15 Gato Gonzalez, Atlantic City (Wins Vacant WBA Title)
Oct 3	**Alexis Arguello** *KO* 14 Ray Mancini, Atlantic City
Nov 21	**Alexis Arguello** *KO* 7 Roberto Elizondo, Las Vegas
Dec 5	**Art Frias** (USA) *KO* 8 Claude Noel, Las Vegas

JUNIOR LIGHTWEIGHTS

Dec 10	**Samuel Serrano** *KO* 12 Hikaru Tomonari, Hato Rey, Puerto Rico

FEATHERWEIGHTS

Dec 5	**Salvador Sanchez** *W* 15 Pat Cowdell, Houston

JUNIOR FEATHERWEIGHTS

Oct 3	**Sergio Palma** *W* 15 Vichit Muangroi-et, Buenos Aires

BANTAMWEIGHTS

Sept 22	**Lupe Pintor** *KO* 15 Hurricane Teru, Nagoya, Japan
Dec 10	**Jeff Chandler** *KO* 13 Eijiro Murata, Atlantic City

JUNIOR BANTAMWEIGHTS

Sept 12	**Gustavo Ballas** (ARG) *KO* 8 Sok Chul Bae, Buenos Aires (Wins Vacant WBA Title)
Nov 18	**Chul Ho Kim** *KO* 9 Jackal Maruyama, Pusan, South Korea
Dec 5	**Rafael Pedroza** (PAN) *W* 15 Gustavo Ballas, Panama City

FLYWEIGHTS

Sept 26	**Juan Herrera** (MEX) *KO* 11 Luis Ibarra, Merida, Mexico
Dec 19	**Juan Herrera** *KO* 7 Betulio Gonzalez, Merida, Mexico

JUNIOR FLYWEIGHTS

Oct 11	**Hwan Jin Kim** *W* 15 Alfonso Lopez, Taejon, South Korea
Nov 6	**Hilario Zapata** *KO* 10 Netrnoi S. Vorasingh, Korat, Thailand
Dec 16	**Katsuo Tokashiki** (JAP) *W* 15 Hwan Jin Kim, Sendai, Japan

JANUARY

1982

APRIL

LOW BLOWS FROM EUSEBIO

Watching Juan LaPorte's try at the WBA featherweight champion Eusebio Pedroza, Howie Albert, the challenger's manager, counted 35 low blows. After checking a tape of the fight, he counted more than 50. Then, after watching the tape again...

LaPorte challenged Pedroza on January 24, at the Sands Hotel & Casino in Atlantic City. It was Pedroza's 14th defense, an all-time division record.

For the first six rounds, LaPorte boxed neatly. Then Pedroza, one of boxing's best late-rounds fighters, began backing LaPorte to the ropes and firing both fists to the body. He was penalized by referee Guy Jutras for hitting low in the eighth, and for using his elbows in the 14th.

Despite the point deductions, Pedroza won by unanimous 15-round decision (scores of 144-141, 144-142, and 145-143).

"Pedroza is the dirtiest fighter I ever fought," complained LaPorte.

Countered the champion, "When you're a professional, you don't cry."

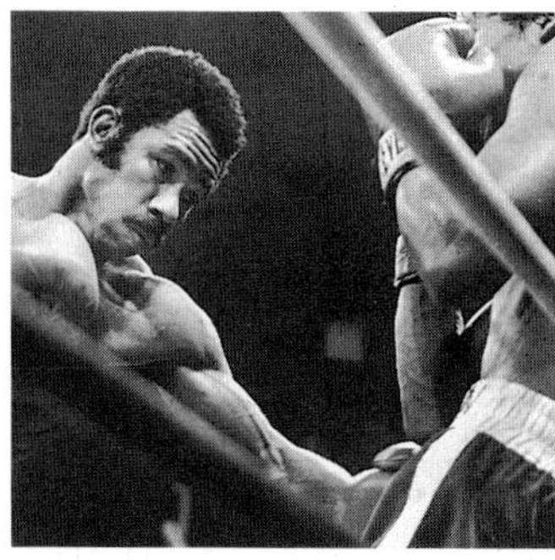

Eusebio Pedroza (left) retained featherweight title vs. Juan LaPorte.

OUT-TOUGHING THE TOUGH GUY

First *no mas*. Now this.

Fourteen months after his inexplicable and unforgivable surrender to Sugar Ray Leonard, Roberto Duran was given an opportunity to become a world champion once more. On January 30, he challenged WBC super welterweight champion Wilfred Benitez at Caesars Palace.

It wasn't that Duran lost – Benitez was a great fighter. It was *how* he lost. Expected to dart in and out and box cautiously, Benitez instead fought with machismo.

"I wanted to beat him at *his* fight, to show him *I* was the champion," he explained.

Both quicker and stronger, Benitez hammered Duran to the body en route to a unanimous 15-round points victory (scores of 144-141, 143-142, and 145-141).

Duran had trained with fervor on Coiba, a penal island 15 miles from Panama. He just hadn't been good enough. At age 30, he was through. Or so it seemed.

Wilfred Benitez (right) was exceedingly sharp in outpointing Roberto Duran over 15 rounds.

WORLD TITLE FIGHTS

CRUISERWEIGHTS

Feb 13 **Osvaldo Ocasio** (PR) *W* 15 Robbie Williams, Johannesburg (Wins Newly Created WBA Title)

Feb 24 **Carlos DeLeon** *KO* 8 Marvin Camel, Atlantic City

LIGHT HEAVYWEIGHTS

Feb 13 **Michael Spinks** *KO* 6 Mustapha Wassaja, Atlantic City

March 21 **Dwight Braxton** *KO* 6 Jerry Martin, Las Vegas

April 11 **Michael Spinks** *KO* 8 Murray Sutherland, Atlantic City

MIDDLEWEIGHTS

March 7 **Marvin Hagler** *KO* 1 William (Caveman) Lee, Atlantic City

JUNIOR MIDDLEWEIGHTS

Jan 30 **Wilfred Benitez** *W* 15 Roberto Duran, Las Vegas

Feb 2 **Davey Moore** (USA) *KO* 6 Tadashi Mihara, Tokyo

April 26 **Davey Moore** *KO* 5 Charlie Weir, Johannesburg

WELTERWEIGHTS

Feb 15 **Sugar Ray Leonard** *KO* 3 Bruce Finch, Reno

JUNIOR WELTERWEIGHTS

March 21 **Aaron Pryor** *KO* 12 Miguel Montilla, Atlantic City

LIGHTWEIGHTS

Jan 30 **Arturo Frias** *Tech Win* 9 Ernesto Espana, Los Angeles

Feb 13 **Alexis Arguello** *KO* 6 Bubba Busceme, Beaumont, TX

JUNIOR LIGHTWEIGHTS

Jan 16 **Rolando Navarette** *KO* 11 Chung Il Choi, Manila

FEATHERWEIGHTS

Jan 24 **Eusebio Pedroza** *W* 15 Juan LaPorte, Atlantic City

JUNIOR FEATHERWEIGHTS

Jan 15 **Sergio Palma** *W* 15 Jorge Lujan, Cordoba, Argentina

March 27 **Wilfredo Gomez** *KO* 6 Juan Meza, Atlantic City

BANTAMWEIGHTS

March 27 **Jeff Chandler** *KO* 6 Johnny Carter, Philadelphia

JUNIOR BANTAMWEIGHTS

Feb 10 **Chul Ho Kim** *KO* 8 Koki Ishii, Taegu, South Korea

April 8 **Jiro Watanabe** (JAP) *W* 15 Rafael Pedroza, Osaka

FLYWEIGHTS

March 20 **Prudencio Cardona** (COL) *KO* 1 Antonio Avelar, Tampico, Mexico

JUNIOR FLYWEIGHTS

Feb 6 **Amado Urzua** (MEX) *KO* 2 Hilario Zapata, Panama City

April 4 **Katsuo Tokashiki** *W* 15 Lupe Madera, Sendai, Japan

April 13 **Tadashi Tomori** (JAP) *W* 15 Amado Ursua, Tokyo

THE RISE AND FALL OF "THE SILVER ASSASSIN"

In South Africa, boxing was big business. And Charlie Weir, a big-punching junior middleweight who was nicknamed "The Silver Assassin," was a big favorite. If he could win the title, it meant big money for everyone.

Initially, at least, there was a problem: Tadashi Mihara was the WBA champion, and Japanese boxers refused to fight in South Africa. As a result, promoter Bob Arum selected Davey Moore, an unrated former amateur star with only nine bouts of pro experience, to dethrone the unexceptional Mihara. In February, he did just that, scoring a sixth-round kayo, and clearing the way for Weir.

On April 26, before a hopeful crowd of more than 45,000 at Ellis Park in Johannesburg, Moore met The Silver Assassin. From the second round through the fifth, the champion scored a total of five knockdowns. After being felled by a straight right in the fifth, the fragile Weir was counted out.

Big surprise: no silver pickings for the former assassin.

Ringside View

JANUARY

Making his first defense, WBC super featherweight champion Rolando Navarette scores a bruising 11th-round knockout of South Korea's Chung Il Choi.

MARCH

In an all-Philadelphia shootout, WBA bantamweight king Jeff Chandler outfights Johnny Carter at close range and keeps the title by sixth-round stoppage.

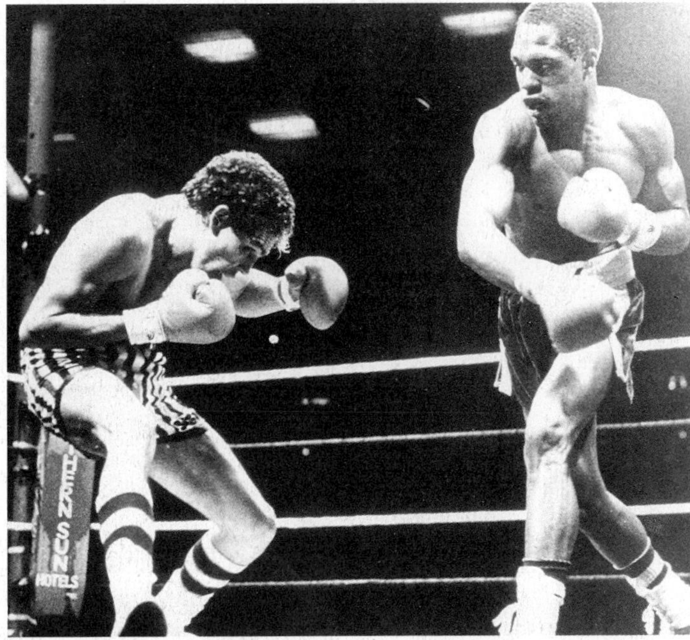

New York's Davey Moore (right) knocked out local hero Charlie Weir in Johannesburg.

A FINCH IN THE HAND...

Having scored title-winning victories over Ayub Kalule and Thomas Hearns, Sugar Ray Leonard could be excused for seeming less than threatened before his welterweight title defense vs. Bruce Finch. Against average competition, you see, Leonard had become good enough to win as he pleased.

Sugar Ray squared off against Finch on February 15, at the Centennial Coliseum in Reno. (It was "The Biggest Little City In The World's" first title fight since Jack Johnson-Jim Jeffries in 1910.)

After a slow first round, Leonard suddenly exploded. He scored two knockdowns in the second, and when Finch fell again in the third, referee Mills Lane halted the mismatch.

Imagine what Leonard might have done had he been motivated.

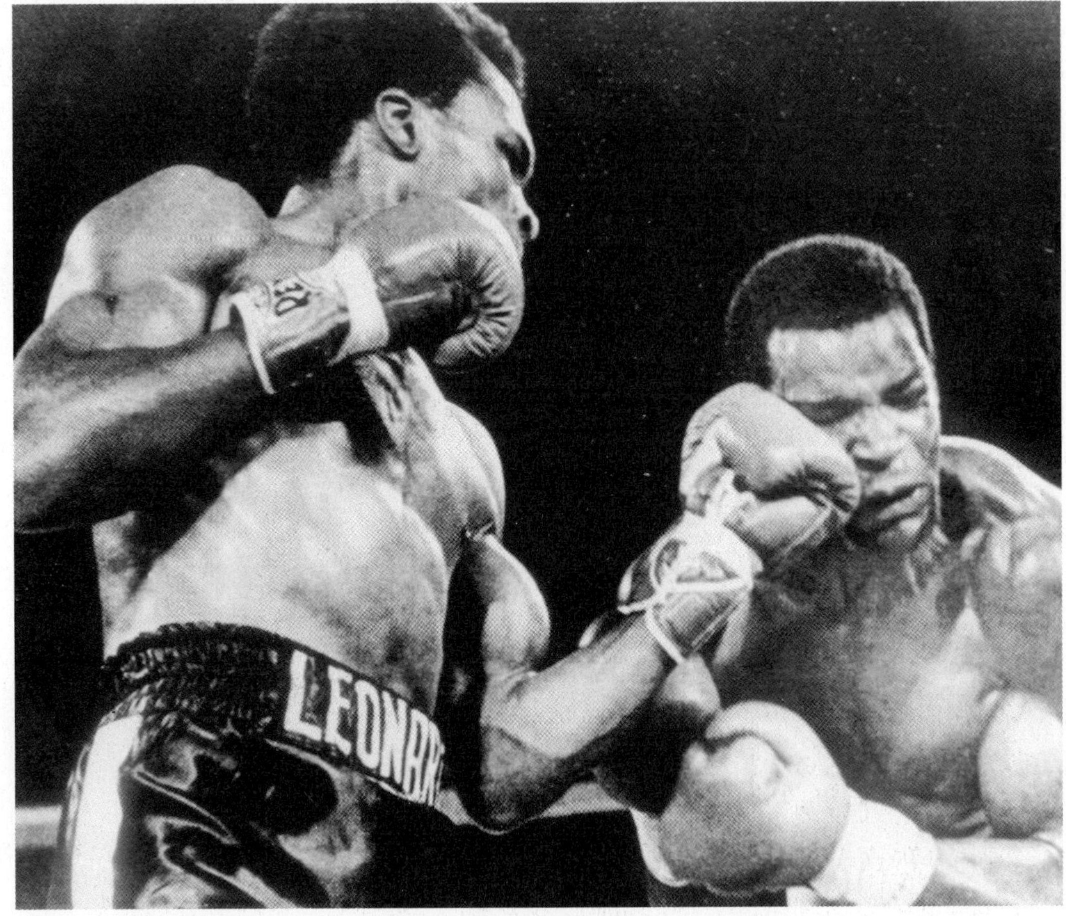

World welterweight king Sugar Ray Leonard (left) stopped challenger Bruce Finch in the third round to retain the title in Reno, Nevada.

MAY

1982

AUGUST

RINGSIDE VIEW

MAY

World welterweight champion Sugar Ray Leonard undergoes surgery to repair a detached retina in his left eye.

A DREAM COMES TRUE – 40 YEARS LATER

In 1941, Lenny Mancini was boxing's top-rated lightweight. Bad timing: he was drafted just before securing a try at world champion Sammy Angott. After the war, he resumed his career, but having been wounded in France, he failed to regain his form.

Forty years later, Ray "Boom Boom" Mancini tried to realize his father's dream when he challenged WBC lightweight champion Alexis Arguello. He was stopped in 14 rounds. Only seven months later, however, he won the WBA crown from Art Frias.

The bout, held on May 8, at the Aladdin Hotel in Las Vegas, was brief and brutal. In the opening round, Mancini was staggered twice and cut over the right eye. Thirty seconds before the bell, he rebounded to drop the champion with two lefts. Hurt and bloodied, Frias backed to the ropes and took 33 straight blows. Referee Richard Greene stepped in.

It was Ray's title, but you can be sure Lenny tried on the championship belt, too.

Ray "Boom Boom" Mancini (left) stopped defending lightweight king Arturo Frias at 2:54 of the first round and became the new champion.

LOTS OF GUTS, BUT NO GLORY

WBC heavyweight champion Larry Holmes' defense vs. Gerry Cooney, fought on June 11 at Caesars Palace, proved that while the lighter weight classes were hotter than ever, nothing can top a heavyweight superfight.

The bout, among the most eagerly anticipated in history, drew a crowd of 29,284, and produced an all-time record gate of $7,293,600. Holmes was the best big man of the day; Cooney was big, powerful, unbeaten... and white. Someone had to fall.

That's just what Cooney did in the second round, when Holmes struck with a right. But the challenger picked himself up and boxed reasonably well until tiring. His punches began to stray low, and referee Mills Lane penalized him twice in the ninth, and again in the 11th.

The end came in the 13th. Holmes drove Cooney to the ropes, and as the gentle giant began to fall, his trainer, Victor Valle, climbed through the ropes and embraced him.

"I'm sorry," Cooney said again and again. Sadly, he would never fully recover his ranking.

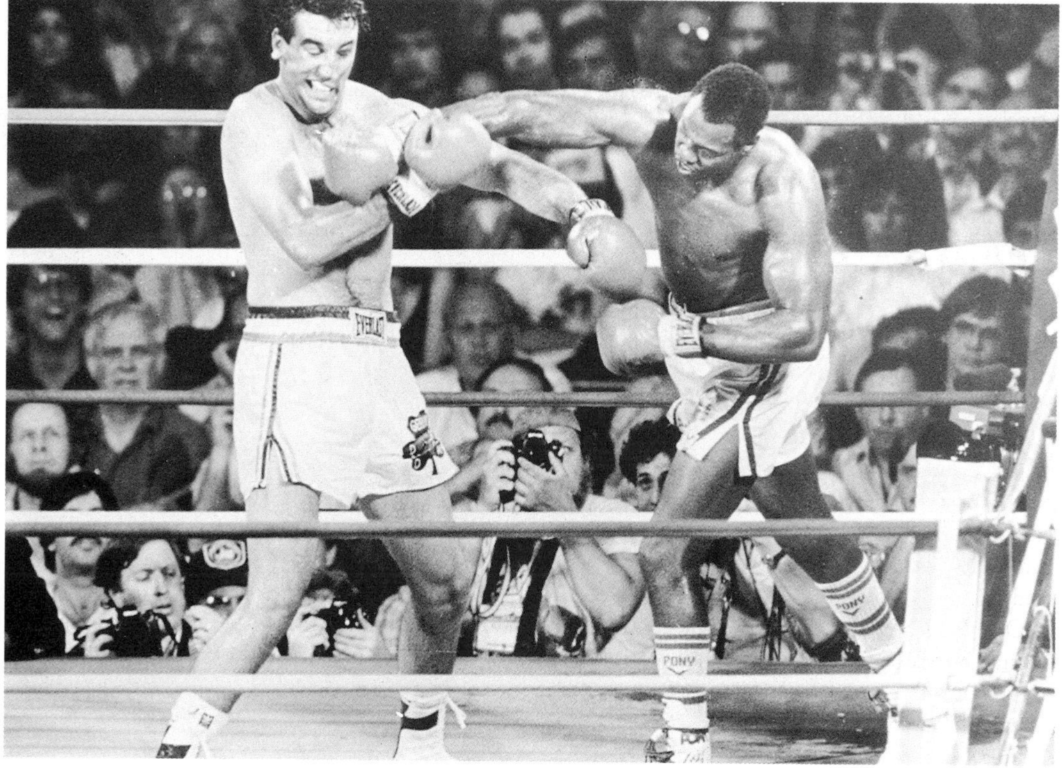

Larry Holmes (right) knocked out Gerry Cooney in the 13th round of a thrilling brawl to retain the world heavyweight title and remain undefeated.

World Title Fights

HEAVYWEIGHTS

June 11 **Larry Holmes** *KO* 13
Gerry Cooney, Las Vegas

CRUISERWEIGHTS

June 27 **ST Gordon** (USA) *KO* 2
Carlos DeLeon, Highland Heights, OH

LIGHT HEAVYWEIGHTS

June 12 **Michael Spinks** *KO* 8
Jerry Celestine, Atlantic City

Aug 7 **Dwight Braxton** *KO* 6
Matthew Saad Muhammad, Philadelphia

JUNIOR MIDDLEWEIGHTS

July 17 **Davey Moore** *KO* 10
Ayub Kalule, Atlantic City

JUNIOR WELTERWEIGHTS

June 26 **Leroy Haley** *W* 15
Saoul Mamby, Highland Heights, OH

July 4 **Aaron Pryor** *KO* 6
Akio Kameda, Cincinnati

LIGHTWEIGHTS

May 8 **Ray Mancini** (USA) *KO* 1
Arturo Frias, Las Vegas

May 22 **Alexis Arguello** *KO* 5
Andrew Ganigan, Las Vegas

July 24 **Ray Mancini** *KO* 6
Ernesto Espana, Warren, OH

JUNIOR LIGHTWEIGHTS

May 29 **Rafael Limon** *KO* 12
Rolando Navarette, Las Vegas

June 5 **Samuel Serrano** *Tech Win* 10
Benedicto Villablanca, Santiago, Chile

FEATHERWEIGHTS

May 8 **Salvador Sanchez** *W* 15
Rocky Garcia, Dallas

July 21 **Salvador Sanchez** *KO* 15
Azumah Nelson, New York City

JUNIOR FEATHERWEIGHTS

June 11 **Wilfredo Gomez** *KO* 10
Juan Antonio Lopez, Las Vegas

June 12 **Leonardo Cruz** (DR) *W* 15
Sergio Palma, Miami Beach

Aug 18 **Wilfredo Gomez** *KO* 8
Roberto Rubaldino, San Juan

BANTAMWEIGHTS

June 3 **Lupe Pintor** *KO* 11
Seung Hoon Lee, Los Angeles

JUNIOR BANTAMWEIGHTS

July 4 **Chul Ho Kim** *D* 15
Raul Valdez, Taejon, South Korea

July 29 **Jiro Watanabe** *KO* 10
Gustavo Ballas, Osaka

FLYWEIGHTS

May 1 **Santos Laciar** *KO* 13
Juan Herrera, Merida, Mexico

July 24 **Freddy Castillo** *W* 15
Prudencio Cardona, Merida, Mexico

Aug 14 **Santos Laciar** *W* 15
Betulio Gonzalez, Maracaibo

JUNIOR FLYWEIGHTS

July 7 **Katsuo Tokashiki** *KO* 8
Masaharu Inami, Tokyo

July 20 **Hilario Zapata** *W* 15
Tadashi Tomori, Kanazawa, Japan

THE TRIUMPH IS FOLLOWED BY THE TRAGEDY

Never was Salvador Sanchez more commanding than on July 21, when he risked the WBC featherweight crown vs. Azumah Nelson at Madison Square Garden. Given that the Mexican was making his ninth defense, and that Ghana's Nelson, a substitute for the injured Mario Miranda, had fought just 13 times, it seemed a mismatch. But it turned out to be a thriller.

Both strong and skilled, Nelson attacked all the way. He was floored in the seventh, but he rose and continued to force a hot pace through the late rounds. Ahead on points, Sanchez scored a second knockdown in the 15th, and halted his game foe at the 1:45 mark.

Three weeks later, on August 12, Sanchez was driving to his training camp when his Porsche collided head-on with a tractor-trailer on a highway north of Mexico City. In an instant, the life of a great fighter, and an immensely popular champion, was snuffed out.

Sanchez was 23 years old.

Salvador Sanchez (right) and Azumah Nelson after Sanchez had scored a 15th-round kayo.

READY OR NOT

When WBA junior middleweight champion Davey Moore was asked whether he was experienced enough to take on a former world champion like Ayub Kalule, the New Yorker replied, "You can have 10 fights and be ready, or you can have 40 fights and not be ready."

On July 17, at Bally's Park Place Casino Hotel in Atlantic City, Moore backed up his words. Kalule opened with a heavy body attack, but during the frequent toe-to-toe exchanges, the hard-punching champion dominated. In the 10th, he landed 20 consecutive blows, and referee Luis Sulbaran finally stepped in to call a halt in his favor at the 2:58 mark.

Call it on-the-job training.

Davey Moore (right) stopped game Ayub Kalule to retain the junior middleweight title.

RINGSIDE VIEW

JUNE

In a stunner, power-punching ST Gordon takes the WBC cruiserweight crown with a second-round stoppage of defending titlist Carlos DeLeon.

JUNE

Irish Leroy Haley wins the WBC super lightweight title by scoring a split 15-round decision over Saoul Mamby.

SEPTEMBER

1982

DECEMBER

RINGSIDE VIEW

DECEMBER

Michael Dokes captures the WBA heavyweight title when referee Joey Curtis issues a controversial first-round stoppage of his bout vs. Mike Weaver.

DECEMBER

Bobby Chacon scores a last-round knockdown en route to a close decision over defending WBC super featherweight champion Bazooka Limon. A vicious slugfest, Chacon-Limon IV is a fitting finale to a year of memorable fights.

FIGHTING TALK

Even when Alexis loses, he'll still be a champion. It's over for me if I lose. For me, it's $4.95 an hour or world champion

AARON PRYOR

WBA junior welterweight champion, before his defense against lightweight king Alexis Arguello

SUGAR RAY COMES FULL CIRCLE

On November 9, world welterweight king Sugar Ray Leonard announced his retirement at the Baltimore Civic Center, where he had turned pro almost six years before. Leonard's parting remark was directed at middleweight champion Marvin Hagler, thought to be the only potential opponent who could motivate Sugar Ray.

"It would be one of the greatest (fights) in the history of boxing," said Sugar Ray. "Unfortunately, it will never happen."

In May, Leonard had undergone surgery to repair a detached retina in his left eye. Through the summer and fall, boxing insiders speculated as to whether he would continue his career. Leonard said that he didn't make a final decision until the night of his announcement.

Among those in attendance was Muhammad Ali, a master of the art of saying goodbye and then coming back.

Sugar Ray should have known: in boxing, you never say never.

Blaming eye problems, Sugar Ray retires.

ALREADY THE FIGHT OF THE DECADE

WBA junior welterweight champion Aaron "The Hawk" Pryor was a 2-1 underdog for his sixth defense, a superstar showdown vs. WBC lightweight king Alexis Arguello. Arguello was attempting to become the first fighter in history to win titles in four divisions. But while Arguello had already secured his place among the all-time greats, The Hawk was fighting to define his career.

Pryor-Arguello came on November 12, before 23,800 fans at the Orange Bowl in Miami. It was a brutal brawl of shifting momentum. Pryor set a quick pace, then, in the middle rounds, backed off and boxed. Arguello landed several crushing rights, but they had no discernible effect.

After Arguello failed to finish Pryor during a 13th-round flurry, he slumped. The Hawk rallied in the 14th, and, in a devastating finish, punched until Arguello fell unconscious. (At the time of the stoppage, Pryor led on two cards.)

There wouldn't be a better fight in the '80s.

Aaron Pryor knocked out Alexis Arguello in the 14th round to retain the junior welterweight title and remain undefeated.

"KILL OR BE KILLED"

Before his challenge of WBA lightweight champion Ray "Boom Boom" Mancini, top-rated South Korean Duk Koo Kim taped a sign on a wall in his hotel room. It read "Kill or be killed."

On November 12, only hours after Alexis Arguello had been knocked out cold by Aaron Pryor, Mancini and Kim answered the opening bell at Caesars Palace. It was a grueling phonebooth war, with Mancini dishing out most of the punishment. He weakened Kim in the 13th, when he landed more than 30 consecutive blows, and dropped him at the start of the 14th. Kim beat the count of referee Richard Greene, but wasn't allowed to fight on. Seconds later, he collapsed and was taken to the hospital.

The 23-year-old Korean underwent 2½ hours of surgery to relieve a blood clot in his brain. He never regained consciousness, and died five days later.

For those in boxing, it was a time to mourn – and examine their consciences.

Five days after he was knocked senseless by Mancini, Korea's Duk Koo Kim (left) died.

IN SUPPORT: THE DUEL OF THE LITTLE GIANTS

The featured bout was supposed to be WBC super welterweight champion Wilfred Benitez vs. Thomas Hearns, but on December 3, at the Superdome in New Orleans, Wilfredo Gomez and Lupe Pintor waged a war for the ages.

While Hearns boxed neatly in scoring a majority 15-round decision over Benitez, WBC super bantamweight champion Gomez and WBC bantamweight king Pintor stood toe to toe all the way. Gomez built up an early lead, but Pintor was rallying when Gomez, his left eye closed, dropped the Mexican twice in the 14th. After the second knockdown, referee Arthur Mercante stepped in. (At the time of the stoppage, Gomez led on two cards.)

The two little giants had come up big.

Wilfredo Gomez kayoed Lupe Pintor in 14 brutal rounds of a junior featherweight title bout.

World Title Fights

HEAVYWEIGHTS

Nov 26	**Larry Holmes** *W* 15 Randall (Tex) Cobb, Houston
Dec 10	**Michael Dokes** (USA) *KO* 1 Mike Weaver, Las Vegas

CRUISERWEIGHTS

Dec 15	**Osvaldo Ocasio** *W* 15 Young Joe Louis, Chicago

LIGHT HEAVYWEIGHTS

Sept 18	**Michael Spinks** *KO* 9 Johnny Davis, Atlantic City
Nov 20	**Dwight Braxton** *KO* 11 Eddie Davis, Atlantic City

MIDDLEWEIGHTS

Oct 30	**Marvin Hagler** *KO* 5 Fulgencio Obelmejias, San Remo, Italy

JUNIOR MIDDLEWEIGHTS

Dec 3	**Thomas Hearns** *W* 15 Wilfred Benitez, New Orleans

JUNIOR WELTERWEIGHTS

Oct 20	**Leroy Haley** *W* 15 Juan Jose Giminez, Cleveland
Nov 12	**Aaron Pryor** *KO* 14 Alexis Arguello, Miami

LIGHTWEIGHTS

Nov 13	**Ray Mancini** *KO* 14 Duk Koo Kim, Las Vegas

JUNIOR LIGHTWEIGHTS

Sept 18	**Rafael Limon** *KO* 7 Chung Il Choi, Los Angeles
Dec 11	**Bobby Chacon** *W* 15 Rafael Limon, Sacramento

FEATHERWEIGHTS

Sept 15	**Juan LaPorte** (PR) *KO* 11 Mario Miranda, New York City (Wins Vacant WBC Title)
Oct 16	**Eusebio Pedroza** *D* 15 Bernard Taylor, Charlotte

JUNIOR FEATHERWEIGHTS

Nov 13	**Leonardo Cruz** *KO* 8 Benito Badilla, San Juan
Dec 3	**Wilfredo Gomez** *KO* 14 Lupe Pintor, New Orleans

BANTAMWEIGHTS

Oct 27	**Jeff Chandler** *KO* 9 Miguel Iriarte, Atlantic City

JUNIOR BANTAMWEIGHTS

Nov 11	**Jiro Watanabe** *KO* 12 Shoji Oguma, Hamanatsu, Japan
Nov 28	**Rafael Orono** *KO* 6 Chul Ho Kim, Seoul

FLYWEIGHTS

Nov 5	**Santos Laciar** *KO* 13 Stephen Muchoki, Copenhagen
Nov 6	**Eleoncio Mercedes** (DR) *W* 15 Freddy Castillo, Los Angeles

JUNIOR FLYWEIGHTS

Sept 18	**Hilario Zapata** *W* 15 Jung Koo Chang, Chongju, South Korea
Oct 10	**Katsuo Tokashiki** *W* 15 Sung Nam Kim, Tokyo
Nov 30	**Hilario Zapata** *KO* 6 Tadashi Tomori, Tokyo

A BAD BOY PROVES GOOD ENOUGH

In 1978 and '79, Roger Mayweather was banned from amateur competitions in his home state of Michigan. It seems that the officials didn't care very much for his habit of taunting his opponents.

As a pro, the bad boy developed a reputation as a good boxer. On January 19, at Hiram Bithorn Stadium in San Juan, he proved good enough to dethrone WBA junior lightweight champion Sammy Serrano.

Over the course of two reigns, Serrano had made 14 defenses. But the 21-year-old Mayweather showed him little respect. When the challenger found it difficult to land his jab, he switched to his right. By the fifth, he had assumed total command.

Late in the seventh, Serrano was staggered, and after 14 years as a pro, he lacked the legs to rebound. The end came one round later, after the local favorite was toppled by a right. Referee Isidro Rodriguez intervened just as Plomito Espinosa, Serrano's manager, began to climb through the ropes.

Having grown up, the bad boy's only habit was winning.

Hard-hitting Roger Mayweather (left) knocked out Sam Serrano in the eighth round.

JANUARY

In the first scheduled 12-round world title fight in decades, WBC super flyweight champion Rafael Orono knocks out Pedro Romero in the fourth.

A CLASS OF ONE

Before middleweight champion Marvin Hagler's sixth defense, Leicester's Tony Sibson figured he had a decent chance of pulling off an upset. After all, Hagler was naturally aggressive, and Sibson, a former British, Commonwealth, and European champion, had a terminator of a left hook.

But he found that Marvelous Marvin could box, too.

Hagler-Sibson was held on February 11, at the Centrum in Worcester, Massachusetts. Moving laterally and leading with a stunner of a jab, the southpaw champion quickly cut Sibson up. (He would take 17 stitches.) Hagler scored two knockdowns in the sixth, and while the challenger picked himself up each time, referee Carlos Padilla waved the bout over at the 2:40 mark.

Said Sibson, "I didn't realize that it was such a jump in class. (But) that class is really a class of just one man."

Britain's Tony Sibson (left) made a gallant bid to dethrone the middleweight champion Marvin Hagler, but Tony was stopped in the sixth round.

MAGRI THE MAGNIFICENT

The early-'80s failed to produce a dominant flyweight. But there were a handful of dominant performances, including Londoner Charlie Magri's effort against defending WBC champion Eleoncio Mercedes.

Magri-Mercedes was held on March 15, at Wembley Arena. The 26-year-old Tunisia-born challenger set a wicked pace, boxed smartly, punched to both the body and head, and accelerated when sensing the end was near.

The turning point came toward the end of the sixth, when Mercedes suffered a six-stitch cut over his left brow. The bout was stopped in the seventh after a second examination by the ringside doctor.

Magri had been flawless. But unfortunately for Charlie, there would be no encore.

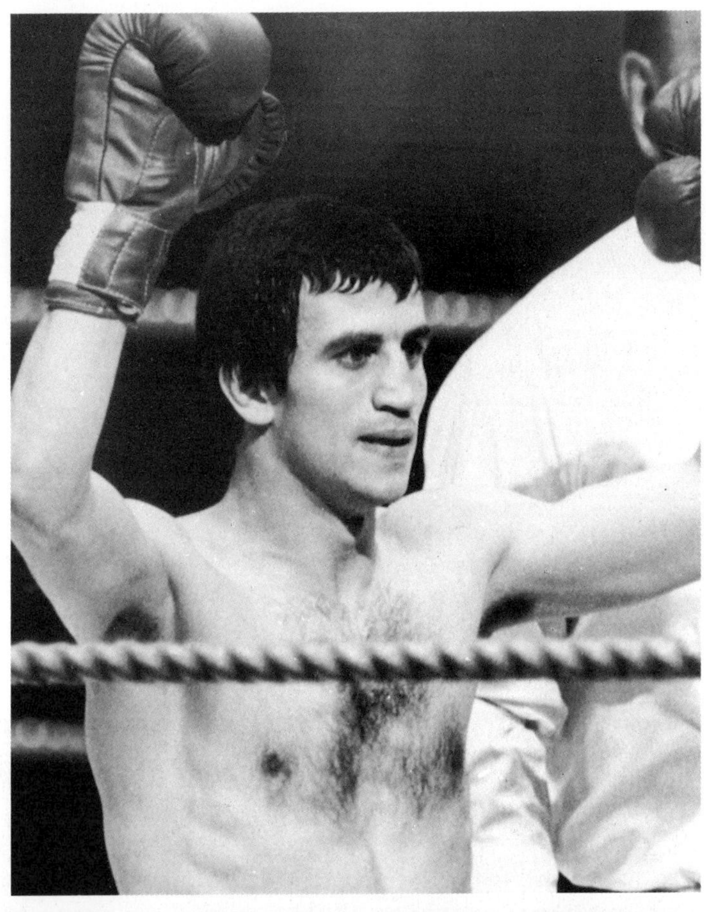

Britain's Charlie Magri after knocking out Eleoncio Mercedes in seventh round to win the flyweight championship of the world.

RINGSIDE VIEW

FEBRUARY

Smooth-boxing Donald Curry wins the vacant WBA welterweight title by rising from the floor to score a decision over South Korea's Jun Sok Hwang.

WORLD TITLE FIGHTS

HEAVYWEIGHTS

March 27	**Larry Holmes** *W* 12 Lucien Rodriguez, Scranton, PA

CRUISERWEIGHTS

Feb 16	**ST Gordon** *KO* 8 Jesse Burnett, East Rutherford, NJ

LIGHT HEAVYWEIGHTS

March 18	**Michael Spinks** *W* 15 Dwight Braxton, Atlantic City

MIDDLEWEIGHTS

Feb 11	**Marvin Hagler** *KO* 6 Tony Sibson, Worcester, MA

JUNIOR MIDDLEWEIGHTS

Jan 29	**Davey Moore** *KO* 4 Gary Guiden, Atlantic City

WELTERWEIGHTS

Feb 13	**Donald Curry** (USA) *W* 15 Jun Sok Hwang, Fort Worth (Wins Vacant WBA Title)
March 19	**Milton McCrory** *D* 12 Colin Jones, Reno (For Vacant WBC Title)

JUNIOR WELTERWEIGHTS

Feb 13	**Leroy Haley** *W* 12 Saoul Mamby, Cleveland
April 2	**Aaron Pryor** *KO* 3 Sang Hyun Kim, Atlantic City

JUNIOR LIGHTWEIGHTS

Jan 19	**Roger Mayweather** (USA) *KO* 8 Samuel Serrano, San Juan
April 20	**Roger Mayweather** *KO* 8 Jorge Alvarado, San Jose, CA

FEATHERWEIGHTS

Feb 20	**Juan LaPorte** *W* 12 Ruben Castillo, Hato Rey, Puerto Rico
April 24	**Eusebio Pedroza** *W* 15 Rocky Lockridge, Liguiria, Italy

JUNIOR FEATHERWEIGHTS

March 16	**Leonardo Cruz** *W* 15 Soon Hyun Chung, Hato Rey, Puerto Rico

BANTAMWEIGHTS

March 13	**Jeff Chandler** *W* 15 Gaby Canizales, Atlantic City

JUNIOR BANTAMWEIGHTS

Jan 31	**Rafael Orono** *KO* 4 Pedro Romero, Caracas
Feb 24	**Jiro Watanabe** *KO* 8 Luis Ibanez, Tsu City, Japan

FLYWEIGHTS

March 4	**Santos Laciar** *KO* 9 Ramon Nery, Cordoba, Argentina
March 15	**Charlie Magri** (ENG) *KO* 7 Eleoncio Mercedes, Wembley

JUNIOR FLYWEIGHTS

Jan 9	**Katsuo Tokashiki** *W* 15 Hwan Jin Kim, Kyoto, Japan
March 26	**Jung Koo Chang** (KOR) *KO* 3 Hilario Zapata, Taejon, South Korea
April 10	**Katsuo Tokashiki** *D* 15 Lupe Madera, Tokyo

COLLECTING HIMSELF – JUST IN TIME

Only minutes before WBA titlist Michael Spinks was called to the ring for his March 18 light heavyweight unification battle vs. WBC champion Dwight Braxton, two-year-old daughter Michelle was brought into the room.

Two months before, Sandy Massey, Michelle's mother, and Spinks' longtime girlfriend, had been killed in a car accident. Michelle's first question to her father was, "Where's mommy?"

"Michael went to pieces," said his trainer, Eddie Futch.

The moment failed to destroy Spinks' focus. Before a crowd of 9,854 at the Atlantic City Convention Center, he boxed beautifully and captured a unanimous 15-round decision (two scores of 144-141, and 144-140).

Following Futch's plan to perfection, Spinks capitalized on his advantages in height and reach by jabbing and hooking, keeping his distance, and moving to his right. His "Spinks Jinx" right hand was never a factor.

Remarkably, neither was Michelle's ill-timed visit.

Michael Spinks (right) and Dwight Braxton.

MAY

1983

AUGUST

RINGSIDE VIEW

AUGUST

Sizzling southpaw Hector "Macho" Camacho wins the vacant WBC super featherweight title by fifth-round TKO over former champion Bazooka Limon.

AUGUST

In a rematch to fill the vacant WBC welterweight title, Milton McCrory scores a split 12-round decision over Wales' Colin Jones. (In March, the fighters had struggled to a draw.)

THE FINAL BELL – JUST IN TIME

It was almost predetermined that Edwin Rosario would become lightweight champion of the world. Dubbed "The Duran of the '80s," the unbeaten 20-year-old sensation was considered the best young fighter from Puerto Rico since Wilfred Benitez. But the title didn't come easy.

On May 1, at Roberto Clemente Coliseum in Hato Rey, Rosario squared off against Mexican southpaw Jose Luis Ramirez for the WBC title that had been vacated by Alexis Arguello. For five rounds, the local favorite boxed brilliantly. But Ramirez was strong, if nothing else. He began a rally in the sixth, and backed up Rosario until the final bell.

Rosario barely hung on to capture a unanimous but disputed decision by three scores of 115-113. The bout was contested over the WBC's new championship distance of 12 rounds. Had it been scheduled for 15, the era of Edwin Rosario might never have begun.

Edwin Rosario (right) was hard-pressed to decision Mexico's Jose Luis Ramirez in 12 rounds.

THE BRAWLING 130-POUND WARS, CONTINUED

In the early-'80s, every title fight involving junior lightweights Rolando Navarette, Cornelius Boza-Edwards, Bobby Chacon, and Bazooka Limon was wilder than the one before it.

On May 15, WBC champion Chacon defended vs. former conqueror Boza at Caesars Palace. It was a bombs-away brawl. Boza was downed in the first, second, and 12th, and scored a knockdown of his own in the third. Chacon suffered hideous cuts over both eyes, and survived two examinations from the ringside doctor.

Fighting strongly off the ropes, the indomitable champion went on to capture a unanimous decision (totals of 115-112, 115-113, and 117-111). He had earned it with his blood.

Bobby Chacon (left) won a unanimous 12-round decision over Cornelius Boza-Edwards.

FIGHTING TALK

Boy, what a fight! I wish I could've seen it

BOBBY CHACON
WBC super featherweight champion, after his decision victory over Cornelius Boza-Edwards

DOUBLE TROUBLE IN THE DESERT

WBC champion Larry Holmes was the best heavyweight in the world. WBA champion Michael Dokes was the heir apparent. On May 20, at the Dunes Hotel in Las Vegas, the co-titlists defended on the same card.

Holmes barely survived against upstart Tim Witherspoon, scoring a 12-round split decision (totals of 118-111, 115-113, and 114-115). During a late rally, 'Spoon negated Holmes' jab, and repeatedly scored with overhand rights. By the finish, Holmes' right eye was swollen and black and blue.

Dokes, too, squeezed by. Rematched with Mike Weaver, whom he had dethroned five months earlier, the WBA titlist struggled to a majority 15-round draw (scores of 143-143, 144-144, and 145-141 for Dokes). The heavyweights went toe to toe in the first round, then settled into the rhythm of a draining infight. At the final bell, Weaver seemed far fresher.

The top 10 suddenly seemed a lot closer to the throne.

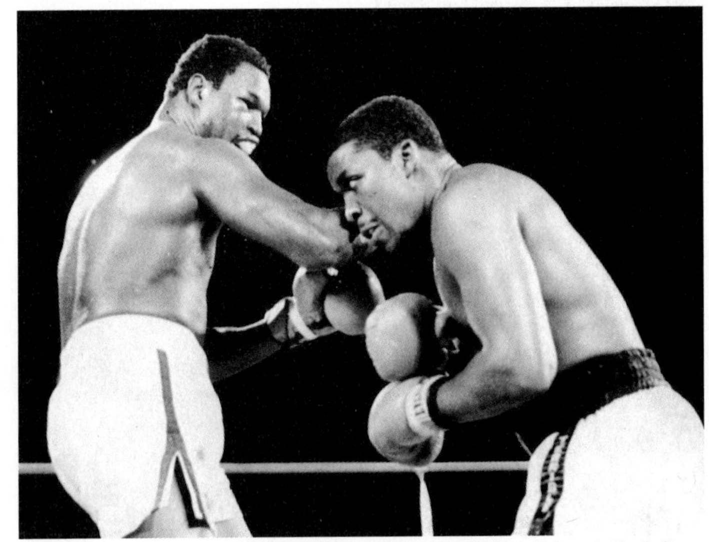

Challenger Tim Witherspoon (right) forced heavyweight champion Larry Holmes to the limit.

"I'VE RETURNED TO BE ROBERTO DURAN"

After consecutive losses to Wilfred Benitez and Kirkland Laing, Roberto Duran was dismissed as yesterday's fighter. But matchmaker Teddy Brenner convinced promoter Bob Arum to give the legendary Panamanian one more chance.

Duran's crossroads kayo of Pipino Cuevas led to a try at unbeaten WBA junior middleweight champion Davey Moore. The bout came on June 16 (Duran's 32nd birthday), before an energized sell-out crowd of 20,061 at Madison Square Garden to see if the legend could come all the way back.

A 5-2 underdog, Duran issued a terrific beating, closing Moore's right eye, battering him to the body, flooring him in the seventh, and finishing him in the eighth. After the bout was stopped, the weeping victor was lifted high as his fans sang *Happy Birthday*. The celebration lasted well into the night.

Said the newly crowned champion, "I've returned to be Roberto Duran. It's been a long time."

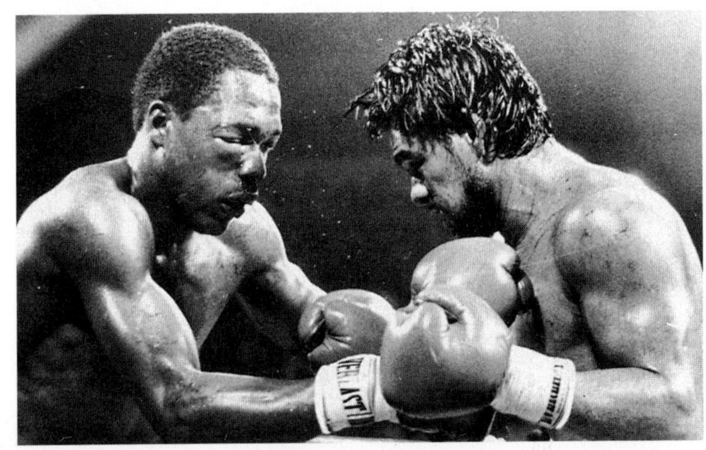

Roberto Duran (right) knocked out Davey Moore to annex the junior middleweight crown.

WORLD TITLE FIGHTS

HEAVYWEIGHTS

May 20	**Michael Dokes** *D* 15 Mike Weaver, Las Vegas
May 20	**Larry Holmes** *W* 12 Tim Witherspoon, Las Vegas

CRUISERWEIGHTS

May 20	**Osvaldo Ocasio** *W* 15 Randy Stephens, Las Vegas
July 17	**Carlos DeLeon** *W* 12 ST Gordon, Las Vegas

MIDDLEWEIGHTS

May 27	**Marvin Hagler** *KO* 4 Wilford Scypion, Providence

JUNIOR MIDDLEWEIGHTS

June 16	**Roberto Duran** *KO* 8 Davey Moore, New York City

WELTERWEIGHTS

Aug 13	**Milton McCrory** *W* 12 Colin Jones, Las Vegas (Wins Vacant WBC Title)

JUNIOR WELTERWEIGHTS

May 18	**Bruce Curry** (USA) *W* 12 Leroy Haley, Las Vegas
July 7	**Bruce Curry** *KO* 7 Hidekazu Akai, Osaka

LIGHTWEIGHTS

May 1	**Edwin Rosario** (PR) *W* 12 Jose Luis Ramirez, Hato Rey, Puerto Rico

JUNIOR LIGHTWEIGHTS

May 15	**Bobby Chacon** *W* 12 Cornelius Boza-Edwards, Las Vegas
Aug 7	**Hector Camacho** (USA) *KO* 5 Rafael Limon, San Juan (Wins Vacant WBC Title)
Aug 17	**Roger Mayweather** *KO* 1 Benedicto Villablanca, Las Vegas

FEATHERWEIGHTS

June 25	**Juan LaPorte** *W* 12 Johnny de la Rosa, Hato Rey, Puerto Rico

JUNIOR FEATHERWEIGHTS

June 15	**Jaime Garza** (USA) *KO* 2 Bobby Berna, Los Angeles (Wins Vacant WBC Title)
Aug 26	**Leonardo Cruz** *W* 15 Cleo Garcia, Santa Domingo

JUNIOR BANTAMWEIGHTS

May 9	**Rafael Orono** *W* 12 Raul Valdez, Caracas
June 23	**Jiro Watanabe** *W* 15 Roberto Ramirez, Sendai, Japan

FLYWEIGHTS

May 5	**Santos Laciar** *KO* 2 Shuichi Hozumi, Shizuoka, Japan
July 17	**Santos Laciar** *KO* 1 Hi Sup Shin, Cheju-do, South Korea

JUNIOR FLYWEIGHTS

June 11	**Jung Koo Chang** *KO* 2 Masaharu Iha, Taegu, South Korea
July 10	**Lupe Madera** (MEX) *Tech Win* 4 Katsuo Tokashiki, Tokyo

SEPTEMBER

1983

DECEMBER

A SUDDEN AND INEXPLICABLE TRAGEDY

The death of Kiko Bejines came with no explanations. The California bantamweight had taken no prior beatings. Moreover, his bout against veteran Albert Davila, fought for the vacant WBC 118-pound crown on September 1, at the Olympic Auditorium in Los Angeles, was rather tame. After 11 rounds, Bejines led on two cards, and was even on the third. Early in the 12th, the light-hitting Davila scored a knockdown with a right. Bejines beat the count of referee Waldemar Schmidt, but wasn't allowed to continue. Then he collapsed.

Bejines subsequently underwent 3½ hours of surgery to relieve pressure on his brain, during which doctors removed part of his frontal lobe and skull. On September 4, he was pronounced dead. He was 20 years old.

"This should be the happiest moment of my life," said Davila, who had won the title on his fourth try. "But I can't enjoy it right now."

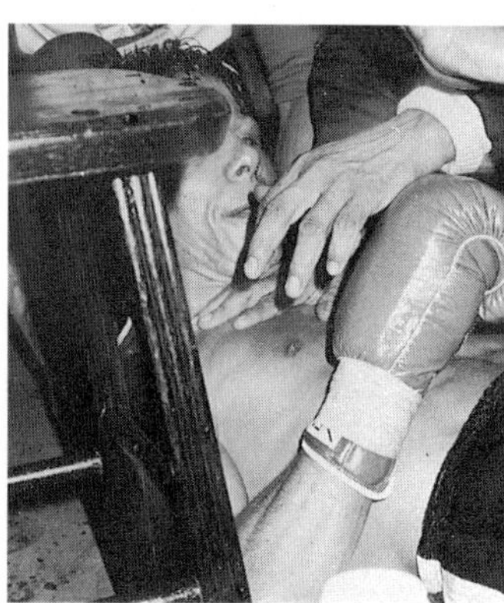

Kiko Bejines collapsed and later died.

WHAT'S LEFT IS GERRIE'S RIGHT

Heavyweight Gerrie Coetzee fired the kind of cross that could derail a locomotive. Nonetheless, he was 0-for-2 in world title fights. Worse yet, he had broken his "bionic" right hand an incredible 10 times. Clearly, it was time for a two-fisted approach.

Enter West Coast trainer Jackie McCoy, who worked on developing Coetzee's jab and hook. On September 23, at the Richfield (Ohio) Coliseum, the South African's improved left served him well during his challenge of WBA king Michael Dokes.

Dokes, a 5-1 favorite, won the first four rounds, and opened a wide cut over his opponent's right eye. But Coetzee scored a flash knockdown in the fifth, after which Dokes seemed to lose interest. Landing with both hands, Coetzee moved ahead on the cards. He finished his work at the end of the 10th with – what else? – two booming rights.

Postscript: the knockout blows hurt Coetzee almost as much as Dokes; he had fractured his right hand one more time.

South Africa's Gerrie Coetzee holds up the championship belt after knocking out Dokes.

MARVELOUS IS JUST GOOD ENOUGH

Before the middleweight title fight between champion Marvin Hagler and Roberto Duran, *KO* magazine asked 25 experts to pick the winner. The results: Hagler 25, Duran 0.

The supposed mismatch took place on November 10, before a curious crowd of 14,600 at Caesars Palace. Hagler was a 4-1 favorite to retain the crown for the eighth time. But he had trained to counterpunch, and when Duran opened cautiously, Marvelous Marvin failed to adjust.

"Duran waited and waited and waited for Marvin to lead," said Goody Petronelli, Hagler's trainer.

A tactical fight saw Hagler landing in combination, and Duran responding mostly with his right. After 13 rounds, the challenger led on points. But Hagler forged ahead by sweeping the last two stanzas.

The decision was unanimous for the champion (scores of 144-142, 146-145, and 144-143). The experts had been right, albeit for all the wrong reasons.

Marvin Hagler (right) overpowered Roberto Duran and captured a unanimous 15-round decision.

MARVIS DOESN'T START SMOKIN' LIKE DAD

Joe Frazier was a legend. But Marvis Frazier was unproven, and when Smokin' Joe matched his eager son with WBC heavyweight champion Larry Holmes, insiders cringed.

Holmes met Frazier on November 25, at Caesars Palace. The WBC refused to sanction the bout because Frazier wasn't ranked in the top 10. (Holmes would subsequently vacate the title and secure instant recognition from the fledgling IBF.)

The champion had fought 311 pro rounds to Frazier's 54. His experience surfaced in the first round. A right dropped Frazier, and after he rose, Holmes punched freely while motioning for referee Mills Lane to step in. Lane complied at the 2:57 mark.

Marvis Frazier was a nice kid. But he'd never be a legend.

RINGSIDE VIEW

SEPTEMBER

In an eagerly anticipated rematch, WBA junior welterweight champion Aaron Pryor again stops Alexis Arguello, halting the triple crown champion in round 10.

DECEMBER

WBA bantamweight champion Jeff Chandler avenges a non-title bout defeat by scoring a seventh-round TKO over Oscar Muniz.

Larry Holmes uses an open glove to hold off Marvis Frazier. Moments later, at 2:57 of the first round, the referee stopped the fight.

WORLD TITLE FIGHTS

HEAVYWEIGHTS

Sept 10	**Larry Holmes** *KO* 5 Scott Frank, Atlantic City
Sept 23	**Gerrie Coetzee** (SA) *KO* 10 Michael Dokes, Richfield, OH
Nov 25	**Larry Holmes** *KO* 1 Marvis Frazier, Las Vegas

CRUISERWEIGHTS

Sept 21	**Carlos DeLeon** *KO* 4 Yaqui Lopez, San Jose, CA
Dec 13	**Marvin Camel** *KO* 5 Roddy MacDonald, Halifax, Canada (Wins Vacant IBF Title)

LIGHT HEAVYWEIGHTS

Nov 25	**Michael Spinks** *KO* 10 Oscar Rivadeneyra, Vancouver

MIDDLEWEIGHTS

Nov 10	**Marvin Hagler** *W* 15 Roberto Duran, Las Vegas

WELTERWEIGHTS

Sept 3	**Donald Curry** *KO* 1 Roger Stafford, Marsala, Italy

JUNIOR WELTERWEIGHTS

Sept 9	**Aaron Pryor** *KO* 10 Alexis Arguello, Las Vegas
Oct 19	**Bruce Curry** *W* 12 Leroy Haley, Las Vegas

LIGHTWEIGHTS

Sept 15	**Ray Mancini** *KO* 9 Orlando Romero, New York City

JUNIOR LIGHTWEIGHTS

Nov 18	**Hector Camacho** *KO* 5 Rafael Solis, Hato Rey, Puerto Rico

FEATHERWEIGHTS

Oct 22	**Eusebio Pedroza** *W* 15 Jose Caba, St. Vincent, Italy

JUNIOR FEATHERWEIGHTS

Dec 4	**Bobby Berna** (PHI) *KO* 10 Seung In Suh, Seoul (Wins Vacant IBF Title)

BANTAMWEIGHTS

Sept 1	**Albert Davila** (USA) *KO* 12 Kiko Bejines, Los Angeles (Wins Vacant WBC Title)
Sept 11	**Jeff Chandler** *KO* 10 Eijiro Murata, Tokyo
Dec 17	**Jeff Chandler** *KO* 7 Oscar Muniz, Atlantic City

JUNIOR BANTAMWEIGHTS

Oct 6	**Jiro Watanabe** *Tech Win* 11 Soon Chun Kwon, Osaka
Oct 29	**Rafael Orono** *KO* 5 Orlando Maldonado, Caracas
Nov 27	**Payao Poontarat** (THA) *W* 12 Rafael Orono, Pattaya, Thailand
Dec 10	**Joo Do Chun** (KOR) *KO* 5 Ken Kasugai, Osaka (Wins Vacant IBF Title)

FLYWEIGHTS

Sept 27	**Frank Cedeno** (PHI) *KO* 6 Charlie Magri, Wembley
Dec 24	**Soon Chun Kwon** *KO* 5 Rene Busayong, Seoul (Wins Vacant IBF Title)

JUNIOR FLYWEIGHTS

Sept 10	**Jung Koo Chang** *W* 12 German Torres, Taejon, South Korea
Oct 23	**Lupe Madera** *W* 12 Katsuo Tokashiki, Sapporo
Dec 10	**Dodie Penalosa** (PHI) *KO* 12 Satoshi Shingaki, Osaka (Wins Vacant IBF Title)

JANUARY

1984

APRIL

BRUCE ON THE LOOSE

On January 29, at the Civic Center in Beaumont, Texas, undefeated New Yorker Bill Costello hooked his way to a 10th-round TKO over defending WBC super lightweight champion Bruce Curry. Slow and unresponsive, Curry seemed a tired fighter.

"He was punching like a girl," said his trainer, Jesse Reid.

Two days later, Curry felt a surge of energy. Having blamed Reid for the loss, the brawler exploded into the Golden Gloves Gym in Las Vegas and challenged his longtime handler to a fist fight. Accustomed to Curry's outbursts, Reid initially declined. But after Curry persisted, the men squared off. Reid almost immediately opened a 15-stitch cut that Curry had suffered during his loss to Costello. The fighter ran to his car and reemerged with a gun. With Reid diving for cover, Curry fired a single shot. He missed the trainer by a few feet, and then left.

Curry subsequently underwent a state-ordered psychiatric evaluation. His championship run had come to a pathetic end.

RINGSIDE VIEW

FEBRUARY

After twice losing in tries for the featherweight title, Rocky Lockridge takes the WBA junior lightweight crown with a one-punch, first-round kayo of Roger Mayweather.

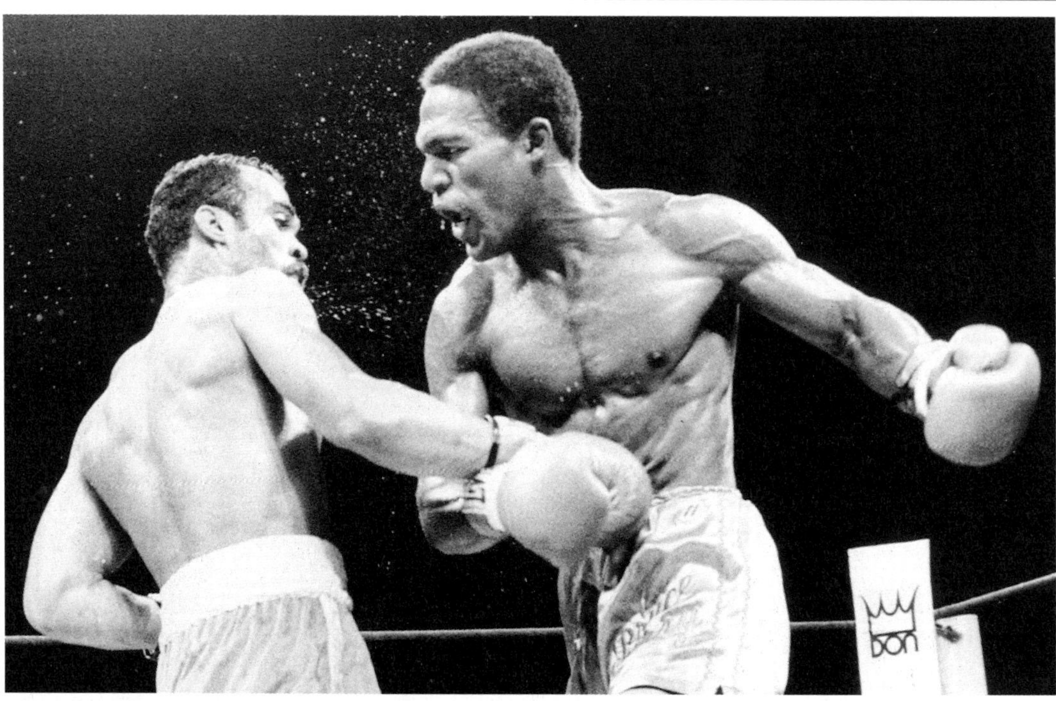

Bill Costello (left) kayoed Bruce Curry in the 10th round to win the junior welterweight title and remain undefeated.

WORLD TITLE FIGHTS

HEAVYWEIGHTS

March 9 **Tim Witherspoon** (USA) *W* 12
Greg Page, Las Vegas
(Wins Vacant WBC Title)

CRUISERWEIGHTS

March 9 **Carlos DeLeon** *W* 12
Anthony Davis, Las Vegas

LIGHT HEAVYWEIGHTS

Feb 25 **Michael Spinks** *W* 12
Eddie Davis, Atlantic City

MIDDLEWEIGHTS

March 30 **Marvin Hagler** *KO* 10
Juan Roldan, Las Vegas

JUNIOR MIDDLEWEIGHTS

Feb 11 **Thomas Hearns** *W* 12
Luigi Minchillo, Detroit

March 11 **Mark Medal** (USA) *KO* 5
Earl Hargrove, Atlantic City
(Wins Vacant IBF Title)

WELTERWEIGHTS

Jan 14 **Milton McCrory** *KO* 6
Milton Guest, Sterling Heights, MI

Feb 4 **Donald Curry** *W* 15
Marlon Starling, Atlantic City

April 15 **Milton McCrory** *KO* 6
Gilles Elbilia, Detroit

April 21 **Donald Curry** *KO* 8
Elio Diaz, Fort Worth

JUNIOR WELTERWEIGHTS

Jan 22 **Johnny Bumphus** (USA) *W* 15
Lorenzo Garcia, Atlantic City
(Wins Vacant WBA Title)

Jan 29 **Bill Costello** (USA) *KO* 10
Bruce Curry, Beaumont, TX

LIGHTWEIGHTS

Jan 14 **Ray Mancini** *KO* 3
Bobby Chacon, Reno

Jan 30 **Charlie Brown** (USA) *W* 15
Melvin Paul, Atlantic City
(Wins Vacant IBF Title)

March 17 **Edwin Rosario** *KO* 1
Roberto Elizondo, San Juan

April 15 **Harry Arroyo** (USA) *KO* 14
Charlie (Choo Choo) Brown, Atlantic City

JUNIOR LIGHTWEIGHTS

Feb 26 **Rocky Lockridge** (USA) *KO* 1
Roger Mayweather, Beaumont, TX

April 22 **Hwan Kil Yuh** (KOR) *W* 15
Rod Sequenan, Seoul
(Wins Vacant IBF Title)

FEATHERWEIGHTS

March 4 **Min Keun Oh** *KO* 2
Joko Arter, Seoul
(Wins Vacant IBF Title)

March 31 **Wilfredo Gomez** *W* 12
Juan LaPorte, Hato Rey, Puerto Rico

JUNIOR FEATHERWEIGHTS

Feb 22 **Loris Stecca** (ITA) *KO* 12
Leonardo Cruz, Milan

April 15 **Seung In Suh** (KOR) *KO* 10
Bobby Berna, Seoul

BANTAMWEIGHTS

April 7 **Richard Sandoval** (USA) *KO* 15
Jeff Chandler, Atlantic City

April 16 **Satoshi Shingaki** (JAP) *KO* 8
Elmer Magallano, Nara, Japan
(Wins Vacant IBF Title)

JUNIOR BANTAMWEIGHTS

Jan 28 **Joo Do Chun** *KO* 12
Prayurasak Muangsurin, Seoul

March 15 **Jiro Watanabe** *KO* 15
Celso Chavez, Osaka

March 17 **Joo Do Chun** *KO* 1
Diego de Villa, Kwangju, South Korea

March 28 **Payao Poontarat** *KO* 10
Guty Espadas, Bangkok

FLYWEIGHTS

Jan 18 **Frank Cedeno** *KO* 2
Koji Kobayashi, Tokyo

Jan 28 **Santos Laciar** *W* 15
Juan Herrera, Marsala, Italy

Feb 25 **Soon Chun Kwon** *Tech Win* 12
Roger Castillo, Seoul

April 9 **Gabriel Bernal** (MEX) *KO* 2
Koji Kobayashi, Tokyo

JUNIOR FLYWEIGHTS

March 13 **Jung Koo Chang** *W* 12
Sot Chitalada, Pusan, South Korea

TOUGHEST EASY FIGHT

World light heavyweight champion Michael Spinks' eighth defense was his toughest. Or his easiest, depending on whose scorecard you believed.

On February 25, Spinks met 32-year-old veteran Eddie Davis at Resorts International Hotel in Atlantic City. The champion capitalized on his reach advantage to control the first half of the bout. Then Davis rallied, hurting Spinks in the eighth, ninth, and 10th rounds.

The bout went the 12-round distance, and the unanimous decision confused everyone, including the judges. Larry Hazzard and Joe Cortez had Spinks far ahead, scoring 118-111 and 119-109, respectively. Carol Castellano, however, saw it 115-114. Had the judges watched the same fight?

"Michael is on a pedestal; he's overrated," complained Davis. "You can beat him, but you can't beat the guys on the sidelines with (the) pencils."

MARCH

Tim Witherspoon captures the vacant WBC heavyweight title by scoring a majority 12-round decision over Greg Page.

Michael Spinks (right) retained the crown with a unanimous decision over durable Eddie Davis.

AN UNFITTING FAREWELL

Pound for pound, WBA bantamweight champion Jeff Chandler was among the best fighters in the world. Which made his one-sided TKO loss to Richard Sandoval all the more perplexing.

Chandler faced Sandoval on April 7, at the Sands Hotel in Atlantic City. The unbeaten challenger confronted "Joltin' Jeff" from the start, and took round after round. In fact, Chandler spent most of the stretch run complaining to referee Arthur Mercante about butts.

The Philadelphian suffered the first knockdown of his career in the 11th, and was rescued after sponging nine consecutive punches in the 15th. The end of the bout also turned out to be the end of his career.

Richie Sandoval (left) became new bantamweight king by kayoing Jeff Chandler.

THE CIVIL WAR OF PUERTO RICO

The biggest fight in the history of Puerto Rico took place on March 31, when WBC featherweight champion Juan Laporte defended against former junior featherweight titlist Wilfredo Gomez at the Roberto Clemente Coliseum in Hato Rey. LaPorte was Puerto Rico-born, but based in New York City. Gomez had never left the island. Care to guess which fighter was the people's choice?

The first six rounds were competitive. The second half of the bout, however, belonged to Gomez. He punched sharply to the head and body, and closed the champion's right eye. LaPorte repeatedly backed to the ropes and covered up. And when he did attack, Gomez slipped almost all of the punches.

After 12 rounds, Gomez was crowned by unanimous decision (scores of 118-110, 117-111, and 119-113). The master was a champion again, and all of Puerto Rico loved him for it.

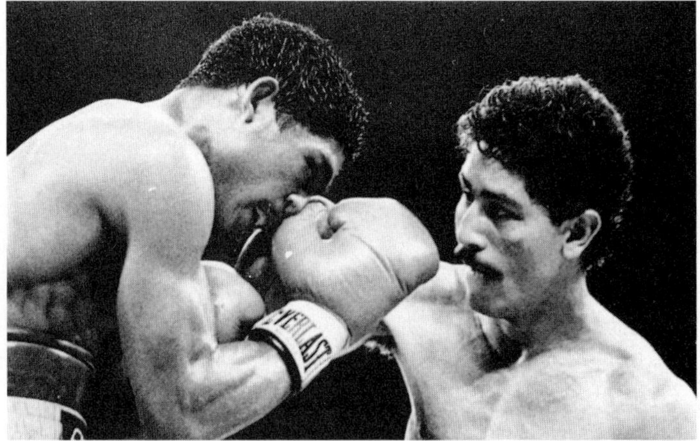

Wilfredo Gomez (right) was crowned the new featherweight king by decisioning Juan LaPorte.

MAY

1984

AUGUST

SHUFFLING CHAMPS IN BUFFALO

On June 1, WBA lightweight champion Ray Mancini and WBA junior welterweight king Johnny Bumphus lost their respective titles at the Memorial Coliseum in Buffalo. The night's biggest loser, however, didn't even lace up his gloves. Unbeaten IBF 140-pound champion Aaron Pryor was in search of big-money fights, and both Mancini and Bumphus had been prospective opponents.

Mancini boxed well for six rounds against switch-hitting Rastafarian Livingstone Bramble, but was subsequently pounded into a bloody mess. Incredibly, he was ahead on two cards when rescued in round 14 by Marty Denkin.

Slick southpaw Bumphus outclassed Hatcher until "The Mad Dog" got angry following an after-the-bell exchange in round 10. He floored a fading Bumphus in the 11th, and seconds later, referee Johnny LoBianco called what most ringsiders felt was a premature halt. On a night of upsets, Aaron Pryor had watched his future pass him by.

Ringside View

MAY

Entering the ring with a career mark of 9-9-1, Dominican Francisco Quiroz wins the WBA junior flyweight title with a ninth-round kayo of Lupe Madera.

MAY

Victor Callejas dethrones WBA junior featherweight champion Loris Stecca via eighth-round kayo.

MAY

Fighting for the first time in more than two years, Sugar Ray Leonard rises from the first knockdown of his career and halts Kevin Howard in the ninth round. Immediately after the bout, Leonard re-retires.

Livingstone Bramble (right) after stopping Ray "Boom Boom" Mancini in the 14th round to win the lightweight title. It was Ray's second loss.

World Title Fights

HEAVYWEIGHTS

Aug 31 **Pinklon Thomas** (USA) *W* 12
Tim Witherspoon, Las Vegas

CRUISERWEIGHTS

May 5 **Osvaldo Ocasio** *KO* 15
John Odhiambo, Guaynabo, Puerto Rico

June 2 **Carlos DeLeon** *W* 12
Bash Ali, Oakland

JUNIOR MIDDLEWEIGHTS

June 15 **Thomas Hearns** *KO* 2
Roberto Duran, Las Vegas

JUNIOR WELTERWEIGHTS

June 1 **Gene Hatcher** (USA) *KO* 11
Johnny Bumphus, Buffalo

June 22 **Aaron Pryor** *W* 15
Nick Furlano, Toronto

July 15 **Bill Costello** *W* 12
Ronnie Shields, Kingston, NY

LIGHTWEIGHTS

June 1 **Livingstone Bramble** (VI) *KO* 14
Ray Mancini, Buffalo

June 23 **Edwin Rosario** *W* 15
Howard Davis Jr., Hato Rey, Puerto Rico

JUNIOR LIGHTWEIGHTS

June 12 **Rocky Lockridge** *KO* 11
Tae Jin Moon, Anchorage

FEATHERWEIGHTS

May 27 **Eusebio Pedroza** *W* 15
Angel Levy Mayor, Maracaibo

June 10 **Min Keun Oh** *W* 15
Kelvin Lampkins, Seoul

JUNIOR FEATHERWEIGHTS

May 26 **Jaime Garza** *KO* 3
Felipe Orozco, Miami Beach

May 26 **Victor Callejas** (PR) *KO* 8
Loris Stecca, Guaynabo, Puerto Rico

July 8 **Seung In Suh** *KO* 4
Cleo Garcia, Seoul

BANTAMWEIGHTS

May 26 **Albert Davila** *KO* 11
Enrique Sanchez, Miami Beach

Aug 4 **Satoshi Shingaki** *W* 15
Joves de la Puz, Naha City, Japan

JUNIOR BANTAMWEIGHTS

May 26 **Joo Do Chun** *KO* 6
Felix Marquez, Wonju, South Korea

July 5 **Jiro Watanabe** *W* 12
Payao Poontarat, Osaka
(Wins WBC Title)

July 20 **Joo Do Chun** *KO* 7
William Develos, Pusan, South Korea

FLYWEIGHTS

May 19 **Soon Chun Kwon** *W* 15
Ian Clyde, Daejon, South Korea

June 1 **Gabriel Bernal** *KO* 11
Antoine Montero, Nimes, France

JUNIOR FLYWEIGHTS

May 13 **Dodie Penalosa** *KO* 9
Jae Hong Kim, Seoul

May 19 **Francisco Quiroz** (DR) *KO* 9
Lupe Madera, Maracaibo

Aug 18 **Jung Koo Chang** *KO* 9
Katsuo Tokashiki, Pohang, South Korea

Aug 18 **Francisco Quiroz** *KO* 2
Victor Sierra, Panama City

HIT MAN DOESN'T MISS

It was possible to envision Roberto Duran losing a fight. It was even possible, after the *No Mas* incident, to envision him quitting. But Duran flat on the canvas, knocked out cold? Not in our lifetime. Then again...

On June 15 at Caesars Palace, WBC super lightweight champion Thomas Hearns defended against the 34-year-old Duran, who had recently been stripped of the WBA title for failing to defend against Mike McCallum. The bout was over in a flash. Striking quickly and savagely, Hearns scored two knockdowns in the first round and opened a cut over Duran's left eye. Early in the second, he gunned a right that exploded on Duran's jaw. Boom! Duran toppled face-first and lay still for referee Carlos Padilla's full count.

"The Hit Man has been on vacation," said Hearns. "But the right I threw today is one of the hardest I've ever thrown."

No one had to ask Duran if he agreed.

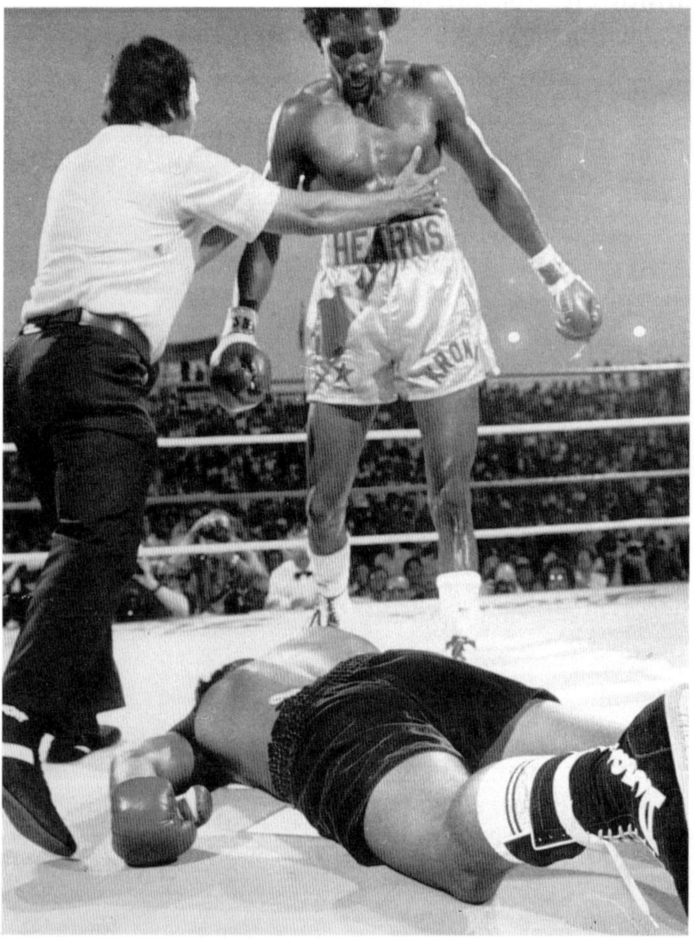

Thomas Hearns knocked out Roberto Duran to retain the junior middleweight championship.

ONE HOOK WAS ALL IT TOOK

"I was destined to be a champion," lightweight Howard Davis Jr. once said. "I've known that since I was 16 years old."

Four years after Davis was named the outstanding fighter of the 1976 Olympics, he lost on points to then-WBC champion Jim Watt. His second chance came on June 23, when he challenged WBC champion Edwin Rosario at the Roberto Clemente Coliseum in Hato Rey, Puerto Rico. He came within 15 seconds of victory.

The New Yorker suffered a second-round knockdown, but turned the fight with a straight right in the third. Usually overcautious, he backed Rosario up and took the middle rounds.

After 11 rounds, the fight was even. Davis won the first two minutes of the 12th, but with 15 seconds left in the fight, he got caught by a hook. The knockdown proved to be the difference in Rosario's split decision victory (scores of 115-114, 117-113, and 113-114).

Davis, it seemed, was destined to be frustrated.

Edwin Rosario (left) outpointed Howard Davis to retain the lightweight title in a close bout.

PINKY AND THE BLINKING 'SPOON

Only in boxing: at age 14, Pinklon Thomas was a heroin addict. At age 26, he was a hero.

On August 31, Thomas, seen as a 2-1 underdog, challenged WBC heavyweight champion Tim Witherspoon at the Riviera Hotel in Las Vegas. Upset with his purse of $400,000, 'Spoon was seeing green when he should have been thinking Pink. He allowed Thomas to dominate with his division-best jab, and kept blinking and complaining about thumbing. However, referee Richard Steele was unsympathetic.

"Witherspoon was getting hit by good, clean jabs," he said.

Thomas took the title by majority 12-round verdict (scores of 116-112, 115-112, and 114-114), meaning Pink was in.

Tim Witherspoon (right) started fast in title defense against Pinklon Thomas, but lost.

SEPTEMBER

1984

DECEMBER

RINGSIDE VIEW

NOVEMBER

Mexico's Juan "Kid" Meza recovers from a knockdown to score a first-round kayo over defending WBC super bantamweight champion Jaime Garza. It is a major upset; entering the bout, Garza is 40-0 (38).

DECEMBER

Underachiever Greg Page finally begins to realize his potential, as he captures the WBA heavyweight title with an eighth-round kayo of Gerrie Coetzee.

BIRTH OF A MEXICAN LEGEND

In retrospect, it's almost unbelievable: not only was 19-year-old Mario Martinez the betting favorite over countryman Julio Cesar Chavez, but he was the fan favorite, too.

On September 13, the Mexicans clashed for the vacant WBC super featherweight title at the Olympic Auditorium in Los Angeles. Chavez was 36-0, but Martinez had been more heavily hyped, primarily because he held a victory over former champion Rolando Navarette.

The fighters engaged in a breathless brawl. Martinez charged forward, and Chavez countered with short, straight blows. By the middle rounds, his technique began to pay off; Martinez was bleeding from the nose and a cut above his right eye.

Toward the end of the eighth, Chavez pummeled his fading foe, puncuating his flurry with two big rights. Referee John Thomas stepped in at thc 2:59 mark.

"I think," understated Chavez, "I got some new fans tonight."

Mexico's 22-year-old Julio Cesar Chavez (right) knocked out Mario Martinez in the eighth round to win the vacant junior lightweight title.

WORLD TITLE FIGHTS

HEAVYWEIGHTS

Nov 9 **Larry Holmes** *KO* 12 James (Bonecrusher) Smith, Las Vegas

Dec 1 **Greg Page** (USA) *KO* 8 Gerrie Coetzee, Sun City

CRUISERWEIGHTS

Oct 6 **Lee Roy Murphy** (USA) *KO* 14 Marvin Camel, Billings, MT

Dec 1 **Piet Crous** (SA) *W* 15 Osvaldo Ocasio, Sun City

Dec 20 **Lee Roy Murphy** *KO* 12 Young Joe Louis, Chicago

MIDDLEWEIGHTS

Oct 19 **Marvin Hagler** *KO* 3 Mustafa Hamsho, New York City

JUNIOR MIDDLEWEIGHTS

Sept 15 **Thomas Hearns** *KO* 3 Fred Hutchings, Saginaw, MI

Oct 19 **Mike McCallum** (JAM) *W* 15 Sean Mannion, New York City (Wins Vacant WBA Title)

Nov 2 **Carlos Santos** (PR) *W* 15 Mark Medal, New York City

Dec 1 **Mike McCallum** *KO* 14 Luigi Minchillo, Milan

WELTERWEIGHTS

Sept 22 **Donald Curry** *KO* 6 Nino LaRocca, Monte Carlo

JUNIOR WELTERWEIGHTS

Nov 3 **Bill Costello** *W* 12 Saoul Mamby, Kingston, NY

Dec 15 **Gene Hatcher** *W* 15 Ubaldo Sacco, Fort Worth

LIGHTWEIGHTS

Sept 1 **Harry Arroyo** *KO* 8 Charlie (White Lightning) Brown, Struthers, OH

Nov 3 **Jose Luis Ramirez** (MEX) *KO* 4 Edwin Rosario, San Juan

JUNIOR LIGHTWEIGHTS

Sept 13 **Julio Cesar Chavez** (MEX) *KO* 8 Mario Martinez, Los Angeles (Wins Vacant WBC Title)

Sept 16 **Hwan Kil Yuh** *KO* 6 Sakda Galaxy, Pohang, South Korea

FEATHERWEIGHTS

Dec 8 **Azumah Nelson** (GHA) *KO* 11 Wilfredo Gomez, San Juan

JUNIOR FEATHERWEIGHTS

Nov 3 **Juan (Kid) Meza** (MEX) *KO* 1 Jaime Garza, Kingston, NY

BANTAMWEIGHTS

Sept 22 **Richard Sandoval** *W* 15 Edgar Roman, Monte Carlo

Dec 15 **Richard Sandoval** *KO* 8 Cardenio Ulloa, Miami Beach

JUNIOR BANTAMWEIGHTS

Nov 21 **Khaosai Galaxy** (THA) *KO* 6 Eusebio Espinal, Bangkok (Wins Vacant WBA Title)

Nov 29 **Jiro Watanabe** *KO* 11 Payao Poontarat, Kumamoto, Japan

FLYWEIGHTS

Sept 7 **Soon Chun Kwon** *KO* 12 Joaquin Flores, Chongju, South Korea

Sept 15 **Santos Laciar** *KO* 10 Prudencio Cardona, Cordoba, Argentina

Oct 8 **Sot Chitalada** (THA) *W* 12 Gabriel Bernal, Bangkok

Dec 8 **Santos Laciar** *W* 15 Hilario Zapata, Buenos Aires

JUNIOR FLYWEIGHTS

Nov 16 **Dodie Penalosa** *W* 15 Chum Hwan Choi, Quezon City

Dec 15 **Jung Koo Chang** *W* 12 Tadashi Kuramochi, Pusan, South Korea

A RUNNER TURNS GUNNER

In March, Mark Medal had won the newly created IBF junior middleweight title by outbrawling Earl Hargrove. His first defense figured to be a different kind of fight. On November 2, he faced Puerto Rico's Carlos Santos at Madison Square Garden's Felt Forum. Bad enough Santos was a southpaw. But he was also a runner.

On this night, however, Santos stood and fought, which helped make a great fight. There was drama in almost every round: Santos scored a knockdown in the first; Medal suffered a torn lip in the second; the 154-pounders went toe to toe throughout the fifth; Medal opened a wide cut over Santos' right eye in the 13th; seemingly out on his feet in the 14th, Medal dropped the challenger with a desperate hook.

At the final bell, the fighters – and the fans – were exhausted. Santos took the title by unanimous and deserved decision (scores of 142-140, 146-138, and 147-139). And he had done so without giving Medal the runaround.

Carlos Santos is paraded around the ring by fellow Puerto Ricans after decisioning Mark Medal.

AZUMAH TURNS BAZOOKA INTO A PALOOKA

It seemed a fair question: how could WBC featherweight champion Wilfredo "Bazooka" Gomez fight so brilliantly in winning the title from Juan LaPorte, and then appear so impotent in defending it against Azumah Nelson? The answer was quite simple: Nelson was a much better fighter than LaPorte.

Azumah dethroned Gomez on December 8, at Hiram Bithorn Stadium in San Juan. The Ghanian set the tone by fearlessly attacking. He backed off during the middle stanzas, then reaccelerated before scoring two knockdowns in the 11th. Referee Octavio Meyran counted Gomez out at the 2:59 mark.

At least on this night, Nelson was a much better fighter than Wilfredo Gomez, too.

GONE IN SAN JUAN

Edwin Rosario would become a three-time lightweight king and a two-division champion, but his chance to be "The Duran of the '80s" ended on November 3, when he defended the WBC 135-pound crown vs. Jose Luis Ramirez.

In May 1983, Rosario had won the vacant title by barely outlasting Ramirez in a distance fight. The rematch was short and explosive. The 21-year-old champion felled his rival in the first and second rounds, and was a punch or two away from scoring a shockingly quick kayo. But Ramirez took command early in the third.

Late in the fourth, the Mexican southpaw drove Rosario into a corner and poured in a dozen powerpunches. Out on his feet, the champion turned away from the onslaught.

It was his way of saying *no mas*.

Jose Luis Ramirez (left) stopped Edwin Rosario in fourth round to win the lightweight crown. It was Rosario's first defeat in 21 fights.

JANUARY

1985

APRIL

THE AWESOME AUSSIE

In the flyweight competition at the 1984 Olympics, Australia's Jeff Fenech had a realistic chance of winning the gold. After losing a controversial decision before the medal round, he returned home with something to prove to the world.

It didn't take him long. Only six months after turning pro, the 20-year-old cyclone challenged IBF bantamweight titlist Satoshi Shingaki at the Hordren Pavilion in Moore Park, New South Wales. It was a mismatch from the start; Fenech smothered the Japanese, winning every round until Shingaki succumbed in the ninth.

It wasn't the gold, but at least a lot of green was sure to follow.

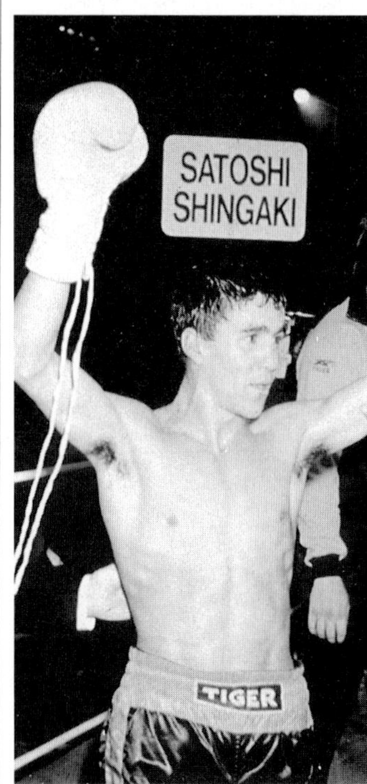

Jeff Fenech after stopping Satoshi Shingaki to become new bantamweight king.

A COP AND HIS TOUGH BEAT

In his hometown of Youngstown, Ohio, Harry Arroyo was a part-time volunteer policeman. On January 12, he was off-duty. Too bad, because he could've used a night stick and handcuffs during his confrontation with Terrence Alli.

Making his second defense of the IBF lightweight title, Arroyo met Alli at Bally's Hotel in Atlantic City. The energetic challenger set a torrid pace, and jumped into the lead when he floored "Dirty Harry" with a looping right in round two.

Alli didn't slow down until the halfway mark. Arroyo began to land to the body, and by the 10th round, he had pulled even on the cards. In the 11th, a huge right shook Alli, and half-a-dozen followup punches felled him. He beat the count of referee Tony Perez, but when Arroyo added another right, the fight was waved over.

For the cop from Youngstown, it had been an arresting performance.

Harry Arroyo (left) stopped Terrence Ali in the 11th round to retain the lightweight crown.

BIGGEST LITTLE HEART IN BOXING

In 1982, Ray "Boom Boom" Mancini won the WBA lightweight title for his father. On February 16, at the Lawlor Events Center in Reno, he tried to regain it from Livingstone Bramble, who had taken it eight months earlier.

"This one," he said, "is for me."

A 2-1 underdog, Mancini came frustratingly close to pulling off an upset. In order to last the 15-round distance, he had to survive a cut above his right eye, a left eye that swelled shut, and three visits from the ringside physician.

Boom Boom boxed far better than he had in losing the title. Still, he was outfought; Bramble landed 674 punches to Mancini's 381. His unyielding spirit captured the crowd, but not the judges, all of whom scored for Bramble by a single point (two totals of 143-142, and 144-143).

Mancini hadn't won back the title, but he had certainly regained his self-respect.

Lightweight champion Livingstone Bramble decisioned Ray "Boom Boom" Mancini (left).

A WAR FOR THE AGES

It can be argued that a battle lasting only seven minutes and 52 seconds shouldn't be rated with the greatest fights in history. Maybe so. But the first three minutes of the middleweight title fight between Marvin Hagler and Thomas Hearns was probably the greatest round of all-time.

On April 15, Hagler and WBC super welterweight titlist Hearns tested wills at Caesars Palace. It was Hearns' gameplan to box, but at the opening bell, the champion attacked as if already desperate.

"I started slugging," explained Hearns, "because I had to."

The fighters rocked each other, refusing to relent until the bell. Hagler showed a bad cut over his right eye, and Hearns had fractured two bones in his right hand. The second round was only slightly tamer. In the third, Hagler, motivated by a mid-round examination by the ringside physician, accelerated once more. Hearns rose from the fight's only knockdown, but referee Richard Steele wouldn't let him continue.

Marvin Hagler (right) was devastating in stopping Thomas Hearns in the third round to retain the undisputed world middleweight championship.

WORLD TITLE FIGHTS

HEAVYWEIGHTS

March 15 **Larry Holmes** *KO* 10
David Bey, Las Vegas

April 29 **Tony Tubbs** (USA) *W* 15
Greg Page, Buffalo

CRUISERWEIGHTS

March 30 **Piet Crous** *KO* 3
Randy Stephens, Sun City

LIGHT HEAVYWEIGHTS

Feb 23 **Michael Spinks** *KO* 3
David Sears, Atlantic City

MIDDLEWEIGHTS

April 15 **Marvin Hagler** *KO* 3
Thomas Hearns, Las Vegas

WELTERWEIGHTS

Jan 19 **Donald Curry** *KO* 4
Colin Jones, Birmingham, England

March 9 **Milton McCrory** *W* 12
Pedro Vilella, Paris

JUNIOR WELTERWEIGHTS

Feb 16 **Bill Costello** *W* 12
Leroy Haley, Kingston, NY

March 2 **Aaron Pryor** *W* 15
Gary Hinton, Atlantic City

LIGHTWEIGHTS

Jan 12 **Harry Arroyo** *KO* 11
Terrence Alli, Atlantic City

Feb 16 **Livingstone Bramble** *W* 15
Ray Mancini, Reno

April 6 **Jimmy Paul** (USA) *W* 15
Harry Arroyo, Atlantic City

JUNIOR LIGHTWEIGHTS

Jan 27 **Rocky Lockridge** *KO* 6
Kamel Bou-Ali, Riva del Garda, Italy

Feb 15 **Lester Ellis** (AUT) *W* 15
Hwan Kil Yuh, Melbourne

April 19 **Julio Cesar Chavez** *KO* 6
Ruben Castillo, Inglewood

April 26 **Lester Ellis** *KO* 13
Rod Sequenan, Melbourne

FEATHERWEIGHTS

Feb 2 **Eusebio Pedroza** *W* 15
Jorge Lujan, Panama City

April 7 **Min Keun Oh** *W* 15
Irving Mitchell, Pusan, South Korea

JUNIOR FEATHERWEIGHTS

Jan 3 **Ji Won Kim** (KOR) *KO* 10
Seung Il Suh, Seoul

Feb 2 **Victor Callejas** *W* 15
Seung Hoon Lee, Hato Rey, Puerto Rico

March 30 **Ji Won Kim** *W* 15
Dario Palacios, Suwon, South Korea

April 19 **Juan (Kid) Meza** *KO* 6
Mike Ayala, Inglewood

BANTAMWEIGHTS

April 26 **Jeff Fenech** (AUT) *KO* 9
Satoshi Shingaki, Moore Park, Australia

JUNIOR BANTAMWEIGHTS

Jan 6 **Joo Do Chun** *KO* 15
Kwang Gu Park, Ulsan, South Korea

March 6 **Khaosai Galaxy** *KO* 7
Dong Chun Lee, Bangkok

FLYWEIGHTS

Jan 25 **Soon Chun Kwon** *D* 15
Chong Kwan Chung, Daejon, South Korea

Feb 20 **Sot Chitalada** *KO* 5
Charlie Magri, London

April 14 **Soon Chun Kwon** *KO* 3
Shinobu Kawashima, Pohang, South Korea

JUNIOR FLYWEIGHTS

March 29 **Joey Olivo** (USA) *W* 15
Francisco Quiroz, Miami Beach

April 27 **Jung Koo Chang** *W* 12
German Torres, Ulsan, South Korea

MAY

1985

AUGUST

THE ROCK WAS NO LOCK

In what many observers viewed as the robbery of the decade, Rocky Lockridge lost the WBA junior lightweight title to former two-division champion Wilfredo Gomez by majority 15-round decision. The controversial battle took place on May 19, at the Roberto Clemente Coliseum in Hato Rey.

It was a critical bout for Puerto Rico's Gomez, who wanted to prove to his countrymen that his December 1984 kayo loss to Azumah Nelson had not finished him. Against Lockridge, the 28-year-old challenger started well and finished strongly. In between, however, he was battered. In fact, in the 10th round, a stoppage seemed imminent.

After the decision was announced (scores of 146-142, 145-144, and 144-144), Gomez said, "I owe this title to Pepe Cordero." He didn't know how right he was: it was the local promoter and WBA power broker who had assigned the judges.

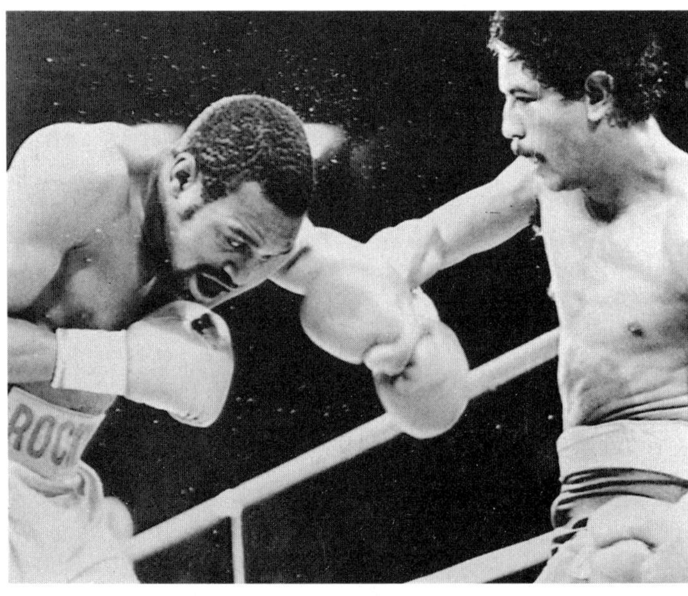

Lockridge (left) lost the junior lightweight title to Gomez by an outrageous decision.

TRUTH AND CONSEQUENCE

Carl "The Truth" Williams had engaged in only 16 pro fights, but Larry Holmes didn't dare take him lightly. Chasing a pair of cherished records, the IBF heavyweight champion couldn't afford to stumble. Holmes was 47-0, and only two wins from tying Rocky Marciano's unmatched mark of 49-0. Moreover, he had made 19 successful defenses, six shy of Joe Louis' all-time record of 25.

Holmes defended against Williams on May 20, at the Lawlor Events Center in Reno. The challenger stood 6'5", and possessed an incredible reach of 85 inches. For the first time in years, Holmes was faced with an opponent who could outjab him.

Williams boxed smartly until being hurt by a body shot in the ninth. Holmes dominated the late rounds, and managed to keep the crown by scores of 146-139 (twice) and a more realistic 143-142. At age 35, he was still winning his race against Father Time.

WORLD TITLE FIGHTS

HEAVYWEIGHTS

May 20 **Larry Holmes** *W* 15
Carl Williams, Reno

June 15 **Pinklon Thomas** *KO* 8
Mike Weaver, Las Vegas

CRUISERWEIGHTS

June 6 **Alfonzo Ratliff** (USA) *W* 12
Carlos DeLeon, Las Vegas

July 27 **Dwight (Braxton) Qawi** *KO* 11
Piet Crous, Sun City

LIGHT HEAVYWEIGHTS

June 6 **Michael Spinks** *KO* 8
Jim MacDonald, Las Vegas

JUNIOR MIDDLEWEIGHTS

June 1 **Carlos Santos** *W* 15
Louis Acaries, Paris

July 28 **Mike McCallum** *KO* 8
David Braxton, Miami

WELTERWEIGHTS

July 14 **Milton McCrory** *KO* 3
Carlos Trujillo, Monte Carlo

JUNIOR WELTERWEIGHTS

July 21 **Ubaldo Sacco** (ARG) *KO* 9
Gene Hatcher, Campione d'Italia, Italy

Aug 21 **Lonnie Smith** (USA) *KO* 8
Bill Costello, New York City

LIGHTWEIGHTS

June 30 **Jimmy Paul** *KO* 14
Robin Blake, Las Vegas

Aug 10 **Hector Camacho** *W* 12
Jose Luis Ramirez, Las Vegas

JUNIOR LIGHTWEIGHTS

May 19 **Wilfredo Gomez** *W* 15
Rocky Lockridge, Hato Rey, Puerto Rico

July 7 **Julio Cesar Chavez** *KO* 2
Roger Mayweather, Las Vegas

July 12 **Barry Michael** (AUT) *W* 15
Lester Ellis, Melbourne

FEATHERWEIGHTS

June 8 **Barry McGuigan** (IRE) *W* 15
Eusebio Pedroza, London

JUNIOR FEATHERWEIGHTS

June 28 **Ji Won Kim** *KO* 4
Bobby Berna, Pusan, South Korea

Aug 18 **Lupe Pintor** *W* 12
Juan (Kid) Meza, Mexico City

BANTAMWEIGHTS

May 4 **Daniel Zaragoza** (MEX) *W Disq* 7
Freddie Jackson, Oranjestad, Aruba (Wins Vacant WBC Title)

Aug 9 **Miguel Lora** (COL) *W* 12
Daniel Zaragoza, Miami

Aug 23 **Jeff Fenech** *KO* 4
Satoshi Shingaki, Sydney

JUNIOR BANTAMWEIGHTS

May 3 **Elly Pical** (IDO) *KO* 8
Joo Do Chun, Djakarta

May 9 **Jiro Watanabe** *W* 12
Julio Soto Solano, Tokyo

July 17 **Khaosai Galaxy** *KO* 5
Rafael Orono, Bangkok

Aug 25 **Elly Pical** *KO* 3
Wayne Mulholland, Djakarta

FLYWEIGHTS

May 6 **Santos Laciar** *W* 15
Antoine Montero, Grenoble

June 22 **Sot Chitalada** *D* 12
Gabriel Bernal, Bangkok

July 17 **Soon Chun Kwon** *D* 15
Chong Kwan Chung, Masan, South Korea

JUNIOR FLYWEIGHTS

July 28 **Joey Olivo** *W* 15
Moon Jin Choi, Seoul

Aug 4 **Jung Koo Chang** *W* 12
Francisco Montiel, Seoul

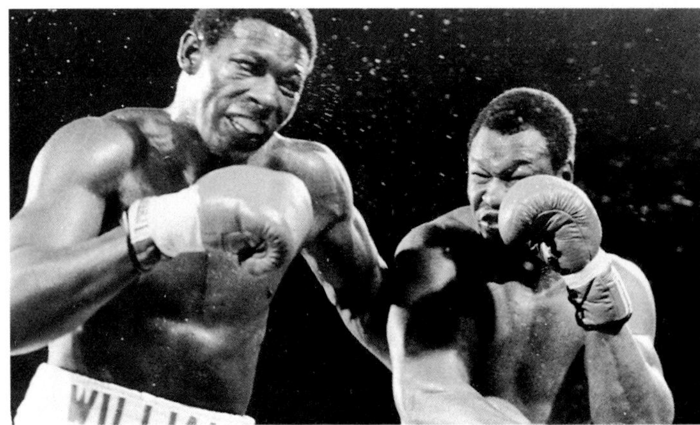

Defending heavyweight king Larry Holmes (right) outpointed Carl "The Truth" Williams.

BARRY DOES THE FIGHTING FOR THE IRISH

Whenever Irish featherweight Barry McGuigan was scheduled for a match, the beleaguered citizens of Belfast shared a saying: "Let Barry do the fighting."

On June 8, McGuigan did enough fighting at the Queen's Park Rangers Stadium in West London to take the WBA featherweight crown from Eusebio Pedroza. It was no easy task: Pedroza was making his 20th defense.

A week before the fight, the challenger, who banked on a finely tuned hook, pulled a ligament in his left arm. But with the Panamanian looking for the hook, McGuigan was able to score with his right.

The fight was close until the seventh, when McGuigan scored a knockdown. He hurt Pedroza again in the ninth and 13th, each time with a cross, and went on to take a unanimous 15-round decision by totals of 149-139, 147-140, and 148-138.

Ireland's national hero Barry McGuigan floored Eusebio Pedroza in the seventh round and went on to win an easy 15-round decision.

MACHO TIME AND AGAIN

After Hector Camacho took the WBC lightweight title by outpointing Jose Luis Ramirez, "The Macho Man" issued a proclamation: "From now on, I'm going to dominate this game." Ironically, it would be his last dominant performance.

The fellow southpaws clashed on August 10, at the Riviera Hotel in Las Vegas. Ramirez chugged forward throughout, but couldn't hope to cope with Camacho's speed. The outcome was never in doubt; Camacho scored a knockdown in the third, controlled the middle rounds, and cruised down the stretch. After 12 rounds, the scoring was unanimous: 118-111, 119-112, and 119-109.

But how much longer would it be Macho Time?

RINGSIDE VIEW

JULY

WBC super featherweight champion Julio Cesar Chavez retains the title for the second time, crushing former king Roger Mayweayther in two rounds.

AUGUST

Colombia's multitalented Miguel "Happy" Lora takes the WBC bantamweight title by scoring a unanimous 12-round decision over Daniel Zaragoza.

Trigger-fisted Hector "Macho" Camacho (left) dazzled Jose Luis Ramirez over 12 rounds.

SEPTEMBER

1985

DECEMBER

TAKING THE TITLE, AND MAKING HISTORY

On September 21, at the Riviera Hotel in Las Vegas, Michael Spinks made history. In the process, he denied Larry Holmes an opportunity to do the same.

Bulked up by a 4,500-calorie diet, the 29-year-old Spinks, 200, became the first light heavyweight champion to win the heavyweight crown. Archie Moore, Billy Conn, and Bob Foster were among those who had failed to accomplish that feat. But Spinks, backtracking and then attacking with an unpredictable whirlwind attack, dethroned the fading 35-year-old Holmes, 221½, by close but unanimous 15-round verdict (two scores of 143-142, and 145-142).

Larry Holmes (left) lost the first fight in his 12-year career, as well as the heavyweight crown, when outpointed in 15 rounds by Michael Spinks.

Had Holmes, a 6-1 favorite, pulled out a victory, he would have tied Rocky Marciano's all-time unbeaten mark of 49-0. Instead, he was 48-1 – and bitter.

"Rocky Marciano," he said, "couldn't carry my jockstrap."

The quote would come back to haunt Holmes. And so would Michael Spinks.

RINGSIDE VIEW

OCTOBER

England's once-beaten Frank Bruno wins the European heavyweight title with a fourth-round kayo of Anders Eklund in Wembley.

DECEMBER

South Korea's Myung Woo Yuh wins the WBA junior flyweight title, scoring a split 15-round decision over Joey Olivo.

DECEMBER

J.B. Williamson captures the vacant WBC light heavyweight title with a unanimous 12-round verdict over California-based Prince Mamah Mohammed, a legitimate heir to a kingdom in Ghana.

TIPPING OVER COWDELL

In December 1981, England's Pat Cowdell had troubled then-WBC featherweight champion Salvador Sanchez, losing a split 15-round decision. On October 12, the 32-year-old European champion secured his second title opportunity, facing WBC 126-pound champion Azumah Nelson at Birmingham's National Exhibition Centre. The bout suggested that what works against one opponent may prove meaningless against another.

Cowdell opened by scoring with jabs. But Nelson quickly timed him, and then answered with a left uppercut. Boom! Cowdell collapsed, and referee Octavio Meyran counted him out.

Azumah Nelson is hugged by his wife after he knocked out Britain's Pat Cowdell in the first.

World Title Fights

HEAVYWEIGHTS

Sept 21 **Michael Spinks** *W* 15
Larry Holmes, Las Vegas

CRUISERWEIGHTS

Sept 21 **Bernard Benton** (USA) *W* 12
Alfonzo Ratliff, Las Vegas

Oct 19 **Lee Roy Murphy** *KO* 12
Chisanda Mutti, Monte Carlo

LIGHT HEAVYWEIGHTS

Dec 10 **J.B. Williamson** (USA) *W* 12
Prince Mamah Mohammed, Inglewood
(Wins Vacant WBC Title)

Dec 21 **Slobodan Kacar** (YUG) *W* 15
Eddie Mustafa Muhammad, Pesaro, Italy
(Wins Vacant IBF Title)

WELTERWEIGHTS

Dec 6 **Donald Curry** *KO* 2
Milton McCrory, Las Vegas
(Unifies World Title)

JUNIOR LIGHTWEIGHTS

Sept 21 **Julio Cesar Chavez** *W* 12
Dwight Pratchett, Las Vegas

Oct 19 **Barry Michael** *KO* 4
Jin Shik Choi, Darwin, Australia

FEATHERWEIGHTS

Sept 6 **Azumah Nelson** *KO* 5
Juvenal Ordenes, Miami

Sept 28 **Barry McGuigan** *KO* 9
Bernard Taylor, Belfast

Oct 12 **Azumah Nelson** *KO* 1
Pat Cowdell, Birmingham, England

Nov 29 **Ki Yung Chung** (KOR) *KO* 15
Min Keun Oh, Chonju, South Korea

JUNIOR FEATHERWEIGHTS

Oct 9 **Ji Won Kim** *KO* 1
Seung Il Suh, Seoul

Nov 8 **Victor Callejas** *KO* 7
Loris Stecca, Rimini, Italy

BANTAMWEIGHTS

Dec 2 **Jeff Fenech** *W* 15
Jerome Coffee, Sydney

JUNIOR BANTAMWEIGHTS

Sept 17 **Jiro Watanabe** *KO* 7
Kazuo Katsuma, Osaka

Dec 13 **Jiro Watanabe** *KO* 5
Suk Hwan Yun, Taegu, South Korea

Dec 23 **Khaosai Galaxy** *KO* 2
Edgar Monserrat, Bangkok

FLYWEIGHTS

Oct 5 **Hilario Zapata** *W* 15
Alonzo Gonzalez, Panama City

Dec 20 **Soon Chun Kwon** (KOR) *KO* 4
Chong Kwan Chung, Pusan, South Korea

JUNIOR FLYWEIGHTS

Oct 12 **Dodie Penalosa** *KO* 3
Yani Dokolamo, Djakarta

Nov 10 **Jung Koo Chang** *W* 12
Jorge Cano, Daejon, South Korea

Dec 8 **Myung Woo Yuh** (KOR) *W* 15
Joey Olivo, Taegu, South Korea

IF WE HADN'T SEEN IT...

A double knockdown? In a championship fight? Had a Hollywood scriptwriter dared suggest it, he would've been sent home.

On October 19, IBF cruiserweight champion Lee Roy Murphy met Zambia's Chisanda Mutti at the Louis II Stadium in Monte Carlo. It was an engrossing battle, with the stylish Mutti boxing smartly, and the stocky Murphy banking on his crunching power.

Mutti hurt the American in the fourth and sixth, and floored him in the ninth. After 11 rounds of a scheduled 15, the challenger was in front on points.

In the 12th, the fighters simultaneously landed big rights. Both crashed to the canvas. Reaching for the ropes, Murphy managed to climb to his feet. Mutti made it to his knees, but failed to beat referee Larry Hazzard's 10-count.

The fight was over. And no one believed it.

FROM STAR TO SUPERSTAR

It takes exceptional opposition to elevate a fighter from star to superstar. WBA welterweight champion Donald Curry, 23-0, flaunted a diverse attack and an air-tight defense. But until he knocked out WBC champion Milton McCrory, 28-0, he had failed the giant jump in status.

Before their unification showdown, held on December 6, at the Hilton Hotel in Las Vegas, Curry and McCrory traded barbs.

"I'm going to take your string-bean heart first," promised Curry, "and then I'll knock you out."

That's exactly what he did. In the first round, Curry, a 4-1 favorite, stunned McCrory and forced him to hold. In the second, he dropped "The Ice Man" with a solid hook. McCrory rose, only to be met by a crunching straight right. This time, he lay supine for 2½ minutes.

From star to superstar. Timing is everything, and Donald Curry's timing had been perfect.

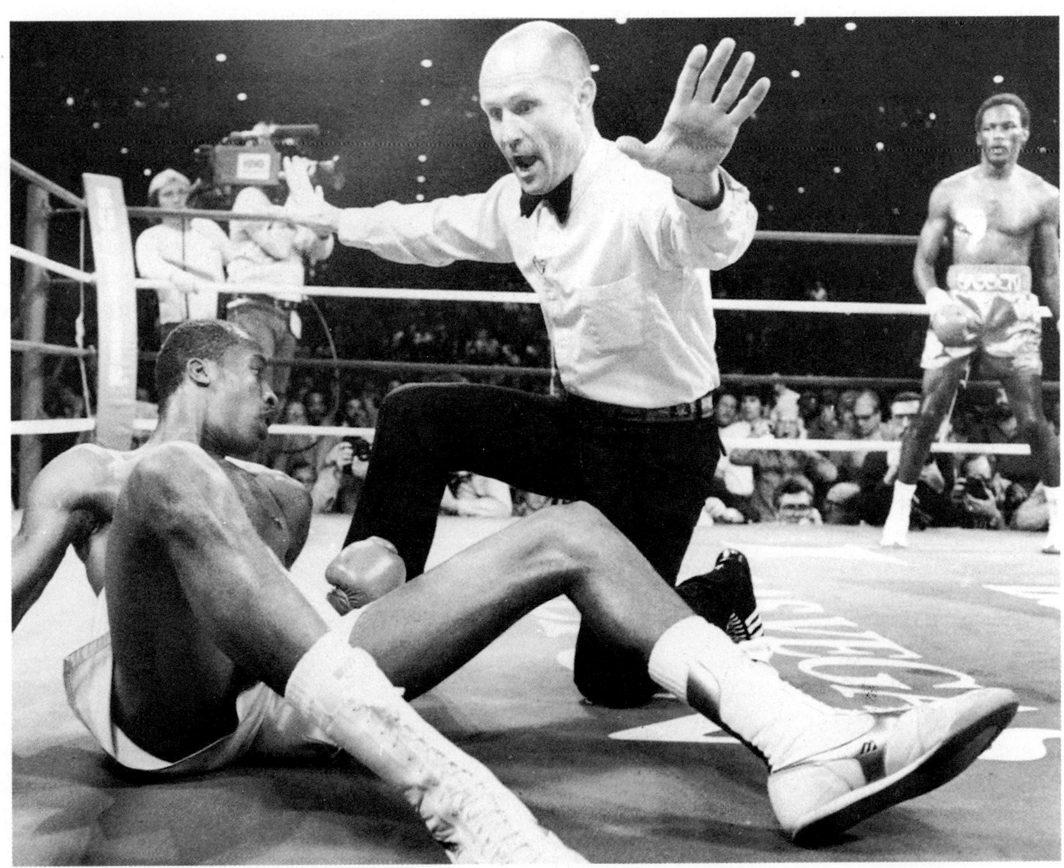

Donald Curry watches Milton McCrory being counted out in the second round. Curry became the undisputed welterweight champion.

JANUARY

1986

APRIL

THE TAMING OF THE BEAST

Middleweight champion Marvin Hagler knocked out John Mugabi in the 11th to retain the crown. It was Mugabi's first defeat.

No matter what John Mugabi was asked before his date with world middleweight champion Marvin Hagler, the unbeaten Ugandan gave the same answer: "I knock him out."

Mugabi's power (26 kayos in 26 wins) and Hagler's rock-hard chin made their title fight, held on March 10 at Caesars Palace, one of the most intriguing matchups of the year. Adding to the bout's significance: it was Hagler's 12th defense. The division record of 14 was held by Carlos Monzon.

Mugabi tried to keep his promise, but Hagler's skills were far too advanced. Dominating with his jab, the southpaw weakened The Beast, almost stopped him in the sixth, and finished him with several rights in the 11th. Referee Mills Lane counted an exhausted Mugabi out at the 1:29 mark.

"I took the toughest opponent out there," said Hagler after the fight, "a guy with all those knockouts, and I destroyed him."

Not only that, but he knocked him out, too.

RINGSIDE VIEW

FEBRUARY

Marvin Johnson, 31, becomes a three-time light heavyweight champion, capturing the vacant WBA title with a seventh-round TKO of Leslie Stewart.

MARCH

In a major upset, Canada's Trevor Berbick dethrones WBC heavyweight champion Pinklon Thomas by unanimous 15-round decision.

MARCH

Frank Bruno positions himself for a try at the heavyweight title by scoring a 110-second stoppage of former WBA champion Gerrie Coetzee in Wembley.

NO FOOD, NO FIGHT

Having engaged in a series of non-title bouts, WBA bantamweight champion Richard Sandoval hadn't made the limit of 118 pounds in over a year. On March 10, underneath the Hagler-Mugabi bout at Caesars Palace, he risked the crown against Texas hooker Gaby Canizales.

Struggling to reduce from 128 pounds, Sandoval stopped eating two days before the fight. Less than 24 hours before the opening bell, he was still 122. He reduced to 117¾ by the weigh-in, but was clearly spent.

Facing limited resistance, Canizales scored one knockdown in the first, another in the fifth, and three more in the seventh. After his fifth fall, Sandoval lay motionless on the canvas and stopped breathing for 90 seconds.

Fortunately, there was no massive hemorrhaging, and while the fighter was hospitalized, brain surgery wasn't necessary. Sandoval would never fight again, of course. Given what might have been, however, that was a small price to pay.

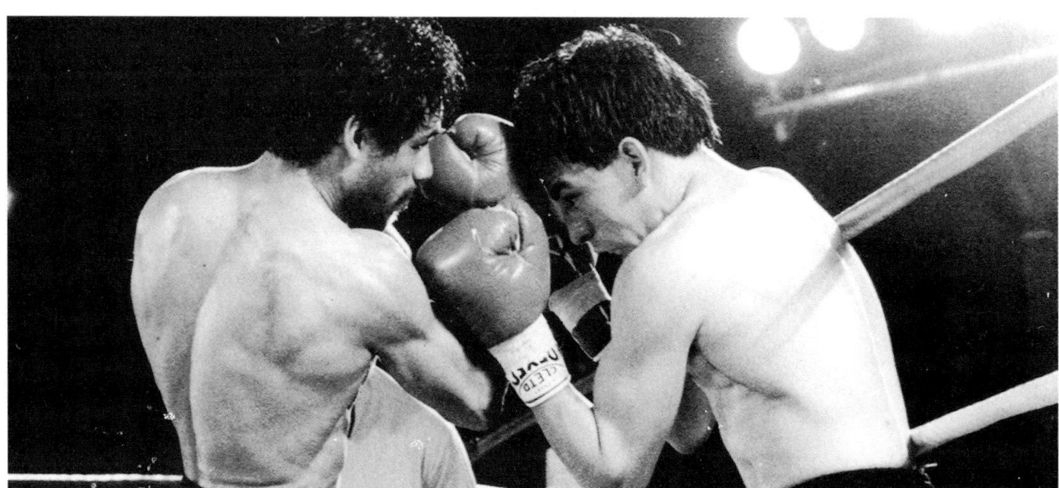
Gaby Canizales (left) overpowered defending bantamweight king Richard Sandoval before scoring a seventh-round knockout to win the title.

THE SPINKS JINX, PART II

Heavyweight champion Michael Spinks knew that his April 19 rematch with Larry Holmes, fought at the Hilton Center in Las Vegas, was going to be especially physical. Holmes didn't want to end his career by losing twice to a blown-up light heavyweight. Even if that blown-up light heavyweight was one of the best fighters of the '80s.

At the start of the first round, the 36-year-old challenger flaunted his muscle by flinging Spinks to the canvas. His point made, he proceeded to try and win back the title. But he broke his right thumb in round three, and while hurting Spinks on at least three occasions, he failed to follow up.

"I know, I didn't go after him," Holmes said of his best opportunity, which had come in round 14. "Not with his awkward style and the determination he had. The more I hit him, the more he fought back."

After 15 rounds, Spinks kept the crown by what most observers felt was an undeserved split decision (scores of 144-141, 144-142, and 141-144). That Holmes was a bitter loser was to be expected. After all, he had always been a bitter winner.

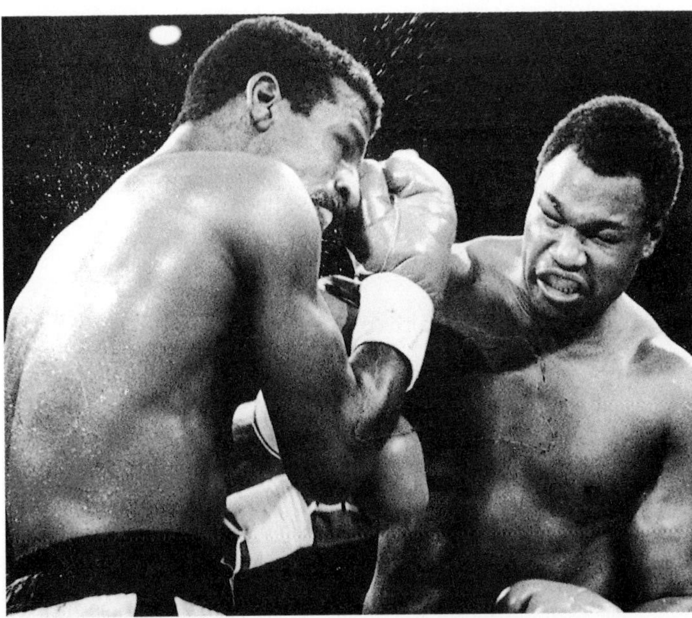

Michael Spinks (left) again outpointed Larry Holmes, this time retaining the title.

Dennis Andries after winning the light heavyweight title from J.B. Williamson by decision.

WORLD TITLE FIGHTS

HEAVYWEIGHTS

Date	Fight
Jan 17	**Tim Witherspoon** *W* 15 Tony Tubbs, Atlanta
March 22	**Trevor Berbick** (CAN) *W* 15 Pinklon Thomas, Las Vegas
April 19	**Michael Spinks** *W* 15 Larry Holmes, Las Vegas

CRUISERWEIGHTS

Date	Fight
March 22	**Dwight Qawi** *KO* 6 Leon Spinks, Reno
March 22	**Carlos DeLeon** *W* 15 Bernard Benton, Las Vegas
April 19	**Lee Roy Murphy** *KO* 9 Dorcey Gaymon, San Remo, Italy

LIGHT HEAVYWEIGHTS

Date	Fight
Feb 9	**Marvin Johnson** *KO* 7 Leslie Stewart, Indianapolis (Wins Vacant WBA Title)
April 30	**Dennis Andries** (ENG) *W* 15 J.B. Williamson, Edmonton, England

MIDDLEWEIGHTS

Date	Fight
March 10	**Marvin Hagler** *KO* 11 John Mugabi, Las Vegas

WELTERWEIGHTS

Date	Fight
March 9	**Donald Curry** *KO* 2 Eduardo Rodriguez, Fort Worth

JUNIOR WELTERWEIGHTS

Date	Fight
March 15	**Patrizio Oliva** (ITA) *W* 15 Ubaldo Sacco, Monte Carlo
April 26	**Gary Hinton** (USA) *W* 15 Reyes Cruz, Lucca, Italy (Wins Vacant IBF Title)

LIGHTWEIGHTS

Date	Fight
Feb 16	**Livingstone Bramble** *KO* 11 Tyrone Crawley, Reno

FEATHERWEIGHTS

Date	Fight
Feb 15	**Barry McGuigan** *KO* 14 Danilo Cabrera, Dublin
Feb 16	**Ki Yung Chung** *KO* 7 Tyrone Jackson, Ulsan, South Korea
Feb 25	**Azumah Nelson** *W* 15 Marcos Villasana, Inglewood

JUNIOR FEATHERWEIGHTS

Date	Fight
Jan 18	**Samart Payakaroon** (THA) *KO* 5 Lupe Pintor, Bangkok

BANTAMWEIGHTS

Date	Fight
Feb 8	**Miguel Lora** *W* 12 Wilfredo Vasquez, Miami Beach
March 10	**Gaby Canizales** (USA) *KO* 7 Richard Sandoval, Las Vegas

JUNIOR BANTAMWEIGHTS

Date	Fight
Feb 15	**Cesar Polanco** (DR) *W* 15 Elly Pical, Djakarta
March 30	**Gilberto Roman** (MEX) *W* 12 Jiro Watanabe, Itami City, Japan

FLYWEIGHTS

Date	Fight
Jan 31	**Hilario Zapata** *W* 15 Javier Lucas, Panama City
Feb 22	**Sot Chitalada** *W* 12 Freddy Castillo, El Kuwait, Kuwait
April 7	**Hilario Zapata** *W* 15 Shuichi Hozumi, Nirasaki, Japan
April 27	**Bi Won Chung** (KOR) *W* 15 Chon Kwan Chung, Pusan, South Korea

JUNIOR FLYWEIGHTS

Date	Fight
March 9	**Myung Woo Yuh** *W* 15 Jose DeJesus, Suwon, South Korea
April 13	**Jung Koo Chang** *W* 12 German Torres, Kwangju, South Korea

THE THIRTYSOMETHING CHAMP

Not all of boxing's world champions are smooth, disciplined boxers with swelling entourages and sterling amateur backgrounds. Fortunately, there's always room for a Dennis Andries.

On April 30, Andries, a British-based Guyanan, challenged WBC light heavyweight champion J.B. Williamson at Picketts Lock Centre in North London. The 32-year-old local favorite wasn't pretty to watch, but he never allowed his opponents to look good either. The champion, a classic boxer, was forced to brawl, and Andries' strength and determination proved to be the difference. After 12 tough rounds, the challenger took the title by split scores of 116-114, 118-116, and 113-115.

At the postfight press conference, Andries declared, "I'm not 32, I'm 37." No one knew whether he was serious. But he had certainly performed like a fighter who had waited a lifetime to reach the top. And however old he was, he was far from finished yet.

MAY

1986

AUGUST

THE DESERT SHOWS NO MERCY

Barry McGuigan's arrival in America was greeted with a level of enthusiasm rarely accorded fighters from overseas. The media hailed the 25-year-old Irishman as not just as an excellent boxer, but a budding superstar.

McGuigan was scheduled to defend the WBA featherweight title against Fernando Sosa. After it was discovered that the challenger had two detached retinas, he was replaced by Steve Cruz, a once-beaten Texan who supplemented his ring earnings by working for $6.50 an hour as a plumber's helper.

On June 23, McGuigan, a 5-1 favorite, and Cruz met outdoors at Caesars Palace. At fight time, it was 110 degrees. The heat didn't seem to bother the champion, who outworked Cruz for most of their fast-paced, highly competitive battle. But "Battlin' Barry" faded badly in the late rounds. Cruz scored a knockdown in the 10th, and with McGuigan dehydrated and lifeless, two more in the 15th. The last round decided the fight; Cruz took the crown by unanimous scores of 143-142, 142-141, and 143-139.

Barry McGuigan (left) and Steve Cruz.

A LITTLE LESS MACHO FOR HECTOR

After the 12 toughest rounds of his professional career, WBC lightweight champion Hector "Macho" Camacho sighed, "If this is macho, I don't want no part of it."

On June 13, Camacho was extremely fortunate to leave the hallowed Madison Square Garden ring with his title belt. His opponent, powerpunching former champion Edwin Rosario, wobbled him in the fifth and 11th rounds, opened a cut on his left eyelid, and drew blood from his nose. Camacho barely survived.

The Macho Man started well, and did enough in the middle rounds to impress the judges. He retained the title by split verdict (two scores of 115-113, and 113-114). The totals drew boos from the crowd. And a ringside poll of boxing writers favored Rosario by 13-6, with 6 votes for a draw.

For the first time in 29 fights, someone had hit Camacho back.

A real macho fighter would have welcomed it. But no one said a nickname had to be accurate.

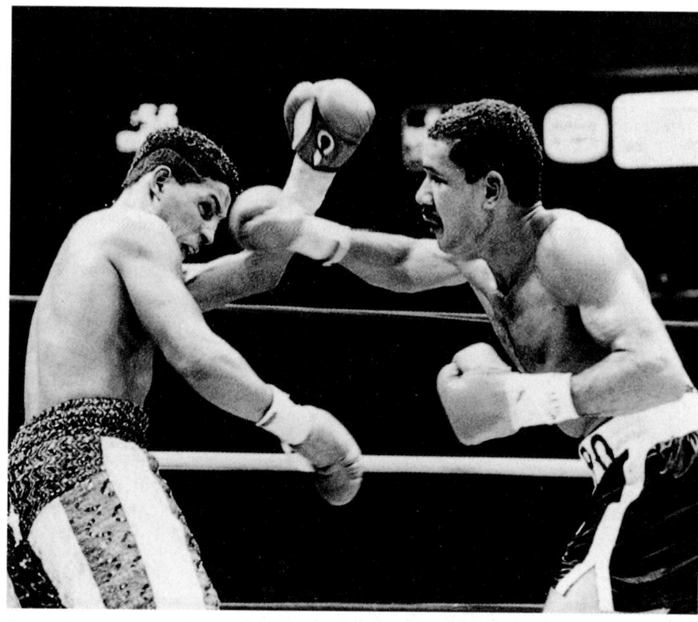

Hector "Macho" Camacho (left) survived a battering to retain the lightweight crown.

WORLD TITLE FIGHTS

HEAVYWEIGHTS

July 19 **Tim Witherspoon** *KO* 11
Frank Bruno, Wembley

CRUISERWEIGHTS

July 12 **Evander Holyfield** (USA) *W* 15
Dwight Qawi, Atlanta

Aug 10 **Carlos DeLeon** *KO* 8
Michael Greer, Giardini Naxos, Italy

JUNIOR MIDDLEWEIGHTS

June 4 **Buster Drayton** (USA) *W* 15
Carlos Santos, East Rutherford, NJ

June 23 **Thomas Hearns** *KO* 8
Mark Medal, Las Vegas

Aug 23 **Mike McCallum** *KO* 2
Julian Jackson, Miami Beach

Aug 24 **Buster Drayton** *KO* 10
Davey Moore, Juan les Pins, France

JUNIOR WELTERWEIGHTS

May 5 **Rene Arredondo** (MEX) *KO* 5
Lonnie Smith, Los Angeles

July 24 **Tsuyoshi Hamada** (JAP) *KO* 1
Rene Arredondo, Tokyo

LIGHTWEIGHTS

June 4 **Jimmy Paul** *W* 15
Cubanito Perez, East Rutherford, NJ

June 13 **Hector Camacho** *W* 12
Edwin Rosario, New York City

Aug 15 **Jimmy Paul** *W* 15
Darryll Tyson, Detroit

JUNIOR LIGHTWEIGHTS

May 15 **Julio Cesar Chavez** *KO* 5
Faustino Barrios, Paris

May 23 **Barry Michael** *KO* 4
Mark Fernandez, Melbourne

May 24 **Alfredo Layne** (PAN) *KO* 9
Wilfredo Gomez, Hato Rey, Puerto Rico

June 13 **Julio Cesar Chavez** *KO* 7
Refugio Rojas, New York City

Aug 3 **Julio Cesar Chavez** *W* 12
Rocky Lockridge, Monte Carlo

Aug 23 **Barry Michael** *W* 15
Najib Daho, Manchester

FEATHERWEIGHTS

May 18 **Ki Yung Chung** *W* 15
Richard Savage, Taegu, South Korea

June 22 **Azumah Nelson** *KO* 10
Danilo Cabrera, San Juan

June 23 **Steve Cruz** (USA) *W* 15
Barry McGuigan, Las Vegas

Aug 30 **Ki Yung Chung** *KO* 10
Antonio Rivera, Pusan, South Korea

JUNIOR FEATHERWEIGHTS

June 1 **Ji Won Kim** *KO* 2
Rudy Casicas, Inchon, South Korea

BANTAMWEIGHTS

June 4 **Bernardo Pinango** (VEN) *W* 15
Gaby Canizales, East Rutherford, NJ

July 18 **Jeff Fenech** *KO* 14
Steve McCrory, Sydney

Aug 23 **Miguel Lora** *KO* 6
Enrique Sanchez, Miami Beach

JUNIOR BANTAMWEIGHTS

May 15 **Gilberto Roman** *W* 12
Edgar Monserrat, Paris

July 5 **Elly Pical** *KO* 3
Cesar Polanco, Djakarta

July 18 **Gilberto Roman** *W* 12
Ruben Condori, Salta, Argentina

Aug 30 **Gilberto Roman** *D* 12
Santos Laciar, Cordoba, Argentina

FLYWEIGHTS

July 5 **Hilario Zapata** *W* 15
Dodie Penalosa, Manila

Aug 2 **Hi Sup Shin** (KOR) *KO* 15
Bi Won Chung, Inchon, South Korea

JUNIOR FLYWEIGHTS

June 14 **Myung Woo Yuh** *KO* 12
Tomohiro Kiyuna, Inchon, South Korea

GOOD AS GOLD? EVEN BETTER

There was a time that Evander Holyfield couldn't box four hard rounds without huffing and puffing. On July 12, at the Omni in his hometown of Atlanta, the *cause celebre* of the 1984 Olympics was asked to go 15 hard rounds in order to dethrone WBA cruiserweight champion Dwight Qawi. It was his 11th fight.

At the Games, Holyfield had settled for a bronze medal; his knockout of New Zealand's Kevin Barry, having come a split second after the referee had ordered a break, resulted in a disqualification. In the pro ranks, however, "The Real Deal" was encouraged to punch whenever he liked. Against Qawi, he delivered a total of 1,290 blows. But the champion managed to work his way inside, and the fighters traded furiously.

"I felt he'd get tired by the sixth or seventh round," said Holyfield, "but he didn't. So I had to put out, put out, put out."

The challenger was rewarded with a split decision (scores of 144-140, 147-138, and 141-143). A huff, a puff, and the right stuff had been enough.

Evander Holyfield (right) won a split decision over Dwight Muhammad Qawi.

RINGSIDE VIEW

MAY

Mexico's Rene Arredondo, a big hitter, and the younger brother of former junior lightweight champion Ricardo Arredondo, wins the WBC super lightweight title with a fifth-round kayo of "Lightning" Lonnie Smith.

AUGUST

WBA junior middleweight champion Mike McCallum survives a toe-to-toe first round and keeps the crown by halting Julian Jackson in round two.

A SPOON-FED DEFEAT FOR THE MAN OF MUSCLE

WBA champion Tim Witherspoon, 234, was slow and bloated. Body-beautiful challenger Frank Bruno, 228, was strong, eager, and chiseled from stone. If a British heavyweight was ever going to be crowned world champion...

On July 19, 'Spoon defended against the immensely popular Bruno before 40,000 hopeful fans at Wembley Stadium. After the first five rounds, the local favorite seemed en route to victory. He matched 'Spoon jab for jab, scored with the occasional right, and determined the tempo.

But in the middle rounds, 'Spoon began to land his overhand right. Having gone the distance only once, Bruno faded, and in the 11th, he met a disastrous fate. 'Spoon struck with four consecutive rights, prompting chief handler Terry Lawless to toss a towel into the ring. Referee Isidro Rodriguez stepped in at the 2:57 mark.

Was it possible that a British heavyweight was never going to be crowned world champion?

Britain's popular Frank Bruno failed in an attempt to win the heavyweight championship when hammered into submission by Tim Witherspoon.

SEPTEMBER

1986

DECEMBER

A ROSARIO IS A ROSARIO IS A...

Every generation has a fighter like Edwin Rosario. Tout him as a future hall of famer and he'll fight without fire. But dismiss him as faded or finished and he'll go and score an upset.

On September 26, at Abel Holz Stadium in Miami Beach, Rosario was a 7-2 underdog vs. WBA lightweight champion Livingstone Bramble. It was the Puerto Rican's first fight since his controversial points loss to WBC champion Hector Camacho. (On the same card, Camacho had retained his share of the title by decisoning Cornelius Boza-Edwards.) Rosario desperately needed a win; he was running out of champions to challenge.

Little happened in the first round. But in the second, Rosario fired a hook that shook the steel-chinned Bramble. What followed was a brutal minute-long assault.

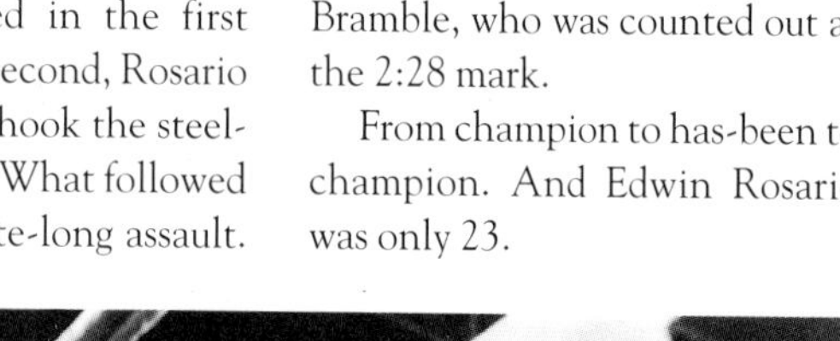

Finally, a right hand dropped Bramble, who was counted out at the 2:28 mark.

From champion to has-been to champion. And Edwin Rosario was only 23.

World Title Fights

HEAVYWEIGHTS

Sept 6	**Michael Spinks** *KO* 4 Steffen Tangstad, Las Vegas
Nov 22	**Mike Tyson** (USA) *KO* 2 Trevor Berbick, Las Vegas
Dec 12	**James (Bonecrusher) Smith** *KO* 1 Tim Witherspoon, New York City

CRUISERWEIGHTS

Oct 25	**Rickey Parkey** (USA) *KO* 10 Lee Roy Murphy, Marsala, Italy

LIGHT HEAVYWEIGHTS

Sept 6	**Bobby Czyz** (USA) *KO* 5 Slobodan Kacar, Las Vegas
Sept 10	**Dennis Andries** *KO* 9 Tony Sibson, London
Sept 20	**Marvin Johnson** *KO* 13 Jean-Marie Emebe, Indianapolis
Dec 26	**Bobby Czyz** *KO* 1 David Sears, West Orange, NJ

JUNIOR MIDDLEWEIGHTS

Oct 25	**Mike McCallum** *KO* 9 Said Skouma, Paris
Dec 5	**Duane Thomas** (USA) *KO* 3 John Mugabi, Las Vegas (Wins Vacant WBC Title)

WELTERWEIGHTS

Sept 27	**Lloyd Honeyghan** (ENG) *KO* 7 Donald Curry, Atlantic City

JUNIOR WELTERWEIGHTS

Sept 6	**Patrizio Oliva** *KO* 3 Brian Brunette, Naples
Oct 30	**Joe Manley** (USA) *KO* 10 Gary Hinton, Hartford
Dec 2	**Tsuyoshi Hamada** *W* 12 Ronnie Shields, Tokyo

LIGHTWEIGHTS

Sept 26	**Edwin Rosario** *KO* 2 Livingstone Bramble, Miami Beach
Sept 26	**Hector Camacho** *W* 12 Cornelius Boza-Edwards, Miami Beach
Dec 5	**Greg Haugen** (USA) *W* 15 Jimmy Paul, Las Vegas

JUNIOR LIGHTWEIGHTS

Sept 27	**Brian Mitchell** (SA) *KO* 10 Alfredo Layne, Sun City
Dec 12	**Julio Cesar Chavez** *W* 12 Juan LaPorte, New York City

JUNIOR FEATHERWEIGHTS

Dec 10	**Samart Payakaroon** *KO* 12 Juan (Kid) Meza, Bangkok

BANTAMWEIGHTS

Oct 4	**Bernardo Pinango** *KO* 10 Ciro de Leva, Turin, Italy
Nov 15	**Miguel Lora** *W* 12 Albert Davila, Barranquilla
Nov 22	**Bernardo Pinango** *KO* 15 Simon Skosana, Johannesburg

JUNIOR BANTAMWEIGHTS

Nov 1	**Khaosai Galaxy** *KO* 5 Israel Contreras, Willemstad, Curacao
Dec 3	**Elly Pical** *KO* 10 Dong Chun Lee, Djakarta
Dec 19	**Gilberto Roman** *W* 12 Kong Payakaroon, Bangkok

FLYWEIGHTS

Sept 13	**Hilario Zapata** *W* 15 Alberto Castro, Panama City
Nov 22	**Hi Sup Shin** *KO* 13 Henry Brent, Chunchon, South Korea
Dec 7	**Hilario Zapata** *W* 15 Claudemir Dias, Salvador, Brazil
Dec 10	**Sot Chitalada** *W* 12 Gabriel Bernal, Bangkok

JUNIOR FLYWEIGHTS

Sept 13	**Jung Koo Chang** *W* 12 Francisco Montiel, Daejon, South Korea
Nov 30	**Myung Woo Yuh** *W* 15 Mario DeMarco, Seoul
Dec 7	**Jum Hwan Choi** (KOR) *W* 15 Cho Woon Park, Pusan, South Korea (Wins Vacant IBF Title)
Dec 14	**Jung Koo Chang** *KO* 5 Hideyuki Ohashi, Inchon, South Korea

Ringside View

SEPTEMBER

South Africa's Brian Mitchell survives a rocky start and wins the WBA junior lightweight title by stopping Alfredo Layne in the 10th round. With the WBA prohibiting title fights in his homeland, Mitchell will have to defend only on the road.

DECEMBER

In a shocker, substitute Bonecrusher Smith captures the WBA heavyweight title with a first-round annihilation of Tim Witherspoon.

Edwin Rosario (right) stopped Livingstone Bramble in the second round of a one-sided bout.

Tim Witherspoon after being kayoed by "Bonecrusher" Smith in WBA heavyweight title bout.

A HONEY OF AN UPSET

British boxing history: Ted (Kid) Lewis. Alan Minter. And on September 27, Lloyd Honeyghan.

In an upset that ranked with the decade's biggest surprises, the Jamaican-born, London-based Honeyghan won the unified welterweight crown by dethroning 6-1 favorite Donald Curry at Caesars Hotel in Atlantic City. He also became only the third British fighter in history to win a world title in the USA.

Undefeated Lloyd Honeyghan (right) stopped Donald Curry to win world welterweight title.

Defending for the eighth time, Curry offered little resistance. "I knew from the first round he was gone," said Honeyghan.

In the fifth, the European champion issued a beating. And in the sixth, he opened a 20-stitch cut over Curry's left eye with what appeared to be a butt, but was ruled a punch. The ringside physician, acting in conjunction with Curry's corner, stopped the fight before the start of round seven.

Curry was supposed to be a legend-in-the-making. Honeyghan had not only made history, but altered it, too.

THE COWERING BEAST

Duane Thomas after kayoing John Mugabi to become new junior middleweight champion.

With John Mugabi coming off 11 tough rounds vs. middleweight champion Marvin Hagler, oddsmakers figured "The Beast" would have little trouble with Kronk contender Duane Thomas. The junior middleweights met for the vacant WBC title on December 5 at Caesars Palace. Mugabi was made a 4-1 favorite. But on a night of upsets – on the same card, Greg Haugen dethroned the IBF lightweight champion Jimmy Paul – he lost in a most unbeastly manner.

Mugabi began by overpowering Thomas. In the third, however, the underdog released a hook that landed on Mugabi's left eye. Several followup blows sent The Beast to the ropes, where he turned his back and began pawing his eye. Left with no choice, referee Carlos Padilla called a halt.

Mugabi's pain was real; he had suffered an orbital fracture below the eye. But he got no sympathy from promoter Bob Arum.

"What rematch?" Arum said. "He got punched in the eye and he quit. That's boxing."

MURDEROUS INTENTIONS

Before WBC heavyweight champion Trevor Berbick's first defense, he dismissed his heavily hyped opponent: "Being ugly and mean is not enough to beat me."

Did he ever underestimate Mike Tyson!

Berbick and the 20-year-old Tyson clashed on November 22 at the Hilton Center in Las Vegas. Already a phenomenon, Tyson 27-0 (25), was made a 4-1 favorite. Still, his victory made eyes pop.

By the end of the first round, the stoic assassin was punishing the 34-year-old Berbick with powerful and sizzling combinations. "I was throwing hydrogen bombs," he explained. "Every punch had murderous intentions."

In the second, a hook toppled the usually sturdy champion, and later in the round, another hook left him falling over himself. Referee Mills Lane intervened.

At age 12, Tyson had been discovered by his mentor, the late Cus D'Amato. Eight years later, he was crowned the youngest heavyweight champion in history. D'Amato, who had been sure, had also been right.

Undefeated Mike Tyson becomes the youngest heavyweight champion of all-time.

Barry McGuigan

RARE indeed is a fighter whose appeal transcends the ring. Over the course of the modern era, only a handful of champions, most notably Muhammad Ali and Joe Louis, dare command a world stage.

What made Barry McGuigan both remarkable and unique is that while he lacked the credentials of the ring immortals, he was, in his own way, as significant as any fighter of his time. Perhaps the best way to put it is that when McGuigan fought, there was peace.

Born on February 28, 1961, Patrick Finbar (Barry) McGuigan was one of eight children raised by Pat and Kate McGuigan. Pat worked as a railway worker, bus conductor, and, ultimately, professional singer. Kate ran a grocery store in Clones, County Monaghan, Ireland, at which Barry bulked up by carrying 50-pound bags of potatoes with either hand. One day, he found a pair of boxing gloves in a closet. We can only presume that the first punch he threw was a left hook.

"When I was six stone (84 pounds)," McGuigan recalled, "I could knock guys spark out with one punch. Other boys could sting an opponent, but I would flatten them."

No Irish boxer ever captured the hearts and souls of his countrymen as did Ulster's Patrick Finbar McGuigan, popularly beloved as "Barry."

In 1977, after McGuigan won the All-Ireland tournament, he was described by *Boxing News* as "a 16-year-old with a big future." He gradually advanced to international competition, and represented his homeland at the 1980 Olympic Games in Moscow. Boxing in the 125-pound class, he was outpointed by Zambia's Wilfred Kabunda in his second bout of the competition.

A natural puncher with big hands and a considerable reach, McGuigan was forever working to perfect his hook. He was considered a hot pro prospect despite his failure in Moscow, and after being wooed by Mickey Duff, Terry Lawless, and the biggest names in British boxing, he signed with the urbane Barney Eastwood, a millionaire from Belfast who owned a string of betting shops.

With trainer Eddie Shaw in his corner, McGuigan turned pro on May 10, 1981, at the Dalymount Park soccer grounds in Dublin. His opponent, Jamaica's Selvin Bell, had 42 losses in 58 fights, and McGuigan, 20, finished business in two rounds. He also won his second bout by kayo, but in his third test, he was shocked by journeyman Peter Eubanks, who outpointed him over eight rounds by the referee's score of 78½-78. McGuigan wouldn't lose again for five years.

One of the victories, however, brought more pain than a dozen unanswered blows. In McGuigan's 12th pro bout, he scored a sixth-round knockout of Young Ali. En route to the dressing room, Ali collapsed and fell into a coma, from which he never recovered. Six months later, on December 13, 1982, Ali died in his native Nigeria.

"I couldn't believe that I could kill somebody, with my own hands," McGuigan said.

After a bout with depression, McGuigan returned to the ring, and on April

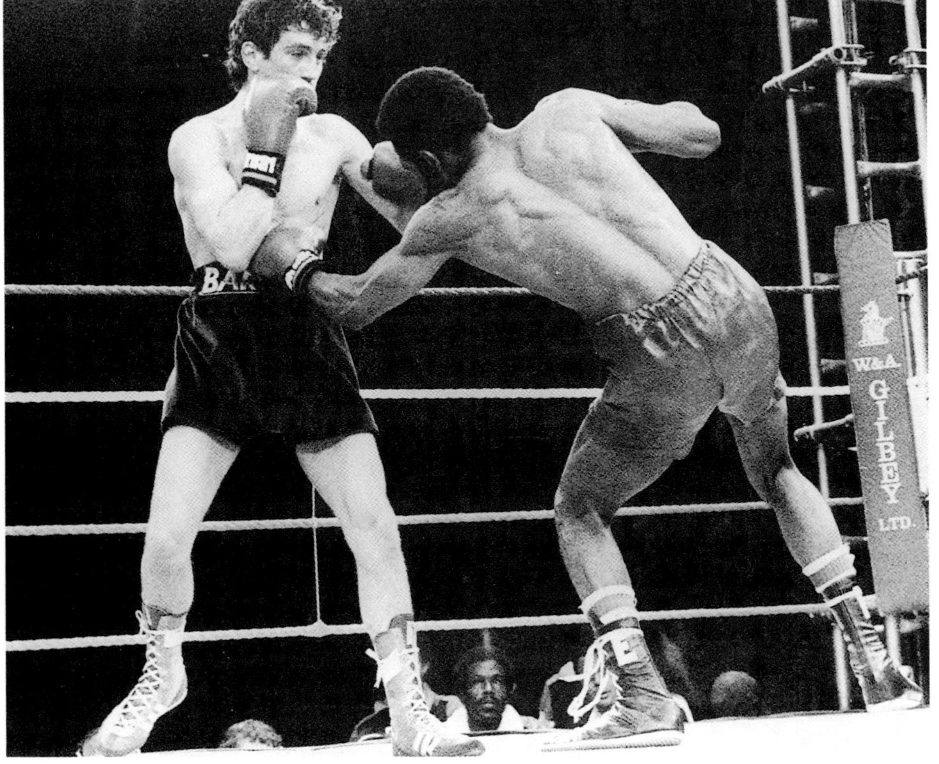

Barry's victory over Panama's Eusebio Pedroza (right) in London, June 8, 1985, earned him the WBA featherweight title and set off week-long celebrations in Ireland.

12, 1983, he won the vacant British featherweight title by stopping the unexceptional Vernon Penprase in two rounds. In order to qualify for the fight, McGuigan had to apply for British citizenship, which, Eastwood feared, would alienate the fighter's base of Irish supporters. But as would be the case when his fights became special events, McGuigan's natural charisma and unaffected charm served to unite all of those who watched him.

"I know who I am; I'm Irish, and I'll always be Irish," he said.

He was also Catholic, and his wife, Sandra, was Protestant. During his brief career, Belfast, which sits only 75 miles from Clones, was a battleground. But at least four or five times a year, both sides, Catholic and Protestant, agreed to "let McGuigan do the fighting."

And the fighting was all in his favor. On November 16, 1983, McGuigan added the vacant European 126-pound title to his resume, rising from the canvas to kayo Italy's Valerio Nati in six rounds. After studying an action photo of the legendary Alexis Arguello, McGuigan had perfected his hook; Nati was taken to the hospital with three cracked ribs.

On June 30, 1984, McGuigan thrilled 7,000 fans at Belfast's King's Hall, as well as a U.S. television audience, with a dominant fifth-round knockout of New York fringe contender Paul DeVorce. Eight months later, the competition was stiffer. But McGuigan was also better, and he survived the bombs of former world champion Juan LaPorte to win a 10-round decision.

The victory broke McGuigan's 18-bout kayo streak, but it also boosted him to 25-1 (22), and clearly established him as the premier threat to world champions Azumah Nelson (WBC) and Eusebio Pedroza (WBA). Eastwood was able to convince the fading Pedroza to travel to London – a division record purse of more than $1-million was far too appealing to reject – and on June 8, 1985, before 25,000 fanatical McGuigan supporters at the Loftus Road Stadium, the slick Panamanian defended the crown for the 20th and final time.

Over 15 rounds, McGuigan proved that he was much more than a one-dimensional

Professional career dates 1981-86; 1988-89
Contests 35
Won 32
Lost 3
Drawn 0
Knockouts 28
World Featherweight Champion 1985-1986

hooker. He boxed well, scored most often with his right, and, in the seventh round, floored the champion en route to a commanding decision victory. *Boxing News* described it as "the greatest (performance) in a British ring since Randolph Turpin's win over Sugar Ray Robinson 34 years ago."

Immediately after the decision was announced, McGuigan was relatively subdued. In a voice choking with emotion, he told BBC-TV's Harry Carpenter, "There's one thing I've been thinking about all week. I want to dedicate this world title to the young lad who fought me in 1982, Young Ali. At least it wasn't an ordinary fighter who beat him, but a world champion."

McGuigan returned home to a joyous parade, but he wasn't fully content. A growing rift with Eastwood was gnawing at him; he wasn't satisfied with the manner in which the manager handled his affairs. Over the next several months, communication gradually broke down, and lawsuits and counter suits were filed. (So affected was McGuigan by his ugly and highly publicized split with Eastwood that after his retirement, he began an effort to unionize British boxers. That effort succeeded in 1993.)

McGuigan successfully defended the title twice, knocking out classy American Bernard Taylor in six rounds, and halting stubborn Dominican Danilo Cabrera in 14. But in his third defense, he encountered a new and difficult foe – the 110-degree heat of Las Vegas – and succumbed on points to substitute Steve Cruz after 15 action-packed rounds. McGuigan lost 12 pounds of body fluid and was badly dehydrated by the late stages, but it took two last-round knockdowns for 5-2 underdog Cruz to secure the verdict. After the bout, the suddenly former champion was hospitalized in a semi-delirious state until the IV took effect.

The loss to Cruz cost McGuigan his title, but the loss of his father, who died of lymphoma in June 1987, cost him his spirit. There would be four comeback bouts, but after defeating Julio Miranda in December 1988, McGuigan sensed the finish. He retired at age 28 after being stopped on cuts by Jim McDonnell on May 31, 1989. He promised to initiate no further comebacks, and so far, has kept his word.

McGuigan had done the fighting. It was time for him to enjoy the peace.

McGuigan (right) met the great Roberto Duran before making what proved to be his disastrous American debut against Steve Cruz, in which he lost the featherweight crown.

JANUARY

1987

APRIL

A DIFFERENT KIND OF EXCUSE

IBF junior welterweight champion Joe Manley suffered from lactose intolerance. Regrettably, he wasn't always careful about his diet. His lack of discipline cost him on March 4, when he defended vs. former European champion Terry Marsh inside of a circus tent in the unbeaten challenger's hometown of Basildon, England.

Manley weighed in at 138½, but by fight time, vomiting and diarrhea had dropped him to 134. Sensing his opponent's lack of strength, Marsh immediately attacked. Manley initially fought back, then began to clinch. By the eighth, he was surviving on instinct. Marsh scored knockdowns in the ninth and 10th, and after the champion's second fall, referee Randy Neuman stepped in at the 20-second mark.

There was no denying that Marsh took advantage of his opportunity. But in truth, Manley had been the first champion in history to be beaten by milk, cheese, and ice cream.

RINGSIDE VIEW

MARCH

WBC heavyweight champion Mike Tyson adds the WBA crown by scoring a unanimous 12-round decision over a reluctant Bonecrusher Smith.

Mike Tyson (right) decisioned "Bonecrusher" Smith to win WBA title and retain WBC crown.

Terry Marsh (left) stopped Joe Manley in the 10th round to win the junior welterweight crown.

THE HUNT OF THE HIT MAN

It was Thomas Hearns' goal to become the first fighter to win world titles at four different weights. On March 7, the former welterweight and junior middleweight champion took the third and perhaps most difficult step by challenging WBC light heavyweight king Dennis Andries at Cobo Arena in "The Hit Man's" hometown of Detroit.

Hearns scaled 173¾, and wore the weight well. He retained enough speed and quickness to outmaneuver Andries, and carried his power, too, scoring six knockdowns.

Andries opened a cut over Hearns' left eye in round two, but that was his sole highlight. Hearns felled the Guyana-born, England-based champion four times in the sixth, once in the ninth, and again in the 10th, at which point referee Ariel Herrera waved off the fight.

The Hit Man had no intention of defending the crown. "I've got to go back to the middleweight division," he said.

History was beckoning.

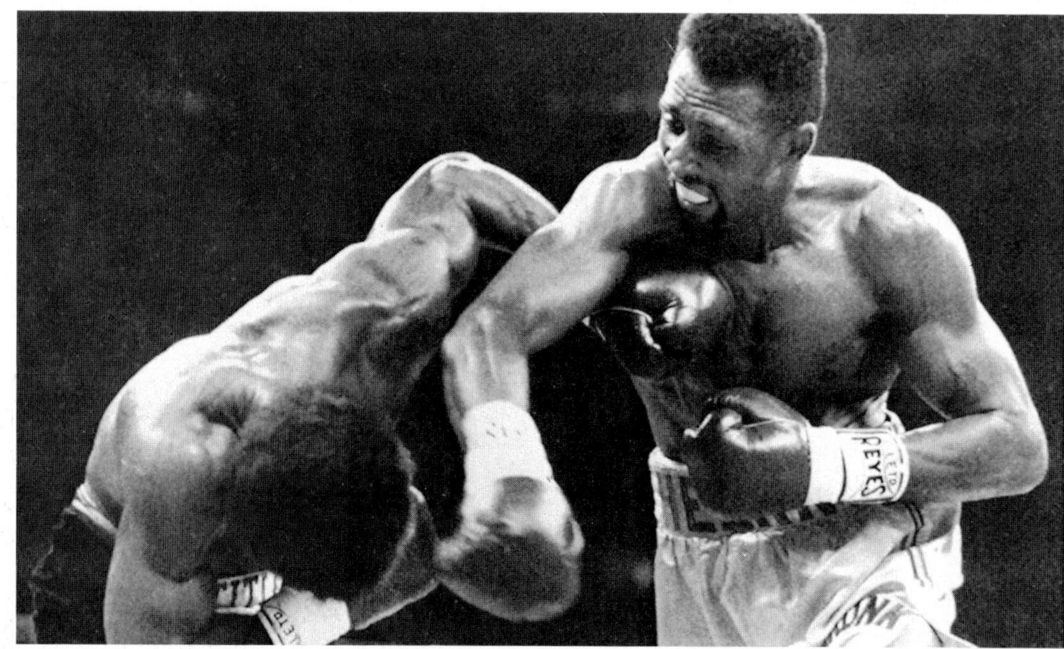

Thomas Hearns (right) stopped Britain's Dennis Andries in the 10th to win his third world championship, the WBC light heavyweight crown.

THE CONTINUING MIRACLE OF SUGAR RAY

Sugar Ray Leonard's umpteenth comeback brought his ultimate test. Inactive for almost three years, the 30-year-old former champion returned for a singular reason: to defeat Marvelous Marvin Hagler. It seemed that Leonard's reach was exceeding his grasp; Hagler had made 12 defenses of the middleweight title, and was unbeaten over 11 years. But a lesser challenge wouldn't have motivated Sugar Ray.

In one of the most anticipated duels of the decade, Leonard and Hagler squared off on April 6, before 15,336 at Caesars Palace. Hagler, a 3-1 favorite, showed far too much patience over the first four rounds. He worked his way inside in the fifth, and the rest of the battle, including a thrilling round nine, featured frequent shifts of momentum. Hagler landed the harder blows, and Leonard the flashier flurries.

After 12 rounds, Leonard was awarded a split decision (scores of 115-113, a ridiculous 118-110, and 113-115).

"He wanted it so bad," said Sugar Ray's brother, Kenny. "That's what kept him going."

RINGSIDE VIEW

MARCH

In the flyweight fight of the decade, Colombia's Fidel Bassa retains the WBA title with a 13th-round stoppage of Irish challenger Dave McAuley. Bassa, downed twice in the ninth, was behind on all three cards at the time of the stoppage.

MARCH

Ending a 10-year retirement, former heavyweight champion George Foreman, 38, kayos Steve Zouski in four rounds.

Sugar Ray Leonard (left) was awarded a split 12-round decision over Marvelous Marvin Hagler.

WORLD TITLE FIGHTS

HEAVYWEIGHTS

March 7 **Mike Tyson** *W* 12
Bonecrusher Smith, Las Vegas
(Wins WBA Title; Retains WBC Title)

CRUISERWEIGHTS

Feb 14 **Evander Holyfield** *KO* 7
Henry Tillman, Reno

Feb 21 **Carlos DeLeon** *KO* 4
Angelo Rottoli, Bergamo, Italy

March 28 **Rickey Parkey** *KO* 12
Chisanda Mutti, Lido de Camaiore, Italy

LIGHT HEAVYWEIGHTS

Feb 21 **Bobby Czyz** *KO* 2
Willie Edwards, Atlantic City

March 7 **Thomas Hearns** *KO* 10
Dennis Andries, Detroit

SUPER MIDDLEWEIGHTS

Jan 25 **Chong Pal Park** *KO* 15
Doug Sam, Seoul

MIDDLEWEIGHTS

April 6 **Sugar Ray Leonard** *W* 12
Marvin Hagler, Las Vegas

JUNIOR MIDDLEWEIGHTS

March 27 **Buster Drayton** *KO* 10
Said Skouma, Cannes

April 19 **Mike McCallum** *KO* 10
Milton McCrory, Phoenix

WELTERWEIGHTS

Feb 6 **Mark Breland** (USA) *KO* 7
Harold Volbrecht, Atlantic City
(Wins Vacant WBA Title)

Feb 22 **Lloyd Honeyghan** *KO* 2
Johnny Bumphus, Wembley

April 18 **Lloyd Honeyghan** *W* 12
Maurice Blocker, London

JUNIOR WELTERWEIGHTS

Jan 10 **Patrizio Oliva** *W* 15
Gato Gonzalez, Agrigento, Italy

March 4 **Terry Marsh** (ENG) *KO* 10
Joe Manley, Basildon, England

JUNIOR LIGHTWEIGHTS

March 27 **Brian Mitchell** *D* 15
Jose Rivera, San Juan

April 18 **Julio Cesar Chavez** *KO* 3
Tomas DaCruz, Nimes, France

FEATHERWEIGHTS

March 6 **Antonio Esparragoza** (VEN) *KO* 12
Steve Cruz, Fort Worth

March 7 **Azumah Nelson** *KO* 6
Mauro Gutierrez, Las Vegas

JUNIOR FEATHERWEIGHTS

Jan 16 **Louie Espinoza** (USA) *KO* 4
Tommy Valoy, Phoenix
(Wins Vacant WBA Title)

Jan 18 **Seung Hoon Lee** (KOR) *KO* 9
Prayurasak Muangsurin, Pohang, South Korea
(Wins Vacant IBF Title)

April 5 **Seung Hoon Lee** *KO* 10
Jorge Diaz, Seoul

BANTAMWEIGHTS

Feb 3 **Bernardo Pinango** *W* 15
Frankie Duarte, Inglewood

March 29 **Takuya Muguruma** (JAP) *KO* 5
Azael Moran, Moriguchi, Japan
(Wins Vacant WBA Title)

JUNIOR BANTAMWEIGHTS

Jan 30 **Gilberto Roman** *KO* 9
Antoine Montero, Montpellier, France

Feb 28 **Khaosai Galaxy** *KO* 14
Elly Pical, Jakarta

March 20 **Gilberto Roman** *W* 12
Frank Cedeno, Calexico, Mexico

FLYWEIGHTS

Feb 13 **Fidel Bassa** (COL) *W* 15
Hilario Zapata, Barranquilla

Feb 22 **Dodie Penalosa** (PHI) *KO* 5
Hi Sup Shin, Inchon, South Korea

April 25 **Fidel Bassa** *KO* 13
Dave McAuley, Belfast

JUNIOR FLYWEIGHTS

March 1 **Myung Woo Yuh** *KO* 1
Eduardo Tunon, Seoul

March 29 **Jum Hwan Choi** *W* 15
Tacy Macalos, Suwon, South Korea

April 19 **Jung Koo Chang** *KO* 6
Efren Pinto, Inchon, South Korea

MAY

1987

AUGUST

THE ONE AND ONLY

In May, Tony Tucker won the vacant IBF heavyweight title by stopping Buster Douglas. (Michael Spinks had been stripped for fighting Gerry Cooney.) The victory should have guaranteed the unbeaten champion a lucrative and promising future. But all it brought was a dark date with Mike Tyson.

On August 1, at the Hilton Center in Las Vegas, Tucker and WBA-WBC champion Tyson met to unify the title for the first time in almost 10 years. The 6'5" Tucker, 35-0, was a talented boxer-puncher. But against "Iron Mike," he was given almost no chance; Tyson answered the bell an 8-1 favorite.

It was a forgettable fight. Tucker started by staggering Tyson with a left uppercut 20 seconds into the bout. After fracturing his right hand in round two, however, the underdog threatened no more. He boxed well in spurts, but Tyson's aggressiveness and superior strength eliminated any chance of an upset. He took a unanimous 12-round verdict by 119-111, 118-113, and 116-112.

Tyson (left) wins unanimous 12-round decision over Tony Tucker to become unified champ.

WORLD TITLE FIGHTS

HEAVYWEIGHTS

May 30 **Mike Tyson** *KO* 6
Pinklon Thomas, Las Vegas

May 30 **Tony Tucker** (USA) *KO* 10
Buster Douglas, Las Vegas
(Wins Vacant IBF Title)

Aug 1 **Mike Tyson** *W* 12
Tony Tucker, Las Vegas
(Unifies World Title)

CRUISERWEIGHTS

May 15 **Evander Holyfield** *KO* 3
Rickey Parkey, Las Vegas
(Wins IBF Title; Retains WBA Title)

Aug 15 **Evander Holyfield** *KO* 11
Osvaldo Ocasio, St. Tropez

LIGHT HEAVYWEIGHTS

May 3 **Bobby Czyz** *KO* 6
Jim MacDonald, Atlantic City

May 23 **Leslie Stewart** (TRI) *KO* 9
Marvin Johnson, Port-of-Spain, Trinidad

SUPER MIDDLEWEIGHTS

May 3 **Chong Pal Park** *W* 15
Lindell Holmes, Inchon

July 26 **Chong Pal Park** *KO* 4
Emmanuel Otti, Kwangju, South Korea

JUNIOR MIDDLEWEIGHTS

June 27 **Matthew Hilton** (CAN) *W* 15
Buster Drayton, Montreal

July 12 **Lupe Aquino** (USA) *W* 12
Duane Thomas, Bordeaux, France

July 18 **Mike McCallum** *KO* 5
Donald Curry, Las Vegas

WELTERWEIGHTS

Aug 22 **Marlon Starling** (USA) *KO* 11
Mark Breland, Columbia, SC

Aug 30 **Lloyd Honeyghan** *KO* 1
Gene Hatcher, Marbella, Spain

JUNIOR WELTERWEIGHTS

July 1 **Terry Marsh** *KO* 6
Akio Kameda, London

July 4 **Juan Coggi** (ARG) *KO* 3
Patrizio Oliva, Ribera, Italy

July 22 **Rene Arredondo** *KO* 6
Tsuyoshi Hamada, Tokyo

LIGHTWEIGHTS

June 7 **Vinny Pazienza** (USA) *W* 15
Greg Haugen, Providence

July 19 **Jose Luis Ramirez** *W* 12
Terrence Alli, St. Tropez
(Wins Vacant WBC Title)

Aug 11 **Edwin Rosario** *KO* 8
Juan Nazario, Chicago

JUNIOR LIGHTWEIGHTS

July 31 **Brian Mitchell** *KO* 14
Francisco Fernandez, Panama City

Aug 9 **Rocky Lockridge** *KO* 8
Barry Michael, Windsor

Aug 21 **Julio Cesar Chavez** *W* 12
Danilo Cabrera, Tijuana

FEATHERWEIGHTS

July 26 **Antonio Esparragoza** *KO* 10
Pascual Aranda, Houston

Aug 29 **Azumah Nelson** *W* 12
Marcos Villasana, Los Angeles

JUNIOR FEATHERWEIGHTS

May 8 **Jeff Fenech** *KO* 4
Samart Payakaroon, Sydney

July 10 **Jeff Fenech** *KO* 5
Greg Richardson, Sydney

July 15 **Louie Espinoza** *KO* 15
Manuel Vilchez, Phoenix

July 19 **Seung Hoon Lee** *KO* 5
Leon Collins, Pohang, South Korea

Aug 15 **Louie Espinoza** *KO* 9
Mike Ayala, San Antonio

BANTAMWEIGHTS

May 15 **Kelvin Seabrooks** (USA) *KO* 5
Miguel Maturana, Cartagena
(Wins Vacant IBF Title)

May 24 **Chan Young Park** (KOR) *KO* 11
Takuya Muguruma, Moriguchi, Japan

July 4 **Kelvin Seabrooks** *KO* 9
Thierry Jacob, Calais, France

July 25 **Miguel Lora** *KO* 4
Antonio Avelar, Key Biscayne, FL

JUNIOR BANTAMWEIGHTS

May 16 **Santos Laciar** *KO* 11
Gilberto Roman, Reims, France

May 17 **Tae Il Chang** (KOR) *W* 15
Soon Chun Kwon, Pusan, South Korea
(Wins Vacant IBF Title)

Aug 8 **Baby Sugar Rojas** (COL) *W* 12
Santos Laciar, Miami

FLYWEIGHTS

Aug 15 **Fidel Bassa** *D* 15
Hilario Zapata, Panama City

JUNIOR FLYWEIGHTS

June 7 **Myung Woo Yuh** *KO* 15
Benedicto Murillo, Pusan, South Korea

June 28 **Jung Koo Chang** *KO* 10
Agustin Garcia, Inchon, South Korea

July 5 **Jum Hwan Choi** *KO* 4
Toshihiko Matsuda, Seoul

Aug 9 **Jum Hwan Choi** *KO* 3
Azadin Anhar, Jakarta

STRAWWEIGHTS

June 14 **Kyung Yun Lee** (KOR) *KO* 2
Masaharu Kawakami, Bujok, South Korea
(Wins Newly Created IBF Title)

RINGSIDE VIEW

MAY

WBA cruiserweight champion Evander Holyfield partially unifies the title by knocking out IBF champion Rickey Parkey in the third round of a slugfest. "The Real Deal's" next target: WBC champion Carlos DeLeon.

JUNE

Vinny Pazienza wins the IBF lightweight title by rallying down the stretch and scoring a controversial 15-round decision over Greg Haugen.

JUNE

Canada's Matthew Hilton thrills an overflow Montreal Forum crowd by unanimously outpointing durable IBF junior middleweight champion Buster Drayton over 15 rounds.

Matthew Hilton wins the junior middleweight title by outpointing Buster Drayton.

CLASHING AT THE CROSSROADS

In boxing, age is a relative thing. WBA junior middleweight champion Mike McCallum, 30, was on the rise; former welterweight titlist Donald Curry, 25, was on the decline. Still, the result of their July 18 battle, fought at Caesars Palace, was somewhat of a surprise.

Making his sixth defense, McCallum had the game, but lacked Curry's name. What he needed was a highlight-film knockout. Early in the bout, it seemed that he would be the victim; in the second, Curry blasted the champion with a left-right. "It was the closest to the canvas I ever came," McCallum acknowledged.

Upon recovering, McCallum began to set up his foe for a sneak hook. In the fifth, Curry dropped his hands to protect his ribs, and McCallum struck. Boom! A tremendous left stretched Curry for referee Richard Steele's full count. Spectacular, indeed.

Said the victor, "Do you think everybody knows who Mike McCallum is now?"

Mike McCallum (left) knocked out Donald Curry to retain the junior middleweight title.

WAY OFF THE MARK

The Class of '84 produced several world champions. The valedictorian, gold medal winner Mark Breland, was supposed to be the best and the brightest. In fact, one boxing writer even touted him as the next Sugar Ray Robinson.

Breland won his first title easily enough, stopping Harold Volbrecht to capture the vacant WBA welterweight crown. But his August 22 defense vs. clever veteran Marlon Starling, held at the Township Auditorium in Columbia, South Carolina, represented his first legitimate test.

Breland entered the ring with torn cartilage in his left ribcage, and while he boxed reasonably well, he appeared fragile. Whenever Starling worked inside, Breland either slipped to the canvas, or was pushed. He fell no less than eight times.

Behind on points, Starling broke through in the 11th. He moved the champion to the ropes, and then exploded with a crunching hook. Boom! Breland barely beat the count of referee Tony Perez, but wasn't allowed to continue.

Can there be an ending to a legend that never really began?

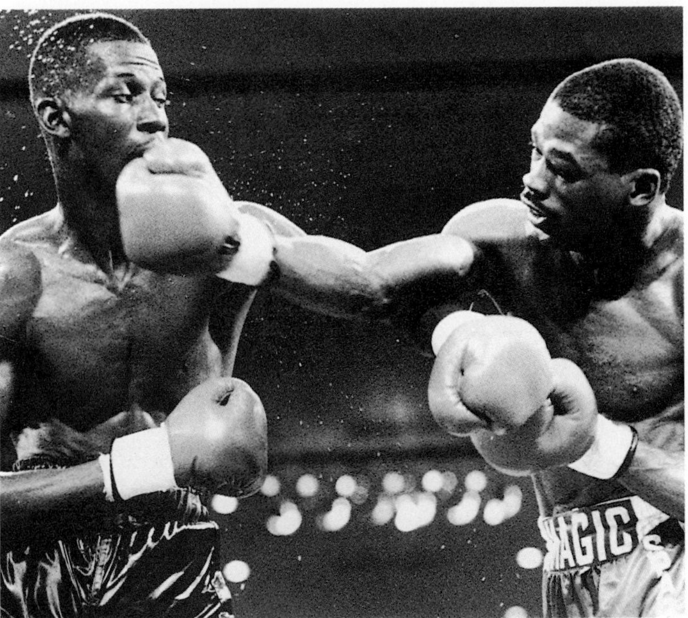

Marlon Starling (right) was trailing on all scorecards when he knocked out Mark Breland.

SEPTEMBER

1987

DECEMBER

THE BEATING ON THE BOARDWALK

Heavyweight champion Mike Tyson was generally respectful of his opponents. But that never stopped him from destroying them. On October 16, at Convention Hall in Atlantic City, he demonstrated what he could do to a fighter he didn't respect. It was a frightening spectacle.

At the 1984 Olympics, Tyrell Biggs won a gold medal. Tyson, on the other hand, had failed to qualify for the Games. And for seven rounds, he took his frustrations out on the challenger. Biggs boxed beautifully for three minutes. Then Tyson went to work. He cut his rival on the left brow, the right cheek, the mouth, and the bridge of the nose, pummeled him to the body, and, despite Biggs' nine-inch reach advantage, outjabbed him.

Biggs' ability to take a punch prolongued the beating. In the seventh, he finally fell. After the round's second knockdown, referee Tony Orlando called a halt.

Too bad; no doubt Tyson would have liked it to have lasted a whole lot longer.

Heavyweight champion Mike Tyson (right) overpowered brave, durable Tyrell Biggs.

FIGHTING TALK

I was hitting him with punches to the body, and he was making noises. It was somewhat like a woman screaming

MIKE TYSON
on his fight with Tyrell Biggs

WORLD TITLE FIGHTS

HEAVYWEIGHTS

Oct 16 **Mike Tyson** *KO 7*
Tyrell Biggs, Atlantic City

CRUISERWEIGHTS

Dec 5 **Evander Holyfield** *KO 4*
Dwight Qawi, Atlantic City

LIGHT HEAVYWEIGHTS

Sept 5 **Virgil Hill** (USA) *KO 4*
Leslie Stewart, Atlantic City

Oct 29 **Charles Williams** (USA) *KO 9*
Bobby Czyz, Las Vegas

Nov 21 **Virgil Hill** *W 12*
Rufino Angulo, Paris

Nov 27 **Don Lalonde** (CAN) *KO 2*
Eddie Davis, Port-of-Spain, Trinidad
(Wins Vacant WBC Title)

SUPER MIDDLEWEIGHTS

Dec 6 **Chong Pal Park** *KO 2*
Jesus Gallardo, Pusan, South Korea

MIDDLEWEIGHTS

Oct 10 **Frank Tate** (USA) *W 15*
Michael Olajide, Las Vegas
(Wins Vacant IBF Title)

Oct 23 **Sumbu Kalambay** (ZAI) *W 15*
Iran Barkley, Livorno, Italy
(Wins Vacant WBA Title)

Oct 29 **Thomas Hearns** *KO 4*
Juan Domingo Roldan, Las Vegas

JUNIOR MIDDLEWEIGHTS

Oct 2 **Gianfranco Rosi** (ITA) *W 12*
Lupe Aquino, Perugia, Italy

Oct 16 **Matthew Hilton** *KO 2*
Jack Callahan, Atlantic City

Nov 21 **Julian Jackson** (VI) *KO 3*
In Chul Baek, Las Vegas
(Wins Vacant WBA Title)

WELTERWEIGHTS

Oct 28 **Jorge Vaca** (MEX) *Tech Dec 8*
Lloyd Honeyghan, Wembley

JUNIOR WELTERWEIGHTS

Nov 12 **Roger Mayweather** *KO 6*
Rene Arredondo, Los Angeles

LIGHTWEIGHTS

Oct 10 **Jose Luis Ramirez** *KO 5*
Cornelius Boza-Edwards, Paris

Nov 21 **Julio Cesar Chavez** *KO 11*
Edwin Rosario, Las Vegas

JUNIOR LIGHTWEIGHTS

Oct 3 **Brian Mitchell** *W 15*
Daniel Londas, Gravelines, France

Oct 25 **Rocky Lockridge** *KO 10*
Johnny de la Rosa, Tucson

Dec 19 **Brian Mitchell** *KO 8*
Salvatore Curcetti, Capo D'Orlando, Italy

JUNIOR FEATHERWEIGHTS

Oct 16 **Jeff Fenech** *Tech Dec 4*
Carlos Zarate, Sydney

Nov 28 **Julio Gervacio** (DR) *W 12*
Louie Espinoza, San Juan

Dec 27 **Seung Hoon Lee** *W 15*
Jose Sanabria, Pohang, South Korea

BANTAMWEIGHTS

Oct 4 **Wilfredo Vasquez** (PR) *KO 10*
Chan Young Park, Seoul

Nov 18 **Kelvin Seabrooks** *KO 4*
Ernie Cataluna, San Cataldo, Italy

Nov 27 **Miguel Lora** *W 12*
Ray Minus, Miami Beach

JUNIOR BANTAMWEIGHTS

Oct 12 **Khaosai Galaxy** *KO 3*
Byung Kwan Chung, Bangkok

Oct 17 **Elly Pical** *W 15*
Tae Il Chang, Jakarta

Oct 24 **Baby Sugar Rojas** *KO 4*
Gustavo Ballas, Miami

FLYWEIGHTS

Sept 5 **Sot Chitalada** *KO 4*
Rae Ki Ahn, Bangkok

Sept 5 **Chang Ho Choi** (KOR) *KO 11*
Dodie Penalosa, Quezon City

Dec 18 **Fidel Bassa** *W 12*
Felix Marti, Cartagena

JUNIOR FLYWEIGHTS

Sept 20 **Myung Woo Yuh** *KO 8*
Rodolfo Blanco, Inchon, South Korea

Dec 13 **Jung Koo Chang** *W 12*
Isidro Perez, Taejon, South Korea

STRAWWEIGHTS

Oct 18 **Hiroki Ioka** (JAP) *W 12*
Mai Thonburifarm, Osaka
(Wins Newly Created WBC Title)

Ringside View

SEPTEMBER

Virgil Hill, a forgotten member of the record-setting 1984 U.S. Olympic team, wins the WBA light heavyweight title with a fourth-round stoppage of Leslie Stewart.

NOVEMBER

Julio Cesar Chavez wins his second world title, and recognition as one of the best fighters in boxing, by scoring an 11th-round TKO over defending WBA lightweight champion Edwin Rosario.

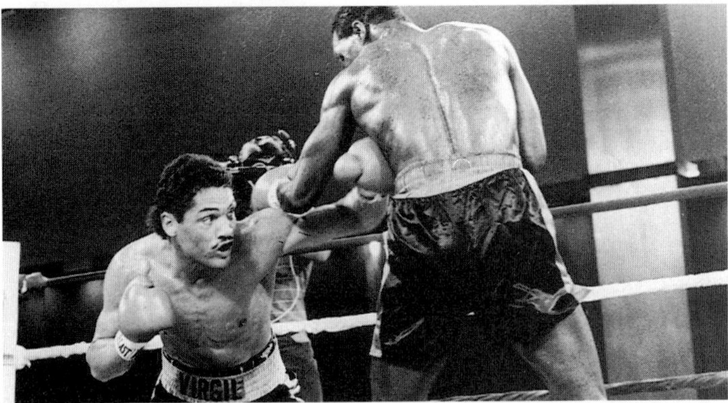

Virgil Hill (left) knocked out Leslie Stewart in their WBA light heavyweight title match.

WINNING NUMBER FOUR, AND LOOKING FOR MORE

Thomas Hearns had suffered knockout losses to Sugar Ray Leonard and Marvin Hagler. But on October 29, at the Hilton Center in Las Vegas, he secured what he perceived to be a measure of revenge.

Matched against Argentina's Juan Roldan in a battle for the vacant WBC middleweight crown, "The Hit Man" attempted to become the first fighter in history to win titles in four different divisions. Armed with a seven-inch reach advantage, it was Hearns' plan to jab from long range. Roldan charged from his corner, however, and immediately initiated a brawl.

It seemed only Hearns' punches counted. He scored two knockdowns in the first round, one in the second, and another in the fourth, when Roldan was counted out by referee Mills Lane.

"I have something that Ray Leonard doesn't have," said Hearns. "I have something that Marvin Hagler doesn't have. And I have something no man in the history of boxing has. I'm a very proud young man right now."

Thomas Hearns (right) flattened Juan Roldan.

A MOST UNTIMELY BUTT TURNS HONEY SOUR

It seemed that as suddenly as Lloyd Honeyghan conquered the world, he fell from grace. On October 28, the British welterweight defended the WBC crown vs. Mexican veteran Jorge Vaca at Wembley Arena's Grand Hall.

The first three rounds were furious, with Vaca taking Honeyghan's best shots and answering with plenty of his own. The pace slowed until late in the seventh.

In the fateful eighth, the fighters accidentally clashed heads, and Vaca began pouring blood from a cut over his right eye. The bout was immediately stopped. According to WBC rules, the fight was decided by the cards. The key: referee Henry Elespuru's deduction of a point from Honeyghan for the butt. The penalty propelled Vaca to a split decision victory (scores of 67-65, 67-66, and 65-67).

There would be a rematch, but for Honeyghan, the fire was now just a flame.

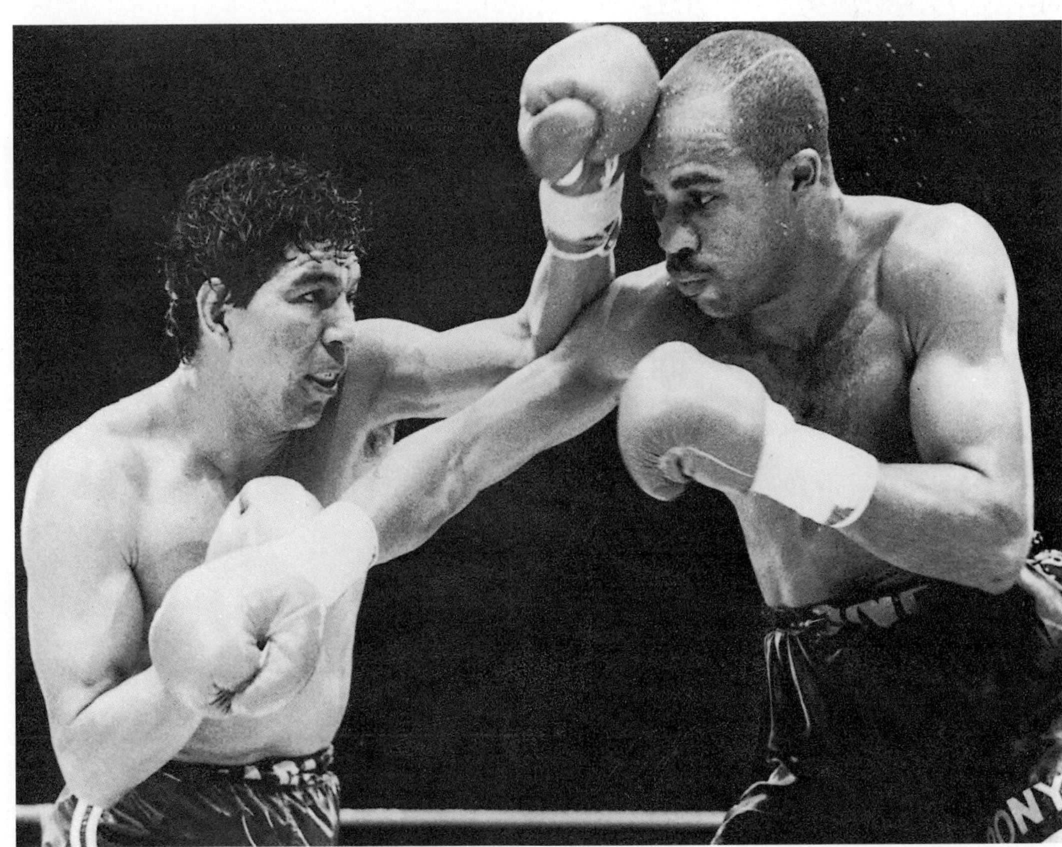

Mexico's Jorge Vaca (left) won after being unable to continue because of a butt from defending welterweight king Lloyd Honeyghan.

JANUARY

1988

APRIL

NO WAY TO TREAT A GRANDFATHER

Why would a rich and famous grandfather risk his limbs against as destructive a physical force as Mike Tyson? Because proud fighters need to go out on their shields.

On January 22, at Convention Hall in Atlantic City, world heavyweight champion Tyson, 21, defended against comebacking former champion Larry Holmes, 38. It was Holmes' first fight since April 1986, when he lost a bitter decision in his rematch vs. Michael Spinks.

Holmes planned to frustrate Tyson with his ring smarts, but his only effective tactic was clinching. So eager that he had punched a hole in his dressing room wall, Tyson exploded in the fourth. Capitalizing on Holmes' tendency to carry his left hand low, the champion scored three knockdowns. After the third, referee Joe Cortez waved the bout over.

"He went out fighting," Tyson said. "Even after that last knockdown, he was willing to get up."

Larry Holmes (left) proved he still had the heart of a champion, but not his old resilience, when Mike Tyson knocked him out in the fourth round.

RINGSIDE VIEW

APRIL

Evander Holyfield unifies the cruiserweight title with an eighth-round stoppage of longtime WBC champion Carlos DeLeon.

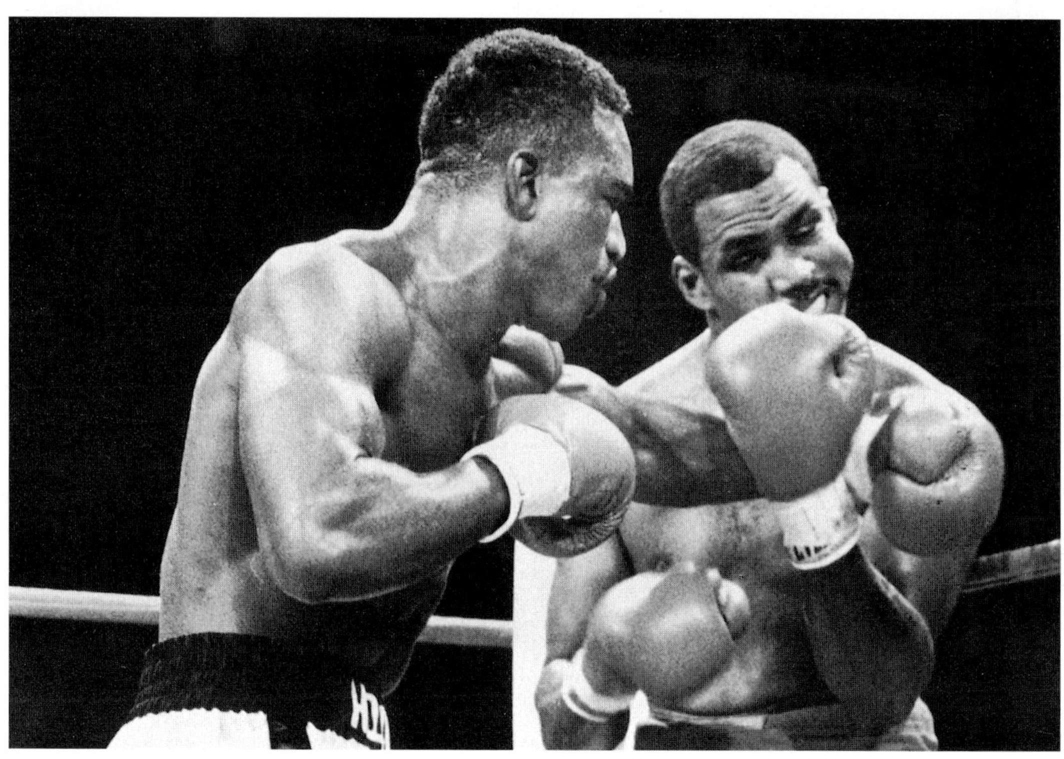
Evander Holyfield (left) and Carlos DeLeon.

POWER SURGE, THEN A BROWN-OUT

The winner said of the loser, "He's got speed, he's got power. The guy was unbelievable. I never fought anyone like this."

What, then, could have been said of the winner?

On April 23, a pair of young American punchers, Simon Brown and Tyrone Trice, met for the vacant IBF welterweight title at the Palais Des Sport in Berck-Sur-Mer, France. It was an action-packed bout, and a strong candidate for fight of the year.

Trice left the starting gate in stride, and in round two, floored his foe with a hook. Brown needed several rounds to recover. He began to box from a distance in the fifth, and made sure to pound Trice's body whenever inside.

Drained by his own intensity, Trice faded in the late rounds. He was downed in the 12th, and again in the 14th, with referee Steve Smoger stepping in at the 2:29 mark. (After 13 rounds, Trice was ahead on two of the three cards.)

Trice had indeed been unbelievable. Unbelievably, Brown had been better.

RINGSIDE VIEW

MARCH

Lloyd Honeyghan regains his form – and the WBC welterweight title – by scoring a third-round kayo of Jorge Vaca.

AN AMERICAN IN PARIS

Don't tell Pernell Whitaker that the French are hospitable to American tourists. On March 12, the unbeaten Olympic gold medalist challenged Mexican ex-patriot and fellow southpaw Jose Luis Ramirez at the Stade de Levallois in the WBC lightweight champion's adopted hometown of Paris. It was a trip "Sweet Pea" would like to forget.

For six rounds, the 24-year-old Whitaker befuddled Ramirez with speed and movement. At some point during the middle rounds, he fractured his oft-injured left hand. He landed less frequently down the stretch, and clinched often, but continued to defend himself well.

"I thought I had a shutout," he said.

The judges disagreed; they scored for Ramirez with split scores of 118-113, 116-115, and 113-117.

The verdict caused a furor. Shelly Finkel, Whitaker's co-manager, accused WBC President Jose Sulaiman and promoter Don King of fixing the fight. The WBC responded by suing for libel. The bottom line: Ramirez kept the title – at the expense of boxing's image.

Jose Luis Ramirez received a "gift" decision.

WORLD TITLE FIGHTS

HEAVYWEIGHTS

Jan 22 **Mike Tyson** *KO* 4
Larry Holmes, Atlantic City

March 21 **Mike Tyson** *KO* 2
Tony Tubbs, Tokyo

CRUISERWEIGHTS

Jan 22 **Carlos DeLeon** *W* 12
Jose Maria Burlon, Atlantic City

April 9 **Evander Holyfield** *KO* 8
Carlos DeLeon, Las Vegas
(Unifies World Title)

LIGHT HEAVYWEIGHTS

April 3 **Virgil Hill** *KO* 11
Jean-Marie Emebe, Bismarck, ND

SUPER MIDDLEWEIGHTS

March 1 **Chong Pal Park** *KO* 5
Polly Pasireron, Chonju, South Korea

March 11 **Graciano Rocchigiani** *KO* 8
Vincent Boulware, Dusseldorf
(Wins Vacant IBF Title)

MIDDLEWEIGHTS

Feb 7 **Frank Tate** *KO* 10
Tony Sibson, Staffordshire

March 5 **Sumbu Kalambay** *W* 12
Mike McCallum, Pesaro, Italy

JUNIOR MIDDLEWEIGHTS

Jan 3 **Gianfranco Rosi** (ITA) *KO* 7
Duane Thomas, Genoa, Italy

WELTERWEIGHTS

Feb 5 **Marlon Starling** *W* 12
Fujio Ozaki, Atlantic City

March 29 **Lloyd Honeyghan** *KO* 3
Jorge Vaca, Wembley

April 16 **Marlon Starling** *D* 12
Mark Breland, Las Vegas

April 23 **Simon Brown** (JAM) *KO* 14
Tyrone Trice, Berck-Sur-Mer, France
(Wins Vacant IBF Title)

JUNIOR WELTERWEIGHTS

Feb 14 **Buddy McGirt** (USA) *KO* 12
Frankie Warren, Corpus Christi
(Wins Vacant IBF Title)

March 24 **Roger Mayweather** *KO* 3
Mauricio Aceves, Los Angeles

LIGHTWEIGHTS

Feb 6 **Greg Haugen** *W* 15
Vinny Pazienza, Atlantic City

March 12 **Jose Luis Ramirez** *W* 12
Pernell Whitaker, Paris

April 11 **Greg Haugen** *Tech Dec* 11
Miguel Santana, Tacoma

April 16 **Julio Cesar Chavez** *KO* 6
Rodolfo Aguilar, Las Vegas

JUNIOR LIGHTWEIGHTS

Feb 29 **Azumah Nelson** *W* 12
Mario Martinez, Inglewood
(Wins Vacant WBC Title)

April 2 **Rocky Lockridge** *W* 15
Harold Knight, Atlantic City

April 26 **Brian Mitchell** *W* 12
Jose Rivera, Madrid

FEATHERWEIGHTS

Jan 23 **Calvin Grove** (USA) *KO* 4
Antonio Rivera, Gamaches, France

March 7 **Jeff Fenech** *KO* 10
Victor Callejas, Sydney
(Wins Vacant WBC Title)

JUNIOR FEATHERWEIGHTS

Feb 27 **Bernardo Pinango** *W* 12
Julio Gervacio, San Juan

Feb 29 **Daniel Zaragoza** *KO* 10
Carlos Zarate, Inglewood

BANTAMWEIGHTS

Jan 17 **Wilfredo Vasquez** *D* 12
Takuya Muguruma, Osaka

Feb 6 **Kelvin Seabrooks** *KO* 2
Fernando Beltran, Paris

April 30 **Miguel Lora** *W* 12
Lucio Lopez, Cartagena

JUNIOR BANTAMWEIGHTS

Jan 26 **Khaosai Galaxy** *W* 12
Kongthoranee Payakaroon, Bangkok

Feb 20 **Elly Pical** *W* 15
Raul Diaz, Pontianak, Indonesia

April 8 **Gilberto Roman** *W* 12
Baby Sugar Rojas, Miami Beach

FLYWEIGHTS

Jan 16 **Rolando Bohol** (PHI) *W* 12
Chang Ho Choi, Manila

Jan 31 **Sot Chitalada** *KO* 6
Hideaki Kamishiro, Osaka

March 26 **Fidel Bassa** *W* 12
Dave McAuley, Belfast

JUNIOR FLYWEIGHTS

Jan 10 **Leo Gamez** (VEN) *W* 12
Bong Jun Kim, Pusan, South Korea

Feb 7 **Myung Woo Yuh** *W* 12
Willy Salazar, Seoul

March 24 **Samuth Sithnarvepol** *KO* 11
Pretty Boy Lucas, Bangkok
(Wins Vacant IBF Title)

STRAWWEIGHTS

Jan 31 **Hiroki Ioka** *KO* 12
Kyung Yun Lee, Osaka

April 24 **Rafael Gamez** *KO* 3
Kenji Yokozawa, Tokyo

MAY

1988

AUGUST

MAKING A HIT ON THE HIT MAN

Middleweight contender Iran Barkley was South Bronx-tough, which isn't like any other kind of tough. No one less indigant could have survived the fury of Thomas Hearns.

WBC middleweight champion Hearns defended vs. Barkley on June 6, at the Hilton Center in Las Vegas. It seemed like a massacre-in-the-making; Hearns landed every jab, cross, hook, and uppercut, and after only two rounds, Barkley was bleeding from the lower lip and cuts over both eyes.

"My corner said, 'You're bleeding,'" Barkley stated. "I said, 'I ain't got time to bleed.'"

When "The Hit Man" opened the third with a body attack, Barkley began to double over. Then he answered with a million-to-one shot of a right. Hearns wobbled, and the challenger added another right. Boom! Hearns got up, but Barkley knocked him back down, and through the ropes, with a hook. Referee Richard Steele didn't bother to count.

That's South Bronx-tough.

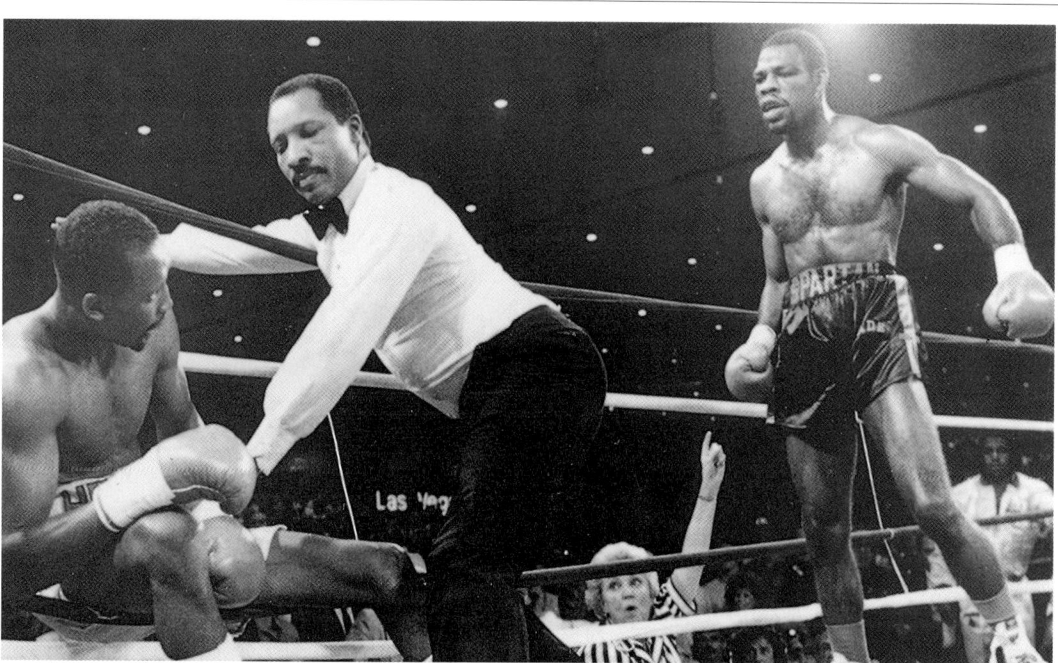

Thomas Hearns is rendered helpless in the third round of his middleweight championship bout with the murderous-hitting Iran Barkley.

RINGSIDE VIEW

JUNE

Former WBA junior middleweight champion Davey Moore, 28, is killed when an unoccupied car rolls over him in the driveway of his New Jersey home.

WORLD TITLE FIGHTS

HEAVYWEIGHTS

June 27 **Mike Tyson** *KO* 1
Michael Spinks, Atlantic City

LIGHT HEAVYWEIGHTS

May 29 **Don Lalonde** (CAN) *KO* 5
Leslie Stewart, Port of Spain, Trinidad

June 6 **Virgil Hill** *W* 12
Ramzi Hassan, Las Vegas

June 10 **Prince Charles Williams** *KO* 11
Richard Caramanolis, Annecy, France

SUPER MIDDLEWEIGHTS

May 23 **Fulgencio Obelmejias** (VEN) *W* 12
Chong Pal Park, Suanbo, South Korea

June 3 **Graciano Rocchigiani** *W* 15
Nicky Walker, Berlin

MIDDLEWEIGHTS

June 6 **Iran Barkley** (USA) *KO* 3
Thomas Hearns, Las Vegas

June 12 **Sumbu Kalambay** *W* 12
Robbie Sims, Ravenna, Italy

July 28 **Michael Nunn** (USA) *KO* 9
Frank Tate, Las Vegas

JUNIOR MIDDLEWEIGHTS

July 8 **Donald Curry** *KO* 9
Gianfranco Rosi, San Remo, Italy

July 30 **Julian Jackson** *KO* 3
Buster Drayton, Atlantic City

WELTERWEIGHTS

July 16 **Simon Brown** *KO* 3
Jorge Vaca, Kingston, Jamaica

July 29 **Lloyd Honeyghan** *KO* 5
Yung Kil Chung, Atlantic City

July 29 **Tomas Molinares** (COL) *KO* 6
Marlon Starling, Atlantic City

JUNIOR WELTERWEIGHTS

May 7 **Juan Coggi** *KO* 2
Sang Ho Lee, San Patrignano, Italy

June 6 **Roger Mayweather** *W* 12
Harold Brazier, Las Vegas

July 31 **Buddy McGirt** *KO* 1
Howard Davis Jr., New York City

JUNIOR LIGHTWEIGHTS

June 25 **Azumah Nelson** *KO* 9
Lupe Suarez, Atlantic City

July 23 **Tony Lopez** (USA) *W* 12
Rocky Lockridge, Sacramento

FEATHERWEIGHTS

May 17 **Calvin Grove** *W* 15
Myron Taylor, Atlantic City

June 23 **Antonio Esparragoza** *D* 12
Marcos Villasana, Los Angeles

Aug 4 **Jorge Paez** (MEX) *W* 15
Calvin Grove, Mexicali

Aug 12 **Jeff Fenech** *KO* 5
Tyrone Downes, Melbourne

JUNIOR FEATHERWEIGHTS

May 20 **Jose Sanabria** *KO* 6
Moises Fuentes, Bucaramanga, Colombia

May 28 **Juan Jose Estrada** (MEX) *W* 12
Bernardo Pinango, Tijuana

May 29 **Daniel Zaragoza** *D* 12
Seung Hoon Lee, Seoul

Aug 21 **Jose Sanabria** *W* 12
Vincenzo Belcastro, Capo D'Orlando, Italy

BANTAMWEIGHTS

May 9 **Kaokor Galaxy** (THA) *W* 12
Wilfredo Vasquez, Bangkok

July 9 **Orlando Canizales** (USA) *KO* 15
Kelvin Seabrooks, Atlantic City

Aug 1 **Miguel Lora** *W* 12
Albert Davila, Inglewood

Aug 14 **Sung Kil Moon** (KOR) *Tech. Dec* 6
Kaokor Galaxy, Seoul

JUNIOR BANTAMWEIGHTS

July 9 **Gilberto Roman** *KO* 5
Yoshiyuki Uchida, Kawagoe, Japan

FLYWEIGHTS

May 6 **Rolando Bohol** *W* 15
Cho Woon Park, Manila

July 24 **Yong Kang Kim** (KOR) *W* 12
Sot Chitalada, Pohang, South Korea

JUNIOR FLYWEIGHTS

June 12 **Myung Woo Yuh** *W* 12
Jose DeJesus, Taejon, South Korea

June 27 **Jung Koo Chang** *KO* 8
Hideyuki Ohashi, Tokyo

Aug 28 **Myung Woo Yuh** *KO* 6
Putt Ohyuthanakorn, Pusan, South Korea

STRAWWEIGHTS

June 5 **Hiroki Ioka** *D* 12
Napa Kiatwanchai, Osaka

Aug 29 **Samuth Sithnarvepol** *W* 15
In Kyu Hwang, Bangkok

"ONCE AND FOR ALL" KNOCKOUT

Big? The *challenger* was paid $13.5-million. Quick? The singing of the National Anthem took two seconds longer than the fight. Brutal? Historians began comparing the winner to the greatest fighters in history.

On June 27, world heavyweight champion Mike Tyson, 21, and unbeaten title claimant Michael Spinks, 31, dueled before a crowd of 21,785 at the Atlantic City Convention Hall. (Spinks had been stripped of the IBF title for fighting Gerry Cooney.) The showdown was billed as "Once And For All."

Tyson proved he was the baddest man on the planet. As intense as ever, he forced Spinks to fight. At the one-minute mark, the challenger was backed to the ropes and dropped by a right to the chest. Having suffered the first knockdown of his career, Spinks rose at four. After referee Frank Cappuccino's mandatory count, he was greeted by a hellacious right hand to the jaw. That was it; the fourth-shortest title fight in heavyweight history was over in 91 seconds.

Mike Tyson. Once, and for always.

Michael Spinks, former undefeated champion, tried to regain the crown from undefeated Mike Tyson, but didn't last a single round.

NO CLOWNING AROUND

Boxing had never seen anything quite like Mexican featherweight Jorge Paez, who did backflips and moonwalks, fought with his hands by his sides, and paid his barber to shave messages on his head. Oh, yeah, Paez, who grew up performing in his grandmother's circus, could fight a little, too.

On August 4, "Maromero" challenged IBF champion Calvin Grove before 12,000 fans at the Plaza de Toros Calafia bullring in Mexicali. The ringside temperature about 125 degrees, the challenger wisely conserved his energy.

Behind on points, Paez exploded just in time. He scored three knockdowns in the 15th round, a dramatic rally which gave him a majority decision by scores of 143-140, 142-140, and 142-142. (It was boxing's last scheduled 15-round title fight.)

Even the bearded lady was dancing in the aisles.

Colorful Jorge Paez, the new champion.

RINGSIDE VIEW

JULY

Colombia's Tomas Molinares wins the WBA welterweight crown by knocking out Marlon Starling with a punch that clearly lands after the bell ending the sixth round.

JULY

In a thrilling duel, Orlando Canizales wins the IBF bantamweight title with a 15th-round stoppage of gutty Kelvin Seabrooks.

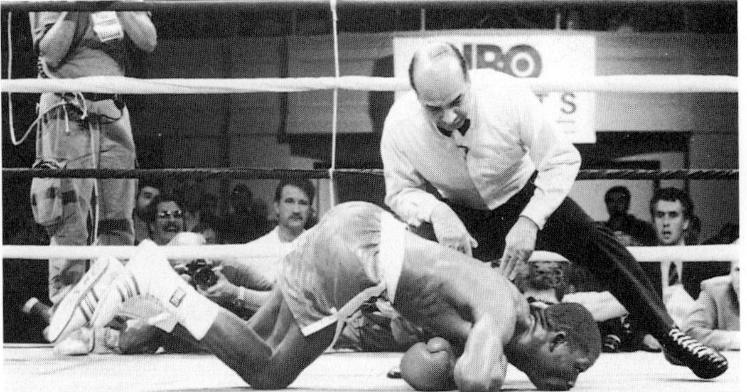

Marlon Starling was flattened by Tomas Molinares in sixth round of welterweight title bout.

SEPTEMBER

1988

DECEMBER

“THE KID” DOESN’T KID A ROUND

Like Mozart, boxing prodigy Meldrick Taylor wasted little time in establishing himself as an exceptional talent. At age 17, the Philadelphian won a gold medal at the 1984 Olympics. And at age 21, he won his first pro title, stopping IBF junior welterweight champion Buddy McGirt in the 12th round.

On September 3, Taylor, a 9-5 underdog, challenged McGirt at Harrah’s Marina-Hotel in Atlantic City. His only anxious moment came in the first round, when McGirt connected with a right. “The Kid” shook, rattled, and rolled, but didn’t fall. The rest of the fight was his.

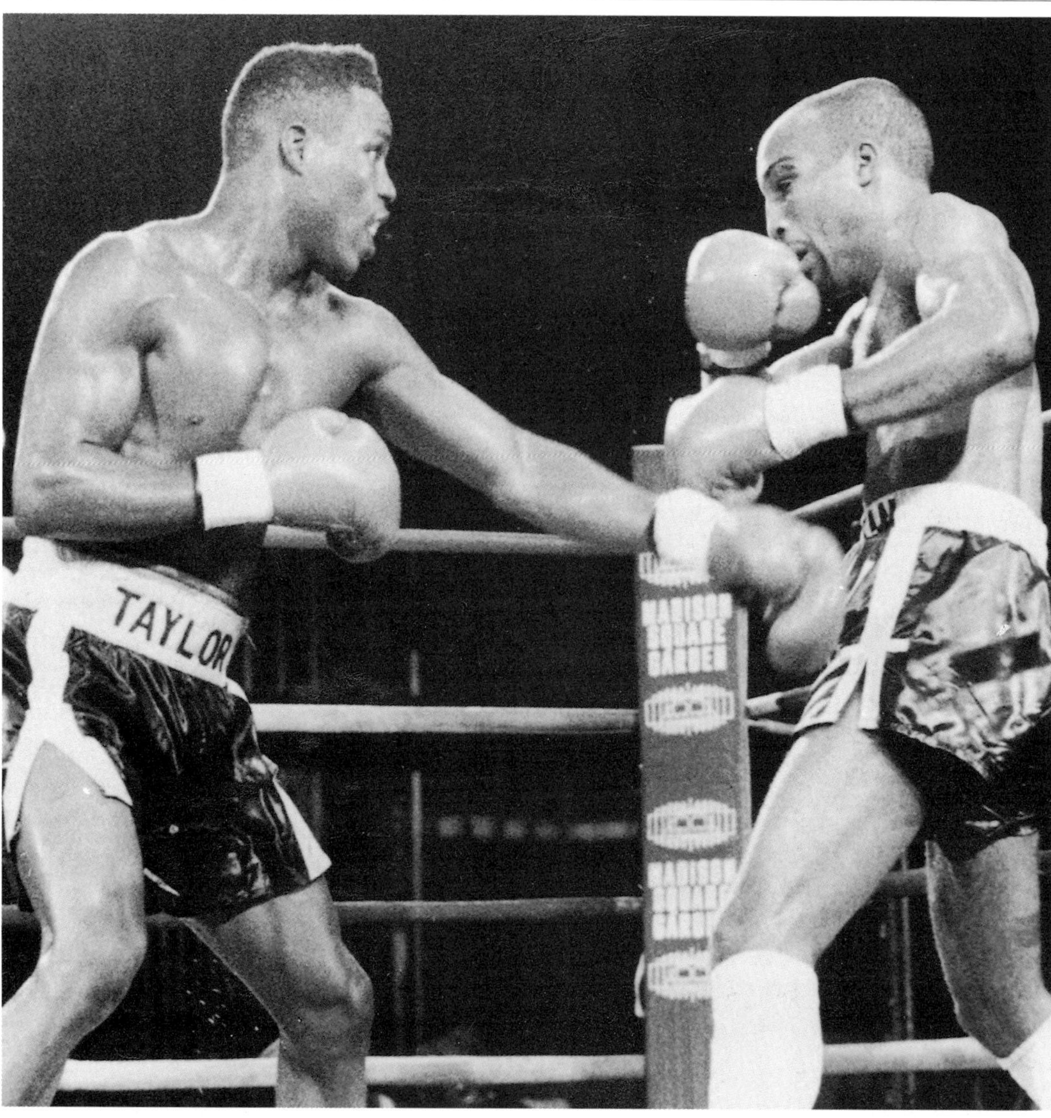

Meldrick Taylor (left) remained undefeated when he stopped James “Buddy” McGirt in the 12th round to win the junior welterweight title.

McGirt simply couldn’t match Taylor’s remarkable hand speed. The champion was battered in the late rounds and eventually rescued in the 12th by his manager, Al Certo, who climbed through the ropes and brought a stoppage at the 2:00 mark.

“I was prepared to fight until my heart busted or my brain busted,” McGirt later said.

If necessary, Taylor would surely have accommodated him.

A MOST FRIENDLY BEATING

Both WBA lightweight champion Julio Cesar Chavez and WBC titlist Jose Luis Ramirez hailed from Culiacan, Mexico. They were friends and neighbors. On October 29, however, they became rivals in a bout that partially unified the 135-pound crown.

A prohibitive favorite, Chavez willingly mixed with his southpaw opponent, who was considered the strongest and sturdiest lightweight in the world. The infighting was fierce, with Chavez dominating from rounds three through seven. “J.C. Superstar” seemed en route to victory when, in round 11, an unintentional butt opened an ugly gash on Ramirez’ forehead.

“It was a deep cut, all the way to the scalp,” explained Dr. Flip Homansky. “They weren’t going to get it closed.”

The bout was immediately halted, and after the scorecards were gathered, Chavez was declared the winner by unanimous scores of 96-94, 98-91, and 95-93.

They could go back to being friends again.

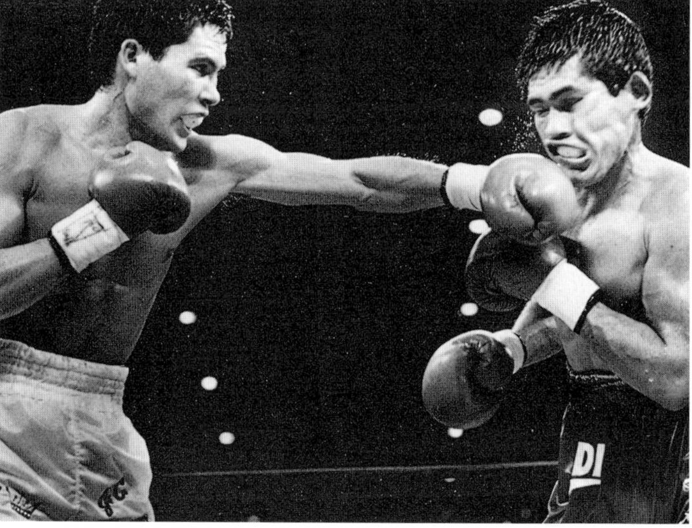
Chavez (left) won by technical decision over Ramirez to partly unify the crown.

COLLECTING TITLES IS A HOBBY FOR LEONARD

Everyone in boxing wanted to fight Sugar Ray Leonard for one good reason: a date with Sir Sugar meant a career-best payday.

After Leonard defeated Marvin Hagler, he allowed the suspense to build. Who would be next? More than one year passed before he chose WBC light heavyweight champion Don Lalonde. "The Golden Boy's" reward: a purse of more than $5-million. Leonard's motivation: a chance to enter the recordbooks by winning titles in his fourth and fifth divisions. (The bout was contested for Lalonde's crown, and also the newly created WBC super middleweight title, by Leonard insisting on the bout being made at 168 pounds.)

On November 7, Leonard and Lalonde traded blows at Caesars Palace. The champion's big weapon was his right cross, and in the fourth, Sugar Ray was floored. But then he slowly gained control. The end came in the ninth, only seconds after Leonard was stung by a series of blows. He scored two brutal knockdowns, bringing referee Richard Steele's intervention at the 2:30 mark.

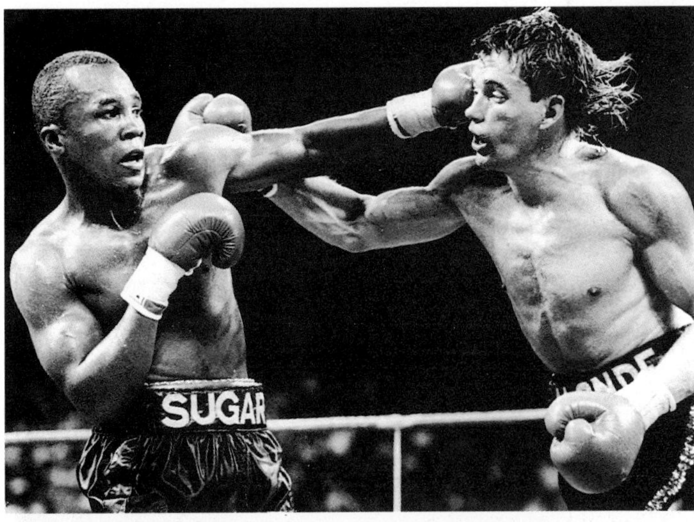

Sugar Ray Leonard (left) stopped Canada's Donny Lalonde in the ninth round.

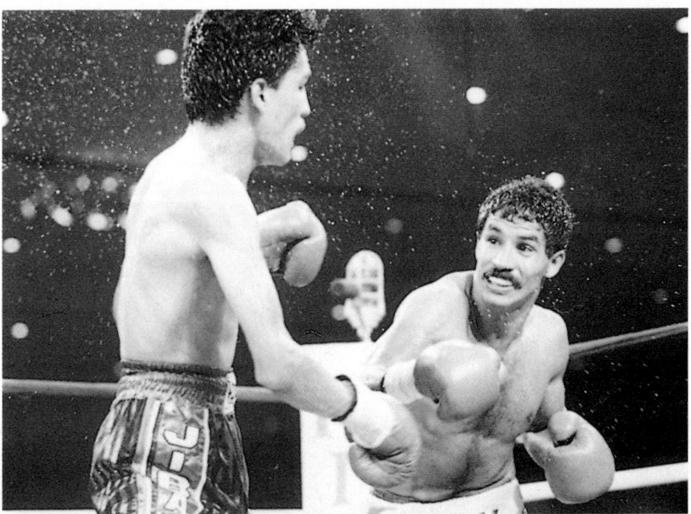

Raul Perez (left) outboxed Miguel Lora over 12 rounds to take the bantamweight title.

WORLD TITLE FIGHTS

LIGHT HEAVYWEIGHTS

Oct 21	**Prince Charles Williams** *KO* 3 Rufino Angulo, Villenave d'Ornon, France
Nov 7	**Sugar Ray Leonard** *KO* 9 Don Lalonde, Las Vegas
Nov 11	**Virgil Hill** *KO* 10 Willie Featherstone, Bismarck, ND

SUPER MIDDLEWEIGHTS

Oct 7	**Graciano Rocchigiani** *KO* 11 Chris Reid, Berlin
Nov 7	**Sugar Ray Leonard** *KO* 9 Don Lalonde, Las Vegas (Wins Vacant WBC Title)

MIDDLEWEIGHTS

Nov 4	**Michael Nunn** *KO* 8 Juan Roldan, Las Vegas
Nov 8	**Sumbu Kalambay** *KO* 7 Doug DeWitt, Monte Carlo

JUNIOR MIDDLEWEIGHTS

Nov 4	**Robert Hines** (USA) *W* 12 Matthew Hilton, Las Vegas

WELTERWEIGHTS

Oct 14	**Simon Brown** *W* 12 Mauro Martelli, Lausanne, Switzerland

JUNIOR WELTERWEIGHTS

Sept 3	**Meldrick Taylor** (USA) *KO* 12 Buddy McGirt, Atlantic City
Sept 22	**Roger Mayweather** *KO* 12 Gato Gonzalez, Los Angeles
Nov 7	**Roger Mayweather** *W* 12 Vinny Pazienza, Las Vegas

LIGHTWEIGHTS

Oct 28	**Greg Haugen** *KO* 10 Gert Bo Jacobsen, Copenhagen
Oct 29	**Julio Cesar Chavez** *Tech Dec* 11 Jose Luis Ramirez, Las Vegas

JUNIOR LIGHTWEIGHTS

Oct 27	**Tony Lopez** *W* 12 John-John Molina, Sacramento
Nov 2	**Brian Mitchell** *W* 12 Jim McDonnell, Southwark, England
Dec 10	**Azumah Nelson** *KO* 3 Sydney Dal Rovere, Accra

FEATHERWEIGHTS

Nov 5	**Antonio Esparragoza** *KO* 8 Jose Marmolejos, Marsala, Italy
Nov 30	**Jeff Fenech** *KO* 5 Georgie Navarro, Melbourne

JUNIOR FEATHERWEIGHTS

Sept 26	**Jose Sanabria** *KO* 10 Fabrice Benichou, Nogent-Sur Marne, France
Oct 16	**Juan Jose Estrada** *KO* 11 Takuya Muguruma, Moriguchi, Japan
Nov 11	**Jose Sanabria** *KO* 6 Thierry Jacob, Gravelines, France
Nov 26	**Daniel Zaragoza** *KO* 5 Valerio Nati, Forli, Italy

BANTAMWEIGHTS

Oct 29	**Raul Perez** (MEX) *W* 12 Miguel Lora, Las Vegas
Nov 27	**Sung Kil Moon** *KO* 7 Edgar Monserrat, Seoul
Nov 29	**Orlando Canizales** *KO* 1 Jimmy Navarro, San Antonio

JUNIOR BANTAMWEIGHTS

Sept 4	**Gilberto Roman** *W* 12 Kiyoshi Hatanaka, Nagoya
Sept 4	**Elly Pical** *W* 12 Ki Chang Kim, Surabaya, Indonesia
Oct 9	**Khaosai Galaxy** *KO* 8 Chang Ho Choi, Seoul
Nov 7	**Gilberto Roman** *W* 12 Baby Sugar Rojas, Las Vegas

FLYWEIGHTS

Oct 2	**Fidel Bassa** *W* 12 Ray Medel, San Antonio
Oct 5	**Duke McKenzie** (ENG) *KO* 11 Rolando Bohol, Wembley
Nov 12	**Yong Kang Kim** *W* 12 Emil Matsushima, Chongju, South Korea

JUNIOR FLYWEIGHTS

Nov 4	**Tacy Macalos** (PHI) *W* 12 Jum Hwan Choi, Seoul
Nov 6	**Myung Woo Yuh** *KO* 7 Udin Beharrudin, Seoul
Dec 11	**German Torres** (MEX) *W* 12 Soon Jung Kang, Kimhae, South Korea (Wins Vacant WBC Title)

STRAWWEIGHTS

Nov 13	**Napa Kiatwanchai** (THA) *W* 12 Hiroki Ioka, Osaka

JANUARY

1989

APRIL

FINDING PEACE BY MAKING WAR

With his life swirling out of control, heavyweight champion Mike Tyson found solace only in the ring. Consider:

* He was estranged from his manager, Bill Cayton, who was feuding with promoter Don King.

* He had fired his longtime trainer, Kevin Rooney, who, he believed, had sided with Cayton.

* He had gone through a very public divorce from actress Robin Givens.

* He had broken his right hand in a streetfight with heavyweight Mitch Green.

* He had knocked himself unconscious after driving into a tree.

On February 25, Tyson ended the longest layoff of his career – eight months – by defending against British hero Frank Bruno at the Las Vegas Hilton. Less than 30 seconds into the first round, the challenger was flat on the canvas, courtesy of a right to the jaw. Bruno fought back with vigor, however, and lasted until the fifth, when an overanxious Tyson finished him with a devastating flurry. Referee Richard Steele halted the bout at 2:55.

At which point Tyson again had to face the rest of his life.

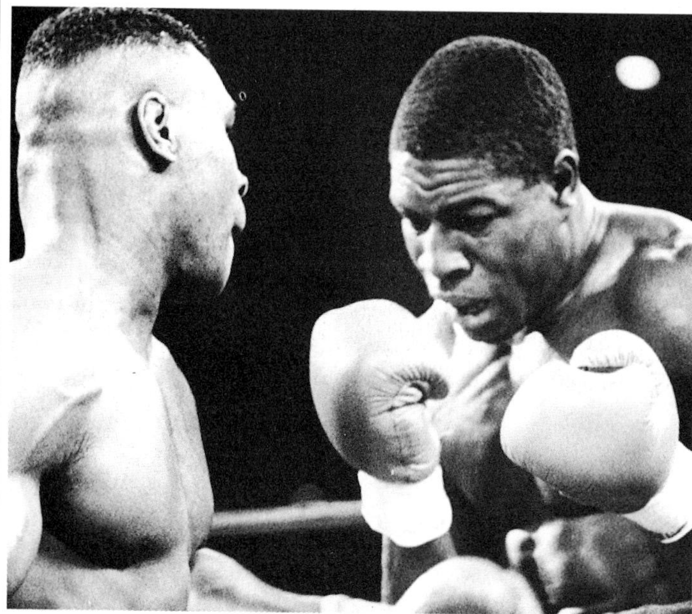

Frank Bruno (right) made a gallant effort, but was stopped by Mike Tyson in the fifth round.

Boxing master Pernell Whitaker (left) decisioned Greg Haugen in a lightweight title bout.

WORLD TITLE FIGHTS

HEAVYWEIGHTS

Feb 25 **Mike Tyson** *KO* 5
Frank Bruno, Las Vegas

CRUISERWEIGHTS

March 25 **Taoufik Belbouli** (FRA) *KO* 8
Michael Greer, Casablanca
(Wins Vacant WBA Title)

LIGHT HEAVYWEIGHTS

Feb 21 **Dennis Andries** *KO* 5
Tony Willis, Tucson
(Wins Vacant WBC Title)

March 4 **Virgil Hill** *W* 12
Bobby Czyz, Bismarck, ND

SUPER MIDDLEWEIGHTS

Jan 27 **Graciano Rocchigiani** *W* 12
Sugarboy Malinga, Berlin

MIDDLEWEIGHTS

Feb 24 **Roberto Duran** *W* 12
Iran Barkley, Atlantic City

March 25 **Michael Nunn** *KO* 1
Sumbu Kalambay, Las Vegas

JUNIOR MIDDLEWEIGHTS

Feb 5 **Darrin Van Horn** (USA) *W* 12
Robert Hines, Atlantic City

Feb 11 **Rene Jacquot** (FRA) *W* 12
Donald Curry, Grenoble

Feb 25 **Julian Jackson** *KO* 8
Francisco DeJesus, Las Vegas

WELTERWEIGHTS

Feb 4 **Mark Breland** *KO* 1
Seung Soon Lee, Las Vegas
(Wins Vacant WBA Title)

Feb 4 **Marlon Starling** *KO* 9
Lloyd Honeyghan, Las Vegas

Feb 18 **Simon Brown** *KO* 3
Jorge Maysonet, Budapest

April 22 **Mark Breland** *KO* 5
Rafael Pineda, Atlantic City

April 27 **Simon Brown** *KO* 7
Al Long, Washington, D.C.

JUNIOR WELTERWEIGHTS

Jan 21 **Meldrick Taylor** *KO* 7
John Meekins, Atlantic City

Jan 21 **Juan Coggi** *W* 12
Harold Brazier, Vasto, Italy

April 29 **Juan Coggi** *W* 12
Akinobu Hiranaka, Vasto, Italy

LIGHTWEIGHTS

Feb 18 **Pernell Whitaker** (USA) *W* 12
Greg Haugen, Hampton, VA

April 30 **Pernell Whitaker** *KO* 3
Louie Lomeli, Norfolk

JUNIOR LIGHTWEIGHTS

Feb 11 **Brian Mitchell** *KO* 8
Salvatore Bottiglieri, Capo D'Orlando, Italy

Feb 25 **Azumah Nelson** *KO* 12
Mario Martinez, Las Vegas

March 5 **Tony Lopez** *W* 12
Rocky Lockridge, Sacramento

FEATHERWEIGHTS

March 26 **Antonio Esparragoza** *KO* 10
Mitsuru Sugiya, Kawasaki, Japan

March 30 **Jorge Paez** *KO* 11
Calvin Grove, Mexicali

April 8 **Jeff Fenech** *W* 12
Marcos Villasana, Melbourne

JUNIOR FEATHERWEIGHTS

March 10 **Fabrice Benichou** (FRA) *W* 12
Jose Sanabria, Limoges, France

April 4 **Juan Jose Estrada** *KO* 10
Jesus Poll, Inglewood

BANTAMWEIGHTS

Feb 19 **Sung Kil Moon** *KO* 5
Chiaki Kobayashi, Taejon, South Korea

March 9 **Raul Perez** *W* 12
Lucio Lopez, Los Angeles

JUNIOR BANTAMWEIGHTS

Jan 15 **Khaosai Galaxy** *KO* 2
Tae Il Chang, Samut Prakarn, Thailand

Feb 25 **Elly Pical** *W* 12
Mike Phelps, Podium Block, Singapore

April 8 **Khaosai Galaxy** *W* 12
Kenji Matsumura, Yokohama, Japan

FLYWEIGHTS

March 5 **Yong Kang Kim** *W* 12
Leopard Tamakuma, Aomori, Japan

March 8 **Duke McKenzie** *KO* 4
Tony DeLuca, London

April 15 **Fidel Bassa** *KO* 6
Julio Gudino, Barranquilla

JUNIOR FLYWEIGHTS

Feb 12 **Myung Woo Yuh** *KO* 10
Katsumi Komiyama, Chongju, South Korea

March 19 **Yul Woo Lee** (KOR) *KO* 9
German Torres, Taejon, South Korea

STRAWWEIGHTS

Feb 11 **Napa Kiatwanchai** *W* 12
John Arief, Korat, Thailand

March 23 **Samuth Sithnarvepol** *D* 12
Nico Thomas, Jakarta

April 16 **Bong Jun Kim** *KO* 7
Agustin Garcia, Pohang, South Korea

SEVENTEEN YEARS LATER, AND ANOTHER TITLE

Roberto Duran won his first world title in 1972. Seventeen years later, he captured his fourth crown, outpointing WBC middleweight champion Iran Barkley on February 24 at the Convention Center in Atlantic City. It was the longest stretch between championships in boxing history.

Duran, 37, proved once more that he was the ultimate warrior. A trim and ready 156¼ pounds, he fought with high energy and an unyielding spirit.

"It was his heart," said Barkley. "It just wouldn't go."

Both fighters performed at their best. Barkley gained an edge in the eighth, when he spun Duran with an explosive right. But the Panamanian roared back in the 11th, scoring the bout's only knockdown with a series of crosses to the jaw.

Duran became the first Latin fighter to win titles in four divisions when he was awarded a split decision (scores of 118-112, 116-112, and 113-116). Each triumph, it seemed, had been more amazing and certainly more unexpected than the one before it.

Roberto Duran jolts Iran Barkley in the fifth round of a scheduled 12-round fight, which Duran won by split decision to capture the middleweight crown, his fourth title in 17 years.

"SECOND TO" NUNN: AND KALAMBAY IS FLOORED IN THE FIRST

Tell Sumbu Kalambay that Michael Nunn can't punch and he'll look at you quizzically. Someone gave him that monster of a headache, and he's pretty sure it was Nunn.

On March 25, Kalambay challenged Nunn for the IBF middleweight title at the Las Vegas Hilton. The bout was originally scheduled as a partial unification, but Kalambay was stripped of the WBA crown for failing to defend against Herol Graham, whom he had already beaten.

The undefeated champion, a southpaw, entered the ring a 5-1 favorite. After only 88 seconds of action, those who backed him were lining up at the cashier's window. Timing Kalambay's jab, Nunn waited for the perfect opportunity and then countered with an overhand left. Boom! Kalambay tried to rise, but pitched forward at Richard Steele's count of eight.

Said Nunn in a most sarcastic tone, "Runners aren't supposed to punch."

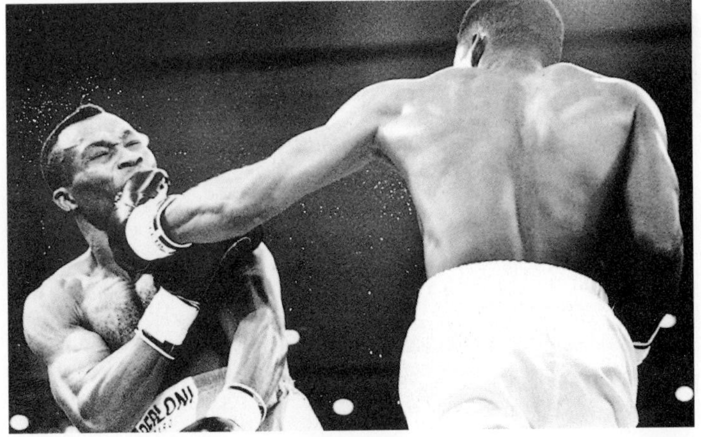

Michael Nunn's perfect left hand kayoed Sumbu Kalambay in the first round of their title bout.

MAY

1989

AUGUST

TOMMY'S UNOFFICIAL REDEMPTION

"For eight years it's been on my mind to beat this man," Thomas Hearns said of Sugar Ray Leonard.

Having craved a rematch ever since September 1981, when Leonard had stopped him in the 14th round, "The Hit Man" challenged for Sugar Ray's WBC super middleweight title on June 12 at Caesars Palace, Las Vegas.

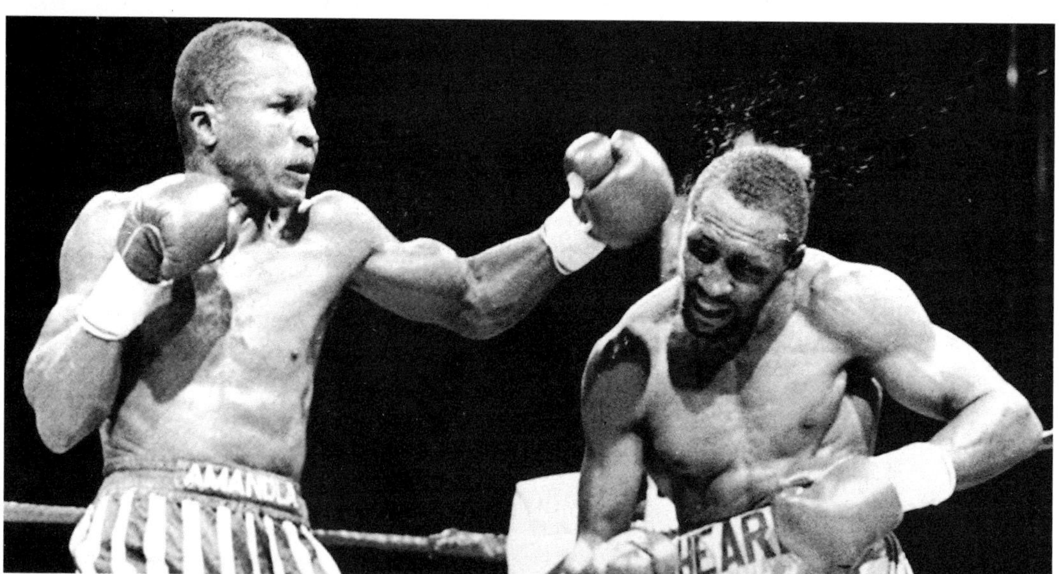

Sugar Ray Leonard (left) was pressed to the limits to retain the super middleweight crown against old rival Thomas Hearns.

Most observers thought his chance for redemption had come too late; both fighters were fading, but Hearns was seemingly a bout or two from the end. As a result, Sugar Ray Leonard was made a 3-1 favorite.

While the fighters may have lacked the sharpness of their primes, their struggle was nonetheless memorable. Hearns scored with his jab, hurt Leonard in the seventh and 12th rounds, and downed him with right hands in the third and 11th.

Sugar Ray exploded in the fifth and ninth rounds, and staged a furious rally in the last minute of the fight. It was enough to salvage an unpopular and split 12-round draw (scores of 113-112 for Hearns, 113-112 for Leonard, and 112-112).

But at least Hearns had won peace of mind.

WORLD TITLE FIGHTS

HEAVYWEIGHTS

July 21 **Mike Tyson** *KO* 1
Carl Williams, Atlantic City

CRUISERWEIGHTS

May 17 **Carlos DeLeon** *KO* 9
Sammy Reeson, London
(Wins Vacant WBC Title)

June 3 **Glenn McCrory** (ENG) *W* 12
Patrick Lumumba, Stanley, England
(Wins Vacant IBF Title)

LIGHT HEAVYWEIGHTS

May 27 **Virgil Hill** *KO* 7
Joe Lasisi, Bismarck, ND

June 24 **Jeff Harding** (AUT) *KO* 12
Dennis Andries, Atlantic City

June 25 **Prince Charles Williams** *KO* 10
Bobby Czyz, Atlantic City

SUPER MIDDLEWEIGHTS

May 28 **In Chul Baek** (KOR) *KO* 11
Fulgencio Obelmejias, Seoul

June 12 **Sugar Ray Leonard** *D* 12
Thomas Hearns, Las Vegas

MIDDLEWEIGHTS

May 10 **Mike McCallum** *W* 12
Herol Graham, Kensington, England
(Wins Vacant WBA Title)

Aug 14 **Michael Nunn** *W* 12
Iran Barkley, Reno

JUNIOR MIDDLEWEIGHTS

July 8 **John Mugabi** (UGA) *KO* 1
Rene Jacquot, Cergy-Pointoise, France

July 15 **Gianfranco Rosi** *W* 12
Darrin Van Horn, Atlantic City

July 30 **Julian Jackson** *KO* 2
Terry Norris, Atlantic City

JUNIOR WELTERWEIGHTS

May 13 **Julio Cesar Chavez** *KO* 10
Roger Mayweather, Inglewood

LIGHTWEIGHTS

July 9 **Edwin Rosario** *KO* 6
Anthony Jones, Atlantic City
(Wins Vacant WBA Title)

Aug 20 **Pernell Whitaker** *W* 12
Jose Luis Ramirez, Norfolk
(Retains IBF Title; Wins WBC Title)

JUNIOR LIGHTWEIGHTS

June 18 **Tony Lopez** *KO* 8
Tyrone Jackson, Lake Tahoe

July 2 **Brian Mitchell** *Tech Dec* 9
Jackie Beard, Crotone, Italy

FEATHERWEIGHTS

May 21 **Jorge Paez** *D* 12
Louie Espinoza, Phoenix

June 2 **Antonio Esparragoza** *KO* 6
Jean-Marc Renard, Namur, Belgium

Aug 6 **Jorge Paez** *W* 12
Steve Cruz, El Paso

JUNIOR FEATHERWEIGHTS

June 10 **Fabrice Benichou** *KO* 5
Fransie Badenhorst, Frosinone, Italy

June 22 **Daniel Zaragoza** *W* 12
Paul Banke, Inglewood

July 10 **Juan Jose Estrada** *W* 12
Luis Mendoza, Tijuana

Aug 31 **Daniel Zaragoza** *KO* 10
Frankie Duarte, Inglewood

BANTAMWEIGHTS

June 24 **Orlando Canizales** *KO* 11
Kelvin Seabrooks, Atlantic City

July 9 **Kaokor Galaxy** *W* 12
Sung Kil Moon, Bangkok

Aug 26 **Raul Perez** *KO* 8
Cardenio Ulloa, Talcahueno, Chile

JUNIOR BANTAMWEIGHTS

June 5 **Gilberto Roman** *W* 12
Juan Carazo, Inglewood

July 29 **Khaosai Galaxy** *KO* 10
Alberto Castro, Surin, Thailand

FLYWEIGHTS

June 3 **Sot Chitalada** *W* 12
Yong Kang Kim, Trang, Thailand

June 7 **Dave McAuley** (IRE) *W* 12
Duke McKenzie, Wembley

JUNIOR FLYWEIGHTS

May 2 **Muangchai Kittikasem** (THA) *W* 12
Tacy Macalos, Bangkok

June 11 **Myung Woo Yuh** *W* 12
Mario DeMarco, Chunan, South Korea

June 25 **Humberto Gonzalez** (MEX) *W* 12
Yul Woo Lee, Chongju, South Korea

STRAWWEIGHTS

June 10 **Napa Kiatwanchai** *KO* 11
Hiroki Ioka, Osaka

June 17 **Nico Thomas** (IND) *W* 12
Samuth Sithnarvepol, Jakarta

Aug 6 **Bong Jun Kim** *W* 12
Sam Joong Lee, Samchongpo, South Korea

ROCKY PLUS CROCODILE DUNDEE

Asked to explain his toughness, Australian light heavyweight Jeff Harding quipped, "It comes from biting off crocodile heads." There was no way, however, to explain his grit during his challenge of WBC champion Dennis Andries.

Harding's moment came on June 24, at the Atlantic City Convention Center. The one-time beach bum took the bout on five weeks notice, replacing Don Lalonde, who had suddenly retired. At first, it seemed too big of a task. Andries landed right hands at will, sending the challenger down under in the fifth, breaking his nose in the 10th, and cutting him over both eyes. But Harding endured, and by the late rounds, his body attack began to slow the 35-year-old champion.

Entering the 12th and final round, Harding trailed on all three cards. But he had just begun to fight. He punched, and then punched some more, and an exhausted Andries fell twice. There were no objections when referee Joe Cortez halted the bout.

Jeff Harding (left) stopped Dennis Andries to become the new light heavyweight king.

"THE TRUTH" HURTS AS TYSON TELLS IT

Sounding more like a Shakespearean actor than a prize fighter, heavyweight champion Mike Tyson once said, "How dare they challenge me with their primitive skills."

The skills of Carl "The Truth" Williams were hardly primitive; the top-ranked contender had an 85-inch reach and one of the best jabs in boxing. But his chin was sensitive, and against "Iron Mike," that was a fatal flaw.

A 13-1 favorite, Tyson made a quick strike. Midway through the first round, he slipped a Williams left and countered with a hook brought up from the floor. Boom! The blow smashed into the side of the challenger's head and sent Williams sprawling. He picked himself up at referee Randy Neumann's count of eight, but was relieved of further action.

"He was wobbly," Neumann said of what many observers believed to be a premature stoppage. "His eyes were blank; his expression was blank."

That's the kind of damage Mike Tyson could do with one punch. And that's the truth.

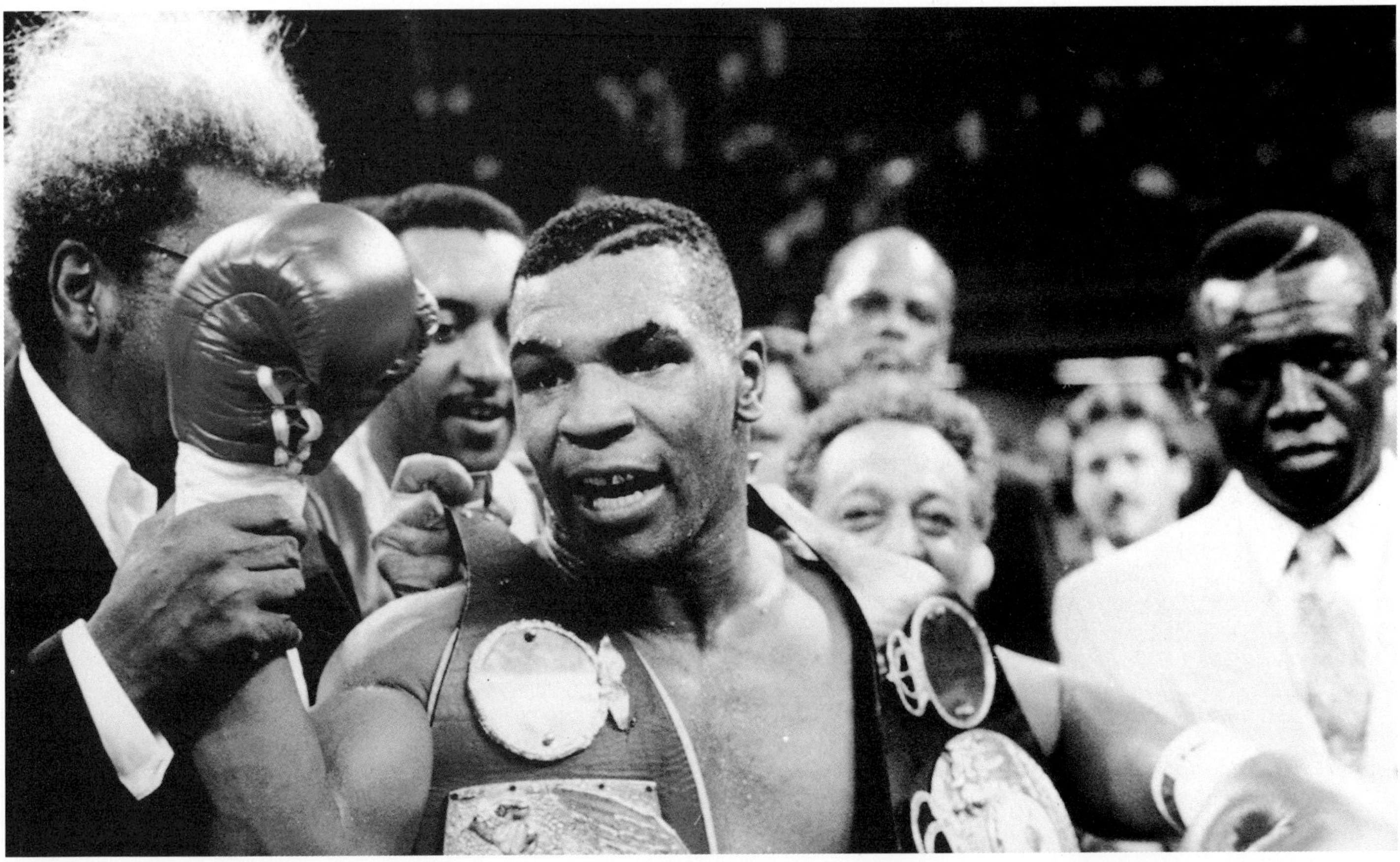

Promoter Don King (face covered by glove) raises Mike Tyson's hand after Mike knocked out Carl "The Truth" Williams at 93 seconds of the first round to retain the heavyweight crown.

SEPTEMBER

1989

DECEMBER

CHEERS, JEERS, AND BEER

IBF junior lightweight champion Tony Lopez was a special fighter not because of his speed, skill, or power, but rather his ability to attract local fans to his bouts. Boxing had few hometown attractions. When Lopez fought, however, the citizens of Sacramento always came to watch him.

On October 7, those fans became an embarrassment. Lopez defended at the Arco Arena vs. Puerto Rico's John-John Molina, whom he had previously edged by hotly disputed decision. This time, the champion was jinxed. By the third round, his right eye was closed; by the fifth, his left eye was cut; and by the seventh, he was bleeding from the nose. Molina built a sizable points lead.

Lopez didn't object when referee Dr. James Jen Kin stopped the blood-letting in the 10th. His fans, however, went wild, tossing beer and debris into the ring. By the time order was restored, most ringsiders were soaked.

Call it hometown disadvantage.

"John-John" Molina (left) became the new champion when he stopped Tony Lopez.

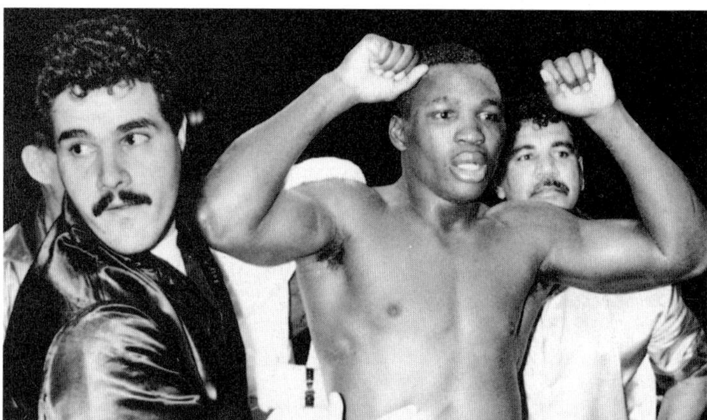

New cruiserweight king Robert Daniels after beating Dwight Qawi on a split decision.

World Title Fights

CRUISERWEIGHTS

Oct 21 **Glenn McCrory** *KO* 11
Siza Makhatini, Langbourgh, England

Nov 27 **Robert Daniels** (USA) *W* 12
Dwight Qawi, Nogent-sur-Marne, France
(Wins Vacant WBA Title)

LIGHT HEAVYWEIGHTS

Oct 24 **Virgil Hill** *KO* 1
James Kinchen, Bismarck, ND

Oct 24 **Jeff Harding** *KO* 2
Tom Collins, Brisbane

SUPER MIDDLEWEIGHTS

Oct 8 **In Chul Baek** *KO* 11
Ronnie Essett, Seoul

Dec 7 **Sugar Ray Leonard** *W* 12
Roberto Duran, Las Vegas

JUNIOR MIDDLEWEIGHTS

Oct 27 **Gianfranco Rosi** *W* 12
Troy Waters, St. Vincent, Italy

WELTERWEIGHTS

Sept 15 **Marlon Starling** *W* 12
Yung Kil Chung, Hartford

Sept 20 **Simon Brown** *KO* 2
Bobby Joe Young, Rochester

Oct 13 **Mark Breland** *KO* 2
Mauro Martelli, Geneva

Nov 9 **Simon Brown** *W* 12
Luis Santana, Springfield, MA

Dec 10 **Mark Breland** *KO* 4
Fujio Ozaki, Tokyo

JUNIOR WELTERWEIGHTS

Sept 11 **Meldrick Taylor** *W* 12
Courtney Hooper, Atlantic City

Nov 18 **Julio Cesar Chavez** *KO* 10
Sammy Fuentes, Las Vegas

Dec 16 **Julio Cesar Chavez** *KO* 3
Alberto Cortes, Mexico City

JUNIOR LIGHTWEIGHTS

Sept 28 **Brian Mitchell** *KO* 7
Irving Mitchell, Lewiston, ME

Oct 7 **John-John Molina** (PR) *KO* 10
Tony Lopez, Sacramento

Nov 5 **Azumah Nelson** *KO* 12
Jim McDonnell, London

FEATHERWEIGHTS

Sept 16 **Jorge Paez** *KO* 2
Jose Maria Lopez, Mexico City

Sept 22 **Antonio Esparragoza** *KO* 5
Fili Montoya, Mexicali

Dec 9 **Jorge Paez** *KO* 6
Lupe Gutierrez, Reno

JUNIOR FEATHERWEIGHTS

Oct 7 **Fabrice Benichou** *W* 12
Ramon Cruz, Bordeaux, France

Dec 3 **Daniel Zaragoza** *W* 12
Chan Yong Park, Inchon, South Korea

Dec 11 **Jesus Salud** (USA) *W Disq* 9
Juan Jose Estrada, Inglewood

BANTAMWEIGHTS

Oct 18 **Luisito Espinosa** (PHI) *KO* 1
Kaokor Galaxy, Bangkok

Oct 23 **Raul Perez** *W* 12
Diego Avila, Inglewood

JUNIOR BANTAMWEIGHTS

Sept 12 **Gilberto Roman** *W* 12
Santos Laciar, Inglewood

Oct 14 **Juan Polo Perez** (COL) *W* 12
Elly Pical, Roanoke, VA

Oct 31 **Khaosai Galaxy** *KO* 12
Kenji Matsumura, Kobe, Japan

Nov 7 **Nana Konadu** (GHA) *W* 12
Gilberto Roman, Mexico City

FLYWEIGHTS

Sept 30 **Jesus Rojas** (VEN) *W* 12
Fidel Bassa, Barranquilla

Nov 8 **Dave McAuley** *W* 12
Dodie Penalosa, Wembley

JUNIOR FLYWEIGHTS

Sept 24 **Myung Woo Yuh** *KO* 11
Kenbun Taiho, Suanbo, South Korea

Oct 6 **Muangchai Kittikasem** *KO* 7
Tacy Macalos, Bangkok

Dec 9 **Humberto Gonzalez** *W* 12
Jung Koo Chang, Taegu, South Korea

STRAWWEIGHTS

Sept 21 **Eric Chavez** (PHI) *KO* 5
Nico Thomas, Jakarta

Oct 22 **Bong Jun Kim** *KO* 9
John Arief, Pohang, South Korea

Nov 12 **Jum Hwan Choi** (KOR) *KO* 12
Napa Kiatwanchai, Seoul

"NO MAS INDEED!" WAS THE FANS' VERDICT

At the start of Sugar Ray Leonard-Roberto Duran III, the fans were chanting "Doo-ran! Doo-ran!" At the finish, they were screaming "Bull——! Bull——!"

For nine years, Duran had waited for a rubber match. Before the bout, former light heavyweight champion Jose Torres made a shrewd observation. "The question is whether it was more important (for him) to *get* the fight than to *win* it," he said.

The bout, fought for Sugar Ray's WBC super middleweight title, came on December 7, at the sparkling new Mirage in Las Vegas. Duran, 38, seemed in reasonable condition, but performed as if he had just awakened from a deep sleep. Leonard boxed and moved, and while he suffered 60 stitches worth of cuts produced by various butts, he won almost every round. The scores: 119-109, 116-111, and 120-110.

The wait hadn't been worth it. For Duran, or anyone else.

In the third match of their torrid series, Sugar Ray Leonard (right) won a unanimous 12-round decision over Roberto Duran to retain super middleweight title.

ANYTHING KONADU CAN DO ROMAN COULD (IF HE TRAINED)

There was no denying that Mexico's Gilberto Roman rated with the best lighter-weight fighters of his era. The WBC super flyweight champion boxed out of a textbook, and frustrated his opponents with a subtle defense. Only trouble was, Roman didn't always train with discipline. On November 7, he paid a terrible and predictable price for his laziness.

Making his 13th defense, the champion defended at the Arena Mexico against Ghana's Nana Konadu, a stablemate of Azumah Nelson. Konadu, a virtual unknown, quickly introduced himself. He floored Roman in the first, twice in the third, and twice more in the fourth. After this, Roman needed all his skill to last the 12-round distance, but he never threatened the bigger, taller, quicker challenger.

The scoring, of course, was lopsided, with Konadu taking the crown by totals of 116-109, 118-104, and 119-103. Perhaps Roman had learned a lesson. But some lessons come too late.

RINGSIDE VIEW

OCTOBER

WBC light heavyweight champion Jeff Harding retains the crown with a second-round stoppage of veteran British bomber Tom Collins.

NOVEMBER

Robert Daniels wins the vacant WBA cruiserweight title by scoring a split 12-round decision over former champion Dwight Muhammad Qawi.

Australian Jeff Harding stopped Tom Collins.

RING DECADE

1990-1993

IN THE early-'80s, boxing fans were spoiled by a string of great fights. One followed the other, creating a most wonderful monotony. Unfortunately the rest of the decade couldn't maintain the pace.

Fight for fight, and fighter for fighter, the early-'90s won't be remembered as particularly special. But over the first three years of the decade, a series of events, both in the ring and out, drew a maelstrom of emotions. For boxing fans, first came wonder, then resignation, and, finally, hope.

Before three months had been played out, we saw a pair of fights that reminded us just how unpredictable the sport could be. On February 11, 1990, in Tokyo, unified world heavyweight champion Mike Tyson, 37-0, defended against 42-1 underdog Buster Douglas, a reasonably talented veteran who had consistently lacked conditioning and courage. It was Tyson, however, who was poorly prepared, and as a result, Douglas managed the unthinkable. Rising from an eighth-round knockdown (so much for his lack of heart), the challenger closed Tyson's left eye and knocked him down and out in the 10th. Like Sonny Liston and George Foreman before him, Tyson was a mere mortal. It took the greatest upset in history to prove it.

Only five weeks later, junior welterweight champions Julio Cesar Chavez (WBC) and Meldrick Taylor (IBF) left an international audience breathless. The unbeaten challengers clashed on March 17 in Las Vegas. Quicker, faster, perhaps even stronger, Taylor outgunned his Mexican rival and seemed en route to an inspired victory. But the indomitable Chavez rallied in the last round and scored a desperation knockdown with 16 seconds to go. Taylor rose at referee Richard Steel's count of six, but was not allowed to continue. The stoppage, the most controversial of all-time, came with Taylor ahead on the cards and two seconds remaining!

"No way in hell should he have stopped a fight of this magnitude," cried Taylor. "I saw a beaten fighter," countered Steele. "His eyes and condition were telling me that he had enough."

Massive Brooklyn-born Riddick Bowe struck gold in racking up his 32nd consecutive victory when he outpointed Evander Holyfield and became heavyweight king.

A third fight brought no storybook ending, but a fascinating storyline, and, like Douglas-Tyson and Chavez-Taylor, a sense of wonderment. On April 19, 1991, undisputed heavyweight champion Evander Holyfield, who had been an easy kayo winner of Douglas, made his first defense against 42-year-old former champion George Foreman. That Big George manoeuvered his way into a try at the title was due more to his everyman, middle-aged appeal than his accomplishments during his unlikely comeback. That aside, his gutty distance performance, though a losing one, both pleased and relieved the pay-per-view audience, which made Holyfield-Foreman one of the most successful promotions in history.

Lennox Lewis rocketed to worldwide fame when he knocked out heavily favored Razor Ruddock. When undisputed heavyweight king Riddick Bowe side-stepped Lewis' solidly justified challenge, the WBC stripped Bowe of the title and proclaimed Lewis champion, giving Britain its first heavyweight king since Bob Fitzsimmons.

If Foreman was all fun and wonder, Tyson had become a most grim and sobering reality. A pair of comeback wins over dangerous contender Razor Ruddock again placed him at the foot of the throne, and he was established as a clear choice to unseat Holyfield. But the bout was first postponed because of an injury to Tyson's ribs, and then cancelled for a far more serious reason.

In September 1991, Tyson was indicted by a grand jury in Indianapolis, Indiana, for the July rape of Desiree Washington, an 18-year-old contestant at the Miss Black America Pageant. The story hit boxing like one of Tyson's thudding hooks, and boxing

Trigger-fisted, hard-punching Julio Cesar Chavez has never lost in 85 fights, an unsurpassed record that puts him in a class with the greatest of all-time.

fans were left shaking their heads in bitter resignation.

Tyson's trial ran every other story off the front page. On February 10, 1992, almost exactly two years after he had fallen at the feet of Douglas, the 25-year-old former champion was found guilty. His sentence: six-to-10 years. Tyson was most likely to serve about three years; in Indiana, an inmate receives one day off his sentence for each day of exemplary service.

"I have always thought he was on the road to self destruction," said Randy Gorion, Chairman of the New York State Athletic Commission. "There was just too much rage inside of him."

With its biggest hero redefined as a convicted felon, boxing badly needed a boost. Instead came another black eye. On February 8, two days before Tyson was found guilty, IBF middleweight champion James Toney retained the title by split decision over clubfighter Dave Tiberi. Having struggled to make weight, Toney fought poorly. By the late rounds, he was dehydrated. Many ringsiders thought Tiberi deserved the verdict, and ABC-TV analyst Alex Wallau, one of the most respected voices in the sport, called the decision "disgusting" and "cruel."

So enraged was William Roth, a Senator from Tiberi's home state of Delaware, that he co-sponsored a bill to create a federal boxing commission. In conduction with the proposed legislation came two days of hearings, held in August by the Senate's Permanent Subcommittee on Investigations. The headline-making testimony served to remind the public just how ugly the business of boxing was. (It was anticipated that Congress would consider Roth's bill some time in 1993.)

Those hoping that the 1992 Summer Olympics would bring relief were disappointed. A ridiculous computerized scoring system overshadowed even the finest of gold medal-winning performances.

Under the scoring rules, the fighter landing the most punches would be awarded the decision. For a punch to register, three of the five judges had to strike a pad (blue for one fighter, red for the other) on their keyboard within one second of one another. The idea was to replace the subjectivity of scoring with a more exact method. It was an embarrassing failure. (One judge, Ghana's Keith Dadzie, was suspended after scoring two bouts 0-0.) Several obvious winners were denied victory, and the boxing competition became a laughingstock.

Once again, boxing had displayed the uncanny knack of landing a crushing blow to its own chin. Nonetheless, the last three months of 1992 brought hope. Illuminating the three-ring circus of Barcelona was lightweight gold medal winner Oscar De La Hoya, a Mexican-American from Los Angeles. De La Hoya was paid a $1-million signing bonus to turn pro, and after he won his first three pro bouts with the skills and charisma of a young Sugar Ray Leonard, he was being projected as a world titlist by the end of 1993, and a multi-division champion soon after that.

"He's a terrific talent, probably the most I've ever seen at this age," said *Los Angeles Times* boxing columnist Earl Gustkey.

Another terrific talent emerged on November 13, when Riddick Bowe took the world heavyweight title from Holyfield. Bowe had the size (6'5", 235 pounds), power, and personality to fit the title. But until his demanding battle vs. Holyfield, he had never displayed the heart.

Two weeks before Bowe's sensational triumph, Britain's Lennox Lewis brutally kayoed Ruddock to emerge as the top contender. A bout with Bowe, whom he had stopped in the gold medal bout at the 1988 Olympics, was signed and sealed, but not delivered. Until it materializes, WBA-IBF champion Bowe and Lewis, who was named WBC champion after Bowe opted to fight Michael Dokes, will attempt to hype their inevitable showdown with a victory or two apiece.

With De La Hoya, Bowe, and Lewis joining established stars Chavez, Buddy McGirt, Pernell Whitaker, and Terry Norris, boxing in the '90s settled into strong hands. There have never been any ills a couple of superstars and superfights couldn't cure.

Terry Norris is judged by many experts to be a better fighter, pound for pound, than Julio Cesar Chavez. A Norris-Chavez battle could well prove to be the fight of the decade.

Oscar De La Hoya, the only American to win the gold at the 1992 Olympics, displayed such extraordinary skill and promise that he was paid $1-million before he even turned pro.

JANUARY

1990

APRIL

THE UPSET OF THE CENTURY

His mother had just died. He was separated from his wife. The mother of his son was seriously ill.

And James "Buster" Douglas had to fight Mike Tyson.

On February 11, world heavyweight champion Tyson, a 42-1 favorite, defended against the underachieving Douglas at the Tokyo Dome. But this wasn't the Tyson who had steamrolled 37 consecutive opponents. Flat and poorly conditioned, the champion was outboxed from the start. The 6'4" Douglas closed Tyson's left eye with ramrod jabs, and punished him with straight rights.

Tyson almost saved the title by dropping Douglas with an eighth-round uppercut. But Buster rebounded to pummel "Iron Mike" in the 10th. The final blow was a hook, and with Tyson struggling to regain his feet, referee Octavio Meyran counted him out at the 1:23 mark. (After nine rounds, the bout was even on points.)

No one could decide which was more shocking: That Tyson was no longer heavyweight champion, or that Douglas was.

In one of history's greatest upsets, "Buster" Douglas ended Mike Tyson's undefeated streak.

JANUARY

In a crossroads heavyweight battle of comebacking heavyweights, former world champion George Foreman, 40, crushes Gerry Cooney in two rounds.

FEBRUARY

IBF featherweight champion Jorge Paez retains the title with a controversial and split 12-round decision over tireless puncher Troy Dorsey.

WORLD TITLE FIGHTS

HEAVYWEIGHTS

Feb 11 **Buster Douglas** (USA) *KO* 10
Mike Tyson, Tokyo

CRUISERWEIGHTS

Jan 27 **Carlos DeLeon** *D* 12
Johnny Nelson, Sheffield

March 22 **Jeff Lampkin** (USA) *KO* 3
Glenn McCrory, Gateshead

LIGHT HEAVYWEIGHTS

Jan 7 **Prince Charles Williams** *KO* 8
Frankie Swindell, Atlantic City

Feb 25 **Virgil Hill** *W* 12
David Vedder, Bismarck, ND

March 18 **Jeff Harding** *KO* 11
Nestor Giovannini, Atlantic City

SUPER MIDDLEWEIGHTS

Jan 13 **In Chul Baek** *KO* 7
Yoshiaki Tajima, Ulsan, South Korea

Jan 27 **Lindell Holmes** (USA) *W* 12
Frank Tate, New Orleans
(Wins Vacant IBF Title)

March 30 **Christophe Tiozzo** *KO* 6
In Chul Baek, Lyon, France

MIDDLEWEIGHTS

Feb 3 **Mike McCallum** *W* 12
Steve Collins, Boston

April 14 **Mike McCallum** *KO* 11
Michael Watson, London

April 14 **Michael Nunn** *W* 12
Marlon Starling, Las Vegas

JUNIOR MIDDLEWEIGHTS

March 31 **Terry Norris** (USA) *KO* 1
John Mugabi, Tampa

April 14 **Gianfranco Rosi** *KO* 7
Kevin Daigle, Monte Carlo

WELTERWEIGHTS

March 3 **Mark Breland** *KO* 3
Lloyd Honeyghan, London

April 1 **Simon Brown** *KO* 10
Tyrone Trice, Washington, D.C.

JUNIOR WELTERWEIGHTS

March 17 **Julio Cesar Chavez** *KO* 12
Meldrick Taylor, Las Vegas

March 24 **Juan Coggi** *W* 12
Jose Luis Ramirez, Ajaccio, Corsica

LIGHTWEIGHTS

Feb 3 **Pernell Whitaker** *W* 12
Freddie Pendleton, Atlantic City

April 4 **Juan Nazario** (PR) *KO* 8
Edwin Rosario, New York City

JUNIOR LIGHTWEIGHTS

Jan 28 **John-John Molina** *KO* 6
Lupe Suarez, Atlantic City

March 14 **Brian Mitchell** *W* 12
Jackie Beard, Grosseto, Italy

FEATHERWEIGHTS

Feb 4 **Jorge Paez** *W* 12
Troy Dorsey, Las Vegas

April 7 **Jorge Paez** *W* 12
Louie Espinoza, Las Vegas

JUNIOR FEATHERWEIGHTS

March 10 **Welcome Ncita** (SA) *W* 12
Fabrice Benichou, Tel Aviv

April 23 **Paul Banke** (USA) *KO* 9
Daniel Zaragoza, Los Angeles

BANTAMWEIGHTS

Jan 22 **Raul Perez** *W* 12
Gaby Canizales, Los Angeles

Jan 24 **Orlando Canizales** *W* 12
Billy Hardy, Sunderland, England

JUNIOR BANTAMWEIGHTS

Jan 20 **Sung Kil Moon** *Tech Dec* 9
Nana Konadu, Seoul

March 29 **Khaosai Galaxy** *KO* 5
Cobra Ari Blanca, Bangkok

April 21 **Robert Quiroga** (USA) *W* 12
Juan Polo Perez, Sunderland, England

FLYWEIGHTS

Jan 30 **Sot Chitalada** *W* 12
Ric Siodoro, Bangkok

March 10 **Yul Woo Lee** *W* 12
Jesus Rojas, Seoul

March 17 **Dave McAuley** *W* 12
Louis Curtis, Belfast

JUNIOR FLYWEIGHTS

Jan 14 **Myung Woo Yuh** *KO* 7
Hisashi Takashima, Seoul

Jan 19 **Muangchai Kittikasem** *KO* 3
Jeung Jai Lee, Bangkok

March 24 **Humberto Gonzalez** *KO* 3
Francisco Tejedor, Mexico City

April 10 **Muangchai Kittikasem** *W* 12
Abdi Pohan, Bangkok

April 29 **Myung Woo Yuh** *W* 12
Leo Gamez, Seoul

STRAWWEIGHTS

Feb 7 **Hideyuki Ohashi** (JAP) *KO* 9
Jeum Hwan Choi, Tokyo

Feb 10 **Bong Jun Kim** *KO* 4
Petchai Chuvatana, Seoul

Feb 22 **Phalan Lukmingkwan** (THA) *KO* 7
Eric Chavez, Bangkok

WINNING WITH TWO SECONDS TO SPARE

Billed as the first great fight of the '90s, the junior welterweight title unification pitting Julio Cesar Chavez (WBC) vs. Meldrick Taylor (IBF) turned out to be the decade's first great controversy.

On March 17, the unbeaten stars met at the Hilton Center in Las Vegas. Expected to box, Taylor surprised his Mexican foe by outgunning him at close range.

"He was faster than I was," acknowledged Chavez. "He was stronger."

Chavez was outpunched, but his blows were more telling; Taylor's face swelled and his lip was torn, forcing him to swallow nearly two pints of his own blood.

With three minutes remaining, Taylor led on two of the three cards. But he was staggered late in the 12th, and with 16 seconds left, Chavez felled him with a straight right. Taylor picked himself up at referee Richard Steele's count of six, but wasn't allowed to continue; Steele stopped the fight with two seconds left.

"I was not going to let him take another punch," he said.

Not even for two seconds.

George Foreman knocked out Gerry Cooney.

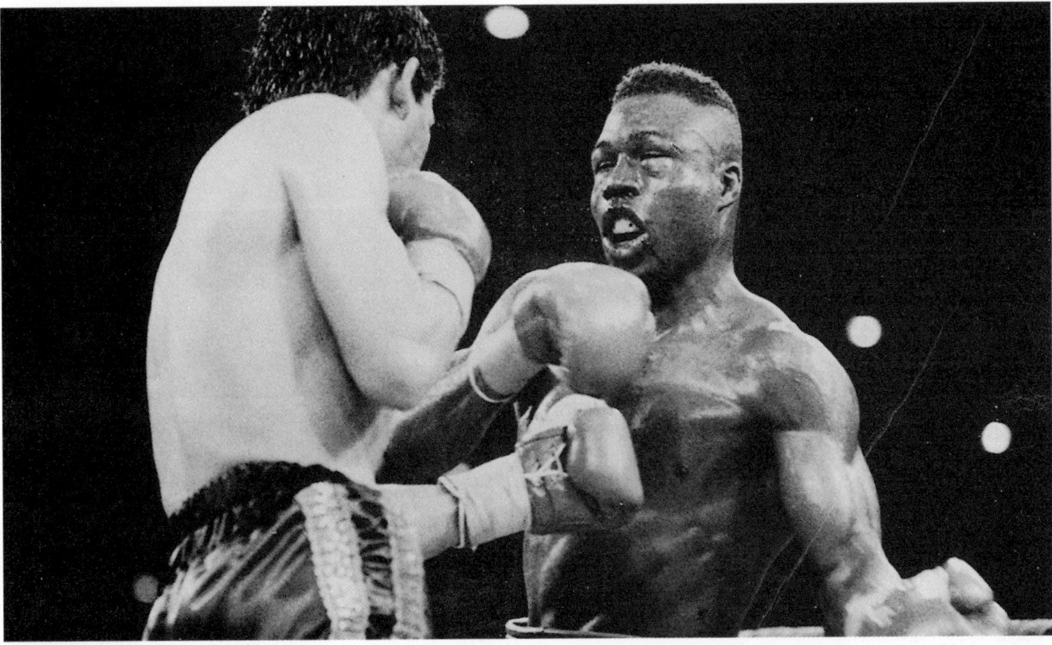

In one of the most exciting and controversial fights of recent years, Julio Cesar Chavez (left) stopped Meldrick Taylor with only two seconds left.

FEASTING ON THE BEAST

A valuable lesson wasn't wasted on 22-year-old Terry Norris. In 1989, the California-based junior middleweight became overconfident during his challenge of WBA champion Julian Jackson. Ouch! In the second round, he was finished by one punch. The lesson learned: if you open your guns, make sure you finish your man.

Norris' second chance came on March 31, when he was matched with WBC titlist John "The Beast" Mugabi at the Sun Dome in the champion's adopted hometown of Tampa. The bout lasted 167 seconds. Norris outslugged the slugger, staggering him with a hook, and then downing him with a flurry. When Mugabi rose, he fought back with fire. Just when he seemed ready to explode, he was blasted by an overhand right. The Beast fell face-first and remained flat for several minutes. It was vivid testimony that Terry Norris had learned to finish.

Terry Norris (left) knocked out John Mugabi in the first round and won the junior middleweight title.

MAY

1990

AUGUST

BAD BREATH, AND A GOOD JAB

Before WBC and IBF lightweight champion Pernell Whitaker defended against WBC super featherweight titlist Azumah Nelson, he was told by trainer George Benton to "box him like you got bad breath." So *that* explained the garlic odor in his dressing room.

Whitaker knew just what Benton meant, and on May 19, at Caesars Palace, he executed his fight plan to perfection. Smoothly keeping his distance, "Sweet Pea" jabbed and used subtle lateral movement. Nelson, seeking his third championship, was reduced to a hunter unable to locate his prey.

Nelson had mild success in the late rounds, but could never land in combination. ("He hit me so hard one time," said Whitaker, "I think I saw my two sons. And they weren't even at the fight.") Still, Whitaker kept the crown by the surprisingly close scores of 116-114, 115-113, and 116-111.

RINGSIDE VIEW

JUNE

Mexico's Marcos Villasana becomes a world champion in his fifth try, capturing the vacant WBC featherweight title with an eighth-round TKO of England's plucky Paul Hodkinson.

Marcos Villasana (left) stopped Paul Hodkinson in the eighth to win the featherweight crown.

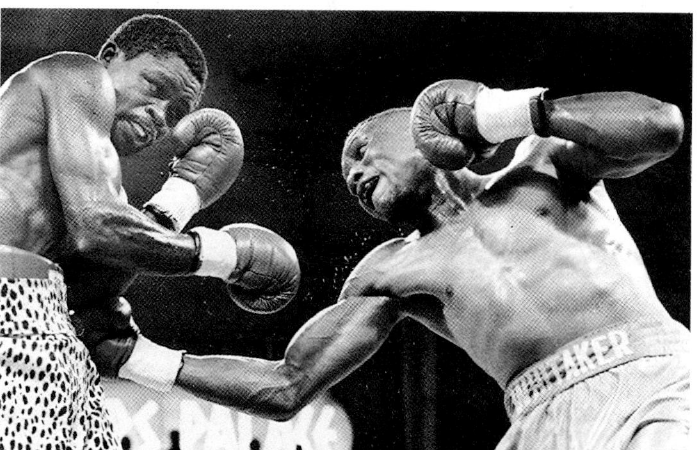

Trigger-fisted Pernell Whitaker (right) was always a step ahead of Azumah Nelson.

WORLD TITLE FIGHTS

CRUISERWEIGHTS

July 19 **Robert Daniels** *W* 12 Craig Bodzianowski, Seattle

July 27 **Massimiliano Duran** (ITA) *W Disq* 11 Carlos De Leon, Capo d'Orlando, Italy

July 29 **Jeff Lampkin** *KO* 8 Siza Makhathini, St. Petersburg, FL

LIGHT HEAVYWEIGHTS

July 7 **Virgil Hill** *W* 12 Tyrone Frazier, Bismarck, ND

July 28 **Dennis Andries** *KO* 7 Jeff Harding, Melbourne

SUPER MIDDLEWEIGHTS

July 19 **Lindell Holmes** *KO* 9 Carl Sullivan, Seattle

July 20 **Christophe Tiozzo** *KO* 8 Paul Whittaker, Aries, France

JUNIOR MIDDLEWEIGHTS

July 13 **Terry Norris** *W* 12 Rene Jacquot, Annecy, France

July 21 **Gianfranco Rosi** *W* 12 Darrin Van Horn, Marino, Italy

WELTERWEIGHTS

July 8 **Aaron Davis** (USA) *KO* 9 Mark Breland, Reno

Aug 19 **Maurice Blocker** (USA) *W* 12 Marlon Starling, Reno

JUNIOR WELTERWEIGHTS

Aug 17 **Loreto Garza** (USA) *W* 12 Juan Coggi, Nice

LIGHTWEIGHTS

May 19 **Pernell Whitaker** *W* 12 Azumah Nelson, Las Vegas

Aug 11 **Pernell Whitaker** *KO* 1 Juan Nazario, Stateline, NV (Unifies World Title)

JUNIOR LIGHTWEIGHTS

May 20 **Tony Lopez** *W* 12 John-John Molina, Reno

FEATHERWEIGHTS

May 13 **Antonio Esparragoza** *W* 12 Chan Mok Park, Seoul

June 2 **Marcos Villasana** (MEX) *KO* 8 Paul Hodkinson, Manchester (Wins Vacant WBC Title)

July 8 **Jorge Paez** *D* 12 Troy Dorsey, Las Vegas

JUNIOR FEATHERWEIGHTS

May 26 **Luis Mendoza** *D* 12 Ruben Palacios, Cartagena (For Vacant IBF Title)

June 2 **Welcome Ncita** *KO* 7 Ramon Cruz, Rome

Aug 17 **Paul Banke** *KO* 12 Ki Jun Lee, Seoul

BANTAMWEIGHTS

May 7 **Raul Perez** *KO* 9 Gerardo Martinez, Inglewood

May 30 **Luisito Espinosa** *KO* 8 Hurley Snead, Bangkok

June 10 **Orlando Canizales** *KO* 2 Paul Gonzales, El Paso

Aug 14 **Orlando Canizales** *KO* 5 Eddie Rangel, Saratoga Springs, NY

JUNIOR BANTAMWEIGHTS

June 9 **Sung Kil Moon** *KO* 8 Gilberto Roman, Seoul

June 30 **Khaosai Galaxy** *KO* 8 Shunichi Nakajima, Chiang Mai, Thailand

FLYWEIGHTS

May 1 **Sot Chitalada** *W* 12 Carlos Salazar, Bangkok

July 28 **Leopard Tamakuma** *KO* 10 Yul Woo Lee, Tokyo

JUNIOR FLYWEIGHTS

June 4 **Humberto Gonzalez** *KO* 3 Carlos Monzote, Inglewood

July 23 **Humberto Gonzalez** *KO* 5 Jung Keun Lim, Inglewood

July 29 **Michael Carbajal** (USA) *KO* 7 Muangchai Kittikasem, Phoenix

Aug 26 **Humberto Gonzalez** *KO* 8 Jorge Rivera, Cancun, Mexico

STRAWWEIGHTS

May 13 **Bong Jun Kim** *W* 12 Silverio Barcenas, Seoul

June 8 **Hideyuki Ohashi** *W* 12 Napa Kiatwanchai, Tokyo

June 24 **Phalan Lukmingkwan** *W* 12 Joe Constantino, Bangkok

Aug 15 **Phalan Lukmingkwan** *W* 12 Eric Chavez, Bangkok

SUPER DUPER SUPERMAN SEES IT THROUGH

Aaron Davis couldn't see Mark Breland. But that didn't mean that he couldn't beat him.

On July 8, the unbeaten Davis, humbly nicknamed "Superman," challenged fellow New Yorker and WBA welterweight champion Breland at Harrah's Reno. It was a sloppy and uneven fight, albeit an exciting one. Davis staggered the champion with jabs in rounds one and two, and floored him with a combination in the third. By then, however, the challenger, an 8-1 underdog, was squinting through a swollen and badly discolored right eye. Despite his early-rounds success, a stoppage seemed imminent.

Said Davis, "I kept telling the doctors, 'Please don't stop the fight.'"

Bloodied but game, Breland gained control in the eighth, hammering Davis with several straight rights. But Superman was strong enough to survive, and late in the ninth, a haymaker of a right drove Breland down for referee Mills Lane's full count. It was the final chapter in his disappointing championship career.

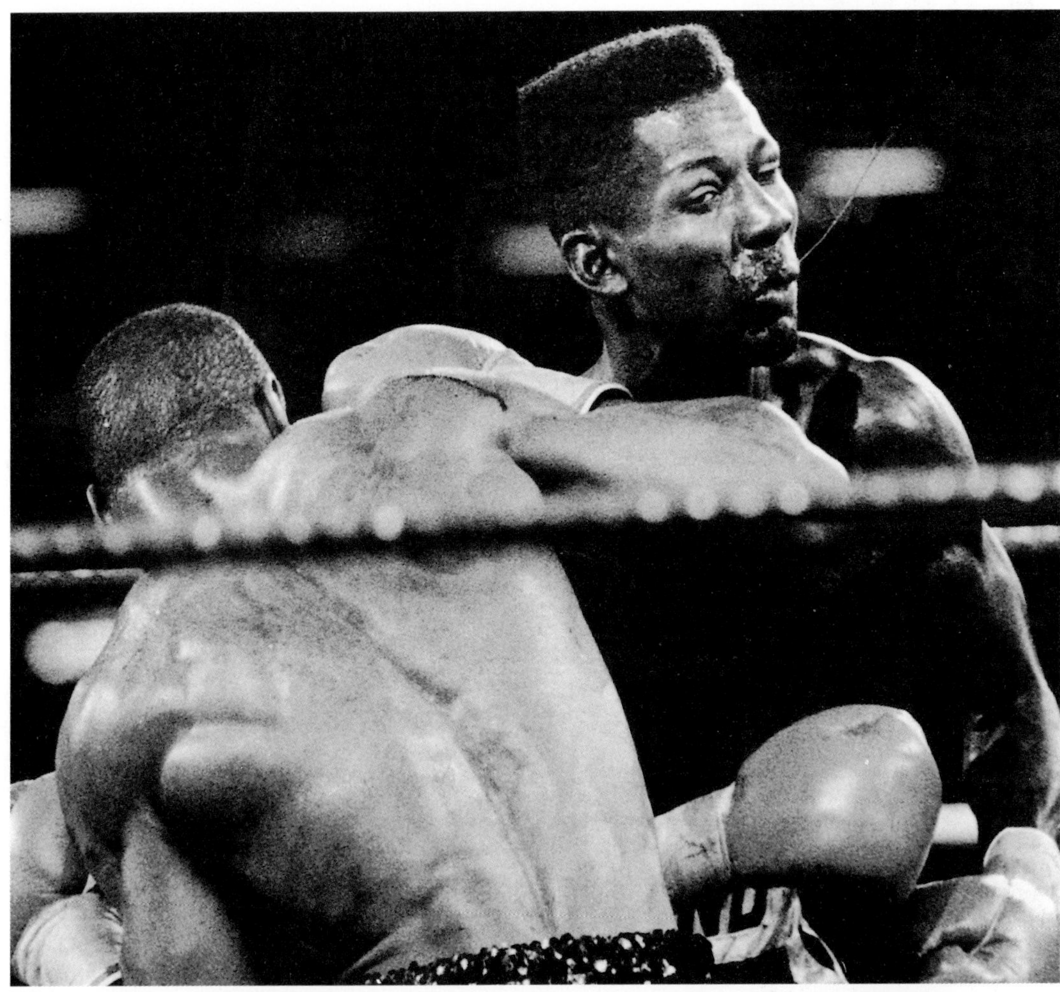

Aaron Davis delivers a blow with four seconds left in the ninth round that knocked out defending welterweight champion Mark Breland.

LITTLE HANDS OF STONE PUNCHES TOWARD BIG DREAMS OF GLORY

Boxing's first million-dollar flyweight? Michael Carbajal hardly seemed a likely candidate. The Olympic class of 1988 featured high profile fighters like Riddick Bowe, Andrew Maynard, and Roy Jones. Carbajal, a silver medalist, was quiet and shy. But "Little Hands of Stone" – his idol was Roberto Duran – could really fight.

On July 29, the unbeaten junior flyweight challenged IBF champion Muangchai Kittikasem at the Veteran's Memorial Coliseum in Carbajal's hometown of Phoenix. The Thai fought gallantly, but Carbajal took advantage of his shaky chin. Kittikasem fell twice in the fourth, was issued a standing-eight count in the sixth, and crashed again at the start of the seventh, at which point referee Bobby Ferrara called a halt.

Afterward, promoter Bob Arum spoke glowingly of the new champion, claiming that Carbajal would someday fight for $1-million. Frivolous hype? Perhaps. But little fighters can have big dreams.

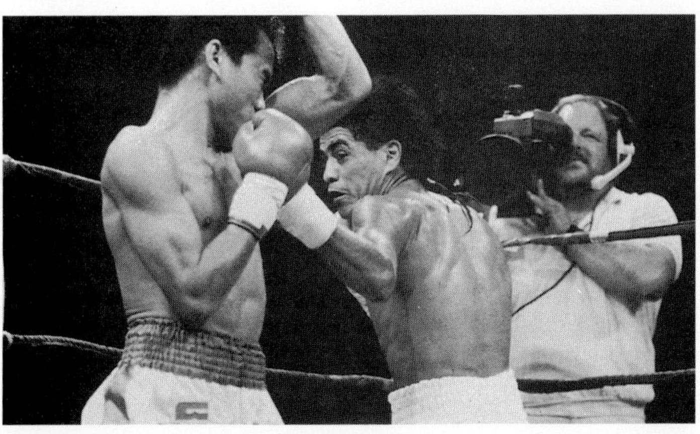

Michael Carbajal (right) stopped Muangchai Kittikasem to become junior flyweight champion.

RINGSIDE VIEW

JUNE

Former junior bantamweight champion Gilberto Roman, 28, is killed when his car smashes into a tractor-trailer near Mexico City.

JULY

Dennis Andries regains the WBC light heavyweight title by knocking out arch-rival Jeff Harding in the seventh round. Harding had dethroned Andries in June 1989.

SEPTEMBER

1990

DECEMBER

BLUBBERY BUSTER AND A BODY BEAUTIFUL

Success didn't go to Buster Douglas' head. Instead, it headed straight for his stomach. The heavyweight champion trained for his first defense, for which he was paid a record $24.1-million, by sitting in a sauna and ordering room-service pizza. (No, we're not kidding.) Meanwhile, former cruiserweight champion Evander Holyfield was working out with two trainers, two bodybuilders, a fitness specialist, and a ballet instructor.

On fight night at the Mirage (October 25), Holyfield scaled 208, and Douglas a rubbery 246. (He had been 231 for his title-winning effort vs. Mike Tyson.) For two rounds, nothing happened. In the third, Douglas led with a right uppercut. Holyfield took a half-step back and countered with a textbook right. Boom! Referee Mills Lane counted Douglas out at the 1:10 mark.

"I don't know if he could've gotten up," said Lane, "but he sure never tried."

The pizza must have been weighing him down.

Undefeated Evander Holyfield knocked out James "Buster" Douglas in the third round to become the new heavyweight champion of the world.

RINGSIDE VIEW

NOVEMBER

Badly outboxed for three rounds, Julian Jackson wins the vacant WBC middleweight title in the fourth by crushing British southpaw Herol Graham with a single right hand.

THE YO-YO APPROACH

If you watched all of Dave McAuley's bouts, you'd swear that flyweights were the most exciting fighters in the world. In 1987, the Irishman and Fidel Bassa engaged in the 112-pound Fight of the Decade. And on September 15, at King's Hall in Belfast, he kept the IBF title under the most unusual of circumstances.

McAuley's opponent, Colombia's Rodolfo Blanco, scored four knockdowns, dropping the champion twice in the second, once in the third, and for a final time in the 11th. McAuley answered only once, downing Blanco in round nine, but still managed to win by unanimous 12-round decision (117-113, 113-111, and 115-110).

"To go out and win the last round as easily as he did," said Eastwood, McAuley's manager, "proved what a great champion he really is. I've never known any man who fights as well when hurt. His well of courage is deep!"

Dave McAuley (left) and Rodolfo Blanco after Dave retained the flyweight title by decision in a magnificent bout.

RINGSIDE VIEW

DECEMBER

In a major surprise, Filipino Rolando Pascua captures the WBC light flyweight crown with a sixth-round kayo of the previously unbeaten Humberto Gonzalez.

Gonzalez after being stopped by Pascua.

FIGHTING FOR THE HOME TURF

At middleweight, at least, the British didn't need the rest of the world. Contenders Chris Eubank, Nigel Benn, and Michael Watson were engaged in a hot round robin.

On November 18, at the National Exhibition Centre in Birmingham, Eubank and Benn partook in a gut-wrenching duel. Eubank was the boxer, and Benn the puncher. But the contest came down to heart.

Both fighters were hurt early. Eubank gained a slight edge in the middle rounds, closing his opponent's left eye. Benn rebounded to score a flash knockdown.

The end came in the ninth, after Eubank broke through with a left-right and a followup flurry. Referee Richard Steele rescued a defenseless Benn at the 2:56 mark.

"I never felt pain like I felt tonight," Eubank said afterward. "If all boxers were as powerful as him, I would quit."

Britain's Chris Eubank (left) stopped countryman Nigel Benn in the ninth round.

WORLD TITLE FIGHTS

HEAVYWEIGHTS

Oct 25 **Evander Holyfield** *KO* 3
Buster Douglas, Las Vegas

CRUISERWEIGHTS

Nov 22 **Robert Daniels** *D* 12
Taoufik Belbouli, Madrid

Dec 8 **Massimiliano Duran** *W Disq* 12
Anaclet Wamba, Ferrara, Italy

LIGHT HEAVYWEIGHTS

Oct 10 **Dennis Andries** *KO* 4
Sergio Merani, London

SUPER MIDDLEWEIGHTS

Nov 23 **Christophe Tiozzo** *KO* 2
Danny Morgan, Cergy Pontoise, France

Dec 15 **Mauro Galvano** (ITA) *W* 12
Dario Matteoni, Monte Carlo
(Wins Vacant WBC Title)

Dec 16 **Lindell Holmes** *W* 12
Sugar Boy Malinga, Marino, Italy

MIDDLEWEIGHTS

Oct 18 **Michael Nunn** *KO* 10
Donald Curry, Paris

Nov 24 **Julian Jackson** *KO* 4
Herol Graham, Benalmadena, Spain

JUNIOR MIDDLEWEIGHTS

Nov 30 **Gianfranco Rosi** *W* 12
Rene Jacquot, Marsala, France

JUNIOR WELTERWEIGHTS

Dec 1 **Loreto Garza** *W Disq* 11
Vinny Pazienza, Sacramento

Dec 8 **Julio Cesar Chavez** *KO* 3
Kyung Duk Ahn, Atlantic City

JUNIOR LIGHTWEIGHTS

Sept 22 **Tony Lopez** *W* 12
Jorge Paez, Sacramento

Sept 29 **Brian Mitchell** *W* 12
Frankie Mitchell, Aosta, Italy

Oct 13 **Azumah Nelson** *W* 12
Juan LaPorte, Sydney

FEATHERWEIGHTS

Sept 30 **Marcos Villasana** *KO* 8
Javier Marquez, Mexico City

JUNIOR FEATHERWEIGHTS

Sept 11 **Luis Mendoza** *KO* 3
Ruben Palacios, Miami
(Wins Vacant IBF Title)

Sept 29 **Welcome Ncita** *KO* 8
Gerardo Lopez, Aosta, Italy

Oct 18 **Luis Mendoza** *W* 12
Fabrice Benichou, Paris

Nov 5 **Pedro Decima** (ARG) *KO* 4
Paul Banke, Inglewood

BANTAMWEIGHTS

Sept 14 **Raul Perez** *D* 12
Pepillo Valdez, Culiacan, Mexico

Nov 29 **Luisito Espinosa** *W* 12
Thalerngsak Sithbaobay, Bangkok

Dec 17 **Raul Perez** *KO* 8
Candelario Carmona, Tijuana

JUNIOR BANTAMWEIGHTS

Sept 29 **Khaosai Galaxy** *KO* 6
Yong Kang Kim, Suphan Buri, Thailand

Oct 6 **Robert Quiroga** *KO* 3
Vuyani Nene, Pagliara, Italy

Oct 20 **Sung Kil Moon** *W* 12
Kenji Matsumura, Seoul

Dec 9 **Khaosai Galaxy** *KO* 6
Ernesto Ford, Petchabun, Thailand

FLYWEIGHTS

Sept 9 **Sot Chitalada** *KO* 11
Richard Clarke, Kingston

Sept 15 **Dave McAuley** *W* 12
Rodolfo Blanco, Belfast

Nov 24 **Sot Chitalada** *W* 12
Jung Koo Chang, Seoul

Dec 6 **Leopard Tamakuma** *W* 12
Jesus Rojas, Aomori, Japan

JUNIOR FLYWEIGHTS

Nov 10 **Myung Woo Yuh** *W* 12
Leo Gamez, Seoul

Dec 8 **Michael Carbajal** *KO* 4
Leon Salazar, Scottsdale, AZ

Dec 19 **Rolando Pascua** (PHI) *KO* 6
Humberto Gonzalez, Inglewood

STRAWWEIGHTS

Oct 25 **Ricardo Lopez** (MEX) *KO* 5
Hideyuki Ohashi, Tokyo

Nov 3 **Bong Jun Kim** *W* 12
Silverio Barcenas, Taegu, South Korea

Dec 20 **Phalan Lukmingkwan** *D* 12
Pretty Boy Lucas, Bangkok

JANUARY

1991

APRIL

STOP ME WHEN IT HURTS

Simon Brown beat up his best friend. Mike Tyson beat up just another enemy. And Richard Steele got pumelled by the press.

On March 18, welterweight champions Brown (IBF) and Maurice Blocker (WBA) partially unified the title at The Mirage in Las Vegas. The fighters lived near one another, trained together, and socialized with each other's families. Why, then, were they fighting?

"Money," explained Blocker, "makes you do crazy things."

The welters traded mercilessly until the 10th, when the stronger Brown scored a knockdown, and a subsequent stoppage.

As for Tyson, the former champion downed Razor Ruddock in the second and third rounds. The Razor rallied in the sixth, but in the seventh, Tyson connected with a right-left. Ruddock fell against the ropes, and referee Richard Steele elected to call a halt.

The premature stoppage prompted a postfight melee featuring Tyson's trainer, Rich Giachetti, and Ruddock's promoter, Murad Muhammad. Somehow, Steele managed to escape unscathed.

RINGSIDE VIEW

JANUARY

Meldrick Taylor wins his second world title, capturing the WBA welterweight crown with a unanimous 12-round decision over Aaron Davis.

MARCH

In an attempt to partially unify the junior lightweight title, champions Brian Mitchell (WBA) and Tony Lopez (IBF) struggle to a well-fought 12-round draw.

Meldrick Taylor (right) won his second title by decisioning Davis in welterweight title go.

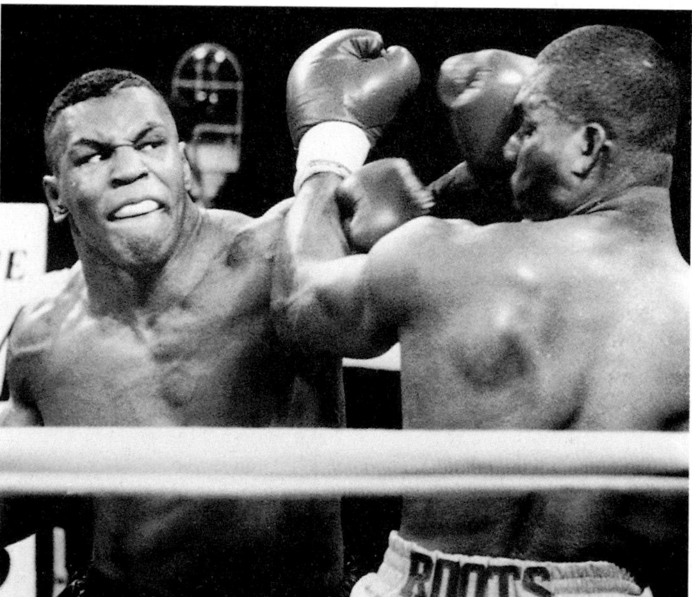

Ex-heavyweight champ Mike Tyson (left) won by TKO over Razor Ruddock.

RE-RE-RE-RETIRING RAY

His lower lip torn and his left eye swollen, Sugar Ray Leonard asked for the ring microphone and announced, "This was my last fight." He meant it, too. His fourth (or fifth?) retirement would be for real.

Leonard's exit turned out to be no different from countless others. On February 9, the 34-year-old former champion fought for the first time at Madison Square Garden. His opponent, 23-year-old WBC super welterweight titlist Terry Norris, proved far too sharp. Leonard was felled in rounds two and seven, and barely hung on to last the 12-round distance. The unanimous scores reflected Norris' dominance: 120-104, 119-103, and 116-110.

"I had to find out for myself," said Leonard. "It just wasn't there."

Sugar Ray's final mark: 36-2-1 (25). He was boxing's only five-division champion, and, in the '80s, the Fighter of the Decade. Moreover, he had earned his "Sugar Ray" nickname.

Terry Norris (right) gave 34-year-old Sugar Ray Leonard a brutal 12-round beating.

World Title Fights

HEAVYWEIGHTS

April 19 **Evander Holyfield** *W* 12
George Foreman, Atlantic City

CRUISERWEIGHTS

March 8 **Bobby Czyz** *W* 12
Robert Daniels, Atlantic City

LIGHT HEAVYWEIGHTS

Jan 6 **Virgil Hill** *W* 12
Mike Peak, Bismarck, ND

Jan 12 **Prince Charles Williams** *W* 12
Mwehu Beya, St. Vincent, Italy

Jan 19 **Dennis Andries** *W* 12
Guy Waters, Adelaide, Australia

April 20 **Prince Charles Williams** *KO* 2
James Kinchen, Atlantic City

SUPER MIDDLEWEIGHTS

March 7 **Lindell Holmes** *W* 12
Antoine Byrd, Madrid

April 5 **Victor Cordoba** (PAN) *KO* 9
Christophe Tiozzo, Marseille

MIDDLEWEIGHTS

April 1 **Mike McCallum** *W* 12
Sumbu Kalambay, Monte Carlo

JUNIOR MIDDLEWEIGHTS

Feb 9 **Terry Norris** *W* 12
Sugar Ray Leonard, New York City

Feb 23 **Gilbert Dele** (GUA) *KO* 7
Carlos Elliott, Point-a-Pitre, Guadeloupe
(Wins Vacant WBA Title)

March 16 **Gianfranco Rosi** *W* 12
Ron Amundsen, Saint Vincent, Italy

WELTERWEIGHTS

Jan 19 **Meldrick Taylor** *W* 12
Aaron Davis, Atlantic City

March 18 **Simon Brown** *KO* 10
Maurice Blocker, Las Vegas
(Wins IBF Title; Retains WBC Title)

JUNIOR WELTERWEIGHTS

March 18 **Julio Cesar Chavez** *KO* 4
John Duplessis, Las Vegas

LIGHTWEIGHTS

Feb 23 **Pernell Whitaker** *W* 12
Anthony Jones, Las Vegas

JUNIOR LIGHTWEIGHTS

March 15 **Brian Mitchell** *D* 12
Tony Lopez, Sacramento
(For WBA & IBF Titles)

FEATHERWEIGHTS

March 30 **Yung Kyun Park** (KOR) *W* 12
Antonio Esparragoza, Kwangju, South Korea

April 11 **Marcos Villasana** *KO* 6
Rafael Zuniga, Mexico City

JUNIOR FEATHERWEIGHTS

Jan 19 **Luis Mendoza** *KO* 8
Noree Jockygym, Bangkok

Feb 3 **Kiyoshi Hatanaka** (JAP) *KO* 8
Pedro Decima, Nagoya, Japan

Feb 27 **Welcome Ncita** *W* 12
Baby Sugar Rojas, Saint Vincent, Italy

April 21 **Luis Mendoza** *W* 12
Carlos Uribe, Cartagena

BANTAMWEIGHTS

Feb 25 **Greg Richardson** (USA) *W* 12
Raul Perez, Inglewood

JUNIOR BANTAMWEIGHTS

Jan 26 **Robert Quiroga** *W* 12
Vincenzo Belcastro, Capo d'Orlando, Italy

March 16 **Sung Kil Moon** *KO* 4
Nana Konadu, Zaragoza, Spain

April 6 **Khaosai Galaxy** *KO* 5
Jae Suk Park, Samut Songkram, Thailand

FLYWEIGHTS

Feb 15 **Muangchai Kittikasem** (THA) *KO* 6
Sot Chitalada, Ayuthaya, Thailand

March 14 **Elvis Alvarez** (COL) *W* 12
Leopard Tamakuma, Tokyo

JUNIOR FLYWEIGHTS

Feb 17 **Michael Carbajal** *KO* 2
Macario Santos, Las Vegas

March 17 **Michael Carbajal** *W* 12
Javier Varguez, Las Vegas

March 25 **Melchor Cob Castro** (MEX) *KO* 10
Rolando Pascua, Inglewood

April 28 **Myung Woo Yuh** *KO* 10
Kajkong Danphoothai, Masan, South Korea

STRAWWEIGHTS

Feb 2 **Hi Yong Choi** (KOR) *W* 12
Bong Jun Kim, Pusan, South Korea

BATTLE OF THE AGES

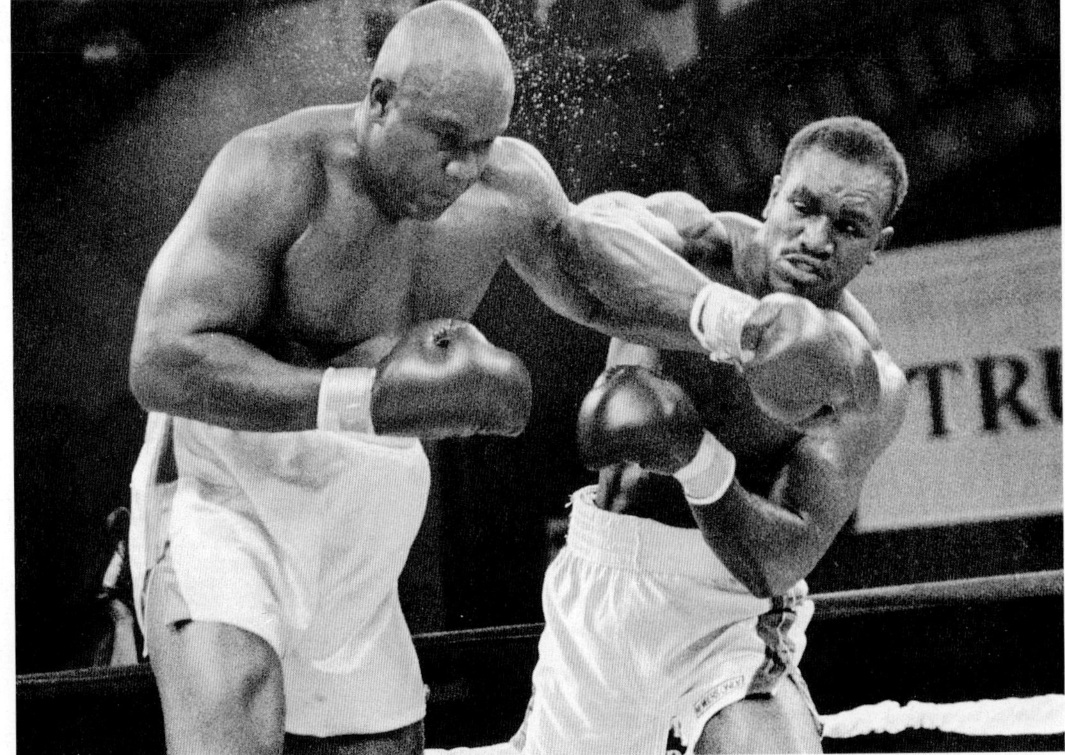

Big George Foreman (left) was the crowd's favorite, but defending heavyweight champ Evander Holyfield was easily the winner.

This was the fight everyone was waiting for?

* World heavyweight champion Evander Holyfield was 28. Comebacking former champion George Foreman was 42.

* Training with big barbells, Holyfield weighed 208 pounds. Training with Big Macs, Big George scaled 257.

* Holyfield had risen from cruiserweight and tackled household names like Michael Dokes, Alex Stewart, and Buster Douglas. Foreman had risen from the ashes and wiped out no-names like Mike Jameson, Ken Lakusta, and Terry Anderson.

On April 19, at the Atlantic City Convention Center, Holyfield kept the title by unanimous 12-round decision (scores of 116-109, 115-112, and 117-110). It was Foreman, however, who became America's Fighter. Gutty throughout, he absorbed all of Holyfield's combinations and remained a threat until the bell.

"Thank you for the opportunity," he said to the champion, suggesting that life indeed does begin at 40.

MAY

1991

AUGUST

"LIGHTS OUT," THE PARTY'S OVER

For five rounds, IBF middleweight champion Michael Nunn speared James "Lights Out" Toney with southpaw jabs, crossed with sharp lefts, and leaned away from the challenger's counterpunches. Still, Toney exuded confidence.

"He's breathing like a freight train," he told his corner. "I got him."

On May 10, Toney and Nunn dueled at John O'Donnell Stadium in the champion's hometown of Davenport, Iowa. By the seventh round, Toney, 22, began crashing right hands onto Nunn's chin. Still, the 20-1 underdog was far behind on points. Only a miraculous finish was going to save him.

Such a finish came in the 11th. Perhaps overly concerned with all those right hands, Nunn got clocked by a monster hook. Boom! Nunn lifted himself up by referee Denny Nelson's count of nine. When Toney again drove him to his knees, however, the bout was stopped.

The era of Michael Nunn was over. Had it ever really started?

In a major upset, James Toney (left) knocked out Michael Nunn in the 11th round.

RINGSIDE VIEW

JUNE

Thomas Hearns, 32-year-old underdog, wins the light heavyweight title for the second time, unanimously outpointing WBA champion Virgil Hill over 12 rounds.

Thomas Hearns after decisioning Virgil Hill.

WORLD TITLE FIGHTS

CRUISERWEIGHTS

July 20 **Anaclet Wamba** *KO* 11
Massimiliano Duran, Palermo, Italy

Aug 9 **Bobby Czyz** *W* 12
Bash Ali, Atlantic City

LIGHT HEAVYWEIGHTS

June 3 **Thomas Hearns** *W* 12
Virgil Hill, Las Vegas

July 20 **Prince Charles Williams** *KO* 3
Vincent Boulware, San Remo, Italy

SUPER MIDDLEWEIGHTS

May 18 **Darrin Van Horn** *KO* 11
Lindell Holmes, Verbania, Italy

July 27 **Mauro Galvano** *W* 12
Ron Essett, Capo d'Orlando, Italy

Aug 17 **Darrin Van Horn** *KO* 3
John Jarvis, Irvine, CA

MIDDLEWEIGHTS

May 10 **James Toney** (USA) *KO* 11
Michael Nunn, Davenport, IA

June 29 **James Toney** *W* 12
Reggie Johnson, Las Vegas

JUNIOR MIDDLEWEIGHTS

May 5 **Gilbert Dele** *W* 12
Jun Sok Hwang, Paris

June 1 **Terry Norris** *KO* 8
Donald Curry, Palm Springs, CA

July 13 **Gianfranco Rosi** *W* 12
Glenn Wolfe, Avezzano, Italy

Aug 17 **Terry Norris** *KO* 1
Brett Lally, San Diego

WELTERWEIGHTS

June 1 **Meldrick Taylor** *W* 12
Luis Garcia, Palm Springs, CA

JUNIOR WELTERWEIGHTS

June 14 **Edwin Rosario** *KO* 3
Loreto Garza, Sacramento

LIGHTWEIGHTS

July 27 **Pernell Whitaker** *W* 12
Poli Diaz, Norfolk

JUNIOR LIGHTWEIGHTS

June 28 **Azumah Nelson** *D* 12
Jeff Fenech, Las Vegas

June 28 **Joey Gamache** (USA) *KO* 10
Jerry Ngobeni, Lewiston, ME
(Wins Vacant WBA Title)

July 12 **Tony Lopez** *KO* 6
Lupe Gutierrez, Lake Tahoe

FEATHERWEIGHTS

June 3 **Troy Dorsey** (USA) *KO* 1
Alfred Rangel, Las Vegas
(Wins Vacant IBF Title)

June 15 **Yung Kyun Park** *KO* 6
Masuaki Takeda, Seoul

Aug 12 **Manuel Medina** (MEX) *W* 12
Troy Dorsey, Inglewood

Aug 15 **Marcos Villasana** *W* 12
Ricardo Cepeda, Marbella, Spain

JUNIOR FEATHERWEIGHTS

May 30 **Luis Mendoza** *KO* 7
Joao Cardosa, Madrid

June 14 **Daniel Zaragoza** *W* 12
Kiyoshi Hatanaka, Nagoya

June 15 **Welcome Ncita** *W* 12
Hurley Snead, San Antonio

Aug 24 **Daniel Zaragoza** *W* 12
Chun Huh, Seoul

BANTAMWEIGHTS

May 4 **Orlando Canizales** *KO* 8
Billy Hardy, Laredo, TX

May 20 **Greg Richardson** *W* 12
Victor Rabanales, Inglewood

JUNIOR BANTAMWEIGHTS

June 15 **Robert Quiroga** *W* 12
Akeem Anifowoshe, San Antonio

July 20 **Sung Kil Moon** *KO* 5
Ernesto Ford, Seoul

July 20 **Khaosai Galaxy** *KO* 5
David Griman, Bangkok

FLYWEIGHTS

May 11 **Dave McAuley** *W* 12
Pedro Feliciano, Belfast

May 18 **Muangchai Kittikasem** *KO* 12
Jung Koo Chang, Seoul

June 1 **Yong Kang Kim** *W* 12
Elvis Alvarez, Seoul

JUNIOR FLYWEIGHTS

May 10 **Michael Carbajal** *W* 12
Hector Patri, Davenport, IA

June 3 **Humberto Gonzalez** *W* 12
Melchor Cob Castro, Las Vegas

STRAWWEIGHTS

May 19 **Ricardo Lopez** *KO* 8
Kimio Hirano, Shizuoka, Japan

June 15 **Hi Yong Choi** *W* 12
Sugar Ray Mike, Seoul

July 2 **Phalan Lukmingkwan** *W* 12
Abdi Pohan, Bangkok

RINGSIDE VIEW

JUNE

Former three-time lightweight champion Edwin Rosario shocks defending WBA junior welterweight champion Loreto Garza with a series of right hands and wins by third-round TKO.

TWO BRAWLS, BUT NO ONE FALLS

It was a dream doubleheader: WBC super featherweight champion Azumah Nelson vs. Jeff Fenech, and the Mike Tyson-Razor Ruddock rematch, held on June 28, at The Mirage in Las Vegas.

Nelson-Fenech was a natural; Azumah was an accomplished champion, and Fenech was seeking his fourth world title. Their battle was contested on the challenger's terms – in close, and against the ropes. Fenech, stronger throughout, staggered Nelson in the 12th round. But the judges scored a split draw (totals of 115-113 Fenech, 116-112 Nelson, and 114-114).

Tyson-Ruddock II was a typical heavyweight slugfest, featuring dull stretches, then sudden and explosive exchanges. "Iron Mike" scored knockdowns in rounds two and four, closed the Razor's left eye, broke his jaw, and punched low. He had to settle, however, for a unanimous 12-round decision (two scores of 114-108, and 113-109).

Australia's undefeated Jeff Fenech (right) cried when, at the end of 12 rounds, his title bout with Azumah Nelson was ruled a draw. Almost everybody thought Jeff had won easily.

LOSES ON POINTS, BUT WINS FIGHT

It was one of those lighter-weight gems, a fantastic fight seen by far too few fans. On June 15, IBF junior bantamweight champion Robert Quiroga defended vs. Las Vegas-based Nigerian "Kid" Akeem Anifowoshe at the HemisFair Arena in San Antonio.

Both unbeaten 115-pounders were primed for the performances of their lives. For 12 rounds, Quiroga and Akeem blasted each other at a highly accelerated pace. There were no knockdowns, and the decision could have gone either way. As it turned out, hometown favorite Quiroga managed to hang on to the crown by unanimous scores of 116-112 (twice) and 115-114.

One minute after the verdict was announced, Akeem began vomiting blood. Then he collapsed into a coma. "For all practical purposes," said Dr. Gerardo Zavala, "the man was dying in the ring."

Akeem, 22, was rushed to the hospital, where he underwent surgery to relieve the pressure on his brain. He would never fight again, but his life was saved.

A happy ending? Fortunately, it wasn't an ending at all.

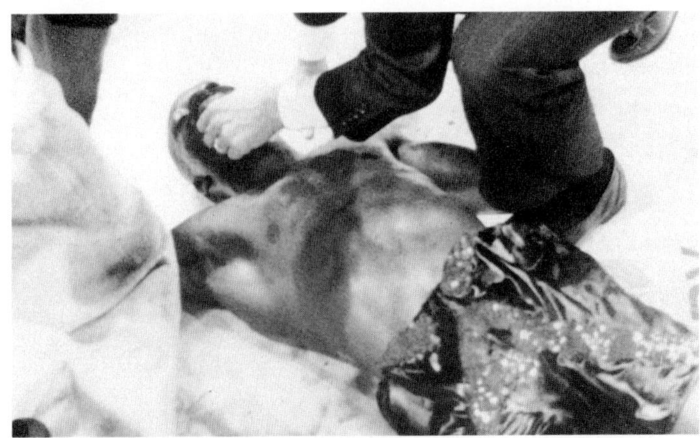

Kid Akeem collapsed after losing a decision to Robert Quiroga. Surgery saved his life.

SEPTEMBER

1991

DECEMBER

A CLASSIC WITH A TRAGIC TWIST

If one of the requisites of a great fight is constant shifts in momentum, then the rematch between British super middleweights Chris Eubank and Michael Watson was a classic.

In June, Eubank had edged Watson via close decision. The return was held on September 21, at White Hart Lane in London. Watson forced the action and landed more blows. Eubank countered with the harder punches. Every round was close.

Late in the 11th, Watson, ahead on points, felled his countryman with a right. As Eubank rose, Watson moved in for the finish – and walked into a tremendous right uppercut. Boom! Now *Watson* was down! He regained his feet and was saved by the bell.

Eubank punched freely at the start of the 12th, bringing referee Roy Francis' stoppage. Moments later, Watson collapsed and fell into a coma. Emergency surgery was performed. Still, his recovery took several months. He was lucky to be alive.

Chris Eubank, winner of the tragic bout.

RINGSIDE VIEW

SEPTEMBER

James Warring makes history, winning the vacant IBF cruiserweight title with a 24-second kayo of James Pritchard. It is the fastest knockout in title fight history.

SEPTEMBER

Former heavyweight champion Mike Tyson is indicted for rape and two counts of deviate sexual behavior. The charges stem from an incident in July, during the Miss Black America beauty pageant in Indianapolis.

ALMOST CLUBBED BY THE SUB FOR A SUB

On November 8, world heavyweight champion Evander Holyfield was scheduled to defend vs. Mike Tyson. After Tyson fell out with separated rib cartilege, Francesco Damiani stepped in. Then Damiani got hurt. The promoters called Smokin' Bert Cooper, who took the bout on six days notice.

The fight came on November 23, at The Omni in the champion's hometown of Atlanta. When "The Real Deal" downed his foe with a first-round body shot, a blowout seemed imminent.

Holyfield won every minute of every round, except for a scare in the third. After 32-1 underdog Cooper struck with a series of rights, Holyfield began to fall. He grabbed to ropes to remain upright, and referee Mills Lane correctly ruled a knockdown – the first of Holyfield's career.

The champion regained command in the fourth, and stopped Cooper with a 21-punch flurry in the seventh. But guess which part of the fight made the highlight films?

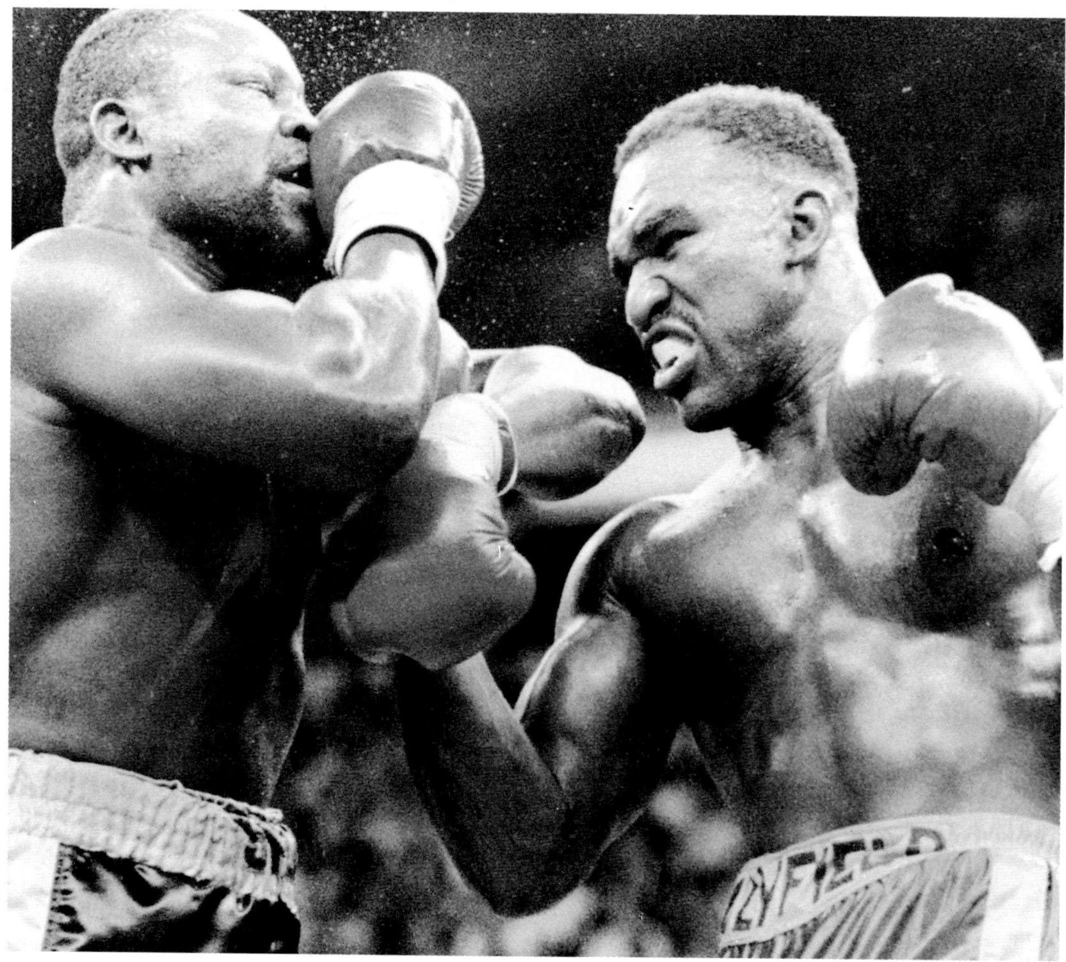

Evander Holyfield (right) stopped Bert Cooper in the seventh round to retain the world heavyweight crown. But it wasn't easy for the champion.

REMEMBER, MARVIN'S WATCHING

The middleweight title fight pitting IBF champion James Toney vs. former WBA king Mike McCallum was attractive enough to draw Marvin Hagler to ringside. Marvelous Marvin's attendance was symbolic; the winner would be the leading candidate to become the Hagler of the '90s.

Champion James Toney (right) retained the title against skillful Mike McCallum.

The slugfest, held on December 13 at the Atlantic City Convention Center, was a candidate for Fight of the Year. Cast in the role of puncher, Toney boxed strongly. McCallum, the consummate technician, unashamedly brawled. The bout became a battle of right hands, with neither 160-pounder gaining a clear edge.

Entering the 12th round, McCallum led on two of the cards. But Toney rallied, and at the final bell, he was punishing his opponent along the ropes. The bout was scored a draw (totals of 116-112 Toney, 115-113 McCallum, and 114-114). Most observers, however, thought Toney deserved the verdict.

Marvelous Marvin's reaction? Suffice to say the former champion isn't easy to impress.

RINGSIDE VIEW

OCTOBER

Former lightweight champion Vinny Pazienza jumps all the way to junior middleweight and dethrones WBA titlist Gilbert Dele by 12th-round TKO.

Vinny Pazienza (right) stopped Gilbert Dele.

WORLD TITLE FIGHTS

HEAVYWEIGHTS

Nov 23 **Evander Holyfield** *KO* 7
Bert Cooper, Atlanta

CRUISERWEIGHTS

Sept 6 **James Warring** (USA) *KO* 1
James Pritchard, Salemi, Italy

Nov 15 **James Warring** *KO* 5
Donnell Wingfield, Roanoke, VA

Dec 13 **Anaclet Wamba** *KO* 11
Massimiliano Duran, Paris

LIGHT HEAVYWEIGHTS

Sept 11 **Jeff Harding** *W* 12
Dennis Andries, London

Oct 19 **Prince Charles Williams** *KO* 2
Freddy Delgado, Williamsburg, VA

SUPER MIDDLEWEIGHTS

Dec 13 **Victor Cordoba** *KO* 11
Vincenzo Nardiello, Paris

MIDDLEWEIGHTS

Sept 14 **Julian Jackson** *KO* 1
Dennis Milton, Las Vegas

Oct 12 **James Toney** *KO* 4
Francesco Dell'Aquila, Monte Carlo

Dec 13 **James Toney** *D* 12
Mike McCallum, Atlantic City

JUNIOR MIDDLEWEIGHTS

Oct 3 **Vinny Pazienza** *KO* 12
Gilbert Dele, Providence

Nov 21 **Gianfranco Rosi** *W* 12
Gilbert Baptist, Perugia, Italy

Dec 13 **Terry Norris** *W* 12
Jorge Castro, Paris

WELTERWEIGHTS

Oct 4 **Maurice Blocker** *W* 12
Glenwood Brown, Atlantic City
(Wins Vacant IBF Title)

Nov 29 **Buddy McGirt** *W* 12
Simon Brown, Las Vegas

JUNIOR WELTERWEIGHTS

Sept 14 **Julio Cesar Chavez** *W* 12
Lonnie Smith, Las Vegas

Dec 7 **Rafael Pineda** (COL) *KO* 9
Roger Mayweather, Reno

LIGHTWEIGHTS

Oct 5 **Pernell Whitaker** *W* 12
Jorge Paez, Reno

JUNIOR LIGHTWEIGHTS

Sept 13 **Brian Mitchell** *W* 12
Tony Lopez, Sacramento

Nov 22 **Genaro Hernandez** (USA) *KO* 9
Daniel Londas, Epernay, France
(Wins Vacant WBA Title)

FEATHERWEIGHTS

Sept 14 **Yung Kyun Park** *W* 12
Eloy Rojas, Seoul

Nov 13 **Paul Hodkinson** (ENG) *W* 12
Marcos Villasana, Belfast

Nov 18 **Manuel Medina** *Tech. Dec* 9
Tom Johnson, Inglewood

JUNIOR FEATHERWEIGHTS

Oct 7 **Raul Perez** *W* 12
Luis Mendoza, Inglewood

Dec 9 **Daniel Zaragoza** *W* 12
Paul Banke, Los Angeles

BANTAMWEIGHTS

Sept 19 **Joichiro Tatsuyoshi** (JAP) *KO* 11
Greg Richardson, Tokyo

Sept 22 **Orlando Canizales** *W* 12
Fernie Morales, Indio, CA

Oct 19 **Israel Contreras** (VEN) *KO* 5
Luisito Espinosa, Manila

Dec 21 **Orlando Canizales** *KO* 11
Ray Minus, Laredo, TX

JUNIOR BANTAMWEIGHTS

Dec 22 **Khaosai Galaxy** *W* 12
Armando Castro, Bangkok

Dec 22 **Sung Kil Moon** *KO* 6
Torsak Pongsupa, Inchon, South Korea

FLYWEIGHTS

Sept 7 **Dave McAuley** *KO* 10
Jacob Matlala, Belfast

Oct 5 **Yong Kang Kim** *W* 12
Leo Gamez, Inchon, South Korea

Oct 25 **Muangchai Kittikasem** *W* 12
Alberto Jiminez, Bangkok

JUNIOR FLYWEIGHTS

Dec 16 **Hiroki Ioka** *W* 12
Myung Woo Yuh, Osaka

STRAWWEIGHTS

Oct 21 **Phalan Lukmingkwan** *W* 12
Andy Tabanas, Bangkok

Oct 26 **Hi Yong Choi** *W* 12
Bong Jun Kim, Seoul

Dec 22 **Ricardo Lopez** *W* 12
Kyung Yun Lee, Inchon, South Korea

Mike Tyson

Professional career dates 1985-1992
Contests 42
Won 41
Lost 1
Drawn 0
Knockouts 36
World Heavyweight Champion 1986-1990

WHEN he was about as big as a thumb, Mike Tyson was regularly beaten up by the bullies of his neighborhood, who called him "little fairy boy." He didn't fight back until the day one of them grabbed his pet pigeon from his hands and twisted its head off.

Tyson came to understand such simple, passionless violence, and has spent the better part of his life trying to punch his opponents' heads off. With his career having been interrupted – if not ended – by a jail term for rape, he may never join Johnson, Dempsey, Louis, Marciano, and Ali in the heavyweight pantheon. But even if he never fights again, he will be remembered as the embodiment of ring rage and power.

On June 30, 1966, Michael Gerard Tyson was born in the Bedford-Stuyvesant section of Brooklyn, New York. His mother, Lorna Tyson, and father, Jimmy Kirkpatrick, never married. They had two other children. Kirkpatrick, a construction worker, left the family when Tyson was two. Eight years later, Lorna moved the family to Brownsville, which was among the most crime-infested neighborhoods of New York. It wasn't long before Tyson was contributing to its reputation; by the age of 13, he had been arrested 38 times.

Tyson was sent upstate to the Tryon School in Johnstown, New York, about 200 miles from the city, where he met Bobby Stewart, a member of the staff and a former amateur boxer. Stewart introduced him to boxing. After Tyson showed an inclination, a private showing was arranged for Cus D'Amato, who had guided Floyd Patterson and Jose Torres to world titles. Less than a year later, Tyson was living with D'Amato, who instantly became his mentor, and soon after, his legal guardian.

"A boy comes to me with a spark of interest," D'Amato once said. "I feed the spark and it becomes a flame. I feed the flame and it becomes a fire. I feed the fire and it becomes a roaring blaze."

Realizing that his aggressive, quick-fisted heavyweight was ideally suited for the pro game, D'Amato minimized Tyson's amateur career. Tyson won his share of titles, but at the 1984 Olympic Trials, he was beaten by eventual gold medal winner Henry Tillman. At that point, D'Amato turned his protege over to co-managers Jim Jacobs and Bill Cayton, who made no mistakes in moving him toward the biggest prize in sports.

Fighting as often as three times per month, Tyson quickly gained an international reputation. He turned pro on March 6, 1985, knocking out Hector Mercedes in one round, and stopped his first 19 foes.

Victim number 18 was respected club-fighter Jesse Ferguson, whom Tyson kayoed in his network TV debut.

"In the fourth round, I saw the opening for that uppercut," Tyson said of his best punch. "I always try to catch them on the tip of the nose because I try to push the bone into the brain."

No one had ever before put it quite that way.

After being extended by James Tillis and Mitch Green, Tyson began another knockout streak. His 30-second kayo of Marvis Frazier was the fastest stoppage in the history of network television, and his annihilations of Jose Ribalta and Alfonzo Ratliff were no less brutal. By the fall of 1986, Tyson was without doubt a top-rated contender.

On November 22, 1986, "Iron Mike," at the age of 20, became the youngest champion in division history when he dethroned WBC titlist Trevor Berbick by second-round kayo. In his next bout, he added the WBA title by outpointing a reluctant Bonecrusher Smith. After crushing Pinklon Thomas, he unified the title on August 1, 1987, with a unanimous 12-round decision over IBF champion Tony Tucker. Was Mike Tyson indestructible? Unbeat-

Heavyweight champion Mike Tyson arriving at Heathrow Airport, London, in 1987, adorned with a collection of championship belts and an oversized bowler.

able? Invincible? He seemed nothing less.

Tyson continued his reign of terror with three consecutive knockouts. In October 1987, he punished Tyrell Biggs over seven rounds. ("I could have knocked him out in the third round," he said, "but I did it very slowly; I wanted him to remember it for a long time.") In January 1988, he finished a comebacking Larry Holmes in four. And two months later, he crushed another former champion, Tony Tubbs, in two.

The biggest victory of Tyson's career also marked the beginning of his downfall. It can be argued that the Tyson who knocked out Michael Spinks on June 27, 1988, would have been competitive with any heavyweight in history. Spinks was unbeaten and highly skilled. Nonetheless, he lasted all of 91 seconds. Tyson floored him twice, first with a right to the body, then for the count with a right to the jaw.

The champion didn't fight again until February 1989. His life had always been a simple cycle: train, fight, celebrate, then return to the gym. But in February 1988, he had married TV actress Robin Givens, and that summer, their union began to crumble in a most public way. Rumors spread that Tyson beat his wife, and in a nationally televised interview, he sat quietly as Givens said "Michael is a manic-depressive. He is. That's just a fact." The marriage would last 16 months.

Also that summer, Tyson, having teamed with promoter Don King, sued to break his contract with Cayton. (Jacobs had died in March). Moreover, he fractured his right hand in a late-night Harlem street brawl with Mitch Green. The champion's life seemed to be unraveling.

There would be two more successful defenses, a fifth-round kayo of Frank Bruno, and a first-round demolition of Carl Williams. But then Tyson was the loser in the greatest upset in the 90 years of the modern era.

On February 11, Tyson faced the undistinguished but physically gifted James (Buster) Douglas in Tokyo. Only one Las Vegas sports book bothered to list odds; Tyson was a 42-1 favorite. But he wasn't prepared mentally or physically, and Douglas took advantage. By the middle rounds, he began to punish the champion, and after rising from an eighth-round knockdown, he resumed his attack. In the 10th, the challenger jolted Tyson with a right uppercut. He followed with a left-right-left hook combination, and for the first time in Tyson's career, he had been knocked down. He had regained his feet by the time that referee Octavio Meyran had counted to nine, but wasn't allowed to continue.

Tyson has a split personality; a real-life Jekyll and Hyde. He can charm an audience, as he did at a 1989 press conference, then instantly turn into a terrifying brute capable of just about anything.

"Losing is part of this business," Tyson said. Don King was not as gracious as Tyson in defeat; he complained that after being felled, Douglas had received a long count. Fortunately, the controversy quickly dissipated.

Tyson recovered reasonably well. In a pair of comeback bouts, he scored first-round kayos of Tillman and Alex Stewart, and in March 1991, he stopped the power-punching Razor Ruddock in seven. In the rematch, Ruddock lasted the 12-round distance, but absorbed a terrific beating.

Tyson had climbed to the top of the ratings, and a try at undefeated champion Evander Holyfield was all but guaranteed. (In Douglas' first defense, he had been crushed by Holyfield.) The bout was signed, and then rescheduled after Tyson suffered a rib injury. But it would never come off. In July 1991, Tyson was accused of rape by Desiree Washington, an 18-year-old contestant at the Miss Black American pageant. That September, he was indicted by an Indianapolis, Indiana, grand jury for rape, confinement, and two counts of criminal deviant conduct. And on February 10, 1992, Mike Tyson, age 25, was found guilty; he received a sentence of six years, and four years suspended. (Tyson will serve a minimum of three years at the Indiana Youth Center; in the state, inmates reduce time served by one day for each day of good behavior.)

Once number one in all of boxing, Tyson was now prisoner number 922335. Perhaps predictably, the roaring blaze had raged out of control.

Master promoter Don King (left) became not only Tyson's manager-promoter, but also the guiding influence in the champion's life. But when this picture of the pair was taken, Tyson was no longer champion. They are arriving in New York after the long flight from Tokyo, where Mike has been knocked out by Buster Douglas in the upset of the century.

JANUARY

1992

APRIL

RINGSIDE VIEW

FEBRUARY

Former heavyweight champion Larry Holmes, 42, passes the toughest test of his comeback by outpointing unbeaten contender Ray Mercer over 12 rounds.

THE REMATCH IS NO REPLAY

Before Azumah Nelson-Jeff Fenech II, both fighters talked tough. "The only way they're going to take (Nelson) home to Ghana is in a body bag," threatened Fenech.

"Tell Fenech he is playing with fire," responded Azumah, "and it will burn him."

In June 1991, Fenech had outworked Nelson, but was denied the WBC super featherweight crown – and his fourth world title – when the judges scored a draw. The return was held on March 1, before 37,000 fans at Princes Park in Melbourne. Almost no one picked the 33-year-old Nelson to win. But he was proud and he performed at his very best.

Fenech was floored in the first, second, and eighth rounds. He fought with passion, but his aggressiveness was neutralized by the champion's jabs and pinpoint powerpunches. Referee Arthur Mercante rescued the challenger, and broke the hearts of his countrymen, by calling a halt at the 2:20 mark of the eighth.

Australians mourned as one.

CHARGED, INDICTED, CONVICTED

At 10:52 p.m. on February 10, almost exactly two years after he lost the world heavyweight title, Mike Tyson, 25, was convicted of rape. In Courtroom 4 of the Marion County (Indiana) Supreme Court, a jury deliberated for 9½ hours before coming to a verdict.

The front-page trial lasted two weeks and included 49 witnesses. Tyson's downfall: the night of July 19, 1991, when he brought Desiree Washington, an 18-year-old contestant in the Miss Black America beauty pageant, to his room at the Canterbury Hotel in Indianapolis. Washington charged that Tyson raped her. Tyson claimed they engaged in consentual sex. The jury believed the former.

Judge Patricia Gifford would subsequently sentence Tyson to six years' imprisonment. It was conceivable that he would not have to serve more than three years; one day would be reduced for each day of exemplary service.

The last chapter? Only time will tell. And Mike Tyson is counting the days.

Former heavyweight champion Mike Tyson is led away by officers after a jury convicted him of raping an 18-year-old beauty queen.

Azumah Nelson walks to a neutral corner after dropping Jeff Fenech. Nelson won by TKO in the eighth round.

THE HIT MAN FADES AGAINST THE BLADE

As he neared the twilight of his career, Thomas Hearns focused on a single goal: to avenge his three career losses. In June 1989, he gained redemption by brawling to a draw with Sugar Ray Leonard. There would be no rematch with the retired Marvin Hagler. But on March 20, one final opportunity came at Caesars Palace, with a return with Iran Barkley, who had kayoed him in 1988.

Barkley rose in weight in an effort to capture Hearns' WBA light heavyweight crown. It was Hearns' plan to box and move, but "The Blade" forced him into a phone booth brawl.

A short hook downed Hearns in the fourth. That aside, it was a grueling battle, with Barkley cut on top of the head, and Hearns' face swollen almost beyond recognition. After 12 rounds, the judges scored for Barkley by split scores of 115-113, 114-113, and 113-114.

Revenge? Hearns had been forced to settle for survival.

RINGSIDE VIEW

FEBRUARY

Dehydrated and suffering from cramps, IBF middleweight champion James Toney barely retains the title, scoring a hotly disputed and split 12-round decision over Dave Tiberi.

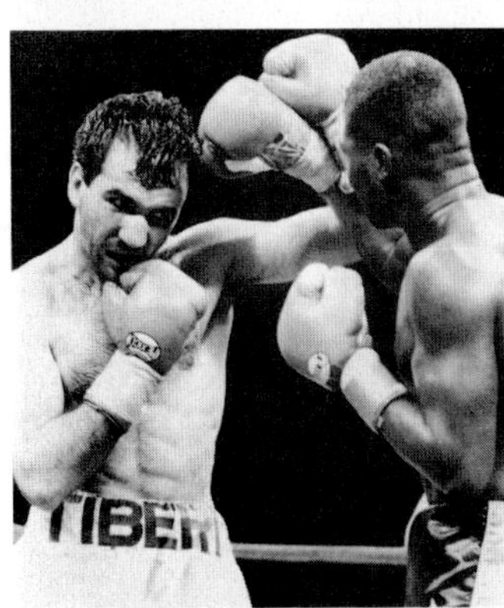

Toney (right) won split decision over Tiberi.

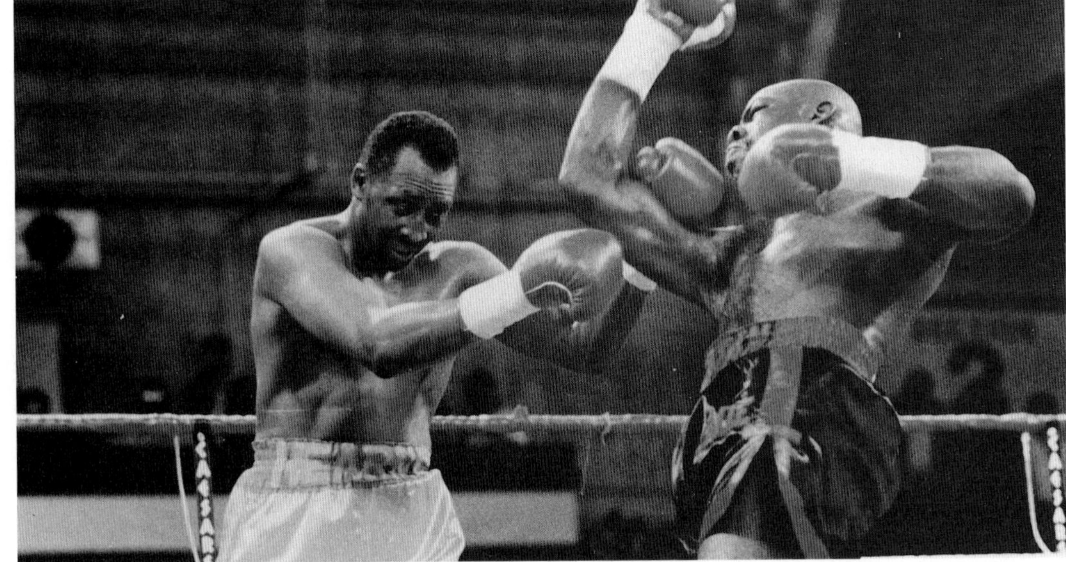

Defending light heavyweight champion Thomas Hearns (left) lost the crown by a 12-round split decision to Iran Barkley.

WORLD TITLE FIGHTS

LIGHT HEAVYWEIGHTS

March 20 **Iran Barkley** *W* 12
Thomas Hearns, Las Vegas

SUPER MIDDLEWEIGHTS

Jan 10 **Iran Barkley** *KO* 2
Darrin Van Horn, New York City

Feb 6 **Mauro Galvano** *W* 12
Juan Carlos Gimenez, Marchino, Italy

MIDDLEWEIGHTS

Feb 8 **James Toney** *W* 12
Dave Tiberi, Atlantic City

Feb 15 **Julian Jackson** *KO* 1
Ismael Negron, Las Vegas

April 10 **Julian Jackson** *KO* 5
Ron Collins, Mcxlco City

April 11 **James Toney** *W* 12
Glenn Wolfe, Las Vegas

April 22 **Reggie Johnson** (USA) *W* 12
Steve Collins, East Rutherford, NJ
(Wins Vacant WBA Title)

JUNIOR MIDDLEWEIGHTS

Feb 22 **Terry Norris** *KO* 9
Carl Daniels, San Diego

April 9 **Gianfranco Rosi** *KO* 6
Angel Hernandez, Celano, Italy

WELTERWEIGHTS

Jan 18 **Meldrick Taylor** *W* 12
Glenwood Brown, Philadelphia

JUNIOR WELTERWEIGHTS

April 10 **Akinobu Hiranaka** (JAP) *KO* 1
Edwin Rosario, Mexico City

April 10 **Julio Cesar Chavez** *KO* 5
Angel Hernandez, Mexico City

JUNIOR LIGHTWEIGHTS

Feb 22 **John-John Molina** *KO* 4
Jackie Gunguluza, Sun City
(Wins Vacant IBF Title)

Feb 25 **Genaro Hernandez** *W* 12
Omar Catari, Inglewood

March 1 **Azumah Nelson** *KO* 8
Jeff Fenech, Melbourne

FEATHERWEIGHTS

Jan 25 **Yung Kyun Park** *KO* 9
Seiji Asakawa, Seoul

March 14 **Manuel Medina** *W* 12
Fabrice Benichou, Antibes, France

April 25 **Paul Hodkinson** *KO* 3
Steve Cruz, Belfast

April 25 **Yung Kyun Park** *KO* 11
Koji Matsumoto, Ansan, South Korea

JUNIOR FEATHERWEIGHT

March 20 **Thierry Jacob** (FRA) *W* 12
Daniel Zaragoza, Calais, France

March 27 **Wilfredo Vasquez** *KO* 3
Raul Perez, Mexico City

April 18 **Welcome Ncita** *W* 12
Jesus Salud, Trevilio, Italy

BANTAMWEIGHTS

March 15 **Eddie Cook** (USA) *KO* 5
Israel Contreras, Las Vegas

March 30 **Victor Rabanales** (MEX) Tech. Dec. 9
Yong Hoon Lee, Inglewood
(Wins Interim WBC Title)

April 2 **Orlando Canizales** *W* 12
Francisco Alvarez, Paris

JUNIOR BANTAMWEIGHTS

Feb 16 **Robert Quiroga** *W* 12
Carlos Mercado, Salerno, Italy

April 10 **Katsuya Onizuka** (JAP) *W* 12
Thalerngsak Sithbaobay, Tokyo
(Wins Vacant WBA Title)

FLYWEIGHTS

Feb 28 **Muangchai Kittikasem** *KO* 9
Sot Chitalada, Sumut Prakan, Thailand

March 24 **Yong Kang Kim** *KO* 6
Jonathan Penalosa, Inchon, South Korea

JUNIOR FLYWEIGHTS

Jan 27 **Humberto Gonzalez** *W* 12
Domingo Sosa, Inglewood

Feb 15 **Michael Carbajal** *W* 12
Marcos Pacheco, Phoenix

March 31 **Hiroki Ioka** *W* 12
Noel Tunacao, Kitakyushi, Japan

STRAWWEIGHTS

Feb 22 **Hi Yong Choi** *KO* 10
Yuichi Hosono, Seoul

Feb 23 **Phalan Lukmingkwan** *KO* 2
Felix Naranjo, Bangkok

March 16 **Ricardo Lopez** *W* 12
Pretty Boy Lucas, Mexico City

MAY

1992

AUGUST

TREATING HIS ELDER WITH TOO MUCH RESPECT

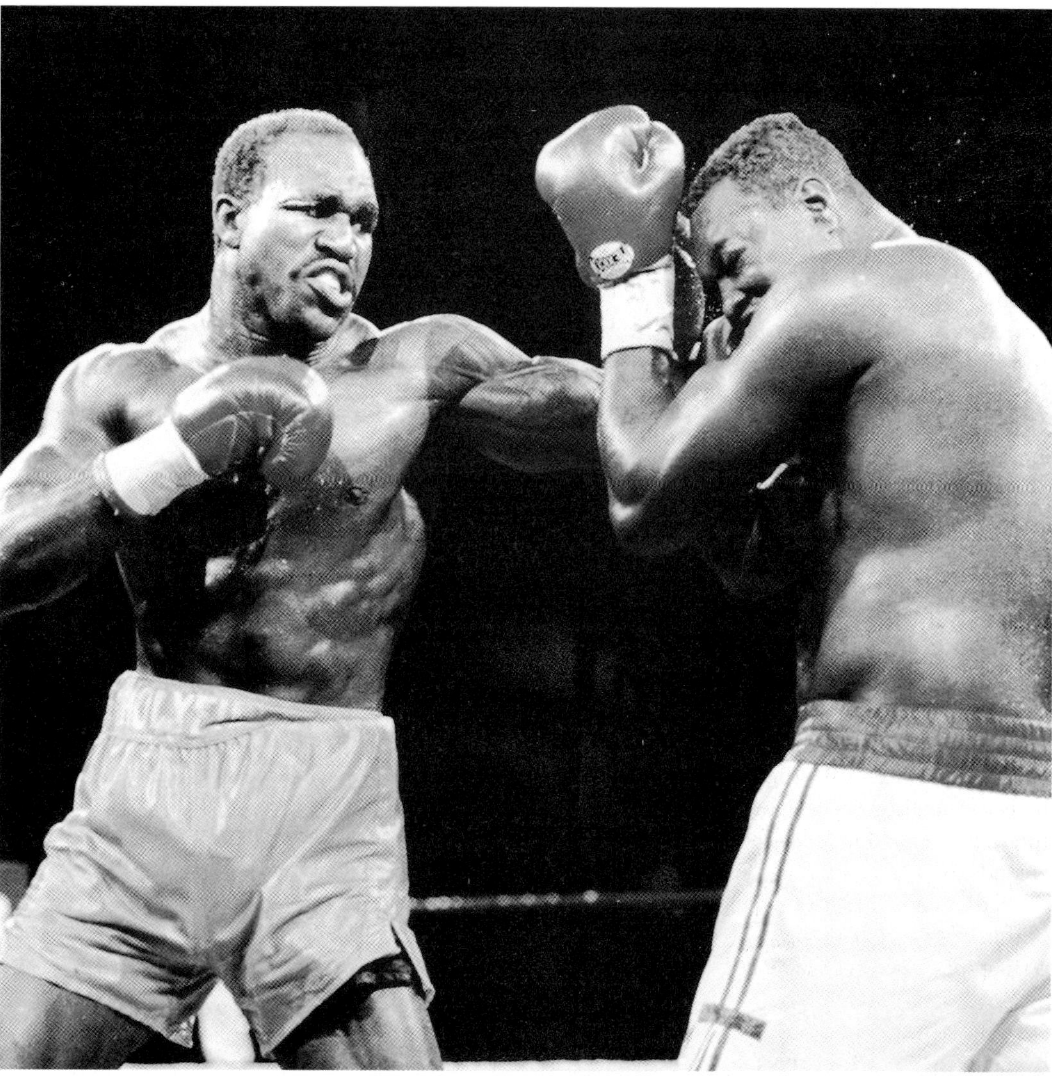
Former heavyweight king Larry Holmes (right) tried desperately to regain the crown, but reigning champion Evander Holyfield was far too strong.

After world heavyweight champion Evander Holyfield failed to kayo George Foreman, the reviews were mixed. After all, even at age 42, Big George was dangerous. But when Holyfield was extended 12 rounds by another 42-year-old, grandfather Larry Holmes, the media spared no insults.

Holyfield-Holmes came on June 19, at Caesars Palace. For the first six rounds, Holmes lay against the ropes in hopes of landing the occasional right. Though Holyfield was busier, he enjoyed limited success.

"Larry Holmes had more than I thought he had," he said. "He was able to turn his body when I hit him. His body was so slippery."

At the end of the sixth, Holmes missed with a right, but followed through with his elbow and opened a 12-stitch cut on the champion's right eyelid. Holyfield wisely fought the remainder of the bout in ring center, and scored often enough to keep the championship by unanimous decision (two totals of 116-112, and 117-111).

The critics had been hoping for something more.

POUND-FOR-POUND BOUND TO SUPERSTARDOM

With 17 divisions and three alphabet organizations, boxing has made room for 51 world champions. But only one of those champions can claim the unofficial title of best fighter, pound-for-pound, in the world. On May 9, WBC super welterweight champion Terry Norris moved toward the top of the pound-for-pound ratings by knocking out WBA welterweight king Meldrick Taylor at The Mirage in Las Vegas.

"Tonight was a signature fight for Terry Norris," said promoter Dan Duva. "He's going to be the superstar of the '90s."

Norris, who was risking his crown, entered the ring with the word KNOCKOUT shaved into his hair. It didn't take long for Taylor to get the message. The Philadelphian stood in front of "Terrible Terry," but lacked the strength to trade punch for punch. Norris slowly gained control, then scored two fourth-round knockdowns, bringing referee Mills Lane's intervention at the 2:55 mark.

Pound-for-pound, it was a perfect performance.

Terry Norris (right) staggers Meldrick Taylor seconds before the fight was stopped in the fourth.

THE SECOND-GENERATION CHAMP

In 1956, Floyd Patterson won the world heavyweight title. It took him 36 years to top that thrill. On June 23, at the Knickerbocker Arena in Albany, New York, Tracy Patterson, Floyd's adopted son, won the WBC super bantamweight crown with a second-round TKO of French southpaw Thierry Jacob. Never before had a father and son won world titles.

"This is the proudest moment of my life," said Floyd. "His (championship) was a lot more important than mine."

It couldn't have come much easier. Tracy started carefully, but toward the end of the first round, he began landing every right he threw. Jacob was downed with 10 seconds to go, and after another knockdown in round two, referee Arthur Mercante Jr. stopped the bout at the 50-second mark.

Floyd had adopted Tracy in 1985. His son's success was vivid testimony to just how significant a positive role model can be.

WORLD TITLE FIGHTS

HEAVYWEIGHTS

June 19 **Evander Holyfield** *W* 12
Larry Holmes, Las Vegas

CRUISERWEIGHTS

May 8 **Bobby Czyz** *W* 12
Don Lalonde, Las Vegas

May 16 **James Warring** *W* 12
Johnny Nelson, Fredericksburg, VA

June 30 **Anaclet Wamba** *KO* 5
Andrei Rudenko, Paris

July 30 **Al Cole** (USA) *W* 12
James Warring, Stanhope, NJ

LIGHT HEAVYWEIGHTS

June 5 **Jeff Harding** *KO* 8
Chris Tiozzo, Marseille

MIDDLEWEIGHTS

Aug 1 **Julian Jackson** *W* 12
Thomas Tate, Las Vegas

Aug 29 **James Toney** *W* 12
Mike McCallum, Reno

JUNIOR MIDDLEWEIGHTS

May 9 **Terry Norris** *KO* 4
Meldrick Taylor, Las Vcgas

July 11 **Gianfranco Rosi** *W* 12
Gilbert Dele, Monte Carlo

WELTERWEIGHTS

June 25 **Buddy McGirt** *W* 12
Patrizio Oliva, Naples

Aug 28 **Maurice Blocker** *W* 12
Luis Garcia, Atlantic City

JUNIOR WELTERWEIGHTS

May 22 **Rafael Pineda** *KO* 7
Clarence Coleman, Mexico City

July 18 **Pernell Whitaker** *W* 12
Rafael Pineda, Las Vegas

Aug 1 **Julio Cesar Chavez** *KO* 4
Frankie Mitchell, Las Vegas

LIGHTWEIGHTS

June 12 **Joey Gamache** *KO* 8
Chil Sung Chun, Portland, ME
(Wins Vacant WBA Title)

Aug 24 **Miguel Angel Gonzalez** (MEX) *KO* 10
Wilfrido Rocha, Mexico City
(Wins Vacant WBC Title)

Aug 29 **Fred Pendleton** *Tech. Draw* 2
Tracy Spann, Reno
(For Vacant IBF Title)

JUNIOR LIGHTWEIGHTS

July 15 **Genaro Hernandez** *W* 12
Masuaki Takeda, Tokyo

Aug 22 **John-John Molina** *KO* 4
Fornando Caicedo, Bayamon, Puerto Rico

FEATHERWEIGHTS

July 27 **Manuel Medina** *KO* 10
Fabrizio Cappai, Capo D'Orlando, Italy

Aug 29 **Yung Kyun Park** *W* 12
Giovanni Nieves, Kyongju, South Korea

JUNIOR FEATHERWEIGHTS

June 23 **Tracy Patterson** (USA) *KO* 2
Thierry Jacob, Albany, NY

June 27 **Wilfredo Vasquez** *W* 12
Freddy Cruz, Gorle, Italy

BANTAMWEIGHTS

May 17 **Victor Rabanales** *KO* 4
Luis Alberto Campo, Tuxtla, Mexico

July 27 **Victor Rabanales** *W* 12
Chang Kyun Oh, Inglewood

JUNIOR BANTAMWEIGHTS

July 4 **Sung Kil Moon** *KO* 8
Armando Salazar, Seoul

July 11 **Robert Quiroga** *W* 12
Jose Ruiz, Las Vegas

FLYWEIGHTS

June 11 **Rodolfo Blanco** (COL) *W* 12
Dave McAuley, Bilbao, Spain

June 23 **Yuri Arbachakov** (CIS) *KO* 8
Muangchai Kittikasem, Tokyo

JUNIOR FLYWEIGHTS

June 7 **Humberto Gonzalez** *KO* 12
Kwang Sun Kim, Seoul

June 15 **Hiroki Ioka** *W* 12
Bong Jun Kim, Osaka

STRAWWEIGHTS

June 14 **Hi Yong Choi** *KO* 3
Rommel Lawas, Inchon, South Korea

June 14 **Phalan Lukmingkwan** *KO* 8
Said Iskandar, Bangkok

Aug 22 **Ricardo Lopez** *KO* 5
Singprasert Kittikasem, Ciudad Madero, Mexico

Tracy Patterson displays junior featherweight championship belt after beating Thierry Jacob.

RINGSIDE VIEW

JUNE

Japan-based flyweight Yuri Arbachakov becomes boxing's first Russian-born world champion when he dethrones WBC champion Muangchai Mittikasem by eighth-round kayo.

JULY

Former undisputed lightweight champion Pernell Whitaker rises in weight and captures the IBF junior welterweight title with a unanimous 12-round decision over Rafael Pineda.

Yuri Arbachakov after his world title win.

SEPTEMBER

1992

DECEMBER

HE PROVES HE'S MACHO AFTER ALL

Tall men are sometimes "Shorty" and fat men "Bones." Hector Camacho was nicknamed "Macho," and over the course of his roller-coaster career, he fought with less and less bravado.

On September 12, however, the former two-division champion displayed commendable courage during his challenge of WBC super lightweight champion Julio Cesar Chavez before a crowd of 19,100 at the Thomas & Mack Center in Las Vegas. Chavez, 81-0 and 21-0 in world title fights, was the prohibitive favorite, and won accordingly, taking a unanimous 12-round decision by scores of 117-111, 119-110, and 120-107. Nonetheless, it was Camacho who showed his mettle by absorbing a terrible beating and lasting the distance.

In the challenger's corner after the 10th round, it was suggested that Camacho surrender. He refused, and the punishment was extended for six more minutes. By the final bell, Camacho's left eye was closed, there was a nasty cut over his right eye, and his nose dripped blood.

"The pressure he put on me was amazing," he said.

That Chavez retained the title was no surprise. Not so with Camacho's gritty effort. We never knew "The Macho Man" had it in him.

Hector "Macho" Camacho.

Crisanto Espana kayoed Meldrick Taylor.

RINGSIDE VIEW

OCTOBER

In London, a Belfast-based Panamanian Crisanto Espana wins the WBA welterweight title by knocking out a faded Meldrick Taylor in round eight.

OCTOBER

Former junior lightweight champion Tony Lopez captures his second title, coming from behind to knock out hometown favorite and defending WBA lightweight champion Joey Gamache in Portland, Maine.

WORLD TITLE FIGHTS

HEAVYWEIGHTS

Nov 13 **Riddick Bowe** (USA) *W* 12
Evander Holyfield, Las Vegas

CRUISERWEIGHTS

Oct 16 **Anaclet Wamba** *W* 12
Andrew Maynard, Paris

LIGHT HEAVYWEIGHTS

Sept 29 **Virgil Hill** *W* 12
Frank Tate, Bismarck, ND
(Wins Vacant WBA Title)

SUPER MIDDLEWEIGHTS

Sept 12 **Michael Nunn** *W* 12
Victor Cordoba, Las Vegas

Oct 3 **Nigel Benn** (GB) *KO* 3
Mauro Galvano, Marchino, Italy

Dec 12 **Nigel Benn** *KO* 11
Nicky Piper, London

MIDDLEWEIGHTS

Oct 27 **Reggie Johnson** *W* 12
Lamar Parks, Houston

JUNIOR MIDDLEWEIGHTS

Dec 21 **Julio Cesar Vasquez** (ARG) *KO* 1
Hitoshi Kamiyama, Buenos Aires
(Wins Vacant WBA Title)

WELTERWEIGHTS

Oct 31 **Crisanto Espana** (VEN) *KO* 8
Meldrick Taylor, London

JUNIOR WELTERWEIGHTS

Sept 9 **Morris East** (PHI) *KO* 11
Akinobu Hiranaka, Tokyo

Sep 12 **Julio Cesar Chavez** *W* 12
Hector Camacho, Las Vegas

LIGHTWEIGHTS

Dec 5 **Miguel Angel Gonzalez** *W* 12
Darryll Tyson, Mexico City

JUNIOR LIGHTWEIGHTS

Nov 7 **Azumah Nelson** *W* 12
Calvin Grove, Stateline, NV

Nov 20 **Genaro Hernandez** *KO* 6
Yuji Watanabe, Tokyo

FEATHERWEIGHTS

Sept 12 **Paul Hodkinson** *KO* 10
Fabrice Benichou, Blagnac, France

Oct 23 **Manuel Medina** *W* 12
Moussa Sangaree, Gravelines, France

Dec 19 **Yung Kyun Park** *W* 12
Ever Beleno, Changwon, South Korea

JUNIOR FEATHERWEIGHTS

Dec 2 **Kennedy McKinney** (USA) *KO* 11
Welcome Ncita, Tortoli, Sardinia

Dec 5 **Tracy Patterson** *D* 12
Daniel Zaragoza, Berck-Sur-Mer, France

Dec 5 **Wilfredo Vasquez** *KO* 8
Thierry Jacob, Berck-Sur-Mer, France

BANTAMWEIGHTS

Sep 17 **Orlando Canizales** *W* 12
Samuel Duran, Bozeman, MT

Sep 17 **Victor Rabanales** *KO* 9
Joichiro Tatsuyoshi, Osaka
(Unifies WBC Title)

Oct 10 **Eleicer Julio** (COL) *W* 12
Eddie Cook, Cartagena

JUNIOR BANTAMWEIGHTS

Sept 11 **Katsuya Onizuka** *KO* 5
Kenichi Matsumura, Tokyo

Oct 31 **Sung Kil Moon** *W* 12
Greg Richardson, Seoul

Dec 11 **Katsuya Onizuka** *W* 12
Armando Castro, Tokyo

FLYWEIGHTS

Scp 26 **Aquiles Guzman** (VEN) *W* 12
Yong Kang Kim, Pohang, South Korea

Oct 20 **Yuri Arbachakov** *W* 12
Yun Un Chin, Tokyo

Nov 29 **Phichit Sithbangprachan** (THA) *KO* 3
Rodolfo Blanco, Bangkok

JUNIOR FLYWEIGHTS

Sep 14 **Humberto Gonzalez** *KO* 2
Napa Kiatwanchai, Inglcwood

Nov 18 **Myung Woo Yuh** *W* 12
Hiroki Ioka, Osaka

Dec 7 **Humberto Gonzalez** *W* 12
Melchor Cob Castro, Inglewood

Dec 12 **Michael Carbajal** *KO* 8
Robinson Cuesta, Phoenix

STRAWWEIGHTS

Sept 6 **Manny Melchor** (PHI) *W* 12
Phalan Lukmingkwan, Bangkok

Oct 11 **Ricardo Lopez** *KO* 2
Rocky Lim, Tokyo

Oct 14 **Hideyuki Ohashi** *W* 12
Hi Yong Choi, Tokyo

Dec 10 **Rattanapol Sorvorapin** (THA) *W* 12
Manny Melchor, Bangkok

THE GREAT BRITISH HOPE TAKES THE TITLE

Razor Ruddock was a big puncher. Lennox Lewis was a big question mark. When the heavyweight contenders squared off on October 31st at Earls Court in London, most of the 13,000 in attendance who fancied Lewis, it seemed, were thinking with their hearts. There hadn't been a British world heavyweight champion since Bob Fitzsimmons in 1899. Lewis, a gold medalist at the 1988 Olympics, seemed a legitimate hope. Still, Ruddock answered the opening bell a 2-1 favorite, based primarily on his 19 rounds of rumbling with former champion Mike Tyson. Lewis' resume was nowhere near as impressive.

The fight lasted less than four minutes. With 10 seconds remaining in the first round, Lewis unleashed his powerpunch, a straight right, and Ruddock crashed.

"I just fired it like a gunshot," he said.

Two more knockdowns followed in the second, and referee Joe Cortez called a halt at the 46-second mark.

Lewis couldn't have known it at the time, but he had just won the WBC version of the title. Two weeks after the fight, Riddick Bowe took the undisputed title from Evander Holyfield. When he and Lewis were unable to agree on a fight, Bowe ceremoniously tossed his WBC belt into a trash can. As a result Lewis was retroactively named champion.

Officially, at least, Britain's wait was over.

Glassy-eyed Razor Ruddock can't regain his feet after being pole-axed and knocked out by Lennox Lewis.

BOWE'S POINTED ARROWS

Riddick Bowe was bigger than heavyweight champion Evander Holyfield, taller, and with a longer reach. He had a better jab, more power, and at least as strong a chin. But it was Holyfield who was favored to win their showdown, which took place on November 13 at the Thomas & Mack Center in Las Vegas. That was because the biggest and best heavyweight title fights are usually decided by heart, Holyfield's greatest asset. Bowe was thought to be lacking.

Holyfield and Bowe fought at a middleweight's pace, testing each other in the Fight of the Year.

"Regardless of how much pressure I put on him," said Holyfield, "no matter how tired he got, he came back."

After boxing in round one, Holyfield collided with the challenger on the inside. By the middle rounds, the 6'5", 235-pound Bowe began to take control. In the unforgettable 10th, he almost finished his foe, only to hang on when Holyfield managed a dramatic comeback. But there was no turnaround after Bowe scored a knockdown in the 11th. He went on to take a unanimous decision by scores of 117-110 twice and 115. In defeat, Holyfield had earned respect. In victory, Bowe had earned the opportunity for greatness.

Riddick Bowe (left) outpoints Evander Holyfield over 12 rounds to become the new world heavyweight king.

APPENDIX

A Miscellaneous Compilation of Title Fight Statistics

Rocky Marciano is the only world champion to retire unbeaten. On April 27, 1956, the heavyweight champion exited with a record of 49-0 (43).

Mike Tyson became the youngest heavyweight champion in history when, in 1986, at 20, he surpassed Floyd Patterson's record by one year.

HEAVIEST BOXERS TO FIGHT FOR THE HEAVYWEIGHT TITLE

1. **Primo Carnera, 270** (W 15 Tommy Loughran, March 1, 1934, Miami)

2. **Primo Carnera, 263½** (KO by 11 Max Baer, June 14, 1934, Long Island City, NY)

3. **Primo Carnera, 260½** (KO 6 Jack Sharkey, June 29, 1933, Long Island City, NY)

4. **Primo Carnera, 259½** (W 15 Paolino Uzcudun, October 22, 1933, Rome)

5. **George Foreman, 257** (L 12 Evander Holyfield, April 19, 1991, Atlantic City)

6. **Abe Simon, 255** (KO by 6 Joe Louis, March 27, 1942, New York City)

7. **(tie) Abe Simon, 254½** (KO by 13 Joe Louis, March 21, 1941, Detroit)

7. **(tie) Leroy Jones, 254½** (KO by 8 Larry Holmes, March 31, 1980, Las Vegas)

9. **Buddy Baer, 250** (KO by 1 Joe Louis, January 9, 1942, New York City)

10. **Buster Douglas, 246** (KO by 3 Evander Holyfield, October 25, 1990, Las Vegas)

Thai junior welterweight **Saensak Muangsurin** holds the all-time record for winning a world title in the least number of bouts. On July 15, 1975, he scored an eighth-round stoppage of defending WBC super lightweight champion Perico Fernandez in Bangkok. It was the former kickboxer's third pro fight.

SHORTEST TITLE FIGHTS IN HISTORY

Heavyweight: James J. Jeffries KO 1 (0:55) Jack Finnegan, April 6, 1900, Detroit

Cruiserweight: James Warring KO 1 (0:24) James Pritchard, September 6, 1991, Salemi, Italy

Light Heavyweight: Gus Lesnevich KO 1 (1:58) Billy Fox, March 5, 1948, New York City

Super Middleweight: Chong Pal Park No-Contest 2 (1:10) Lindell Holmes, July 6, 1986, Chungju, South Korea

Middleweight: Julian Jackson KO 1 (0:50) Ismael Negron, February 15, 1992, Las Vegas

Junior Middleweight: Koichi Wajima KO 1 (1:49) Domenico Tiberia, May 7, 1972, Tokyo

Welterweight: Lloyd Honeyghan KO 1 (0:45) Gene Hatcher, August 30, 1987, Marbella, Spain

Junior Welterweight: Akinobu Hiranaka KO 1 (1:32) Edwin Rosario, April 10, 1992, Mexico City

Lightweight: Tony Canzoneri KO 1 (1:06) Al Singer, November 14, 1930, New York City

Junior Lightweight: Flash Elorde KO 1 (1:20) Harold Gomes, August 17, 1960, San Francisco

Featherweight: Kuniaki Shibata KO 1 (2:04) Raul Cruz, June 3, 1971, Tokyo

Junior Featherweight: Ji Won Kim KO 1 (1:06) Seung Il Suh, October 19, 1985, Seoul

Bantamweight: Sixto Escobar KO 1 (1:49) Indian Quintana, October 13, 1936, New York City

Junior Bantamweight: Joo Do Chun KO 1 (2:35) Diego de Villa, March 17, 1984, Kwangju, South Korea

Flyweight: Spider Pladner KO 1 (0:58) Frankie Genaro, March 2, 1929, Paris

Junior Flyweight: Myung Woo Yuh KO 1 (2:46) Eduardo Tunon, March 1, 1987, Seoul

Strawweight: Kyung Yun Lee KO 2 (0:31) Masaharu Kawakami, June 14, 1987, Bujok, South Korea

FIGHTERS WHO HAVE WON WORLD TITLES IN MORE THAN TWO DIVISIONS

5–Sugar Ray Leonard (world welterweight, WBA junior middleweight, WBC middleweight, WBC super middleweight, WBC light heavyweight)

4–Thomas Hearns (WBA welterweight, WBC super welterweight, WBC middleweight, WBA & WBC light heavyweight)

4–Roberto Duran (world lightweight, WBC welterweight, WBA junior middleweight, WBC middleweight)

3–Bob Fitzsimmons (world middleweight, world light heavyweight, world heavyweight)

3–Tony Canzoneri (world featherweight, world lightweight, world junior welterweight)

3–Barney Ross (world lightweight, world junior welterweight, world welterweight)

3–Henry Armstrong* (world featherweight, world lightweight, world welterweight)

3–Emile Griffith (welterweight, EBU junior middleweight, middleweight)

3–Wilfred Benitez (WBA junior welterweight, WBC welterweight, WBC super welterweight)

3–Alexis Arguello (WBA featherweight, WBC super featherweight, WBC lightweight)

3–Wilfredo Gomez (WBC super bantamweight, WBC featherweight, WBA junior lightweight)

3–Jeff Fenech (IBF bantamweight, WBC super bantamweight, WBC featherweight)

3–Julio Cesar Chavez (WBC super featherweight, WBA & WBC lightweight, IBF & WBC super lightweight)

3–Iran Barkley (WBC middleweight, IBF super middleweight, WBA light heavyweight)

3–Pernell Whitaker (world lightweight, IBF junior welterweight, WBC welterweight)

*Armstrong simultaneously held all three titles

In the modern era, there has never been a southpaw heavyweight champion. Only two left-handers have challenged for the crown, **Karl Mildenberger** in 1966 (KO by 12 Muhammad Ali), and **Richard Dunn** in 1976 (KO by 5 Muhammad Ali).

BEHIND ON POINTS, THEY SCORED A LAST-ROUND KAYO TO WIN

Jake LaMotta KO 15 (2:47) Laurent Dauthuille, September 13, 1950, Detroit (Retains World Middleweight Title)

Oscar Albarado KO 15 (1:57) Koichi Wajima, June 4, 1974, Tokyo (Wins WBA Junior Middleweight Title)

Mike Weaver KO 15 (2:15) John Tate, March 31, 1980, Knoxville, Tennessee (Wins WBA Heavyweight Title)

Jeff Harding KO 12 (1:23) Dennis Andries, June 24, 1989, Atlantic City (Wins WBC Light Heavyweight Title)

Julio Cesar Chavez KO 12 (2:58) Meldrick Taylor, March 17, 1990, Las Vegas (Retains WBC Super Lightweight Title; Wins IBF Junior Welterweight Title)

Humberto Gonzalez KO 12 (0:55) Kwang Sun Kim, June 7, 1992, Seoul (Retains WBC Junior Flyweight Title)

The last world title fight scheduled for more than 15 rounds was **Joe Louis-Bob Pastor,** scheduled for 20 rounds, and held on September 20, 1939, in Detroit. Louis retained the heavyweight title by 11th-round kayo.

Roberto Duran holds the record for the longest span between world titles. On June 26, 1972, he won the WBA lightweight crown by stopping Ken Buchanan in the 14th round. Almost 17 years later, on February 24, 1989, he won the WBC middleweight title by outpointing Iran Barkley over 12 rounds.

Henry Armstrong held three world championships simultaneously, at a time when there were only eight major weight divisions.

The all-time record for longest unbeaten streak at the start of a career is held by flyweight champion **Jimmy Wilde**, who fought 98 bouts before suffering his first defeat; the longest winning streak at the start of a career is held by triple-crown champion **Julio Cesar Chavez**, who, as of March 15, 1993, had won 85 consecutive bouts.

MOST SUCCESSFUL CONSECUTIVE TITLE DEFENSES

Heavyweight: Joe Louis-25

Cruiserweight: Evander Holyfield-5

Light Heavyweight: Bob Foster-14

Super Middleweight: Chong Pal Park-8

Middleweight: Carlos Monzon-14

Junior Middleweight: Gianfranco Rosi-10

Welterweight: Henry Armstrong-19

Junior Welterweight: Antonio Cervantes-10

Lightweight: Roberto Duran-12

Junior Lightweight: Brian Mitchell-12

Featherweight: Eusebio Pedroza-19

Junior Featherweight: Wilfredo Gomez-17

Bantamweight: Manuel Ortiz-15

Junior Bantamweight: Khaosai Galaxy-19

Flyweight: Miguel Canto-14

Junior Flyweight: Myung Woo Yuh-17

Strawweight: Phalan Lukmingkwan-7

Michael Spinks is the only light heavyweight champion to dethrone a heavyweight king. (On September 22, 1985, he scored a unanimous 15-round decision over IBF titleholder Larry Holmes.) The 175-pound champions who had tried and failed: Philadelphia Jack O'Brien, Georges Carpentier, John Henry Lewis, Billy Conn, Joey Maxim, Archie Moore, and Bob Foster.

Joe Louis, whose 11 years, 8 months reign as heavyweight champion and 25 successful title defenses are records that will probably stand forever.

LONGEST TITLE REIGNS

Heavyweight: Joe Louis
(11 years, 7 months)

Cruiserweight: Ossie Ocasio
(2 years, 9 months)

Light Heavyweight: Archie Moore
(9 years, 2 months)

Super Middleweight: Chong Pal Park
(3 years, 6 months)

Middleweight: Carlos Monzon
(6 years, 9 months)

Junior Middleweight: Thomas Hearns
(3 years, 9 months)

Welterweight: (tie) Freddie Cochrane
(4 years, 6 months) **Jose Napoles** (4 years, 6 months)

Junior Welterweight: Bruno Arcari
(4 years, 6 months)

Lightweight: Roberto Duran
(6 years, 7 months)

Junior Lightweight: Flash Elorde
(7 years, 3 months)

Featherweight: Eusebio Pedroza
(7 years, 2 months)

Junior Featherweight: Wilfredo Gomez
(5 years, 10 months)

Bantamweight: Panama Al Brown
(5 years, 11 months)

Junior Bantamweight: Khaosai Galaxy
(7 years, 1 month)

Flyweight: Jimmy Wilde
(7 years, 4 months)

Junior Flyweight: Myung Woo Yuh
(6 years, 0 months)

Strawweight: Phalan Lukmingkwan
(2 years, 7 months)

The youngest fighter to win a world title was **Wilfred Benitez**, who, on March 6, 1976, scored a split 15-round decision over defending WBA junior welterweight champion Antonio Cervantes in San Juan. Benitez was 17½ years old. The oldest fighter to compete in a world title bout was **Archie Moore**, who, on June 10, 1961, retained the light heavyweight crown with a unanimous 15-round decision over Giulio Rinaldi. Moore was a very unofficial 47½ years old.

WORLD CHAMPIONS WHO HAVE BOXED THE MOST TITLE FIGHT ROUNDS

1. **Emile Griffith-339**
2. **Abe Attell-337**
3. **Hilario Zapata-303**
4. **Sugar Ray Robinson-288**
5. **Muhammad Ali-270**
6. **(tie) Eusebio Pedroza-266**
6. **(tie) Miguel Canto-266**
8. **Manuel Ortiz-260**
9. **Tony Canzoneri-259**
10. **Larry Holmes-254**

Four fighters won the world title in their fifth tries (within the same division). They are heavyweight **Jersey Joe Walcott,** featherweight **Marcos Villasana,** flyweight **Susumu Hanagata,** and junior flyweight **German Torres.**

BIBLIOGRAPHY

Joe Louis: Black Hero In White America, by Chris Mead (Charles Scribner's Sons)

Joe Louis: 50 Years An American Hero, by Joe Louis Barrow, Jr. and Barbara Munder (McGraw-Hill Book Company, 1988)

The Great Book Of Boxing, by Harry Mullan (Crescent Books, 1987)

Jack Kid Berg: The Whitechapel Windmill, by John Harding with Jack Berg (Robson Books, 1987)

The World Heavyweight Boxing Championship, by John D. McCallum (Chilton Book Company, 1974)

Barry McGuigan: The Untold Story, by Barry McGuigan with Gerry Callan and Harry Mullan (Robson Books, 1991)

Muhammad Ali: His Life and Times, by Thomas Hauser (Simon & Schuster, 1991)

Jack Johnson & His Times, by Denzil Batchelor (George Weidenfield & Nicolson Limited, 1956)

The Jewish Boxers' Hall Of Fame, by Ken Blady (Shapolsky Publishers, Inc., 1988)

England's Boxing Heroes, by Frank McGhee (Bloomsbury Publishing Limited, 1988)

In This Corner..., by Peter Heller (Simon & Schuster, 1973)

Mickey Walker: The Toy Bulldog & His Times, by Mickey Walker with Joe Reichler (Random House, 1961)

Sugar Ray, by Sugar Ray Robinson, with Dave Anderson (The Viking Press, 1970)

Leonard The Magnificent, by Nat Fleischer (The O'Brien Suburban Press, 1947)

The Fighters, by Chris Greyvenstein (Sigma Motor Corp., 1981)

Blood Season: Tyson And The World Of Boxing, by Phil Berger (William Morrow and Company, 1989)

Bad Intentions: The Mike Tyson Story, by Peter Heller (New American Library, 1989)

Jack Dempsey: The Manassa Mauler, by Randy Roberts (Louisiana State University Press, 1979)

Boxing Babylon, by Nigel Collins (Citadel Press, 1990)

Fighting Was My Business, by Jimmy Wilde (Michael Joseph Ltd., 1938)

Index

WHY IS MOORE POISON?
25 Cents
NOVEMBER
The RING
World's Most Ignored Boxer, Archie Moore
See Page 3

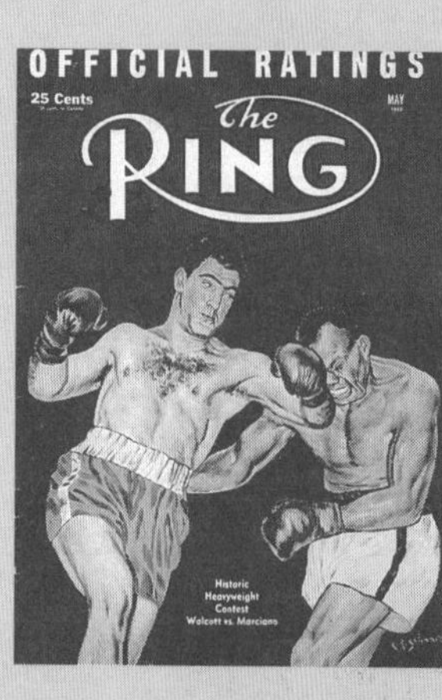
OFFICIAL RATINGS
25 Cents
MAY
The RING
Historic Heavyweight Contest Walcott vs. Marciano

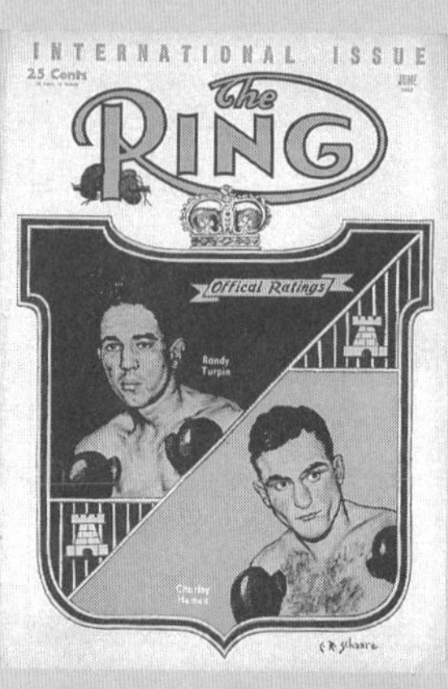
INTERNATIONAL ISSUE
25 Cents
JUNE
The RING
Official Ratings

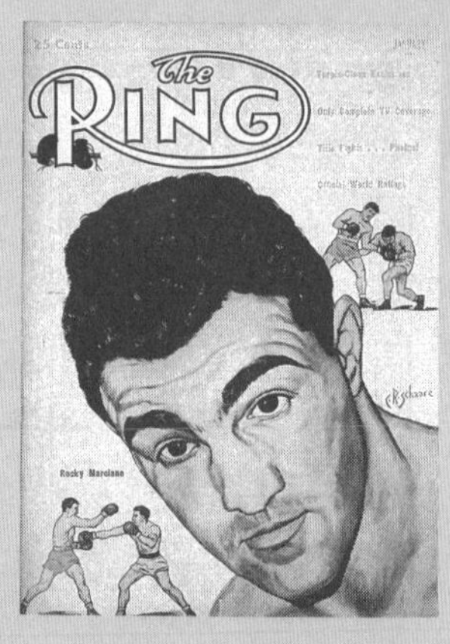
25 Cents
The RING

EXCLUSIVE-PHOTOS -TWO TITLE FIGHTS
FEBRUARY
The RING
35 Cents
ANNUAL ISSUE— 2500 Fighters Rated Year Roundup Complete Wrestling Section
THE ROUND IN 1959 THAT OUTDAZZLED ALL OTHERS— JOHANSSON-PATTERSON
WHICH FIGHT WAS VOTED TOPS?
WHICH WAS 1959'S BIGGEST UPSET?
WHICH BOXER PROGRESSED MORE THAN ANY OTHER
"I Will Fight," Says BASILIO

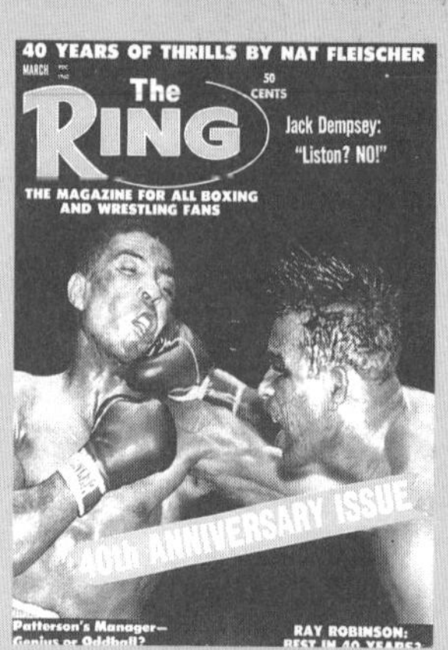
40 YEARS OF THRILLS BY NAT FLEISCHER
MARCH
The RING
50 CENTS
Jack Dempsey: "Liston? NO!"
THE MAGAZINE FOR ALL BOXING AND WRESTLING FANS
40th ANNIVERSARY ISSUE
Patterson's Manager— Genius or Oddball?
RAY ROBINSON: BEST IN 40 YEARS?

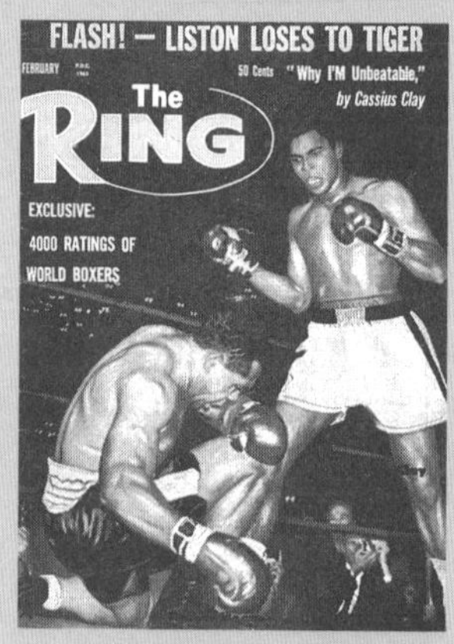
FLASH! — LISTON LOSES TO TIGER
FEBRUARY
The RING
50 Cents
"Why I'M Unbeatable," by Cassius Clay
EXCLUSIVE: 4000 RATINGS OF WORLD BOXERS

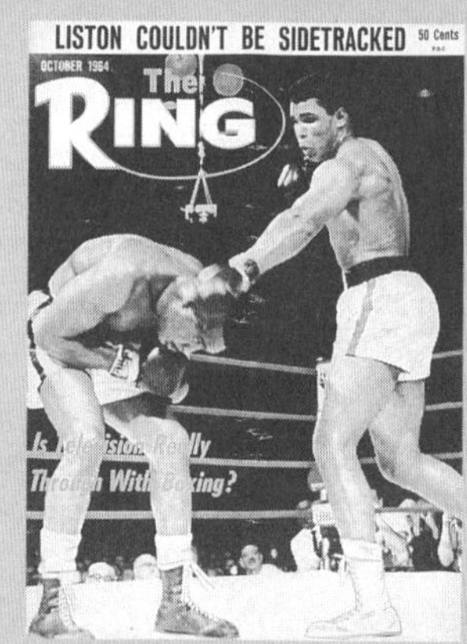
LISTON COULDN'T BE SIDETRACKED
50 Cents
OCTOBER 1964
The RING
Through With Boxing?

JULY 1967
50 Cents
RING
The Era Builders
Dempsey
Louis
Clay
WHO IS OUR NEXT MAN OF DESTINY?
Wild Bull Firpo— Magnificent Failure!
Why Can't Bob Foster Fight For Title???

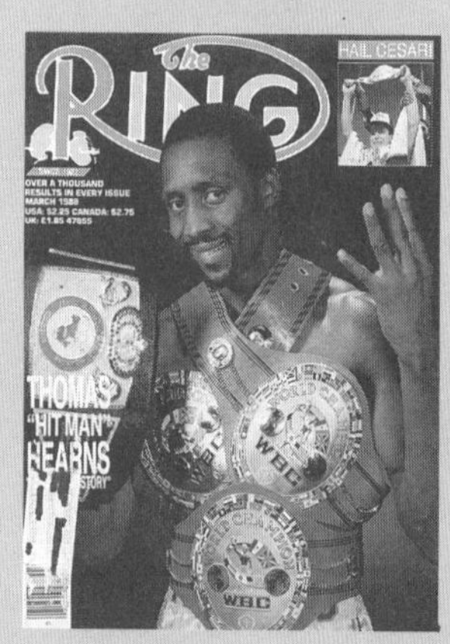
The RING
HAIL CESAR!
OVER A THOUSAND RESULTS IN EVERY ISSUE
THOMAS "HIT MAN" HEARNS
WBC

"FIGHT OR JAIL" CRISIS FOR CLAY
The RING
AUGUST 1968
50 Cents
Ellis False Alarm Or Top Toughie???
DEAD END

IS BENVENUTI'S NUMBER UP ??
The RING
JUNE 1970
60 Cents
STARS WARN FRAZIER ON HIS FUTURE!!!
Heavyweight Champ's Life In Pictures

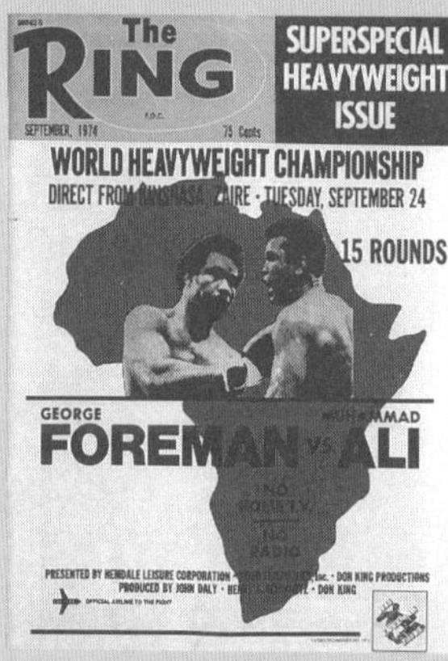
The RING
SUPERSPECIAL HEAVYWEIGHT ISSUE
SEPTEMBER, 1974
75 Cents
WORLD HEAVYWEIGHT CHAMPIONSHIP
TUESDAY, SEPTEMBER 24
15 ROUNDS
GEORGE FOREMAN VS MUHAMMAD ALI

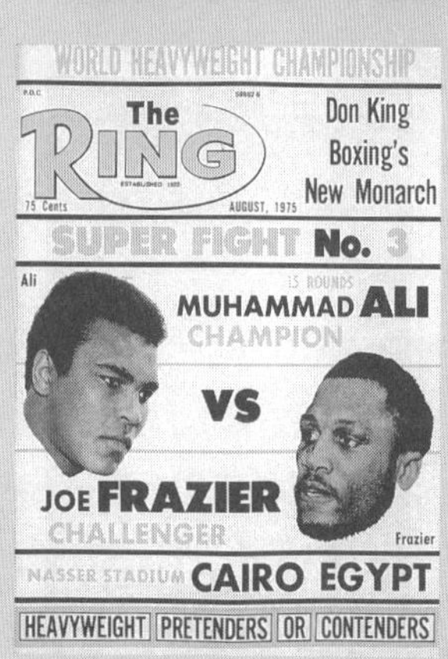
WORLD HEAVYWEIGHT CHAMPIONSHIP
The RING
Don King Boxing's New Monarch
75 Cents
AUGUST, 1975
SUPER FIGHT No. 3
Ali
15 ROUNDS
MUHAMMAD ALI CHAMPION
VS
JOE FRAZIER CHALLENGER
Frazier
NASSER STADIUM CAIRO EGYPT
HEAVYWEIGHT PRETENDERS OR CONTENDERS

The RING
1.50
96 PAGE SOUVENIR ISSUE
FROM RINGSIDE: ALI, NORTON, MONZON, ESCALERA, ZAMORA, VELASQUEZ- PLUS
The Many Faces of the Retired Joe Frazier

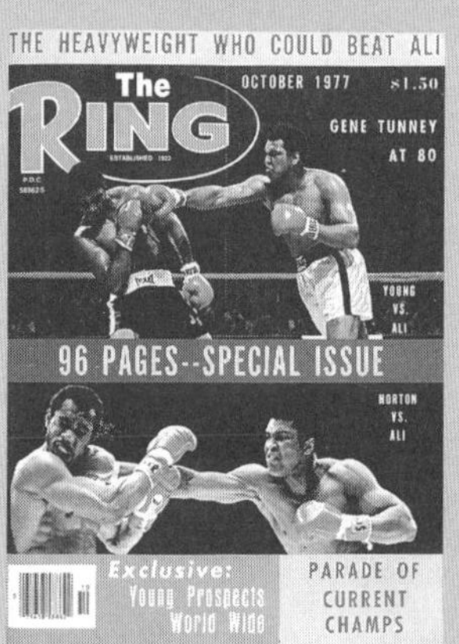
THE HEAVYWEIGHT WHO COULD BEAT ALI
The RING
OCTOBER 1977
$1.50
GENE TUNNEY AT 80
YOUNG VS. ALI
96 PAGES--SPECIAL ISSUE
NORTON VS. ALI
Exclusive: Young Prospects World Wide
PARADE OF CURRENT CHAMPS

The RING
REQUIEM FOR JOE LOUIS
HOW THE WBC AND WBA 'RATE'
THE PACKAGING OF SUGAR RAY LEONARD
THE GUARANTEED HOT CLEANER-UPPER
EXTRA ACTION
PUNCH
AMERICA'S FAVORITE
ONLY $TEN MILLION

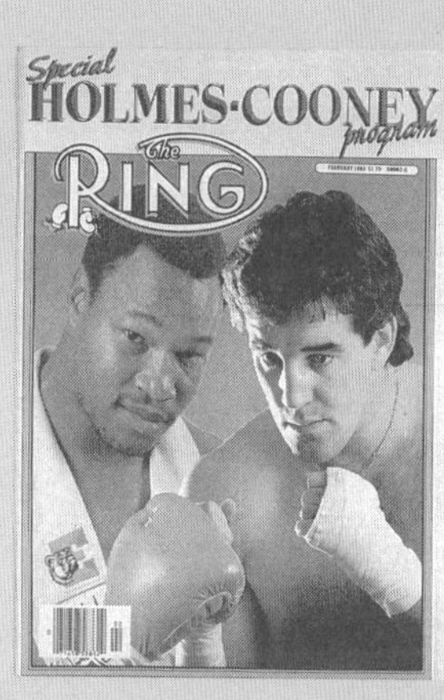
Special HOLMES·COONEY program
The RING

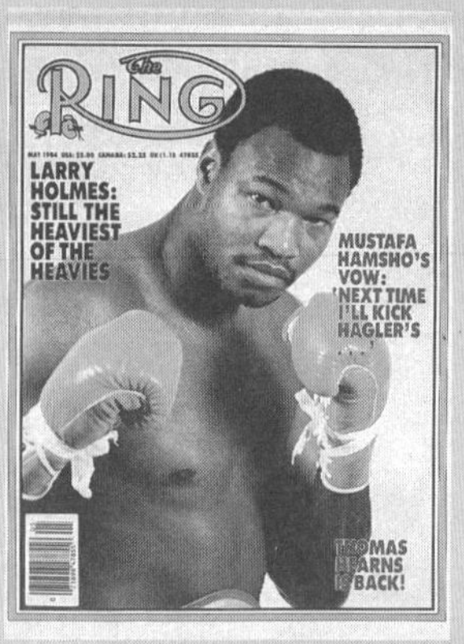
The RING
LARRY HOLMES: STILL THE HEAVIEST OF THE HEAVIES
MUSTAFA HAMSHO'S VOW: 'NEXT TIME I'LL KICK HAGLER'S
THOMAS HEARNS IS BACK!

The RING
SPECIAL HAGLER-HEARNS SOUVENIR PROGRAM INSIDE
HECTOR CAMACHO: THE RETURN OF THE 'MACHO MAN'